Particle Swarm Optimization

Edited by
Aleksandar Lazinica

Particle Swarm Optimization

Edited by Aleksandar Lazinica

Republished by InTech

Janeza Trdine 9, 51000 Rijeka, Croatia

Additional hard copies can be obtained from orders@intechopen.com

Particle Swarm Optimization, Edited by Aleksandar Lazinica
p. cm.
ISBN 978-953-7619-48-0

For EU product safety concerns:
IN TECH d.o.o., Prolaz Marije Krucifikse Kozulić 3, 51000 Rijeka, Croatia,
info@intechopen.com or visit our website at intechopen.com.

Meet the editor

Alex Lazinica is the founder and CEO of IntechOpen. After obtaining a Master's degree in Mechanical Engineering, he continued his PhD studies in Robotics at the Vienna University of Technology. Here he worked as a robotic researcher with the university's Intelligent Manufacturing Systems Group as well as a guest researcher at various European universities, including the Swiss Federal Institute of Technology Lausanne (EPFL). During this time he published more than 20 scientific papers, gave presentations, served as a reviewer for major robotic journals and conferences and most importantly he co-founded and built the International Journal of Advanced Robotic Systems- world's first Open Access journal in the field of robotics. Starting this journal was a pivotal point in his career, since it was a pathway to founding IntechOpen - Open Access publisher focused on addressing academic researchers needs. Alex is a personification of IntechOpen key values being trusted, open and entrepreneurial. Today his focus is on defining the growth and development strategy for the company.

Preface

Particle swarm optimization (PSO) is a population based stochastic optimization technique developed by Dr. Eberhart and Dr. Kennedy in 1995, inspired by social behavior of bird flocking or fish schooling.

PSO shares many similarities with evolutionary computation techniques such as Genetic Algorithms (GA). The system is initialized with a population of random solutions and searches for optima by updating generations. However, unlike GA, PSO has no evolution operators such as crossover and mutation. In PSO, the potential solutions, called particles, fly through the problem space by following the current optimum particles.

This book represents the contributions of the top researchers in this field and will serve as a valuable tool for professionals in this interdisciplinary field.

This book is certainly a small sample of the research activity on Particle Swarm Optimization going on around the globe as you read it, but it surely covers a good deal of what has been done in the field recently, and as such it works as a valuable source for researchers interested in the involved subjects.

Special thanks to all authors, which have invested a great deal of time to write such interesting and high quality chapters.

Aleksandar Lazinica

Contents

1

Novel Binary Particle Swarm Optimization

Mojtaba Ahmadieh Khanesar, Hassan Tavakoli, Mohammad Teshnehlab andMahdi Aliyari Shoorehdeli
K N. Toosi University of Technology
Iran

1. Introduction

Particle swarm optimization (PSO) was originally designed and introduced by Eberhart and Kennedy (Ebarhart, Kennedy, 1995; Kennedy, Eberhart, 1995; Ebarhart, Kennedy, 2001). The PSO is a population based search algorithm based on the simulation of the social behavior of birds, bees or a school of fishes. This algorithm originally intends to graphically simulate the graceful and unpredictable choreography of a bird folk. Each individual within the swarm is represented by a vector in multidimensional search space. This vector has also one assigned vector which determines the next movement of the particle and is called the velocity vector. The PSO algorithm also determines how to update the velocity of a particle. Each particle updates its velocity based on current velocity and the best position it has explored so far; and also based on the global best position explored by swarm (Engelbrecht, 2005; Sadri, Ching, 2006; Engelbrecht, 2002).

The PSO process then is iterated a fixed number of times or until a minimum error based on desired performance index is achieved. It has been shown that this simple model can deal with difficult optimization problems efficiently. The PSO was originally developed for real-valued spaces but many problems are, however, defined for discrete valued spaces where the domain of the variables is finite. Classical examples of such problems are: integer programming, scheduling and routing (Engelbrecht, 2005). In 1997, Kennedy and Eberhart introduced a discrete binary version of PSO for discrete optimization problems (Kennedy, Eberhart, 1997). In binary PSO, each particle represents its position in binary values which are 0 or 1. Each particle's value can then be changed (or better say mutate) from one to zero or vice versa. In binary PSO the velocity of a particle defined as the probability that a particle might change its state to one. This algorithm will be discussed in more detail in next sections.

Upon introduction of this new algorithm, it was used in number of engineering applications. Using binary PSO, Wang and Xiang (Wang & Xiang, 2007) proposed a high quality splitting criterion for codebooks of tree-structured vector quantizers (TSVQ). Using binary PSO, they reduced the computation time too. Binary PSO is used to train the structure of a Bayesian network (Chen et al., 2007). A modified discrete particle swarm optimization (PSO) is successfully used based technique for generating optimal preventive maintenance schedule of generating units for economical and reliable operation of a power system while satisfying system load demand and crew constraints (Yare & Venayagamoorthy, 2007). Choosing optimum input subset for SVM (Zhang & Huo, 2005),

designing dual-band dual-polarized planar antenna (Marandi et. al, 2006) are two other engineering applications of binary PSO. Also some well-known problems are solved using binary PSO and its variations. For example, binary PSO has been used in many applications like Iterated Prisoner's Dilemma (Franken & Engelbrecht, 2005) and traveling salesman (Zhong, et. al. 17).
Although binary PSO is successfully used in number of engineering applications, but this algorithm still has some shortcomings. The difficulties of binary PSO will be discussed, and then a novel binary PSO algorithm will be proposed. In novel binary PSO proposed here, the velocity of a particle is its probability to change its state from its previous state to its complement value, rather than the probability of change to 1. In this new definition the velocity of particle and also its parameters has the same role as in real-valued version of the PSO. This algorithm will be discussed. Also simulation results are presented to show the superior performance of the proposed algorithm over the previously introduced one. There are also other versions of binary PSO. In (Sadri & Ching, 2006) authors add birth and mortality to the ordinary PSO. AMPSO is a version of binary PSO, which employs a trigonometric function as a bit string generator (Pampara et al., 2005). Boolean algebra can also be used for binary PSO (Marandi et al., 2006). Also fuzzy system can be used to improve the capability of the binary PSO as in (Wei Peng et al., 2004).

2. THE PARTICLE SWARM OPTIMIZATION

A detailed description of PSO algorithm is presented in (Engelbrecht, 2005; Sadri, Ching, 2006; Engelbrecht, 2002). Here we will give a short description of the real- valued and binary PSO proposed by Kennedy and Eberhart.

2.1 Real-valued particle swarm optimization

Assume that our search space is d-dimensional, and the i-th particle of the swarm can be represented by a d-dimensional position vector $X_i = (x_{i1}, x_{i2}, ..., x_{id})$. The velocity of the particle is denoted by $V_i = (v_{i1}, v_{i2}, ..., v_{id})$. Also consider best visited position for the particle is $P_{i,best} = (p_{i1}, p_{i2}, ..., p_{id})$ and also the best position explored so far is $P_{g,best} = (p_{g1}, p_{g2}, ..., p_{gd})$. So the position of the particle and its velocity is being updated using following equations:

$$V_i(t+1) = w.V_i(t) + c_1\varphi_1(P_{ibest} - X_i) + c_2\varphi_2(P_{gbest} - X_i) \tag{1}$$

$$x_i(t+1) = x_i(t) + v_i(t+1) \tag{2}$$

Where c_1 and c_2 are positive constants, and $x_i(t+1) = x_i(t) + v_i(t+1)$ are two random variables with uniform distribution between 0 and 1. In this equation, W is the inertia weight which shows the effect of previous velocity vector on the new vector. An upper bound is placed on the velocity in all dimensions $V_{\max}$. This limitation prevents the particle from moving too rapidly from one region in search space to another. This value is usually initialized as a function of the range of the problem. For example if the range of all x_{ij} is [−50,50] then $V_{\max}$ is proportional to 50. P_{ibest} for each particle is updated in each iteration when a better position for the particle or for the whole swarm is obtained. The feature that drives PSO is social interaction. Individuals (particles) within the swarm learn from each other, and based on the knowledge obtained then move to become similar to their "better" previously obtained position and also to their "better" neighbors. Individual within a neighborhood communicate with one other. Based on the communication of a particle within the swarm different neighborhood topologies are defined. One of these topologies which is considered here, is the star topology. In this topology each particle can communicate with every other individual, forming a fully connected social network. In this case each particle is attracted toward the best particle (best problem solution) found by any member of the entire swarm. Each particle therefore imitates the overall best particle. So the P_{gbest} updated when a new best position within the whole swarm is found. The algorithm for the PSO can be summarized as follows:

1. Initialize the swarm X i , the position of particles are randomly initialized within the hypercube of feasible space.
2. Evaluate the performance F of each particle, using its current position Xi (t).
3. Compare the performance of each individual to its best performance so far: $F(X_i) < F(P_{ibest})$.

$$F(P_{ibest}) = F(X_i) \,,\; P_{ibest} = X_i \,,$$

4. Compare the performance of each particle to the global best particle: if $F(X_i) < F(P_{gbest})$

$$F(P_{gbest}) = F(X_i) \,,\; P_{gbest} = X_i$$

5. Change the velocity of the particle according to (1).
6. Move each particle to a new position using equation (2).
7. Go to step 2, and repeat until convergence.

2.2 Binary particle swarm optimization

Kennedy and Eberhart proposed a discrete binary version of PSO for binary problems [4]. In their model a particle will decide on "yes" or " no", "true" or "false", "include" or "not to include" etc. also this binary values can be a representation of a real value in binary search space.

In the binary PSO, the particle's personal best and global best is updated as in real- valued version. The major difference between binary PSO with real-valued version is that velocities of the particles are rather defined in terms of probabilities that a bit will change to one. Using this definition a velocity must be restricted within the range [0,1] . So a map is introduced to map all real valued numbers of velocity to the range [0,1] [4]. The normalization function used here is a sigmoid function as:

$$V'_{ij}(t) = sig(V_{ij}(t)) = \frac{1}{1+e^{-V_{ij}(t)}} \tag{3}$$

Also the equation (1) is used to update the velocity vector of the particle. And the new position of the particle is obtained using the equation below:

$$x_{ij}(t+1) = \begin{cases} 1 \; if & r_{ij} < sig(v_{ij}(t+1)) \\ 0 & otherwise \end{cases} \tag{4}$$

Where r_{ij} is a uniform random number in the range [0,1].

2.3 Main problems with binary PSO

Here two main problems and concerns about binary PSO is discussed the first is the parameters of binary PSO and the second is the problem with memory of binary PSO.

a) Parameters of the binary PSO

It is not just the interpretation of the velocity and particle trajectories that changes for the binary PSO. The meaning and behavior of the velocity clamping and the inertia weight differ substantially from the real-valued PSO. In fact, the effects of these parameters are the opposite of those for the real valued PSO. In fact, the effects of these parameters are the opposite of those for the real-valued PSO (Engelbrecht, 2005).

In real-valued version of PSO large numbers for maximum velocity of the particle encourage exploration. But in binary PSO small numbers for V_{max} promotes exploration, even if a good solution is found. And if V_{max} = 0, then the search changes into a pure random search. Large values for V_{max} limit exploration. For example if V_{max}= 4, then $sig(V_{max})$ = 0.982 is the probability of x_{ij} to change to bit 1.

There is also some difficulties with choosing proper value for inertia weight w . For binary PSO, values of $w<1$ prevents convergence. For values of $-1<w<1$, V_{ij} becomes 0 over time. For which $sig(0)=0$ so for $w<1$ we have $\lim_{t\to\infty} sig(V_{ij}(t))=0.5$. If $w>1$ velocity increases over time and $\lim_{t\to\infty} sig(V_{ij}(t))=0$ so all bits change to 1. If $-1<w$ then $\lim_{t\to\infty} sig(V_{ij}(t))=0$ so the probability that bits change to bit 0 increases.

As discussed in (Engelbrecht, 2005) the inertia weight and its effect is a problem. Also two approaches are suggested there: First is to remove the momentum term. According to (Engelbrecht, 2005), as the change in particle's position is randomly influenced by f/y , so the momentum term might not be needed. This approach is unexplored approach although it is used in (Pampara et al., 2005), but no comparisons are provided there. The second approach is to use a random number for w in the range: (-1,1) . In fact inertia weight has some valuable information about previously found directions found. Removing this term can't give any improvement to the binary PSO and the previous direction will be lost in this manner. Also using a random number for *win* the range (-1, 1) or any range like this can't be a good solution. It is desired that the algorithm is quite insensible to the values selected for *w*. Also using negative values for *w* makes no sense because this term provides the effect of previous directions in the next direction of the particle. Using a negative value for this parameter is not logical.

b) Memory of the binary PSO

Considering equation (4) the next value for the bit is quite independent of the current value of that bit and the value is solely updated using the velocity vector. In real-valued version of PSO the update rule uses current position of the swarm and the velocity vector just determines the movement of the particle in the space.

3. THE NOVEL BINARY PARTICLE SWARM OPTIMIZATION

Here, the P_{ibest} and P_{gbest} of the swarm is updated as in real-valued or binary version. The major difference between this algorithm and other version of binary PSO is the interpretation of velocity. Here, as in real-valued version of PSO, velocity of a particle is the rate at which the particle changes its bit's value. Two vectors for each particle are introduced as: $\vec{V}_i^0$ and $\vec{V}_i^1$. $\vec{V}_i^0$ is the probability of the bits of the particle to change to zero while $\vec{V}_i^1$ is the probability that bits of particle change to one. Since in update equation of these velocities, which will be introduced later, the inertia term is used, these velocities are not complement. So the probability of change in *j-th* bit of *i-th* particle is simply defined as follows:

$$x_{ij}(t+1) = \begin{cases} 1 \ if & r_{ij} < sig(v_{ij}(t+1)) \\ 0 & otherwise \end{cases} \tag{4}$$

In this way the velocity of particle is simply calculated. Also the update algorithm for $\vec{V}_i^0$ and $\vec{V}_i^1$ is as follows: consider the best position visited so far for a particle is P_{ibest} and the global best position for the particle is P_{gbest}. Also consider that the *j-th* bit of *i-th* best particle is one. So to guide the bit *j-th* of *i-th* particle to its best position, the velocity of change to one ($\vec{V}_i^0$) for that particle increases and the velocity of change to zero ($\vec{V}_i^1$) is decreases. Using this concept following rules can be extracted:

$$\begin{aligned}
&If \ P_{ibest}^j = 1 \ Then \ d_{ij,1}^1 = r_1 c_1 \ and \ d_{ij,1}^0 = -r_1 c_1 \\
&If \ P_{ibest}^j = 0 \ Then \ d_{ij,1}^0 = r_1 c_1 \ and \ d_{ij,1}^1 = -r_1 c_1 \\
&If \ P_{gbest}^j = 1 \ Then \ d_{ij,2}^1 = r_2 c_2 \ and \ d_{ij,2}^0 = -r_2 c_2 \\
&If \ P_{gbest}^j = 0 \ Then \ d_{ij,2}^1 = r_2 c_2 \ and \ d_{ij,2}^0 = -r_2 c_2
\end{aligned} \tag{6}$$

Where d_{ij}^1, d_{ij}^0 are two temporary values, r_1 and r_2 are two random variable in the range of (0,1) which are updated each iteration. Also c_1 , c_2 are two fixed variables which are determined by user. Then:

$$\begin{aligned}
V_{ij}^1 &= wV_{ij}^1 + d_{ij,1}^1 + d_{ij,2}^1 \\
V_{ij}^0 &= wV_{ij}^0 + d_{ij,1}^0 + d_{ij,2}^0
\end{aligned} \tag{7}$$

Where w is the inertia term. In fact in this algorithm if the *j-th* bit in the global best variable is zero or if the *j-th* bit in the corresponding personal best variable is zero the velocity (V_{ij}^0) is increased. And the probability of changing to one is also decreases with the same rate. In addition, if the j-th bit in the global best variable is one V_{ij}^1 is increased and V_{ij}^0 decreases.

In this approach previously found direction of change to one or change to zero for a bit is maintained and used so particles make use of previously found direction. After updating velocity of particles, $\vec{V}_i^0$ and $\vec{V}_i^1$, the velocity of change is obtained as in (5). A normalization process is also done. Using sigmoid function as introduced in (3). And then the next particles state is computed as follows:

$$\begin{aligned}
V_{ij}^1 &= wV_{ij}^1 + d_{ij,1}^1 + d_{ij,2}^1 \\
V_{ij}^0 &= wV_{ij}^0 + d_{ij,1}^0 + d_{ij,2}^0
\end{aligned} \tag{7}$$

Where $\bar{x}_{ij}(t)$ is the 2's complement of $x_{ij}(t)$. That is, if $x_{ij} = 0$ then $\bar{x}_{ij} = 1$ and if $x_{ij} = 1$ then $\bar{x}_{ij} = 0$. And r_{ij} is a uniform random number between 0 and 1.

The meaning of the parameters used in velocity equation, are exactly like those for the real-valued PSO. The inertia weight used here maintains the previous direction of bits of particle to the personal best bit or global best bit whether it is 1 or 0. Also the meaning of velocity is the same as meaning of the velocity in real-valued version of PSO which is the rate of change in particle's position. Also as in real-valued PSO if the maximum velocity value considered is large, random search will happen. Small values for maximum velocity cause the particle to move less. Here also the previous states of the bits of the particles are taking into account. Using the equation (7) the previous value of the particle is taken into account, while in binary PSO just velocity determined the next value of particle. So, better performance and better learning from experiments in this algorithm is achieved. Experimental results in the next section support these complain. The algorithm proposed here for the binary PSO can be summarized as follows:

1. Initialize the swarm X i , the position of particles are randomly initialized within the hypercube. Elements of X i are randomly selected from binary values 0 and 1.
2. Evaluate the performance F of each particle, using its current position Xi (t) .
3. Compare the performance of each individual to its best performance so far: if if $F(X_i) < F(P_{ibest})$.

$$F(P_{ibest}) = F(X_i)$$
$$P_{ibest} = X_i$$

4. Compare the performance of each particle to the global best particle: $F(X_i) < F(P_{gbest})$:

$$F(P_{gbest}) = F(X_i)$$
$$P_{gbest} = X_i$$

5. Change the velocity of the particle, $\vec{V}_i^0$ and $\vec{V}_i^1$ according to (6,7).
6. Calculate the velocity of change of the bits, $\vec{V}_i^c$ as in (5).
7. Generate the random variable r_{ij} in the range: (0,1). Move each particle to a new position using equation (8).
8. Go to step 2, and repeat until convergence.

4. EXPERIMENTAL RESULTS

In this section we will compare the performance of proposed binary PSO and the binary PSO proposed by Kennedy and Eberhart in (Kennedy & Ebarhart, 1997) and the binary PSO used in (Tasgetiren & Liang,2007). In our experiments we investigated methods on the minimization of test functions set which is proposed in (Kennedy & Ebarhart, 1997). The functions used here are: Sphere, Rosenbrock, Griewangk and Rastrigin which are represented in equations (9-12) respectively. The global minimum of all of these functions is zero. The expression of these test functions are as follows:

$$f_1(X) = \sum_{i=1}^{N} x_i^2 \tag{9}$$

$$f_2(X) = \sum_{i=1}^{N-1} (100(x_{i+1} - x_i^2)^2 + (x_i - 1)^2) \tag{10}$$

$$f_3(X) = \frac{1}{4000} \sum_{i=1}^{N} x_i^2 - \prod_{i=1}^{N} \cos\frac{x_i}{\sqrt{i}} + 1 \tag{11}$$

$$f_4(X) = \sum_{i=1}^{N} (x_i^2 - 10\cos(2\pi x_i) + 10) \tag{12}$$

These functions have been used by many researchers as benchmarks for evaluating and comparing different optimization algorithms. In all of these functions N is the dimension of our search space. In our experiments the range of the particles were set to [-50 ,50] and 20 bits are used to represent binary values for the real numbers. Also population size is 100 and the number of iteration assumed to be 1000. The different values assumed in tests for *N* are 3, 5,10, where N is the dimension of solution space. As it is shown in Table (1-8), the results are quite satisfactory and much better than the algorithms proposed in (Kennedy & Ebarhart, 1997) and (Tasgetiren & Liang,2007). As it was mentioned earlier, the method proposed here uses the previous direction found effectively and velocity has the same interpretation as the real-valued PSO, which is the rate of changes. The method of selecting inertia weight in binary PSO proposed in (Kennedy & Ebarhart, 1997) is still a problem (Engelbrecht, 2005). But removing the inertia weight is also undesirable because the previous direction is completely losses. In fact the previous velocities of a particle contain some information about the direction to previous personal best and global bests of the particle and surely have some valuable information which can help us faster and better find the solution. But in the proposed algorithm the effect of previous direction and also the effect of previous state of the system is completely taken into account. The results obtained here quite support the idea.

5. CONCLUSION

In this study a new interpretation for the velocity of binary PSO was proposed, which is the rate of change in bits of particles. Also the main difficulty of older version of binary PSO which is choosing proper value for *wis* solved. The previous direction and previous state of each particle is also taken into account and helped finding good solutions for problems. This approach tested and returned quite satisfactory results in number of test problems. The binary PSO can be used in variety of applications, especially when the values of the search space are discrete like decision making, solving lot sizing problem, the traveling salesman problem, scheduling and routing.

Dimension of input space	The Novel Binary PSO	Binary PSO as (Kennedy 1997)	Binary PSO as (Tasgetiren 2007)
N=3	6.82 x10^{-9}	0.06	0.15
N=5	1. 92 x10^{-6}	7.96	22.90
N=10	0.11	216.61	394.71

Table 1. The results of best global best of minimization for sphere function

Dimension of input space	The Novel Binary PSO	Binary PSO as (Kennedy 1997)	Binary PSO as (Tasgetiren 2007)
N=3	2.57 x10^{-8}	9.21	0.15
N=5	5.29 x10^{-4}	171.54	224.40
N=10	1.98	1532.90	1718.3

Table 2. The results of best mean of personal bests for sphere function

Dimension of input space	The Novel Binary PSO	Binary PSO as (Kennedy 1997)	Binary PSO as (Tasgetiren2007)
N=3	0.09	0.93	0.86
N=5	2.25	1406	3746
N=10	32.83	1.3094x10^{6}	1.523x10^{6}

Table 3. The results of best global best of minimization for Rosenbrock function

Dimension of input space	The Novel Binary PSO	Binary PSO as (Kennedy 1997)	Binary PSO as (Tasgetiren2007)
N=3	0.52	837.62	2945.8
N=5	2.52	304210	6000503
N=10	367.84	3.62 x10^{7}	5.02 x10^{7}

Table 4. The results of best mean of personal bests for Rosenbrock function

Dimension of input space	The Novel Binary PSO	Binary PSO as (Kennedy 1997)	Binary PSO as (Tasgetiren2007)
N=3	2.09 x10^{9}	3.00 x10^{-3}	0.03
N=5	7.4 x10^{3}	0.21	0.15
N=10	0.06	0.83	1.03

Table 5. The results of best global best of minimization for Grienwangk function

Dimension of input space	The Novel Binary PSO	Binary PSO as (Kennedy 1997)	Binary PSO as (Tasgetiren2007)
N=3	3.78 x10^{-8}	0.17	0.20
N=5	0.012	0.58	0.66
N=10	0.30	1.39	1.43

Table 6. The results of best mean of personal bests for Grienwangk function

Dimension of input space	The Novel Binary PSO	Binary PSO as (Kennedy 1997)	Binary PSO as (Tasgetiren2007)
N=3	1.35 $\times 10^{-6}$	2.67	3.71
N=5	3.40 $\times 10^{-3}$	25.88	51.32
N=10	10.39	490.82	539.34

Table 7. The results of best global best of minimization for Rastrigrin function

Dimension of input space	The Novel Binary PSO	Binary PSO as (Kennedy 1997)	Binary PSO as (Tasgetiren2007)
N=3	6.51 $\times 10^{-6}$	32.03	46.79
N=5	0.38	215.59	268.40
N=10	39.14	1664.3	1820.2

Table 8. The results of best mean of personal bests for Rastrigrin function

6. REFERENCES

R. Eberhart, and J. Kennedy, (1995) A New Optimizer Using Particles Swarm Theory, *Proc. Sixth International Symposium on Micro Machine and Human Science* (Nagoya, Japan), IEEE Service Center, Piscataway, NJ, pp. 39-43,

J. Kennedy, and R Eberhart, (1995), Particle Swarm Optimization, *IEEE Conference on Neural Networks*, pp. 1942-1948, (Perth, Australia), Piscataway, NJ, IV, 1995.

J. Kennedy and R. Eberhart. Swarm Intelligence. Morgan Kaufmann Publishers, Inc., San Francisco, CA, 2001.

Kennedy, J.; Eberhart, R.C. (1997), A discrete binary version of the particle swarm algorithm, *IEEE Conference on Systems, Man, and Cybernetics*, 1997.

A. P. Engelbrecht. (2005),Fundamentals of Computational Swarm Intelligence. Wiley, 2005

J. Sadri, and Ching Y. Suen, (2006), A Genetic Binary Particle Swarm Optimization Model, *IEEE Congress on Evolutionary Computation*, Vancouver, BC, Canada, 2006

M. Fatih Tasgetiren. & Yun-Chia Liang, (2007), A Binary Particle Swarm Optimization Algorithm for Lot Sizing Problem *Journal of Economic and Social Research* vol 5. Elsevier pp. 1-20

A. P. Engelbrecht, (2002), computational Intelligence, John Wiley and Sons, 2002 Pampara,

G., Franken, N. ,Engelbrecht, A.P. (2005), Combining particle swarm optimisation with angle modulation to solve binary problems, *IEEE Congress on Evolutionary Computation*, 2005 pp 89-96

Marandi, A., Afshinmanesh, F., Shahabadi, M., Bahrami, F., (2006), Boolean Particle Swarm Optimization and Its Application to the Design of a Dual-Band Dual-Polarized Planar Antenna, *CEC 2006*, pp. 3212-3218

Franken, N., Engelbrecht, A.P., (2005), Particle swarm optimization approaches to coevolve strategies for the iterated prisoner's dilemma, *IEEE Transactions on Evolutionary Computation*, 2005 pp.562 - 579

Chunkai Zhang; Hong Hu, (2005), Using PSO algorithm to evolve an optimum input subset for a SVM in time series forecasting, *IEEE International Conference on Systems, Man and Cybernetics*, 2005 pp. 3793-3796

Yu-Xuan Wang; Qiao-Liang Xiang, (2007), An Improved Discrete Particle Swarm Optimizer for Fast Vector Quantization Codebook Design, Multimedia and Expo, 2007 *IEEE International Conference on, Issue*, 2-5 July 2007 pp.472 - 475

Heng Xing-Chen, Qin Zheng, Tian Lei, Shao Li-Ping, (2007), Learning Bayesian Network Structures with Discrete Particle Swarm Optimization Algorithm, *Proceedings of the 2007 IEEE Symposium on Foundations of Computational Intelligence*, pp.47-53

Yusuf Yare, Ganesh K. Venayagamoorthy, (2007), Optimal Scheduling of Generator Maintenance using Modified Discrete Particle Swarm Optimization, *Symposium Bulk Power System Dynamics and Control* August, 2007, Charleston, SC, USA

Wen-liang Zhong, Jun Zhang, Wei-neng Chen, (2007), A novel discrete particle swarm optimization to solve traveling salesman problem, *Evolutionary Computation*, 2007. CEC 2007. IEEE Congress on, Singapore, Sept. 2007,pp. 3283-3287.

Wei Pang, Kang-ping Wang, Chun-guang Zhou, Long-jiang Dong, (2004) *Fuzzy* Discrete Particle Swarm Optimization for Solving Traveling Salesman Problem, *Proceedings of the Fourth International Conference on Computer and Information Technology* (CIT04), Volume, Issue, 14-16 Sept. 2004 pp. 796 - 800

2

Swarm Intelligence Applications in Electric Machines

Amr M. Amin and Omar T. Hegazy
Power and Electrical Machines Department, Faculty of Engineering – Helwan University
Egypt

1. Introduction

Particle Swarm Optimization (PSO) has potential applications in electric drives. The excellent characteristics of PSO may be successfully used to optimize the performance of electric machines in many aspects.

In this chapter, a field-oriented controller that is based on Particle Swarm Optimization is presented. In this system, the speed control of two asymmetrical windings induction motor is achieved while maintaining maximum efficiency of the motor. PSO selects the optimal rotor flux level at any operating point. In addition, the electromagnetic torque is also improved while maintaining a fast dynamic response. A novel approach is used to evaluate the optimal rotor flux level by using Particle Swarm Optimization. PSO method is a member of the wide category of Swarm Intelligence methods (SI). There are two speed control strategies will demonstrate in next sections. These are field-oriented controller (FOC), and FOC based on PSO. The strategies are implemented mathematically and experimental. The simulation and experimental results have demonstrated that the FOC based on PSO method saves more energy than the conventional FOC method.

In this chapter, another application of PSO for losses and operating cost minimization control is presented for the induction motor drives. Two strategies for induction motor speed control are proposed in this section. These strategies are based on PSO and called maximum efficiency strategy and minimum operating cost Strategy. The proposed technique is based on the principle that the flux level in a machine can be adjusted to give the minimum amount of losses and minimum operating cost for a given value of speed and load torque.

In the demonstrated systems, the flux and torque hysteresis bands are the only adjustable parameters to achieve direct torque control (DTC) of induction motors. Their selection greatly influences the inverter switching loss, motor harmonic loss and motor torque ripples, which are the major performance criteria. In this section, the effects of flux and torque hysteresis bands are investigated and optimized by the particle swarms optimization technique. A DTC control strategy with variable hysteresis bands, which improves the drive performance compared to the classical DTC, is presented.

Online Artificial Neural Networks (ANNs) could be also trained based on PSO optimized data. Here the fast response of ANN is used to optimize the operating conditions of the machine.

It is very important to note that, these applications were achieved without any additional hardware cost, because the PSO is a software scheme. Consequently, PSO has positive promises for a wide range of variable speed drive applications.

2. Losses Minimization of Two Asymmetrical Windings Induction Motor

In this section, applying field orientation based on Particle Swarm Optimization (PSO) controls the speed of two-asymmetrical windings induction motor is the first application of PSO. The maximum efficiency of the motor is obtained by the evaluation of optimal rotor flux at any operating point. In addition, the electro-magnetic torque is also improved while maintaining a fast dynamic response. In this section, a novel approach is used to evaluate the optimal rotor flux level. **This approach is based on Particle Swarm Optimization (PSO). This section presents two speed control strategies. These are field-oriented controller (FOC) and FOC based on PSO.** The strategies are implemented mathematically and experimental. The simulation and experimental results have demonstrated that the FOC based on PSO method saves more energy than the conventional FOC method.
The two asymmetrical windings induction motor is treated as a two-phase induction motor (TPIM). It is used in many low power applications, where three–phase supply is not readily available. This type of motor runs at an efficiency range of 50% to 65% at rated operating conditions [1, 2].
The conventional field-oriented controller normally operates at rated flux at any values with its torque range. When the load is reduced considerably, the core losses become so high causing poor efficiency. If significant energy savings are required, it is necessary to optimize the efficiency of the motor. The optimum efficiency is obtained by the evaluation of the optimal rotor flux level . This flux level is varied according to the torque and the speed of the operating point.
PSO is applied to evaluate the optimal flux. It has the straightforward goal of minimizing the total losses for a given load and speed. It is shown that the efficiency is reasonably close to optimal.

2.1 Mathematical Model of the Motor

The d-q model of an unsymmetrical windings induction motor in a stationary reference frame can be used for a dynamic analysis. This model can take in account the core losses. The d-q model as applied to TPIM is described in [1, 2]. The equivalent circuit is shown in fig. 1. The machine model may be expressed by the following voltage and flux linkage equations :
Voltage Equations:

$$v_{qs} = r_m \, i_{qs} + p\lambda_{qs} \tag{1}$$

$$v_{ds} = r_a \, i_{ds} + p\lambda_{ds} \tag{2}$$

$$0 = r_r i_{qr} - (1/k) * \omega_r \lambda_{dr} + p\lambda_{qr} \tag{3}$$

$$0 = r_R\ i_{ds} + \ k * \omega_r\ \lambda_{qr}\ +\ p\lambda_{dr} \tag{4}$$

$$0 = -\,i_{qfe}\,R_{qfe} + L_{mq}(\,p\,i_{qs} + p\,i_{qr} - p\,i_{qfe}\,) \tag{5}$$

$$0 = -\,i_{dfe}\,R_{dfe} + \ L_{md}\ (\,p\,i_{ds} + p\,i_{dr} - p\,i_{dfe}\,) \tag{6}$$

Flux Linkage Equations:

$$\lambda_{qs} = L_{lm}\,i_{qs} + L_{mq}\,(i_{qs} + i_{qr} - i_{qfe}) \tag{7}$$

$$\lambda_{ds} = L_{la}\,i_{ds} + L_{md}\,(i_{ds} + i_{dr} - i_{dfe}) \tag{8}$$

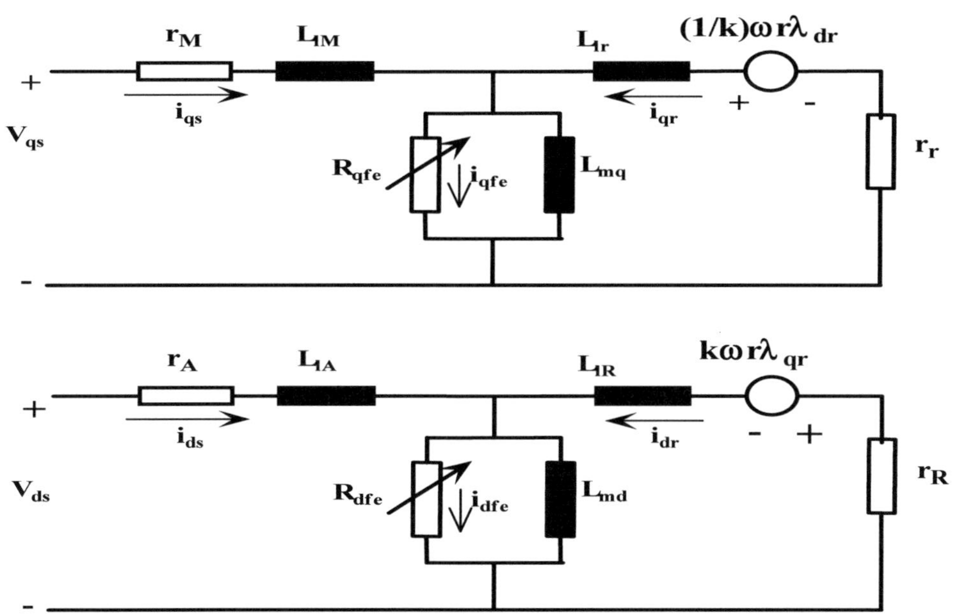

Figure 1. The d-q axes two-phase induction motor Equivalent circuit with iron losses [5]

$$\lambda_{qr} = L_{lr}\,i_{qr} + L_{mq}\,(\,i_{qs} + i_{qr} - i_{qfe}\,) \tag{9}$$

$$\lambda_{dr} = L_{lR}\,i_{dr} + L_{md}\,(\,i_{ds} + i_{dr} - i_{dfe}\,) \tag{10}$$

Electrical torque equation is expressed as:

$$Te = \frac{P}{2}(\,k\,L_{mq}\,i_{dr}(\,i_{qs} + i_{qr} - i_{qfe}\,) - \frac{1}{k}L_{md}\,i_{qr}(\,i_{ds} + i_{dr} - i_{qfe}\,) \tag{11}$$

Dynamic equation is given as follows:

$$Te - T_l = j_m p\omega_r + B_m \omega_r \tag{12}$$

2.2 Field-Oriented Controller [FOC]

The stator windings of the motor are unbalanced. The machine parameters differ from the d axis to the q axis. The waveform of the electromagnetic torque demonstrates the unbalance of the system. The torque in equation (11) contains an AC term; it can be observed that two values are presented for the referred magnetizing inductance. It is possible to eliminate the AC term of electro-magnetic torque by an appropriate control of the stator currents. However, these relations are valid only in linear conditions. Furthermore, the model is implemented using a non-referred equivalent circuit, which presumes some complicated measurement of the magnetizing mutual inductance of the stator and the rotor circuits [3]. The indirect field-oriented control scheme is the most popular scheme for field-oriented controllers. It provides decoupling between the torque of flux currents. The electric torque must be a function of the stator currents and rotor flux in synchronous reference frame [6]. Assuming that the stator currents can be imposed as:

$$i^s_{ds} = i^s_{ds1} \tag{13}$$

$$i^s_{qs} = k\, i^s_{qs1} \tag{14}$$

Where: $k = M_{srd}/M_{srq}$

$$T_e = \frac{P}{2L_r}\left[M_{sqr} i^s_{qs} \lambda^s_{dr} - M_{sdr} i^s_{ds} \lambda^s_{qr}\right] \tag{15}$$

By substituting the variables $\mathbf{i_{ds}}$, and $\mathbf{i_{qs}}$ by auxiliary variables $\mathbf{i_{ds1}}$, and $\mathbf{i_{qs1}}$ into (15) the torque can be expressed by

$$T_e = \frac{PM_{sdr}}{2L_r}\left[i^s_{qs1} \lambda^s_{dr} - i^s_{ds1} \lambda^s_{qr}\right] \tag{16}$$

In synchronous reference frame, the electromagnetic torque is expressed as :

$$T_e = \frac{PM_{sdr}}{2L_r}\left[i^e_{qs1} \lambda^e_{dr} - i^e_{ds1} \lambda^e_{qr}\right] \tag{17}$$

$$T_e = \frac{PM_{sdr}}{2L_r}\left[i^e_{qs1} \lambda^e_{r}\right] \tag{18}$$

$$i^{e}_{ds1} = \frac{\lambda^{e}_{r}}{M_{sdr}} \tag{19}$$

$$\omega_{e} - \omega_{r} = \frac{M_{sdr}}{\tau_{r} * \lambda_{r}} i^{e}_{qs1} \tag{20}$$

2.3 Model with the Losses of two asymmetrical windings induction motor

Finding the losses expression for the two asymmetrical windings induction motor with losses model is a very complex. In this section, a simplified induction motor model with iron losses will be developed [4]. For this purpose, it is necessary to transform all machine variables to the synchronous reference frame. The voltage equations are written in expanded form as follows:

$$v^{e}_{qs} = r_{m} i^{e}_{qs} + L_{lm} \frac{di^{e}_{qs}}{dt} + L_{mq} \frac{di^{e}_{qm}}{dt} + \omega_{e}(L_{la} i^{e}_{ds} + L_{md} i^{e}_{dm}) \tag{21}$$

$$v^{e}_{ds} = r_{a} i^{e}_{ds} + L_{la} \frac{di^{e}_{ds}}{dt} + L_{md} \frac{di^{e}_{dm}}{dt} - \omega_{e}(L_{lm} i^{e}_{qs} + L_{mq} i^{e}_{qm}) \tag{22}$$

$$0 = r_{r} i^{e}_{qr} + L_{lr} \frac{di^{e}_{qr}}{dt} + L_{mq} \frac{di^{e}_{qm}}{dt} + \frac{\omega_{sl}}{k}(L_{lR} i^{e}_{dr} + L_{md} i^{e}_{dm}) \tag{23}$$

$$0 = r_{R} i^{e}_{dr} + L_{lR} \frac{di^{e}_{dr}}{dt} + L_{md} \frac{di^{e}_{dm}}{dt} - k * \omega_{sl}(L_{lr} i^{e}_{qr} + L_{mq} i^{e}_{qm}) \tag{24}$$

$$i^{e}_{qs} + i^{e}_{qr} = i^{e}_{qfe} + i^{e}_{qm} \tag{25}$$

$$i^{e}_{ds} + i^{e}_{dr} = i^{e}_{dfe} + i^{e}_{dm} \tag{26}$$

Where:

$$i^{e}_{dfe} = \frac{v^{e}_{qm}}{R_{qfe}}; \; i^{e}_{dfe} = \frac{v^{e}_{dm}}{R_{dfe}}$$

$$v^{e}_{dm} = -\frac{\omega_{e} L_{lr} L_{mqs}}{L_{r}} i^{e}_{qs} \tag{27}$$

$$v_{qm}^{e} = \omega_e L_{mds} i_{ds}^{e} \tag{28}$$

The losses in the motor are mainly:

a. Stator copper losses,
b. Rotor copper losses,
c. Core losses, and
d. Friction losses.

The total electrical losses can be expressed as follows

$$P_{losses} = P_{cu1} + P_{cu2} + P_{cor} \tag{29}$$

Where:

P_{cu1}: Stator copper losses
P_{cu2} : Rotor copper losses
P_{core}: Core losses

The stator copper losses of the two asymmetrical windings induction motor are caused by electric currents flowing through the stator windings. The core losses of the motor due to hysteresis and eddy currents in the stator. The total electrical losses of motor can be rewritten as:

$$P_{losses} = r_m i_{qs}^{e^2} + r_a i_{ds}^{e^2} + r_r i_{qr}^{e^2} + r_R i_{dr}^{e^2} + \frac{v_{qm}^{e^2}}{R_{qfe}} + \frac{v_{dm}^{e^2}}{R_{dfe}} \tag{30}$$

The total electrical losses are obtained as follows:

$$P_{losses} = \left[r_m + \frac{r_r L_{mqs}^2}{L_r^2} + \frac{\omega_e^2 L_{lr}^2 L_{mqs}^2}{L_r^2 R_{dfe}} \right] \left(\frac{T_e^2 L_r^2}{P^2 \left(\frac{L_{mds}}{K} \right)^2 \lambda_r^2} \right) + \left(r_a + \frac{\omega_e^2 L_{mds}^2}{R_{qfe}} \right) \frac{\lambda_r^2}{L_{mds}^2} \tag{31}$$

Where:

$\omega_e = \omega_r + \omega_{sl}$, and ω_{sl} is the slip speed r/sec.

$$\omega_{sl} = \frac{2 T_e * r_r}{P * \lambda_r^2} \tag{32}$$

Equation (31) is the electrical losses formula, which depends on rotor flux (λr) according to operating point (speed and load torque).

Total P_{losses} (TP_{losses}) = P_{losses} + friction power losses

= P_{in} - P_{out}

$$\text{Efficiency } (\eta) = Po / (Po + \text{Total } P_{losses}) \tag{33}$$

Where:
Friction power losses = F $*\omega_r^2$, and
Output power (Po) = $T_L * \omega_r$.
The equation (31) is the cost function, which depends on rotor flux (λ_r) according to the operating point. Figure 2 presents the distribution of losses in motor and its variation with the flux. As the flux reduces from the rated value, the core losses decrease, but the motor copper losses increase. However, the total losses decrease to a minimum value and then increase again. It is desirable to set the rotor flux at the optimal value, so that the efficiency is optimum.

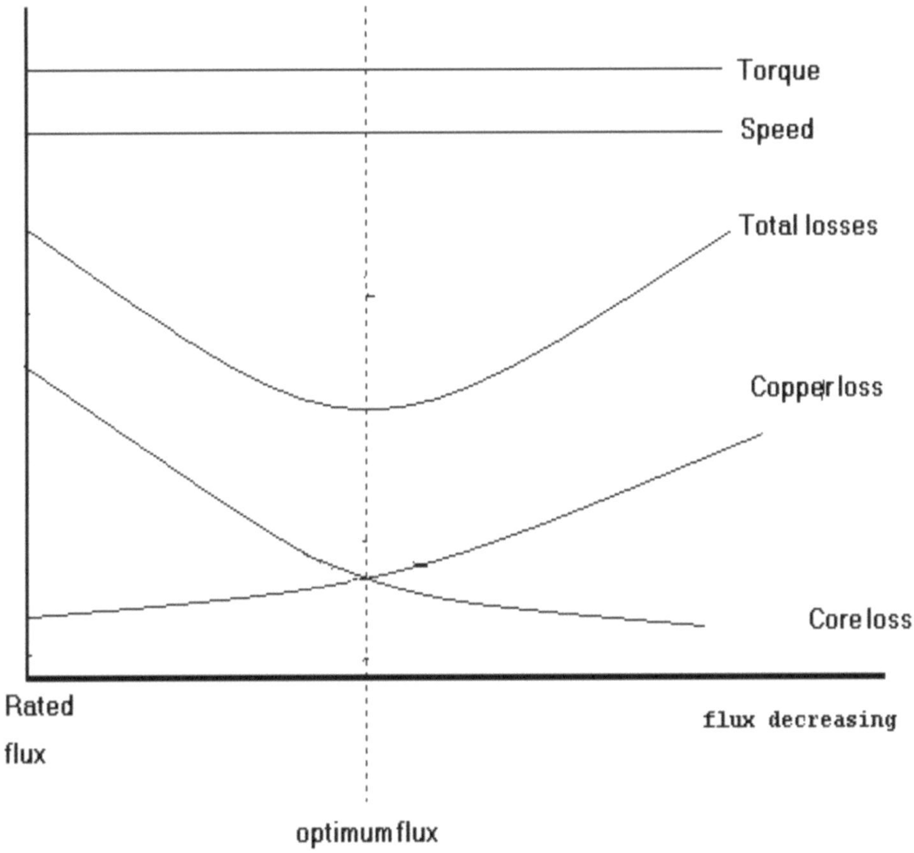

Figure 2. Losses variation of the motor with varying flux

The function of the losses minimization of the motor problem can be formulated as follows:
Minimize Total Losses which are a function of λ , Te , and ωr

- The losses formula is the cost function of PSO. The particle swarm optimization (PSO) technique is used for minimizing this cost function.
- The PSO is applied to evaluate the optimal rotor flux that minimizes the motor losses at any operating point. Figure 3 presents the flowchart of the execution of PSO, which evaluates the optimal flux by using MATLAB /SIMULINK.

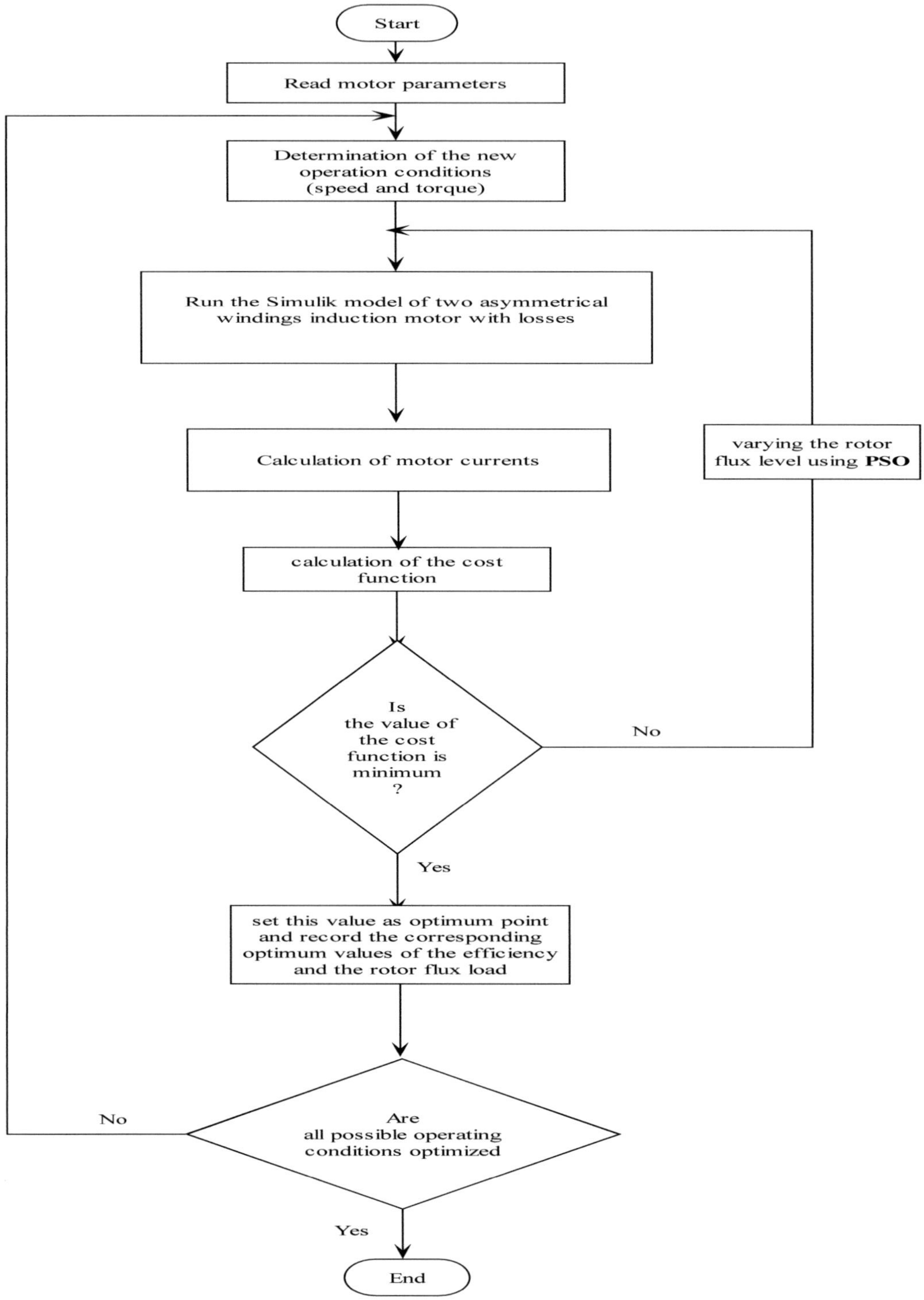

Figure 3. The flowchart of the execution of PSO

The optimal flux is the input of the indirect rotor flux oriented controller. The indirect field-oriented controller generates the required two reference currents to drive the motor corresponding to the optimal flux. These currents are fed to the hysteresis current controller of the two-level inverter. The switching pattern is generated according to the difference between the reference current and the load current through the hysteresis band. Figure 4 shows a whole control diagram of the proposed losses-minimization control system.

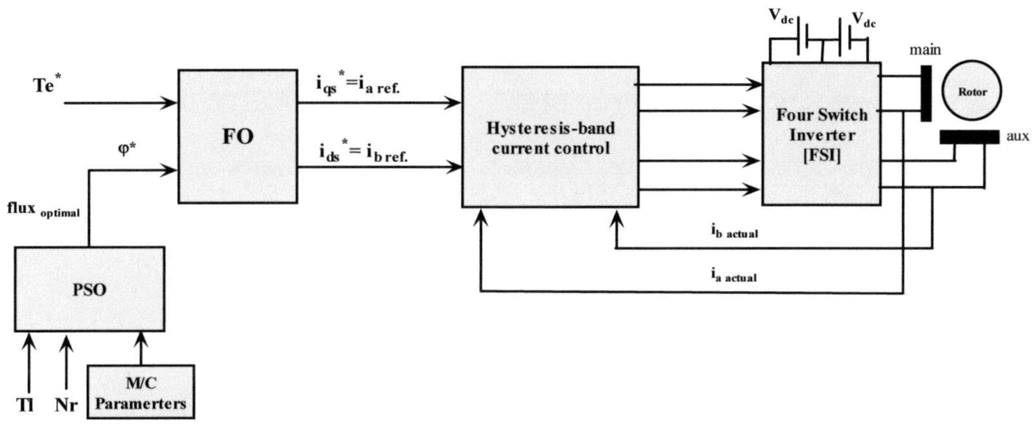

Figure 4. Proposed losses minimization control system

2.4 Simulation study with FOC

The motor used in this study has the following parameters, which were measured by using experimental tests . The FOC module is developed with closed loop speed control. The input of the FOC module is the reference speed and the rated rotor flux. The field-oriented controller generates the required reference currents to drive the motor as shown in fig.5. These currents are based on the flux level, which determines the value of direct current, and the reference torque, which determines the value of quadrature current. The reference torque is calculated according to the speed error. In this section, six-cases of motor operation with FOC are presented.

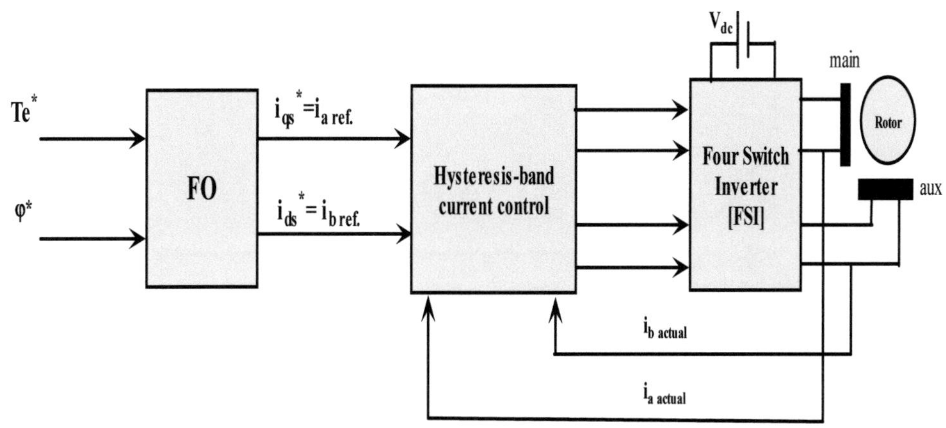

Figure 5. Block diagram of indirect rotor flux oriented control of the motor

Figure 6 shows the performance of the motor at case (1), where the motor is loaded by 0.25p.u. The control technique based on the PI controller has been developed. The proportional (Kp) and integral (Ki) constants of PI controller are chosen by trial and error. The speed-time curve for the motor is shown in fig. 6a. It is noticed that the speed oscillations are eliminated when the FOC is applied to the drive system.
Figure 6b illustrates the developed torque-time curve of the motor. In this figure, the pulsating torque is eliminated.

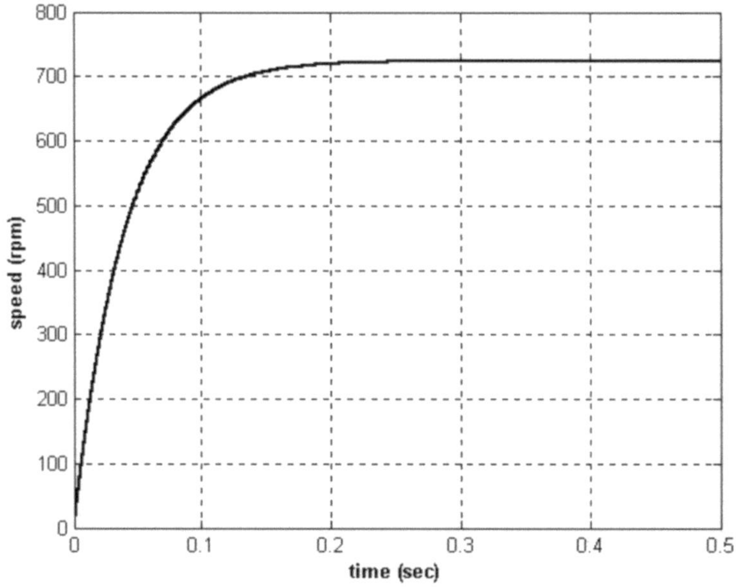

(a)

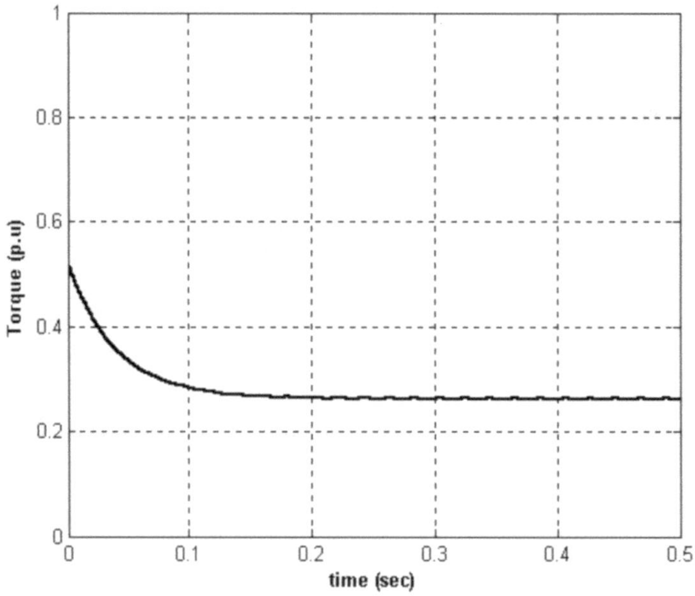

(b)

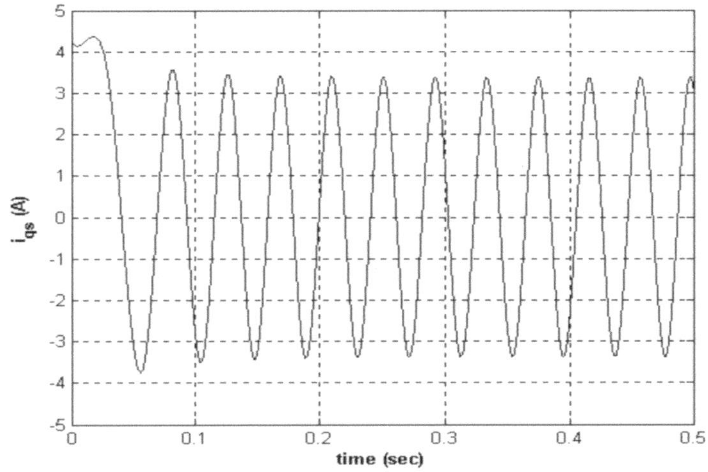

(c)

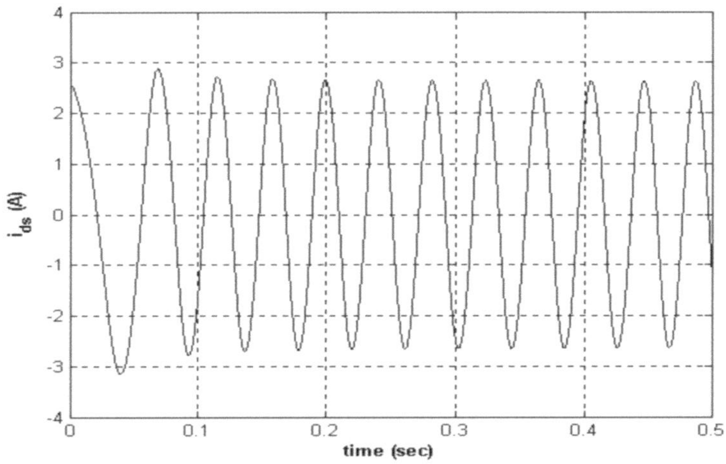

(d)

Figure 6. Simulation results of the motor at case (1), (a) Speed-time curve, (b) Torque-time curve, (c)The stator current in q-axis, (d) the stator current in d-axis

The efficiency is calculated from equation (33). Therefore, the efficiency is found to be equal to 33.85 %. The six-cases are summarized in Table 1.

Torque load (T_L) p.u	Speed (N)	Flux rated p.u	Efficiency (%)
0.25	0.5 N_{rated}	1	33.85
0.375	0.5 N_{rated}	1	36.51
0.5	0.5 N_{rated}	1	48.21
0.6125	0.5 N_{rated}	1	55.15
0.75	0.5 N_{rated}	1	60.175
1	0.5 N_{rated}	1	63.54

Table 1. The summary of the cases

It is clear that, the indirect field-oriented controller with a rated rotor flux generally exhibits poor efficiency of the motor at light load. If significant energy savings need to be obtained, it is necessary to optimize the efficiency of the motor. The optimum efficiency of the motor is obtained by the evaluation of the optimal rotor flux level.

2.5 Losses minimization control scheme

As swarm intelligence is based on real life observations of social animals (usually insects), it is more flexibility and robust than any traditional optimization methods. PSO method is a member of the wide category of swarm intelligence methods (SI). In this section, PSO is applied to evaluate the optimal flux that minimizes the motor losses. The problem can be formulated as follows:

Minimize Total Losses which are a function of λ, Te, and ωr

- The motor used as a two-asymmetrical windings induction motor. The parameters used are shown in Table 2 [10].

Parameters	Value
Population size	10
Max. iter	50
c1	0.5
c2	0.5
Max. weight	1.4
Min. weight	0.1
r1	[0,1]
r2	[0,1]
Lbnd	0.2
upbnd	2

Table 2. PSO Algorithm Parameters

A simplified block diagram of the proposed speed control scheme is shown in fig.7.

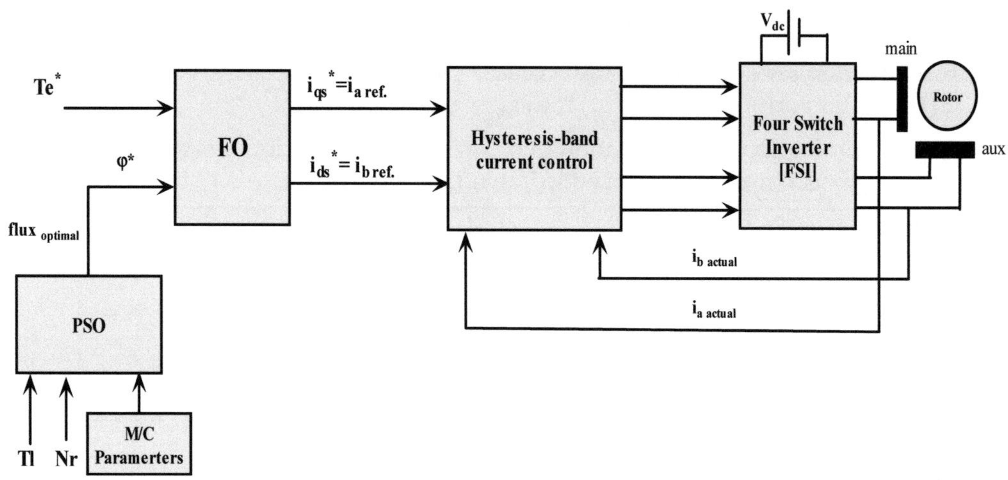

Figure 7. Proposed losses minimization control system

A Four-Switch Inverter (FSI) feeds the two-asymmetrical windings induction motor. The optimal flux is fed to the indirect rotor flux oriented control. The indirect field-oriented control generates the required reference current to drive the motor corresponding to this flux

2.6 Simulation results with FO based on PSO

The optimal rotor flux provides the maximum efficiency at any operating point, next the previous six-cases are repeated by using FOC based on PSO. PSO will evaluate the optimal rotor flux level. This flux is fed to the FOC module. Figure 8 shows the performance of the motor at case (1), when PSO is applied side-by-side FOC.

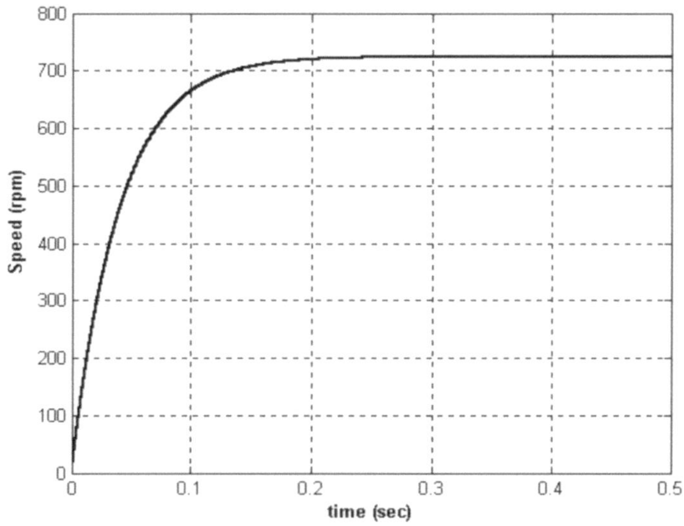

(a)

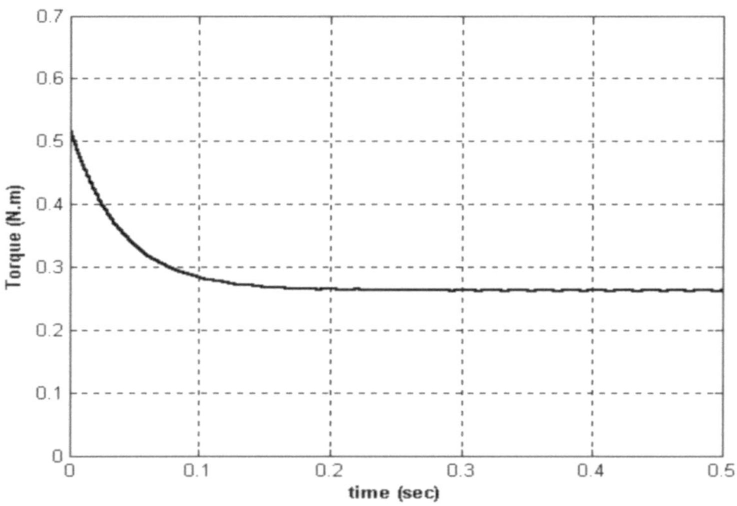

(b)

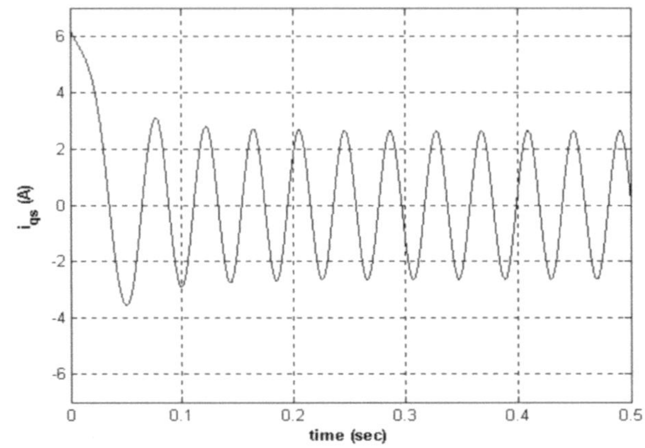

(c)

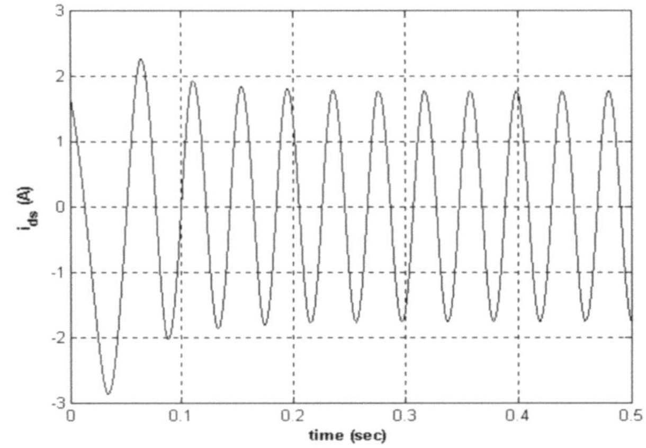

(d)

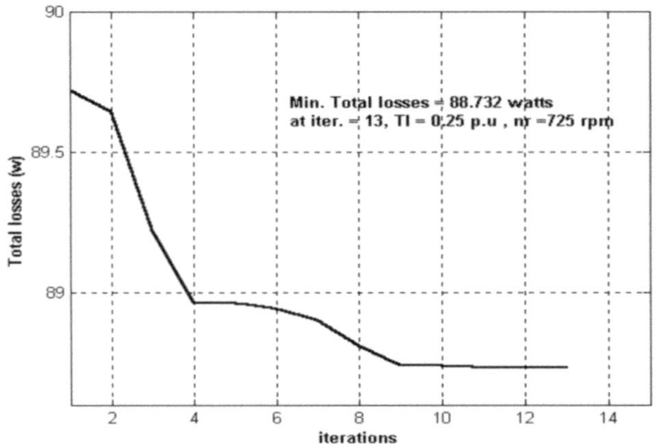

(e)

Figure 8. Simulation results of the motor at case (1). (a) Speed-time curve , (b)Torque-time curve, (c) The stator current in q-axis, (d) The stator current in d-axis, (e) Total Losses against iterations

It is noticed that, the PSO implementation increased the efficiency of the motor to 46.11% at half the rated speed. The six-cases are summarized in Table 3.

Torque load (TL) p.u	Speed (N)	Optimal flux(p.u)	Efficiency (%)
0.25	0.5 Nrated	0.636	46.11
0.375	0.5 Nrated	0.6906	49.15
0.5	0.5 Nrated	0.722	57.11
0.6125	0.5 Nrated	0.761	62.34
0.75	0.5 Nrated	0.8312	65.31
1	0.5 Nrated	0.8722	68.15

Table 3. The summary of the six-cases at optimal flux

In practical system, the flux level based on PSO at different operating points (torque and speed) is calculated and stored in a look up table. The use of look up table will enable the system to work in real time without any delay that might be needed to calculate the optimal point. The proposed controller would receive the operating point (torque and speed) and get the optimum flux from the look up table. It will generate the required reference current. It is noticed that, the efficiency with the FOC based on PSO method is higher than the efficiency with the FOC method only.

2.7 Experimental Results

To verify the validity of the proposed control scheme, a laboratory prototype is built and tested. The basic elements of the proposed experimental scheme are shown in fig. 9 and fig. 10. The experimental results of the motor are achieved by coupling the motor to an eddy current dynamometer. The experimental results are achieved using two control methods:

- Field-Oriented Control [FOC], and
- Field-Oriented Control [FOC] based on PSO.

The reference and the actual motor currents are fed to the hysteresis current controller. The switching pattern of the two-level four-switch inverter [FSI] is generated according to the difference between the reference currents and the load currents. Figure 11 shows the experimental results of the motor with FOC at case (1), where the motor is loaded by Tl = 0.25 p.u.

The measured input power of the motor is about 169 watts, and then the efficiency is calculated about 44.92 %, whereas the efficiency with FOC is 32.30 %. It is noticed that, the PSO implementation increased the efficiency of the motor by 12.62 %. The cases are summarized in Table 4 as follows.

Cases	FOC			FOC with PSO		
	Flux p.u	Power Input	η (%)	Flux p.u	Power Input	η (%)
(1)	1	235	32.3	0.636	169	44.92
(2)	1	323	35.2	0.690	243	47.06

Table 5 the summary of the two-cases

The improvement of the efficiency in case (1) is around 12.62 % when PSO is applied. The improvement of the efficiency in case (2) is around 11.84 %, where the motor is loaded by Tl = 0.375 p.u. These results demonstrate that, the FOC based on PSO method saves more energy than conventional FOC method. Thus, the efficiency with PSO is improved than it's at FOC.

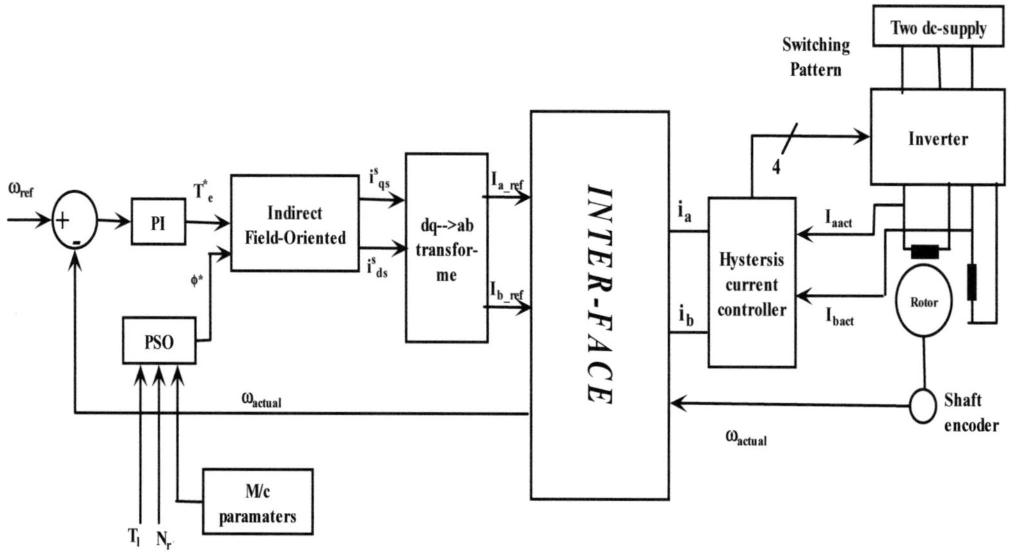

Figure 9. Block diagram of the proposed drive system

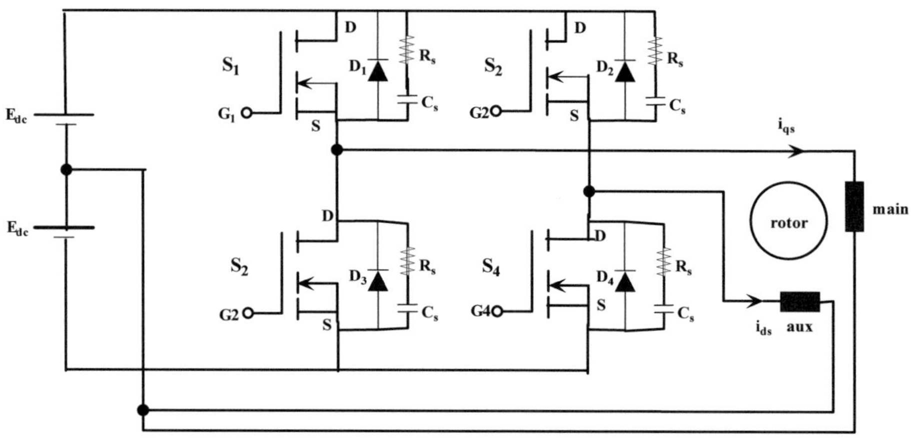

Figure 10. The power circuit of Four Switch inverter [FSI]

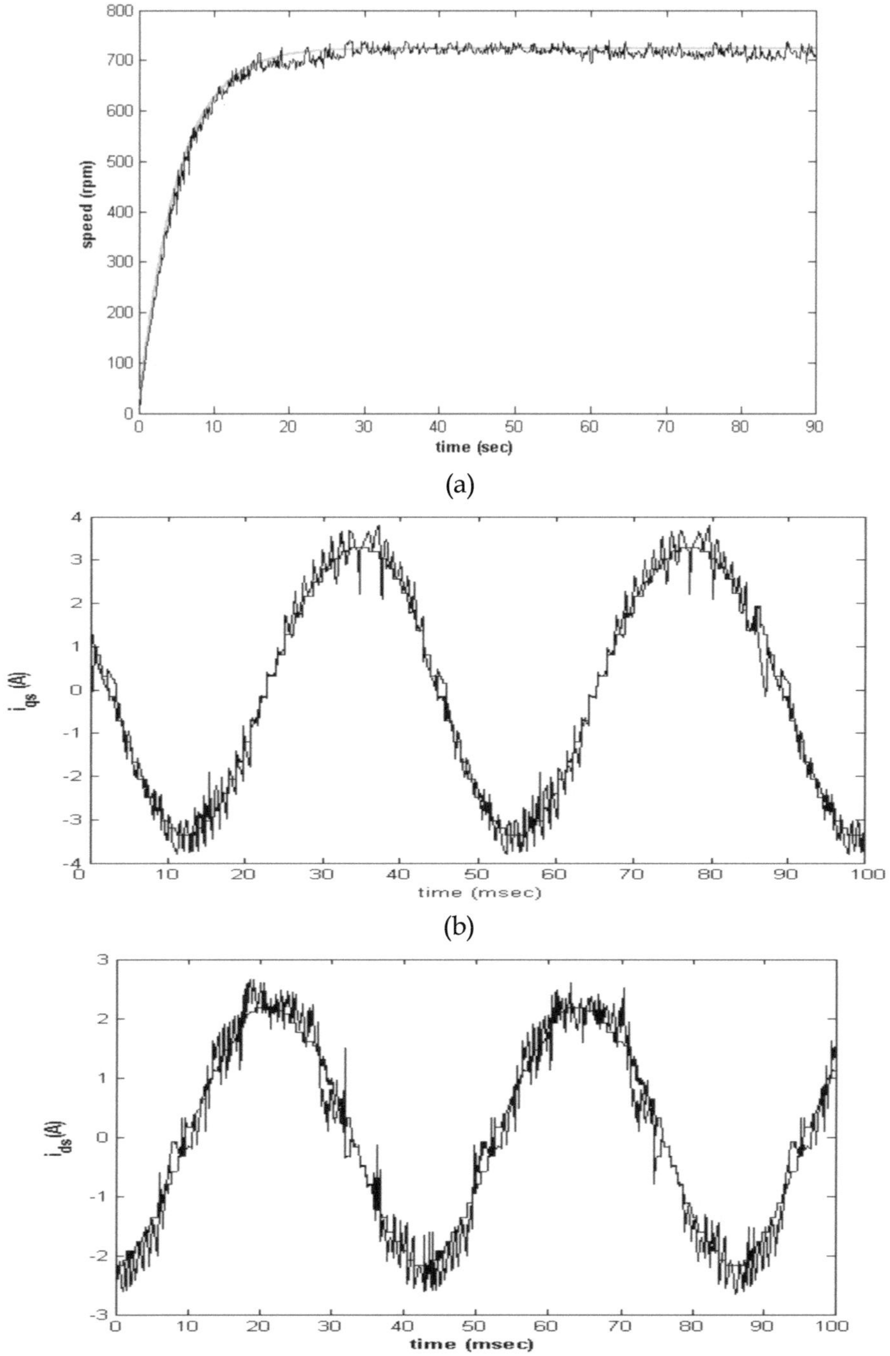

(c)

Figure 11. Experimental results of FOC method. (a)The reference and actual speed, (b) The reference and actual current in q-axis, (c) The reference and actual current in d-axis

The measured total input power of the motor is 235 watts. The efficiency is calculated from equation (33). The efficiency is found to be equal to 32.30 %. Figure 11 shows the experimental result of the motor with FOC based on PSO at case (1).

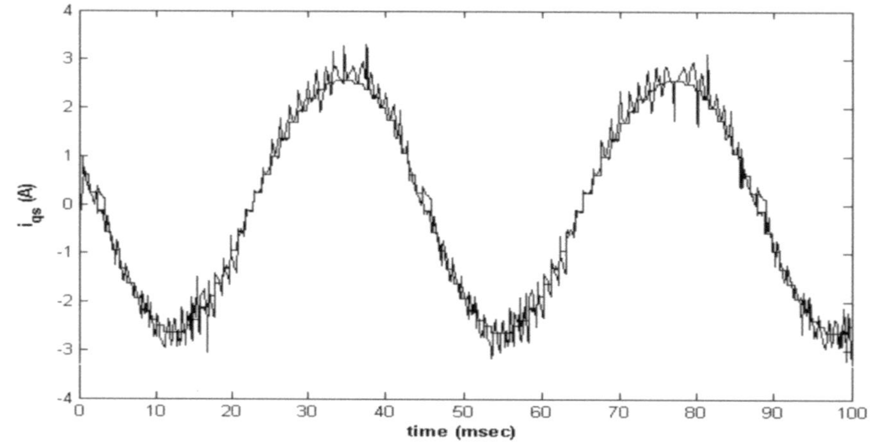

(a)

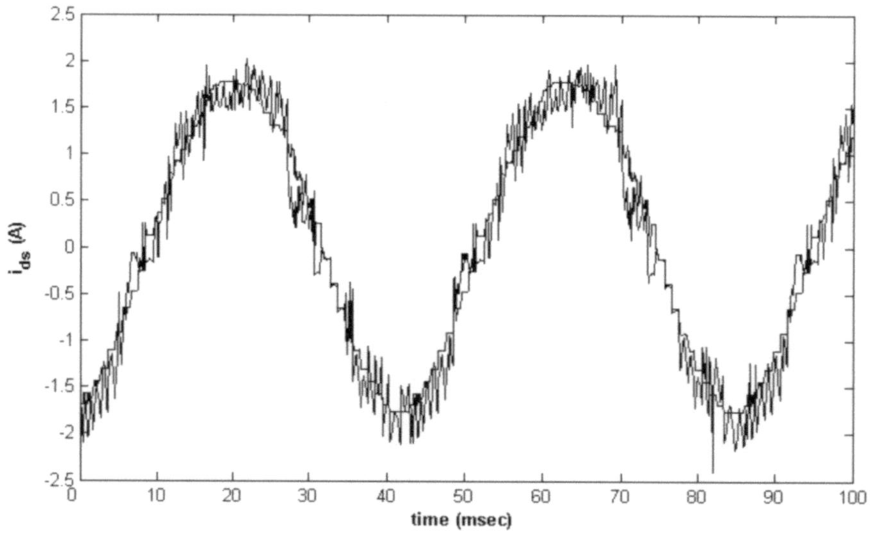

(b)

Figure 11. Experimental results of FOC method based on PSO. (a) The reference and actual current in q-axis, (b)The reference and actual current in d-axis

3. Maximum Efficiency and Minimum Operating Cost of Induction motors

This section presents another application of PSO for losses and operating cost minimization control in the induction motor drives. In this paper, two strategies for induction motor speed control are proposed. Those two strategies are based on PSO and called Maximum

Efficiency Strategy and Minimum Operating Cost Strategy. The proposed technique is based on the principle that the flux level in the machine can be adjusted to give the minimum amount of losses and minimum operating cost for a given value of speed and load torque. The main advantages of the proposed technique are; its simple structure and its straightforward maximization of induction motor efficiency and its operating cost for a given load torque. As will be demonstrated, PSO is so efficient in finding the optimum operating machine's flux level. The optimum flux level is a function of the machine operating point.

Simulation results show that a considerable energy and cost savings are achieved in comparison with the conventional method of operation under the condition of constant voltage to frequency ratio [5, 6].

It is estimated that, electric machines consume more than 50% of the world electric energy generated. Improving efficiency in electric drives is important, mainly, for two reasons: economic saving and reduction of environmental pollution. Induction motors have a high efficiency at rated speed and torque. However, at light loads, the iron losses increase dramatically, reducing considerably the efficiency. The main induction motor losses are usually split into 5 components: stator copper losses, rotor copper losses, iron losses, mechanical losses, and stray losses.

The efficiency that decreases with increasing losses can be improved by minimizing the losses. Copper losses reduce with decreasing the stator and the rotor currents, while the core losses essentially increase with increasing air-gap flux density. A study of the copper and core losses components reveals that their trends conflict. When the core losses increase, the copper losses tends to decrease. However, for a given load torque, there is an air-gap flux density at which the total losses is minimized. Hence, electrical losses minimization process ultimately comes down to the selection of the appropriate air-gap flux density of operation. Since the air-gap flux density must be variable when the load is changing, control schemes in which the (rotor, air-gap) flux linkage is constant will yield sub-optimal efficiency operation especially when the load is light. Then to improve the motor efficiency, the flux must be reduced when it operates under light load conditions by obtaining a balance between copper and iron losses.

The challenge to engineers, however, is to be able to predict the appropriate flux values at any operating points over the complete torque and speed range which will minimize the machines losses, hence maximizing the efficiency. In general, there are three different approaches to improve the induction motor efficiency especially under light-load conditions.

a. **Losses Model Controller (LMC)**

This controller depends on a motor losses model to compute the optimum flux analytically. The main advantage of this approach is its simplicity and it does not require extra hardware. In addition, it provides smooth and fast adaptation of the flux, and may offer optimal performance during transient operation. However, the main problem of this approach is that it requires the exact values of machine parameters. These parameters include the core losses and the main inductance flux saturation, which are unknown to the users and change considerably with temperature, saturation, and skin effect. In addition, these parameters may vary due to changes in the operating conditions. However, with continuing improvement of evolutionary parameter determination algorithms, the disadvantages of motor parameters dependency are slowly disappearing.

b. **Search Controller (SC)**

This controller measures the input power of the machine drive regularly at fixed time intervals and searches for the flux value, which results in minimum power input for given values of speed and load torque [5]. This particular method does not demand knowledge of the machine parameters and the search procedure is simple to implement.
However, some disadvantages appear in practice, such as continuous disturbances in the torque, slow adaptation (7sec.), difficulties in tuning the algorithm for a given application, and the need for precise load information. In addition, the precision of the measurements may be poor due to signal noise and disturbances. This in turn may cause the SC method to give undesirable control performance. Moreover, nominal flux is applied in transient state and is tuned after the system reaches steady state to an optimal value by numerous increments, thus lengthening the optimization process. Therefore, the SC technique may be slow in obtaining the optimal point. In addition, in real systems, it may not reach a steady state and so cause oscillations in the air gap flux that result in undesirable torque disturbances. For these reasons, this is not a good method in industrial drives.

c. **Look Up Table Scheme**

It gives the optimal flux level at different operating points. This table, however, requires costly and time-consuming prior measurements for each motor . In this section, a new control strategy uses the loss model controller based on PSO is proposed. This strategy is simple in structure and has the straightforward goal of maximizing the efficiency for a given load torque. The resulting induction motor efficiency is reasonably close to optimal. It is well known that the presence of uncertainties ,the rotor resistance, for instance makes the result no more optimal. Digital computer simulation results are obtained to demonstrate the effectiveness of the proposed method.

3.1 Differences between PSO and Other Evolutionary Computation (EC) Techniques

The most striking difference between PSO and the other evolutionary algorithms is that PSO chooses the path of cooperation over competition. The other algorithms commonly use some form of decimation, survival of the fittest. In contrast, the PSO population is stable and individuals are not destroyed or created. Individuals are influenced by the best performance of their neighbors. Individuals eventually converge on optimal points in the problem domain. In addition, the PSO traditionally does not have genetic operators like crossover between individuals and mutation, and other individuals never substitute particles during the run. Instead, the PSO refines its search by attracting the particles to positions with good solutions. Moreover, compared with genetic algorithms (GAs), the information sharing mechanism in PSO is significantly different. In GAs, chromosomes share information with each other. So the whole population moves like a one group towards an optimal area. In PSO, only Gbest (or Pbest) gives out the information to others. It is a one-way information sharing mechanism. The evolution only looks for the best solution. In PSO, all the particles tend to converge to the best solution quickly, comparing with GA, even in the local version in most cases [7, 8].

3.2 Definition of Operating Strategies

The following definitions are useful in subsequent analyses. Referring to the analysis of the induction motor presented in [3], the per-unit frequency is

$$a = \frac{\omega_e}{\omega_b} = \frac{\omega_s + \omega_r}{\omega_b} \tag{34}$$

The slip is defined by

$$s = \frac{\omega_s}{\omega_e} = \frac{\omega_s}{\omega_s + \omega_r} \tag{35}$$

The rotor current is given by

$$I_r' = \frac{\phi_m}{\sqrt{\left(\frac{r_r'}{sa}\right)^2 + X_{lr}'^2}} \tag{36}$$

The electromagnetic torque is given by

$$T_e = \frac{\left(\frac{r_r'}{sa}\right)}{\left(\frac{r_r'}{sa}\right)^2 + X_{lr}'^2}\phi_m^2 \tag{37}$$

The stator current is related to the air gap flux and the electromagnetic torque as:

$$I_s = \sqrt{\left(s_1\phi_m + s_2\phi_m^3 + s_3\phi_m^5\right)^2 + C_L\frac{T_e^2}{\phi_m^2}} \tag{38}$$

Where

$$C_L = 1 + 2 \times \frac{x_{lr}'}{x_m}$$

The air gap flux is related to the electromagnetic torque as:

$$\phi_m = \sqrt{\frac{sa}{r_r'}}\sqrt{\left(\frac{r_r'}{sa}\right)^2 + x_{lr}'^2}\sqrt{T_e} \tag{39}$$

The efficiency is defined as the output power divided by the electric power supplied to the stator (inverter losses are included):

$$\eta = \frac{P_{out}}{P_{in}} \tag{40}$$

3.1.1 Maximum Efficiency Strategy

In MES (Maximum Efficiency Strategy), the slip frequency is adjusted so that the efficiency of the induction motor drive system is maximized.
The induction motor losses are the following:

1. **Copper losses:** these are due to flow of the electric current through the stator and rotor windings and are given by:

$$P_{cu} = r_s I_s^2 + r_r' I_r'^2 \tag{41}$$

2. **Iron losses**: these are the losses due to eddy current and hysteresis, given by

$$P_{core} = k_e\left(1 + s^2\right) a^2 \ \phi_m^2 + k_h\left(1 + s\right) a \ \phi_m^2 \tag{42}$$

3. **Stray losses**: these arise on the copper and iron of the motor and are given by:

$$P_s = C_{str} \ \omega_r^2 \ I_r'^2 \tag{43}$$

4. **Mechanical losses**: these are due to the friction of the machine rotor with the bearings and are given by

$$P_{f\omega} = C_{f\omega} \ \omega_r^2 \tag{44}$$

5. **Inverter losses :** The approximate inverter loss as a function of stator current is given by:

$$P_{inv} = K_{1inv} \ i_s^2 + K_{2inv} \ i_s \tag{45}$$

Where: K_{1inv}, K_{2inv} are coefficients determined by the electrical characteristics of a switching element where: K_{1inv}= 3.1307e-005, K_{2inv}=0.0250.
The total power losses are expressed as:

$$\begin{aligned} P_{losses} &= P_{cu} + P_{core} + P_s + P_{fw} + P_{inv} = \left[r_s I_s^2 + r_r' I_r'^2\right] + \\ &+ \left[k_e\left(1 + s^2\right) a^2 \ \phi_m^2\right] + \left[k_h\left(1 + s\right) a \ \phi_m^2\right] + \left[C_{str} \ \omega_r^2 \ I_r'^2\right] + \\ &+ \left[C_{f\omega} \ \omega_r^2\right] + \left[K_{1inv} \ i_s^2 + K_{2inv} \ i_s\right] \end{aligned} \tag{46}$$

The output power is given by:

$$P_{out} = T_l \times \omega_r \tag{47}$$

The input power is given by:

$$\begin{aligned} P_{in} = P_{out} + P_{losses} &= \left[r_s I_s^2 + r_r' I_r'^2\right] + \left[k_e\left(1 + s^2\right) a^2\ \phi_m^2\right] + \\ &+ \left[k_h\left(1 + s\right) a\ \phi_m^2\right] + \left[C_{str}\ \omega_r^2\ I_r'^2\right] + \left[C_{f\omega}\ \omega_r^2\right] + \\ &+ \left[K_{1inv}\ i_s^2 + K_{2inv}\ i_s\right] + T_l \times \omega_r \end{aligned} \tag{48}$$

The efficiency is expressed as:

$$\eta = \frac{\left(T_e \times \omega_r\right)}{\left(\begin{aligned} &\left(r_s I_s^2 + r_r' I_r'^2\right) + \left(k_e\left(1 + s^2\right) a^2\ \phi_m^2\right) + \\ &+ \left(k_h\left(1 + s\right) a\ \phi_m^2\right) + \left(C_{str}\ \omega_r^2\ I_r'^2\right) + \\ &+ \left(C_{f\omega}\ \omega_r^2\right) + \left(K_{1inv}\ i_s^2 + K_{2inv}\ i_s\right) + \left(T_l \times \omega_r\right) \end{aligned}\right)} \tag{49}$$

The efficiency maximization of the induction motor problem can be formulated as follows:

$$\text{Maximize}\ \ \eta\left(T_e, \omega_s, \omega_r\right) \tag{50}$$

The maximization should observe the fact that the amplitude of the stator current and flux cannot exceed their specified maximum point.

3.2.2 Minimum Operating Cost Strategy

In Minimum Operating cost Strategy (MOCS), the slip frequency is adjusted so that the operating cost of the induction motor is minimized. The operating cost of the induction machine should be calculated over the whole life cycle of the machine. That calculation can be made to evaluate the cost of the consumed electrical energy. The value of average energy cost considering the power factor penalties can be determined by the following stages:

1. If $0 \le PF < 0.7$

$$C = C_0\left[1 + \left(\frac{0.9 - PF}{0.01}\right) \times \frac{1}{100}\right] \tag{51}$$

2. If 0.7 ≤ PF ≤ 0.92, If PF ≥ 0.9, PF = 0.9

$$C = C_0 \left[1 + \left(\frac{0.9 - PF}{0.01} \right) \times \frac{0.5}{100} \right] \quad (52)$$

3. If 0.9 ≤ PF ≤ 1, If 0.95 ≤ PF ≤ 1, PF = 0.95

$$C = C_0 \left[1 + \left(\frac{0.9 - PF}{0.01} \right) \times \frac{0.5}{100} \right] \quad (53)$$

If the average energy cost C is calculated, it can be used to establish the present value of losses. The total cost of the machine is the sum of its initial cost plus the present worth value of losses and maintenance costs.

$$PW_L = C \times T \times N \times P_{out} \times \left[\frac{1}{\eta} - 1 \right] \quad (54)$$

Where:
PW_L = present worth value of losses
C_0 = energy cost (L.E/KwH), L.E is the Egyptian Pound
C = modified energy cost (L.E/KwH)
T = running time per year (Hrs / year)
N = evaluation life (years)
P_{out} = the output power (Kwatt)
η = the efficiency
The operating cost minimization of the induction motor problem can be formulated as follows:

$$\text{Minimize} \quad PW_L(T_e, \omega_s, \omega_r) \quad (55)$$

The optimization in each case should observe the fact that the amplitude of the stator current and flux cannot exceed their specified maximum.

3.3 Simulation Results

The simulation is carried out on a three-phase, 380 V, 1-HP, 50 Hz, and 4-pole, squirrel cage induction motor. The motor parameters are R_s=0.0598, X_{ls}=0.0364, X_m=0.8564, X_{lr}=0.0546, R_r=0.0403, K_e=0.0380, K_h=0.0380, C_{str} =0.0150, Cfw=0.0093, S1=1.07, S_2=-0.69, S_3=0.77. For cost analysis, the following values were assumed: C_0=0.05, N=15, T=8000. Figure 12 shows the efficiency variation with respect to the rotor and slip speed at various levels of load torque. At certain load torque and rotor speed, a certain value of slip frequency at which the maximum efficiency occurs is optimal. The task of PSO controller is to find that value of slip at which the maximum efficiency occurs. At certain load torque and rotor speed, the PSO controller determines the slip frequency ω_s at which the maximum efficiency and minimum operating cost occur. The block diagram of the optimization process based on

PSO is shown in fig.13. In the proposed controller, the PSO algorithm receives the rotor speed, load torque, and the fitness function (efficiency equation).
The PSO determines the slip frequency at which the maximum efficiency or minimum operating cost occurs at that rotor speed and load torque. Figures (14) and (15) show the efficiency of the machine as a function of the load torque and rotor speed under constant voltage to frequency ratio strategy and field oriented control strategy. From these figures it is obvious that, the efficiency decreases substantially when either the torque or rotor speed is small. On the other hand, fig. 16 shows the efficiency versus the load torque and rotor speed using the proposed technique (MES). This figure shows a great improving in efficiency especially at light loads and small rotor speed. To observe the improvements in efficiency using the suggested PSO controller, fig. 17 shows the efficiency of the selected machine for all operating conditions using conventional methods (constant voltage to frequency ratio, field oriented control strategy) and using the proposed PSO controller at different rotor speed levels, $W_r = 0.2$ PU, and $W_r = 1$ PU respectively. This figure shows that a considerable energy saving is achieved in comparison with the conventional method (field oriented control strategy and constant voltage to frequency ratio). Table (1) shows the efficiency comparison using few examples of operating points.

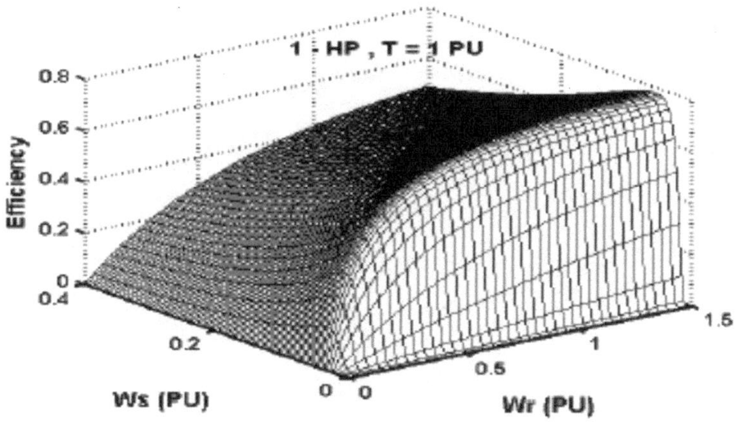

Figure 12. Efficiency versus rotor speed and slip speed at load torque $T_L = 1$ PU

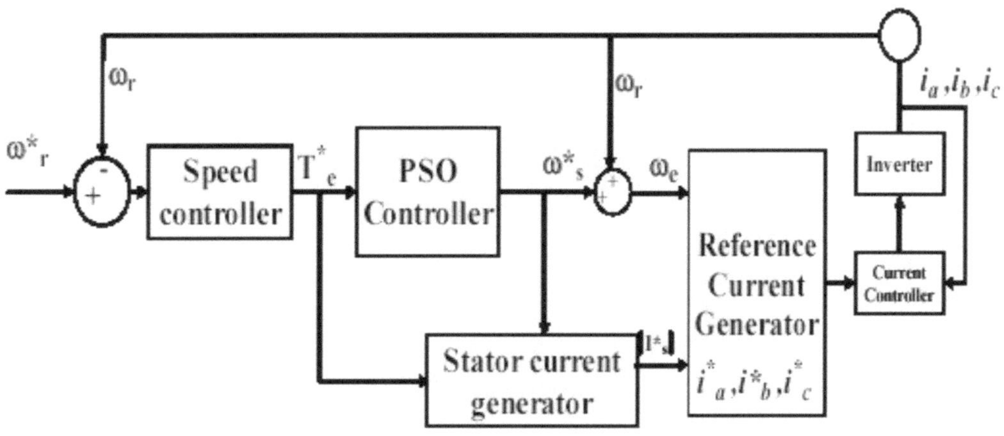

Figure 13. The proposed drive system based on PSO

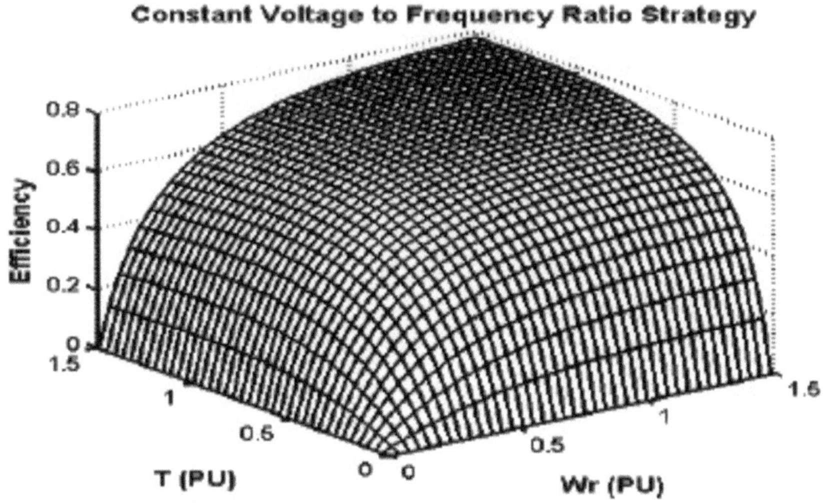

Figure 14. Efficiency versus rotor speed and load torque under constant voltage to frequency ratio strategy

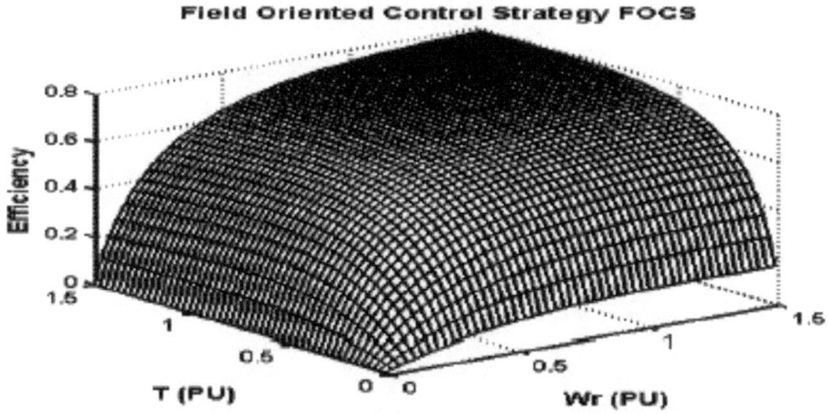

Figure 15. Efficiency versus rotor speed and load torque under field Oriented control strategy

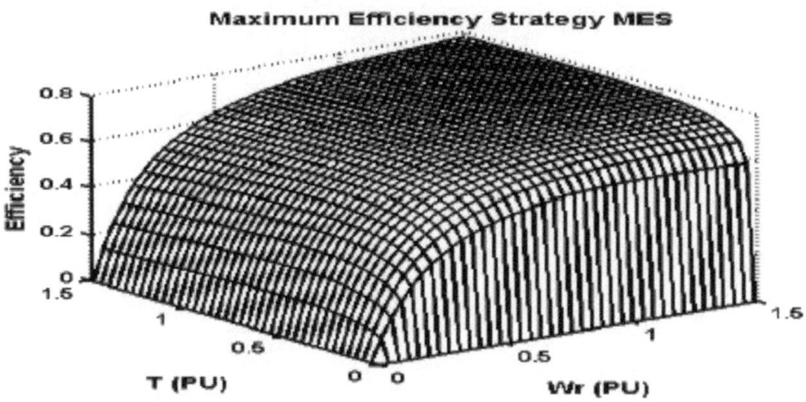

Figure 8. Efficiency versus rotor speed and load torque using the Proposed PSO controller (MES)

Efficiency comparison for $\omega_r = 1$ PU				
T (PU)	Constant voltage to frequency ratio	Field oriented control	Maximum efficiency strategy	Minimum Operating Cost Strategy
0.2	0.5003	0.5330	0.7217	0.7193
0.4	0.6482	0.6730	0.7506	0.7485
0.6	0.7100	0.7271	0.7598	0.7584
0.8	0.7384	0.7494	0.7618	0.7608
1	0.7508	0.7569	0.7603	0.7595
1.2	0.7544	0.7566	0.7568	0.7562

Table 1. Some examples of efficiency comparison under different Load torque levels and $W_r = 1$ PU

Figure (10) compares the efficiency of the induction motor drive system under the maximum efficiency strategy with the minimum operating cost strategy at $W_r = 0.2$ PU and $W_r = 1$ PU, respectively. It is obvious from the figure that the efficiency is almost the same for both strategies for all operating points. On the other hand, fig. 11 shows the percentage of the operating cost saving for the two strategies for $W_r = 0.2$ and $W_r = 1$ PU respectively. The percentage of the operating cost saving is calculated according to the following equation:

$$Saving = \frac{PW_{IMOCS} - PW_{IMES}}{PW_{IMES}} \times 100\ \% \quad (56)$$

Where: PW_{IMES} is the present worth value of losses under MES, and PW_{IMOCS} is the present worth value of losses under MOCS. It is obvious from fig (11) that the saving has a noticeable value especially at light loads and rated speed that can as high as 11.2 %. It is clear that the PWL using the minimum operating cost strategy is less than the PWL using the maximum efficiency strategy. This difference in operating cost is shown in table (2). The reason for that difference is due to the difference in their power factor values. The difference in power factor values is shown in fig.12.

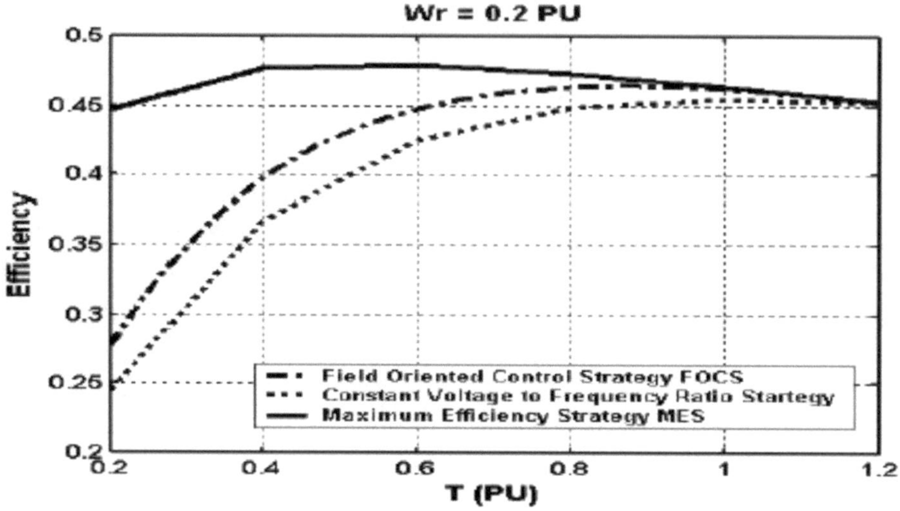

(a)

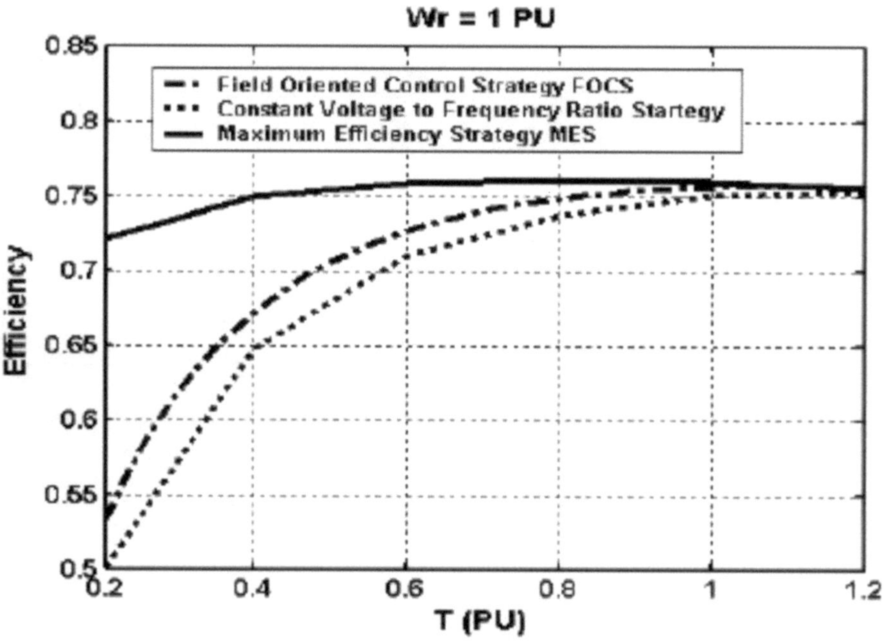

(b)

Figure 9. The efficiency of the induction motor using the maximum efficiency strategy compared with the efficiency using the conventional methods (field oriented control strategy and constant voltage to frequency ratio) for different rotor speed levels. (a) W_r = 0.2 PU, (b) W_r= 1 PU

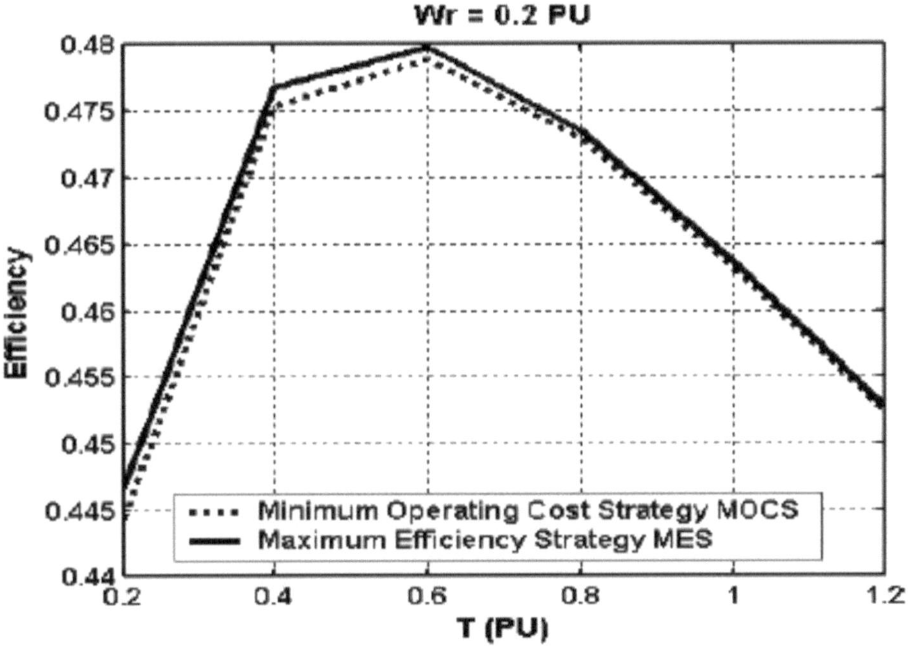

(a)

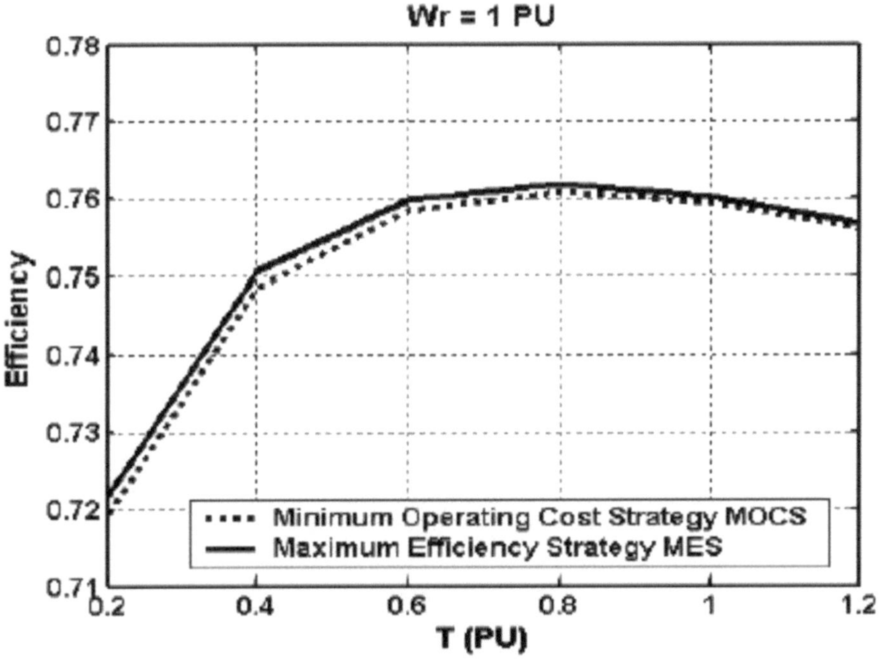

Figure 10. the efficiency of the induction motor using the maximum efficiency strategy compared with the efficiency using minimum operating cost strategy for different rotor speed levels. (a) Wr = 0.2 PU, (b) Wr= 1 PU

Operating cost comparison (L.E) for $\omega_r = 1$ PU				
T (PU)	Constant voltage to frequency ratio	Field oriented control	Maximum efficiency strategy	Minimum Operating Cost Strategy
0.2	1496494	1300954	432108	383515
0.4	1486907	1308896	742514	661747
0.6	1547089	1391272	1040340	937485
0.8	1669655	1539698	1343879	1224637
1	1848908	1748378	1535790	1529263
1.2	1914440	1870885	1860518	1854120

Table 2. Some examples of operating cost comparison under different load torque levels and Wr = 1 PU

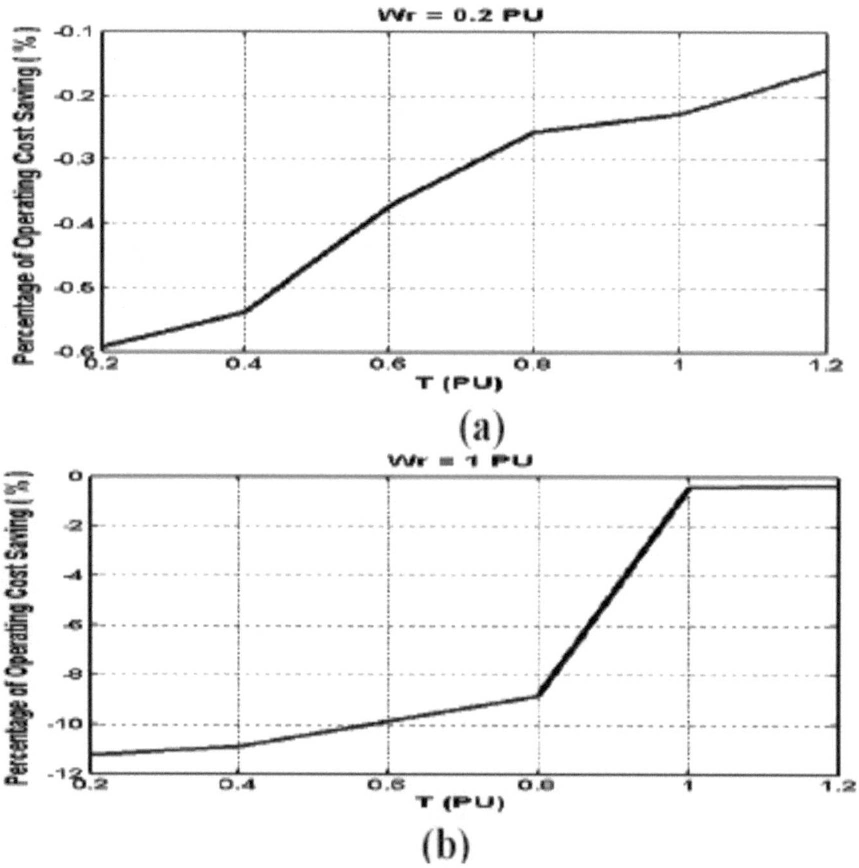

Figure 11. the PW_L using maximum efficiency strategy compared with the PWL using the minimum operating cost strategy for different rotor speed levels.
(a) Wr = 0.2 PU, (b) Wr= 1 PU

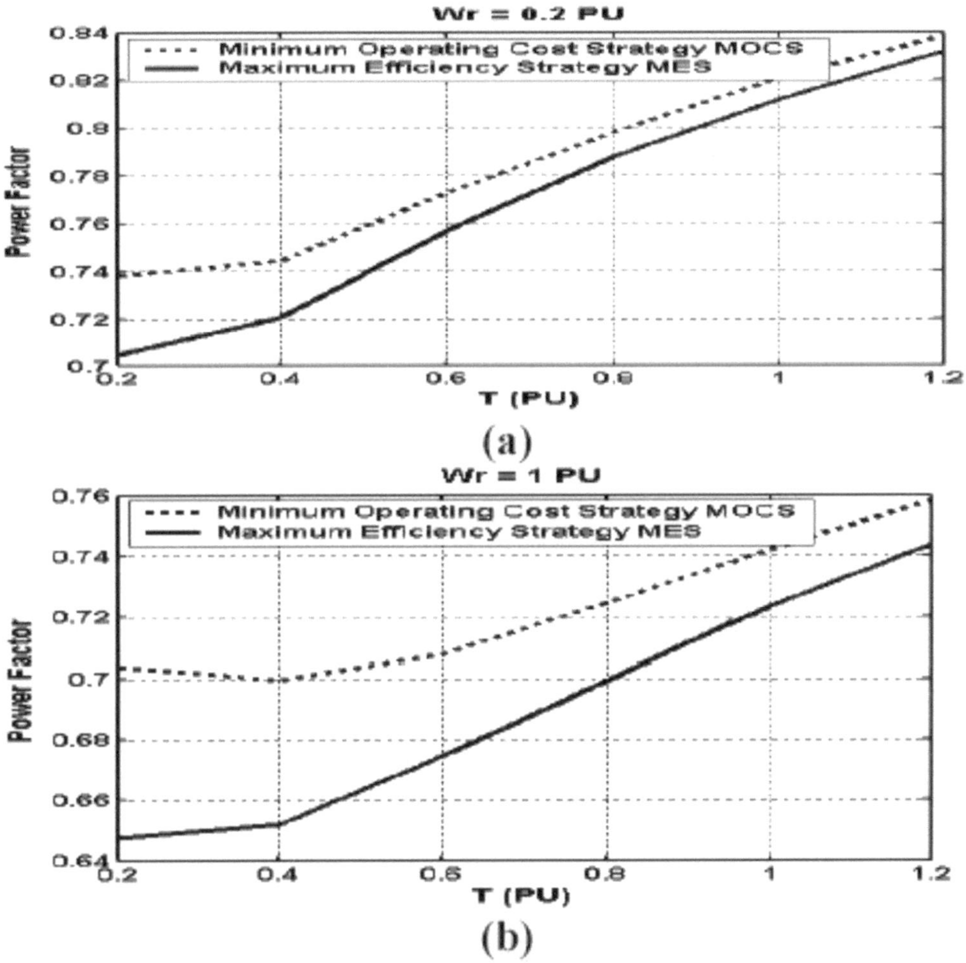

Figure 12. The Power factor of the induction motor using the maximum efficiency strategy compared with the Power factor using minimum operating cost strategy for different rotor speed levels, (a) Wr = 0.2 PU, (b) Wr= 1 PU

Finally, this section presents the application of PSO for losses and operating cost minimization control in the induction motor drives. Two strategies for induction motor speed control are proposed. Those two strategies are based on PSO and called Maximum Efficiency Strategy and Minimum Operating Cost Strategy. The proposed PSO-controller adaptively adjusts the slip frequency such that the drive system is operated at the minimum loss and minimum operating cost. It was found that the optimal system slip changes with variations in speed and load torque. When comparing the proposed strategy with the conventional methods field oriented control strategy and constant voltage to frequency ratio), It was found that a significant efficiency improvement It was found that a significant efficiency improvement is found at light loads for all speeds. On the other hand, small efficiency improvement is achieved at near rated loads. Finally, when comparing the MOCS with MES, it was found that, the saving in PW_L using the MOCS is greater than that of the MES, especially at light loads and rated speed.

4. Particle Swarm Optimized Direct Torque Control of Induction Motors

The flux and torque hysteresis bands are the only adjustable parameters in direct torque control (DTC) of induction motors. Their selection greatly influences the inverter switching loss, motor harmonic loss and motor torque ripples, which are major performance criteria. In this section, the effects of flux and torque hysteresis bands on these criteria are investigated and optimized via the minimization, by the particle swarm optimization (PSO) technique, of a suitably selected cost function. A DTC control strategy with variable hysteresis bands, which improves the drive performance compared to the classical DTC, is proposed. Online operating Artificial Neural Networks (ANNs) use the offline optimum values obtained by PSO, to modify the hysteresis bands in order to improve the performance. The implementation of the proposed scheme is illustrated by simulation results [9].

In this section, the effects of flux and torque hysteresis bands on inverter switching loss, motor harmonic loss and motor torque ripple of induction motor are investigated. To reduce speed and torque ripples it is desirable to make the hysteresis band as small as possible, thus increasing the switching frequency, which results in reduced efficiency of the drive by enlarging the inverter switching and motor harmonic losses. Hence, these hysteresis bands should be optimized in order to achieve a suitable compromise between efficiency and dynamic performance. In order to find their optimum values at each operating condition, a cost function combining losses and torque ripples is defined and optimized. A DTC control strategy with variable hysteresis bands is proposed, such that the optimum hysteresis band values are used at each operating condition. The proposed method combines the emerging Particle Swarm Optimization (PSO) for offline optimization of the cost function and the ANN technique for online determination of the suitable hysteresis band values at the operating point.

4.1 DTC Performance Cost Function Optimization

The design of the DTC involves the selection of suitable hysteresis band. In this section, the hysteresis band is selected so that it results in an optimal performance cost function. Since the optimal hysteresis bands depend on the operating conditions, the optimization procedure is implemented via PSO at several operating conditions that covers the possible working conditions of the drive system [9, 10, 11]. Fig. 13 shows the flow chart of the optimization method. A computer model of the overall drive system has been developed using MATLAB/SIMULINK software. The simulations have been performed for a 10 Hp induction motor (the motor parameters are given in the appendix). The cost function is expressed as follows:

$$C(\Delta Te,\ \Delta\lambda s)= W_1\, P_{IL} + W_2\, P_c + W_3 \Delta T \tag{57}$$

Where:

ΔTe: is the torque hysteresis band,

$\Delta\lambda s$: is the flux hysteresis band,

P_{IL}: is inverter switching loss,

P_C: is core loss, and

W_i : is a designer specified weighting factor.

The weighting terms are selected to be $W_1 = 0.2$, $W_2 = 0.2$ and $W_3 = 0.6$. The reduction of torque ripples is the most important objective of the optimization. In the thirty-six different operating conditions, corresponding to the combination of six different speed and six different load torque values, are considered. The harmonic spectrum of the motor stator flux is calculated up to 30th harmonic and the Simulink model is run for 2.5 seconds. For PSO, the following parameters are used: Size of the swarm = 10, maximum number of iterations = 100, maximum inertia weight's value = 1.2, minimum inertia weight's value = 0.1, $C_1 = C_2 = 0.5$,lower and upper bound for initial position of the swarm are 0 and 20 respectively maximum initial velocities value = 2 and the weight vary linearly from 1.2 to 0.1. Table 1 presents the optimum torque and flux hysteresis bands (TB, and FB respectively) obtained by PSO.

T_l / ω_r	0		1/5		2/5		3/5		4/5		5/5	
	T.B	F.B	T.B	F.B	T.B	F.B	T.B	F.B	T.B	F.B	T.B	F.B
6/6	17.9	4.99	15.6	1.35	16.0	4.44	14.0	5.73	9.40	6.76	19.3	5.14
5/6	12.4	1.45	13.2	0.70	4.64	0.31	3.32	0.48	10.6	0.80	15.1	3.21
4/6	4.48	4.78	14.6	5.61	13.2	13.3	15.9	12.7	15.0	12.3	4.01	1.04
3/6	8.04	6.28	14.4	8.31	9.29	15.5	18.0	16.4	0.949	17.9	7.80	8.44
2/6	15.1	11.1	7.72	15.3	16.2	8.79	6.04	6.19	14.4	3.97	14.4	3.57
1/6	2.75	6.61	18.5	19.0	16.2	5.23	14.0	5.32	9.63	4.23	12.7	1.36

Table 3. The optimum hysteresis bands obtained by PSO optimization process

4.2 Neural Network Controller For DTC

In the previous section, PSO is used as an offline optimization technique that determines the optimal values of the hysteresis bands. These bands depend on loading conditions. To ensure keeping the drive system running at the optimal performance cost function, the hysteresis band must be changed online depending on the current operating conditions. Neural networks (NNs) have good approximation ability and can interpolate and extrapolate its training data. Hence, to achieve the online selection of the hysteresis bands, two neural networks are trained by the offline optimum results obtained by PSO for flux and torque bands respectively. The inputs of these NN are the desired motor speed and the desired load torque.

The two considered NN's are Feed-forward type networks. Each NN has two inputs, one output, and two layers. The flux neural network has 8 neurons in the input layer and one neuron in the output layer. The torque neural network has 9 neurons in the input layer and one neuron in the output layer. The activation function of the hidden layer is log sigmoid while the output layer is linear. For both networks, the Neural Network Matlab Toolbox is used for the training. The training algorithm selected is Levenberg-Marquarbt back propagation, the adaptation learning function is "trains" sequential order incremental update, and the performance function is the sum-squared error.

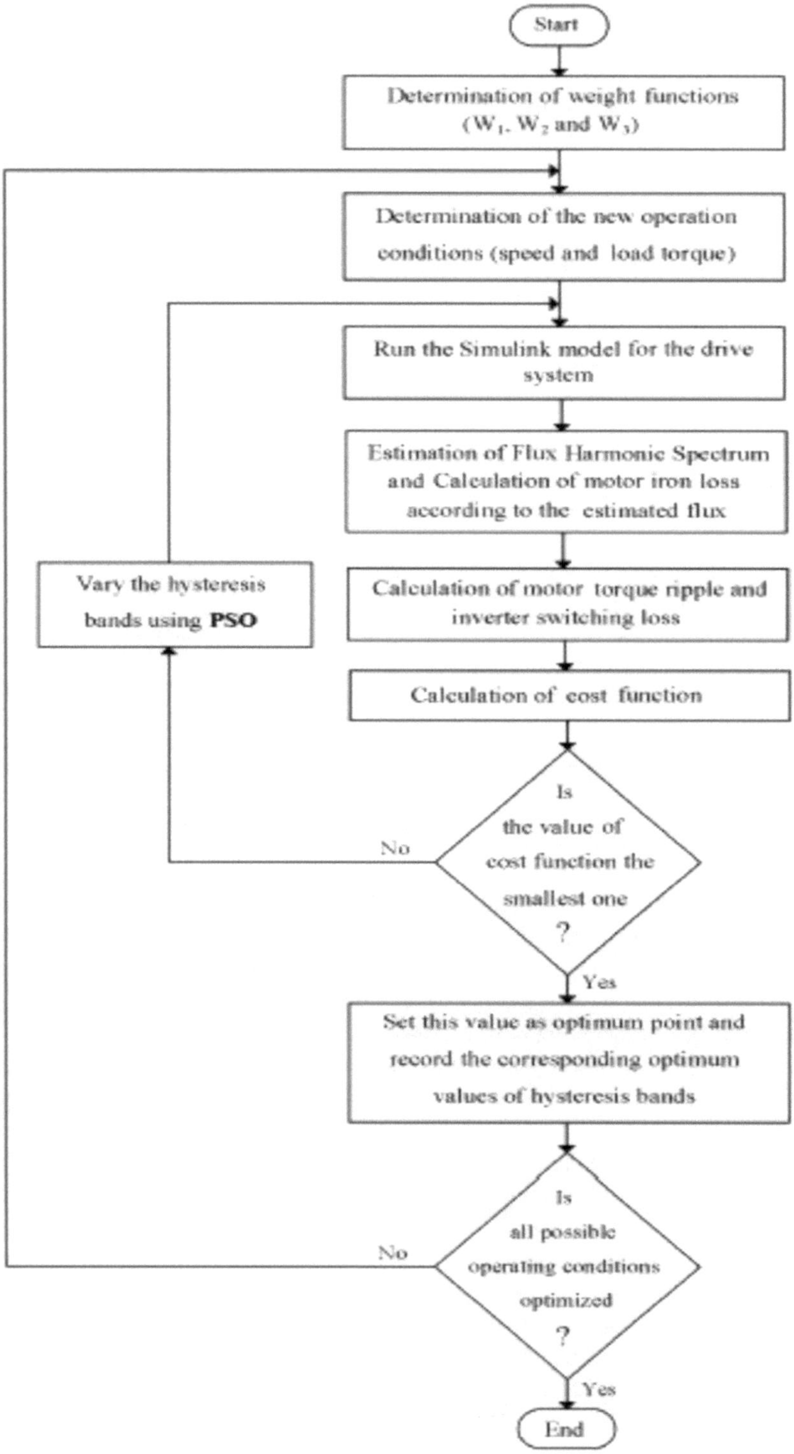

Figure 13. The flow chart of the optimization process

4.3 Comparison Between Classical and the Neural Network Controller for DTC

Simulations have been performed for the above mentioned 10 Hp induction motor to compare between the classical and the neural network controller for direct torque controlled IM. For classical DTC the results have been obtained for flux and torque hysteresis band amplitude equal to 2 %. In neural network Controller the above flux and torque neural networks are used to set the optimal hysteresis bands. Fig. 14 and Fig. 15 show the simulation results for the classical and the neural network controller respectively for a test run that covers wide operating range. It is clear that, the proposed scheme achieves a considerable reduction in inverter switching loss, motor harmonic loss, and motor torque ripple of the direct torque controlled induction motor drives compared to the Classical DTC. Table 4 shows the comparison between classical DTC and NN DTC

	Swt. Loss	Iron Loss	T. Ripples	Cost Fun.
Classical DTC	0.4169	0.7606	0.9568	0.80958
NN optimized DTC	0.3545	0.6706	0.4522	0.47634

Table 4. Comparison between classical and NN controller for DTC

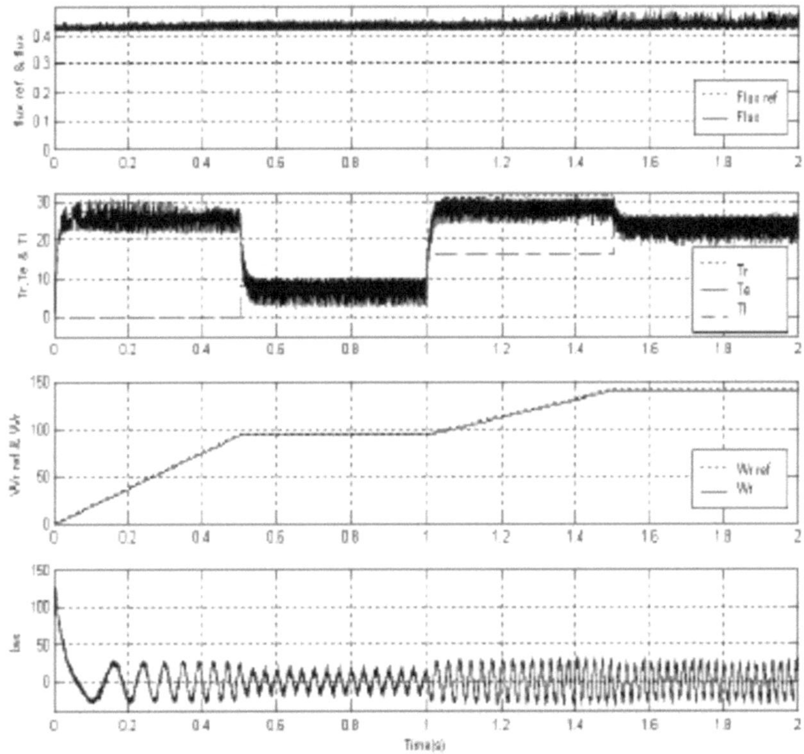

Figure 14. The classical direct torque controlled IM simulation results

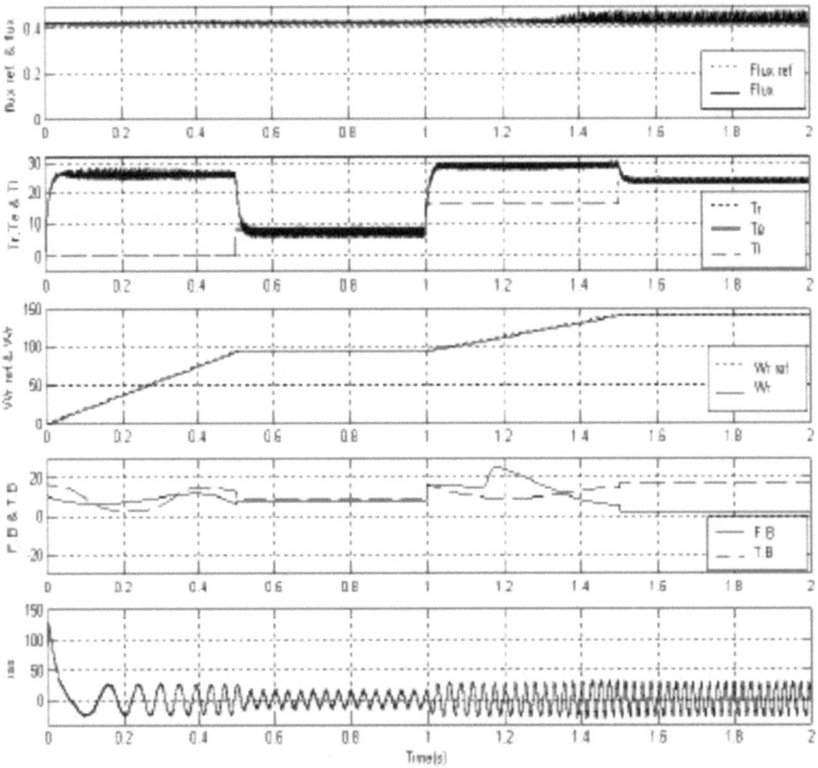

Figure 15. The neural network direct torque controlled IM simulation results

Finally, the DTC control strategy with variable hysteresis bands, which improves the drive performance compared to the classical DTC, is proposed. Particle swarm optimization is used offline to minimize a cost function that represents the effect of the hysteresis band on the inverter switching loss, motor harmonic loss and motor torque ripples at different operating conditions. Online operating ANNs use the offline optimum values obtained by PSO, to decide the suitable hysteresis bands based on the current operating condition. Simulation results indicate the validity of the proposed scheme in achieving better performance of the drive system in a wide operating range.

5. Index I

List of principal symbols

ω_e	: *synchronous speed*
ω_r	: *rotor speed*
p	: *differential operator*
r_m, r_a	: *main, auxiliary stator windings resistance*
r_r	: *rotor winding resistance*
$R_{feq,d}$	: *equivalent iron-loss resistance(d and q axis)*
L_{lm}, L_{la}	: *main, auxiliary stator leakage inductance*

L_{md}, L_{mq}	: *magnetizing inductance (d& q axis)*
L_{lr}	: *rotor leakage inductance*
K	: *turns ratio auxiliary/main windings*
T_e	: *electromagnetic torque*
J	: *inertia of motor*
$\lambda_{ds,qs}$	: *stator flux(d and q axis)*
$\lambda_{dr,qr}$	: *rotor flux(d and q axis)*
$V_{ds,qs}$	: *stator voltage (d and q axis)*
$i_{ds,qs}$	: *stator current (d and q axis)*
M	: *mutual inductance*

6. References

A. M. A. Amin, M. I. Korfally, A. A. Sayed, and O.T. M.Hegazy, Losses Minimization of Two Asymmetrical Windings Induction Motor Based on Swarm Intelligence, *Proceedings of IEEE- IECON* 06 , pp 1150 - 1155, Paris , France , Nov. 2006 . [1]

A. M. A. Amin, M. I. Korfally, A. A. Sayed, and O.T. M.Hegazy, Swarm Intelligence-Based Controller of Two-Asymmetrical Windings Induction Motor, *accepted for IEEE. EMDC07*, pp 953 -958, Turkey, May 2007. [2]

M. Popescu, A. Arkkio, E. Demeter, D. Micu, V. Navrapescu. Development of an inverter fed two-phase variable speed induction motor drive, in *Conference Records of PEMC'98*, pp.4-132 - 4-136 Sept. 1998, Prague, Czech Republic ISBN–80-01-01832-6. [3]

Ahmed A. A. Esmin, Germano Lambert-Torres, and Antônio C. Zambroni de Souza, A Hybrid Particle Swarm Optimization Applied to Loss Power Minimization *IEEE Transactions on Power Systems*, Vol. 20, No. 2, May 2005. [4]

Radwan H. A. Hamid, Amr M. A. Amin, Refaat S. Ahmed, and Adel A. A. El-Gammal, New Technique For Maximum Efficiency And Minimum Operating Cost Of Induction Motors Based On Particle Swarm Optimization (PSO), *Proceedings of IEEE- IECON 06* , pp 1029 – 1034, Paris , France , Nov. 2006. [5]

Zhao, B.; Guo, C.X.; Cao, Y.J.; A Multiagent-Based Particle Swarm Optimization Approach For Optimal Reactive Power Dispatch,Power Systems, *IEEE Transactions on* Volume 20, Issue 2, May 2005 Page(s):1070 – 1078. [6]

Cui Naxin; Zhang Chenghui; Zhao Min; Optimal Efficiency Control Of Field-Oriented Induction Motor Drive And Rotor Resistance Adaptive Identifying, *Power Electronics and Motion Control Conference*, 2004. IPEMC 2004. The 4th International Volume 1, 2004. [7]

Chakraborty, C.; Hori, Y.; Fast Efficiency Optimization Techniques for the Indirect Vector-Controlled Induction Motor Drives, Industry Applications, *IEEE Transactions on*, Volume: 39, Issue: 4, July-Aug. 2003 Pages: 1070 – [8]

O. S. El-Laban, H. A. Abdel Fattah, H. M. Emara, and A. F. Sakr, Particle Swarm Optimized Direct Torque Control of Induction Motors, *Proceedings of IEEE- IECON 06* , pp 1586 – 1591, Paris , France , Nov. 2006 . [9]

S. Kaboli, M.R. Zolghadri and A. Emadi, Hysteresis Band Determination of Direct Torque Controlled Induction Motor Drives with Torque Ripple and Motor-Inverter Loss Considerations. *Proceeding of the 34th IEEE Power Electronics Specialists Conference*, PESC03, June 2003, pp. 1107,1111. [10]

S. Kaboli, M.R. Zolghadri, S. Haghbin and A. Emadi, Torque Ripple Minimization in DTC of Induction Motor Based on Optimized Flux value Determination, *Proceeding of 29th Conference of IEEE Industrial Electronics Society* IECON03, pp.431-435. [11]

3

Particle Swarm Optimization for HW/SW Partitioning

M. B. Abdelhalim and S. E. -D. Habib
Electronics and Communications Department, Faculty of Engineering - Cairo University
Egypt

1. Introduction

Embedded systems typically consist of application specific hardware parts and programmable parts, e.g. processors like DSPs, core processors or ASIPs. In comparison to the hardware parts, the software parts are much easier to develop and modify. Thus, software is less expensive in terms of costs and development time. Hardware, however, provides better performance. For this reason, a system designer's goal is to design a system fulfilling all system constraints. The co-design phase, during which the system specification is partitioned onto hardware and programmable parts of the target architecture, is called Hardware/Software partitioning. This phase represents one key issue during the design process of heterogeneous systems. Some early co-design approaches [Marrec et al. 1998, Cloute et al. 1999] carried out the HW/SW partitioning task manually. This manual approach is limited to small design problems with small number of constituent modules. Additionally, automatic Hardware/Software partitioning is of large interest because the problem itself is a very complex optimization problem.
Varieties of Hardware/Software partitioning approaches are available in the literature. Following Nieman [1998], these approaches can be distinguished by the following aspects:

1. The complexity of the supported partitioning problem, e.g. whether the target architecture is fixed or optimized during partitioning.
2. The supported target architecture, e.g. single-processor or multi-processor, ASIC or FPGA-based hardware.
3. The application domain, e.g. either data-flow or control-flow dominated systems.
4. The optimization goal determined by the chosen cost function, e.g. hardware minimization under timing (performance) constraints, performance maximization under resource constraints, or low power solutions.
5. The optimization technique, including heuristic, probabilistic or exact methods, compared by computation time and the quality of results.
6. The optimization aspects, e.g. whether communication and/or hardware sharing are taken into account.
7. The granularity of the pieces for which costs are estimated for partitioning, e.g. granules at the statement, basic block, function, process or task level.
8. The estimation method itself, whether the estimations are computed by special estimation tools or by analyzing the results of synthesis tools and compilers.

9. The cost metrics used during partitioning, including cost metrics for hardware implementations (e.g. execution time, chip area, pin requirements, power consumption, testability metrics), software cost metrics (e.g. execution time, power consumption, program and data memory usage) and interface metrics (e.g. communication time or additional resource-power costs).
10. The number of these cost metrics, e.g. whether only one hardware solution is considered for each granule or a complete Area/Time curve.
11. The degree of automation.
12. The degree of user-interaction to exploit the valuable experience of the designer.
13. The ability for Design-Space-Exploration (DSE) enabling the designer to compare different partitions and to find alternative solutions for different objective functions in short computation time.

In this Chapter, we investigate the application of the Particle Swarm Optimization (PSO) technique for solving the Hardware/Software partitioning problem. The PSO is attractive for the Hardware/Software partitioning problem as it offers reasonable coverage of the design space together with O(n) main loop's execution time, where n is the number of proposed solutions that will evolve to provide the final solution.

This Chapter is an extended version of the authors' 2006 paper [Abdelhalim et al. 2006]. The organization of this chapter is as follows: In Section 2, we introduce the HW/SW partitioning problem. Section 3 introduces the Particle Swarm Optimization formulation for HW/SW Partitioning problem followed by a case study. Section 4 introduces the technique extensions, namely, hardware implementation alternatives, HW/SW communications modeling, and fine tuning algorithm. Finally, Section 5 gives the conclusions of our work.

2. HW/SW Partitioning

The most important challenge in the embedded system design is partitioning; i.e. deciding which components (or operations) of the system should be implemented in hardware and which ones in software. The granularity of each component can be a single instruction, a short sequence of instructions, a basic block or a function (procedure). To clarify the HW/SW partitioning problem, let us represent the system by a Data Flow Graph (DFG) that defines the sequencing of the operations starting from the input capture to the output evaluation. Each node in this DFG represents a component (or operation). Implementing a given component in HW or in SW implies different delay/ area/ power/ design-time/ time-to-market/ … design costs. The HW/SW partitioning problem is, thus, an optimization problem where we seek to find the partition (an assignment vector of each component to HW or SW) that minimizes a user-defined global cost function (or functions) subject to given area/ power/ delay …constraints. Finding an optimal HW/SW partition is hard because of the large number of possible solutions for a given granularity of the "components" and the many different alternatives for these granularities. In other words, the HW/SW partitioning problem is hard since the design (search) space is typically huge. The following survey overviews the main algorithms used to solve the HW/SW partitioning problem. However, this survey is by no means comprehensive.

Traditionally, partitioning was carried out manually as in the work of Marrec et al. [1998] and Cloute et al. [1999]. However, because of the increase of complexity of the systems, many research efforts aimed at automating the partitioning as much as possible. The suggested partition approaches differ significantly according to the definition they used to the problem. One of the main differences is whether to include other tasks (such as scheduling where starting times of the components should be determined) as in Lopez-Vallejo et al [2003] and in Mie et al. [2000], or just map components to hardware or software only as in the work of Vahid [2002] and Madsen et al [1997]. Some formulations assign communication events to links between hardware and/or software units as in Jha and Dick [1998]. The system to be partitioned is generally given in the form of task graph, the graph nodes are determined by the model granularity, i.e. the semantic of a node. The node could represent a single instruction, short sequence of instructions [Stitt et al. 2005], basic block [Knudsen et al. 1996], a function or procedure [Ditzel 2004, and Armstrong et al. 2002]. A flexible granularity may also be used where a node can represent any of the above [Vahid 2002; Henkel and Ernst 2001]. Regarding the suggested algorithms, one can differentiate between exact and heuristic methods. The proposed exact algorithms include, but are not limited to, branch-and-bound [Binh et al 1996], dynamic programming [Madsen et al. 1997], and integer linear programming [Nieman 1998; Ditzel 2004]. Due to the slow performance of the exact algorithms, heuristic-based algorithms are proposed. In particular, Genetic algorithms are widely used [Nieman 1998; Mann 2004] as well as simulated annealing [Armstrong et al 2002; Eles et al. 1997], hierarchical clustering [Eles et al. 1997], and Kernighan-Lin based algorithms such as in [Mann 2004]. Less popular heuristics are used such as Tabu search [Eles et al. 1997] and greedy algorithms [Chatha and Vemuri 2001]. Some researchers used custom heuristics, such as Maximum Flow-Minimum Communications (MFMC) [Mann 2004], Global Criticality/Local Phase (GCLP) [Kalavade and Lee 1994], process complexity [Adhipathi 2004], the expert system presented in [Lopez-Vallejo et al. 2003], and Balanced/Unbalanced partitioning (BUB) [Stitt 2008].

The ideal Hardware/Software partitioning tool produces automatically a set of high-quality partitions in a short, predictable computation time. Such tool would also allow the designer to interact with the partitioning algorithm.

De Souza et al. [2003] propose the concepts of "quality requisites" and a method based on Quality Function Deployment (QFD) as references to represent both the advantages and disadvantages of existing HW/SW partitioning methods, as well as, to define a set of features for an optimized partitioning algorithm. They classified the algorithms according to the following criterion:

1. Application domain: whether they are "multi-domain" (conceived for more than one or any application domain, thus not considering particularities of these domains and being technology-independent) or "specific domain" approaches.
2. The target architecture type.
3. Consideration for the HW-SW communication costs.
4. Possibility of choosing the best implementation alternative of HW nodes.
5. Possibility of sharing HW resources among two or more nodes.
6. Exploitation of HW-SW parallelism.
7. Single-mode or multi-mode systems with respect to the clock domains.

In this Chapter, we present the use of the Particle Swarm Optimization techniques to solve the HW/SW partitioning problem. The aforementioned criterions will be implicitly considered along the algorithm presentation.

3. Particle swarm optimization

Particle swarm optimization (PSO) is a population based stochastic optimization technique developed by Eberhart and Kennedy in 1995 [Kennedy and Eberhart 1995; Eberhart and

Kennedy 1995; Eberhart and Shi 2001]. The PSO algorithm is inspired by social behavior of bird flocking, animal hording, or fish schooling. In PSO, the potential solutions, called particles, fly through the problem space by following the current optimum particles. PSO has been successfully applied in many areas. A good bibliography of PSO applications could be found in the work done by Poli [2007].

3.1 PSO algorithm

As stated before, PSO simulates the behavior of bird flocking. Suppose the following scenario: a group of birds is randomly searching for food in an area. There is only one piece of food in the area being searched. Not all the birds know where the food is. However, during every iteration, they learn via their inter-communications, how far the food is. Therefore, the best strategy to find the food is to follow the bird that is nearest to the food.
PSO learned from this bird-flocking scenario, and used it to solve optimization problems. In PSO, each single solution is a "bird" in the search space. We call it "particle". All of particles have fitness values which are evaluated by the fitness function (the cost function to be optimized), and have velocities which direct the flying of the particles. The particles fly through the problem space by following the current optimum particles.
PSO is initialized with a group of random particles (solutions) and then searches for optima by updating generations. During every iteration, each particle is updated by following two "best" values. The first one is the position vector of the best solution (fitness) this particle has achieved so far. The fitness value is also stored. This position is called ***pbest***. Another "best" position that is tracked by the particle swarm optimizer is the best position, obtained so far, by any particle in the population. This best position is the current global best and is called ***gbest***.
After finding the two best values, the particle updates its velocity and position according to equations (1) and (2) respectively.

$$v^i_{k+1} = wv^i_k + c_1 r_1 (pbest^i - x^i_k) + c_2 r_2 (gbest_k - x^i_k) \tag{1}$$

$$x^i_{k+1} = x^i_k + v^i_{k+1} \tag{2}$$

where v^i_k is the velocity of ith particle at the kth iteration, x^i_k is current the solution (or position) of the ith particle. r_1 and r_2 are random numbers generated uniformly between 0 and 1. c_1 is the self-confidence (cognitive) factor and c_2 is the swarm confidence (social) factor. Usually c_1 and c_2 are in the range from 1.5 to 2.5. Finally, w is the inertia factor that takes linearly decreasing values downward from 1 to 0 according to a predefined number of iterations as recommended by Haupt and Haupt [2004].
The 1st term in equation (1) represents the effect of the inertia of the particle, the 2nd term represents the particle memory influence, and the 3rd term represents the swarm (society) influence. The flow chart of the procedure is shown in Fig. 1.
The velocities of the particles on each dimension may be clamped to a maximum velocity $\mathbf{V_{max}}$, which is a parameter specified by the user. If the sum of accelerations causes the velocity on that dimension to exceed $\mathbf{V_{max}}$, then this velocity is limited to $\mathbf{V_{max}}$ [Haupt and Haupt 2004]. Another type of clamping is to clamp the position of the current solution to a certain range in which the solution has valid value, otherwise the solution is meaningless [Haupt and Haupt 2004]. In this Chapter, position clamping is applied with no limitation on the velocity values.

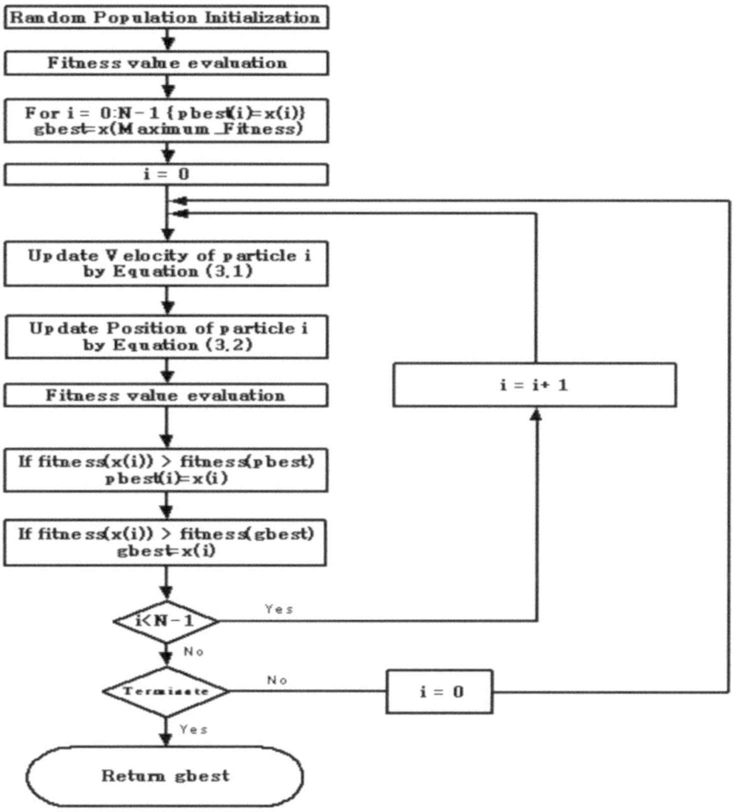

Figure 1. PSO Flow chart

3.2 Comparisons between GA and PSO

The Genetic Algorithm (GA) is an evolutionary optimizer (EO) that takes a sample of possible solutions (individuals) and employs mutation, crossover, and selection as the primary operators for optimization. The details of GA are beyond the scope of this chapter, but interested readers can refer to Haupt and Haupt [2004]. In general, most of evolutionary techniques have the following steps:

1. Random generation of an initial population.
2. Reckoning of a fitness value for each subject. This fitness value depends directly on the distance to the optimum.
3. Reproduction of the population based on fitness values.
4. If requirements are met, then stop. Otherwise go back to step 2.

From this procedure, we can learn that PSO shares many common points with GA. Both algorithms start with a group of randomly generated population and both algorithms have fitness values to evaluate the population, update the population and search for the optimum with random techniques, and finally, check for the attainment of a valid solution.
On the other hand, PSO does not have genetic operators like crossover and mutation. Particles update themselves with the internal velocity. They also have memory, which is important to the algorithm (even if this memory is very simple as it stores only $pbest^i$ and $gbest_k$ positions).

Also, the information sharing mechanism in PSO is significantly different: In GAs, chromosomes share information with each other. So the whole population moves like one group towards an optimal area even if this move is slow. In PSO, only ***gbest*** gives out the information to others. It is a one-way information sharing mechanism. The evolution only looks for the best solution. Compared with GA, all the particles tend to converge to the best solution quickly in most cases as shown by Eberhart and Shi [1998] and Hassan et al. [2004].

When comparing the run-time complexity of the two algorithms, we should exclude the similar operations (initialization, fitness evaluation, and termination) form our comparison. We exclude also the number of generations, as it depends on the optimization problem complexity and termination criteria (our experiments in Section 3.4.2 indicate that PSO needs lower number of generations than GA to reach a given solution quality). Therefore, we focus our comparison to the main loop of the two algorithms. We consider the most time-consuming processes (recombination in GA as well as velocity and position update in PSO).

For GA, if the new generation replaces the older one, the recombination complexity is $O(q)$, where **q** is group size for tournament selection. In our case, **q** equals the **Selection rate*n**, where **n** is the size of population. However, if the replacement strategy depends on the fitness of the individual, a sorting process is needed to determine which individuals to be replaced by which new individuals. This sorting is important to guarantee the solution quality. Another sorting process is needed any way to update the rank of the individuals at the end of each generation. Note that the quick sorting complexity ranges from $O(n^2)$ to $O(n\log_2 n)$ [Jensen 2003, Harris and Ross 2006].

In the other hand, for PSO, the velocity and position update processes complexity is $O(n)$ as there is no need for pre-sorting. The algorithm operates according to equations (1) and (2) on each individual (particle) [Rodriguez et al. 2008].

From the above discussion, GA's complexity is larger than that of PSO. Therefore, PSO is simpler and faster than GA.

3.3 Algorithm Implementation

The PSO algorithm is written in the MATLAB program environment. The input to the program is a design that consists of the number of nodes. Each node is associated with cost parameters. For experimental purpose, these parameters are randomly generated. The used cost parameters are:

A Hardware implementation cost: which is the cost of implementing that node in hardware (e.g. number of gates, area, or number of logic elements). This hardware cost is uniformly and randomly generated in the range from 1 to 99 [Mann 2004].

A Software implementation cost: which is the cost of implementing that node in software (e.g. execution delay or number of clock cycles). This software cost is uniformly and randomly generated in the range from 1 to 99 [Mann 2004].

A Power implementation cost: which is the power consumption if the node is implemented in hardware or software. This power cost is uniformly and randomly generated in the range from 1 to 9. We use a different range for Power consumption values to test the addition of other cost terms with different range characteristics.

Consider a design consisting of **m** nodes. A possible solution (particle) is a vector of **m** elements, where each element is associated to a given node. The elements assume a "0" value (if node is implemented in software) or a "1" value (if the node is implemented in hardware). There are **n** initial particles; the particles (solutions) are initialized randomly.

The velocity of each node is initialized in the range from (-1) to (1), where negative velocity means moving the particle toward 0 and positive velocity means moving the particle toward 1.
For the main loop, equations (1), (2) are evaluated in each loop. If the particle goes outside the permissible region (position from 0 to 1), it will be kept on the nearest limit by the aforementioned clamping technique.
The cost function is called for each particle, the used cost function is a normalized weighted sum of the hardware, software, and power cost of each particle according to equation (3).

$$\mathrm{Cost}=100*\left\{\alpha\frac{\mathrm{HWcost}}{\mathrm{allHWcost}}+\beta\frac{\mathrm{SWcost}}{\mathrm{allSWcost}}+\gamma\frac{\mathrm{POWERcost}}{\mathrm{allPOWERcost}}\right\} \tag{3}$$

where **allHWcost** (**allSWcost**) is the Maximum Hardware (Software) cost when all nodes are mapped to Hardware (Software), and **allPOWERcost** is the average of the power cost of all-Hardware solution and all-Software solution. **α**, **β**, and **γ** are weighting factors. They are set by the user according to his/her critical design parameters. For the rest of this chapter, all the weighting factors are considered equal unless otherwise mentioned. The multiplication by 100 is for readability only.
The **HWCost** (**SWCost**) term represent the cost of the partition implemented in hardware (software), it could represent the area and the delay of the partition (the area and the delay of the software partition). However, the software cost has a fixed (CPU area) term that is independent on the problem size.
The weighted sum of normalized metrics is a classical approach to transform Multi-objective Optimization problems into a single objective optimization [Donoso and Fabregat 2007]
The PSO algorithm proceeds according to the flow chart shown in Fig. 1. For simplicity, the cost value could be considered as the inverse of the fitness where good solutions have low cost values.
According to equations (1) and (2), the particle nodes values could take any value between 0 and 1. However, as a discrete, i.e. binary, partitioning problem, the nodes values must take values of 1 or 0. Therefore, the position value is rounded to the nearest integer [Hassan et al. 2004].
The main loop is terminated when the improvement in the global best solution ***gbest*** for the last number iterations is less than a predefined value (ε). The number of these iterations and the value of (ε) are user controlled parameters.
For GA parameters, the most important parameters are:

- Selection rate which is the percentage of the population members that are kept unchanged while the others go under the crossover operators.
- Mutation rate which is the percentage of the population that undergo the gene alteration process after each generation.
- The mating technique which determines the mechanism of generating new children form the selected parents.

3.4 Results

3.4.1 Algorithms parameters

The following experiments are performed on a Pentium-4 PC with 3GHz processor speed, 1 GB RAM and WinXP operating system. The experiments were performed using MATLAB 7

program. The PSO results are compared with the GA. Common parameters between the two algorithms are as follows:
No. of particles (Population size) **n** = 60, design size **m** = 512 nodes, $\varepsilon = 100 * $ **eps**, where **eps** is defined in MATLAB as a very small (numerical resolution) value and equals $2.2204*10^{-16}$ [Hanselman and Littlefield 2001].
For PSO, $c_1 = c_2 = 2$, w starts at 1 and decreases linearly until reaching 0 after 100 iterations. Those values are suggested in [Shi and Eberhart 1998; Shi and Eberhart 1999; Zheng et al. 2003].
To get the best results for GA, the parameters values are chosen as suggested in [Mann 2004; Haupt and Haupt 2004] where Selection rate = 0.5, Mutation rate = 0.05 , and The mating is performed using randomly selected single point crossover.
The termination criterion is the same for both PSO and GA. The algorithm stops after 50 unchanged iterations, but at least 100 iterations must be performed to avoid quick stagnation.

3.4.2 Algorithm results

Figures 2 and 3 shows the best cost as well as average population cost of GA and PSO respectively.

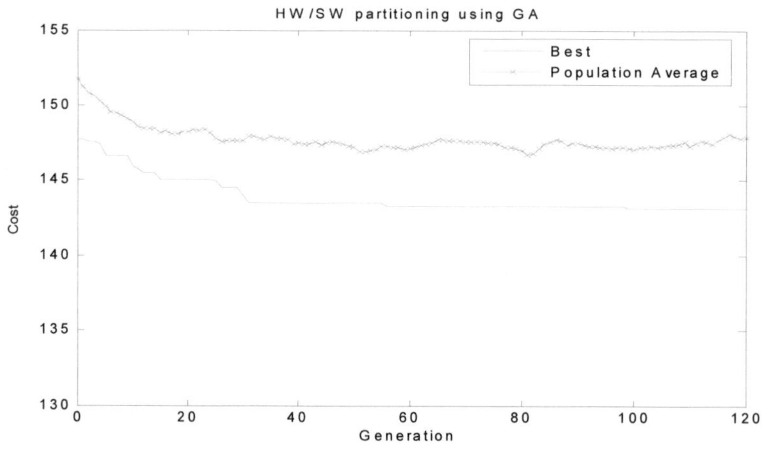

Figure 2. GA Solution

As shown in the figures, the initialization is the same, but at the end, the best cost of GA is 143.1 while for PSO it is 131.6. This result represents around 8% improvement in the result quality in favor of PSO. Another advantage of PSO is its performance (speed), as it terminates after 0.609 seconds while GA terminates after 0.984 seconds. This result represents around 38% improvement in performance in favor of PSO.
The results vary slightly from one run to another due to the random initialization. Hence, decisions based on a single run are doubtful. Therefore, we ran the two algorithms 100 times for the same input and took the average of the final costs. We found the average best cost of GA is 143 and it terminates after 155 seconds, while for the PSO the average best cost was 131.6 and it terminates after 110.6 seconds. Thus, there are 8% improvement in the result quality and 29% speed improvement.

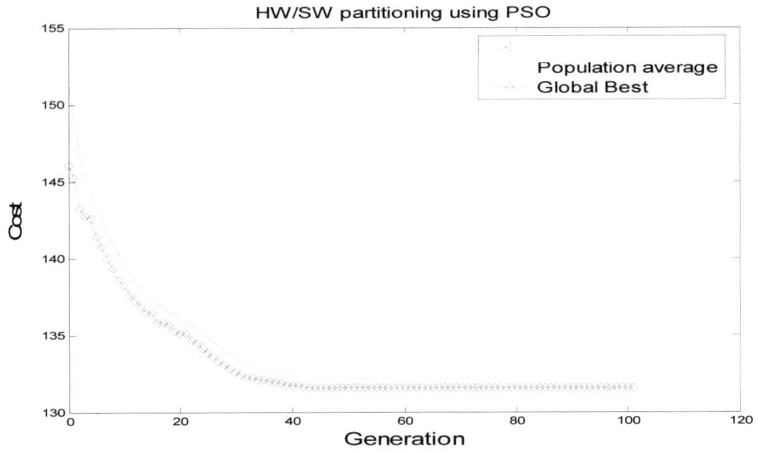

Figure 3. PSO Solution

3.4.3 Improved Algorithms.

To further enhance the quality of the results, we tried cascading two runs of the same algorithm or of different algorithms. There are four possible cascades of this type: GA followed by another GA run (GA-GA algorithm), GA followed by PSO run (GA - PSO algorithm), PSO followed by GA run (PSO-GA algorithm), and finally PSO followed by another PSO run (PSO-PSO algorithm). For these cascaded algorithms, we kept the parameters values the same as in the Section 3.4.1.

Only the last combination, PSO-PSO algorithm proved successful. For GA-GA algorithm, the second GA run is initialized with the final results of the first GA run. This result can be explained as follows. When the population individuals are similar, the crossover operator yields no improvements and the GA technique depends on the mutation process to escape such cases, and hence, it slowly escapes local minimums. Therefore, cascading several GA runs takes a very long time to yield significant improvement in results.

The PSO-GA algorithm did not fair any better. This negative result can be explained as follows. At the end of the first PSO run, the whole swarm particles converge around a certain point (solution) as shown in Fig. 3. Thus, the GA is initialized with population members of close fitness with small or no diversity. In fact, this is a poor initialization of the GA, and hence it is not expected to improve the PSO results of the first step of this algorithm significantly. Our numerical results confirmed this conclusion

The GA-PSO algorithm was not also successful. Figures 4 and 5 depict typical results for this algorithm. PSO starts with the final solutions of the GA stage (The GA best output cost is ~143, and the population final average is ~147) and continues the optimization until it terminates with a best output cost equals ~132. However, this best output cost value is achieved by PSO alone as shown in Fig. 3. This final result could be explained as the PSO behavior is not strongly dependent on the initial particles position obtained by GA due to the random velocities assigned to the particles at the beginning of PSO phase. Notice that, in Fig. 5, the cost increases at the beginning due to the random velocities that force the particles to move away from the positions obtained by GA phase.

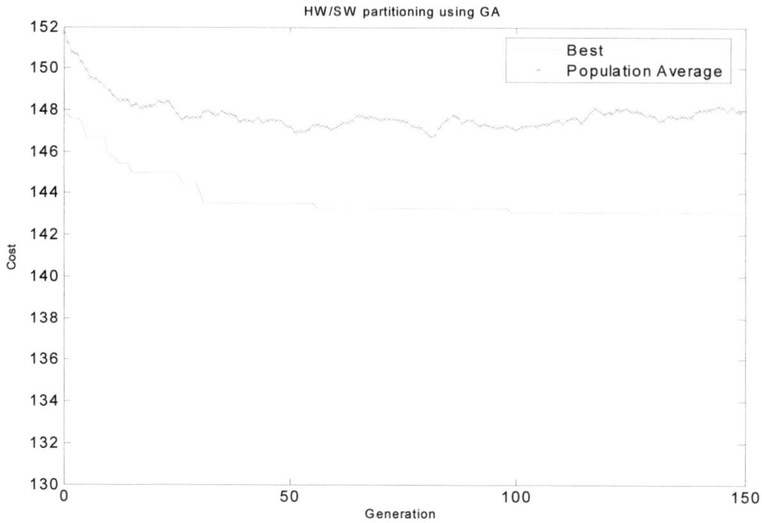

Figure 4. GA output of GA-PSO

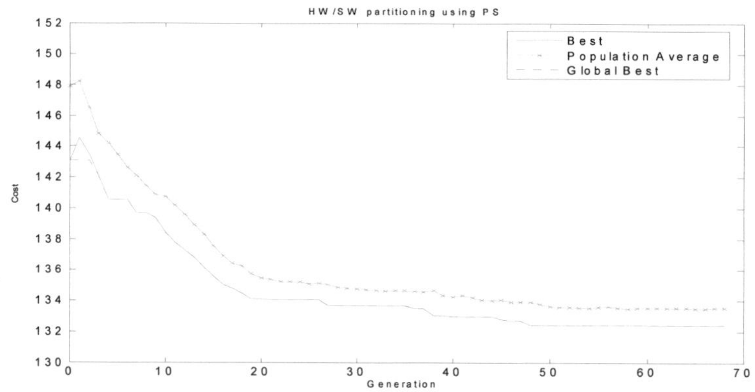

Figure 5. PSO output of GA-PSO

3.4.4 Re-exited PSO algorithm.

As the PSO proceeds, the effect of the inertia factor (**w**) is decreased until reaching 0. Therefore, v_{k+1}^{i} at the late iterations depends only on the particle memory influence and the swarm influence (2nd and 3rd terms in equation (1)). Hence, the algorithm may give non-global optimum results. A hill-climbing algorithm is proposed, this algorithm is based on the assumption that if we take the run's final results (particles positions) and start allover again with (**w**) = 1 and re-initialize the velocity (v) with new random values, and keeping the ***pbest*** and ***gbest*** vectors in the particles memories, the results can be improved. We found that the result quality is improved with each new round until it settles around a certain value. Fig. 6 plots the best cost in each round. The curve starts with cost ~133 and settles at round number 30 with cost value ~116.5 which is significantly below the results obtained in the previous two subsections (about 15% quality improvement). The program performed 100 rounds, but it could be modified to stop earlier by using a different termination criterion (i.e. if the result remains unchanged for a certain number of rounds).

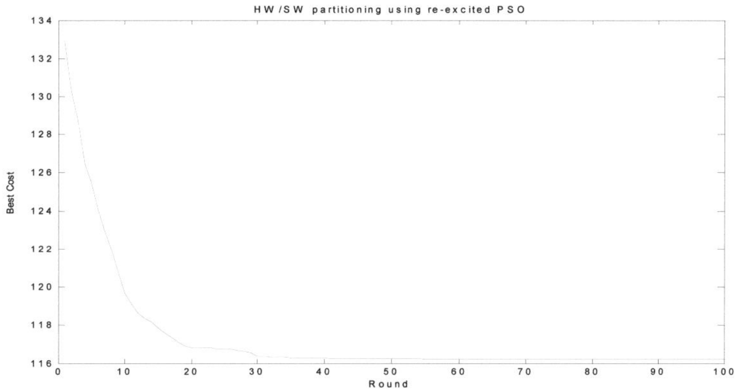

Figure 6. Successive improvements in Re-excited PSO

As the new algorithm depends on re-exciting new randomized particle velocities at the beginning of each round, while keeping the particle positions obtained so far, it allows another round of domain exploration. We propose to name this successive PSO algorithm as the ***Re-excited PSO*** algorithm. In nature, this algorithm looks like giving the birds a big push after they are settled in their best position. This push re-initializes the inertia and speed of the birds so they are able to explore new areas, unexplored before. Hence, if the birds find a better place, they will go there, otherwise they will return back to the place from where they were pushed.

The main reason of the advantage of re-excited PSO over successive GA is as follows: The PSO algorithm is able to switch a single node from software to hardware or vice versa during a single iteration. Such single node flipping is difficult in GA as the change is done through crossover or mutation. However, crossover selects large number of nodes in one segment as a unit of operation. Mutation toggles the value of a random number of nodes. In either case, single node switching is difficult and slow.

This re-excited PSO algorithm can be viewed as a variant of the re-start strategies for PSO published elsewhere. However, our re-excited PSO algorithm is not identical to any of these previously published re-starting PSO algorithms as discussed below.

In Settles and Soule [2003], the restarting is done with the help of Genetic Algorithm operators, the goal is to create two new child particles whose position is between the parents position, but accelerated away from the current direction to increase diversity. The children's velocity vectors are exchanged at the same node and the previous best vector is set to the new position vector, effectively restarting the children's memory. Obviously, our restarting strategy is different in that it depends on pure PSO operators.

In Tillett et al. [2005], the restarting is done by spawning a new swarm when stagnation occurs, i.e. the swarm spawns a new swarm if a new global best fitness is found. When a swarm spawns a new swarm, the spawning swarm (parent) is unaffected. To form the spawned (child) swarm, half of the children particles are randomly selected from the parent swarm and the other half are randomly selected from a random member of the swarm collection (mate). Swarm creation is suppressed when there are large numbers of swarms in

existence. Obviously, our restarting strategy is different in that it depends on a single swarm.
In Pasupuleti and Battiti [2006], the Gregarious PSO or G-PSO, the population is attracted by the global best position and each particle is re-initialized with a random velocity if it is stuck close to the global best position. In this manner, the algorithm proceeds by aggressively and greedily scouting the local minima whereas Basic-PSO proceeds by trying to avoid them. Therefore, a re-initialization mechanism is needed to avoid the premature convergence of the swarm. Our algorithm differs than G-PSO in that the re-initialization strategy depends on the global best particle not on the particles that stuck close to the global best position which saves a lot of computations needed to compare each particle position with the global best one.
Finally, the re-start method of Van den Bergh [2002], the Multi-Start PSO (MPSO), is the nearest to our approach, except that when the swarm converges to a local optima. The MPSO records the current position and re-initialize the positions of the particles. The velocities are not re-initialized as MPSO depends on a different version of the velocity equation that guarantees that the velocity term will never reach zero. The modified algorithm is called Guaranteed Convergence PSO (GCPSO). Our algorithm differs in that we use the velocity update equation defined in Equation (1) and our algorithm re-initializes the velocity and the inertia of the particles but not the positions at the restart.

3.5 Quality and Speed Comparison between GA, PSO, and re-excited PSO

For the sake of fair comparison, we assumed that we have different designs where their sizes range from 5 nodes to 1020 nodes. We used the same parameters as described in previous experiments and we ran the algorithms on each design size 10 times and took the average results. Another stopping criterion is added to the re-excited PSO where it stops when the best result is the same for the last 10 rounds. Fig. 7 represents the design quality improvement of PSO over GA, re-excited PSO over GA, and re-excited PSO over PSO. We noticed that when the design size is around 512, the improvement is about 8% which confirms the quality improvement results obtained in Section 3.4.2.

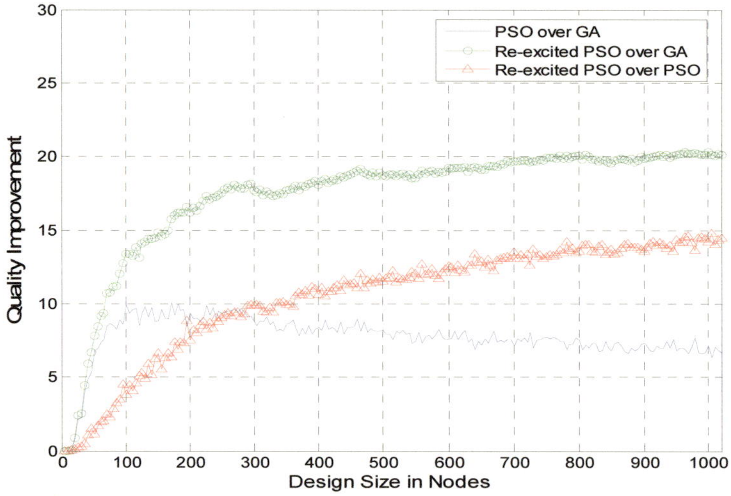

Figure 7. Quality improvement

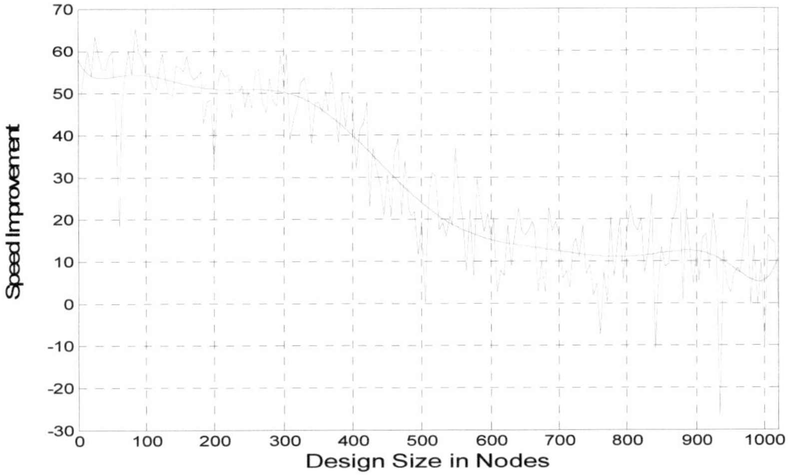

Figure 8. Speed improvement

Fig. 8 represents the performance (speed) improvement of PSO over GA (original and fitted curve, the curve fitting is done using MATLAB Basic Fitting tool). Re-excited PSO is not included as it depends on multi-round scheme where it starts a new round internally when the previous round terminates, while GA and PSO runs once and produces their outputs when a termination criterion is met.

It is noticed that in a few number of points in Fig. 8, the speed improvement is negative which means that GA finishes before PSO, but the design quality in Fig. 7 does not show any negative values. Fig. 7 also shows that, on the average, PSO outperforms GA by a ratio of 7.8% improvements in the result quality and Fig. 8 shows that, on the average, PSO outperforms GA by a ratio 29.3% improvement in speed.

On the other hand, re-excited PSO outperforms GA by an average ratio of 17.4% in design quality, and outperforms normal PSO by an average ratio of 10.5% in design quality. Moreover, Fig. 8 could be divided into three regions. The first region is the small size designs region (lower than 400 nodes) where the speed improvement is large (from 40% to 60%). The medium size design region (from 400 to 600 nodes) depicts an almost linear decrease in the speed improvement from 40% to 10%. The large size design region (bigger than 600 nodes) shows an almost constant (around 10%) speed improvement, with some cases where GA is faster than PSO. Note that most of the practical real life HW/SW partitioning problems belong to the first region where the number of nodes < 400.

3.6 Constrained Problem Formulation

3.6.1 Constraints definition and violation handling

In embedded systems, the constraints play an important role in the success of a design, where hard constraints mean higher design effort and therefore a high need for automated tools to guide the designer in critical design decisions. In most of the cases, the constraints are mainly the software deadline times (for real-time systems) and the maximum available area for hardware. For simplicity, we will refer to them as software constraint and hardware constraint respectively.

Mann [2004] divided the HW/SW partitioning problem into 5 sub-problems (P_1 - P_5). The unconstrained problem (P_5) is discussed in Section 3.3. The P_1 problem involves with both

Hardware and Software constraints. The P_2 (P_3) problem deals with hardware (software) constrained designs. Finally, the P_4 problem minimizes HW/SW communications cost while satisfying hardware and software constraints. The constraints affect directly the cost function. Hence, equation (3) should be modified to account for constraints violations.

In Lopez-Vallejo et al. [2003] three different techniques are suggested for the cost function correction and evaluation:

Mean Square Error minimization: This technique is useful for forcing the solution to meet certain equality, rather than inequality, constraints. The general expression for Mean Square Error based cost function is:

$$\mathrm{MSE\_cost}_i = k_i * \frac{(\mathrm{cost}_i - \mathrm{constraint}_i)^2}{\mathrm{constraint}_i^{\,2}} \tag{4}$$

where $\mathrm{constraint}_i$ is the constraint on parameter i and k_i is a weighting factor. The cost_i is the parameter cost function. cost_i is calculated using the associated term (i.e. area or delay) of the general cost function (3).

Penalty Methods: These methods punish the solutions that produce medium or large constraints violations, but allow invalid solutions close to the boundaries defined by the constraints to be considered as good solutions [Lopez-Vallejo et al. 2003]. The cost function in this case is formulated as:

$$\mathrm{Cost}(x) = \sum_i k_i * \frac{\mathrm{cost}_i(x)}{\mathrm{Totalcost}_i} + \sum_{ci} k_{ci} * \mathrm{viol}(ci, x) \tag{5}$$

where x is the solution vector to be evaluated, k_i and k_{ci} are weighting factors (100 in our case). i denotes the design parameters such as: area, delay, power consumption, etc., ci denotes a constrained parameter, and viol(ci,x) is the correction function of the constrained parameters. viol(ci,x) could be expressed in terms of the percentage of violation defined by :

$$\mathrm{viol}(ci, x) = \begin{cases} 0 & \mathrm{cost}_i(x) < \mathrm{constraint}(ci) \\ \dfrac{\mathrm{cost}_i(x) - \mathrm{constraint}(ci)}{\mathrm{constraint}(ci)} & \mathrm{cost}_i(x) > \mathrm{constraint}(ci) \end{cases} \tag{6}$$

Lopez-Vallejo and Lopez et al. [2003] proposed to use the squared value of viol(ci,x).

The penalty methods have an important characteristic in which there might be invalid solutions with better overall cost than valid ones. In other words, the invalid solutions are penalized but could be ranked better than valid ones.

Barrier Techniques: These methods forbid the exploration of solutions outside the allowed design-space. The barrier techniques rank the invalid solutions worse than the valid ones. There are two common forms of the barrier techniques. The first form assigns a constant high cost to all invalid solutions (for example infinity). This form is unable to differentiate between near-barrier or far-barrier invalid solutions. it also needs to be initialized with at least one valid solution, otherwise all the costs are the same (i.e. ∞) and the algorithm fails. The other form, suggested in Mann [2004], assigns a constant-base barrier to all invalid solutions. This base barrier could be a constant larger than maximum cost produced by any valid solution. In our case for example, from equation (3), each cost term is normalized such that its maximum value is one. Therefore, a good choice of the constant-base penalty is "one" for each violation ("one" for hardware violation, "one" for software violation, and so on).

3.6.2 Constraints modeling

In order to determine the best method to be adopted, a comparison between the penalty methods (first order or second order percentage violation term) and the barrier methods (infinity vs. constant-base barrier) is performed. The details of the experiments are not shown here for the sake of brevity.

Our experiments showed that combining the constant-base barrier method with any penalty method (first-order error or second-order error term) gives higher quality solutions and guarantees that no invalid solutions beat valid ones. Hence, in the following experiments, equation (7) will be used as the cost function form. Our experiments further indicate that the second-order error penalty method gives a slight improvement over first-order one.

For double constraints problem (P_1), generating valid initial solutions is hard and time consuming, and hence, the barrier methods should be ruled out for such problems. When dealing with single constraint problems (P_2 and P_3), one can use the Fast Greedy Algorithm (FGA) proposed by Mann [2004] to generate valid initial solutions. FGA starts by assigning all nodes to the unconstrained side. It then proceeds by randomly moving nodes to the constrained side until the constraint is violated.

$$\mathrm{Cost}(x) = \sum_i k_i * \frac{\mathrm{cost}_i(x)}{\mathrm{Totalcost}_i} + \sum_{ci} k_{ci}(\mathrm{Penalty\_viol}(ci,x) + \mathrm{Barrier\_viol}(ci)) \tag{7}$$

3.6.3 Single constraint experiments

As P_2 and P_3 are treated the same in our formulation, we consider the software constrained problem (P_3) only. Two experiments were performed, the first one with relaxed constraint where the deadline (Maximum delay) is 40% of all-Software solution delay, the second one is a hard real-time system where the deadline is 15% of the all-Software solution delay. The parameters used are the same as in Section 3.4. Fast Greedy Algorithm is used to generate the initial solutions and re-excited PSO is performed for 10 rounds. In the cases of GA and normal PSO only, all results are based on averaging the results of 100 runs.

For the first experiment; the average quality of the GA is ~ 137.6 while for PSO it is ~ 131.3, and for re-excited PSO it is ~ 120. All final solutions are valid due to the initialization scheme used (Fast Greedy Algorithm).

For the second experiment, the average quality of the solution of GA is ~ 147 while for PSO it is ~ 137 and for re-excited PSO it is ~ 129.

The results confirm our earlier conclusion that the re-excited PSO again outperforms normal PSO and GA, and that the normal PSO again outperforms GA.

3.6.4 Double constraints experiments

When testing P_1 problems, the same parameters as the single-constrained case are used except that FGA is not used for initialization. Two experiments were performed: balanced constraints where maximum allowable hardware area is 45% of the area of the all-Hardware solution and the maximum allowable software delay is 45% of the delay of the all-Software solution. The other one is an unbalanced-constraints problem where maximum allowable hardware area is 60% of area of the all-Hardware solution and the maximum allowable software delay is 20% of the delay of the all-Software solution. Note that these constraints are used to guarantee that at least a valid solution exists.

For the first experiment, the average quality of the solution of GA is ~ 158 and invalid solutions are obtained during the first 22 runs out of xx total runs. The best valid solution cost was 137. For PSO the average quality is ~ 131 with valid solutions during all the runs. The best valid solution cost was 128.6. Finally for the re-excited PSO; the final solution quality is 119.5. It is clear that re-excited PSO again outperforms both PSO and GA.

For the second experiment; the average quality of the solution of GA is ~ 287 and no valid solution is obtained during the runs. Note that a constant penalty barrier of value 100 is added to the cost function in the case of a violation. For PSO the average quality is ~ 251 and no valid solution is obtained during the runs. Finally, for the re-excited PSO, the final solution quality is 125 (As valid solution is found in the seventh round). This shows the performance improvement of re-excited PSO over both PSO and GA.

Hence, for the rest of this Chapter, we will use the terms PSO and re-excited PSO interchangeably to refer to the re-excited algorithm.

3.7 Real-Life Case Study

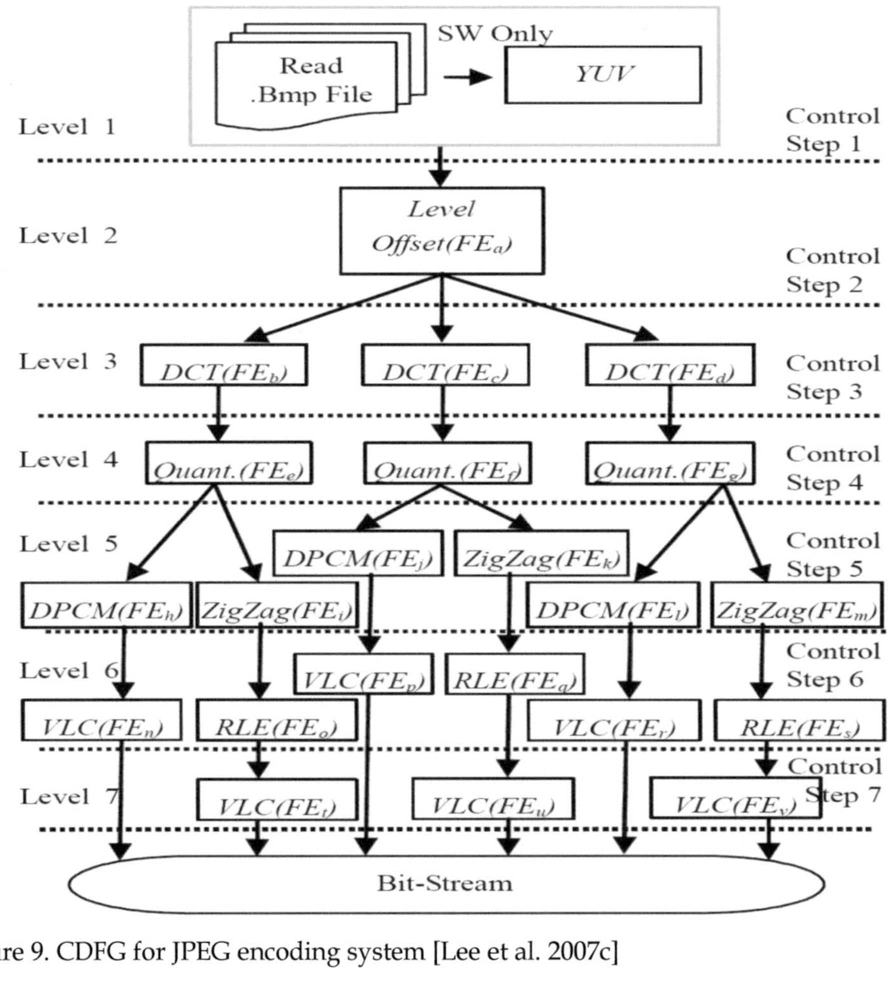

Figure 9. CDFG for JPEG encoding system [Lee et al. 2007c]

To further validate the potential of PSO algorithm for HW/SW partitioning problem we need to test it on a real-life case study, with a realistic cost function terrain. We also wanted to verify our PSO generated solutions against a published "benchmark" design. The HW/SW cost matrix for all the modules of such real life case study should be known. We carried out a comprehensive literature search in search for such case study. Lee et al. [2007c] provided such details for a case study of the well-known Joint Picture Expert Group (JPEG) encoder system. The hardware implementation is written in "Verilog" description language, while the software is written in "C" language. The Control-Data Flow Graph (CDFG) for this implementation is shown in Fig. 9. The authors pre-assumed that the RGB to YUV converter is implemented in SW and will not be subjected to the partitioning process. For more details regarding JPEG systems, interested readers can refer to Jonsson [2005].
Table 1 shows measured data for the considered cost metrics of the system components. Including such table in Lee et al. [2007c] allows us to compare directly our PSO search algorithm with the published ones without re-estimating the HW or SW costs of the design modules on our platform. Also, armed with this data, there is no need to re-implement the published algorithms or trying to obtain them from their authors.

Execution Time		**Cost Percentage**		**Power Consumption**		**Component**
HW(ns)	**SW(us)**	**HW(10^{-3})**	**SW(10^{-3})**	**HW(mw)**	**SW(mw)**	
155.264	9.38	7.31	0.58	4	0.096	**Level Offset (FE_a)**
1844.822	20000	378	2.88	274	45	**DCT (FE_b)**
1844.822	20000	378	2.88	274	45	**DCT (FE_c)**
1844.822	20000	378	2.88	274	45	**DCT (FE_d)**
3512.32	34.7	11	1.93	3	0.26	**Quant (FE_e)**
3512.32	33.44	9.64	1.93	3	0.27	**Quant (FE_f)**
3512.32	33.44	9.64	1.93	3	0.27	**Quant (FE_g)**
5.334	0.94	2.191	0.677	15	0.957	**DPCM (FE_h)**
399.104	13.12	35	0.911	61	0.069	**ZigZag (FE_i)**
5.334	0.94	2.191	0.677	15	0.957	**DPCM(FE_j)**
399.104	13.12	35	0.911	61	0.069	**ZigZag (FE_k)**
5.334	0.94	2.191	0.677	15	0.957	**DPCM (FE_l)**
399.104	13.12	35	0.911	61	0.069	**ZigZag (FE_m)**
2054.748	2.8	7.74	14.4	5	0.321	**VLC (FE_n)**
1148.538	43.12	2.56	6.034	3	0.021	**RLE (FE_o)**
2197.632	2.8	8.62	14.4	5	0.321	**VLC (FE_p)**
1148.538	43.12	2.56	6.034	3	0.021	**RLE (FE_q)**
2197.632	2.8	8.62	14.4	5	0.321	**VLC (FE_r)**
1148.538	43.12	2.56	6.034	3	0.021	**RLE (FE_s)**
2668.288	51.26	19.21	16.7	6	0.018	**VLC (FE_t)**
2668.288	50	1.91	16.7	6	0.018	**VLC (FE_u)**
2668.288	50	1.91	16.7	6	0.018	**VLC (FE_v)**

Table 1. Measured data for JPEG system

The data is obtained through implementing the hardware components targeting ML310 board using Xilinx ISE 7.1i design platform. Xilinx Embedded Design Kit (EDK 7.1i) is used to measure the software implementation costs.
The target board (ML310) contains Virtex2-Pro XC2vP30FF896 FPGA device that contains 13696 programmable logic slices and 2448 Kbytes memory and two embedded IBM Power PC (PPC) processor cores. In general, one slice approximately represents two 4-input Look-Up Tables (LUTs) and two Flip-Flops [Xilinx 2007].
The first column in the table shows the component name (cf. Fig. 9) along with a character unique to each component. The second and third columns show the power consumption in mWatts for the hardware and software implementations respectively. The fourth column shows the software cost in terms of memory usage percentage while the fifth column shows the hardware cost in terms of slices percentage. The last two columns show the execution time of the hardware and software implementations.
Lee et al. [2007c] also provided detailed comparison of their methodology with another four approaches. The main problem is that the target architecture in Lee et al. [2007c] has two processors and allows multi-processor partitioning while our target architecture is based on a single processor. A slight modification in our cost function is performed that allows up to two processors to run on the software part concurrently.
Equation (3) is used to model the cost function after adding the memory cost term as shown in Equation (8)

$$\text{Cost} = 100 * \left\{ \alpha \frac{\text{HWcost}}{\text{allHWcost}} + \beta \frac{\text{SWcost}}{\text{allSWcost}} + \gamma \frac{\text{POWERcost}}{\text{allPOWERcost}} + \eta \frac{\text{MEMcost}}{\text{allMEMcost}} \right\} \quad (8)$$

The added memory cost term (***MEMcost***) and its weight factor (η) account for the memory size (in bits). ***allMEMcost*** is the maximum size (upper-bound) of memory bits i.e., memory size of all software solution.
Another modification to the cost function of Equation (8) is affected if the number of multiprocessors is limited. Consider that we have only two processors. Thus, only two modules can be assigned to the SW side at any control step. For example, in the step 3 of Fig. 9, no more than two DCT modules can be assigned to the SW side. The solution that assigns the three DCT modules of this step to SW side is penalized by a barrier violation term of value "one".
Finally, as more than one hardware component could run in parallel, the hardware delay is not additive. Hence, we calculate the hardware delay by accumulation the maximum delay of each control steps as shown in Fig. 9. In other words, we calculate the critical-path delay.
In Lee et al. [2007c], the results of four different algorithms were presented. However, for the sake brevity, details of such algorithms are beyond the scope of this chapter. We used these results and compared them with our algorithm in Table 2.
In our experiments, the parameters used for the PSO are the population size is fixed to 50 particles, the round terminates after 50 unimproved runs, and 100 runs must run at the beginning to avoid trapping in local minimum. The number of re-excited PSO rounds is selected by the user.
The power constraint is constrained to 600 mW, area and memory are constrained to the maximum available FPGA resources, i.e. 100%, and maximum number of concurrent software tasks is two.

Method	Results *Lev/DCT/Q/DPCM-Zig/ VLC-RLE/VLC*	Execution Time (us)	Memory (KB)	Slice use rate (%)	Power (mW)
FBP [Lee et al. 2007c]	1/001/111/101111/111101/111	20022.26	51.58	53.9	581.39
GHO [Lee et al. 2007b]	1/010/111/111110/111111/111	**20021.66**	**16.507**	54.7	586.069
GA [Lin et al. 2006]	0/010/010/101110/110111/010	20111.26	146.509	47.1	499.121
HOP [Lee et al. 2007a]	0/100/010/101110/110111/010	20066.64	129.68	56.6	599.67
PSO-delay	1/010/111/111110/111111/111	**20021.66**	**16.507**	54.7	586.069
PSO-area	0/100/001/111010/110101/010	20111.26	181.6955	**44.7**	**494.442**
PSO-power	0/100/001/111010/110101/010	20111.26	181.6955	**44.7**	**494.442**
PSO-memory	1/010/111/111110/111111/111	**20021. 66**	**16.507**	54.7	586.069
PSO-NoProc	0/000/111/000000/111111/111	20030.9	34.2328	8.6	189.174
PSO-Norm	0/010/111/101110/111111/111	20030.9	19.98	50.6	521.234

Table 2. Comparison of partitioning results

Different configurations of the cost function are tested for different optimization goals. ***PSO-delay, PSO-area, PSO-power***, and ***PSO-memory*** represent the case where the cost function includes only one term, i.e. delay, area, power, and memory, respectively. ***PSO-NoProc*** is the normal PSO-based algorithm with the cost function shown in equation (7) but the number of processors is unconstrained. Finally, ***PSO-Norm*** is the normal PSO with all constraints being considered, i.e. the same as ***PSO-NoProc*** with maximum number of two processors.

The second column in Table 2 shows the resulting partition where '0' represents software and '1' represents hardware. The vector is divided into sets, each set represents a control step as shown in Fig. 9. The third to fifth columns of this table list the execution time, memory size, % of slices used and the power consumption respectively of the optimum solutions obtained according to the algorithms identified in the first column. As shown in the table, the bold results are the best results obtained for each design metrics.

Regarding PSO performance, all the PSO-based results are found within two or three rounds of the Re-excited PSO. Moreover, for each individual optimization objective, PSO obtains the best result for that specific objective. For example, ***PSO-delay*** obtains the same results as GHO algorithm [ref.] does and it outperforms the other solutions in the execution time and memory utilization and it produces good quality results that meet the constraints. Hence, our cost function formulation enables us to easily select the optimization criterion that suits our design goals.

In addition, ***PSO-a*** and ***PSO-p*** give the same results as they try to move nodes to software while meeting the power and number of processors constraints. On the other hand, ***PSO-del*** and ***PSO-mem*** try to move nodes to hardware to reduce the memory usage and the delay, so their results are similar.

PSO-NoProc is used as a what-if analysis tool, as its results answer the question of what is the optimum number of parallel processors that could be used to find the optimum design.

In our case, obtaining six processors would yield the results shown in the table even if three of them will be used only for one task, namely, the DCT.

4. Extensions

4.1 Modeling Hardware Implementation alternatives

As shown previously, HW/SW partitioning depends on the HW area, delay, and power costs of the individual nodes. Each node represents a grain (from an instruction up to a procedure), and the grain level is selected by the designer. The initial design is usually mapped into a sequencing graph that describes the flow dependencies of the individual nodes. These dependencies limit the maximum degree of parallelism possible between these nodes. Whereas a sequencing graph denotes the partial order of the operations to be performed, the scheduling of a sequencing graph determines the detailed starting time for each operation. Hence, the scheduling task sets the actual degree of concurrency of the operations, with the attendant delay and area costs [De Micheli 1994]. In short, delay and area costs needed for the HW/SW partitioning task are only known accurately post the scheduling task. Obviously, this situation calls for time-wasteful iterations. The other solution is to prepare a library of many implementations for each node and select one of them during the HW/SW partitioning task as the work done by Kalavade and Lee [2002]. Again, such approach implies a high design time cost.

Our approach to solve this egg-chicken coupling between the partitioning and scheduling tasks is as follows: represent the hardware solution of each node by two limiting solutions, HW_1 and HW_2, which are automatically generated from the functional specifications. These two limiting solutions bound the range of all other possible schedules. The partitioning algorithm is then called on to select the best implementation for the individual nodes: SW, HW_1 or HW_2. These two limiting solutions are:

1. **Minimum-Latency solution:** where As-Soon-As-Possible (ASAP) scheduling algorithm is applied to find the fastest implementation by allowing unconstrained concurrency. This solution allows for two alternative implementations, the first where maximum resource-sharing is allowed. In this implementation, similar operational units are assigned to the same operation instance whenever data precedence constraints allow. The other solution, the non-shared parallel solution, forbids resource-sharing altogether by instantiating a new operational unit for each operation. Which of these two parallel solutions yields a lower area is difficult to predict as the multiplexer cost of the shared parallel solution, added to control the access to the shared instances, can offset the extra area cost of the non-shared solution. Our modeling technique selects the solution with the lower area. This solution is, henceforth, referred to as the ***parallel hardware*** solution.
2. **Maximum Latency solution:** where no concurrency is allowed, or all operations are simply serialized. This solution results in the maximum hardware latency and the instantiation of only one operational instance for each operation unit. This solution is, henceforth, referred to as the ***serial hardware*** solution.

To illustrate our idea, consider a node that represents the operation y = (a*b) + (c*d). Fig. 10.a (10.b) shows the parallel (serial) hardware implementations.

From Fig. 10 and assuming that each operation takes only one clock cycle, the first implementation finishes in 2 clock cycles but needs 2 multiplier units and one adder unit. The second implementation ends in 3 clock cycles but needs only one unit for each operation (one adder unit and one multiplier unit). The bold horizontal lines drawn in Fig. 10 represent the clock boundaries.

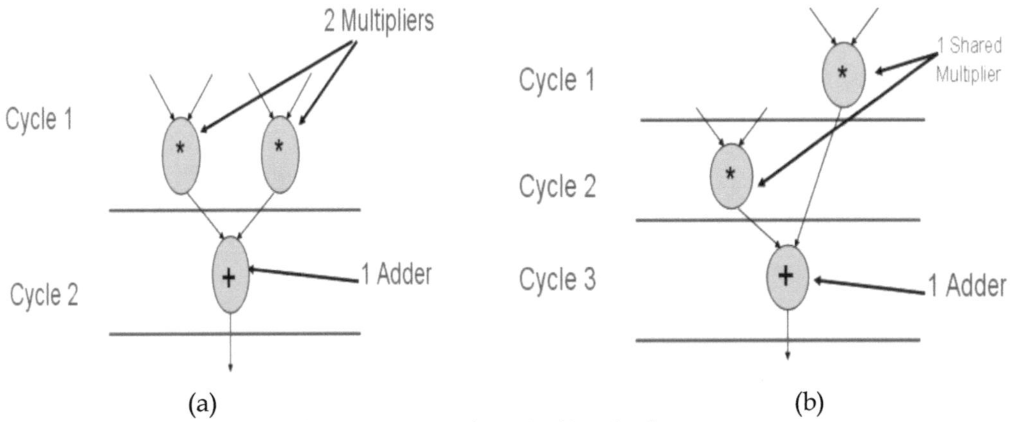

Figure 10. Two extreme implementations of y = (a*b) + (c*d)

In general, the parallel and serial HW solutions have different area and delay costs. For special nodes, these two solutions may have the same area cost, the same delay cost or the same delay and area costs. The reader is referred to Abdelhalim and Habib [2007] for more details on such special nodes.

The use of two alternative HW solutions converts the HW/SW optimization problem from a binary form to a tri-state form. The effectiveness of the PSO algorithm for handling this extended HW/SW partitioning problem is detailed in Section 4.3.

4.2 Communications Cost Modeling

The Communications cost term in the context of HW/SW partitioning represents the cost incurred due to the data and control passing from one node to another in the graph representation of the design. Earlier co-design approaches tend to ignore the effect of HW/SW communications. However, many recent embedded systems are communications oriented due to the heavy amount of data to be transferred between system components.

The communications cost should be considered at the early design stages to provide high quality as well as feasible solutions. The communication cost can be ignored if it is between two nodes on the same side (i.e., two hardware nodes or two software nodes). However, if the two nodes lie on different sides; the communication cost cannot be ignored as it affects the partitioning decisions. Therefore, as communications are based on physical channels, the nature of the channel determines the communication type (class). In general, the HW/SW communications between the can be classified into four classes [Ernest 1997]:

1. Point-to-point communications
2. Bus-based communications
3. Shared memory communications
4. Network-based communications

To model the communications cost, a communication class must be selected according to the target architecture. In general, the model should include one or more of the following cost terms [Luthra et al. 2003]:

1. **Hardware cost:** The area needed to implement the HW/SW interface and associated data transfer delay on the hardware side.

2. **Software cost:** The delay of the software interface driver on the software side.
3. **Memory size:** The size of the dedicated memory and registers for control and data transfers as well as shared memory size.

The terms could be easily modeled within the overall delay, hardware area and memory costs of the system, as shown in equation (8).

4.3 Extended algorithm experiments

As described in Section 3.3, the input to the algorithm is a graph that consists of a number of nodes and number of edges. Each node (edge) is associated with cost parameters. The used cost parameters are:

Serial hardware implementation cost: which is the cost of implementing the node in serialized hardware. The cost includes HW area as well as the associated latency (in clock cycles).

Parallel hardware implementation cost: which is the cost of implementing the node in parallel hardware. The cost includes HW area as well as the associated latency (in clock cycles).

Software implementation cost: the cost of implementing the node in software (e.g. execution clock cycles and the CPU area).

Communication cost: the cost of the edge if it crosses the boundary between the HW and the SW sides (interface area and delay, SW driver delay and shared memory size).

For experimental purposes, these parameters are randomly generated after considering the characteristics of each parameter, i.e. Serial HW area ≤ Parallel HW area, and SW delay ≤ Serial HW delay ≤ Parallel HW delay.

The needed modification is to allow each node in the PSO solution vector to have three values: "0" for software, "1" for serial hardware and "2" for parallel hardware.

The parameters used in the implementation are: No. of particles (Population size) **n** = 50, No. of design size **(m)** = 100 nodes, No. of communication edges **(e)** = 200, No. The number of re-exited PSO rounds set to a predefined value = 50. All other parameters are taken from Section 3.4. The constraints are: Maximum hardware area is 65% of the all-Hardware solution area, and the maximum delay is 25% of the all-Software solution delay.

4.3.1 Results

Three experiments were performed. The first (second) experiment uses the normal PSO with only the serial (parallel) hardware implementation. The third experiment examines the proposed tristate formulation where the hardware is represented by two solutions (serial and parallel solutions). The results are shown in Table 3.

	Area Cost	**Delay Cost**	**Comm. Cost**	**Serial HW nodes**	**Parallel HW nodes**	**SW nodes**
Serial HW	34.9%	**30.52%**	1.43%	99	N/A	1
Parallel HW	57.8%	**29.16%**	32.88%	N/A	69	31
Tri-state formul.	50.64%	23.65%	18.7%	31	55	14

Table 3. Cost result of different hardware alternatives schemes

As shown in this table, the serial hardware solution pushes approximately all nodes to hardware (99 out of 100) but fails to meet the deadline constraint due to the relatively large delay of the serial HW implementations. On the other hand, the parallel HW solution fails to meet the delay constraint due to the relatively large area of parallel HW. Moreover, It has large communications cost. Finally, the tri-state formulation meets the constraints and results in a relatively low communication cost.

4.4 Tuning Algorithm.

As shown in Table 3, the third solution with two limiting HW alternatives has a 23.65% delay. The algorithm could be tuned to push the delay to the constrained value (25%) by moving some hardware-mapped nodes from the parallel HW solution to the serial HW solution. This node switching reduces the hardware area at the expense of increasing the delay cost within the acceptable limits, while the communication cost is unaffected because all the moves are between HW implementations.

1) Find all nodes with parallel HW implementation (***min_delay_set***)
2) Calculate the ***Delay_margin = Delay deadline – PSO Achieved delay***
3) Calculate ***Hardware_range = Node's Max. area – Node's Min. area.***
4) Calculate ***Delay_range = Node's Max. delay – Node's Min. delay.***
5) Create (***dedicated_nodes_list***) with nodes in (***min_delay_set***) sorted in ascending order according to ***Hardware_rang*** such that ***Delay_range<Delay_margin***
6) **While** (***dedicated_nodes_list***) is not empty
 7) Move node with the maximum ***Hardware_range*** to serial HW region.
 8) For many nodes with the same ***Hardware_range***, choose the one with minimum ***Delay_range***
 9) Re-calculate ***Delay_margin***
 10) Update (***dedicated_nodes_list***)
11) **End While**
12) Update (***min_delay_set***)
13) Calculate ***Hardware Sensitivity = Hardware range / Delay range***

Outputs

1. HW/SW partition
2. The remaining ***delay range*** in clock cycles.
3. Remaining parallel hardware nodes and their ***Hardware Sensitivity***

Nodes with high ***Hardware Sensitivity*** could be used along with the ***delay range*** to obtain refined implementations (***Time Constrained Scheduling Problem***)

Figure 11. Tuning heuristic for reducing the hardware area.

The heuristic used to reduce the hardware area is shown Fig. 11. It shares many similarities with the greedy approaches presented by Gupta et al. [1992].
First, the heuristic calculates the extra delay that the system could tolerate and still achieves the deadline constraint (***delay margin***).
It then finds all nodes in parallel HW region with delay range less than delay margin and selects the node with maximum reduction in HW area cost (***hardware range***) to be moved to the serial hardware region. Such selection is carried out to obtain the maximum hardware reduction while still meeting the deadline.

(***delay margin***) is then re-calculated to find the nodes that are movable after the last movement.

After moving all allowable nodes, the remaining parallel HW nodes can not move to the serial HW region due to deadline violation. Therefore, the algorithm reports to the designer with all the remaining parallel HW nodes, their ***Hardware Sensitivity*** (the average hardware decrease due to the increase in the latency by one clock cycle), and the remaining delay margin. The user can, then, select a parallel hardware node or more and make a refined HW implementation with the allowable delay (Time-constrained Scheduling problem [De Micheli 1994]).

The algorithm can be easily modified for the opposite goals, i.e. to account for reducing the delay while still meeting the hardware constraint.

The above algorithm could not start if the PSO terminates with invalid solution. Therefore, we implemented a similar algorithm as a pre-tuning phase but with the opposite goal: moving nodes form serial HW region to parallel HW region to reduce the delay, hence meet the deadline constraint if possible, while minimizing the increase in the hardware area.

4.4.1 Results after using the Tuning Algorithm

Two experiments were done: the first one is the tuning of the results shown in Table 3. The tuning algorithm starts from where PSO ends. The Delay Margin was 1.35% (about 72 clock cycles). At the end of the algorithm, the Delay margin reaches 1 clock cycles, the area decreased to 40.09% and the delay reaches 24.98%. 12 parallel HW nodes were moved to the serial HW implementation. The results show that the area decreases by 10.55% for a very small delay increase (1.33%).

The constraints are modified such that the deadline constraint is reduced to 22% and the maximum area constraint is reduced to 55% to test the pre-tuning phase. PSO terminates with 23.33%delay, 47.68% area, and communications 25.58%. The deadline constraint is violated by 1.33% (about 71 clock cycles). The pre-tuning phase moves nodes from serial HW region into parallel HW region until satisfying the deadline constraints (delay is reduced to 21.95%). It moves 32 nodes and the Area increased to 59.13%. The delay margin becomes 2 clock cycles. Then the normal tuning heuristic starts with that delay margin and moves two nodes back to the serial HW region. The final area is 59% and the final delay is 21.99%. Notice that the delay constraint is met while the area constraint becomes violated.

5. Conclusions

In this chapter, the recent introduction of the Particle Swarm Optimization technique to solve the HW/SW partitioning problem is reviewed, along with its "re-exited PSO" modification. The re-exited PSO algorithm is a recently-introduced restarting technique for PSO. The Re-exited PSO proved to be highly effective for solving the HW/SW partitioning problem.

Efficient cost function formulation is of a paramount importance for an efficient optimization algorithm. Each component in the design must have hardware as well as software implementation costs that guide the optimization algorithm. The hardware cost in our platform is modeled using two extreme implementations that bound all other schedule-dependent implementations. Communications cost between hardware and software domains are then proposed in contrast to other approaches that completely ignore such

term. Finally, a tuning algorithm is proposed to fine tune the results and/or try to meet the constraints if PSO provides violating solutions.
Finally, JPEG encoder system is used as a real-life case study to test the viability of the PSO for solving the HW/SW partitioning problems. This case study compares our results with other published results from the literature. The comparison focuses on the PSO technique only. The results prove that our algorithm provides better or equal results relative to the cited results.
The following conclusions can be made:

- PSO is effective for solving the HW/SW Partitioning Problem. The PSO yields better quality and faster performance relative to the well-known Genetic Algorithm.
- A newly-proposed "Re-exited PSO" restarting technique is effective in escaping local minimum.
- Formulating the HW/SW partitioning problem using the recently proposed two extreme hardware alternatives is effective for solving tightly constrained problems. The introduction of two limiting hardware alternatives provides extra degree of freedom for the designer without penalizing the designer with excessive computational cost.
- Greedy-like Tuning algorithms are useful for refining the PSO results. Such algorithms moves hardware-mapped nodes between their two extreme implementations to refine the solution or even to meet the constraints.
- A JPEG Encoder system is used as a real-life case study to verify the potential of our methodology for partitioning large HW/SW co-design problems.

6. References

Abdelhalim, M. B, Salama, A. E., and Habib S. E. -D. 2006. Hardware Software Partitioning using Particle Swarm Optimization Technique. In The *6th International Workshop on System-on-Chip for Real-Time Applications* (Cairo, Egypt). 189-194.

Abdelhalim, M. B, and Habib S. E. -D. 2007. Modeling communication cost and hardware alternatives in PSO based HW/SW partitioning. In the *19th International Conference on Microelectronics* (Cairo, Egypt). 115-118.

Adhipathi, P. 2004. *Model based approach to Hardware/Software Partitioning of SOC Designs.* MSc Thesis, Virginia Polytechnic Institute and State University, USA.

Armstrong, J.R., Adhipathi, P. J.M. Baker, Jr. 2002. Model and synthesis directed task assignment for systems on a chip. *15th International Conference on Parallel and Distributed Computing Systems* (Cambridge, MA, USA).

Binh, N. N., Imai, M., Shiomi, A., and Hikichi, N. 1996. A hardware/software partitioning algorithm for designing pipelined ASIPs with least gate counts. *Proceedings of 33rd Design Automation Conference* (Las Vegas, NV, USA). 527 - 532.

Chatha, K. S., and Vemuri, R. 2001.MAGELLAN: multiway hardware-software partitioning and scheduling for latency minimization of hierarchical control-dataflow task graphs. *In proceedings of the 9th International Symposium on Hardware/Software Codesign* (Copenhagen, Denmark). 42 – 47.

Cloute, F., Contensou, J.-N., Esteve, D., Pampagnin, P., Pons, P., and Favard, Y. 1999. Hardware/software co-design of an avionics communication protocol interface system: an industrial case study. *In proceedings of the 7th International Symposium on Hardware/Software Codesign* (Rome, Italy). 48-52.

De Micheli, G. 1994. *Synthesis and Optimization of Digital Circuits.* McGraw Hill.

De Souza, D. C., De Barros, M. A., Naviner, L. A. B., and Neto, B. G. A. 2003. On relevant quality criteria for optimized partitioning methods. *In proceedings of 45th Midwest Symposium on Circuits and Systems* (Cairo, Egypt). 1502- 1505.

Ditzel, M. 2004. *Power-aware architecting for data-dominated applications.* PhD thesis, Delft University of Technology, The Netherlands.

Donoso, Y., and Fabregat, R. 2007. *Multi-objective optimization in computer networks using metaheuristics.* Auerbach Publications.

Eberhart, R. C., and Shi, Y. 2001. Particle swarm optimization: developments, applications and resources. In *Processions of 2001 congress on evolutionary computation* (Seoul, Korea). 81-86.

Eberhart, R. C., and Shi, Y. 1998. Comparison between genetic algorithms and particle swarm optimization. *In proceedings of the 7th annual conference on evolutionary programming* (San Diego, CA, USA). 611-616,

Eberhart, R.C., and Kennedy, J. 1995. A new optimizer using particle swarm theory. *Proceedings of the 6th international symposium on micro-machine and human science* (Nagoya, Japan). 39-43.

Eles, P., Peng, Z., Kuchcinski, K., and Doboli, A. 1997. System level HW/SW partitioning based on simulated annealing and tabu search. *Design automation for embedded systems.* Vol. 2, No. 1. 5-32.

Ernest, R. L. 1997. Target architectures in *Hardware/Software Co-Design: principles and practice,* Staunstrup, J. and Wolf W. (eds.). Kluwer Academic publishers. 113-148.

Gupta, R.K., and De Micheli, G. 1992. System-level synthesis using re-programmable components. *In Proceedings of the 3rd European Conference on Design Automation* (Brussels, Belgium). 2-7.

Hanselman, D., and Littlefield, B. 2001. *Mastering MATLAB 6*, Prentice Hall.

Hassan, R., Cohanim, B., de Weck, O., and Venter, G. 2005. A comparison of particle swarm optimization and the genetic algorithm. *1st AIAA Multidisciplinary Design Optimization Specialist Conference* (Austin, Texas).

Haupt, R. L., and Haupt, S. E. 2004. *Practical Genetic Algorithms.* Second Edition, Wiley Interscience.

Henkel, J., and Ernst, R. 2001. An approach to automated hardware/software partitioning using a flexible granularity that is driven by high-level estimation techniques. *IEEE Transactions on Very Large Scale Integration Systems*, Vol. 9, No. 2, 273 - 289.

Jensen, M. T. 2003. Reducing the run-time complexity of multiobjective EAs: The NSGA-II and other algorithms. *IEEE Transactions on Evolutionary Computation,* Vol 7, No. 5, 503-515.

Jha, N. K. and Dick, R. P. 1998. MOGAC: a multiobjective genetic algorithm for hardware-software co-synthesis of distributed embedded systems. *IEEE Transactions on Computer-Aided Design of Integrated Circuits and Systems,* Vol. 17, No. 10. 920 - 935.

Jonsson, B. 2005. *A JPEG encoder in SystemC,* MSc thesis, Lulea University of Technology, Sweden.

Kalavade, A. and Lee, E. A. 1994. A global criticality/local phase driven algorithm for the constrained hardware/software partitioning problem. *In Proceedings of Third International Workshop on Hardware/Software Codesign* (Grenoble, France). 42-48.

Kalavade, A. and Lee, E. A. 2002. The Extended Partitioning Problem: Hardware-software Mapping and Implementation-Bin Selection. In *Readings in hardware/software co-design*, De Micheli, G., Ernest, R. L, and Wolf W.(eds.), Morgan Kaufmann. 293-312.

Kennedy, J., and Eberhart, R.C. 1995. Particle swarm optimization. *In proceedings of IEEE international Conference on Neural Networks* (Perth, Australia). 1942-1948.

Knudsen, P. V., and Madsen, J. 1996. PACE: a dynamic programming algorithm for hardware/software partitioning. *Fourth International Workshop on Hardware/Software Co-Design* (Pittsburgh, PA, USA). 85 - 92.

Lee, T.Y., Fan, Y. H., Cheng, Y. M. Tsai, C. C., and Hsiao, R. S. 2007a. Hardware-Oriented Partition for Embedded Multiprocessor FPGA systems. *In Proceedings of the Second International Conference on Innovative Computing, Information and Control* (Kumamoto, Japan). 65-68.

Lee, T.Y., Fan, Y. H., Cheng, Y. M. Tsai, C. C., and Hsiao, R. S. 2007b. An efficiently hardware-software partitioning for embedded Multiprocessor FPGA system. *In Proceedings of International Multiconference of Engineers and Computer Scientists* (Hong Kong). 346-351.

Lee, T.Y., Fan, Y. H., Cheng, Y. M., Tsai, C. C., and Hsiao, R. S. 2007c. Enhancement of Hardware-Software Partition for Embedded Multiprocessor FPGA Systems. *In Proceedings of the 3rd International Conference on International Information Hiding and Multimedia Signal Processing* (Kaohsiung, Taiwan). 19-22.

Lin, T. Y., Hung, Y. T., and Chang, R. G. 2006. Efficient hardware/software partitioning approach for embedded multiprocessor systems. *In Proceedings of International Symposium on VLSI Design, Automation and Test* (Hsinchu, Taiwan). 231-234.

Lopez-Vallejo, M. and Lopez, J. C. 2003. On the hardware-software partitioning problem: system modeling and partitioning techniques. *ACM transactions on design automation for electronic systems*, Vol. 8, No. 3. 269-297.

Luthra, M., Gupta, S., Dutt, N., Gupta, R., and Nicolau, A. 2003. Interface synthesis using memory mapping for an FPGA platform. *In Proceedings of the 21st International conference on computer design* (San Jose, CA, USA). 140 - 145.

Madsen, J., Gorde, J., Knudsen, P. V. Petersen, M. E., and Haxthausen, A. 1997. lycos: The Lyngby co-synthesis system. *Design Automation of Embedded Systems*, Vol. 2, No. 2. 195-236.

Mann, Z. A. 2004. *Partitioning algorithms for Hardware/Software Co-design*. PhD thesis, Budapest University of Technology and Economics, Hungary.

Marrec, P. L., Valderrama, C. A., Hessel, F., Jerraya, A. A., Attia, M., and Cayrol, O. 1998. Hardware, software and mechanical cosimulation for automotive applications. *proceedings of 9th International Workshop on Rapid System Prototyping* (Leuven, Belgium). 202 - 206.

Mei, B., Schaumont, P., and Vernalde, S. 2000. A hardware/software partitioning and scheduling algorithm for dynamically reconfigurable embedded systems. *In Proceedings of 11th ProRISC* (Veldhoven, Netherlands).

Nieman, R. 1998. *Hardware/Software co-design for data flow dominated embedded systems*. Kluwer Academic publishers.

Pasupuleti, S. and Battiti, R. 2006. The Gregarious Particle Swarm Optimizer (GPSO). *Proceedings of the Genetic and Evolutionary Computation Conference* (Seattle, WA, USA). 67 - 74.

Poli, R. 2007. *Analysis of the publications on the applications of particle swarm optimization applications*. Tech. Rep. CSM-469, Department of Computing and Electronic Systems, University of Essex, Colchester, Essex, UK.

Rodriguez, M, A., and Bollen, J. 2008. *Simulating Network Influence Algorithms Using Particle-Swarms: PageRank and PageRank-Priors*. Available online @ http://arxiv.org/abs/cs.DS/0602002.

Settles, M., and Soule, T. 2003, A hybrid GA/PSO to evolve artificial recurrent neural networks. *In Intelligent Engineering Systems through Artificial NN* (St. Louis, MO, USA). 51-56.

Shi, Y, and Eberhart, R. C. 1999. Empirical study of particle swarm optimization. *In Proceedings of the 1999 Congress on Evolutionary Computation* (Washington, DC, USA). 1945-1950.

Shi, Y, and Eberhart, R. C. 1998. Parameter selection in particle swarm optimization. *In Proceedings of 7th Annual Conference on Evolutionary Computation* (New York, NY, USA). 591-601.

Stitt, G. 2008. Hardware/Software Partitioning with Multi-Version Implementation Exploration, *In Proceedings ofGreat Lakes Symposium in VLSI* (Orlando, FL, USA). 143-146.

Stitt, G., Vahid, F., McGregor, G., and Einloth, B. 2005. Hardware/Software Partitioning of Software Binaries: A Case Study of H.264 Decoder. *IEEE/ACM CODES+ISSS'05* (New York, NY, USA). 285 - 290.

Tillett, J., Rao, T.M., Sahin, F., and Rao, R. 2005, Darwinian particle swarm optimization. *Proceedings of the 2nd Indian Intl. Conference on Artificial Intelligence* (Pune, Indi). 1474-1487.

Vahid, F. 2002.Partitioning Sequential Programs for CAD using a Three-Step Approach. *ACM Transactions on Design Automation of Electronic Systems*, Vol. 7, No. 3. 413-429.

Van den Bergh, F. 2002. *An Analysis of Particle Swarm Optimizer*. PhD thesis, Department of Computer Science, University of Pretoria, South Africa.

Xilinx Inc., 2007. *Virtex-II Pro and Virtex-II Pro X Platform FPGAs: Complete Data Sheet.*

Zheng, Y. L., Ma, L. H., Zhang, L. Y., and Qian, J. X. 2003. On the convergence analysis and parameter selection in particle swarm optimization. *In Proceedings of the 2nd International Conference on Machine Learning and Cybernetics* (Xi-an, China). 1802 - 1807.

Zou, Y. Zhuang, Z., and Cheng, H. HW-SW partitioning based on genetic algorithm. 2004. *In Proceedings of Congress on Evolutionary Computation* (Anhui, China). 628- 633.

4

Particle Swarms in Statistical Physics*

Andrei Băutu [1] and Elena Băutu [2]
[1] "Mircea cel Batrân" Naval Academy, [2] "Ovidius" University
Romania

1. Introduction

Statistical physics is the area of physics which studies the properties of systems composed of many microscopic particles (like atoms and molecules). When combined, the interactions between these particles produce the macroscopic features of the systems. The systems are usually characterized by a very large number of variables and the limited possibilities for observing the properties of the components of the system. For these reasons, solving problems arisen in Statistical Physics with analytical approaches is usually ineffective and sometimes impossible. However, statistical approaches (such as Monte Carlo simulation) can provide acceptable approximations for solutions of these problems. Moreover, recent studies showed that nature inspired metaheuristics (like Genetic Algorithms, Evolutionary Strategies, Particle Swarm Optimization, etc) can also be used to simulate, analyse, and optimize such systems, providing fast and accurate results. Apart from physical implications, problems from Statistical Physics are also important in fields like biology, chemistry, mathematics, communications, economy, sociology, etc.

We will present two important problems from Statistical Physics and discuss how one can use Particle Swarm Optimization (PSO) to tackle them. First, we will discuss how the real-valued version of PSO can be used to minimize the energy of a system composed of repulsive point charges confined on a sphere. This is known as the Thomson problem and it is included in Stephen Smale's famous list of 18 unsolved mathematical problems to be solved in the 21st century. This problem also arises in biology, chemistry, communications, economy, etc.

Latter on, we will discuss how the binary version of PSO can be used to search ground states of Ising spin glasses. Spin glasses are materials that simultaneously present ferromagnetic and anti-ferromagnetic interactions among their atoms. A ground state of a spin glass is a configuration of the system in which this has the lowest energy possible. Besides its importance for Statistical Physics, this problem has applications in neural network theory, computer science, biology, etc.

2. The Basics of Particle Swarm Optimization

Particle Swarm Optimization (PSO) is a metaheuristic inspired by the behaviour of social creatures, which interact between them in order to achieve a common goal. Such behaviour

---

* This work was in part supported by CNCSIS grants TD 254/2008 and TD 199/2007.

can be noticed in flocks of birds searching for food or schools of fish trying to avoid predators (Eberhart & Kennedy, 1995).

The philosophy of PSO is based on the evolutionary cultural model, which states that in social environments individuals have two learning sources: individual learning and cultural transmission (Boyd & Richerson, 1988). Individual learning is an important feature in static and homogeneous environments, because one individual can learn many things about the environment from a single interaction with it. However, if the environment is dynamic or heterogeneous, then that individual needs many interactions with the environment before it gets to know it. Because a single individual might not get enough chances to interact with such environment, cultural transmission (meaning learning from the experiences of others) becomes a requisite, too. In fact, individuals that have more chances to succeed in achieving their goals are the ones that combine both learning sources, thus increasing their gain in knowledge.

In order to solve any problem with PSO, we need to define a fitness function which will be used to measure the quality of possible solutions for that problem. Then, solving the original problem is equivalent to optimizing parameters of the fitness function, such that we find one of its minimum or maximum values (depending on the fitness function). By using a set of possible solutions, PSO will optimize our fitness function, thus solving our original problem. In PSO terms, each solution is called a particle and the set of particles is called a swarm. Particles gather and share information about the problem in order to increase their quality and hopefully become the optimum solution of the problem. Therefore, the driving force of PSO is the collective swarm intelligence (Clerc, 2006).

The fitness function generates a problem landscape in which each possible solution has a corresponding fitness value. We can imagine that similar to birds foraging in their environment, the PSO particles move in this landscape searching locations with higher rewards and exchanging information about these locations with their neighbours. Their common goal is to improve the quality of the swarm. During the search process the particles change their properties (location, speed, memory, etc) to adapt to their environment.

3. Particle Swarm Optimization and the Thompson problem

In 1904, while working on his plum pudding model of the atom, the British physicist Joseph John Thomson stated the following problem: what is the minimum energy configuration of N electrons confined on the surface of a sphere? Obviously, each two electrons repel each other with a force given by Coulomb's law:

$$F = \frac{q_e^2}{4\pi\varepsilon_0}\frac{1}{d^2}, \tag{1}$$

where ε_0 is the electric constant of vacuum, q_e is the charge on a single electron, and d is the distance between the two electrons. Because of these forces, each electron will try to get as far as possible from the others. However, being confined on the surface of the sphere, they will settle for a system configuration with minimum potential energy. The potential energy of a system with N electrons is:

$$U(S)=\frac{q_e^2}{4\pi\varepsilon_0}\sum_{j=1}^{N-1}\sum_{i=j+1}^{N}\frac{1}{d_{ij}}, \tag{2}$$

where we consider the electrons numbered in some random fashion, and d_{ij} is the distance between electrons i^{th} and j^{th} in the system configuration S. Any configuration with minimum potential energy is called a "ground state" of the system.

Over the years, various generalizations for the Thomson problem have also been studied from different aspects. The most common generalization involves interactions between particles with arbitrary potentials. Bowick studied a system of particles constrained to a sphere and interacting by a $d^{-\gamma}$ potential, with $0<\gamma<2$ (Bowick et al, 2002). Travesset studied the interactions of the particles on topologies other than the 2-sphere (Travesset, 2005). Levin studied the interactions in a system with $N-1$ particles confined on the sphere and 1 particle fixed in the centre of the sphere (Levin & Arenzon, 2003). In general, finding the ground state of a system of N repulsive point charges constrained to the surface of the 2-sphere is a long standing problem, which was ranked 7 in Stephen Smale's famous list (Smale, 2000) of 18 unsolved mathematical problems to be solved in the 21st century, along with other famous problems, like the Navier-Stokes equations, Hilbert's sixteenth problem and the P=NP problem.

Apart from physics, the Thomson problem arises in various forms in many other fields: biology (determining the arrangements of the protein subunits which comprise the shells of spherical viruses), telecommunications (designing satellite constellations, selecting locations for radio relays or access points for wireless communications), structural chemistry (finding regular arrangements for proteins S-layers), mathematics, economy, sociology, etc. From an optimization point of view, the Thomson problem is of great interest to computer scientists also, because it provides an excellent test bed for new optimization algorithms, due to the exponential growth of the number of minimum energy configurations and to their characteristics.

The Thomson problem can be solved exactly for small values of N point charges on the surface of a sphere or a torus. However, for large values of $N>8$, exact solutions are not known. The configurations found so far for such values display a great variety of geometrical structures. The best known solutions so far for such systems were identified with numerical simulations, using methods based on Monte Carlo simulations, evolutionary algorithms, simulated annealing, etc (Carlson et al., 2003; Morris et al., 1996; Perez-Garrido et al., 1996; Pang, 1997). PSO for the Thompson problem was first introduced in (Băutu & Băutu, 2007).

We will present in the following how the real-valued version of PSO can be used to tackle the Thomson problem. In order to avoid confusion, we will use the term "point charges" to refer to physical particles on the sphere (electrons, for example) and "particles" to refer to the data structures used by the PSO algorithm.

As mentioned in the previous section, in order to use a PSO algorithm we need to define a function that will measure the quality of solutions encoded by particles. One can think of many such functions for the Thompson problem, but a simple and quick solution is to use the potential energy of a system. We can save some computation time if we ignore the physical constants and use a simplified version of (2) for our fitness function:

$$F(P) = \sum_{j=1}^{N-1} \sum_{i=j+1}^{N} \frac{1}{d_{ij}} \tag{3}$$

where N is the number of point charges in the system, d_{ij} is the Euclidian distance between point charges i and j, encoded by the particle P. If we represent our system configuration in 3D space using a Cartesian coordinate system, then we need to handle $3N$ real values, for the values on the Ox, Oy and Oz axis of each particle (see Figure 1). We will also need to explicitly enforce the sphere surface constraints which require additional computation time.

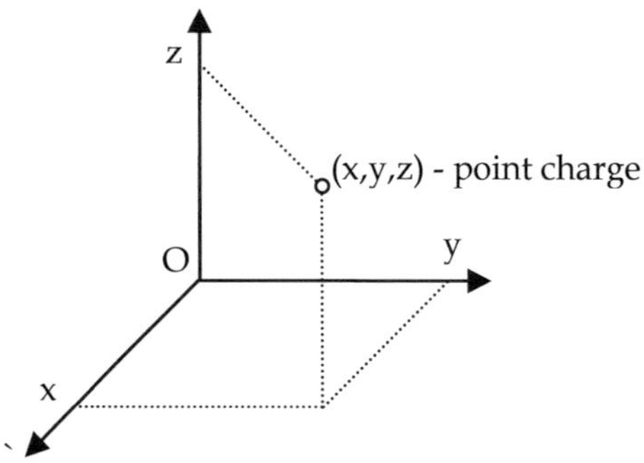

Figure 1. Point charge represented in 3D Cartesian coordinate system

The memory requirements can be reduced and the computation overhead for constraint enforcing can be avoided, if we scale our system to the unit sphere and represent its configuration using a Spherical coordinate system. In this way, the sphere surface constraint is implicitly enforced and since r is constant, the system configuration is encoded with only $2N$ real values, representing the azimuth ϕ and elevation θ angles (see Figure 2).

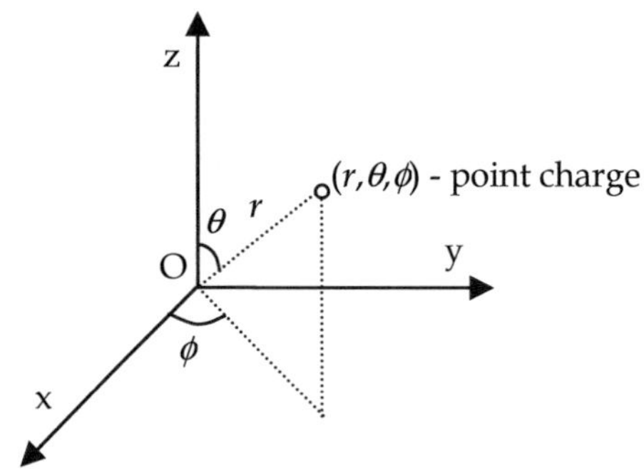

Figure 2. Point charge represented in 3D Spherical coordinate system

In this case, the distance between point charges i and j located on the surface of the unit sphere is

$$d_{ij} = \sqrt{2 - 2[\cos\phi_i \cos\phi_j + \sin\phi_i \sin\phi_j \cos(\theta_i - \theta_j)]}\,, \tag{4}$$

where $\phi_1, \phi_2 \in [-\pi, \pi]$ is the azimuth angle and $\theta_i, \theta_j \in [-\pi/2, \pi/2]$ is the elevation angle. Thus, PSO particles move in the search space $[0,1]^{2N}$ and the location $x \in [0,1]^{2N}$ of a particle decodes into a system configuration with:

$$\phi_i = 2\pi x_{2i-1} - \pi \tag{5}$$

$$\theta_i = \pi x_{2i} - \pi/2 \tag{6}$$

With this setup in place, the PSO algorithm begins with a swarm of particles randomly scattered around the search space. This generic initialization method could be replaced with a problem specific one (spherical initialization, for example). Each particle has a set of neighbours with which it will exchange information. An iterative process begins, which updates the properties of the particles. On each iteration each particle use the information from its own memory and the information gathered from its neighbours to update its properties. The equation used for updating the speed is:

$$v_t = \omega v_{t-1} + \phi_1 R_1 (p_{t-1} - x_{t-1}) + \phi_2 R_2 (g_{t-1} - x_{t-1}), \tag{7}$$

where v_t is the speed at iteration t, x_t is the location of the particle at iteration t, p_t is the best location the particle has found until iteration t, g_t is the best location the neighbours of the particle found up to the iteration t. The individual learning and cultural transmission factors (ϕ_1 and ϕ_2) control the importance of the personal and neighbour's experience on the search process. Note that although they share the same notation, these are parameters of the algorithm and are distinct and not related to the azimuth angles of the point charges. Because the importance of individual learning and cultural transmission is unknown, the learning factors are weighted by random values $R_1, R_2 \in [0,1)$. Usually the speed is bounded by some v_{max} parameter to prevent it from increasing too much because of these random values.

With the updated speed vector and the old position of the particle, the new position is computed with:

$$x_t = x_{t-1} + v_t \Delta t, \tag{8}$$

for $\Delta t = 1$ iteration.

Based on the previous discussion, the PSO algorithm used for the Thomson problem is summarized in Figure 3. The algorithm is very simple and requires basic programming skills to be implemented in any programming language. It has many parameters that can be tuned in order to achieve high performance results. The tuning process of these parameters is beyond the purpose of this chapter. For now, let's consider the following setup: $\omega = 0.9$ – will allow the algorithm to avoid rapid changes in the trajectories of the particles; $\phi_1 = \phi_2 = 2$ – gives equal weight to individual and social learning; iterations = 500 – for small and medium size systems, this should be enough for the particles to discover and focus on good solutions; $M = 2N$ – increases the swarm size with the size of the system.

```
Initialize M random particles
for t = 1 to iterations
    for each particle
        Update v_t according to (7)
        Update x_t according to (8)
        Decode x_t using (5) and (6)
        Evaluate x_t using (3) and (4)
        Update p_t and g_t according to their definition
    next
next
return solution from the particle with smaller fitness
```

Figure 3. PSO algorithm for the Thomson problem

Performing 10 runs of the algorithm from Figure 3 for systems with different sizes, we obtained the results presented in Table 1:

N	Minimum known energy	Energy of PSO solution
2	0.500000000	0.500000000
3	1.732050808	1.732050808
4	3.674234614	3.674234614
5	6.474691495	6.474691495
6	9.985281374	9.985281374
7	14.452997414	14.452987365
8	19.675287861	19.675287861
9	25.759986531	25.759986599
10	32.716949460	32.717003657
15	80.670244114	80.685310397
20	150.881568334	150.953443814
25	243.812760299	243.898092955
30	359.603945904	359.901863399
35	498.569872491	499.018395878
40	660.675278835	661.666117852
45	846.188401061	847.129739052
50	1055.182314726	1056.517970873

Table 1. Minimum energies for Thomson problem found in experiments

From the results in Table 1, one can see that this simple PSO algorithm can provide high quality estimates for the ground states of various instances of the Thomson problem. The algorithm can be further improved not only in its parameters, but also in its structure (using a more advanced initialization method, for example). Obviously, the Particle Swarm Optimization algorithm can be applied for generalized forms of Thomson problem and other related problems, not only from Statistical Physics, but other domains, too.

4. Binary Particle Swarm Optimization and Ising Spin Glasses

Matter is composed of atoms and each atom carries a spin, meaning the magnetic moment of the microscopic magnetic field around the atom generated by the motion of the electrons around its nucleus.

If we heat a metal object higher than the Curie point of its material, the object will loose its ferromagnetic properties and become paramagnetic. At that point, the spins of the atoms change randomly so erratic that at any time they can point with equal probability to any possible direction. In this case, the individual microscopic magnetic fields generated by the spins cancel each other out, such that there is no macroscopic magnetic field (Huang, 1987).

When the temperature is lower than the Curie point, in some metals (iron and nickel, for example) the spins of the atoms tend to be polarized in the same direction, producing a measurable macroscopic magnetic field. This is called "ferromagnetic" behaviour. By contrast, below the Curie point, in spin glasses only some pairs of neighbouring spins prefer to be aligned, while the others prefer to be anti-aligned, resulting two types of interactions between atoms: ferromagnetic and anti-ferromagnetic. Because of this mix of interactions, these systems are called disordered (den Hollander & Toninelli, 2005).

In the past, condensed matter physics has focused mainly on ordered systems, where symmetry and regularity lead to great mathematical simplification and clear physical insight. Over the last decades, spin glasses became a thriving area of research in condensed matter physics, in order to understand disordered systems. Spin glasses are the most complex kind of condensed state encountered so far in solid state physics (De Simone et al., 1995). Some examples of spin glasses are metals containing random magnetic impurities (called disordered magnetic alloys), such as gold with small fractions of iron added (AuFe).

Apart from their central role in Statistical Physics, where they are the subject of extensive theoretical, experimental and computational investigation, spin glasses also represent a challenging class of problems for testing optimization algorithms. The problem is interesting because of the properties of spin glass systems, such as symmetry or large number of plateaus (Pelikan & Goldberg, 2003).

From an optimization point of view, the main objective is to find the minimum energy for a given spin glass system (Hartmann, 2001; Pelikan & Goldberg, 2003; Fischer, 2004; Hartmann & Weigt, 2005). System configurations with the lowest energy are called ground states and thus the problem of minimizing the energy of spin glass instances can be formulated as the problem of finding ground states of these instances (Pelikan et al., 2006). The main difficulties when searching for ground states of spin glasses come from the many local optima in the energy landscape which are surrounded by high-energy neighbouring configurations (Pelikan & Goldberg, 2003).

The Ising model is a simplified description of ferromagnetism, yet it is extremely important because other systems can be mapped exactly or at least approximately to it. Its applications range from neural nets and protein folding to flocking birds, beating heart cells and more. It was named after the German physicist Ernst Ising who first discussed it in 1925, although it was suggested in 1920 by his Ph.D. advisor, Wilhelm Lenz. Ising used it as a mathematical model for phase transitions with the goal of explaining how long-range correlations are generated by local interactions.

The Ising model can be formulated for any dimension in graph-theoretic terms. Let us consider a spin glass system with N spins and no external magnetic field. The interaction graph $G=(V,E)$ associated with the system has the vertex set $V=\{v_1,\dots,v_N\}$. Each vertex

$i \in V$ can be in one of two states $S_i \in \{-1,1\}$. Edges in this graph represent bonds between adjacent atoms in the spin glass system. Each edge $ij \in E$ has assigned a coupling constant, denoted by $J_{ij} \in \{-J, J\}$; an edge exists between vertices *i* and *j* if the interaction between atoms *i* and *j* is not zero. In the classic model, this graph is a standard "square" lattice in one, two, or three dimensions. Therefore, each atom has two, four, or six nearest neighbours, respectively (see Figure 4). However, various papers present research done on larger dimensions (Hartmann, 2001).

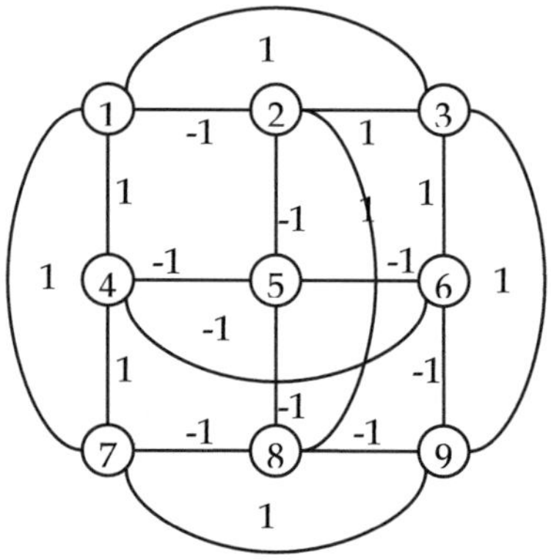

Figure 4. Two dimensional Ising spin glass system

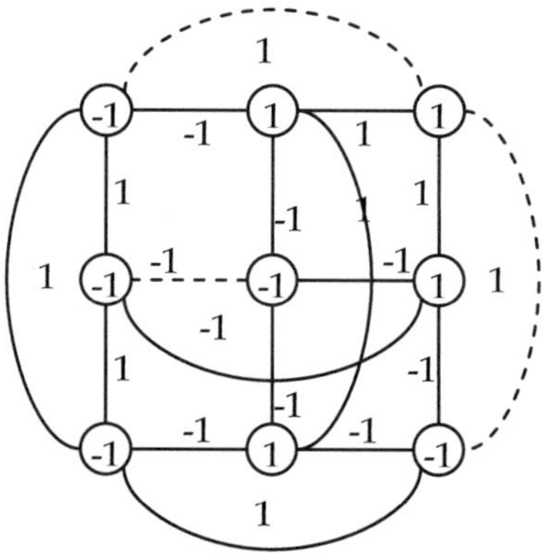

Figure 5. Ground state of the system from Figure 4 (values inside circles represent the states of the spins; dashed lines represent unsatisfied bonds)

For a system configuration S, the interaction between neighbouring vertices *i* and *j* contributes an amount of $-J_{ij}S_iS_j$ to the total energy of the system, expressed as the Hamiltonian:

$$H(S) = -\sum_{ij \in E} J_{ij} S_i S_j \,. \tag{9}$$

The sign of J_{ij} gives the nature of the interaction between neighbours *i* and *j*. If J_{ij} is positive, the interaction is ferromagnetic. Having the two neighbours in the same state ($S_i = S_j$) decreases the total energy. If J_{ij} is negative, the interaction between neighbours *i* and j is anti-ferromagnetic. The decrease in total energy is obtained if they have opposite states. When all coupling constants are positive (or negative), a lowest-energy configuration is obtained when all vertices have the same state. This is the case of ferromagnetic materials. When the coupling constants are a mix of positive and negative values, as is the case for spin glasses, finding the "ground state" is a very difficult problem. A ground state of the system from Figure 4 is presented in Figure 5.

The two-dimensional Ising model of ferromagnetism has been solved exactly by Onsager (Onsager, 1944). The most common configurations in the literature are 2D Ising spin glasses on a grid with nearest neighbour interactions. In the case of no periodic boundary conditions and no exterior magnetic field, the problem reduces to finding a minimum weight cut in a planar graph for which polynomial time algorithms exist (Orlova & Dorfman, 1972; Goodman & Hedetniemi, 1973; Hadlock, 1975). Barahona showed that finding a ground state for the three-value coupling constant ($J_{ij} \in \{-1,0,1\}$) on a cubic grid is equivalent to finding a maximum set of independent edges in a graph for which each vertex has degree 3 (Barahona, 1982). He also showed that computing the minimum value of the Hamiltonian of a spin glass with an external magnetic field,

$$H(S) = -\sum_{ij \in E} J_{ij} S_i S_j - h \sum_{i \in V} S_0 S_i \,, \tag{10}$$

is equivalent to solving the problem of finding the largest set of disconnected vertices in a planar, degree-3 graph. This means that finding ground states for three-dimensional spin glasses on the standard square lattice and for planar spin glasses with an external field are NP-complete problems. Istrail showed that the essential ingredient for the NP-completeness of the Ising model is the non planarity of the graph (Istrail, 2000).

Particle Swarm Optimization was introduced as a technique for numerical optimization and has proved to be very efficient on many real-valued optimization problems. Because finding the ground state of a spin glass system in the Ising model is a combinatorial problem, we need to apply a modified version of PSO. We will use the binary version of PSO (Kennedy & Eberhard, 1997). In this case, the ith component of the position vector of a particle encodes the state of the ith spin in the system (0 means down, 1 means up), while the ith component of the velocity vector determines the confidence of the particle that the ith spin should be up.

On each iteration of the search process, each particle updates its velocity vector (meaning its confidence that the spins should be up) using (7). After that, the particle's position vector (meaning its decision about spins being up or down) it updated using the component-wise formula:

$$x_{ti} = \begin{cases} 1, \text{if } R < \left(1 + \exp(-v_{ti})\right)^{-1} \\ 0, \text{otherwise} \end{cases} \tag{11}$$

where $R \in [0,1)$ is a random value. Once a particle's position is known, its profit can be computed by:

$$F(x_t) = -\sum_{1 \le i < j \le N} J_{ij} \left(2x_{ti} - 1\right)\left(2x_{tj} - 1\right), \tag{12}$$

With such fitness function, lower values indicate better solutions. Obviously, this fitness function is inspired by the Hamiltonian given in (9) and can be adapted easily to external magnetic field environments using (10).

Based on the previous discussion, the Binary PSO algorithm used for the Ising spin glass problem is presented in Figure 6. A more advanced PSO algorithm for this problem is described in (Băutu et al., 2007). It combines the PSO algorithm with a local optimization technique which allows the resulting hybrid algorithm to fine tune candidate solutions.

Initialize M random particles
for t = 1 to iterations
    for each particle
        Update v_t according to (7)
        Update x_t according to (11)
        Evaluate x_t using (12)
        Update p_t and g_t according to their definition
    next
next
return solution from the particle with smaller fitness

Figure 6. PSO algorithm for the Ising spin glass problem

In order to test this algorithm, one can use a spin grass system generator, like the Spin Glass Server (SGS). SGS can be used to solve exactly 2D and 3D systems with small sizes or to generate systems for testing. It is available online at http://www.informatik.uni-koeln.de/ls_juenger/research/sgs/sgs.html.

N	SGS minimum energy per spin	PSO minimum energy per spin
64 / 3D	-1.6875	-1.6875
64 / 3D	-1.7500	-1.7500
64 / 3D	-1.8750	-1.8750
125 / 3D	-1.7040	-1.6720
125 / 3D	-1.7680	-1.7360
125 / 3D	-1.7360	-1.7040

Table 2. Minimum energies for Ising spin glasses found in experiments

Table 2 presents the energy per spin values obtained for 3D systems of 4x4x4 and 5x5x5 spins using (13). They will give you an idea about the performance of the binary PSO on this type of problems. The actual values depend on the spin system for which the algorithm is used.

$$E(x_t) = \frac{F(x_t)}{N} \tag{13}$$

The results from table 2 were obtained without any tuning of the PSO parameters: the individual and social learning factors are $\phi_1 = \phi_2 = 2$ and the inertia factor is $\omega = 0.9$. The number of iterations is twice the number of spins, and the number of particles is three times the number of spins. SGS provides the minimum energy for these systems using a branch-and-cut algorithm (De Simone et al., 1995).

5. Conclusions

This chapter presented the basic traits of Particle Swarm Optimization and its applications for some well known problems in Statistical Physics. Recent research results presented in the literature for these problems prove that PSO can find high quality solutions in reasonable times (Băutu et al, 2007; Băutu & Băutu, 2008). However, many questions are still open: how do the parameters setups relate to the problems tackled? how can we improve the basic PSO to get state of the are results? how can we tackle very large size systems?

6. References

Barahona, F. (1982). On the Computational Complexity of Ising Spin Glass Models, *Journal of Physics A: Mathematical and General*, 15(10), Oct. 1982, pp. 3241-3253

Băutu, A., Băutu, E. & Luchian, H. (2007). Particle Swarm Optimization Hybrids for Searching Ground States of Ising Spin Glasses, *Proceedings of the Ninth International Symposium on Symbolic and Numeric Algorithms for Scientific Computing*, Timisoara, Romania, pp. 415-418, ISBN 0-7695-3078-8, IEEE Computer Society

Băutu, A. & Băutu, E. (2007). Energy Minimization Of Point Charges On A Sphere With Particle Swarms, *7th International Balkan Workshop on Applied Physics*, Constantza, Jul. 2007

Băutu, A. & Băutu, E. (2008). Searching Ground States of Ising Spin Glasses with Genetic Algorithms and Binary Particle Swarm Optimization, *Nature Inspired Cooperative Strategies for Optimization (NICSO 2007)*, vol. 129, May 2008, pp. 85-94, ISBN 978-3-540-78986-4, Springer, Berlin

Bowick, M., Cacciuto, A., Nelson, D.R. & Travesset, A. (2002). Crystalline Order on a Sphere and the Generalized Thomson Problem, *Physical Review Letters*, 89(18), Oct. 2002, pp. 185502, ISSN 0031-9007

Boyd, R. & Richerson, P.J. (1988). *Culture and the Evolutionary Process*, University of Chicago Press, ISBN 0226069338, Chicago

Carlson, J., Chang, S.Y., Pandharipande, V.R. & Schmidt, K.E. (2003). Superfluid Fermi Gases with Large Scattering Length, *Physical Review Letters*, 91(5), Aug. 2003, pp. 050401, ISSN 0031-9007

Clerc, M. (2006). *Particle Swarm Optimization*, Hermes Science Publishing Ltd., ISBN 1905209045, London

De Simone, C., Diehl, M., Junger, M., Mutzel, P. Reinelt, G., & Rinaldi, G. (1995). Exact ground states of Ising spin glasses: New experimental results with a branch and cut algorithm, *Journal of Statistical Physics*, 80(2), Jul. 1995, pp. 487-496, ISSN 0022-4715

Eberhart, R. & Kennedy, J. (1995). A new optimizer using particle swarm theory, *Proceedings of the Sixth International Symposium on Micro Machine and Human Science*, pp. 39-43, ISBN 0-7803-2676-8, Nagoya, Oct. 1995, IEEE Press, Piscataway

Fischer, S. (2004). A Polynomial Upper Bound for a Mutation-Based Algorithm on the Two-Dimensional Ising Model, *Proceedings of GECCO-2004, Part I*, pp. 1100-1112, ISBN 3-540-22344-4, Genetic and Evolutionary Computation, Jun. 2004, Springer, Berlin

Goodman, S. & Hedetniemi, S. (1973). Eulerian walks in graphs, *SIAM Journal on Computing*, 2(2), Mar. 1973, pp. 16-27, SIAM, ISSN 0097-5397

Hadlock, F. (1975) Finding a Maximum Cut of a Planar Graph in Polynomial Time, *SIAM Journal on Computing*, 4(3), Sep.1975, pp. 221-225, SIAM, ISSN 0097-5397

Hartmann, A.K. (2001). Ground-State Clusters of Two-, Three- and Four-dimensional ±J Ising Spin Glasses, *Physical Review E*, 63(2), Jan. 2001, pp. 016106, ISSN 0031-9007

Hartmann, A.K. & Weigt, M. (2005). *Phase Transitions in Combinatorial Optimization Problems: Basics, Algorithms and Statistical Mechanics*, Wiley, ISBN 3-527-40473-5, New York

den Hollander, F., Toninelli, F. (2005). Spin glasses: A mystery about to be solved, *Eur. Math. Soc. Newsl.*, vol. 56, pp. 13-17, 2005

Huang, K. (1987) *Statistical Mechanics, 2nd ed.*, Wiley, ISBN 0471815187, New York

Istrail, S. (2000). Universality of Intractability of the Partition Functions of the Ising Model Across Non-Planar Lattices, *Proceedings of the STOC00*, pp. 87-96, ISBN 1-58113-184-4, 32nd ACM Symposium on the Theory of Computing, May 2000, ACM Press

Kennedy, J. & Eberhart, R.C. (1997). A discrete binary version of the particle swarm algorithm, *Proceedings of the World Multiconference on Systemics, Cybernetics and Informatics*, vol. 5, IEEE International Conference on Systems, Man, and Cybernetics, pp. 4104-4109, ISBN 0-7803-4053-1, IEEE Press, Piscataway

Levin, Y. & Arenzon, J.J. (2003) Why charges go to the surface: A generalized Thomson problem, *Europhysics Letters*, 63(3), Aug. 2003, pp. 415-418, ISSN 0295-5075

Morris, J.R., Deaven, D.M. & Ho, K.M. (1996). Genetic-algorithm energy minimization for point charges on a sphere, *Phys. Rev. B*, 53(4), pp. 1740-1743, ISSN 0163-1829

Onsager, L. (1944). Crystal statistics in a two-dimensional model with an order-disorder transition, *Physical Review*, 65(3), Feb. 1944, pp. 117-149

Orlova, G.I. & Dorfman, Y.G. (1972). Finding the maximum cut in a graph, *Engr. Cybernetics*, 10, pp. 502-506

Pang, T. (1997). *An Introduction to Computational Physics*, Cambridge University Press, ISBN 0521825695, New York

Pelikan, M. & Goldberg, D.E. (2003). Hierarchical BOA Solves Ising Spin Glasses and MAXSAT, *Proceedings of GECCO-2003*, pp. 1271-1282, ISBN 3-540-40603-4, Genetic and Evolutionary Computation, Jul. 2003, Springer, Berlin

Pelikan, M. Hartmann, A.K., & Sastry, K. (2006). Hierarchical BOA, Cluster Exact Approximation, and Ising Spin Glasses, *Proceedings of PPSN 2006*, pp. 122-131, ISBN 978-3-540-38990-3, Parallel Problem Solving from Nature - IX, Springer, Berlin

Perez-Garrido, A., Ortuno, M., Cuevas, E. & Ruiz, J. (1996). Many-particle jumps algorithm and Thomson's problem, *Journal of Physics A: Mathematical and General*, 29(9), May 1996, pp. 1973-1978, ISSN 0305-4470

Smale, S. (2000), Mathematical problems for the next century, In: *Mathematics: frontiers and perspectives*, V.I. Arnold, M. Atiyah, P. Lax, B. Mazur (Ed.), pp. 271-294, American Mathematical Society, ISBN 0821820702, Providence, USA

Travesset, A. (2005). Ground state of a large number of particles on a frozen topography, *Physical Review E*, 72(3), September, 2005, pp. 036110, ISSN 0031-9007

5

Individual Parameter Selection Strategy for Particle Swarm Optimization

Xingjuan Cai, Zhihua Cui, Jianchao Zeng and Ying Tan
Division of System Simulation and Computer Application, Taiyuan University of Science and Technology
P.R.China

1. Brief Survey of Particle Swarm Optimization

With the industrial and scientific developments, many new optimization problems are needed to be solved. Several of them are complex multi-modal, high dimensional, non-differential problems. Therefore, some new optimization techniques have been designed, such as genetic algorithm (Holland, 1992), ant colony optimization (Dorigo & Gambardella, 1997), etc. However, due to the large linkage and correlation among different variables, these algorithms are easily trapped to a local optimum and failed to obtain the reasonable solution.

Particle swarm optimization (PSO) (Eberhart & Kennedy, 1995; Kennedy & Eberhart, 1995) is a population-based, self-adaptive search optimization method motivated by the observation of simplified animal social behaviors such as fish schooling, bird flocking, etc. It is becoming very popular due to its simplicity of implementation and ability to quickly converge to a reasonably good solution (Shen et al., 2005; Eberhart & Shi, 1998; Li et al., 2005).

In a PSO system, multiple candidate solutions coexist and collaborate simultaneously. Each solution called a "particle", flies in the problem search space looking for the optimal position to land. A particle, as time passes through its quest, adjusts its position according to its own "experience" as well as the experience of neighboring particles. Tracking and memorizing the best position encountered build particle's experience. For that reason, PSO possesses a memory (i.e. every particle remembers the best position it reached during the past) . PSO system combines local search method (through self experience) with global search methods (through neighboring experience), attempting to balance exploration and exploitation.

A particle status on the search space is characterized by two factors: its position and velocity, which are updated by following equations:

$$\overrightarrow{v_j}(t+1) = w\overrightarrow{v_j}(t) + c_1 r_1(\overrightarrow{p_j}(t) - \overrightarrow{x_j}(t)) + c_2 r_2(\overrightarrow{p_g}(t) - \overrightarrow{x_j}(t)) \tag{1}$$

$$\overrightarrow{x_j}(t+1) = \overrightarrow{x_j}(t) + \overrightarrow{v_j}(t+1) \tag{2}$$

where $\overrightarrow{v_j}(t)$ and $\overrightarrow{x_j}(t)$ represent the velocity and position vectors of particle *j* at time *t*, respectively. $\overrightarrow{p_j}(t)$ means the best position vector which particle *j* had been found, as well as $\overrightarrow{p_g}(t)$ denotes the corresponding best position found by the whole swarm. Cognitive coefficient c_1 and social coefficient c_2 are constants known as acceleration coefficients, and r_1 and r_2 are two separately generated uniformly distributed random numbers in the range [0, 1]. To keep the moving stability, a limited coefficient v_{max} is introduced to restrict the size of velocity.

$$|v_{jk}(t+1)| \leq v_{max} \tag{3}$$

The first part of (1) represents the previous velocity, which provides the necessary momentum for particles to roam across the search space. The second part, known as the "cognitive" component, represents the personal thinking of each particle. The cognitive component encourages the particles to move toward their own best positions found so far. The third part is known as the "social" component, which represents the collaborative effect of the particles, in finding the global optimal solution. The social component always pulls the particles toward the global best particle found so far.

Since particle swarm optimization is a new swarm intelligent technique, many researchers focus their attentions to this new area. One famous improvement is the introduction of the inertia weight (Shi & Eberhart, 1998a), similarly with temperature schedule in the simulated annealing algorithm. Empirical results showed the linearly decreased setting of inertia weight can give a better performance, such as from 1.4 to 0 (Shi & Eberhart, 1998a), and 0.9 to 0.4 (Shi & Eberhart, 1998b, Shi & Eberhart, 1999). In 1999, Suganthan (Suganthan,1999) proposed a time-varying acceleration coefficients automation strategy in which both c_1 and c_2 are linearly decreased during the course of run. Simulation results show the fixed acceleration coefficients at 2.0 generate better solutions. Following Suganthan's method, Venter (Venter, 2002) found that the small cognitive coefficient and large social coefficient could improve the performance significantly. Further, Ratnaweera (Ratnaweera et al., 2004) investigated a time-varying acceleration coefficients. In this automation strategy, the cognitive coefficient is linearly decreased during the course of run, however, the social coefficient is linearly increased inversely.

Hybrid with Kalman filter, Monson designed a new Kalman filter particle swarm optimization algorithm (Monson & Seppi, 2004) . Similarly, Sun proposed a new quantum particle swarm optimization (Sun et al., 2004) in 2004. From the convergence point, Cui designed a global convergence algorithm — stochastic particle swarm optimization (Cui & Zeng, 2004). There are still many other modified methods, such as fast PSO (Cui et al., 2006a), predicted PSO (Cui et al.,2006b), etc. The details of these algorithms can be found in corresponding references.

The PSO algorithm has been empirically shown to perform well on many optimization problems. However, it may easily get trapped in a local optimum for high dimensional multi-modal problems. With respect to the PSO model, several papers have been written on the subject to deal with premature convergence, such as the addition of a queen particle (Mendes et al., 2004), the alternation of the neighborhood topology (Kennedy, 1999), the introduction of subpopulation and giving the particles a physical extension (Lovbjerg et al., 2001), etc. In this paper, an individual parameter selection strategy is designed to improve the performance when solving high dimensional multi-modal problems.

The rest of this chapter is organized as follows: the section 2 analyzes the disadvantages of the standard particle swarm optimization parameter selection strategies; the individual inertia weight selection strategy is designed in section 3; whereas section 4 provides the cognitive parameter selection strategy. In section 5, the individual social parameter selection strategies is designed. Finally, conclusion and future research are discussed.

2. The Disadvantages of Standard Particle Swarm Optimization

Partly due to the differences among individuals, swarm collective behaviors are complex processes. Fig.l and Fig.2 provide an insight of the special swarm behaviors about birds flocking and fish schooling. For a group of birds or fish families, there exist many differences. Firstly, in nature, there are many internal differences among birds (or fish), such as ages, catching skills, flying experiences, and muscles' stretching, etc. Furthermore, the lying positions also provide an important influence on individuals. For example, individuals, lying in the side of the swarm, can make several choices differing from center others. Both of these differences mentioned above provide a marked contribution to the swarm complex behaviors.

Figure 1. Fish's Swimming Process

Figure 2. Birds' Flying Process

For standard particle swarm optimization, each particle maintains the same flying (or swimming) rules according to (1), (2) and (3). At each iteration, the inertia weight w, cognitive learning factor c_1 and social learning factor c_2 are the same values within the whole swarm, thus the differences among particles are omitted. Since the complex swarm behaviors can emerge the adaptation, a more precise model, incorporated with the differences, can provide a deeper insight of swarm intelligence, and the corresponding algorithm may be more effective and efficient. Inspired with this method, we propose a new algorithm in which each particle maintains personal controlled parameter selection setting.

3. Individual Inertia weight Selection Strategy

Without loss of generality, this paper consider the following problem:

$$min\ f(\vec{X}) \qquad \vec{X} \in D \subseteq R^n \tag{4}$$

From the above analysis, the new variant of PSO in this section will incorporate the personal differences into inertia weight of each particle (called PSO-IIWSS, in briefly) (Cai et al., 2008), providing a more precise model simulating the swarm behaviors. However, as a new modified PSO, PSO-IIWSS should consider two problems listed as follows:

1. How to define the characteristic differences of each particle?
2. How to use the characteristic difference to control inertia weight, so as to affect its behaviors?

3.1 How to define the characteristic differences?

If the fitness value of particle u is better than which of particle m, the probability that global optima falls into u's neighborhood is larger than that of particle m. In this manner, the particle u should pay more attentions to exploit its neighborhood. On the contrary, it may tend to explore other region with a larger probability than exploitation. Thus the information index is defined as follows:

The information index - score of particle u at time t is defined as

$$Score_u(t) = \frac{f(x_{worst}(t)) - f(x_u(t))}{f(x_{worst}(t)) - f(x_{best}(t))} \tag{5}$$

where $x_{worst}(t)$ and $x_{best}(t)$ are the worst and best particles' position vectors at time t, respectively.

3.2 How to use the characteristic differences to guild its behaviors?

Since the coefficients setting can control the particles' behaviors, the differences may be incorporated into the controlled coefficients setting to guide each particle's behavior. The allowed controlled coefficients contain inertia weight w, two accelerators c_1 and c_2. In this section, inertia weight w is selected as a controlled parameter to reflect the personal characters. Since w is dependent with each particle, we use $w_u\ (t)$ representing the inertia weight of particle u at time t.

Now, let us consider the adaptive adjustment strategy of inertia weight $w_u(t)$. The following part illustrates three different adaptive adjustment strategies.

Inspired by the ranking selection mechanism of genetic algorithm (Mich ale wicz, 1992), the first adaptive adjustment of inertia weight is provided as follows:

The inertia weight $w_u(t)$ of particle u at time t is computed by

$$w_u(t) = w_{low}(t) + (w_{high}(t) - w_{low}(t)) \times (1 - Score_j(t)) \tag{6}$$

where $w_{low}(t)$ and $w_{high}(t)$ are the lower and upper bounds of the swarm at time t.
This adaptive adjustment strategy states the better particles should tend to exploit its neighbors, as well as the worse particles prefer to explore other region. This strategy implies the determination of inertia weight of each particle, may provide a large selection pressure.
Compared with ranking selection, fitness uniform selection scheme (FUSS) is a new selection strategy measuring the diversity in phenotype space. FUSS works by focusing the selection intensity on individuals which have uncommon fitness values rather than on those with highest fitness as is usually done, and the more details can be found in (Marcus, 2002). Inspired by FUSS, the adaptive adjustment strategy two aims to provide a more chance to balance exploration and exploitation capabilities.
The inertia weight $w_u(t)$ of particle u at time t is computed by

$$w_u(t) = w_{low}(t) + (w_{high}(t) - w_{low}(t)) \times (1 - Score_{rand}(t)) \tag{7}$$

where $w_{low}(t)$ and $w_{high}(t)$ are the lower and upper bounds of the swarm at time t. $Score_{rand}(t)$ is defined as follows.

$$Score_{rand}(t) = \{Score_s(t) \| r - f(x_s(t))| \leq |r - f(x_i(t))|, i = 1, ..., s-1, s+1, ..., n\} \tag{8}$$

where r is a random number sampling uniformly between $f(x_{best}(t))$ and $f(x_{worst}(t))$.
Different from ranking selection and FUSS strategies which need to order the whole swarm, tournament strategy (Blickle & Thiele, 1995) is another type of selection strategy, it only uses several particles to determine one particle's selection probability. Analogized with tournament strategy, the adaptive adjustment strategy three is designed with local competition, and defined as follows:
The inertia weight $w_u(t)$ of particle u at time t is computed by

$$w_u(t) = \begin{cases} w_{low}(t) + (w_{high}(t) - w_{low}(t)) \times (1 - Score_{r_1}(t)), & \text{if } f(x_{r_1}) < f(x_{r_2}) \\ w_{low}(t) + (w_{high}(t) - w_{low}(t)) \times (1 - Score_{r_2}(t)), & \text{otherwise} \end{cases} \tag{9}$$

where $w_{low}(t)$ and $w_{high}(t)$ are the lower and upper bounds of the swarm at time t. $x_{r_1}(t)$ and $x_{r_1}(t)$ are two random selected particles uniformly.

3.3 The Step of PSO-IIWSS

The step of PSO-IIWSS is listed as follows.

- Step 1. Initializing each coordinate $x_{jk}(0)$ to a value drawn from the uniform random distribution on the interval $[x_{min}, x_{max}]$, for $j = 1,2, ..., s$ and $k = 1,2, ..., n$. This distributes the initial position of the particles throughout the search space. Where s is the value of the swarm, n is the value of dimension. Initializing each $v_{jk}(0)$ to a value drawn from the uniform random distribution on the interval $[-v_{max}, v_{max}]$, for all j and k. This distributes the initial velocity of the particles.
- Step 2. Computing the fitness of each particle.
- Step 3. Updating the personal historical best positions for each particle and the swarm;

- Step 4. Determining the best and worst particles at time *t*, then, calculate the score of each particle at time *t*.
- Step 5. Computing the inertia weight value of each particle according to corresponding adaptive adjustment strategy one,two and three (section 3.2, respectively) .
- Step 6. Updating the velocity and position vectors with equation (1),(2) and (3) in which the inertia w is changed with $w_j(t)$.
- Step 7. If the stop criteria is satisfied, output the best solution; otherwise, go step 2.

3.4 Simulation Results

3.4.1 Selected Benchmark Functions

In order to certify the efficiency of the PSO-IIWSS, we select five famous benchmark functions to testify the performance, and compare PSO-IIWSS with stan-
dard PSO (SPSO) and Modified PSO with time- varying accelerator coefficients (MPSO_TVAC) (Ratnaweera et al, 2004). Combined with different adaptive adjustment strategy of inertia weight one, two and three, the corresponding versions of PSO-IIWSS are called PSO-IIWSS1, PSO-IIWSS2, PSO-IIWSS3, respectively.
Sphere Modal:

$$f_1(x) = \sum_{j=1}^{n} x_j^2$$

where $|x_j| \leq 100.0$, and

$$f_1(x^*) = f_1(0, 0, ..., 0) = 0.0$$

Schwefel Problem 2.22:

$$f_2(x) = \sum_{j=1}^{n} |x_j| + \prod_{k=1}^{n} |x_k|$$

where $|x_j| \leq 10.0$, and

$$f_2(x^*) = f_2(0, 0, ..., 0) = 0.0$$

Schwefel Problem 2.26:

$$f_3(x) = -\sum_{j=1}^{n} (x_j \sin(\sqrt{|x_j|}))$$

where $|x_j| \leq 500.0$, and

$$f_3(x^*) = f_3(420.9687, 420.9687, ..., 420.9687) \approx -12569.5$$

Ackley Function:

$$f_4(x) = -20exp(-0.2\sqrt{\frac{1}{n}\sum_{j=1}^{n} x_j^2}) - exp(\frac{1}{n}\sum_{k=1}^{n} \cos 2\pi x_k) + 20 + e$$

where $|x_j| \leq 32.0$, and

$$f_4(x^*) = f_4(0, 0, ..., 0) = 0.0$$

Hartman Family:

$$f_5(x) = -\sum_{i=1}^{4} c_i exp[-\sum_{j=1}^{3} a_{ij}(x_j - p_{ij})^2]$$

where $x_j \in [0.0,1.0]$, and a_{ij} is satisfied with the following matrix.

$$\begin{pmatrix} 3 & 10 & 30 \\ 0.1 & 10 & 35 \\ 3 & 10 & 30 \\ 0.1 & 10 & 35 \end{pmatrix}$$

p_{ij} is satisfied with the following matrix.

$$\begin{pmatrix} 0.3687 & 0.1170 & 0.2673 \\ 0.4699 & 0.4387 & 0.7470 \\ 0.1091 & 0.8732 & 0.5547 \\ 0.03815 & 0.5743 & 0.8828 \end{pmatrix}$$

c_i is satisfied with the following matrix.

$$\begin{pmatrix} 1 \\ 1.2 \\ 3 \\ 3.2 \end{pmatrix}$$

$$f_5(x^*) = f_5(0.114, 0.556, 0.852) = -3.86$$

Sphere Model and Schwefel Problem 2.22 are unimodel functions. Schwefel Problem 2.26 and Ackley function are multi-model functions with many local minima,as well as Hartman Family with only several local minima.

3.4.2 Parameter Setting

The coefficients of SPSO,MPSO_TVAC and PSO-IIWSS are set as follows:

The inertia weight w is decreased linearly from 0.9 to 0.4 with SPSO and MPSO_TVAC, while the inertia weight lower bounds of PSO-IIWSS is set 0.4, and the upper bound of PSO-IIWSS is set linearly from 0.9 to 0.4. Two accelerator coefficients c_1 and c_2 are both set to 2.0 with SPSO and PSO-IIWSS, as well as in MPSO_TVAC, c_1 decreases from 2.5 to 0.5,while c_2

increases from 0.5 to 2.5. Total individuals are 100 except Hartman Family with 20, and v_{max} is set to the upper bound of domain.The dimensions of Sphere Model, Schwefel Problem 2.22,2.26 and Ackley Function are set to 30,while Hartman Family's is 3.Each experiment the simulation runs 30 times while each time the largest evolutionary generation is 1000 for Sphere Model, Schwefel Problem 2.22, Schwefel Problem 2.26, and Ackley Function, and due to small dimensionality, Hartman Family is set to 100.

3.4.3 Performance Analysis

Table 1 to 5 are the comparison results of five benchmark functions under the same evolution generations respectively.The average mean value and average standard deviation of each algorithm are computed with 30 runs and listed as follows.

From the Tables, PSO-IIWSSI maintains a better performance than SPSO and MPSO_TVAC with the average mean value. For unimodel functions, PSO-IIWSS3 shows preferable convergence capability than PSO-IIWSS2,while vice versa for the multi-model functions.

From Figure 1 and 2,PSO-IIWSSI and PSO-IIWSS3 can find the global optima with nearly a line track, while PSO-IIWSSI owns the fast search capability during the whole course of simulation for figure 3 and 4. PSO-IIWSS2 shows the better search performance with the increase of generations. In one word, PSO-IIWSSI owns a better performance within the convergence speed for all functions nearly.

Algorithm	Average Mean Value	Average Standard Deviation
SPSO	9.9512e-006	1.4809e-005
MPSO_TVAC	4.5945e-018	1.9379e-017
PSO-IIWSSI	1.4251e-023	1.8342e-023
PSO-IIWSS2	1.2429e-012	2.8122e-012
PSO-IIWSS3	1.3374e-019	6.0570e-019

Table 1. Simulation Results of Sphere Model

Algorithm	Average Mean Value	Average Standard Deviation
SPSO	7.7829e-005	7.5821e-005
MPSO_TVAC	3.0710e-007	1.0386e-006
PSO-IIWSSI	2.4668e-015	2.0972e-015
PSO-IIWSS2	1.9800e-009	1.5506e-009
PSO-IIWSS3	3.2359e-012	4.1253e-012

Table 2. Simulation Results of Schwefel Problem 2.22

Algorithm	Average Mean Value	Average Standard Deviation
SPSO	-6.2474e+003	9.2131e+002
MPSO_TVAC	-6.6502e+003	6.0927e+002
PSO-IIWSSI	-7.7455e+003	8.0910e+002
PSO-IIWSS2	-6.3898e+003	9.2699e+002
PSO-IIWSS3	-6.1469e+003	9.1679e+002

Table 3. Simulation Results of Schwefel Problem 2.26

Algorithm	Average Mean Value	Average Standard Deviation
SPSO	8.8178e-004	6.8799e-004
MPSO_TVAC	1.8651e-005	1.0176e-004
PSO-IIWSS1	2.9940e-011	4.7552e-011
PSO-IIWSS2	3.8672e-007	5.6462e-007
PSO-IIWSS3	3.3699e-007	5.8155e-007

Table 4. Simulation Results of Ackley Function

Algorithm	Average Mean Value	Average Standard Deviation
SPSO	-3.7507e+000	1.0095e-001
MPSO_TVAC	-3.8437e+000	2.9505e-002
PSO-IIWSS1	-3.8562e+000	1.0311e-002
PSO-IIWSS2	-3.8511e+000	1.6755e-002
PSO-IIWSS3	-3.8130e+000	5.2168e-002

Table 5. Simulation Results of Hartman Family

3.5 Individual non-linear inertia weight selection strategy (Cui et al., 2008)

3.5.1 PSO-IIWSS with Different Score Strategies (PSO-INLIWSS)

As mentioned above, the linearly decreased score strategy can not reflect the truly complicated search process of PSO. To make a deep insight of action for score, three non-linear score strategies are designed in this paper. These three strategies are unified to a power function, which is set to the following equation:

$$Score_u(t) = \{1 - [\frac{f(x_{worst}(t)) - f(x_u(t))}{f(x_{worst}(t)) - f(x_{best}(t))}]^{k_1}\}^{k_2} \tag{10}$$

where k_1 and k_2 are two integer numbers.

Figure 3 shows the trace of linear and three non-linear score strategies, respectively. In Figure 1, the value $f(x_{best}(t))$ is set 1, as well as $f(x_{worst}(t))$ is 100. When k_1 and k_2 are both set to 1, it is just the score strategy proposed in [?], which is also called strategy one in this paper. While $k_1 > 1$ and $k_2 = 1$, this non-linear score strategy is called strategy two here. And strategy three corresponds to $k_1 = 1$ and $k_2 > 1$, strategy four corresponds to $k_1 > k_2 > 1$. Description of three non-linear score strategies are listed as follows: Strategy two: the curve $k_1 = 2$ and $k_2 = 1$ in Figure 3 is an example of strategy two. It can be seen this strategy has a lower score value than strategy one. However, the increased ratio of score is not a constant value. For those particles with small fitness values, the corresponding score values are smaller than strategy one, and they pay more attention to exploit the region near the current position. However, the particles tends to make a local search is larger than strategy one due to the lower score values. Therefore, strategy two enhances the local search capability.

Strategy three: the curve $k_1 = 1$ and $k_2 = 2$ in Figure 3 is an example of strategy three. As we can see, it is a reversed curve compared with strategy two. Therefore, it enhances the global search capability.

Strategy four: the curve $k_1 = 2$ and $k_2 = 5$ in Figure 3 is an example of strategy four. The first part of this strategy is similar with strategy two, as well as the later part is similar with strategy three. Therefore, it augments both the local and global search capabilities.

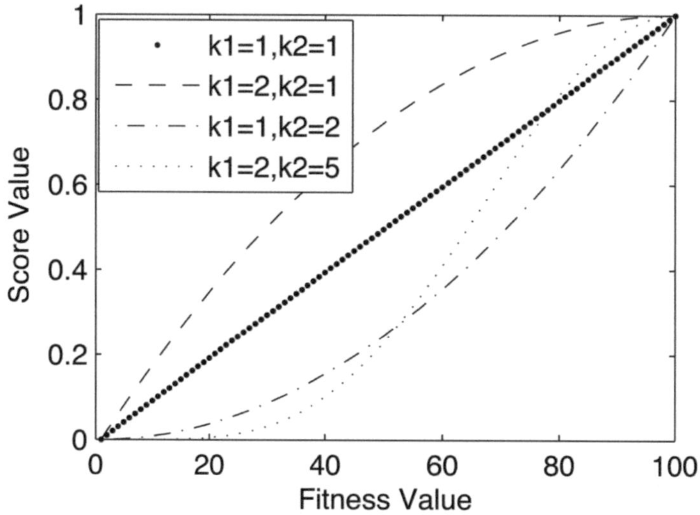

Figure 3. Illustration of Score Strategies

The step of PSO-INLIWSS with different score strategies are listed as follows.

- Step 1. Initializing the position and velocity vectors of the swarm, and de termining the historical best positions of each particle and its neighbors;
- Step 2. Determining the best and worst particles at time t with the following definitions.

$$x_{best}(t) = \arg\min\{f(x_j(t)), j = 1, 2, ..., s\} \tag{11}$$

and

$$x_{worst}(t) = \arg\max\{f(x_j(t)), j = 1, 2, ..., s\} \tag{12}$$

- Step 3. Calculate the score of each particle at time t with formula (10) using different strategies.
- Step 4. Calculating the PSO-INLIWSS inertia weight according to formula (6);
- Step 5. Updating the velocity and position vectors according to formula (1), (2) and (3);
- Step 6. Determining the current personal memory (historical best position);
- Step 7. Determining the historical best position of the swarm;
- Step 8. If the stop criteria is satisfied, output the best solution; otherwise, go step 2.

3.5.2 Simulation Results

To certify the efficiency of the proposed non-linear score strategy, we select five famous benchmark functions to test the performance, and compared with standard PSO (SPSO), modified PSO with time- varying accelerator coefficients (MPSO-TVAC) (Ratnaweera et al., 2004), and comprehensive learning particle swarm optimization (CLPSO) (Liang et al., 2006). Since we adopt four different score strategies, the proposed methods are called PSO-INLIWSS1 (with strategy one, in other words, the original linearly PSO-IIWSS1), PSO-INLIWSS2 (with strategy two), PSO-INLIWSS3 (with strategy three) and PSO-INLIWSS4 (with strategy four), respectively. The details of the experimental environment and results are explained as follows.

In this paper, five typical unconstraint numerical benchmark functions are used to test. They are: Rosenbrock, Schwefel Problem 2.26, Ackley and two Penalized functions.
Rosenbrock Function:

$$f_1(x) = \sum_{j=1}^{n-1}[100(x_{j+1} - x_j^2)^2 + (x_j - 1)^2]$$

where $|x_j| \leq 30.0$, and

$$f_1(x^*) = f_1(1, 1, ..., 1) = 0.0$$

Schwefel Problem 2.26:

$$f_2(x) = -\sum_{j=1}^{n}(x_j \sin(\sqrt{|x_j|}))$$

where $|x_j| \leq 500.0$, and

$$f_2(x^*) = f_2(420.9687, 420.9687, ..., 420.9687) \approx -12569.5$$

Ackley Function:

$$f_3(x) = -20exp(-0.2\sqrt{\frac{1}{n}\sum_{j=1}^{n} x_j^2}) - exp(\frac{1}{n}\sum_{k=1}^{n}\cos 2\pi x_k) + 20 + e$$

where $|x_j| \leq 32.0$, and

$$f_3(x^*) = f_3(0, 0, ..., 0) = 0.0$$

Penalized Function l:

$$f_4(x) = \frac{\pi}{30}\{10\sin^2(\pi y_1) + \sum_{i=1}^{n-1}(y_i - 1)^2[1 + 10\sin^2(\pi y_{i+1})] + (y_n - 1)^2\} + \sum_{i=1}^{n} u(x_i, 10, 100, 4)$$

where $|x_j| \leq 50.0$, and

$$u(x_i, a, k, m) = \begin{cases} k(x_i - a)^m, & \text{if } x_i > a \\ 0, & \text{if } -a \leq x_i \leq a \\ k(-x_i - a)^m, & \text{if } x_i < -a \end{cases}$$

$$y_i = 1 + \frac{1}{4}(x_i + 1)$$

$$f_4(x^*) = f_4(1, 1, ..., 1) = 0.0$$

Penalized Function 2:

$$f_5(x) = 0.1\{\sin^2(3\pi x_1) + \sum_{i=1}^{n-1}(x_i - 1)^2[1 + \sin^2(3\pi x_{i+1})]$$
$$+(x_n - 1)^2[1 + \sin^2(2\pi x_n)]\} + \sum_{i=1}^{n} u(x_i, 5, 100, 4)$$

where $|x_j| \leq 50.0$, and

$$f_5(x^*) = f_5(1, 1, ..., 1) = 0.0$$

Generally, Rosenbrock is viewed as a unimodal function, however, in recent literatures, several numerical experiments (Shang & Qiu, 2006) have been made to show Rosenbrock is a multi-modal function with only two local optima when dimensionality between 4 to 30. Schwefel problem 2.26, Ackley, and two penalized functions are multi-model functions with many local minima.

The coefficients of SPSO, MPSO-TVAC, and PSO-INLIWSS are set as follows: inertia weight w is decreased linearly from 0.9 to 0.4 with SPSO and MPSO-TVAC, while the inertia weight lower bounds of all version of PSO-INLIWSS are both set to 0.4, and the upper bounds of PSO-INLIWSS are both set linearly decreased from 0.9 to 0.4. Two accelerator coefficients c_1 and c_2 are set to 2.0 with SPSO and PSO-INLIWSS, as well as in MPSO-TVAC, c_1 decreases from 2.5 to 0.5, while c_2 increases from 0.5 to 2.5. Total individuals are 100, and the velocity threshold v_{max} is set to the upper bound of the domain. The dimensionality is 30. In each experiment, the simulation run 30 times, while each time the largest iteration is 50 x *dimension*.

Algorithm	Mean Value	Std Value
SPSO	5.6170e+001	4.3584e+001
MPSO-TVAC	3.3589e+001	4.1940e+001
CLPSO	5.1948e+001	2.7775e+001
PSO-INLIWSS1	2.3597e+001	2.3238e+001
PSO-INLIWSS2	3.4147e+001	2.9811e+001
PSO-INLIWSS3	4.0342e+001	3.2390e+001
PSO-INLIWSS4	3.1455e+001	2.4259e+001

Table 6. The Comparison Results for Rosenbrock

Algorithm	Mean Value	Std Value
SPSO	-6.2762e+003	1.1354e+003
MPSO-TVAC	-6.7672e+003	5.7050e+002
CLPSO	-1.0843e+004	3.6105e+002
PSO-INLIWSS1	-7.7885e+003	1.1526e+003
PSO-INLIWSS2	-7.2919e+003	1.1476e+003
PSO-INLIWSS3	-9.0079e+003	7.1024e+002
PSO-INLIWSS4	-9.0064e+003	9.6881e+002

Table 7. The Comparison Results for Schwefel Problem 2.26

For Rosenbrock (see Table 6), because there is an additional local optimum near (-1, 0, 0,...,0), the performance of the MPSO-TVAC, PSO-INLIWSS1 and PSO-INLIWSS4 are better than others. We also perform several other unimodel and multi-modal functions with only few local optima, the PSO-INLIWSS1 are always the best one within these seven algorithms.
For Schwefel problem 2.26 (Table 7) and Ackley (Table 8), the performance of PSO-INLIWSS3 and PDPSO4 are nearly the same. Both of them are better than others.
However, for two penalized functions (Table 9 and 10), the performance of PSO-INLIWSS3 is not the same as the previous two, although PSO-INLIWSS4 is still stable and better than others. As we known, both of these two penalized functions has strong linkage among dimensions. This implies PSO-INLIWSS4 is more suit for multi-modal problems.
Based on the above analysis, we can draw the following two conclusions:
(l) PSO-INLIWSSl (the original version of PSO-IIWSS1) is suit for unimodel and multi-modal functions with a few local optima;
(2) PSO-INLIWSS4 is the most stable and effective among three score strategies. It is fit for multi-modal functions with many local optima especially for linkages among dimensions;

Algorithm	Mean Value	Std Value
SPSO	5.8161e-006	4.6415e-006
MPSO-TVAC	7.5381e-007	3.3711e-006
CLPSO	5.6159e-006	4.9649e-006
PSO-INLIWSS1	4.2810e-014	4.3890e-014
PSO-INLIWSS2	1.1696e-011	1.2619e-011
PSO-INLIWSS3	2.2559e-014	8.7745e-015
PSO-INLIWSS4	2.1493e-014	7.8195e-015

Table 8. The Comparison Results for Ackley

Algorithm	Mean Value	Std Value
SPSO	6.7461e-002	2.3159e-001
MPSO-TVAC	1.8891e-017	6.9756e-017
CLPSO	1.0418e-002	3.1898e-002
PSO-INLIWSS1	1.6477e-025	4.7735e-025
PSO-INLIWSS2	6.2234e-026	1.6641e-025
PSO-INLIWSS3	2.4194e-024	7.6487e-024
PSO-INLIWSS4	2.2684e-027	4.4964e-027

Table 9. The Comparison Results for Penalized Functionl

Algorithm	Mean Value	Std Value
SPSO	5.4943e-004	2.4568e-003
MPSO-TVAC	9.3610e-027	4.1753e-026
CLPSO	1.1098e-007	2.6748e-007
PSO-INLIWSS1	4.8692e-027	1.3533e-026
PSO-INLIWSS2	2.8092e-028	5.6078e-028
PSO-INLIWSS3	9.0765e-027	2.5940e-026
PSO-INLIWSS4	8.2794e-028	1.6562e-027

Table 10. The Comparison Results for Penalized Function2

4. Individual Cognitive Selection Strategy

Because each particle maintains two types of performance at time *t*: the fitness value $f(\overrightarrow{p}_j(t))$ of historical best position found by particle *j* and that of current position $f(\overrightarrow{x}_j(t))$, respectively. Similarly, two different rewards of environment are also designed associated with $f(\overrightarrow{p}_j(t))$ and $f(\overrightarrow{x}_j(t))$. For convenience, the reward based upon $f(\overrightarrow{p}_j(t))$ is called the self-learning strategy one, and the other one is called the self-learning strategy two. The details of these two strategies are explained as follows.

4.1 Self-learning Strategy One

Let us suppose $\overrightarrow{P}(t) = (\overrightarrow{p}_1(t), \overrightarrow{p}_2(t), ..., \overrightarrow{p}_n(t))$ is the historical best position vector of the swarm at time *t*, where *n* and $\overrightarrow{p_j}(t)$ denote the dimensionality and the historical best position found by particle *j* until time *t*.
The expectation limitation position of particle *j* of standard version of PSO is

$$E\{lim_{t\to\infty}\overrightarrow{x}_j(t)\} = \frac{c_1\overrightarrow{p}_j + c_2\overrightarrow{p}_g}{c_1 + c_2} \tag{13}$$

if c_1 and $\overrightarrow{p_j}(t)$ are constant values. Thus, a large c_1 makes the $E\{lim_{t\to\infty}\overrightarrow{x}_j(t)\}$ moving towards $\overrightarrow{p}_j$, and exploits near $\overrightarrow{p}_j$ with more probability, and vice versa. Combined the better $\overrightarrow{p_j}(t)$ implies the more capability of which global optima falls into, the cognitive coefficient is set as follows.

$$c_{1,j}(t) = c_{low} + (c_{high} - c_{low}) \times Reward1_j(t) \tag{14}$$

where c_{low}, and c_{high} are two predefined lower and upper bounds to control this coefficient. $Reward1_j(t)$ is defined

$$Reward1_j(t) = \begin{cases} 1 \quad , & \text{if } f_{worst} = f_{best}, \\ \frac{f_{worst} - f(\overrightarrow{p}_j(t)))}{f_{worst} - f_{best}}, & \text{otherwise} . \end{cases} \tag{15}$$

where f_{worst} and f_{best} denote the worst and best values among $f(\overrightarrow{P}(t))$.

4.2 Self-learning Strategy Two

Let us suppose $\overrightarrow{X}(t) = (\overrightarrow{x}_1(t), \overrightarrow{x}_2(t), ..., \overrightarrow{x}_n(t))$ is the population at time *t*, where *n*, $\overrightarrow{x_j}(t)$ denote the dimensionality and the position of particle *j* at time *t*.
Different from strategy one, if the performance $\overrightarrow{x_j}(t)$ is better than $\overrightarrow{x}_k(t)$ (*j* and *k* are arbitrary chosen from the population), the probability of global optimal fallen near $\overrightarrow{x_j}(t)$ is larger than $\overrightarrow{x}_k(t)$, thus, particle *j* should exploit near its current position with a larger probability than particle *k*. It means $c_{1,j}(t)$ should be less than $c_{1,k}(t)$ to provide little affection of historical best position $\overrightarrow{p_j}(t)$, and the adjustment is defined as follows

$$c_{1,j}(t) = c_{low} + (c_{high} - c_{low}) \times Reward2_j(t) \tag{16}$$

where $Reward2_j(t)$ is defined as

$$Reward2_j(t) = \begin{cases} 0 \quad , & \text{if } f_{worst} = f_{best}, \\ \frac{f(\vec{x}_j(t)) - f_{best}}{f_{worst} - f_{best}}, & \text{otherwise.} \end{cases} \tag{17}$$

where f_{worst} and f_{best} denote the worst and best values among $f(\vec{X}(t))$.

4.3 Mutation Strategy

To avoid premature convergence, a mutation strategy is introduced to enhance the ability escaping from the local optima.

This mutation strategy is designed as follows. At each time, particle j is uniformly random selected within the whole swarm, as well as the dimensionality k is also uniformly random selected, then, the $v_{jk}(t)$ is changed as follows.

$$v_{jk}(t) = \begin{cases} 0.5 \times x_{max} \times r_1 \quad , & \text{if } r_2 < 0.5, \\ -0.5 \times x_{max} \times r_1 & \text{otherwise.} \end{cases} \tag{18}$$

where r_1 and r_2 are two random numbers generated with uniform distribution within 0 and 1.

4.4 The Steps of PSO-ILCSS

For convenience, we call the individual Linear Cognitive Selection Strategy(Cai X.J. et al.,2007;Cai X.J. et al.,2008) as ILCSS, and the corresponding variant is called PSO-ILCSS. The detailed steps of PSO-ILCSS are listed as follows.

- Step 1. Initializing each coordinate x_{jk} (0) and v_{jk} (0) sampling within [x_{min}, x_{max}], and [0, v_{max}], respectively, determining the historical best position by each particle and the swarm.
- Step 2. Computing the fitness of each particle.
- Step 3. For each dimension k of particle j, the personal historical best position p_{jk} (t) is updated as follows.

$$p_{jk}(t) = \begin{cases} x_{jk}(t), & \text{if } f(x_j(t)) < f(p_j(t-1)) \ , \\ p_{jk}(t-1) \quad , & \text{otherwise.} \end{cases} \tag{19}$$

- Step 4. For each dimension k of particle j, the global best position p_{gk} (t) is updated as follows.

$$p_{gk}(t) = \begin{cases} p_{jk}(t), & \text{if } f(p_j(t)) < f(p_g(t-1)) \ , \\ p_{gk}(t-1) \quad , & \text{otherwise.} \end{cases} \tag{20}$$

- Step 5. Selecting the self-learning strategy:if strategy one is selected, computing the cognitive coefficient $c_{1,j}$ (t) of each particle according to formula (14) and (15); otherwise, computing cognitive coefficient $c_{1,j}$ (t) with formula (16) and (17).
- Step 6. Updating the velocity and position vectors with equations (l)-(3).
- Step 7. Making mutation operator described in section 4.3.
- Step 8. If the criteria is satisfied, output the best solution; otherwise, goto step 2.

4.5 Simulation Results

Five famous benchmark functions are used to test the proposed algorithm's efficiency. They are Schwefel Problem 2.22,2.26, Ackley, and two different Penalized Functions, the global optima is 0 except Schwefel Problem 2.26 is -12569.5, while Schwefel Problem 2.22 is unimodel function. Schwefel Problem 2.26,Ackley function and two Penalized Functions are multi-model functions with many local minima.

In order to certify the efficiency, four different versions are used to compare: PSO-ILCSS with self-learning strategy one (PSO-ILCSSI), PSO-ILCSS with self-learning strategy two (PSO-ILCSS2),standard PSO (SPSO) and Modified PSO with time-varying accelerator coefficients (MPSO-TVAC) (Ratnaweera et al., 2004).

The coefficients of SPSO,MPSO-TVAC,PSO-ILCSS1 and PSO-ILCSS2 are set as follows: the inertia weight w is decreased linearly from 0.9 to 0.4. Two accelerator coefficients c_1 and c_2 are both set to 2.0 with SPSO, and in MPSO-TVAC, ci decreased from 2.5 to 0.5,while c_2 increased from 0.5 to 2.5. In PSO-ILCSSI and PSO-ILCSS2, the lower bounds c_{low} of c_1 set to 1.0, and the upper bound c_{high} set to linearly decreased from 2.0 to 1.0, while c_2 is set to 2.0. Total individual is 100, and the dimensionality is 30, and v_{max} is set to the upper bound of domain. In each experiment,the simulation run 30 times, while each time the largest evolutionary generation is 1000.

Table 2 is the comparison results of five benchmark functions under the same evolution generations. The average mean value and average standard deviation of each algorithm are computed with 30 runs and listed as follows.

Function	Algorithm	Average Mean Value	Average Standard Deviation
Fl	SPSO	6.6044e-005	4.7092e-005
	MPSO-TVAC	3.0710e-007	1.0386e-006
	PSO-ILCSS1	2.1542e-007	3.2436e-007
	PSO-ILCSS2	9.0189e-008	1.3398e-007
F2	SPSO	-6.2474e+003	9.2131e+002
	MPSO-TVAC	-6.6502e+003	6.0927e+002
	PSO-ILCSS1	-8.1386e+003	6.2219e+002
	PSO-ILCSS2	-8.0653e+003	7.2042e+002
F3	SPSO	1.9864e-003	6.0721e-003
	MPSO-TVAC	1.8651e-005	1.0176e-004
	PSO-ILCSS1	3.8530e-008	3.8205e-008
	PSO-ILCSS2	1.3833e-008	1.0414e-008
F4	SPSO	4.3043e-002	6.6204e-002
	MPSO-TVAC	1.7278e-002	3.9295e-002
	PSO-ILCSS1	9.1694e-012	3.4561e-011
	PSO-ILCSS2	9.7771e-014	4.9192e-013
F5	SPSO	4.3662e-003	6.3953e-003
	MPSO-TVAC	3.6624e-004	2.0060e-003
	PSO-ILCSS1	9.4223e-013	3.9129e-012
	PSO-ILCSS2	4.6303e-015	1.0950e-014

Table 11. The Comparison Results of Benchmark Function

From the Table 2, PSO-ILCSSI and PSO-ILCSS2 both maintain better performances than SPSO and MPSO-TVAC no matter the average mean value or standard deviation. The dynamic performances of PSO-ILCSSI and PSO-ILCSS2 are near the same with SPSO and MPSO-TVAC in the first stage, although PSO-ILCSSI and PSO-ILCSS2 maintains quick global search capability in the last period. In one words, the performances of PSO-ILCSSI and PSO-ILCSS2 surpasses slightly than which of MPSO-TVAC and SPSO a little for unimodel functions, while for the multi-model functions, PSO-ILCSSI and PSO-ILCSS2 show preferable results.

5. Individual Social Selection Strategy

5.1 Individual Linear Social Selection Strategy (ILSSS)

Similarly with cognitive parameter, a dispersed control manner (Cai et al., 2008) is introduced, in which each particle selects its social coefficient value to decide the search direction: $\vec{p}_j$ or $\vec{p_g}$.

Since the literatures only consider the extreme value $\vec{p_g}$, however, they neglect the differences between $\vec{p}_j$ and $\vec{p_g}$. These settings lose some information maybe useful to find the global optima or escape from a local optima. Thus, we design a new index by introducing the performance differences, and the definition is provided as follows:

$$Grade_u(t) = \frac{f_{worst}(t) - f(x_u(t))}{f_{worst}(t) - f_{best}(t)} \tag{21}$$

where $f_{worst}(t)$ and $f_{best}(t)$ are the worst and best fitness values of the swarm at time t, respectively. Occasionally, the swarm converges onto one point, that means $f_{worst}(t) = f_{best}(t)$. In this case, the value $Grade_u(t)$ of arbitrary particle u is set to 1. $Grade_u(t)$ is an information index to represent the differences of particle u at time t, according to its fitness value of the current position. The better the particle is, the larger $Grade_u(t)$ is, and vice versa.

As we known, if the fitness value of particle u is better than which of particle m, the probability that global optima falls into m's neighborhood is larger than that of particle m. In this manner, the particle u should pay more attentions to exploit its neighborhood. On the contrary, it may tend to explore other region with a larger probability than exploitation. Thus, for the best solution, it should make complete local search around its historical best position, as well as for the worst solution, it should make global search around $\vec{p_g}$. Then, the dispersed social coefficient of particle j at time t is set as follows:

$$c_{2,j}(t) = c_{low} + (c_{up} - c_{low}) \times Grade_j(t) \tag{22}$$

where c_{up} and c_{low}, are two predefined numbers, and $c_{2,j}(t)$ represents the social coefficient of particle j at time t.

5.2 Individual Non-linear Social Selection Strategy(INLSSS)

As mentioned before, although the individual linear social parameter selection strategy improves the performance significantly, however, its linear manner can not meet the complex optimization tasks. Therefore, in this section, we introduce four different kinds of non-linear manner, and investigate the affection for the algorithm's performance.

Because there are fruitful results about inertia weight, therefore, an intuitive and simple method is to introduce some effective non-linear manner of inertia weight into the study of social parameter automation. Inspired by the previous literatures (Chen et al., 2006; Jiang & Etorre, 2005), four different kinds of nonlinear manner are designed.

The first non-linear social automation strategy is called parabola opening downwards strategy :

$$c_{2,j}(t) = c_{start} - (c_{start} - c_{end}) \times (\frac{t}{MAX\_ITER})^2 \times Grade_j(t) \quad (23)$$

The second non-linear social automation strategy is called parabola opening upwards strategy:

$$\begin{aligned} c_{2,j}(t) &= c_{start} + (c_{start} - c_{end}) \times (\frac{t}{MAX\_ITER})^2 \\ &-(c_{start} - c_{end}) \times \frac{2t}{MAX\_ITER} \times Grade_j(t) \end{aligned} \quad (24)$$

The third non-linear social automation strategy is called exponential curve strategy:

$$c_{2,j}(t) = c_{end} \cdot (\frac{c_{start}}{c_{end}})^{\frac{1}{1+10\frac{t}{MAX\_ITER}}} \times Grade_j(t) \quad (25)$$

The fourth non-linear social automation strategy is called negative-exponential strategy:

$$c_{2,j}(t) = c_{start} \times e^{-\frac{t}{MAX\_ITER}} \times Grade_j(t) \quad (26)$$

5.3 The Steps of PSO-INLSSS

The detail steps of PSO-INLSSS are listed as follows:

- Step 1. Initializing each coordinate x_j^k and v_j^k sampling within $[x_{min}, x_{max}]$ and $[-v_{max}, v_{max}]$, respectively.
- Step 2. Computing the fitness value of each particle.
- Step 3. For $k'th$ dimensional value of $j'th$ particle, the personal historical best position p_j^k is updated as follows.

$$p_j^k = \begin{cases} x_j^k, & \text{if } f(\overrightarrow{x}_j) < f(\overrightarrow{p}_j) \text{ ,} \\ p_j^k & \text{, otherwise.} \end{cases} \quad (27)$$

- Step 4. For $k'th$ dimensional value of $j'th$ particle, the global best position p_g^k is updated as follows.

$$p_g^k = \begin{cases} p_j^k, & \text{if } f(\overrightarrow{p}_j) < f(\overrightarrow{p}_g) \text{ ,} \\ p_g^k & \text{, otherwise.} \end{cases} \quad (28)$$

- Step 5. Computing the social coefficient $c_{2,j}$ value of each particle according to formula (23)- (26).
- Step 6. Updating the velocity and position vectors with equation (1)-(3) in which social coefficient c_2 is changed with $c_{2,j}$.
- Step 7. Making mutation operator described in section 4.3.
- Step 8. If the criteria is satisfied, output the best solution; otherwise, goto step 2.

5.4 Simulation Results

To testify the performance of these four proposed non-linear social parameter automation strategies, three famous benchmark functions are chosen to test the performance, and compared with standard PSO (SPSO), modified PSO with time- varying accelerator coefficients (MPSO-TVAC) (Ratnaweera et al., 2004) and individual social selection strategy (PSO-ILSSS). Since we adopt four different non-linear strategies, the proposed methods are called PSO-INLSSS-1 (with strategy one), PSO-INLSSS-2 (with strategy two), PSO-INLSSS-3 (with strategy three) and PSO-INLSSS-4 (with strategy four), respectively. The details of the experimental environment and results are explained as follows.

5.4.1 Benchmarks

In this paper, three typical unconstraint numerical benchmark functions are used to test.
Rastrigin Function:

$$f_1(x) = \sum_{j=1}^{n}[x_j^2 - 10cos(2\pi x_j) + 10]$$

where $|x_j| \leq 5.12$, and

$$f_1(x^*) = f_6(0, 0, ..., 0) = 0.0$$

Ackley Function:

$$f_2(x) = -20exp(-0.2\sqrt{\frac{1}{n}\sum_{j=1}^{n} x_j^2})$$

$$-exp(\frac{1}{n}\sum_{k=1}^{n}\cos 2\pi x_k) + 20 + e$$

where $|x_j| \leq 32.0$, and

$$f_2(x^*) = f_3(0, 0, ..., 0) = 0.0$$

Penalized Function:

$$f_3(x) = 0.1\{\sin^2(3\pi x_1) + \sum_{i=1}^{n-1}(x_i - 1)^2[1 + \sin^2(3\pi x_{i+1})]$$

$$+(x_n - 1)^2[1 + \sin^2(2\pi x_n)]\} + \sum_{i=1}^{n} u(x_i, 5, 100, 4)$$

where $|x_j| \leq 50.0$, and

$$u(x_i, a, k, m) = \begin{cases} k(x_i - a)^m, & \text{if } x_i > a \\ 0, & \text{if } -a \leq x_i \leq a \\ k(-x_i - a)^m, & \text{if } x_i < -a \end{cases}$$

$$y_i = 1 + \frac{1}{4}(x_i + 1)$$

$$f_3(x^*) = f_8(1, 1, ..., 1) = 0.0$$

5.4.2 Parameter Settings

The coefficients of SPSO, MPSO-TVAC, PSO-ILSSS and PSO-INLSSS are set as follows:
The inertia weight w is decreased linearly from 0.9 to 0.4 within SPSO, MPSO-TVAC, PSO-ILSSS and PSO-INLSSS. Accelerator coefficients c_1 and c_2 are set to 2.0 within SPSO, as well as in MPSO-TVAC, ci decreases from 2.5 to 0.5, while c_2 increases from 0.5 to 2.5. For PSO-ILSSS and PSO-INLSSS, cognitive parameter c_1 is fixed to 2.0, while social parameter c_2 is decreased, whereas the lower bounds of c_2 is set to 1.0, and the upper bounds is set from 2.0 decreased to 1.0. Total individuals are 100, and the velocity threshold v_{max} is set to the upper bound of the domain. The dimensionality is 30 and 50. In each experiment, the simulation run 30 times, while each time the largest iteration is 50 x *dimension.*

5.4.3 Performance Analysis

The comparison results of these three famous benchmarks are listed as Table 12-14, in which *Dim.* represents the dimension, *Alg.* represents the corresponding algorithm, *Mean* denotes the average mean value, while *STD* denotes the standard variance.
For Rastrigin Function (Table 12), the performances of all non-linear PSO-INLSSS algorithms are worse than PSO-ILSSS when dimension is 30, although they are better than SPSO and MPSO-TVAC. However, with the increased dimensionality, the performance of non-linear modified variant PSO-INLSSS surpasses that of PSO-ILSSS, for example, the best performance is achieved by PSO-INLSSS-3. This phenomenon implies that non-linear strategies can exactly affect the performance.
For Ackley Function (Table 13) and Penalized Function (Table 14), the performance of PSO-INLSSS-3 always wins. Based on the above analysis, we can draw the following two conclusions:
PSO-INLSSS-3 is the most stable and effective among four non-linear strategies. It is especially suit for multi-modal functions with many local optima especially.

Dim.	*Alg.*	Mean	STD
30	SPSO	1.7961e+001	4.2276e+000
	MPSO-TVAC	1.5471e+001	4.2023e+000
	PSO-ILSSS	6.4012e+000	5.0712e+000
	PSO-INLSSS-1	6.8676e+000	3.1269e+000
	PSO-INLSSS-2	8.2583e+000	2.3475e+000
	PSO-INLSSS-3	8.8688e+000	1.7600e+000
	PSO-INLSSS-4	1.0755e+001	4.2686e+000
50	SPSO	3.9958e+001	7.9258e+000
	MPSO-TVAC	3.8007e+001	7.0472e+000
	PSO-ILSSS	1.5380e+001	5.5827e+000
	PSO-INLSSS-1	1.4329e+001	4.7199e+000
	PSO-INLSSS-2	1.5623e+001	4.4020e+000
	PSO-INLSSS-3	1.3740e+001	4.3426e+000
	PSO-INLSSS-4	2.1975e+001	5.6844e+000

Table 12. Comparison Results for Rastrigin Function

6. Conclusion and Future Research

This chapter proposes a new model incorporated with the characteristic differences for each particle, and the individual selection strategy for inertia weight, cognitive learning factor and social learning factor are discussed, respectively. Simulation results show the individual selection strategy maintains a fast search speed and robust. Further research should be made on individual structure for particle swarm optimization.

Dim.	*Alg.*	Mean	STD
30	SPSO	5.8161e-006	4.6415e-006
	MPSO-TVAC	7.5381e-007	3.3711e-006
	PSO-ILSSS	4.7853e-011	9.1554e-011
	PSO-INLSSS-1	1.8094e-011	1.8533e-011
	PSO-INLSSS-2	1.1870e-011	2.0876e-011
	PSO-INLSSS-3	5.2100e-013	5.5185e-013
	PSO-INLSSS-4	3.2118e-010	2.2272e-010
50	SPSO	1.7008e-004	1.2781e-004
	MPSO-TVAC	4.4132e-002	1.9651e-001
	PSO-ILSSS	1.5870e-008	1.7852e-008
	PSO-INLSSS-1	2.3084e-008	3.6903e-008
	PSO-INLSSS-2	1.1767e-008	1.3027e-008
	PSO-INLSSS-3	4.7619e-010	1.4337e-009
	PSO-INLSSS-4	3.4499e-008	4.7674e-008

Table 13. Comparison Results for Ackley Function

Dim.	*Alg.*	Mean	STD
30	SPSO	5.4943e-004	2.45683e-003
	MPSO-TVAC	9.3610e-027	4.1753e-026
	PSO-ILSSS	5.1601e-023	1.7430e-022
	PSO-INLSSS-1	6.0108e-020	1.5299e-019
	PSO-INLSSS-2	4.5940e-021	6.2276e-021
	PSO-INLSSS-3	9.7927e-024	1.6162e-023
	PSO-INLSSS-4	1.0051e-016	1.9198e-016
50	SPSO	6.4279e-003	1.0769e-002
	MPSO-TVAC	4.9270e-002	2.0248e-001
	PSO-ILSSS	1.6229e-017	3.9301e-017
	PSO-INLSSS-1	6.2574e-015	1.3106e-014
	PSO-INLSSS-2	1.6869e-014	3.3596e-014
	PSO-INLSSS-3	6.2959e-018	5.6981e-018
	PSO-INLSSS-4	8.0886e-013	3.7972e-013

Table 14. Comparison Results for Penalized Function

7. Acknowledgement

This chapter is supported by National Natural Science Foundation of China under Grant No.60674104, and also supported by Doctoral Scientific Research Starting Foundation of Taiyuan University of Science and Technology under Grant No.20082010.

8. References

Holland, J.H. (1992). *Adaptation in natural and artificial systems: an introductory analysis with application to biology, control, and artificial intelligence,* 2nd Edition, Cambridge, MA: MIT Press. [1]

Dorigo, M. & Gambardella, L.M. (1997) Ant colony system: a cooperative learning approach to the traveling salesman problem, *IEEE Transactions on Evolutionary Computation,* Vol.1, No.l, 53-66. [2]

Eberhart, R.C. & Kennedy, J. (1995). A new optimizer using particle swarm theory, *Proceedings of 6th International Symposium on Micro Machine and Human Science,* pp.39-43. [3]

Kennedy, J. & Eberhart, R.C. (1995). Particle swarm optimization, *Proceedings of IEEE International Conference on Neural Networks,* pp. 1942-1948. [4]

Shen, H.Y.; Peng, X.Q.; Wang, J.N. & Hu, Z.K. (2005). A mountain clustering based on improved PSO algorithm, *Lecture Notes on Computer Science 3612,* Changsha, China, pp.477-481. [5]

Eberhart, R.C. & Shi, Y. (1998). Extracting rules from fuzzy neural network by particle swarm optimization, *Proceedings of IEEE International Conference on Evolutionary Computation,* Anchorage, Alaska, USA. [6]

Li, Q.Y.; Shi, Z.P.; Shi, J. & Shi, Z.Z. (2005). Swarm intelligence clustering algorithm based on attractor, *Lecture Notes on Computer Science 3612,Changsha,* China, pp.496-504. [7]

Shi, Y. & Eberhart, R.C. (1998a). A modified particle swarm optimizer, *Proceedings of the IEEE International Conference on Evolutionary Computation,* Anchorage, Alaska, USA,pp.69-73. [8]

Shi Y. & Eberhart R.C. (1998b). Parameter selection in particle swarm optimization, *Proceedings of the 7th Annual Conference on Evolutionary Programming,* pp.591-600. [9]

Shi Y. & Eberhart R.C. (1999). Empirical study of particle swarm optimization, *Proceedings of the Congress on Evolutionary Computation,* pp. 1945-1950. [10]

Suganthan P.N. (1999). Particle swarm optimizer with neighbourhood operator, *Proceedings of the Congress on Evolutionary Computation,* pp. 1958-1962. [11]

Venter, G. (2002). Particle swarm optimization, *Proceedings of 43rd AIAA/ASME/ASCE/AHS/ASC Structure, Structures Dynamics and Materials Conference,* pp.22-25. [12]

Ratnaweera, A.; Halgamuge, S.K. & Watson, H.C. (2004). Self-organizing hierarchical particle swarm opitmizer with time-varying acceleration coefficients, *IEEE Transactions on Evolutionary Computation,* Vol.8, No.3, 240-255. [13]

Monson, C.K. & Seppi, K.D. (2004). The Kalman swarm: a new approach to particle motion in swarm optimization, *Proceedings of the Genetic and Evolutionary Computation Conference,pp.* 140-150. [14]

Sun, J. et al. (2004). Particle swarm optimization with particles having quantum behavior, *Proceedings of the IEEE Congress on Evolutionary Computation,* pp.325-331. [15]

Cui, Z.H. & Zeng, J.C. (2004). A guaranteed global convergence particle swarm optimizer, *Lecture Notes in Artificial Intelligence,* vol.3066, Sweden, pp.762-767. [16]

Cui, Z.H.; Zeng, J.C. & Sun, G.J. (2006a). A fast particle swarm optimization, *International Journal of Innovative Computing, Information and Control,* Vol.2, No.6,pp.l365-1380. [17]

Cui, Z.H.; Cai, X.J.; Zeng, J.C. & Sun, G.J. (2006b). Predicted-velocity particle swarm optimization using game-theoretic approach, *Lecture Notes in Computer Science,* vol.4115, Kunming, China, pp.145-154. [18]

Mendes, R.; Kennedy, J. & Neves, J. (2004). The fully informed particle swarm: simper, maybe better, *IEEE Transactions on Evolutionary Computation,* Vol.8, No.3, pp.204-210. [19]

Kennedy, J. (1999). Small worlds and mega-minds: effects of neighborhood topology on particle swarm performance, *Poceedings of the 1999 Congress on Evolutionary Computation,* pp.1931-1938. [20]

Løvbjerg, M.; Rasmussen, T.K. & Krink, T. (2001). Hybrid particle swarm optimiser with breeding and subpopulations, *Proceedings of the third Genetic and Evolutionary Computation Conference.* [21]

Cai, X.J.; Cui, Z.H.; Zeng, J.C. & Tan Y. (2007a). Performance-dependent adaptive particle swarm optimization, *International Journal of Innovative Computing, Information and Control,* Vol.3, No.GB, 1697-1706. [22]

Michalewicz, Z. (1992). *Genetic Algorithm+ Data Structures =Evolution Programs,* Springer-Verlag, Berlin. [23]

Marcus, H. (2002). Fitness uniform selection to preserve genetic diversity, *Proceedings of IEEE Congress on Evolutionary Computation,* pp.783-388. [24]

Blickle, T. & Thiele, L. (1995). A mathematical analysis of tournament selection, *Proceedings of the Sixth International Conference on Genetic Algorithms,* San Francisco, California, pp.9-16. [25]

Cui, Z.H; Cai, X.J. & Zeng J.C. (2008). Some Non-linear Score Strategies in *PDPSO, ICIC Express Letters* Vol.2, No.3. [26]

Liang, J.J.; Qin, A.K.; Suganthan, P.N. & Baskar, S. (2006). Comprehensive learning particle swarm optimizer for global optimization of multimodal functions, *IEEE Transactions on Evolutionary Computation,* Vol.10, No.3, 281-295. [27]

Shang, Y.W. & Qiu, Y.H. (2006). A note on the extended Rosenbrock function, *Evolutionary Computation,* Vol.14, No.l, 119-126. [28]

Cai, X.J.; Cui, Z.H.; Zeng, J.C. & Tan Y. (2007b). Self-learning Particle Swarm Optimization Based on Environmental FeedbackProceerfzngs *of the Second International Conference on Innovative Computing, Information and Control (ICICIC2007),* Japan. [29]

Cai, X.J.; Cui Z.H.; Zeng, J.C. & Tan, Y. (2008). Particle Swarm Optimization with Self-adjusting Cognitive Selection Strategy, *International Journal of Innovative Computing, Information and Control (IJICIC),* Vol.4, No.4, 943-952. [30]

Chen, G.M.; Jia, J.Y. & Han, Q. (2006). Study on the Strategy of Decreasing Inertia Weight in Particle Swarm Optimization Algorithm, *Journal of Xi'an Jiao Tong University*, Vol.40, No.l, pp.53-56. (in Chinese) [31]

Jiang, C.W. & Etorre, B. (2005). A self-adaptive chaotic particle swarm algorithm for short term hydroelectric system scheduling in deregulated environment, *Energy Conversion and Management*, Vol.46, No.17, pp.2689-2696. [32]

6

Personal Best Oriented Particle Swarm Optimizer

Chang-Huang Chen[1], Jonq-Chin Hwang[2] and Sheng-Nian Yeh[2]
[1]*Tungnan University,* [2]*National Taiwan University of Science and Technology*
Taipei, Taiwan, ROC

1. Introduction

Optimization problems are frequently encountered in many engineering, economic or scientific fields that engineers or researchers are seeking to minimize cost or time, or to maximize profit, quality or efficiency, of a specific problem. For example, economic dispatch of power generation, optimal allocation of resources for manufacture, design optimal plant to maximize production, and so many which are unable to enumerate completely. In addition, many optimization problems are very complex and hard to solve by conventional gradient-based techniques, particularly the objective function and constraint are not in closed forms. Thus, the development of a good optimization strategy or algorithm is of great value.

In the past decade, particle swarm optimization (PSO) algorithm [Eberhart & Kennedy 1995, Kennedy and Eberhart 1995] attracts many sights around the world due to its powerful searching ability and simplicity. PSO simulates the swarm behavior of birds flocking and fish schooling that swarms work in a collaborative manner to search for foods as efficient and quick as possible. There are three different types of PSO which are frequently encountered in literature. They are constriction type PSO, constant inertia weight PSO and linearly decreasing inertia weight PSO. Each of them has been successfully applied to many optimization problems.

While empirical studies have proven PSO's usefulness as an optimization algorithm, it does not always fit all problems. Sometimes, it may also get stuck on local optimal. In order to improve the performance, many variants of PSO have been proposed. Some of the proposed algorithms adopted new operations and some of the modifications hybridized with other algorithm. Although they are claimed better than original PSO algorithm, most of them will introduce extra mathematical or logical operations, which, in turn, making algorithm more complicate and spending more computing time. Especially, they, in general, did not present any theoretical models to describe its behavior and support such modifications.

Many researchers have devoted to study how PSO works. They intended to discover the implicit properties of PSO and its weakness and strength via theoretical analysis. The first attempt to analysis PSO is made by Kenndey [Kennedy, 1998]. Meanwhile, Ozcan and Mohan showed that a particle in a simple one-dimensional PSO system follows a path defined by a sinusoidal wave with random amplitude and frequency. However, the effects of inertia weight are not addressed in that paper [Ozcan & Mohan, 1999]. In order to analyze the dynamics of PSO, Yasuda proposed a generalized reduced model of PSO accounting for the inertia weight. The stability analysis is carried out on the basis of both the eigenvalue analysis and numerical simulation [Yasuda et al., 2003]. Trelea has carried out a convergence analysis of PSO and then derived a graphical parameter selection guideline to facilitate choosing parameters [Trelea, 2003].

A formal analysis of the PSO is carried out by Clerc and Kennedy [Clerc & Kennedy, 2002]. By treating the random coefficients as constants, the analysis started from converting the standard stochastic PSO to a deterministic dynamical system. The resulting system was a second-order linear dynamic system whose stability depended on the system's eigenvalues. The parameter space that guarantees stability is also identified. A similar analysis based on deterministic model of the PSO was also carried out in identifying regions in the parameter space that guarantee stability [van den Berg, 2002]. Recently, stochastic convergence analysis of the standard PSO is reported in [Jian, 2007], where a parameter selection guide is also provided to ensure the convergence.

Similar to genetic algorithm or evolutionary algorithm, PSO is also a population-based optimization technique. PSO searches for optimal solution via collaborating with individuals within a swarm of population. Each individual, called particle, is made of two parts, the position and velocity, and proceeds according to two major operations, velocity and position updating rules. Position and velocity represent the candidate solution and step size, a particle will advance in the next iteration, respectively. For an n-dimensional problem and a swarm of m particles, the i-th particle's position and velocity, in general, are denoted as $x_i=[x_{i1}, x_{i2}, \ldots, x_{in}]^T$ and $v_i=[v_{i1}, v_{i2}, \ldots, v_{in}]^T$, for i=1, 2, …, m, respectively, where m is the number of particles, and superscript T stands for the transpose operator. Considering on the inertia weight PSO, the operations of position and velocity are expressed as:

$$v_{id}(t+1) = \omega \cdot v_{id}(t) + c_1 \cdot \mathrm{rnd}(1) \cdot (p_{gd} - x_{id}(t)) + c_2 \cdot \mathrm{rnd}(1) \cdot (p_{id} - x_{id}(t)) \quad (1)$$

$$x_{id}(t+1) = x_{id}(t) + v_{id}(t+1) \quad (2)$$

where ω is the inertia weight; c_1 and c_2 are two positive constants called acceleration constants; rnd(1) is a uniform random number in (0,1); d is the index of dimension; p_g and p_i are the best position ever found by all particles and the best position a particle ever found so far, respectively; t is the iteration count. Hereafter, p_g and p_i will be called the global best and personal best particle of the swarm, respectively, in this chapter.

Personal best oriented particle swarm optimizer (PPSO), also a varient of particle swarm optimization, is a newly developed optimization solver [Chen & Yeh, 2006a]. PPSO uses the same velocity updating rule as PSO. However, the position updating rule is replaced by (3).

$$x_{id}(t+1) = p_{id} + v_{id}(t+1) \quad (3)$$

The modification came from the observation that since p_{id} is the best particle ever found so far, it may locate around the vinicity of the optimal solution. Fotunately, previous studies showed that PPSO performs well both in testing on a suite of benchmark functions and applying to economic dispatch problems of the power system and others [Chen & Yeh, 2006a, 2006b, 2007, 2008]. However, all the results were obtained from emperical studies. The main drawback of PPSO may lie in a fragile theory basis at first galance. No theoretical

analysis has been found in literature, although it not only can help reveal the behavior of particles but also the convergent property of the proposed approach.
This chapter presents a therotical analysis of PPSO. Based on the analysis, the implicit behavior of PPSO will be revealed. Meanwhile, it also provide a guideline for parameters selection. It is well-known that the particle's trajectory of PSO is characterized by a second-order difference equation. However, it will be clear later that a first order difference equation is sufficient to characterize the particle's behavior of PPSO. A simple mathematical model can help one easily grasp the features of PPSO and convergent tendency.

2. Analysis of PPSO

This section intends to construct the mathematical model of PPSO and, based on the developed model, study the property of PPSO. The analysis is started from a simplified deterministic model, a single particle and one dimension case, keeping all the parameters constants. After that, assuming some parameters be uniformly distributed random numbers, a stochastic model is then built to simulate the nature of PPSO in the next section.

2.1 Simple PPSO: one particle and one dimension case

Each particle in PPSO represents a candidate solution of a specific problem. In other words, a particle is a position in a multidimensional search space in which each particle attempts to explore for an optimal solution with respect to a fitness function or objective function. In this section, a simple PPSO is first derived on which the following analysis is based.
The canonical form of PPSO is represented as .

$$v_{id}(t+1) = \omega \cdot v_{id}(t) + \varphi_1 \cdot (p_{gd} - x_{id}(t)) + \varphi_2 \cdot (p_{id} - x_{id}(t)) \tag{4}$$

$$x_{id}(t+1) = v_{id}(t+1) + p_{id} \tag{5}$$

where $\varphi_1 = c_1 \cdot rnd(1)$ and $\varphi_2 = c_2 \cdot rnd(1)$ are two random numbers drawn uniformly from $(0, c_1)$ and $(0, c_2)$, respectively.
Since (4) and (5) operate on each dimension exclusively, for notation simplicity, one can omit the subscript i and d of x_{id} and v_{id}, and retain subscript g and i of p_g and p_i to emphasize the difference between them. The analysis given below considers only one particle and one dimensional case. However, the results can easily be extended to multidimensional case without losing generality.
Eqations (4) and (5) can now be rewritten as:

$$v(t+1) = \omega \cdot v(t) + \varphi_1 \cdot (p_g - x(t)) + \varphi_2 \cdot (p_i - x(t)) \tag{6}$$

$$x(t+1) = v(t+1) + p_i \tag{7}$$

Substituting (6) into (7), one has:

$$x(t+1) = \omega \cdot v(t) + \varphi_1 \cdot (p_g - x(t)) + \varphi_2 \cdot (p_i - x(t)) + p_i \tag{8}$$

Since

$$x(t) = v(t) + p_i \tag{9}$$

It has

$$v(t) = x(t) - p_i \tag{10}$$

and

$$x(t+1) = \omega \cdot (x(t) - p_i) + \varphi_1 \cdot (p_g - x(t)) + \varphi_2 \cdot (p_i - x(t)) + p_i \tag{11}$$

Rearranging (11), it becomes

$$x(t+1) - (\omega - \varphi)x(t) = \varphi_1 \cdot p_g + (1 + \varphi_2 - \omega) \cdot p_i \tag{12}$$

where $\varphi = \varphi_1 + \varphi_2$. Obviously, a first-order linear difference equation is sufficient to characterize the dynamic behaviors of the simple PPSO.

2.2 Deterministic model of PPSO

Now assume that both p_i and p_g are constants. Also assume that φ_1 and φ_2 are two constants. It turns out that the PPSO becomes a deterministic model described by a first-order linear difference equation with constant coefficients. If the right-hand side of (12) is nonzero, it is a nonhomogeneous linear difference equation. The total solution of a nonhomogeneous linear difference equation with constant coefficients is the sum of two parts, the homogeneous solution, which satisfies the difference equation when the right-hand side of the equation is zero, and the particular solution, which satisfies the difference equation with a nonzero function F(t) on the right-hand side.

The homogeneous solution of a difference equation with constant coefficient is of the form $A\lambda^t$, where λ is called the characteristic root of the difference equation and A is a constant to be determined by the boundary (initial) condition.

The homogeneous solution and particlar solution of (12) can be obtained readily

$$x_h(t) = A(\omega - \varphi)^t \tag{13}$$

and

$$x_p(t) = [\varphi_1 \cdot p_g + (1 + \varphi_2 - \omega) \cdot p_i]/(1 + \varphi - \omega) \tag{14}$$

Here, subscript h and p are used to denote the homogeneous solution and particular solution. The total solution of (12) become

$$x(t) = A(\omega - \varphi)^t + p_w \tag{15}$$

where

$$p_w = [\varphi_1 \cdot p_g + (1 + \varphi_2 - \omega) \cdot p_i]/(1 + \varphi - \omega) \tag{16}$$

is called the weighted mean of p_g and p_i. Given the initial condition $x(0)=x_0$, the dynamic property of a particle is completely characterized by

$$x(t) = (x_0 - p_w)(\omega - \varphi)^t + p_w \tag{17}$$

where x_0 is the initial vale of x(t) and A = (x_0 - p_w). Equation (12) and (17) represent the position or trajectory that a particle may explore in implicit and explicit form.

2.2.1 Convergence property of the deterministic PPSO

Apparently, if (ω - ϕ) satisfies the following condition

$$\left|(\omega-\varphi)\right|<1 \tag{18}$$

or

$$-1<(\omega-\varphi)<1 \tag{19}$$

Then

$$\lim_{t\to\infty}\left(x(t)\right)=p_w \tag{20}$$

The limit does exist whenever p_w is an arbitrary point in the search space, i.e., p_w is finite. It is obvious that if $0 < \omega < 1$, it leads to $(1 + \varphi - \omega) > 0$ since $\varphi = \varphi_1 + \varphi_2 > 0$, and the weighted mean p_w is finite.
Hereafter, finite p_w and $0 < \omega < 1$ are assumed, unless stated explicitly. The feasible region in which x(t) is strictly converges for $0<\omega<1$ and $-1<\varphi< 2$ is plotted in Fig.1, where the gray area is the feasible region if stability is concerned, and the dark line on the center corresponds to $\omega = \varphi$.

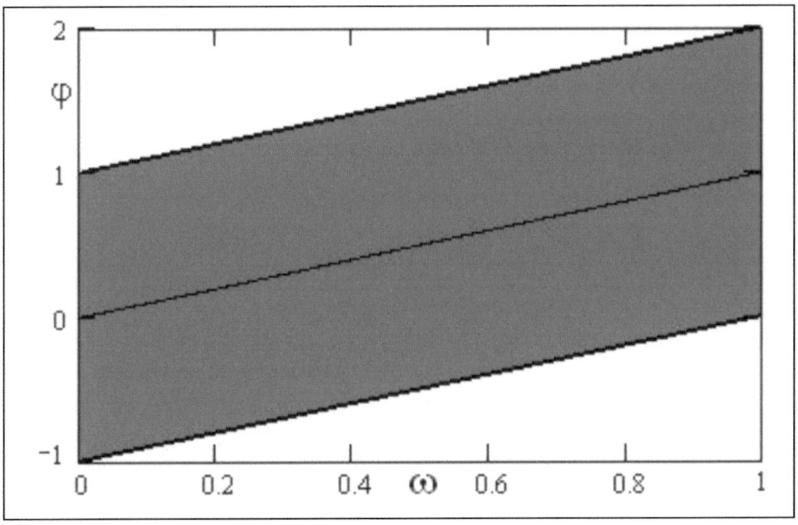

Figure 1. The gray region is the feasible region which particle strictly converges for $0 < \omega < 1$ and $-1< \varphi < 2$. The centered dark-line on the gray area corresponds to $\omega = \varphi$

2.2.2 Step size

The span the particle advances in the next step is calculated using the successive positions at t and (t+1),

$$x(t) = (x_0 - p_w)(\omega - \varphi)^t + p_w \tag{21}$$

and

$$x(t+1) = (x_0 - p_w)(\omega - \varphi)^{t+1} + p_w \tag{22}$$

Define the step size as

$$\begin{aligned} \Delta x(t) &\equiv x(t+1) - x(t) \\ &= (\omega - \varphi - 1)(x_0 - p_w)(\omega - \varphi)^t \end{aligned} \tag{23}$$

Since

$$(x_0 - p_w)(\omega - \varphi)^t = -(p_w - x(t)) \tag{24}$$

It has

$$\Delta x(t) = -(\omega - \varphi - 1) \cdot dx \tag{25}$$

where

$$dx \equiv (p_w - x(t)) \tag{26}$$

is the distance between the current position x(t) and the weighted mean, p_w. Equation (26) tells that the step size is a multiple, defined by $-(\omega - \varphi - 1)$, of the distance between x(t) and p_w. If $-(\omega - \varphi - 1)$ is positive, x(t) moves in aligning with the direction from current position to p_w and, if $-(\omega - \varphi - 1)$ is negative, x(t) moves on the opposite side. The former make particles moving close to p_w and the latter make particles get far way from p_w.
Now, define a step size control factor, δ, as:

$$\delta \equiv -(\omega - \varphi - 1) \tag{27}$$

Then

$$\Delta x(t) = \delta \cdot dx \tag{28}$$

Obviously, how long a particle will advance in next turn is controlled by the step size control factor δ. A large δ makes a particle to move far away from current position and a small value of δ makes a particle moving to nearby area.
Meanwhile, it is interesting to note that if $0 < \delta < 2$, (27) becomes to

$$0 < -(\omega - \varphi - 1) < 2 \tag{29}$$

or

$$-1 < (\omega - \varphi) < 1 \tag{30}$$

This agrees with (19). In other words, if the step size control factor satisfies $0 < \delta < 2$, the deterministic PPSO converges to p_w. Otherwise, it diverges.

Clearly, under condition $0 < \delta < 2$, the deterministic PPSO is stable, otherwise, it is unstable. Since δ is a function of ω and φ, the choices of ω and φ affect the magnitude of the step size control factor, or, in other words, affect the stability of PPSO.

Returning to (30), there are two cases are especially worthy to pay attention:

(a) $0< (\omega - \varphi) < 1$

This case corresponds to

$$0 < -(\omega - \varphi - 1) < 1 \Rightarrow 0 < \delta < 1 \tag{31}$$

In such situation, x(t+1) moves to the region to the left of p_w whenever p_w is greater than x(t), or the region to the right of p_w whenever p_w is less then x(t).

(b) $-1 < (\omega - \varphi) < 0$

This case corresponds to

$$1 < -(\omega - \varphi - 1) < 2 \Rightarrow 1 < \delta < 2 \tag{32}$$

This means that x(t+1) advances to the region to the right of p_w whenever p_w is less than x(t), or the region to the left of p_w whenever p_w is greater then x(t).

These two cases are illustrated in Figs.2 and 3. It is apparent that the step size control factor affects how far the particle moves. Since the step size is proportional to δ, a large δ corresponds to advancing in a large step and small δ corresponds to small step. Moreover, a positive δ makes x(t) move along the direction from x(t) to p_w ,while a negative δ causes it move along the opposite direction. By controlling δ, or equivalently $(\omega - \varphi)$, particles movement will be totally grasped. It is expected that if δ is uniformly changed in (0, 2), then x(t) will vibrate around the center position, p_w, the weighted midpoint of p_g and p_i. This is a very important property of PPSO. Similar phenomenon has been observed [Kennedy, 2003] and verified theoretically in PSO [Clerc & Kennedy, 2002].

2.2.3 Parameters selection

Equation (27) defines the step size control factor. It provides clues for determining parameters. First, confine the step size control factor within $(\delta_{min}, \delta_{max})$, where δ_{min} and δ_{max} are the lower and upper limits of the step size control factor, respectively, it turns out that

$$\delta_{min} < -(\omega - \varphi - 1) < \delta_{max} \tag{33}$$

After proper rearrangement, (33) becomes

$$(\delta_{min} + \omega - 1) < \varphi < (\delta_{max} + \omega - 1) \tag{34}$$

According to (34), once the lower and upper bounds of the step size control factor are specified, the range of φ depends on ω. The most important is that a stable PPSO requires, based on (29), $\delta_{min} = 0$ and $\delta_{max} = 2$. Substituting these two values into into (34), it has

$$\omega - 1 < \varphi < 1 + \omega \tag{35}$$

Equation (35) says that, if φ uniformly varies from $(\omega - 1)$ to $(\omega + 1)$, x(t) will explore the region from $(p_w - dx)$ to $(p_w + dx)$. It also implies that it is possible to use a negative value of φ while PPSO is still stable. This fact has been shown in Fig.1.

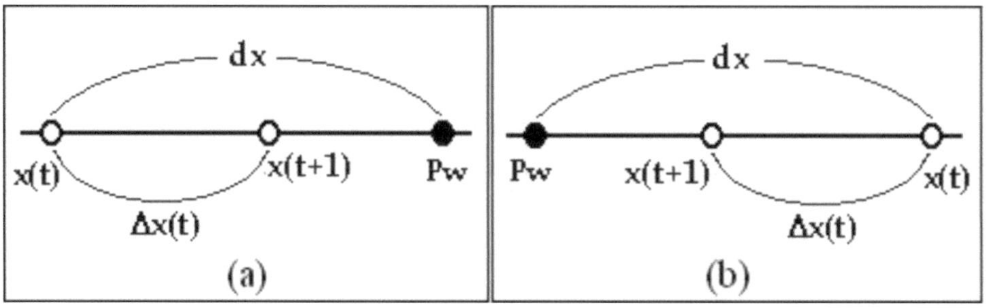

Figure 2. The next position, x(t+1), a particle will move to for $0 < \delta < 1$, (a) $p_w > x(t)$ and (b) $p_w < x(t)$

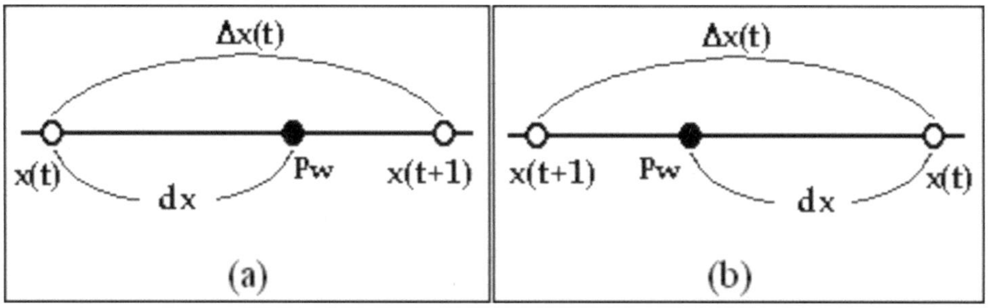

Figure 3. The next position, x(t+1), a particle will move to for $1 < \delta < 2$, (a) $p_w > x(t)$ and (b) $p_w < x(t)$

Since φ_1 and φ_2 are both positive numbers, so is φ. Fig.4 shows the case that φ is positive and is restricted to $0 < \varphi < 2$.
If ω is assigned, from (27), one also has

$$\varphi_{min} + 1 - \omega < \delta < \varphi_{max} + 1 - \omega \tag{36}$$

where φ_{min} and φ_{max} are the lower and upper limits of φ. Thus, one can use (36) to predict the range the particle attempts to explore for a specific range of φ, if ω is given. From (36), one can also readily verify that $\varphi_{min} = \omega - 1$ and $\varphi_{max} = \omega + 1$ result in $\delta = 0$ and 2, respectively, agreeing with (29).
A graph of step size control factor versus ϕ with ω as parameter is plotted in Fig.5 for $0 < \varphi < 2$ and $0 < \omega < 1$. The gray area corresponds to convergent condition since $0 < \delta < 2$. One can use this graph to evaluate whether the selected parameters result in convergence or not.

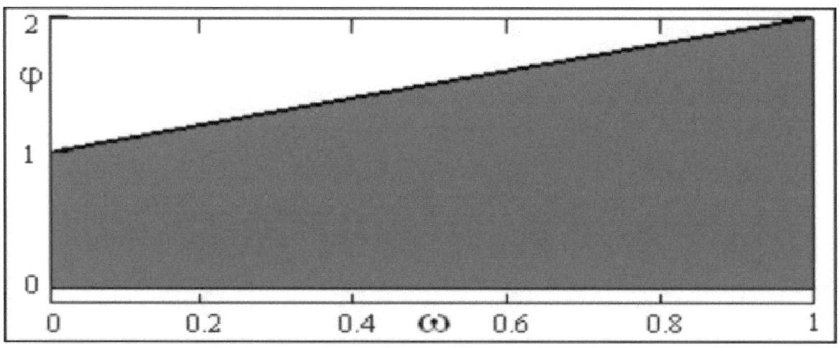

Figure 4. The feasible region for $0 < \omega < 1$ and $0 < \varphi < 2$

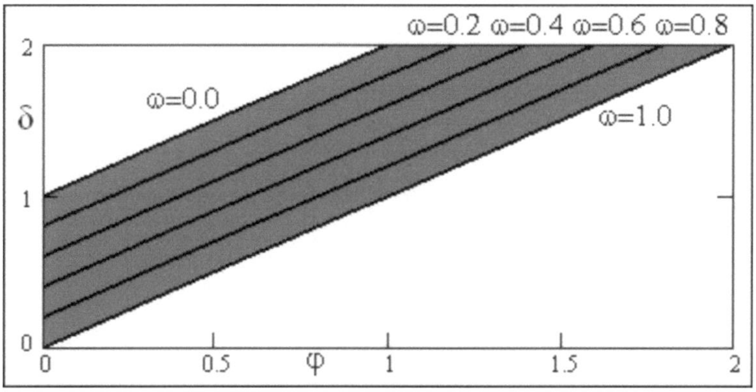

Figure 5. A plot of step size control factor δ versus φ with ω as parameter

2.2.4 Stability

The stability criterion imposed upon the deterministic PPSO is directly obtained from (18), i.e, $|(\omega - \varphi)| < 1$. However, based on (29), an implication of stability means that the step size control factor needs to meet the requirement $0 < \delta < 2$. Hence, stability of the deterministic PPSO can be described by one of the following rules:

(a) $|(\omega - \varphi)| < 1$

or

(b) $0 < -(\omega - \varphi - 1) < 2$

2.2.5 Equilibrium point

According to the above analysis, one can conclude that, for a stable deterministic PPSO, each particle moves in discrete time along the trajectory defined by (12) or (17), with specific step size, and finally settles down at an equilibrium point p_w. The equilibrium point is a function of φ_1 and φ_2. Referring to (16), one can readily verify that if $\varphi_1 > (1 + \varphi_2 - \omega)$, the equilibrium point p_w biases to p_g, and biases to p_i if $\varphi_1 \leq (1 + \varphi_2 - \omega)$. However, the equilibrium point found in PSO is the midpoint of p_g and p_i since $\varphi_1 = \varphi_2$ is usually used in PSO.

3.Stochastic PPSO

Instead of constants, now, restore both φ_1 and φ_2 to be uniform random numbers in $(0, c_1)$ and $(0, c_2)$, respectively. The model of (12) and (17) are still applied except that φ_1 and φ_2 are now two uniform random numbers. Analysis of the dynamic behavior of this stochastic PPSO will be given by extending the analysis provided in the previous section, with the replacement of expectation value for φ_1 and φ_2 as well as $x(t)$ from the probabilistic point of view. In the following analysis, the terms mean value, or simply mean, and expectation value will be used alternatively, in a looser mathematical standard, in the context.

3.1 Convergent property

Considering the explicit representation, Eq.(17), of the trajectory of a particle, since φ_1 and φ_2 are both uniform random numbers, the averaged dynamic behavior of a particle can be observed by its expectation value, i.e.

$$\begin{aligned} E(x(t)) &= E\left((x_0 - p_w)(\omega - \varphi)^t + p_w\right) \\ &= \left(x_0 - E(p_w)\right)\left(\omega - E(\varphi)\right)^t + E(p_w) \end{aligned} \tag{37}$$

where E(x(t)), $E(p_w)$, and $E(\varphi)$ are the expectation value of x(t), p_w and φ, respectively. Here, φ_1 and φ_2 are assumed to be two exclusive uniform random numbers; and $E(\varphi) = E(\varphi_1) + E(\varphi_2)$. Apparently, if the condition

$$1 < \omega - E(\varphi)) < 1 \tag{38}$$

is true, then

$$\lim_{t\to\infty} E(x(t)) = E(p_w) \tag{39}$$

According to (39), the trajectory of each particle converges to a random weighted mean, $E(p_w)$, of p_g and p_i, where

$$\begin{aligned} E(p_w) &= E\left([\varphi_1 \cdot p_g + (1+\varphi_2 - \omega)\cdot p_i]/(1+\varphi-\omega)\right) \\ &= \frac{E(\varphi_1)\cdot p_g + (1+E(\varphi_2)-\omega)\cdot p_i}{1+E(\varphi_1)+E(\varphi_2)-\omega} \end{aligned} \tag{40}$$

Since

$$1+E(\varphi_1)+E(\varphi_2) > \omega \quad \text{if } 0<\omega<1 \tag{41}$$

$E(p_w)$ is finite for $0 < \omega < 1$, $0 < E(\varphi_1)$ and $0 < E(\varphi_2)$ as well as finite p_i and p_g.
Owing to φ_1 and φ_2 are both uniform random numbers in $(0, c_1)$ and $(0, c_2)$, respectively, it has $E(\varphi_1) = 0.5c_1$, $E(\varphi_2) = 0.5c_2$ and $E(\varphi) = E(\varphi_1 + \varphi_2) = 0.5(c_1 + c_2)$. Thus, (40) becomes

$$\begin{aligned} E(p_w) &= \frac{E(\varphi_1)\cdot p_g + (1+E(\varphi_2)-\omega)\cdot p_i}{1+E(\varphi_1)+E(\varphi_2)-\omega} \\ &= \frac{0.5c_1\cdot p_g + (1+0.5c_2-\omega)\cdot p_i}{1+0.5(c_1+c_2)-\omega} \end{aligned} \tag{42}$$

Obviously, for a stochastic model of PPSO, the random weighted mean p_w is different from that obtained by deterministic model of PSO and PPSO. Meanwhile, for $0 < \omega < 1$, $E(p_w)$ bias to p_i. This means that particle will cluster to p_i instead of p_g.

3.2 Step size

Similar to deterministic PPSO, the step size of the stochastic PPSO can be computed by

$$\begin{aligned} E(\Delta x(t)) &= E(x(t+1)) - E(x(t)) \\ &= -(\omega - E(\varphi) - 1)(E(p_w) - E(x(t))) \\ &= -(\omega - 0.5(c_1 + c_2) - 1)E(dx) \end{aligned} \tag{43}$$

where

$$E(dx) = E(p_w) - E(x(t)) \tag{44}$$

For a stochastic PPSO, the mean (expectant) step size a particle will move in next turn is computed from (43), which is a multiple of the mean distance between the random weighted mean $E(p_w)$ and mean current position $E(x(t))$. Similar to deterministic PPSO, the mean step size control factor is defined as

$$E(\delta) = -(\omega - E(\varphi) - 1) \tag{45}$$

The step size and step size control factor are no longer static values but stochastic ones. Furthermore, for $0 < E(\delta) < 2$, from (45), it also has

$$-1 < -(\omega - E(\varphi)) < 1 \tag{46}$$

Actually, (46) is the same as (38). Rearranging (46), one has

$$\omega - 1 < E(\varphi) < 1 + \omega \tag{47}$$

Equations (46) and (47) are similar to (30) and (35), respectively, except that the constant φ ($=\varphi_1 + \varphi_2$) is replaced by sum of the expectation values of two random numbers. As concluded in the previous section, a stable stochastic PPSO equivalently means that the mean step size control factor of each particle's movement must be within the range of $0 < E(\delta) < 2$. In other words, if $E(\varphi)$ lies between $(\omega - 1)$ and $(1 + \omega)$, the system is stable.

3.3 Parameter selection for stochastic PPSO

This subsection discusses how to choose proper parameters for PPSO.

3.3.1 Inertia weight

Recall that $E(\varphi)$ is a positive number since φ is the sum of two uniformly random numbers varying between $(0, c_1)$ and $(0, c_2)$, where c_1 and c_2 are two positive numbers. Now, consider the step size control factor governed by (45) for ω chosen from the following ranges:

(a) $1 < \omega$, it has

$$E(\delta) < E(\varphi) \tag{48}$$

(b) $0 < \omega < 1$, it has

$$E(\varphi) < E(\delta) < 1 + E(\varphi) \tag{49}$$

(c) $-1 < \omega < 0$, it has

$$1 + E(\varphi) < E(\delta) < 2 + E(\varphi) \tag{50}$$

(d) $\omega < -1$, it has

$$2 + E(\varphi) < E(\delta) \tag{51}$$

If $E(\varphi)$ is assigned, Eqs.(48)-(51) specify the average possible value of step size control factor for different choosing ranges of inertia weight ω. For example, if $E(\varphi) = 1.5$, $E(\delta)$ are 1.25, 1.75, 2.75 and 3.75 for ω = 1.25, 0.75, -0.25 and -1.25, respectively. Clearly, it is improper to have a minus value of ω since it will make particle violate the stability rule, i.e., the trajectory of particle diverges.

To have a better vision of parameter selection for $\omega > 1$ and $0 < \omega < 1$, it is better to explain with figure as illustrated in Figs.6 and 7 where the dotted lines represent the domain a particle may visit in next turn for the cases $\omega = 1.25$ and 0.75 under the condition of $E(\varphi) = 1.5$. The cross sign in the midpoint of two ellipses is the center of the search range. Here, only the case that $E(p_w)$ located to the right of $E(x(t))$ is shown. However, similar aspects can be observed for $E(p_w)$ located to the left of $E(x(t))$.

Since $E(\varphi) = 1.5$, the uniform random number φ varies from 0 to 3. The lower and upper step size control factors are -0.25 and 2.75, respectively, for $\omega = 1.25$. These values are calculated using Eq.(27) . It is seen then in Fig.6 that the search area extends from -0.25E(dx) to 2.75E(dx). Although the upper value of $E(\delta)$ is greater than the upper limit of the step size control factor, the expectation value of the step size control factor is 1.25, which obeys the stability rule given in Eq.(38). From Fig.6, one can also find that if ω is greater than unity, particle is possible to search the region to the left of $E(x(t))$. Meanwhile, the greater ω is, the more the search area shift to left of $E(x(t))$, which will reduce diversity of particle because particles move to the vinicity of $E(x(t))$. Now, refer to Fig.7, for $\omega = 0.75$ and $E(\varphi) = 1.5$,the searach domain are in 0.25E(dx) and 3.25E(dx) with mean of 1.75E(dx). This parameter setting also obeys the stability criterion. It seems both cases of parameter choice is proper. However, refer to Eq.(37), the trajectory of a particle is mainly governed by the term $(\omega - E(\varphi))^t$. If $(\omega - E(\varphi))$ is too small, $E(x(t))$ will vanish quickly and particle may get stuck on local optimum. In other words, the value of $(\omega - E(\varphi))$ represents an index for evaluation of the prematurity of particles. Therefore, it is better to have $0 < \omega < 1$, and empirical studies have shown that it is proper to choice of inertia weight in $0.7 < \omega < 0.8$.

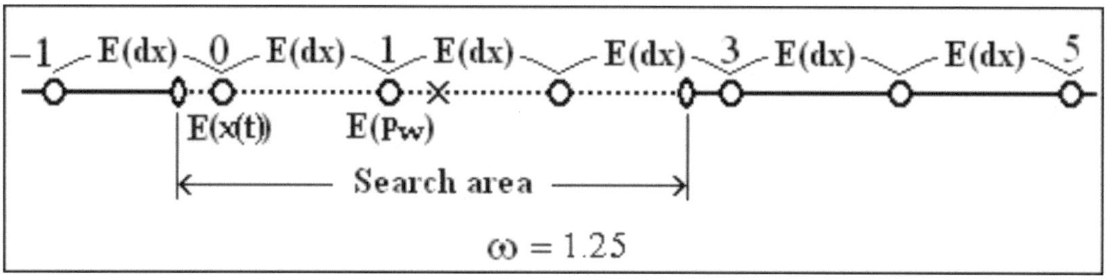

Figure 6. The area the particle will explore for $\omega = 1.25$ and $E(\varphi) = 1.5$

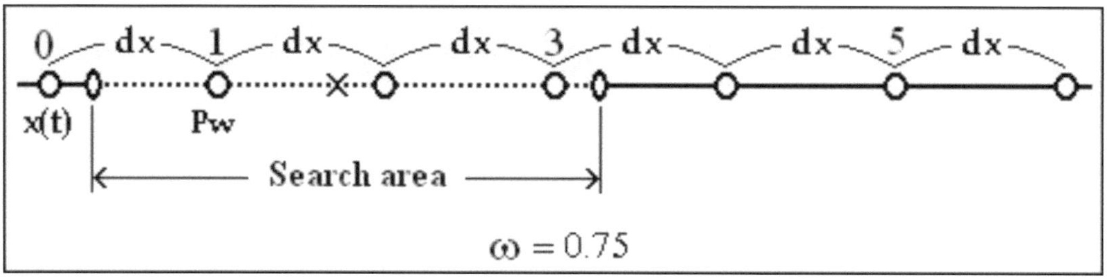

Figure 7. The area the particle will explore for $\omega = 0.75$ and $E(\varphi) = 1.5$

3.3.2 Acceleration coefficient

Recall that c_1 and c_2 are referred to acceleration coefficients, and φ is the sum of two uniform random numbers in $(0, c_1)$ and $(0, c_2)$. The lower and upper limits of φ are then 0 and (c_1+c_2), respectively. To determine c_1 and c_2, it has to consider from three aspects: prematurity, population diversity and particle stability.

If φ varies from 0 to (c_1+c_2) uniformly, from Eq.(27), the lower bound of the step size control factor is determined by the choice of ω, i.e.,

$$\delta_{\min} = -\omega + 1 \tag{52}$$

while the upper bound is set by ω, c_1 and c_2, which is

$$\delta_{\max} = -\omega + (c_1 + c_2) + 1 \tag{53}$$

For simplicity, it usually has c_1=c_2=c, Eq.(53) becomes

$$\delta_{\max} = -\omega + 2c + 1 \tag{54}$$

Accounting for stability, in terms of step size control factor, staibility criterion is descibed as

$$0 < E(\delta) < 2 \tag{55}$$

Approximate the expectation value E(δ) by the average value of δ_{min} and δ_{max}, it has

$$E(\delta) = -\omega + c + 1 \tag{56}$$

Based on (56), one can determine the acceleration coefficients once ω and E(δ) is assigned. For example, let ω = 0.75 and E(δ) = 1.75 (stisfies Eq.(55)), solve Eq.(56) for c. It is obtained c=1.5. The acceleration coefficients are then set to c_1=c_2=1.5. The lower and upper bounds of the step size control factor computed by Eq.(52) and Eq.(54) are 0.25 and 3.25, respectively. The range the particle will search is shown in Fig.7 for this example. It is seen that the search domain stretchs over from 0.25E(dx) to 3.25E(dx), where E(dx) = E(p_w) - E(x(t)) is the distance between expectation values of the random weighted mean, p_w, of p_g and p_i and current particle position x(t).
Of course, this is not the unique parameters setting for PPSO. Frequently, it is required to compare the performances between PSO and PPSO. In such situation, the common used parameters for PSO (ω=0.729, c_1=c_2=1.494) fit to PPSO since E(φ) = 1.494, and E(δ) = 1.765 which satisfies Eq.(55).

3.4 Equilibrium point

Both PPSO and PSO define the particles as potential solutions to a problem in a multi-dimensional space with a memory of its ever found best solution and the best solution among all particles. PPSO generates a sequence of x(t) iteratively, and if x(t) is a stable sequence, it has

$$\lim_{t \to \infty} x(t) = E(p_w) \tag{57}$$

where the random weighted mean E(p_w) defined in (42) is the equilibrium point of the sequence. As an optimization solver, it is expected that E(p_w) is the optimum solution. It is seen from (57) that if p_g = p_i = p, E(p_w) = p. This means that particle settles down at the global best ever found, i.e., PPSO is expected to constantly update the personal best and global best solutions ever found, and finally converges to E(p_w)= p_g = p_i, the optimum solution or near optimum solution of the problem at hand.

Note that the random weighted mean of PSO is defined as [Kennedy, 1999 and van den Bergs, 2003]

$$p_w = \frac{c_1 \cdot p_g + c_2 \cdot p_i}{c_1 + c_2} \tag{58}$$

Oviuously, the particles of PSO and PPSO will converge to different equilibrium points. Therefore, in additon to the equilibrium points, the trajectories of PSO and PPSO are also different since trajectories of PPSO and PSO are characterised by a first-order and second-order difference equations [Trelea, 2003, Yasuda et al., 2003, van den Bergh, 2003], respectively. These are the distinctive features of PSO and PPSO.

4. Example Trajectories

To see the properties between PSO and PPSO, the trajectories the particle traversed are investigated by a primitive PSO and PPSO model, where p_g and p_i are set as two arbitrarily constants. To keep thing simple and have a better observation, trajectories of one dimension are considered here. Both the trajectories are generated with same initial condition, i.e., same initial values for position and velocity. Meanwhile, both PSO and PPSO use the same value for the parameters, ω, c_1 and c_2 that they are set as ω=0.729 and c_1=c_2=1.494. Each of the trajectories is constructed by 10000 points and, for fair comparison, each points is generated using the same random numbers for both PSO and PPSO at each time step.
The pseudo-code for generating the trajectories is shown in Fig.8, where x(t) and y(t) are the positions of PSO and PPSO at time step t; vx(t) and vy(t) represent the velocity of PSO and PPSO, respectively; x(0) and y(0) is the initial positions, vx(0) and vy(0) are the initial velocities of PSO and PPSO, respectively.

```
/* pseudo-code for evaluation PSO and PPSO */
Set ω, c1, c2, pg and pi;
Initialize x(0), y(0), vx(0) and vy(0);
For t=1 to 10000 {
    φ1 = c1 · rnd(1); φ2 = c2 · rnd();
    vx(t) = ω · vx(t−1) + φ1 · (pg − x(t−1)) + φ2 · (pi − x(t−1));
    vy(t) = ω · vy(t−1) + φ1 · (pg − y(t−1)) + φ2 · (pi − y(t−1));
    x(t) = vx(t) + x(t−1);
    y(t) = vy(t) + pi;
}
/* End */
```

Figure 8. Pseudo-code for evaluating the trajectories of PSO and PPSO

Figure 9 and 10 depicted examples of the trajectories of PSO and PPSO. These plots are obtained with p_g, p_i, x(0), y(0) vx(0) and vy(0) that are arbitrarily set to -50, 10, 0, 0, 20 and 20, respectively. The gray lines in the centre of the figures represent the mean values of x(t) and y(t). They are denoted as μ_x and μ_y for x(t) and y(t), respectively. It is seen obviously that both the trajectories of PSO and PPSO randomly vibrate, or oscillate around the mean values within a limited ranges. The mean values are obtained as μ_x = -20.009, and μ_y = -15.288. These two values very close to the theoretical random weighted mean of p_g and p_i, defined in (58) and (42) for PSO and PPSO, which are calculated to be -20 and -15.394.

Furthermore, the minimum and maximum values of x(t) are -697.131 and 706.212, while the minimum and maximum values of y(t) are -713.624 and 676.268.

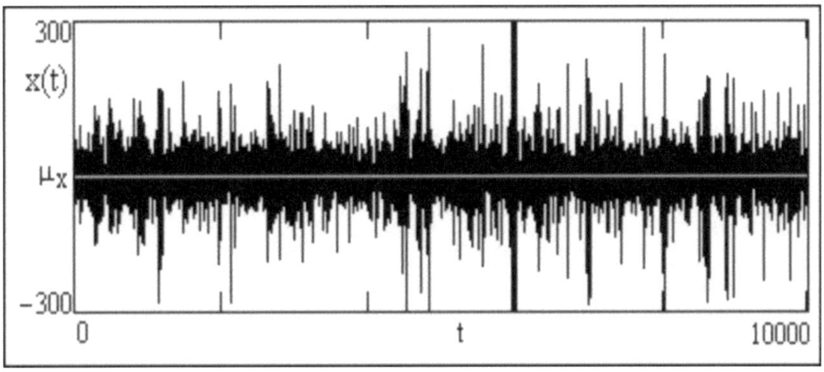

Figure 9. Sample trajectory of x(t) for PSO with p_g=-50, p_i=10, x(0)=0 and vx(0)=20

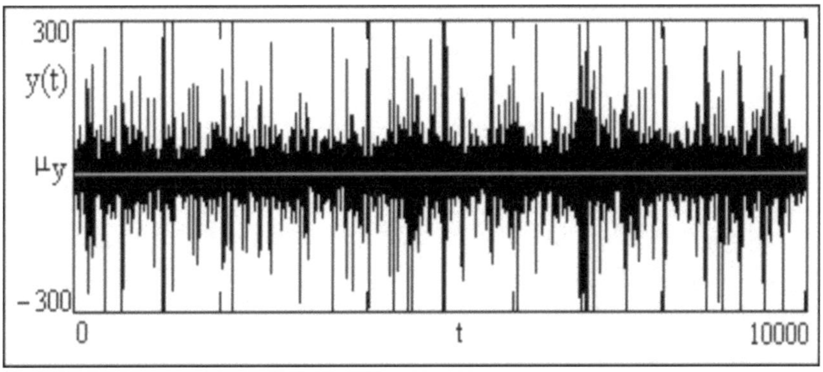

Figure 10. Sample trajectory of y(t) for PPSO with p_g=-50, p_i=10, y(0)=0 and vy(0)=20

Recall that PSO has bell-shaped distribution of the trajectory centred approximately at p_w, i.e., the weighted mean which equals to the midpoint of p_g and p_i [Kennedy, 2003]. This feature also has been observed in PPSO. Refer to Figs.(11) and (12), the histogram plots of the distribution of x(t) and y(t) are illustrated. In these figures, the distributions of the trajectories are drawn in grey lines and the vertical dash-line denoted the mean value of the trajectory. The horizontal and vertical axes represent the values of the trajectory and the occurrences a particle ever explored. The plots of the horizontal axis extend from (μ_x - 3σ_x) to (μ_x + 3σ_x) and (μ_y - 3σ_y) to (μ_y + 3σ_y) for PSO and PPSO, respectively, where σ_x and σ_y are the standard deviations of x(t) and y(t). Obviously, the distribution of the trajectory of the PPSO is also a bell-shaped centred at the random weighted mean. For a comparison, the normal distribution with mean μ_x and standard deviation σ_x for PSO and mean μ_y and standard deviation σ_y for PPSO are drawn in thick solid lines. Clearly, although PSO and PPSO works based on different mathematical models, they have similar dynamic behaviour.

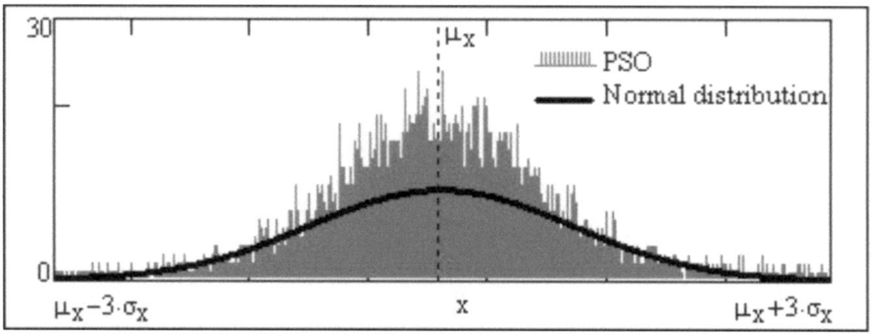

Figure 11. The histogram plot of x(t) for PSO with p_g=-50, p_i=10, x(0)=0 and vx(0)=20

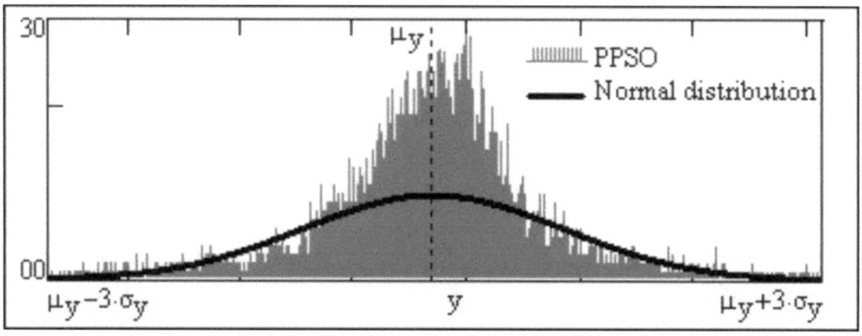

Figure 12. The histogram plot of y(t) for PPSO with p_g=-50, p_i=10, y(0)=0 and vy(0)=20

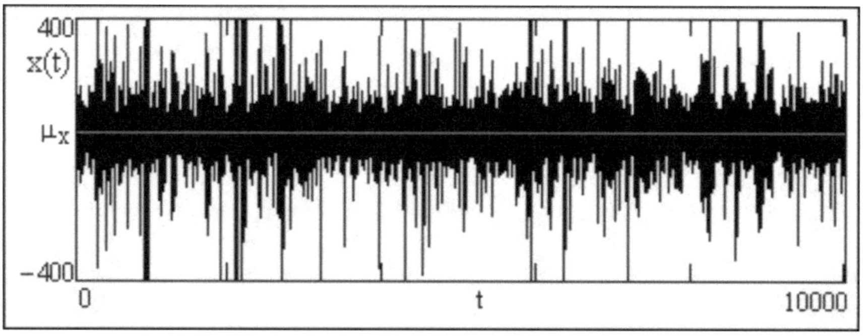

Figure 13. Sample trajectory of x(t) for PSO with p_g = 0, p_i = 100, x(0) = 10 and vx(0) = -2

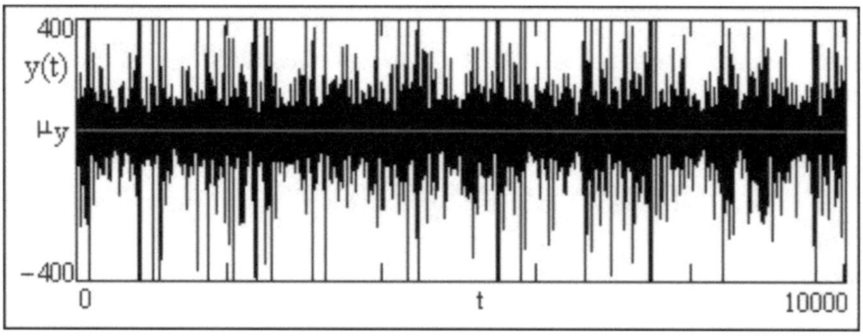

Figure 14. Sample trajectory of y(t) for PPSO with p_g = 0, p_i = 100, y(0) = 10 and vy(0) = -2

Another samples of trajectory for different setting of p_g and p_i as well as initial condition are show in Figs.13 and 14 where p_g, p_i, x(0), y(0) vx(0) and vy(0) are arbitrarily chosen as 0, 100, 10, 10, -2 and -2, respectively. With $p_g = 0$ and $p_i = 100$, the random weighted mean, p_w, of PSO and PPSO are 50 and 57.677. Meanwhile, the mean values, μ_x and μ_y, are 50.588 and 57.609 for PSO and PPSO. The minimum and maximum values are -3.249×10^3 and 3.550×10^3 for x(t) and -1.639×10^3 and 2.941×10^3 for y(t). Apparently, both the trajectories also oscillate around the random weighted mean within a specific domain, which are verified further in the histogram plots shown in Figs.(15) and (16).

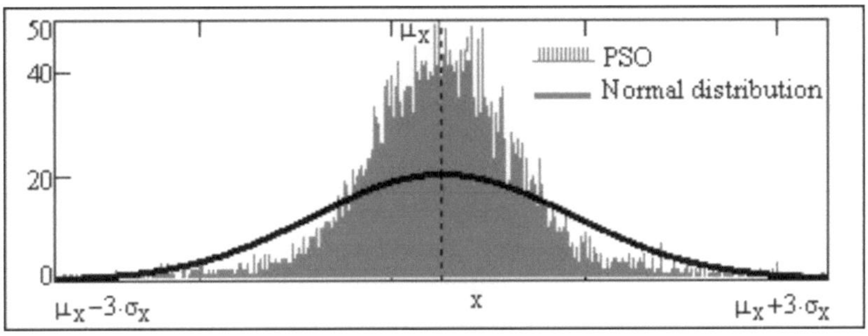

Figure 15. The histogram plot of x(t) for PSO with $p_g = 0$, $p_i = 100$, x(0) = 10 and vx(0) = -2

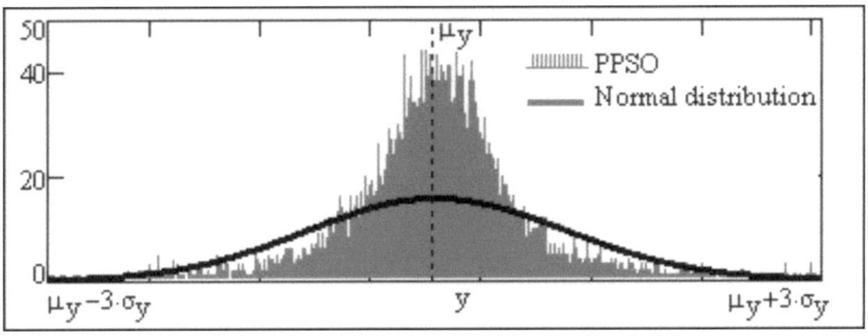

Figure 16. The histogram plot of y(t) for PPSO with $p_g = 0$, $p_i = 100$, y(0) = 10 and vy(0)= -2

5. Conclusion

This chapter intends to provide a theoretical analysis of PPSO to clarify the characteristics of PPSO. The analysis is started from a simplified deterministic model, a single particle and one dimension case, keeping all the parameters constants. After that, assuming the acceleration coefficients as uniformly distributed random numbers, a stochastic model is then built to describe the nature of the PPSO. With the assumption, it is shown that a first-order difference equation is sufficient to describe the dynamic behaviour of the particles. Based on the models, the convergence property is studied and the guidance for parameters selection is provided.

Trajectories comparison between PSO and PPSO are also presented. It is found that, similar to PSO, the particles of PPSO also stochastically explore for optimal solution within a region centered approximately equals to a random weighted mean of the best positions found by an individual (personal best) and its neighbours (global best). Like PSO, bell-shaped distribution of the particle's trajectory is also observed in PPSO. However, the centres of the

distribution of PSO and PPSO are different so that leading to different equilibrium points and, hence, different results and performances.
The results derived in this chapter justify the possibility of PPSO to be an optimization algorithm. Simulation results have been shown that PPSO performs in general better than PSO on a suite of benchmark functions. However, it does not imply that PPSO is a local or global search algorithm even the condition of stability is met. Further research is thus required to improve the search capability.

6. References

Chen, C. H. & Yeh, S. N. (2006a), Personal best oriented constriction type of particle swarm optimization, The *2nd international conference on cybernetics and intelligent systems*, pp. 167-170, Bangkok, Thailand, 7-9 Jun., 2006.

Chen, C. H. & Yeh, S. N. (2006b), Particle swarm optimization for economic power dispatch with valve-point effects, *2006 IEEE PES transmission and distribution conference and exposition : Latin America*, 6 pages, Caracas, Venezuela, 16-19 Aug., 2006.

Chen, C. H. & Yeh, S. N., (2007), Simplified personal best oriented particle swarm optimizer and its applications, The *2nd IEEE Conference on Industrial Electronics and Applications*, pp.2362-2365, Harbin, China, 23-25 May, 2007.

Chen, C. H. & Yeh, S. N. (2008), Personal best oriented particle swarm optimizer for economic dispatch problem with piecewise quadratic cost functions, *International Journal of Electrical Engineering*, vol. 15, no.5, 2008, pp.389-397.

Clerc M. & Kennedy J., (2002), The particle swarm - explosion, stability and convergence in a multidimensional complex space, *IEEE Transaction on Evolutionary Computation*, vol.6, no.1, 2002, pp.58-73.

Eberhart R. C. & Kennedy J. (1995), A new optimizer using particle swarm theory, *Proceedings of the IEEE 6th International Symposium on Micro Machine and Human Science*, pp. 39-43, vol.1, Oct., 1995.

Kennedy J., & Eberhart R. C. (1995), Particle swarm optimization, *Proceedings of the IEEE International Conference on Neural Networks*, pp.1942-1948, vol.4, Perth, Australia, Nov., 1995.

Kennedy J. (1998), The behaviour of particle, *Proceedings of the 7th Annual Conference on Evolutionary Programming*, pp.581-589, 1998.

Kennedy J. (2003), Bare bones particle swarms, *Proceedings of the IEEE Swarm Symposium*, 2003, pp.80-87.

Jiang, M.; Luo Y.P. & Yang S. Y., (2007), Stochastic convergence analysis and parameter selection of the standard particle swarm optimization algorithm, *Information Processing Letters*, vol.102, 2007, pp.8-16.

Ozcan E. & Mohan C. K., (1999), Particle swarm optimization: surfing the waves, *Proceedings of the IEEE Congress on Evolutionary Computation*, pp.1939-1944, vol.3, Jul., 1999.

Trelea I. C., (2003), The particle swarm optimization algorithm: convergence analysis and parameter selection, *Information Processing Letters*, vol.85, 2003, pp.317-325.

van den Bergh F. (2002), Analysis of particle swarm optimization, *Ph.D. dissertation*, University of Pretoria, Pretoria, South Africa, 2002.

Yasuda K., Ide A. & Iwasaki N., (2003), Adaptive particle swarm optimization, pp.1554-1559, *IEEE International Conference on Systems, Man and Cybernetics*, vol.2, Oct., 2003.

7

Particle Swarm Optimization for Power Dispatch with Pumped Hydro

Po-Hung Chen
Department of Electrical Engineering, St. John's University
Taiwan

1. Introduction

Recently, a new evolutionary computation technique, known as particle swarm optimization (PSO), has become a candidate for many optimization applications due to its high-performance and flexibility. The PSO technique was developed based on the social behavior of flocking birds and schooling fish when searching for food (Kennedy & Eberhart, 1995). The PSO technique simulates the behavior of individuals in a group to maximize the species survival. Each particle "flies" in a direction that is based on its experience and that of the whole group. Individual particles move stochastically toward the position affected by the present velocity, previous best performance, and the best previous performance of the group. The PSO approach is simple in concept and easily implemented with few coding lines, meaning that many can take advantage of it. Compared with other evolutionary algorithms, the main advantages of PSO are its robustness in controlling parameters and its high computational efficiency (Kennedy & Eberhart, 2001). The PSO technique has been successfully applied in areas such as distribution state estimation (Naka et al., 2003), reactive power dispatch (Zhao et al., 2005), and electromagnetic devices design (Ho et al., 2006). In the previous effort, a PSO approach was developed to solve the capacitor allocation and dispatching problem (Kuo et al., 2005).

This chapter introduces a PSO approach for solving the power dispatch with pumped hydro (PDWPH) problem. The PDWPH has been reckoned as a difficult task within the operation planning of a power system. It aims to minimize total fuel costs for a power system while satisfying hydro and thermal constraints (Wood & Wollenberg, 1996). The optimal solution to a PDWPH problem can be obtained via exhaustive enumeration of all pumped hydro and thermal unit combinations at each time period. However, due to the computational burden, the exhaustive enumeration approach is infeasible in real applications. Conventional methods (El-Hawary & Ravindranath, 1992; Jeng et al., 1996; Allan & Roman, 1991; Al-Agtash, 2001) for solving such a non-linear, mix-integer, combinatorial optimization problem are generally based on decomposition methods that involve a hydro and a thermal sub-problem. These two sub-problems are usually coordinated by LaGrange multipliers. The optimal generation schedules for pumped hydro and thermal units are then sequentially obtained via repetitive hydro-thermal iterations. A well-recognized difficulty is that solutions to these two sub-problems can oscillate between maximum and minimum generations with slight changes of multipliers (Guan et al., 1994; Chen, 1989). Consequently, solution cost frequently gets stuck at a local optimum rather than at the global optimum. However, obtaining an optimal solution is of priority concern to an electric utility. Even small percentage reduction in production costs typically leads to considerable savings. Obviously, a comprehensive and efficient algorithm for solving the PDWPH problem is still in demand. In the previous efforts, a dynamic programming (DP) approach (Chen, 1989) and a genetic algorithm (GA) technique (Chen & Chang, 1999) have been adopted to solve the PDWPH problem. Although the GA has been successfully applied to solve the PDWPH problem, recent studies have identified some deficiencies in GA performance. This decreased efficiency is apparent in applications in which parameters being optimized are highly correlated (Eberhart & Shi, 1998; Boeringer & Werner, 2004). Moreover, premature convergence of the GA reduces its performance and search capability (Angeline, 1998; Juang, 2004).

This work presents new solution algorithms based on a PSO technique for solving the PDWPH problem. The proposed approach combines a binary version of the PSO technique with a mutation operation. Kennedy and Eberhart first introduced the concept of binary PSO and demonstrated that a binary PSO was successfully applied to solve a discrete binary problem (Kennedy & Eberhart, 1997). In this work, since all Taipower's pumped hydro units are designed for constant power pumping, novel binary encoding/decoding techniques are judiciously devised to model the discrete characteristic in pumping mode as well as the continuous characteristic in generating mode. Moreover, since the basic PSO approach converges fast during the initial period and slows down in the subsequent period and sometimes lands in a local optimum, this work employs a mutation operation that speeds up convergence and escapes local optimums. Representative test results based on the actual Taipower system are presented and analyzed, illustrating the capability of the proposed PSO approach in practical applications.

2. Modeling and Formulation

2.1 List of symbols

DR_i	Down ramp rate limits of thermal unit i.
$F_i^t(P_{si}^t)$	Production costs for P_{si}^t.
I_j^t	Natural inflow into the upper reservoir of pumped hydro plant j in hour t.
N_h	Number of pumped hydro units.
N_s	Number of thermal units.
P_{hj}^t	Power generation (positive) or pumping (negative) of pumped hydro plant j in hour t.
P_L^t	System load demand in hour t.
P_{si}^t	Power generation of thermal unit i in hour t.
Q_j^t	Water discharge of pumped hydro plant j in hour t.
$Q_{j,p}^t$	Water pumping of pumped hydro plant j in hour t.

$R_{hj}^{t}(P_{hj}^{t})$	Spinning reserve contribution of pumped hydro plant *j* for P_{hj}^{t}.
R_{req}^{t}	System's spinning reserve requirements in hour *t*.
$R_{si}^{t}(P_{si}^{t})$	Spinning reserve contribution of thermal unit *i* for P_{si}^{t}.
S_{j}^{t}	Water spillage of pumped hydro plant *j* in hour *t*.
T	Number of scheduling hours.
UR_{i}	Up ramp rate limits of thermal unit *i*.
V_{j}^{t}	Water volume of the upper reservoirs of plant *j* at the end of hour *t*.
$V_{j,l}^{t}$	Water volume of the lower reservoirs of plant *j* at the end of hour *t*.
v_{i}^{k}	Velocity of particle *i* at iteration *k*.
x_{i}^{k}	Position (coordinate) of particle *i* at iteration *k*.

2.2 Modeling a pumped hydro plant

A pumped hydro plant, which consists of an upper and a lower reservoir, is designed to save fuel costs by generating during peak load hours with water in the upper reservoir, which is pumped up from the lower reservoir to the upper reservoir during light load hours (Fig. 1).

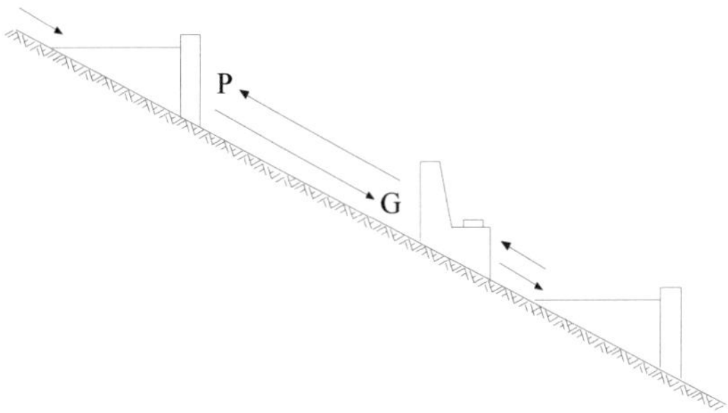

Figure 1. Pumped hydro plant

In generating mode, the equivalent-plant model can be derived using an off-line mathematical procedure that maximizes total plant generation output under different water discharge rates (Wood & Wollenberg, 1996). The generation output of an equivalent pumped hydro plant is a function of water discharged through turbines and the content (or the net head) of the upper reservoir. The general form is expressed as

$$P_{hj}^{t} = f(Q_{j}^{t}, V_{j}^{t-1}) \tag{1}$$

The quadratic discharge-generation function, considering the net head effect, utilized in this work as a good approximation of pumped hydro plant generation characteristics is given as

$$P_{hj}^{t} = \alpha_{j}^{t-1} Q_{j}^{t^{2}} + \beta_{j}^{t-1} Q_{j}^{t} + \gamma_{j}^{t-1} \tag{2}$$

where coefficients α_j^{t-1}, β_j^{t-1}, and γ_j^{t-1} depend on the content of the upper reservoir at the end of hour *t-1*. In this work, the read-in data includes five groups of α, β, γ coefficients that are associated with different storage volume, from minimum to maximum, for the upper reservoir (first quadrant in Fig. 2). Then, the corresponding coefficients for any reservoir volume are calculated using a linear interpolation (Chen, 1989) between the two closest volume.

In pumping mode, since all Taipower's pumped hydro units are designed for constant power pumping, the characteristic function of a pumped hydro plant is a discrete distribution (third quadrant in Fig. 2).

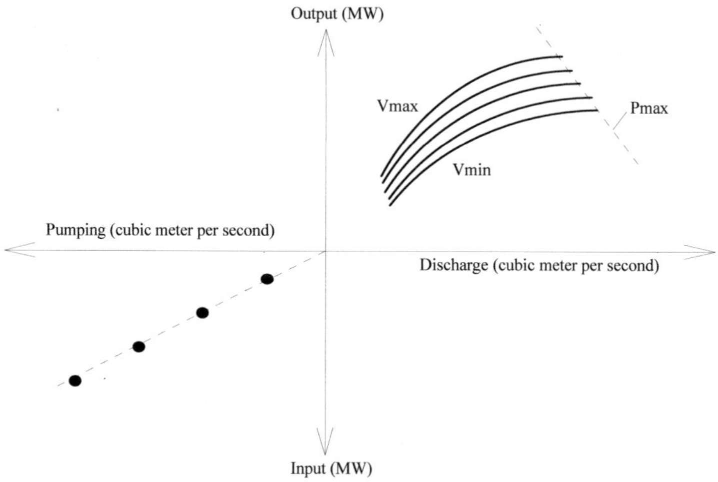

Figure 2. Typical input-output characteristic for a pumped hydro plant

2.3 Objective function and constraints

The pumped hydro scheduling attempts seeking the optimal generation schedules for both pumped hydro and thermal units while satisfying various hydro and thermal constraints. With division of the total scheduling time into a set of short time intervals, say, one hour as one time interval, the pumped hydro scheduling can be mathematically formulated as a constrained nonlinear optimization problem as follows:

$$\textbf{\textit{Problem:}}\ \ Minimize\ \sum_{t=1}^{T}\sum_{i=1}^{N_s} F_i^t(P_{si}^t) \tag{3}$$

Subject to the following constraints:

System power balance

$$\sum_{i=1}^{N_s} P_{si}^t + \sum_{j=1}^{N_h} P_{hj}^t - P_L^t = 0 \tag{4}$$

Water dynamic balance

$$V_j^t = V_j^{t-1} + I_j^t - Q_j^t + Q_{j,p}^t - S_j^t \tag{5}$$

$$V_{j,l}^{t} = V_{j,l}^{t-1} + Q_j^t - Q_{j,p}^t + S_j^t \tag{6}$$

Thermal generation and ramp rate limits

$$Max(\underline{P_{si}}, P_{si}^{t-1} - DR_i) \leq P_{si}^t \leq Min(\overline{P_{si}}, P_{si}^{t-1} + UR_i) \tag{7}$$

Water discharge limits

$$\underline{Q_j} \leq Q_j^t \leq \overline{Q_j} \tag{8}$$

Water pumping limits

$$\underline{Q_{j,p}} \leq Q_{j,p}^t \leq \overline{Q_{j,p}} \tag{9}$$

Reservoir limits

$$\underline{V_j} \leq V_j^t \leq \overline{V_j} \tag{10}$$

$$\underline{V_{j,l}} \leq V_{j,l}^t \leq \overline{V_{j,l}} \tag{11}$$

System's spinning reserve requirements

$$\sum_{i=1}^{N_s} R_{si}^t(P_{si}^t) + \sum_{j=1}^{N_h} R_{hj}^t(P_{hj}^t) \geq R_{req}^t \tag{12}$$

3. Refined PSO Solution Methodology

3.1 Basic PSO technique

Consider an optimization problem of D variables. A swarm of N particles is initialized in which each particle is assigned a random position in the D-dimensional hyperspace such that each particle's position corresponds to a candidate solution for the optimization problem. Let x denote a particle's position (coordinate) and v denote the particle's flight velocity over a solution space. Each individual x in the swarm is scored using a scoring function that obtains a score (fitness value) representing how good it solves the problem. The best previous position of a particle is *Pbest*. The index of the best particle among all particles in the swarm is *Gbest*. Each particle records its own personal best position (*Pbest*), and knows the best positions found by all particles in the swarm (*Gbest*). Then, all particles that fly over the D-dimensional solution space are subject to updated rules for new positions, until the global optimal position is found. Velocity and position of a particle are updated by the following stochastic and deterministic update rules:

$$\begin{aligned} v_i^{k+1} = wv_i^k &+ c_1 Rand(\,) \times (Pbest_i^k - x_i^k) \\ &+ c_2 Rand(\,) \times (Gbest^k - x_i^k) \end{aligned} \tag{13}$$

$$x_i^{k+1} = x_i^k + v_i^{k+1} \tag{14}$$

where w is an inertia weight, c_1 and c_2 are acceleration constants, and $Rand(\,)$ is a random number between 0 and 1.

Equation (13) indicates that the velocity of a particle is modified according to three components. The first component is its previous velocity, v_i^k, scaled by an inertia, w. This component is often known as "habitual behavior." The second component is a linear attraction toward its previous best position, $Pbest_i^k$, scaled by the product of an acceleration constant, c_1, and a random number. Note that a different random number is assigned for each dimension. This component is often known as "memory" or "self-knowledge." The third component is a linear attraction toward the global best position, $Gbest^k$, scaled by the product of an acceleration constant, c_2, and a random number. This component is often known as "team work" or "social knowledge." Fig. 3 illustrates a search mechanism of a PSO technique using the velocity update rule (13) and the position update rule (14).

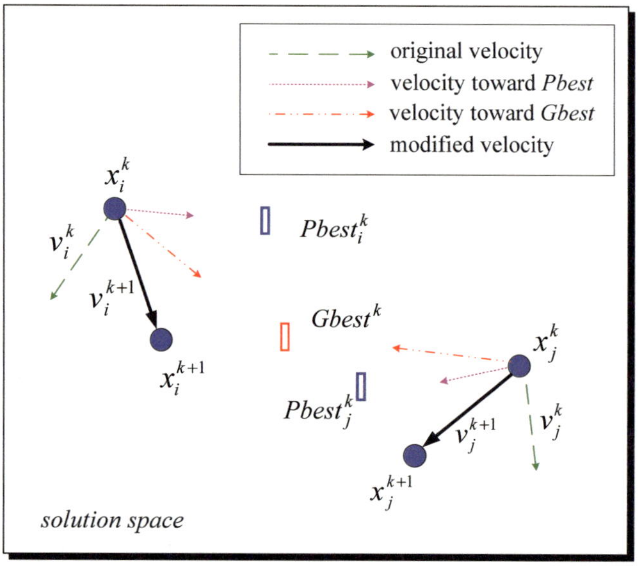

Figure 3. Searching mechanism of a PSO

Acceleration constants c_1 and c_2 represent the weights of the stochastic acceleration terms that push a particle toward *Pbest* and *Gbest*, respectively. Small values allow a particle to roam far from target regions. Conversely, large values result in the abrupt movement of particles toward target regions. In this work, constants c_1 and c_2 are both set at 2.0, following the typical practice in (Eberhart & Shi, 2001). Suitable correction of inertia w in (13) provides a balance between global and local explorations, thereby reducing the number of iterations when finding a sufficiently optimal solution. An inertia correction function called "inertia weight approach (IWA)" (Kennedy & Eberhart, 2001) is utilized in this work. During the IWA, the inertia weight w is modified according to the following equation:

$$w = w_{max} - \frac{w_{max} - w_{min}}{Itr_{max}} \times Itr \tag{15}$$

where w_{max} and w_{min} are the initial and final inertia weights, Itr_{max} is the maximum number of iteration, and Itr is the current number of iteration.

3.2 Binary encoding

For exposition ease, consider a pumped hydro plant with four units. Fig. 4 presents a particle string that translates the encoded parameter-water discharges of each plant into their binary representations.

Hour	1	2	.....	24
	1 0 0 0 1	0 0 0 1 1	.....	1 0 0 1 0

Figure 4. Particle string for a pumped hydro plant with four units

Using a plant's water discharge instead of the plant's generation output, the encoded parameter is more beneficial when dealing with difficult water balance constraints. Each particle string contains 24 sub-strings that represent the solution for hourly discharge/pumping schedules of the pumped hydro plant during a 24-hour period. Each sub-string is assigned the same number of five bits. The first bit is used to identify whether the plant is in generating or pumping mode. The remaining four bits are used to represent a normalized water discharge, q_j^t, in generating mode, or the number of pumping units in pumping mode. In generating mode, the resolution equals $1/2^4$ of the discharge difference from minimum to maximum.

3.3 Decoding of particle string

A particle within a binary PSO approach is evaluated through decoding the encoded particle string and computing the string's scoring function using the decoded parameter. The following steps summarize the detailed decoding procedure.

Step 1. Decode the first bit to determine whether the plant is in generating or pumping mode:

Hour t

b_1	b_2	b_3	b_4	b_5

b_2=b_3=b_4=b_5="0" => "idle mode"
b_1="0" => "pumping mode"
b_1="1" => "generating mode"

Step 2. If in idle mode, P_{hj}^t =0, go to Step 10; if in pumping mode, go to Step 3; if in generating mode, go to Step 6.

Step 3. Decode the remaining four bits of the sub-string to calculate the number of pumping units, N_p^t, and the total volume of pumped water, $Q_{j,p}^t$:

Hour t

0	b_2	b_3	b_4	b_5

$$N_p^t = \sum_{i=2}^{5}(b_i) \qquad b_i \in \{0, 1\} \tag{16}$$

$$Q_{j,p}^t = Q_{j,sp} \times N_p^t \tag{17}$$

where $Q_{j,sp}$ is the constant volume for pumping per unit.

Step 4. Calculate the upper boundary of pumped water:

$$\overline{Q^t_{j,p}} = Min[\overline{Q_{j,p}}, (V^{t-1}_{j,l} - \underline{V_{j,l}})] \tag{18}$$

If the total volume of pumped water exceed the upper boundary, then decrease the number of pumping units until the upper boundary is satisfied.

Step 5. Calculate the MW power for pumping:

$$P^t_{hj} = -\left(P_{j,sp} \times N^t_p\right) \tag{19}$$

where $P_{j,sp}$ is the constant power for pumping per unit. Then go to step 10.

Step 6. Decode the remaining four bits of the sub-string to obtain a normalized discharge, q^t_j, in decimal values:

Hour t

1	b_2	b_3	b_4	b_5
	×	×	×	×
	2^{-1}	2^{-2}	2^{-3}	2^{-4}

$$q^t_j = \sum_{i=2}^{5}\left(b_i \times 2^{-(i-1)}\right) \qquad b_i \in \{0, 1\} \tag{20}$$

Step 7. Calculate the upper boundary of discharge:

$$\overline{Q^t_j} = Min[\overline{Q_j}, (\overline{V_{j,l}} - V^{t-1}_{j,l})] \tag{21}$$

Step 8. Translate the normalized value, q^t_j, to the actual value, Q^t_j:

$$Q^t_j = \underline{Q_j} + q^t_j\left(\overline{Q^t_j} - \underline{Q_j}\right) \tag{22}$$

Step 9. Calculate the generation output, P^t_{hj}, using (2).

Step 10. Calculate the remaining thermal loads, P^t_{rm}:

$$P^t_{rm} = P^t_L - P^t_{hj} \tag{23}$$

Step 11. Continue with computations of the 10 steps from hour 1 to hour 24.

Step 12. Perform the unit commitment (UC) for the remaining thermal load profile, and return the corresponding thermal cost. In this work, a UC package based on the neural network (Chen & Chen, 2006) is used to perform the UC task taking into account fuel costs, start-up costs, ramp rate limits, and minimal uptime/downtime constraints.

Step 13. Translate the corresponding thermal cost into the score of the *i*-th particle using a scoring function (details are found in the next Section).

Step 14. Repeat these 13 steps for each particle from the first to last particle.

3.4 Scoring function

The scoring function adopted is based on the corresponding thermal production cost. To emphasize the "best" particles and speed up convergence of the evolutionary process, the scoring function is normalized into a range of 0–1. The scoring function for the *i*-th particle in the swarm is defined as

$$SCORE(i) = \frac{1}{1 + k_i\left(\frac{cost(i)}{cost(Gbest)} - 1\right)} \tag{24}$$

where *SCORE(i)* is the score (fitness value) of the *i*-th particle; *cost(i)* is the corresponding thermal cost of the *i*-th particle; *cost(Gbest)* is the cost of the highest ranking particle string, namely, the current best particle; and, k_i is a scaling constant (k_i =100 in this study).

3.5 Mutation operation

The basic PSO approach typically converges rapidly during the initial search period and then slows. Then, checking the positions of particles showed that the particles were very tightly clustered around a local optimum, and the particle velocities were almost zero. This phenomenon resulted in a slow convergence and trapped the whole swarm at a local optimum. Mutation operation is capable of overcoming this shortcoming. Mutation operation is an occasional (with a small probability) random alternation of the *Gbest* string, as shown in Fig. 5. This work integrates a PSO technique with a mutation operation providing background variation and occasionally introduces beneficial materials into the swarm to speed up convergence and escape local optimums.

Gbest:	1	1	1	1	1	0	0	.....	0	1	0
			↓								
New Particle:	1	1	0	1	1	0	0	.....	0	1	0

Figure 5. Mutation operation

The solution methodology for solving the pumped hydro scheduling problem using the proposed approach is outlined in the general flow chart (Fig. 6).

4. Test Results

The proposed approach was implemented on a MATLAB software and executed on a Pentium IV 3.0GHz personal computer. Then, the proposed approach was tested for a portion of the Taipower system, which consists of 34 thermal units and the Ming-Hu pumped hydro plant with four units. In addition to the typical constraints listed in Section 2, the Taipower system has three additional features that increase problem difficulty.

a. The Taipower system is an isolated system. Thus it is self-sufficient at all times. The 300MW system's spinning reserve requirement must be satisfied each hour.
b. Thermal units, due to their ramp rate limits, have difficulty handling large load fluctuations, especially at noon lunch break.
c. The lower reservoir of Ming-Hu pumped hydro plant has only a small storage volume.

Table 1 presents detailed data for the Ming-Hu pumped hydro plant. The thermal system consists of 34 thermal units: six large coal-fired units, eight small coal-fired units, seven oil-fired units, ten gas turbine units, and three combined cycle units. For data on the characteristics of the 34-unit thermal system, please refer to (Chen & Chang, 1995).

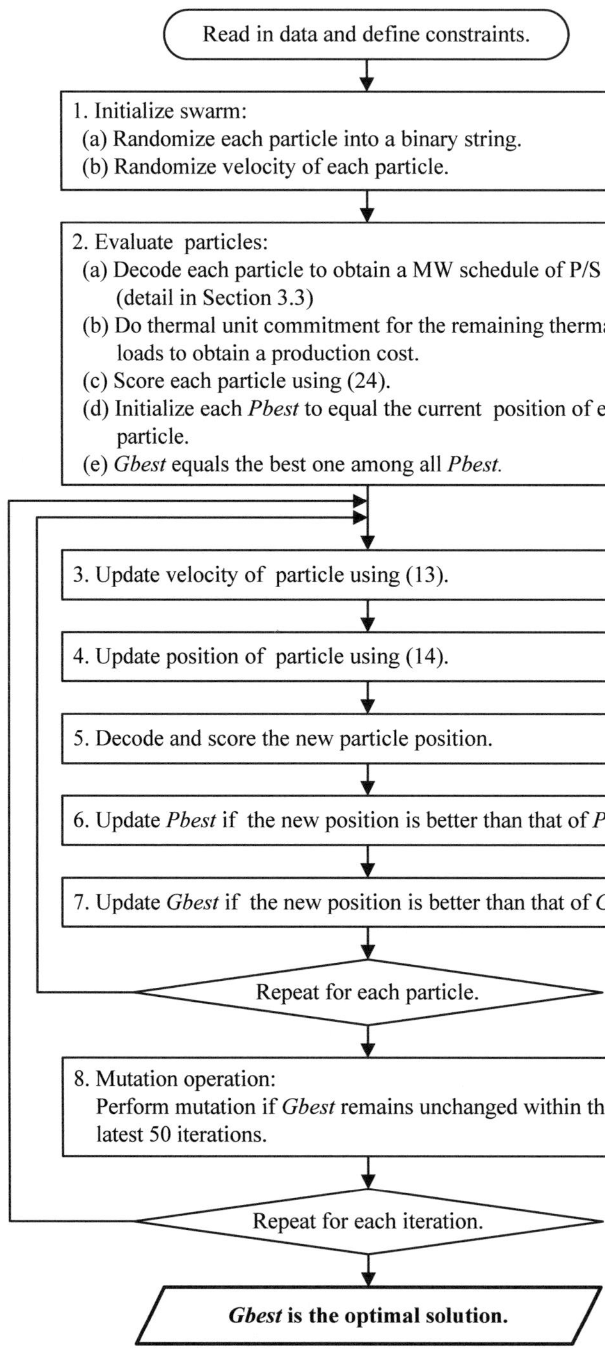

Figure 6. General flow chart of the proposed approach

			Lower Reservoir		
Installed Capacity	Maximal Discharge (m^3/s)	Maximal Pumping (m^3/s)	Maximal Storage ($10^3 m^3$)	Minimal Storage ($10^3 m^3$)	Efficiency
250MW×4	380	249	9,756	1,478	≈0.74

Table 1. Characteristics of the Ming-Hu pumped hydro plant

The proposed approach was tested on a summer weekday whose load profile (Fig. 7) was obtained by subtracting expected generation output of other hydro plants and nuclear units from the actual system load profile. Fig. 8 and 9 present schematics of test results. Fig. 8 shows the total generation/pumping schedules created by the proposed approach. Fig. 9 shows the remaining thermal load profiles. The optimal schedules for pumped hydro units and thermal units are obtained within 3 minutes, satisfying Taipower's time requirement.

To investigate further how the proposed approach and existing methods differ in performance, this work adopts a DP method (Chen, 1989) and a GA method (Chen & Chang, 1999) as the benchmark for comparison. Table 2 summarizes the test results obtained using these three methods.

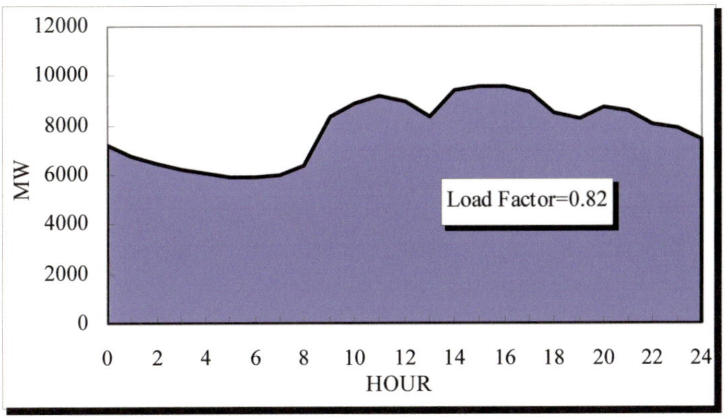

Figure 7. Summer weekday load profile

Several interesting and important observations are derived from this study and are summarized as follows:

a. The generation/pumping profile generally follows the load fluctuation, a finding that is consistent with economic expectations. The Ming-Hu pumped hydro plant generates 3,893 MWh power during peak load hours and pumps up 5,250 MWh power during light load hours, resulting in a cost saving of NT$5.91 million in one day, where cost saving = (cost without pumped hydro) - (cost with pumped hydro).
b. The pumped hydro units are the primary source of system spinning reserve due to their fast response characteristics. The system's spinning reserve requirement accounts for the fact that pumped hydro units do not generate power at their maximum during peak load hours.
c. Variation of water storage in the small lower reservoir is always retained within the maximum and minimum boundaries. The final volume returns to the same as the initial volume.
d. The load factor is improved from 0.82 to 0.88 due to the contribution of the four pumped hydro units.

e. Notably, both cost saving and execution time for the proposed approach are superior to either a DP or a GA method.

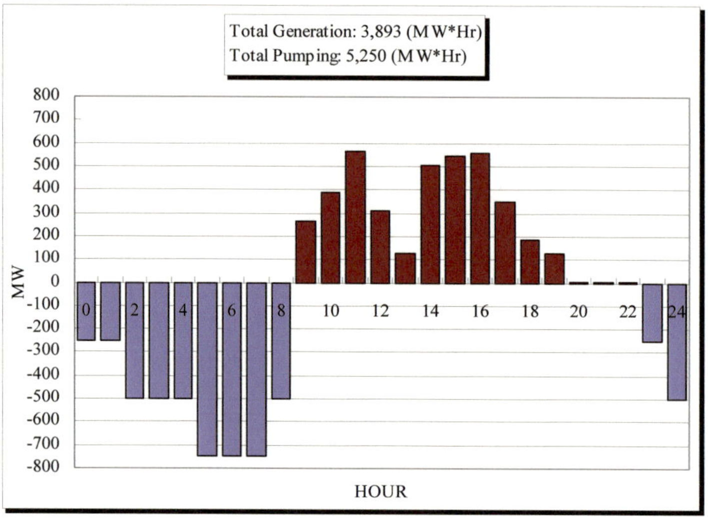

Figure 8. Hourly generation/pumping schedules

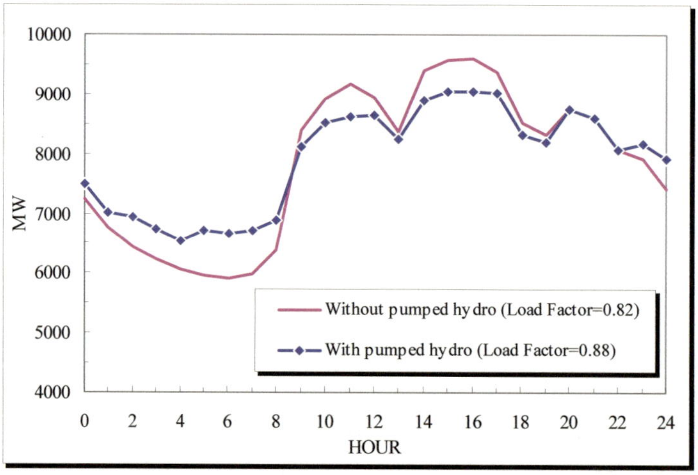

Figure 9. Contrast of two remaining thermal load profiles

Method	Load Factor	Cost Saving (10^3 NT$)	Execution Time (second)
DP	0.87	5,641	336
GA	0.87	5,738	164
RPSO	0.88	5,906	127

Table 2. Performance comparison with existing methods

5. Conclusion

This work presents a novel methodology based on a refined PSO approach for solving the power dispatch with pumped hydro problem. An advantage of the proposed technique is the flexibility of PSO for modeling various constraints. The difficult water dynamic balance constraints are embedded and satisfied throughout the proposed encoding/decoding algorithms. The effect of net head, constant power pumping characteristic, thermal ramp rate limits, minimal uptime/downtime constraints, and system's spinning reserve requirements are all considered in this work to make the scheduling more practical. Numerical results for an actual utility system indicate that the proposed approach has highly attractive properties, a highly optimal solution and robust convergence behavior for practical applications.

6. References

Al-Agtash, S. (2001). Hydrothermal scheduling by augmented Lagrangian: consideration of transmission constraints and pumped-storage units, *IEEE Transactions on Power System*, Vol. 16, pp. 750-756

Allan, R. N. & Roman, J. (1991). Reliability assessment of hydrothermal generation systems containing pumped storage plant, *IEE Proceedings-C, Generation, Transmission, and Distribution*, Vol. 138, pp. 471-478

Angeline, P. J. (1998). Evolutionary optimization versus particle swarm optimization: philosophy and performance differences, *Lecture Notes in Computer Science*, Vol. 1447, pp. 601–610

Boeringer, D. W. & Werner, D. H. (2004). Particle swarm optimization versus genetic algorithms for phased array synthesis, *IEEE Transactions on Antennas Propagation*, Vol. 52, pp. 771-779

Chen, P. H. (1989). Generation scheduling of hydraulically coupled plants, *Master's thesis*, Dept. Elect. Eng., National Tsing-Hua University, Taiwan

Chen, P. H. & Chang, H. C. (1995). Large-scale economic dispatch by genetic algorithm, *IEEE Transactions on Power System*, Vol. 10, pp. 1919-1926

Chen, P. H. & Chang, H. C. (1999). Pumped-storage scheduling using a genetic algorithm, *Proceedings of the Third IASTED International Conference on Power and Energy Systems*, pp. 492-497, USA

Chen, P. H. & Chen, H. C. (2006). Application of evolutionary neural network to power system unit commitment, *Lecture Notes in Computer Science*, Vol. 3972, pp. 1296–1303

Eberhart, R. & Shi, Y. (1998). Comparison between genetic algorithms and particle swarm optimization, *Lecture Notes in Computer Science*, vol. 1447, pp. 611–616

Eberhart, R. & Shi, Y. (2001). Particle swarm optimization: developments, applications and resources, *Proceedings of IEEE International Congress on Evolutionary Computation*, Vol. 1, pp. 81–86

El-Hawary, M. E. & Ravindranath, K. M. (1992). Hydro-thermal power flow scheduling accounting for head variations, *IEEE Transactions on Power System*, Vol. 7, pp. 1232-1238

Guan, X.; Luh, P. B.; Yen, H. & Rogan, P. (1994). Optimization-based scheduling of hydrothermal power systems with pumped-storage units, *IEEE Transactions on Power System*, Vol. 9, pp. 1023-1029

Ho, S. L.; Yang, S.; Ni, G. & Wong, H. C. (2006). A particle swarm optimization method with enhanced global search ability for design optimizations of electromagnetic devices, *IEEE Transactions on Magnetics*, Vol. 42, pp. 1107-1110

Jeng, L. H.; Hsu, Y. Y.; Chang, B. S. & Chen, K. K. (1996). A linear programming method for the scheduling of pumped-storage units with oscillatory stability constraints, *IEEE Transactions on Power System*, Vol. 11, pp. 1705-1710

Juang, C. F. (2004). A hybrid of genetic algorithm and particle swarm optimization for recurrent network design, *IEEE Transactions on Systems, Man, and Cybernetics*, Vol. 34, pp. 997-1006

Kennedy, J. & Eberhart, R. (1995). Particle swarm optimization, *Proceedings of IEEE International Conference on Neural Networks*, Vol. 4, pp. 1942–1948

Kennedy, J. & Eberhart, R. (1997). A discrete binary version of the particle swarm algorithm, *Proceedings of International Conference on Systems, Man, and Cybernetics*, pp. 4104–4109, Piscataway, NJ

Kennedy, J. & Eberhart, R. (2001). *Swarm Intelligence*, Morgan Kaufmann, San Francisco

Kuo, C. C.; Chen, P. H.; Hsu, C. L. & Lin, S. S. (2005). Particle swarm optimization for capacitor allocation and dispatching problem using interactive best-compromise approach, *WSEAS Transactions on System*, Vol. 4, pp. 1563-1572

Naka, S.; Genji, T.; Yura, T. & Fukuyama, Y. (2003). A hybrid particle swarm optimization for distribution state estimation, *IEEE Transactions on Power System*, Vol. 18, pp. 60-68

Wood, A. J. & Wollenberg, B. F. (1996). *Power Generation, Operation, and Control*, 2nd ed., John Wiley & Sons, New York

Zhao, B.; Guo, C. X. & Cao, Y. J. (2005). A multiagent-based particle swarm optimization approach for optimal reactive power dispatch, *IEEE Transactions on Power System*, Vol. 20, pp. 1070-1078

8

Searching for the best Points of interpolation using swarm intelligence techniques

Djerou L.[1], Khelil N.[1], Zerarka A.[1] and Batouche M.[2]
[1]*Labo de Mathématiques Appliquées, Université Med Khider*
[2]*Computer Science Department, CCIS-King Saud University*
[1]*Algeria,* [2]*Saudi Arabia*

1. Introduction

If the values of a function, *f(x)*, are known for a finite set of x values in a given interval, then a polynomial which takes on the same values at these x values offers a particularly simple analytic approximation to *f(x)* throughout the interval. This approximating technique is called polynomial interpolation. Its effectiveness depends on the smoothness of the function being sampled (if the function is unknown, some hypothetical smoothness must be chosen), on the number and choice of points at which the function is sampled.

In practice interpolating polynomials with degrees greater than about 10 are rarely used. One of the major problems with polynomials of high degree is that they tend to oscillate wildly. This is clear if they have many roots in the interpolation interval. For example, a degree 10 polynomial with 10 real roots must cross the x-axis 10 times. Thus, it would not be suitable for interpolating a monotone decreasing or increasing function on such an interval.

In this chapter we explore the advantage of using the Particle Swarm Optimization (PSO) interpolation nodes. Our goal is to show that the PSO nodes can approximate functions with much less error than Chebyshev nodes.

This chapter is organized as follows. In Section 2, we shall present the interpolation polynomial in the Lagrange form. Section 3 examines the Runge's phenomenon; which illustrates the error that can occur when constructing a polynomial interpolant of high degree. Section 4 gives an overview of modern heuristic optimization techniques, including fundamentals of computational intelligence for PSO. We calculate in Subsection 4.2 the best interpolating points generated by PSO algorithm. We make in section 5, a comparison of interpolation methods. The comments and conclusion are made in Section 6.

2. Introduction to the Lagrange interpolation

If $x_0, x_1, \ldots x_n$ are distinct real numbers, then for arbitrary values $y_0, y_1, \ldots y_n$, there is a unique polynomial p_n of degree at most n such that $p_n(x_i) = y_i$ $(0 \leq i \leq n)$ (David Kincaid & Ward Cheney, 2002).

The Lagrange form looks as follows:

$$p_n\left(x\right) = y_0 l_0\left(x\right) + \ldots + y_n l_n\left(x\right) = \sum_{i=0}^{n} y_i l_i\left(x\right) \tag{1}$$

Such that coordinal functions can be expressed in the following

$$l_i\left(x\right) = \prod_{j=0, j\neq i}^{n} \frac{\left(x - x_j\right)}{\left(x_i - x_j\right)} \tag{2}$$

(David Kincaid & Ward Cheney, 2002), (Roland E. et al 1994).
are coordinal polynomials that satisfy

$$l_i(x_j) = \begin{cases} 1, & i=j \\ 0, & i\neq j \end{cases} \tag{3}$$

The Lagrange form gives an error term of the form

$$E_n\left(x\right) = f(x) - p_n\left(x\right) = \frac{f^{(n+1)}\left(c\right)}{\left(n+1\right)!}\phi_n\left(x\right) \tag{4}$$

Where

$$\phi_n\left(x\right) = \prod_{i=0}^{n}\left(x - x_i\right) \tag{5}$$

If we examine the error formula for polynomial interpolation over an interval [a, b] we see that as we change the interpolation points, we change also the locations c where the derivative is evaluated; thus that part in the error also changes, and that change is a "black hole" to us: we never know what the correct value of c is, but only that c is somewhere in the interval [a, b]. Since we wish to use the interpolating polynomial to approximate the Equation (4) cannot be used, of course, to calculate the exact value of the error f – P_n, since c, as a function of x is, in general, not known. (An exception occurs when the (n + 1)st derivative off is constant). And so we are likely to reduce the error by selecting interpolation points $x_0, x_1,\ldots,x_n$ so as to minimize the maximum value of product $\phi_n\left(x\right)$

The most natural idea is to choose them regularly distribute in [a, b].

3. Introduction to the Runge phenomenon and to Chebyshev approximations

3.1 Runge phenomenon

If x_k are chosen to be the points $x_k = a + k\dfrac{b-a}{n} \quad \left(k = 0,\ldots,n\right)$ (means that are equally spaced at a distance $2n + 1$ apart), then the interpolating polynomial $p_n(x)$ need not to converge uniformly on [a, b] as $n \longrightarrow \infty$ for the function f(x).

This phenomenon is known as the Runge phenomenon (RP) and it can be illustrated with the Runge's "bell" function on the interval [-5, 5] (Fig.1).

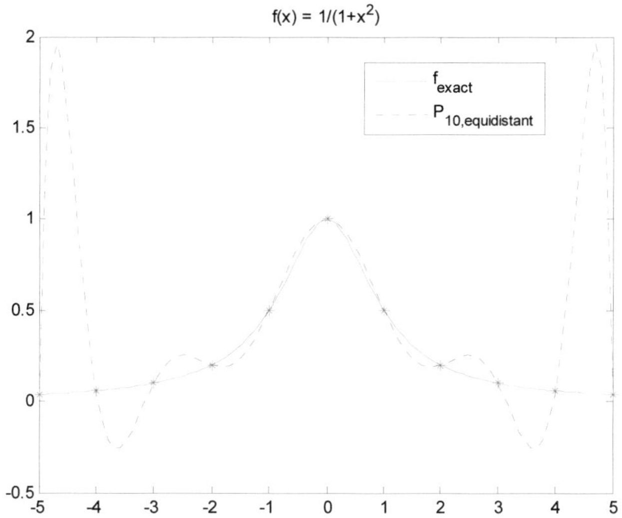

Figure 1. solid blue line: present Runge's "bell" function. dots red line: present the polynomial approximation based on equally 11 spaced nodes

3.2 Chebyshev Nodes

The standard remedy against the RP is Chebyshev -type clustering of nodes towards the end of the interval (Fig.3).

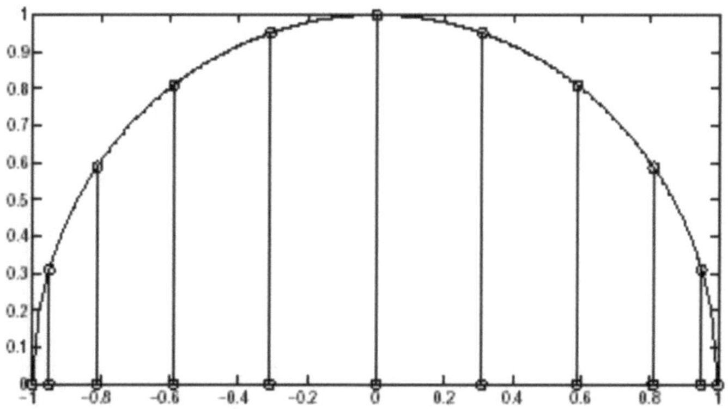

Figure 2. Chebyshev Point Distribution.

To do this, conceptually, we would like to take many points near the endpoints of the interval and few near the middle. The point distribution that minimizes the maximum value of product $\phi_n(x)$ is called the Chebyshev distribution, as shown in (Fig. 2). In the Chebyshev distribution, we proceed as follows:

1. Draw the semicircle on [a, b].

2. To sample $n+1$ points, place n equidistant partitions on the arc.
3. Project each partition onto the x-axis: for j =0, 1… n

$$x_j = \frac{a+b}{2} + \frac{b-a}{2}\cos\left(j\frac{\pi}{n}\right) \quad \text{for } j=0,1\ldots n \tag{6}$$

The nodes x_i that will be used in our approximation are:

Chebyshev nodes
-5.0000
-4.2900
-4.0251
-2.6500
-1.4000
0.0000
1.4000
2.6500
4.0451
4.2900
5.0000

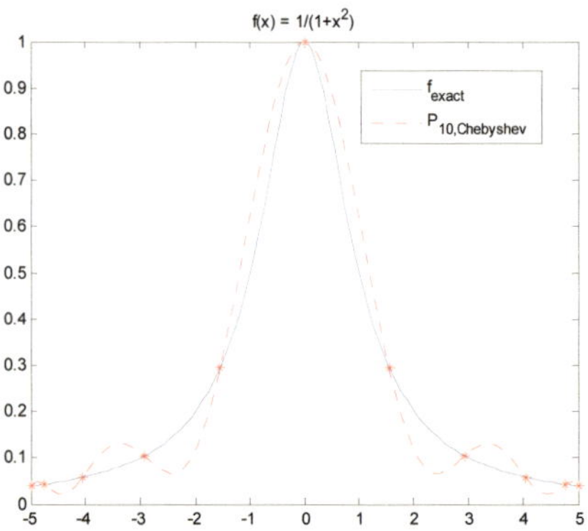

Figure 3. solid blue line: present Runge's "bell" function. dots red line: present the polynomial approximation based on 11 Chebyshev nodes

In this study, we have made some numerical computations using the particle swarm optimization to investigate the best interpolating points and we are showing that PSO nodes provide smaller approximation error than Chebyshev nodes.

4. Particle swarm optimization

4.1 Overview and strategy of particle swarm optimization

Recently, a new stochastic algorithm has appeared, namely 'particle swarm optimization' PSO. The term 'particle' means any natural agent that describes the `swarm' behavior. The PSO model is a particle simulation concept, and was first proposed by Eberhart and Kennedy (Eberhart, R.C. et al. 1995). Based upon a mathematical description of the social behavior of swarms, it has been shown that this algorithm can be efficiently generated to find good solutions to a certain number of complicated situations such as, for instance, the static optimization problems, the topological optimization and others (Parsopoulos, K.E. et al., 2001a); (Parsopoulos, K.E.et al. 2001b); (Fourie, P.C. et al., 2000); (Fourie, P.C. et al., 2001). Since then, several variants of the PSO have been developed (Eberhart,R.C. et al 1996); (Kennedy, J. et al., 1998); (Kennedy, J. et al., 2001); (Shi, Y.H. et al. 2001); (Shi, Y. et al. 1998a.); (Shi, Y.H. et al., 1998b); (Clerc, M. 1999). It has been shown that the question of convergence of the PSO algorithm is implicitly guaranteed if the parameters are adequately selected (Eberhart, R.C. et al.1998); (Cristian, T.I. 2003). Several kinds of problems solving start with computer simulations in order to find and analyze the solutions which do not exist analytically or specifically have been proven to be theoretically intractable.

The particle swarm treatment supposes a population of individuals designed as real valued vectors - particles, and some iterative sequences of their domain of adaptation must be established. It is assumed that these individuals have a social behavior, which implies that the ability of social conditions, for instance, the interaction with the neighborhood, is an important process in successfully finding good solutions to a given problem.

The strategy of the PSO algorithm is summarized as follows: We assume that each agent (particle) i can be represented in a N dimension space by its current position $x_i = \left(x_{i1}, x_{i2}, \ldots, x_{iN}\right)$ and its corresponding velocity. Also a memory of its personal (previous) best position is represented by, $p = \left(p_{i1}, p_{i2}, \ldots, p_{iN}\right)$ called (pbest), the subscript i range from 1 to s, where s indicates the size of the swarm. Commonly, each particle localizes its best value so far (pbest) and its position and consequently identifies its best value in the group (swarm), called also (sbest) among the set of values (pbest).

The velocity and position are updated as

$$v_{ij}^{k+1} = w_j v_{ij}^k + c_1 r_1^k \left[(pbest)_{ij}^k - x_{ij}^k\right] + c_2 r_2^k \left[(sbest)_{ij}^k - x_{ij}^k\right] \tag{7}$$

$$x_{ij}^{k+1} = v_{ij}^{k+1} + x_{ij}^k \tag{8}$$

where are the position and the velocity vector of particle i respectively at iteration k + 1, c_1 et c_2 are acceleration coefficients for each term exclusively situated in the range of 2--4, w_{ij} is the inertia weight with its value that ranges from 0.9 to 1.2, whereas r_1, r_2 are uniform random numbers between zero and one. For more details, the double subscript in the relations (7) and (8) means that the first subscript is for the particle i and the second one is for the dimension j. The role of a suitable choice of the inertia weight w_{ij} is important in the success of the PSO. In the general case, it can be initially set equal to its maximum value, and progressively we decrease it if the better solution is not reached. Too often, in the relation (7), w_{ij} is replaced by w_{ij} / σ, where σ denotes the constriction factor that controls the velocity of the particles. This algorithm is successively accomplished with the following steps (Zerarka, A. et al., 2006):

1. Set the values of the dimension space N and the size s of the swarm (s can be taken randomly).
2. Initialize the iteration number k (in the general case is set equal to zero).
3. Evaluate for each agent, the velocity vector using its memory and equation (7), where pbest and sbest can be modified.
4. Each agent must be updated by applying its velocity vector and its previous position using equation [8].
5. Repeat the above step (3, 4 and 5) until a convergence criterion is reached.

The practical part of using PSO procedure will be examined in the following section, where we'll interpolate Runge's "bell", with two manners; using Chebyshev interpolation approach and PSO approach, all while doing a comparison.

4.2 PSO distribution

So the problem is the choice of the points of interpolation so that quantity $\phi_n\left(x\right)$ deviates from zero on [a, b] the least possible.

Particle Swarm Optimization was used to find the global minimum of the maximum value of product $\phi_n\left(x\right)$, where very x is represented as a particle in the swarm.

The PSO parameter values that were used are given in Table 1.

Parameter	Setting
Population size	20
Number of iterations	500
C1 and C2	0.5
Inertial Weight	1.2 to 0.4
Desired Accuracy	10-5

Table 1. Particle Swarm Parameter Setting used in the present study

The best interpolating points x generated by PSO algorithm for polynomial of degree 5 and 10 respectively for example are:

Chebyshev	Points generated with PSO
-5.0000	-5.0000
-3.9355	-4.0451
-2.9041	-1.5451
0.9000	1.5451
3.9355	4.0451
5.0000	5.0000

Table 2 Polynomial of degree 5

Chebyshev	Points generated with PSO
-5.0000	-5.0000
-4.2900	-4.7553
-4.0251	-4.0451
-2.6500	-2.9389
-1.4000	-1.5451
0.0000	-0.0000
1.4000	1.5451
2.6500	2.9389
4.0451	4.0451
4.2900	4.7553
5.0000	5.0000

Table 3. Polynomial of degree 10

5. Comparison of interpolation methods

How big an effect can the selection of points have? Fig. 4 and Fig. 5 shows Runge's "bell" function interpolated over [-5, 5] using equidistant points, points selected from the Chebyshev distribution, and a new method called PSO. The polynomial interpolation using Chebyshev points does a much better job than the interpolation using equidistant points, but neither does as well as the PSO method.

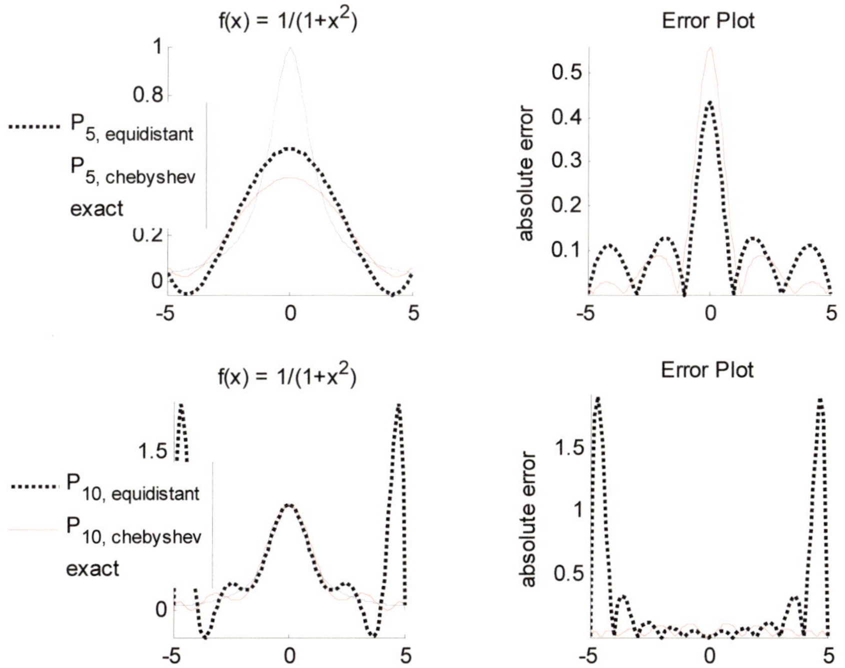

Figure 4. Comparison of interpolation polynomials for equidistant and Chebyshev sample points

Comparing Fig. 4, we see that the maximum deviation of the Chebyshev polynomial from the true function is considerably less than that of Lagrange polynomial with equidistant nodes. It can also be seen that increasing the number of the Chebyshev nodes—or, equivalently, increasing the degree of Chebyshev polynomial—makes a substantial contribution towards reducing the approximation error.
Comparing Fig. 5, we see that the maximum deviation of the PSO polynomial from the true function is considerably less than that of Chebyshev polynomial nodes. It can also be seen that increasing the number of the PSO nodes—or, equivalently, increasing the degree of PSO polynomial—makes a substantial contribution towards reducing the approximation error.

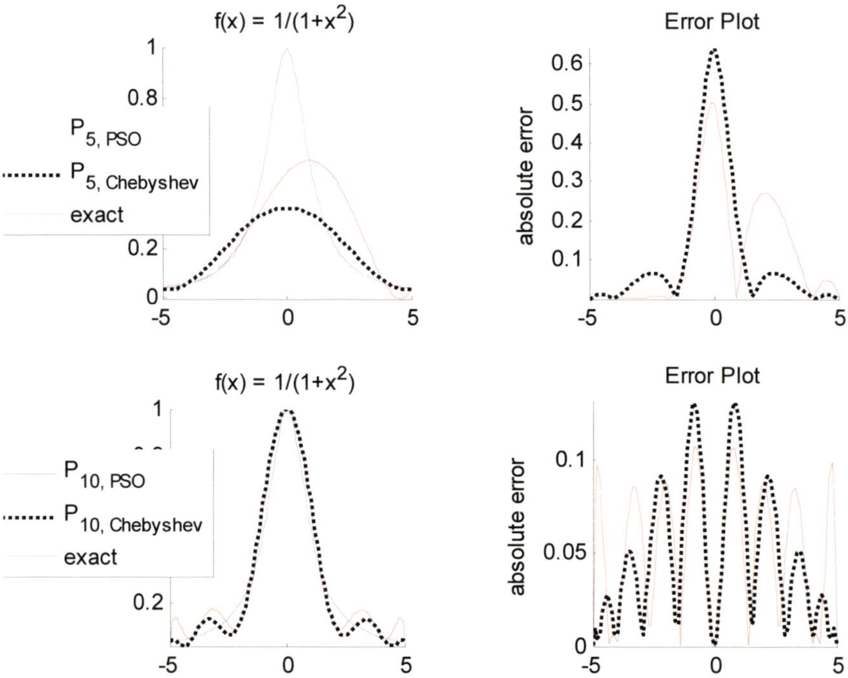

Figure 5. Comparison of interpolation polynomials for PSO and Chebyshev sample points

In this study we take as measure of the error of approximation the greatest vertical distance between the graph of the function and that of the interpolating polynomial over the entire interval under consideration (Fig. 4 and Fig. 5).
The calculation of error gives

Degree	Error points equidistant	Error points Chebychev	Error points PSO
5	0.4327	0.6386	0.5025
10	1.9156	0.1320	0.1076
15	2.0990	0.0993	0.0704
20	58.5855	0.0177	0.0131

Table 2. The error

6. Conclusion

The particle swarm optimization is used to investigate the best interpolating points. Some good results are obtained by using the specific PSO approach. It is now known that the PSO scheme is powerful, and easier to apply specially for this type of problems. Also, the PSO method can be used directly and in a straightforward manner. The performance of the scheme shows that the method is reliable and effective.

7. References

Clerc, M. (1999). The swarm and the queen: towards a deterministic and adaptive particle swarm optimization, *Proceedings of the 1999 IEEE Congress on Evolutionary Computation, pp.1951 – 1957,* Washington DC.

Cristian, T.I. (2003). The particle swarm optimization algorithm: convergence analysis and parameter selection, *Information Processing Letters,* Vol. 85, No. 6, pp.317--325.

David Kincaid and Ward Cheney, (2002). *Numerical Analysis: Mathematics of Scientific Computing*. Brooks/Cole.

Eberhart, R.C. and Kennedy, J. (1995). A new optimizer using particles swarm theory', *Sixth International Symposium on Micro Machine and Human Science,* pp.39--43, *Nagoya,* Japan.

Eberhart, R.C. and Shi, Y. (1998). Parameter selection in particle swarm optimization, in Porto, V.W.,

Eberhart, R.C. et al (1996). Computational Intelligence PC Tools, *Academic Press Professional,* Boston.

Fourie, P.C. and Groenwold, A.A. (2000). Particle swarms in size and shape optimization', *Proceedings of the International Workshop on Multi-disciplinary Design Optimization,* August 7--10, pp.97—106, Pretoria, South Africa.

Fourie, P.C. and Groenwold, A.A. (2001). Particle swarms in topology optimization', *Extended Abstracts of the Fourth World Congress of Structural and Multidisciplinary Optimization,* June 4--8, pp.52, 53, Dalian, China.

Hammer, R. Et al (1995). Numerical Toolbox for Verified Computing I, *Springer Verlag,* Berlin.

Kennedy, J. 1998. The behavior of particles, *Evol. Progr.*, Vol. VII, pp.581-587.

Kennedy J. and Eberhart, R.C, (1995). Particle swarm optimization, *Proc. IEEE Int. Conf. Neural Networks, Piscataway,* NJ, pp.1942--1948, USA.

Kennedy, J. and Eberhart, R.C. (2001). Swarm Intelligence, *Morgan Kaufmann Publishers,* San Francisco.

Kennedy, J. and Spears, W.M. (1998). Matching algorithms to problems: an experimental test of the particle swarm and some genetic algorithms on the multimodal problem generator, *Proceedings of the (1998) IEEE International Conference on Evolutionary Computation,* Anchorage, May 4--9, Alaska.

Kulisch, U. and Miranker, W.L. (1983). A New Approach to Scientific Computation, Academic Press, New York.

L. N. Trefethen. Spectral Methods in Matlab. *SIAM,* (2000). 9, Philadelphia

L. Djerou, M. Batouche, N. Khelil and A.Zerarka, *(2007).* Towards the best points of interpolation using Particles swarm optimization approach, *in proceedings of IEEE Congress of Evolutionary Computing, CEC 2007, pp. 3211-3214, Singapore.*

Maron, M. and Lopez, R. (1991). Numerical Analysis, *Wadsworth Publishing Company*, Belmont, California.

Parsopoulos, K.E. and Vrahatis, M.N. (2001). `Modification of the particle swarm optimizer for locating all the global minima', in Kurkova, V. et al. (Eds.): *Artificial Neural Networks and Genetic Algorithms, Springer*, pp.324--327, New York.

Parsopoulos, K.E. et al, (2001a). Objective function stretching to alleviate convergence to local minima, *Nonlinear Analysis TMA*, Vol. 47, pp.3419--3424.

Parsopoulos, K.E.et al (2001b). Stretching technique for obtaining global minimizers through particle swarm optimization, *Proceedings of the PSO Workshop*, pp.22--29, Indianapolis, USA.

Roland E. Larson, Robert P. Hostetler, Bruch H. Edwards and David E. Heyd, (1994)., *Calculus with Analytic Geometry*. D. C. Heath and Company.

Saravanan, N., Waagen, D. and Eiben, A.E. (Eds.): *Lecture Notes in Computer Science-Evolutionary Programming VII, Springer*, Vol. 1447, pp.591--600.

Shi, Y. and Eberhart, R.C. (1998a). A modified particle swarm optimizer, *Proceedings of the 1998 IEEE International Conference on Evolutionary Computation*, May 4−9, Anchorage, Alaska.

Shi, Y.H. and Eberhart, R.C. (1998b). Parameter selection in particle swarm optimization, Evolutionary Programming VII, *Lecture Notes in Computer Science*, pp.591--600.

Shi, Y.H. and Eberhart, R.C. (2001). Fuzzy adaptive particle swarm optimization', *IEEE Int. Conf. on Evolutionary Computation*, pp.101--106.

Zerarka, A., Khelil, N. (2006). A generalized integral quadratic method: improvement of the solution for one dimensional Volterra integral equation using particle swarm optimization, *Int. J. Simulation and Process Modeling*, Vol. 2, Nos. 1/2, pp.152-163.

9

Particle Swarm Optimization and Other Metaheuristic Methods in Hybrid Flow Shop Scheduling Problem

M. Fikret Ercan
Singapore Polytechnic School of Electrical and Electronic Engineering
Singapore

1. Introduction

Multiprocessor task scheduling is a generalized form of classical machine scheduling where a task is processed by more than one processor. It is a challenging problem encountered in wide range of applications and it is vastly studied in the scheduling literature (see for instance (Chan & Lee, 1999 and Drozdowski, 1996) for a comprehensive introduction on this topic). However, Drozdowski (1996) shows that multiprocessor task scheduling is difficult to solve even in its simplest form. Hence, many heuristic algorithms are presented in literature to tackle multiprocessor task scheduling problem. Jin et al. (2008) present a performance study of such algorithms. However, most of these studies primarily concerned with a single stage setting of the processor environment. There are many practical problems where multiprocessor environment is a flow-shop that is it is made of multiple stages and tasks have to go through one stage to another.

Flow-shop scheduling problem is also vastly studied in scheduling context though most of these studies concerned with single processor at each stage (see for instance Linn & Zhang, 1999, Dauzère-Pérès & Paulli, 1997). With the advances made in technology, in many practical applications, we encounter parallel processors at each stage instead of single processors such as parallel computing, power system simulations, operating system design for parallel computers, traffic control in restricted areas, manufacturing and many others (see for instance (Krawczyk & Kubale, 1985, Lee & Cai, 1999, Ercan & Fung, 2000, Caraffa et. al.,2001)). This particular problem is defined as hybrid flow-show with multiprocessor tasks in scheduling terminology and minimizing the schedule length (makespan) is the typical scheduling problem addressed. However, Brucker & Kramer (1995) show that multiprocessor flow-shop problem to minimize makespan is also NP-hard. Gupta (1988) showed that hybrid flow-shop even with two stages is NP-hard. Furthermore, the complexity of the problem increases with the increasing number of stages.

Multiprocessor task scheduling in a hybrid flow-shop environment has recently gained the attention of the research community. To the best of our knowledge, one of the earliest papers that deal with this problem in the scheduling literature is by Oğuz and Ercan, 1997. However, due to the complexity of the problem, in the early studies (such as (Lee & Cai, 1999, Oğuz et. al., 2003)) researchers targeted two layer flow-shops with multiprocessors. Simple list based heuristics as well as meta-heuristics were introduced for the solution

(Oğuz et al.,2003, Jdrzęjowicz & Jdrzęjowicz,2003, Oğuz et al.,2004). Apparently, a broader form of the problem will have arbitrary number of stages in the flow-shop environment. This is also studied recently and typically metaheuristic algorithms applied to minimize the makespan such as population learning algorithm (Jdrzęjowicz & Jdrzęjowicz, 2003), tabu search (Oğuz et al.,2004), genetic algorithm (Oğuz & Ercan,2005) and ant colony system (Ying & Lin,2006). Minimizing the makespan is not the only scheduling problem tackled; recently Shiau et al. (2008) focused on minimizing the weighted completion time in proportional flow shops.

These metaheuristic algorithms produce impressive results though they are sophisticated and require laborious programming effort. However, of late particle swarm optimization (PSO) is gaining popularity within the research community due to its simplicity. The algorithm is applied to various scheduling problems with notable performance. For instance, Sivanandam et al. (2007) applied PSO to typical task allocation problem in multiprocessor scheduling. Chiang et al. (2006) and Tu et al. (2006) demonstrate application of PSO to well known job shop scheduling problem.

PSO, introduced by Kennedy & Eberhart (1995), is another evolutionary algorithm which mimics the behaviour of flying birds and their communication mechanism to solve optimization problems. It is based on a constructive cooperation between particles instead of survival of the fittest approach used in other evolutionary methods. PSO has many advantages therefore it is worth to study its performance for the scheduling problem presented here. The algorithm is simple, fast and very easy to code. It is not computationally intensive in terms of memory requirements and time. Furthermore, it has a few parameters to tune.

This chapter will present the hybrid flow-shop with multiprocessor tasks scheduling problem and particle swarm optimization algorithm proposed for the solution in details. It will also introduce other well known heuristics which are reported in literature for the solution of this problem. Finally, a performance comparison of these algorithms will be given.

2. Problem definition

The problem considered in this paper is formulated as follows: There is a set J of n independent and simultaneously available jobs where each job is made of Multi-Processor Tasks (*MPT*) to be processed in a multi-stage flow-shop environment, where stage j consists of m_j identical parallel processors ($j=1,2,...,k$). Each $MPT_i \in J$ should be processed on $p_{i,j}$ identical processors simultaneously at stage j without interruption for a period of $t_{i,j}$ ($i=1,2,...,n$ *and* $j=1,2,...,k$). Hence, each $MPT_i \in J$ is characterized by its processing time, $t_{i,j}$, and its processor requirement, $p_{i,j}$. The scheduling problem is basically finding a sequence of jobs that can be processed on the system in the shortest possible time. The following assumptions are made when modeling the problem:

- All the processors are continuously available from time 0 onwards.
- Each processor can handle no more than one task at a time.
- The processing time and the number of processors required at each stage are known in advance.
- Set-up times and inter-processor communication time are all included in the processing time and it is independent of the job sequence.

3. Algorithms

3.1 The basic PSO algorithm

PSO is initialized with a population of random solutions which is similar in all the evolutionary algorithms. Each individual solution flies in the problem space with a velocity which is adjusted depending on the experiences of the individual and the population. As mentioned earlier, PSO and its hybrids are gaining popularity in solving scheduling problems. A few of these works tackle the flow shop problem (Liu et al.,2005) though application to hybrid flow-shops with multiprocessor tasks is relatively new (Ercan & Fung, 2007, Tseng & Liao, 2008).

In this study, we first employed the global model of the PSO (Ercan & Fung, 2007). In the basic PSO algorithm, particle velocity and position are calculated as follows:

$$V_{id}=W\ V_{id} + C_1R_1(P_{id}-X_{id})+C_2R_2(P_{gd}-X_{id}) \tag{1}$$

$$X_{id}=X_{id}+V_{id} \tag{2}$$

In the above equations, V_{id} is the velocity of particle i and it represents the distance traveled from the current position. W is inertia weight. X_{id} represents particle position. P_{id} is the local best solution (also called as "pbest") and P_{gd} is global best solution (also called as "qutgbest"). C_1 and C_2 are acceleration constants which drive particles towards local and global best positions. R_1 and R_2 are two random numbers within the range of [0, 1]. This is the basic form of the PSO algorithm which follows the following steps:

Algorithm 1: The basic PSO

```
Initialize swarm with random positions and velocities;
begin
repeat
  For each particle evaluate the fitness i.e. makespan of the schedule;
  if current fitness of particle is better than Pid then set Pid to current value;
  if Pid is better than global best then set Pgd to current particle fitness value;
  Change the velocity and position of the particle;
until termination = True
end.
```

The initial swarm and particle velocity are generated randomly. A key issue is to establish a suitable way to encode a shedule (or solution) to PSO particle. We employed the method shown by Xia et al.(2006). Each particle consists of a sequence of job numbers representing the n number of jobs on a machine with k number of stages where each stage has m_j identical processors ($j=1,2,...,k$). The fitness of a particle is then measured with the maximum completion time of all jobs. In our earlier work (Oğuz & Ercan,2005), a list scheduling algorithm is developed to map a given job sequence to the machine environment and to compute the maximum completion time (makespan). A particle with the lowest completion time is a good solution.

Figure 1 shows an example to scheduling done by the list scheduling algorithm. In this example, number of jobs is n= 5 and a machine is made of two stages k=2 where each stage contains four identical processors. Table 1 depicts the list of jobs and their processing times and processor requirements at each stage for this example.

Job #	Stage 1 (j=1)		Stage 2 (j=2)	
i	$p_{i,1}$	$t_{i,1}$	$p_{i,2}$	$t_{i,2}$
1	1	1	2	2
2	3	3	4	2
3	3	3	3	2
4	2	1	2	1
5	1	1	1	1

Table 1. Example jobs and their processing time and processor requirements at each stage

For the schedule shown in Figure 1, it is assumed that a job sequence is given as $S_1 = \{2,3,1,4,5\}$. At stage 1, jobs are iteratively allocated to processors from the list starting from time 0 onwards. As job 2 is the first in the list, it is scheduled at time 0. It is important to note that although there are enough available processors to schedule job 1 at time 0 this will violate the precedence relationship established in the list. Therefore, job 1 is scheduled to time instance 3 together with job 3 and this does not violate the precedence relationship given in S_1 . Once all the jobs are scheduled at first stage, a new list is produced for the succeeding stage based on the completion of jobs at previous stage and the precedence relationships given in S_1. In the new list for stage 2, $S_2 = \{2,1,3,4,5\}$, job 1 is scheduled before job 3 since it is available earlier than job 3. At time instance 7, jobs 3, 4 and 5 are all available to be processed. Job 3 is scheduled first since its completion time is earlier at stage 1. Although, there is enough processor to schedule job 5 at time 8 this will again violate the order given in list S_1 , hence it is scheduled together with job 4. In this particular example, jobs 4 and 5 will be the last to be mapped to stage 2 and the over all completion time of tasks will be 10 units.

The parameters of PSO are set based on our empirical study as well as referring to the experiences of other researchers. The acceleration constants C_1 and C_2 are set to 2.0 and initial population of swarm is set to 100. Inertia weight, W, determines the search behavior of the algorithm. Large values for W facilitate searching new locations whereas small values provide a finer search in the current area. A balance can be established between global and local exploration by decreasing the inertia weight during the execution of the algorithm. This way PSO tends to have more global search ability at the beginning and more local search ability towards the end of the execution. In our PSO algorithm, an exponential function is used to set the inertia weight and it is defined as:

$$W = W_{end} + (W_{start} - W_{end})e^{-\frac{x\alpha}{x_{\max}}} \quad (3)$$

where, W_{start} is the starting, W_{end} is the ending inertia values. W_{start} are W_{end} are set as 1.5 and 0.3 respectively. In addition, x shows the current iteration number and x_{max} shows the maximum iteration number which is set to 10000. An integer constant α is used to manipulate the gradient of the exponentially decreasing W value and it is set to 4.

In this application, X_{id} and V_{id} are used to generate and modify solutions therefore they are rounded off to the nearest integer and limited to a maximum value of n which is the maximum number of jobs. That is position coordinates are translated into job sequence in our algorithm and a move in search space is obtained by modifying the job sequence.

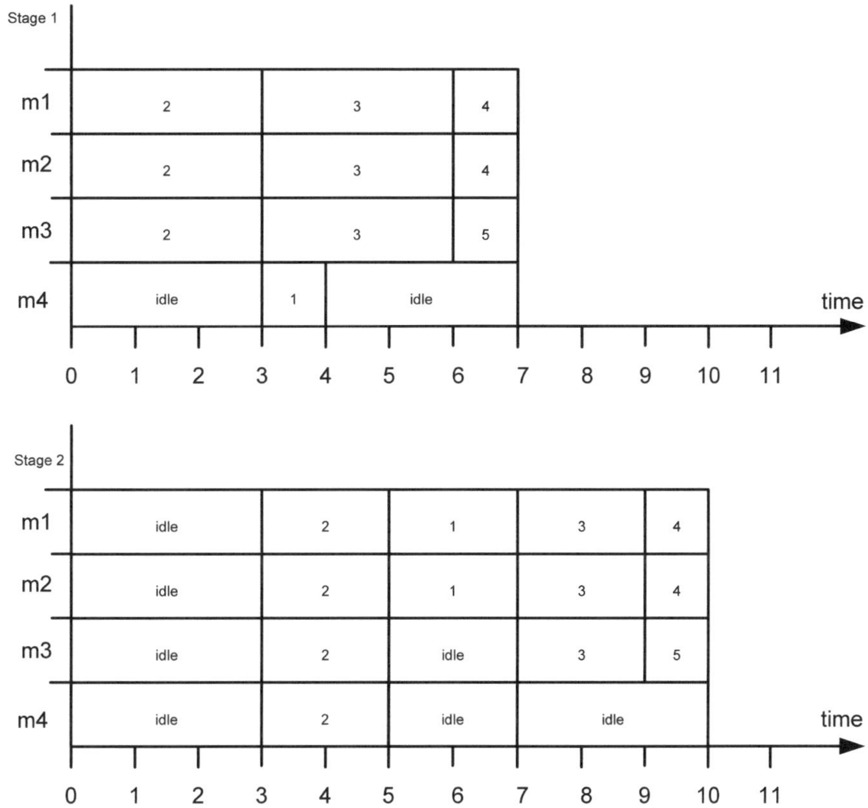

Figure 1. The schedule of job sequence [2, 3, 1, 4, 5] after being allocated to processors of the multilayer system using the list scheduling algorithm. Idle periods of the processors are labeled as idle

3.2 Hybrid PSO algorithms

Although, PSO is very robust and has a well global exploration capability, it has the tendency of being trapped in local minima and slow convergence. In order to improve its performance, many researchers experimented with hybrid PSO algorithms. Poli et al. (2007) give a review on the varations and the hybrids of particle swarm optimisation. Similarly, in scheduling problems, performance of PSO can be improved further by employing hybrid techniques. For instance, Xia & Wu (2006) applied PSO-simulated annealing (SA) hybrid to job shop scheduling problem and test its performance with benchmark problems. Authors conclude that PSO-SA hybrid delivered equal solution quality as compared to other metaheuristic algorithms though PSO-SA offered easier modeling, simplicity and ease of implementation. These findings motivated us to apply PSO and its hybrids to this particular scheduling problem and study its performance.

The basic idea of the hybrid algorithms presented here is simply based on runnign PSO algorithm first and then improving the result by employing a simulated annealing (SA) or tabu search (TS) heuristics. SA and TS introduce a probability to avoid becoming trapped in a local minimum. In addition, by introducing a neighborhood formation and tuning the parameters, it is also possible to enhance the search process. The initial findings of this study are briefly presented in (Ercan,2008). The following pseudo codes show the hybrid algorithms:

Algorithm 2: Hybrid PSO with SA

```
Initialize swarm with random positions and velocities;
   begin
   initialize PSO and SA;
     while (termination !=true)
     do{
      generate swarm;
      compute and find best Pgd;
      }
   set particle that gives best Pgd as initial solution to SA;
      while (Tcurrent>Temp_end)
       do{
       generate neighborhood;
       evaluate and update best solution and temperature;
       }
   end.
```

Algorithm 3: Hybrid PSO with TS

```
Initialize swarm with random positions and velocities;
   begin
   initialize PSO and TS;
      while (termination !=true)
      do{
      generate swarm;
      compute and find best Pgd;
      }
   set particle that gives best Pgd as initial solution to TS;
      while (termination!=true)
       do{
       generate sub set of neighborhoods;
       evaluate and update the best solution;
       update the tabu list;
       }
    end.
```

The initial temperature for PSO-SA hybrid is estimated after 50 randomly permuted neighborhood solutions of the initial solution. A ratio of average increase in the cost to acceptance ratio is used as initial temperature. Temperature is decreased using a simple cooling strategy $T_{current} = \lambda T_{current} -1$. The best value for lambda is experimentally found and set as 0.998. The end temperature is set to 0.01.

A neighbor of the current solution is obtained in various ways.

- Interchange neighborhood: Two randomly chosen jobs from the job list are exchanged.

- Simple switch neighborhood: It is a special case of interchange neighborhood where a randomly chosen job is exchanged with its predecessor.
- Shift neighborhood: A randomly selected job is removed from one position in the priority list and put it into another randomly chosen position.

It is experimentally found that interchange method performs the best amongst all three. The interchange strategy is also found to be the most effective one for generating the sub-neighborhoods for TS.

In the tabu list, a fixed number of last visited solutions are kept. Two methods for updating the tabu list are experimented; elimination of the farthest solution stored in the list, and removing the worst performing solution from the list. In PSO-TS hybrid removing the worst performing solution from the list method is used as it gave a slightly better result.

4. GA algorithm

Genetic algorithms, introduced by Holland (1975), have been widely applied to many scheduling problems in literature (see for instance job-shop environment (Della et al.,1995) and (Dorndorf & Pesch,1995), flow-shop environment (Murata et al., 1996)). Genetic algorithms are also employed in hybrid flow-shops with multiprocessor environment (Oğuz & Ercan, 2005). In this work, authors proposed a new crossover operator, NXO, to be used in the genetic algorithm and compare its performance with well-known PMX crossover. They employed two selection criteria in NXO to minimize the idle time of the processors. Firstly, NXO basically aims to keep the best characteristics of the parents in terms of the neighbouring jobs. That is if two jobs are adjacent to each other in both parents with good fitness values, then NXO tries to keep this structure in the offspring. If there is no such structure, then next criteria is employed in which NXO tries to choose the next job that will fit well in terms of the processor allocations. The results show that the genetic algorithm performs better in terms of the percentage deviation of the solution from the lower bound value when new crossover operator is used along with the insertion mutation. Some of the results from this study are included in this paper for comparison.

5. Other heuristic methods

The ant colony system (Dorigo, 1997) is another popular algorithm which is widely used in optimisation problems. Recently, Ying & Lin (2006) applied ant colony system (ACS) to hybrid flow-shops with multiprocessors tasks. Authors determine the jobs-permutation at the first stage, by ACS approach. Other stages are scheduled using an ordered list which is obtained by referring to completion times of jobs at the previous stage. Authors also apply the same procedure to the inverse problem to obtain the backward schedules. After that they employ a local search approach to improve the best schedule obtained in current iteration. Their computational results show that ACS has better performance compared to TS or GA though their algorithm is not any simpler than that of TS or GA.

Recently, Tseng & Liao (2008) tackled the problem by using particle swarm optimization. Their algorithm differs in terms of encoding scheme to construct a particle, the velocity equation and local search mechanism when compared to the basic PSO and the hybrid PSO algorithms presented here. Based on their published experimental results, PSO algorithm developed by Tseng & Liao (2008) performs well in this scheduling problem. Lately, Ying (2008) applied iterated greedy (IG) heuristic in search of a simpler and more efficient solution. The IG heuristic also shows a notable performance as it's tailored to this particular problem.

6. Experimental results

The performance of all the meta-heuristics described above is tested using intensive computational experiments. Similarly, performance of the basic PSO and the hybrid PSO algorithms, in minimizing the overall completion time of all jobs, is also tested using the same computational experiments. The effects of various parameters such as number of jobs and processor configurations on the performance of the algorithm are also investigated. The results are presented in terms of Average Percentage Deviation (APD) of the solution from the lower bound which is expressed as:

$$APD = \frac{C_{\max} - LB}{LB} \times 100 \qquad (3)$$

Here, C_{max} indicates the completion time of the jobs and LB indicates the lower bound calculated for the problem instance. The lower bounds used in this performance study were developed by Oğuz et al. (2004) and it is given with the following formula:

$$LB = \left\{ \max_{i \in M} \left\{ \min_{j \in J} \sum_{l=1}^{i-1} t_{l,j} \right\} + \frac{1}{m_i} \sum_{j \in J} p_{i,j} \times t_{i,j} + \min_{j \in J} \left\{ \sum_{l=i+1}^{l} t_{l,j} \right\} \right\} \qquad (4)$$

In the above formula, M and J represent the set of stages and set of jobs consecutively. We used the benchmark data available at Oğuz's personal web-site (http://home.ku.edu.tr/~coguz/). Data set contains instances for two types of processor configurations:

(i) **Random processor:** In this problem set, the number of processors in each stage is randomly selected from a set of {1,..., 5}

(ii) **Fixed processor:** In this case identical number of processors assigned at each stage which is fixed to 5 processors.

For both configurations, a set of 10 problem instances is randomly produced for various number of jobs (n=5, 10, 20, 50, 100) and various number of stages (k=2, 5, 8). For each n and k value, the average APD is taken over 10 problem instances.

Table 2 and 3 presents the APD results obtained for the basic PSO and the hybrid PSO algorithms. Furthermore, we compare the results with genetic algorithm developed by Oğuz and Ercan (2005), tabu search by Oğuz et al. (2004), ant colony system developed by Ying and Lin (2006), iterated greedy algorithm (IG) by Ying (2008) and PSO developed by Tseng & Liao (2008). The performance of GA (Oğuz and Ercan,2005) is closely related to the control parameters and the cross over and mutation techniques used. Therefore, in Tables 2 and 3, we include the best results obtained from four different versions of GA reported. The performance comparison given in below tables is fair enough as most of the authors were employing the same problem set. Furthermore, all the algorithms use the same LB. However there are two exceptions. For the GA, authors use an improved version of the LB than the one given in equation 4. In addition, the PSO developed by Tseng & Liao (2008) is tested with different set of problems and with the same LB as in GA. However, these problems also have the same characteristic in terms of number of stage, generation methods for processor and processing time requirements, etc.

From the presented results in Table 2 and 3, it can be observed that TS delivers reasonably good results only in two stage case; whereas GA demonstrates a competitive performance for small to medium size problems. For large number of jobs (such as n=50, 100) and large number of stages (k=8), GA did not outperform ACS, IG or PSO. When we compare ACS with TS and GA, we can observe that it outperforms TS and GA in most of the cases. For instance, it outperforms GA in 8 out of 12 problems in random processor case (Table 2). Among those, the performance improvement was more than %50 in six cases. On the other hand, IG gives a better result when compared to ACS in all most all the cases. The IG heuristic shows notable performance improvement for large problems (n=50 and n=100). For example, in n=100 and k=8 case, IG result is %71 better as compared to GA, %95 compared to TS and %7 compared to ACS.

The basic PSO algorithm presented here approximates to GA and ACS results though it did not show a significant performance improvement. PSO outperformed GA 4 in 12 problems for random processors and 1 in 12 problems for fixed processors. The best performance improvement was 54%. On the other hand, PSO-SA hybrid outperformed GA 7 and ACS 3 in 12 problems. In most of the cases, PSO-SA and PSO-TS outperformed the basic PSO algorithm. Amongst the two hybrids experimented here, PSO-SA gave the best results. The best result obtained with PSO-SA was in 50-jobs, 5-stages case, where the improvement was about 59% when compared to GA but this was still not better than ACS or IG. However, PSO developed by Tseng & Liao (2008) gives much more competitive results. Although thier results are for different set of problems, it can be seen that their algorithm performance improves when the problem size increases. Authors compared their algorithm with GA and ACS using the same set of data and reported that their PSO algorithm supersedes them, in particular for large problems. From the results, it can also be observed that when the number of processors are fixed, that is m_j =5, the scheduling problem becomes more difficult to solve and APD results are relatively higher. This is evident in the given results of different metaheuristic algorithms as well as the basic PSO and the hybrid PSO algorithms presented here. In the fixed processor case, PSO-SA, which is the best performing algorithm among the three PSO algorithms, outperformed GA in 3 out of 12 problems and the best improvement achieved was %34. The performance of ACS is better for large problems though IG is dominant in most of the problems. For the fixed problem case, PSO algorithm developed by (Tseng & Liao, 2008) did not show an exceptional performance when compared to GA or ACS for smaller problems though for large problems (that is n=50 and 100) their PSO algorithm outperforms all.

The execution time of the algorithms is another indicator of the performance though it may not be a fair comparison as different processors and compilers used for each reported algorithm in literature. For instance, the basic PSO and the hybrid PSO algorithms presented here are implemented using Java language and run on a PC with 2GHz Intel Pentium processor (with 1024 MB memory). GA (Oğuz & Ercan, 2005) implemented with C++ and run on a PC with 2GHz Pentium 4 processor (with 256 MB memory), IG (Ying, 2008) with visual C#.net and PC with 1.5GHz CPU and ACS (Ying & Lin, 2006) with Visual C++ and PC with 1.5 GHz Pentium 4 CPU. However, for the sake of completeness we execute GA, the basic PSO and the hybrid PSO on the same computing platform using one easy (k=2, n=10) and one difficult problem (k=8, n=100) for the same termination criterion of 10000 iterations for all the algorithms. Results are reported in Table 4, which illustrates the speed performance of PSO. It can be seen that PSO is approximately 48% to 35% faster than reported GA CPU timings. The fast execution time of PSO is also reported by Tseng and Liao (2008). However, in our case hybrid algorithms were as costly as GA due to computations in SA and TS steps.

k	n	TS (Oğuz et al. 2004)	GA (Oğuz & Ercan, 2005)	ACS (Ying & Lin, 2006)	IG (Ying, 2008)	Basic PSO	PSO-SA	PSO-TS	PSO* (Tseng & Liao, 2008)
	10	3.0	1.60	1.60	1.49	2.7	1.7	2.1	2.8*
2	20	2.88	0.80	1.92	1.87	2.88	1.12	1.92	5.40
	50	2.23	0.69	2.37	2.21	2.38	2.4	2.4	2.30
	100	9.07	0.35	0.91	0.89	1.82	0.82	1.1	1.62
	10	29.42	11.89	9.51	8.73	10.33	9.78	10.4	10.45
5	20	24.40	5.54	3.07	2.97	8.6	3.19	4.53	6.04
	50	10.51	5.11	1.51	1.49	3.31	2.06	2.98	1.44
	100	11.81	3.06	1.05	1.03	2.11	1.05	1.77	2.80
	10	46.53	16.14	16.50	13.91	18.23	16.14	17.5	19.01
8	20	42.47	7.98	6.77	5.83	12.03	6.69	7.03	5.76
	50	21.04	6.03	2.59	2.47	5.98	3.0	4.19	2.91
	100	21.50	4.12	1.33	1.23	8.78	2.11	5.22	1.53

Table 2. APD of the algorithms for 10 random instances. Random processors case ($m_j \sim [1,5]$)
(*) Different problem set

k	n	TS (Oğuz et al. 2004)	GA (Oğuz & Ercan, 2005)	ACS (Ying & Lin, 2006)	IG (Ying, 2008)	Basic PSO	PSO-SA	PSO-TS	PSO* (Tseng & Liao, 2008)
	10	10.82	6.13	12.62	8.85	13.8	10.11	12.8	12.75*
2	20	7.25	7.10	10.73	6.93	10.75	9.59	10.73	6.05
	50	5.80	3.34	8.17	5.66	10.32	7.02	8.82	5.69
	100	5.19	2.87	5.66	5.04	7.43	3.21	6.43	6.56
	10	45.14	11.32	26.09	23.49	29.6	11.32	22.2	19.58
5	20	35.13	10.78	15.11	12.64	19.4	10.77	16.5	12.33
	50	28.64	14.91	13.11	11.29	14.17	13.24	13.86	12.47
	100	26.49	11.02	12.45	10.53	12.45	12.45	12.45	11.49
	10	77.21	25.98	25.14	22.17	30.81	25.83	25.83	33.92
8	20	62.99	24.13	25.18	22.79	26.74	24.34	25.02	24.98
	50	54.25	21.87	22.23	20.71	27.01	23.07	25.11	19.41
	100	36.05	19.46	13.90	12.85	20.39	14.43	17.9	15.93

Table 3. APD of the algorithms for 10 random instances. Fixed processor case ($m_j = 5$)
(*) Different problem set

k	n	GA	PSO	PSO-SA	PSO-TS
2	10	12.14	6.3	13.5	12.94
8	100	2109.9	1388.67	4029.1	3816.3

Table 4. Average CPU time (in seconds) of GA, TS and PSO. Processors setting is m_j=5

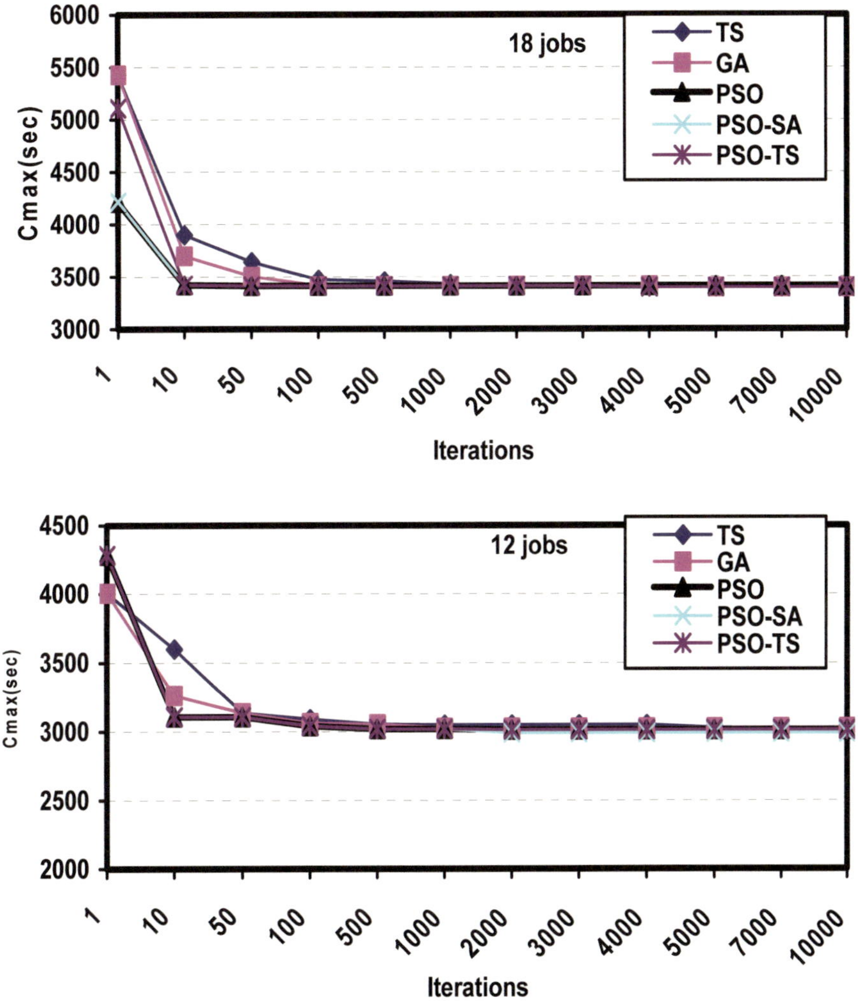

Figure 2. Convergence of TS, GA and PSO algorithms for a machine vision system

Lastly, we run the basic PSO and the hybrid PSO algorithms together with genetic algorithm and tabu search algorithm for the data obtained from a machine-vision system. The system is a multiprocessor architecture designed mainly for machine vision applications. The system comprise of two stages where each stage holds four identical DSP processors from Analog Devices. Data gathered from this system are for 8, 10, 12 and 18 jobs. The number of job is determined by the number of objects to be detected in a given image. The execution time and the processor requirements of parallel algorithms for each job are recorded in order to use them as test problems in our scheduling algorithms. By utilizing this data, which can be obtained from the author, the convergence characteristic of the algorithms is analyzed. As it can be seen from Figure 2, all the algorithms converge very rapidly. However, PSO algorithms converge faster than TS and GA. In addition, PSO-SA finds a slightly better solution for 12 job problem. All the algorithms find a reasonably good solution within 1000 iterations. Hence, for practical application of the scheduling algorithms a small value for termination criteria can be selected.

7. Conclusion

In this chapter, a scheduling problem, defined as hybrid flow-shops with multiprocessor tasks, is presented together with various meta-heuristic algorithms reported for the solution in literature. As the solution to this scheduling problem has merits in practise, endeavour to find a good solution is worthy. The basic PSO and the hybrid PSO algorithms are employed to solve this scheduling problem, as PSO proven to be a simple and effective algorithm applied in various engineering problems. In this particular scheduling problem, a job is made up of interrelated multiprocessor tasks and each multiprocessor task is modelled with its processing requirement and processing time. The objective was to find a schedule in which completion time of all the tasks will be minimal. We observe that basic PSO has a competitive performance as compared to GA and ACS algorithms and superior performance when compared to TS. Considering the simplicity of the basic PSO algorithm, the performance achieved is in fact impressive. When experimented with the hybrids of PSO, it is observed that PSO-SA combination gave the best results. Hybrid methods improved the performance of PSO significantly though this is achieved at the expense of increased complexity. When compared to other published results on this problem, it can be concluded that IG algorithm (Ying, 2008) and PSO given by (Tseng & Liao, 2008) are the best performing algorithms on this problem so far. In terms of effort to develop an algorithm, execution time of algorithm and simplicity to tune it, PSO tops all the other metaheuristics.
As in many practical scheduling problems, it is likely to have precedence constraints among the jobs hence in future study hybrid flow-shops with precedence constraints will be investigated. In addition, PSO may be applied to other scheduling problems and its performance can be exploited in other engineering problems.

8. References

Brucker, P. & Kramer, B. (1995). Shop scheduling problems with multiprocessor tasks on dedicated processors, *Annals of Operations Research*, Vol. 50, 13-27

Caraffa, V.; Ianes, S.; Bagchi, T.P. & Sriskandarajah, C. (2001). Minimizing make-span in blocking flow-shop using genetic algorithms, *International Journal of Production Economics*, Vol. 70, 101-115

Chan, J. & Lee, C. Y. (1999). General multiprocessor task scheduling, *Naval Research Logistics*, Vol. 46, 57-74

Chiang, T. C.; Chang, P.Y. & Huang, Y. M. (2006). Multi-processor tasks with resource and timing constraints using particle swarm optimization, *International Journal of Computer Science and Network Security*, Vol.6, No.4, 71-77

Dauzère-Pérès, S. & Paulli, J. (1997). An integrated approach for modelling and solving the general multiprocessor job-shop scheduling problem using tabu search, *Annals of Operations Research*, Vol. 70, 281-306

Dorigo, M. & Gambardella, L.M.(1997). Ant colony system: a cooperative learning approach to the travelling sales man problem. *IEEE Transaction in Evolutionary Computing*, Vol. 1, 53-66

Drozdowski, M. (1996). Scheduling multiprocessor tasks - an overview, *European Journal of Operational Research*, Vol. 94, 215-230

Ercan, M.F. & Fung, Y.F. (2000). The design and evaluation of a multiprocessor system for computer vision, *Microprocessors and Microsystems*, Vol. 24, 365-377

Ercan, M.F. and Fung, Y.F. (2007). Performance of particle swarm optimisation in scheduling hybrid flow-shops with multi-processor tasks, *Lecture Notes in Computer Science*, Vol. 4706, 309-319

Ercan M. F. (2008). A Performance Comparison of PSO and GA in Scheduling Hybrid Flow-Shops with Multiprocessor Tasks, *ACM Symposium on Applied Computing*, Ceara, Brasil.

Gupta J. N. D. (1988). Two stage hybrid flow shop scheduling problem. *Journal of Operational Research Society*, Vol. 39. No: 4, 359–364.

Holland J. H. (1975). *Adaption in Natural and Artificial Systems*, University of Michigan Press, Ann Arbor

Jdrzęjowicz, J. & Jdrzęjowicz, P. (2003). Population-based approach to multiprocessor task scheduling in multistage hybrid flow shops, *Lecture Notes in Computer Science*, Vol. 2773, 279-286

Jin, S.; Schiavone, G. & Turgut, D. (2008). A performance study of multiprocessor task scheduling algorithms, *Journal of Supercomputing*, Vol. 43, 77–97

Kennedy, J., & Eberhart R. (1995) Particle swarm optimization, *Proceedings of IEEE Int. Conf. on Neural Network*, pp. 1942-1948.

Krawczyk, H. & Kubale, M. (1985). An approximation algorithm for diagnostic test scheduling in multi-computer systems, *IEEE Trans. Computers*, Vol. 34/9, 869-8

Lee, C.Y. & Cai, X. (1999). Scheduling one and two-processors tasks on two parallel processors, *IIE Transactions*, Vol. 31, 445-455

Linn, R. & Zhang, W. (1999). Hybrid flow-shop schedule: a survey, *Computers and Industrial Engineering*, Vol. 37, 57-61 [9]

Liu, B.; Wang, L. & Jin, Y.H. (2005). Hybrid particle swarm optimization for flow shop scheduling with stochastic processing time, *Lecture Notes in Artificial Intelligence*, Vol. 3801, 630-637

Murata, T.; Ishibuchi, H. & Tanaka, H. (1996). Multi-objective genetic algorithm and its application to flow-shop scheduling, *Computers and Industrial Engineering*, Vol. 30, 957-968

Oğuz C. & Ercan M.F. (1997). Scheduling multiprocessor tasks in a two-stage flow-shop environment, *Computers and Industrial Engineering*, Vol. 33, 269-272

Oğuz, C.; Ercan, M.F.; Cheng, T.C.E. & Fung, Y.F. (2003). Heuristic algorithms for multiprocessor task scheduling in a two stage hybrid flow shop, *European Journal of Operations Research*, Vol.149, 390-403

Oğuz, C.; Zinder, Y.; Do., V.; Janiak, A. & Lichtenstein, M. (2004). Hybrid flow-shop scheduling problems with multiprocessor task systems, *European Journal of Operations Research*, Vol.152, 115-131

Oğuz, C. & Ercan, M. F. (2005). A genetic algorithm for hybrid flow-shop scheduling with multiprocessor tasks, *Journal of Scheduling*, Vol. 8, 323-351

Poli, R.; Kennedy, J. & Blackwell, T. (2007). Particle swarm optimization an overview, *Swarm Intelligence*, Vol. 1, No. 3, 33-57.

Salman, A.; Ahmad, I. & Al-Madani, S. (2002). Particle swarm optimization for task assignment problem, *Microprocessors and Microsystems*, Vol. 26, 363-371

Shiau, D.F.; Cheng, S.C. & Huang, Y.M. (2008). Proportionate flexible flow shop scheduling via a hybrid constructive genetic algorithm, *Expert Systems with Applications*, Vol. 34, 1133-1143

Sivanandam, S.N.; Visalakshi, P. and Bhuvaneswari, A. (2007). Multiprocessor scheduling using hybrid particle swarm optimization with dynamically varying inertia, *International Journal of Computer Science & Applications*, Vol. 4, 95-106

Tseng, C.T. & Liao, C.J. (2008), A particle swarm optimization algorithm for hybrid flow-shop scheduling with multiprocessor tasks, *International Journal of Production Research*, Vol. 46, 4655-4670.

Tu, K.; Hao, Z. & Chen, M. (2006). PSO with improved strategy and topology for job shop scheduling, *Lecture Notes in Computer Science*, Vol. 4222, 146-155

Xia, W.J. & Wu, Z.M. (2006). A hybrid particle swarm optimization approach for the job-shop scheduling problem, *International Journal of Advance Manufacturing Technology*, Vol. 29, 360-366

Ying, K.C. & Lin, S.W. (2006). Multiprocessor task scheduling in multistage hybrid flow-shops: an ant colony system approach, *International Journal of Production Research*, Vol. 44, 3161-3177

Ying, K.C. (2008). Iterated greedy heuristic for multiprocessor task scheduling problems, *Journal of the Operations Research Society (online edition)*, 1-8

10

A Particle Swarm Optimization technique used for the improvement of analogue circuit performances

Mourad Fakhfakh[1], Yann Cooren[2], Mourad Loulou[1] and Patrick Siarry[2]
[1]University of Sfax, [2]University of Paris 12
[1]Tunisia, [2]France

1. Introduction

The importance of the analogue part in integrated electronic systems cannot be overstressed. Despite its eminence, and unlike the digital design, the analogue design has not so far been automated to a great extent, mainly due to its towering complexity (Dastidar et al., 2005). Analogue sizing is a very complicated, iterative and boring process whose automation is attracting great attention (Medeiro et al., 1994). The analogue design and sizing process remains characterized by a mixture of experience and intuition of skilled designers (Tlelo-Cuautle & Duarte-Villaseñor, 2008). As a matter of fact, optimal design of analogue components is over and over again a bottleneck in the design flow.
Optimizing the sizes of the analogue components automatically is an important issue towards ability of rapidly designing true high performance circuits (Toumazou & Lidgey, 1993; Conn et al., 1996).
Common approaches are generally either fixed topology ones or/and statistical-based techniques. They generally start with finding a "good" DC quiescent point, which is provided by the skilled analogue designer. After that a simulation-based tuning procedure takes place. However these statistic-based approaches are time consuming and do not guarantee the convergence towards the global optimum solution (Talbi, 2002).
Some mathematical heuristics were also used, such as Local Search (Aarts & Lenstra, 2003), Simulated Annealing (Kirkpatrick et al., 1983; Siarry(a) et al., 1997), Tabu Search (Glover, 1989; Glover, 1990), Genetic Algorithms (Grimbleby, 2000; Dréo et al., 2006), etc. However these techniques do not offer general solution strategies that can be applied to problem formulations where different types of variables, objectives and constraint functions are used. In addition, their efficiency is also highly dependent on the algorithm parameters, the dimension of the solution space, the convexity of the solution space, and the number of variables.
Actually, most of the circuit design optimization problems simultaneously require different types of variables, objective and constraint functions in their formulation. Hence, the abovementioned optimization procedures are generally not adequate or not flexible enough.
In order to overcome these drawbacks, a new set of nature inspired heuristic optimization algorithms were proposed. The thought process behind these algorithms is inspired from

the collective behaviour of decentralized, self-organized systems. It is known as Swarm Intelligence (SI) (Bonabeau et al. 1999). SI systems are typically made up of a population of simple agents (or ''particles'') interacting locally with each other and with their environment. These particles obey to very simple rules, and although there is no centralized control structure dictating how each particle should behave, local interactions between them lead to the emergence of complex global behaviour. Most famous such SIs are Ant Colony Optimization (ACO) (Dorigo et al., 1999), Stochastic Diffusion Search (SDS) (Bishop, 1989) and Particle Swarm Optimization (PSO) (Kennedy & Eberhart, 1995; Clerc, 2006).

PSO, in its current form, has been in existence for almost a decade, which is a relatively short period when compared to some of the well known natural computing paradigms, such as evolutionary computation. PSO has gained widespread demand amongst researchers and has been shown to offer good performance in an assortment of application domains (Banks et al., 2007).

In this chapter, we focus on the use of PSO technique for the optimal design of analogue circuits. The practical applicability and suitability of PSO to optimize performances of such multi-objective problems are highlighted. An example of optimizing performances of a second generation MOS current conveyor (CCII) is presented. The used PSO algorithm is detailed and Spice simulation results, performed using the 'optimal' sizing of transistors forming the CCII and bias current, are presented. Reached performances are discussed and compared to others presented in some published works, but obtained using classical approaches.

2. The Sizing Problem

The process of designing an analogue circuit mainly consists of the following steps (Medeiro et al., 1994) :

- the topology choice: a suitable schematic has to be selected,
- the sizing task: the chosen schematic must be dimensioned to comply with the required specifications,
- The generation of the layout.

Among these major steps, we focus on the second one, i.e. the optimal sizing of analogue circuits.

Actually, analogue sizing is a constructive procedure that aims at mapping the circuit specifications (objectives and constraints on performances) into the design parameter values. In other words, the performance metrics of the circuit, such as gain, noise figure, input impedance, occupied area, etc. have to be formulated in terms of the design variables (Tulunay & Balkir, 2004).

In a generic circuit, the optimization problem consists of finding optimal values of the design parameters. These variables form a vector $\vec{X}^T = \{x_1, x_2, \ \ , x_N\}$ belonging to an N-dimensional design space. This set includes transistor geometric dimensions and passive component values, if any. Hence, performances and objectives involved in the design objectives are expressed as functions of *X*.

These performances may belong to the set of constraints ($\vec{g}(\vec{X})$) and/or to the set of objectives ($\vec{f}(\vec{X})$). Thus, a general optimization problem can be formulated as follows:

$$\begin{aligned} &\textit{minimize} &:\quad & f_i(\vec{X}),\ i \in [1, k] \\ &\textit{such that:} &:\quad & g_j(\vec{X}) \le 0,\ j \in [1, l] \\ &&& h_m(\vec{X}) \le 0,\ m \in [1, p] \\ &&& x_{Li} \le x_i \le x_{Ui},\ i \in [1, N] \end{aligned} \tag{1}$$

k, *l* and *p* denote the numbers of objectives, inequality constraints and equality constraints, respectively. $\vec{x}_L$ and $\vec{x}_U$ are lower and upper boundaries vectors of the parameters.
The goal of optimization is usually to minimize an objective function; the problem for maximizing $\vec{f}(\vec{x})$ can be transformed into minimizing $-\vec{f}(\vec{x})$. This goal is reached when the variables are located in the set of optimal solutions.
For instance, a basic two-stage operational amplifier has around 10 parameters, which include the widths and lengths of all transistors values which have to be set. The goal is to achieve around 10 specifications, such as gain, bandwidth, noise, offset, settling time, slew rate, consumed power, occupied area, CMRR (common-mode rejection ratio) and PSRR (power supply rejection ratio). Besides, a set of DC equations and constraints, such as transistors' saturation conditions, have to be satisfied (Gray & Meyer, 1982).

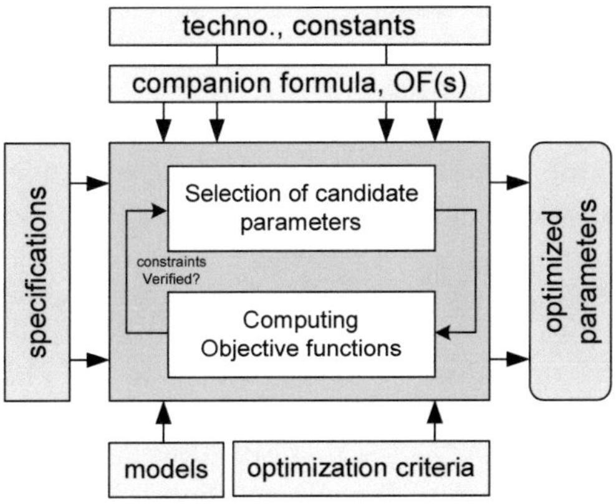

Figure 1. Pictorial view of a design optimization approach

The pictorial flow diagram depicted in Fig. 1 summarizes main steps of the sizing approach.
As it was introduced in section 1, there exist many papers and books dealing with mathematic optimization methods and studying in particular their convergence properties (see for example (Talbi, 2002; Dréo et al., 2006; Siarry(b) et al., 2007)).
These optimizing methods can be classified into two categories: deterministic methods and stochastic methods, known as heuristics.
Deterministic methods, such as Simplex (Nelder & Mead, 1965), Branch and Bound (Doig, 1960), Goal Programming (Scniederjans, 1995), Dynamic Programming (Bellman, 2003)... are effective only for small size problems. They are not efficient when dealing with NP-hard

and multi-criteria problems. In addition, it has been proven that these optimization techniques impose several limitations due to their inherent solution mechanisms and their tight dependence on the algorithm parameters. Besides they rely on the type of objective, the type of constraint functions, the number of variables and the size and the structure of the solution space. Moreover they do not offer general solution strategies.

Most of the optimization problems require different types of variables, objective and constraint functions simultaneously in their formulation. Therefore, classic optimization procedures are generally not adequate.

Heuristics are necessary to solve big size problems and/or with many criteria (Basseur et al., 2006). They can be 'easily' modified and adapted to suit specific problem requirements. Even though they don't guarantee to find in an exact way the optimal solution(s), they give 'good' approximation of it (them) within an acceptable computing time (Chan & Tiwari, 2007). Heuristics can be divided into two classes: on the one hand, there are algorithms which are specific to a given problem and, on the other hand, there are generic algorithms, i.e. metaheuristics. Metaheuristics are classified into two categories: local search techniques, such as Simulated Annealing, Tabu Search ... and global search ones, like Evolutionary techniques, Swarm Intelligence techniques ...

ACO and PSO are swarm intelligence techniques. They are inspired from nature and were proposed by researchers to overcome drawbacks of the aforementioned methods. In the following, we focus on the use of PSO technique for the optimal design of analogue circuits.

3. Overview of Particle Swarm Optimization

The particle swarm optimization was formulated by (Kennedy & Eberhart, 1995). The cogitated process behind the PSO algorithm was inspired by the optimal swarm behaviour of animals such, as birds, fishes and bees.

PSO technique encompasses three main features:

- It is a SI technique; it mimics some animal's problem solution abilities,
- It is based on a simple concept. Hence, the algorithm is neither time consumer nor memory absorber,
- It was originally developed for continuous nonlinear optimization problems. As a matter of fact, it can be easily expanded to discrete problems.

PSO is a stochastic global optimization method. Like in Genetic Algorithms (GA), PSO exploits a population of potential candidate solutions to investigate the feasible search space. However, in contrast to GA, in PSO no operators inspired by natural evolution are applied to extract a new generation of feasible solutions. As a substitute of mutation, PSO relies on the exchange of information between individuals (particles) of the population (swarm).

During the search for the promising regions of the landscape, and in order to tune its trajectory, each particle adjusts its velocity and its position according to its own experience, as well as the experience of the members of its social neighbourhood. Actually, each particle remembers its best position, and is informed of the best position reached by the swarm, in the global version of the algorithm, or by the particle's neighbourhood, in the local version of the algorithm. Thus, during the search process, a global sharing of information takes place and each particle's experience is thus enriched thanks to its discoveries and those of all the other particles. Fig. 2 illustrates this principle.

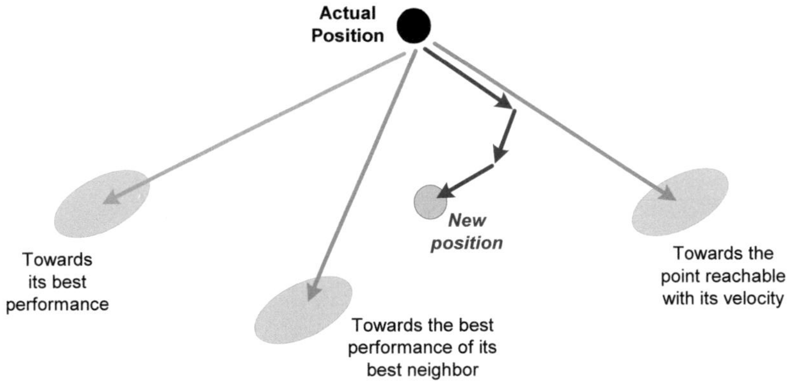

Figure 2. Principle of the movement of a particle

In an N-dimensional search space, the position and the velocity of the ith particle can be represented as $X_i = [x_{i,1}, x_{i,2}, \ldots, x_{i,N}]$ and $V_i = [v_{i,1}, v_{i,2}, \ldots, v_{i,N}]$ respectively. Each particle has its own best location $P_i = [p_{i,1}, p_{i,2}, \ldots, p_{i,N}]$, which corresponds to the best location reached by the ith particle at time *t*. The global best location is named $g = [g_1, g_2, \ldots, g_N]$, which represents the best location reached by the entire swarm. From time *t* to time *t+1*, each velocity is updated using the following equation:

$$v_{i,j}(t+1) = \overbrace{w\, v_{i,j}(t)}^{inertia} + \overbrace{c_1\, r_1 (p_{i,j} - v_{i,j}(t))}^{Personal\ Influence} + \overbrace{c_2\, r_2 (g_i - v_{i,j}(t))}^{Social\ Influence} \quad (2)$$

where *w* is a constant known as inertia factor, it controls the impact of the previous velocity on the current one, so it ensures the diversity of the swarm, which is the main means to avoid the stagnation of particles at local optima. c_1 and c_2 are constants called acceleration coefficients; c_1 controls the attitude of the particle of searching around its best location and c_2 controls the influence of the swarm on the particle's behaviour. r_1 and r_2 are two independent random numbers uniformly distributed in [0,1].

The computation of the position at time *t+1* is derived from expression (2) using:

$$x_{i,j}(t+1) = x_{i,j}(t) + v_{i,j}(t+1) \quad (3)$$

It is important to put the stress on the fact that the PSO algorithm can be used for both mono-objective and multi-objective optimization problems.

The driving idea behind the multi-objective version of PSO algorithm (MO-PSO) consists of the use of an archive, in which each particle deposits its 'flight' experience at each running cycle. The aim of the archive is to store all the non-dominated solutions found during the optimization process. At the end of the execution, all the positions stored in the archive give us an approximation of the theoretical Pareto Front. Fig. 3 illustrates the flowchart of the MO-PSO algorithm. Two points are to be highlighted: the first one is that in order to avoid excessive growing of the storing memory, its size is fixed according to a crowding rule (Cooren et al., 2007). The second point is that computed optimal solutions' inaccuracy crawls in due to the inaccuracy of the formulated equations.

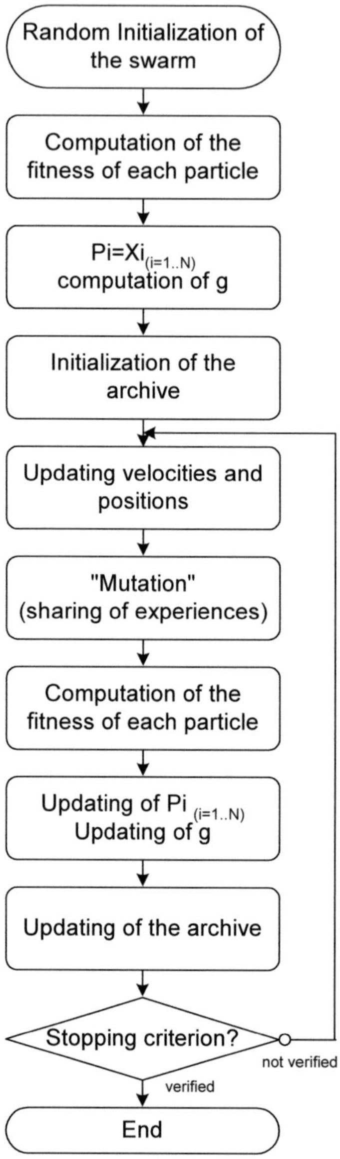

Figure 3. Flowchart of a MO-PSO

In the following section we give an application example dealing with optimizing performances of an analogue circuit, i.e. optimizing the sizing of a MOS inverted current conveyor in order to maximize/minimize performance functions, while satisfying imposed and inherent constraints. The problem consists of generating the trade off surface (Pareto front[1]) linking two conflicting performances of the CCII, namely the high cut-off current frequency and the parasitic X-port input resistance.

[1] Definition of Pareto optimality is given in Appendix.

4. An Application Example

The problem consists of optimizing performances of a second generation current conveyor (CCII) (Sedra & Smith, 1970) regarding to its main influencing performances. The aim consists of maximizing the conveyor high current cut-off frequency and minimizing its parasitic X-port resistance (Cooren et al., 2007).
In the VLSI realm, circuits are classified according to their operation modes: voltage mode circuits or current mode circuits. Voltage mode circuits suffer from low bandwidths arising due to the stray and circuit capacitances and are not suitable for high frequency applications (Rajput & Jamuar, 2007).
In contrary, current mode circuits enable the design of circuits that can operate over wide dynamic ranges. Among the set of current mode circuits, the current conveyor (CC) (Smith & Sedra, 1968; Sedra & Smith, 1970) is the most popular one.
The Current Conveyor (CC) is a three (or more) terminal active block. Its conventional representation is shown in Fig. 4a. Fig. 4b shows the equivalent nullator/norator representation (Schmid, 2000) which reproduces the ideal behaviour of the CC. Fig. 4.c shows a CCII with its parasitic components (Ferry et al. 2002).

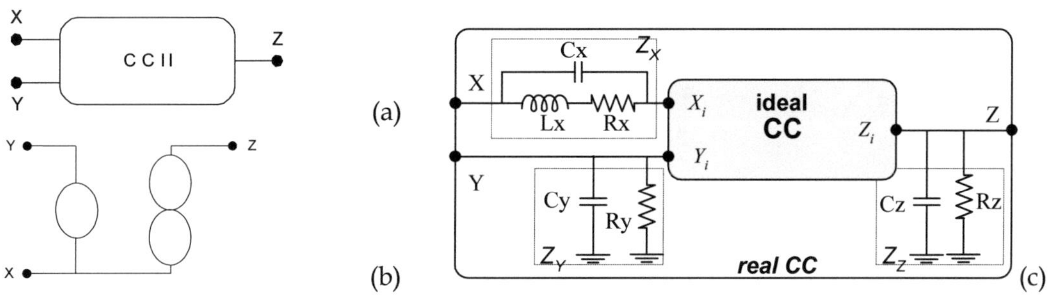

Figure 4. (a) General representation of current conveyor, (b) the nullor equivalency: ideal CC, (c) parasitic components: real CC

Relations between voltage and current terminals are given by the following matrix relation (Toumazou & Lidgey, 1993):

$$\begin{bmatrix} I_Y \\ V_X \\ I_Z \end{bmatrix} = \begin{bmatrix} \frac{1}{(C_Y // R_Y)} & \alpha & 0 \\ \gamma & R_X & 0 \\ 0 & \beta & \frac{1}{(C_Z // R_Z)} \end{bmatrix} \begin{bmatrix} V_Y \\ I_X \\ V_Z \end{bmatrix} \quad (4)$$

For the above matrix representation, α specifies the kind of the conveyor. Indeed, for α =1, the circuit is considered as a first generation current conveyor (CCI). Whereas when α =0, it is called a second generation current conveyor (CCII). β characterizes the current transfer from X to Z ports. For β=+1, the circuit is classified as a positive transfer conveyor. It is considered as a negative transfer one when β=-1. γ=±1: When γ=-1 the CC is said an inverted CC, and a direct CC, otherwise.

Accordingly, the CCII ensures two functionalities between its terminals:

- A Current follower/Current mirror between terminals X and Z.
- A Voltage follower/Voltage mirror between terminals X and Y.

In order to get ideal transfers, CCII are commonly characterized by low impedance on terminal X and high impedance on terminals Y and Z.

In this application we deal with optimizing performances of an inverted positive second generation current conveyor (CCII+) (Sedra & Smith, 1970; Cooren et al., 2007) regarding to its main influencing performances. The aim consists of determining the optimal Pareto circuit's variables, i.e. widths and lengths of each MOS transistor, and the bias current I_0, that maximizes the conveyor high current cut-off frequency and minimizes its parasitic X-port resistance (R_X) (Bensalem et al., 2006; Fakhfakh et al. 2007). Fig. 5 illustrates the CCII+'s MOS transistor level schema.

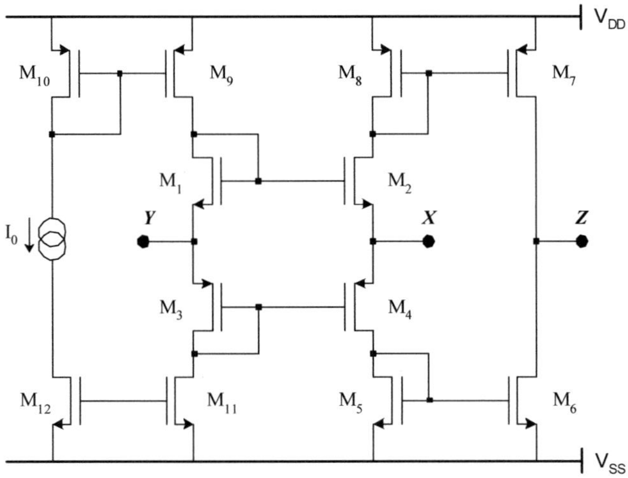

Figure 5. The second generation CMOS current conveyor

Constraints:

- Transistor saturation conditions: all the CCII transistors must operate in the saturation mode. Saturation constraints of each MOSFET were determined. For instance, expression (5) gives constraints on M2 and M8 transistors:

$$\sqrt{\frac{I_0}{K_P W_P / L_P}} \leq \frac{V_{DD}}{2} - |V_{TP}| - \sqrt{\frac{I_0}{K_N W_N / L_N}} \tag{5}$$

  where I_0 is the bias current, $W_{(N,P)}/L_{(N,P)}$ is the aspect ratio of the corresponding MOS transistor. $K_{(N,P)}$ and V_{TP} are technology parameters. V_{DD} is the DC voltage power supply.

Objective functions:

In order to present simplified expressions of the objective functions, all NMOS transistors were supposed to have the same size. Ditto for the PMOS transistors.

- R_X: the value of the X-port input parasitic resistance has to be minimized,
- f_{chi}: the high current cut-off frequency has to be maximized.

Symbolic expressions of the objective functions are not given due to their large number of terms.

PSO algorithm was programmed using C++ software. Table 1 gives the algorithm parameters.

Fig. 6 shows Pareto fronts (R_X vs. *fci*) and optimal variables (W_P vs. W_N) corresponding to the bias current I_0=50µA (6.a, 6.b), 100µA (6.c, 6.d), 150µA (6.e, 6.f), 200µA (6.g, 6.h), 250µA (6.i, 6.j) and 300µA (6.k, 6.l). Where values of L_N, L_P, W_N and W_P are given in µm, I_0 is in µA, R_X in ohms and $fc_{i(min, Max)}$ in GHz.

In Fig. 6 clearly appears the high interest of the Pareto front. Indeed, amongst the set of the non-dominated solutions, the designer can choose, always with respect to imposed specifications, its best solution since he can add some other criterion choice, such as Y-port and/or Z-port impedance values, high voltage cut-off frequency, etc.

Fig. 7 shows Spice simulation results performed for both points corresponding to the edge of the Pareto front, for I_0=100µA, where R_{Xmin}=493 ohms, R_{XMax}=787 ohms, fc_{imin}=0.165 GHz and fc_{iMax}=1.696 GHz.

Swarm size	Number of iterations	*w*	c_1	c_2
20	1000	0.4	1	1

Table 1. The PSO algorithm parameters

Technology	CMOS AMS 0.35 µm
Power voltage supply	V_{SS}=-2.5V, V_{DD}=2.5V

Table 2. SPICE simulation conditions

I_0	W_N	L_N	W_P	L_P	W_N	L_N	W_P	L_P
	R_{Xmin}		fc_{imin}		R_{XMax}		fc_{iMax}	
50	17.21	0.90	28.40	0.50	4.74	0.87	8.40	0.53
	714		0.027		1376		0.866	
100	20.07	0.57	30.00	0.35	7.28	0.55	12.60	0.35
	382		0.059		633		1.802	
150	17.65	0.6	28.53	0.35	10.67	0.59	17.77	0.36
	336		0.078		435		1.721	
200	17.51	0.53	29.55	0.35	12.43	0.53	20.32	0.35
	285		0.090		338		2.017	
250	18.60	0.54	30.00	0.35	15.78	0.55	24.92	0.35
	249		0.097		272		1.940	
300	19.17	0.55	29.81	0.35	17.96	0.54	29.16	0.35
	224		0.107		230		2.042	

Table 3. Pareto trade-off surfaces' boundaries corresponding to some selected results

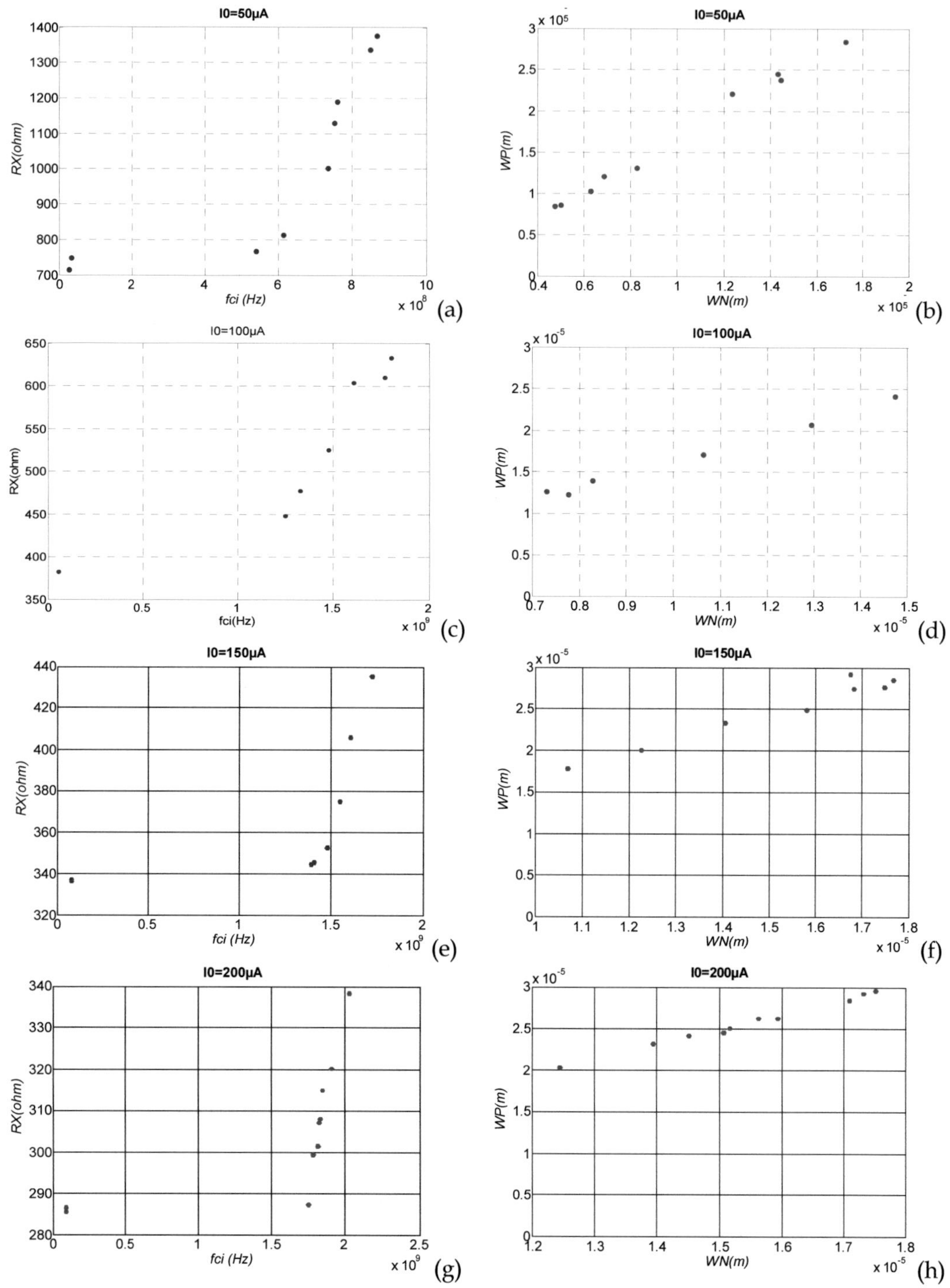
I0=50μA
RX(ohm)
fci (Hz)
x 10^8
(a)
I0=50μA
WP(m)
WN(m)
x 10^5
(b)
I0=100μA
RX(ohm)
fci(Hz)
x 10^9
(c)
I0=100μA
WP(m)
WN(m)
x 10^-5
(d)
I0=150μA
RX(ohm)
fci (Hz)
x 10^9
(e)
I0=150μA
WP(m)
WN(m)
x 10^-5
(f)
I0=200μA
RX(ohm)
fci (Hz)
x 10^9
(g)
I0=200μA
WP(m)
WN(m)
x 10^-5
(h)

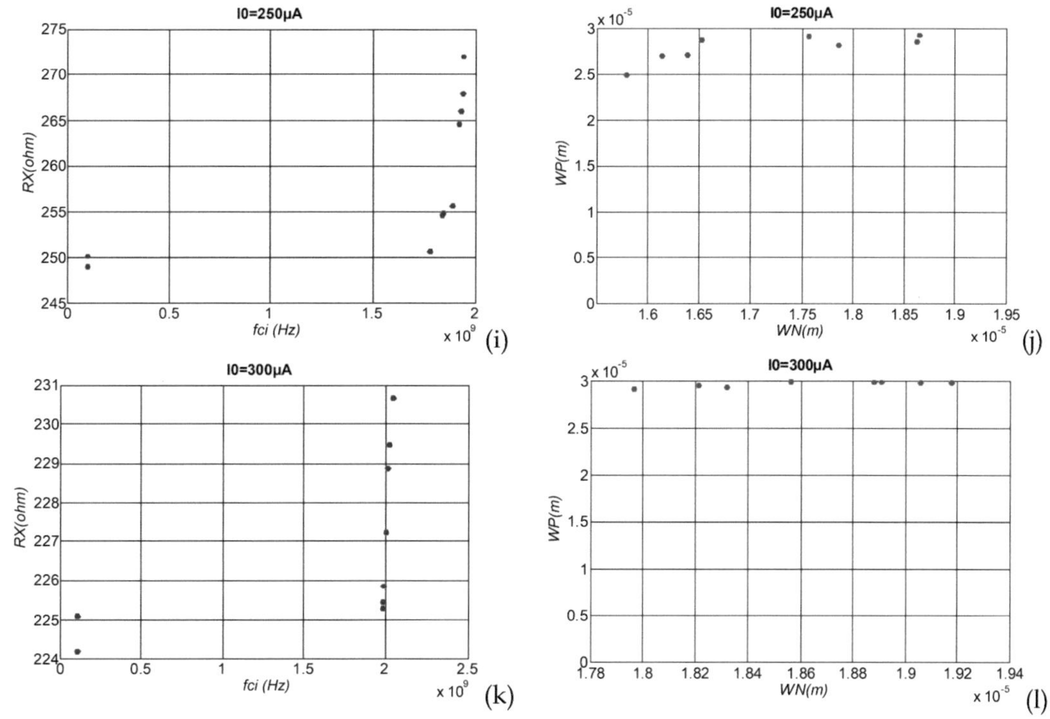

Figure 6. Pareto fronts and the corresponding variables for various bias currents

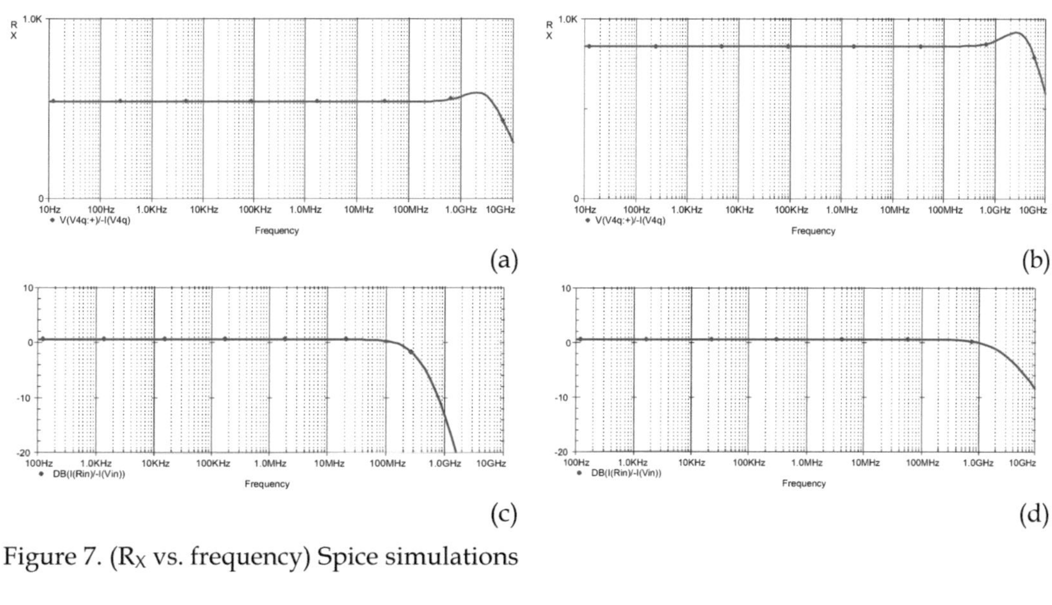

Figure 7. (R_X vs. frequency) Spice simulations

5. Conclusion

The practical applicability and suitability of the particle swarm optimization technique (PSO) to optimize performances of analog circuits were shown in this chapter. An application example was presented. It deals with computing the Pareto trade-off surface in the solution space: parasitic input resistance vs. high current cut-off frequency of a positive second generation current conveyor (CCII+). Optimal parameters (transistors' widths and lengths, and bias current), obtained thanks to the PSO algorithm were used to simulate the CCII+. It was shown that no more than 1000 iterations were necessary for obtaining 'optimal' solutions. Besides, it was also proven that the algorithm doesn't require severe parameter tuning. Some Spice simulations were presented to show the good agreement between the computed (optimized) values and the simulation ones.

6. Appendix

In the analogue sizing process, the optimization problem usually deals with the minimization of several objectives simultaneously. This multi-objective optimization problem leads to trade-off situations where it is only possible to improve one performance at the cost of another. Hence, the resort to the concept of Pareto optimality is necessary.

A vector $\theta = [\theta_1 \cdots \theta_n]^T$ is considered superior to a vector $\psi = [\psi_1 \cdots \psi_n]^T$ if it dominates ψ, i.e., $\theta \prec \psi \Leftrightarrow \underset{i \in \{1,\cdots,n\}}{\forall} (\theta_i \leq \psi_i) \wedge \underset{i \in \{1,\cdots,n\}}{\exists} (\theta_i < \psi_i)$

Accordingly, a performance vector $f^{\bullet}$ is Pareto-optimal if and only if it is non-dominated within the feasible solution space $\Im$, i.e., $\neg \underset{f \in \Im}{\exists} f \prec f^{\bullet}$.

7. References

Aarts, E. & Lenstra, K. (2003) Local search in combinatorial optimization. Princeton University Press.

Banks, A.; Vincent, J. & Anyakoha, C. (2007) A review of particle swarm optimization. Part I: background and development, *Natural Computing Review*, Vol. 6, N. 4 December 2007. DOI 10.1007/s11047-007-9049-5. pp. 467-484.

Basseur, M.; Talbi, E. G.; Nebro, A. & Alba, E. (2006) Metaheuristics for multiobjective combinatorial optimization problems : review and recent issues, report n°5978. National Institute of Research in Informatics and Control (INRIA). September 2006.

Bellman, R. (2003) Dynamic Programming, Princeton University Press, Dover paperback edition.

BenSalem, S; M. Fakhfakh, Masmoudi, D. S., Loulou, M., Loumeau, P. & Masmoudi, N. (2006) A High Performances CMOS CCII and High Frequency Applications, *Journal of Analog Integrated Circuits and Signal Processing*, Springer US, 2006. vol. 49, no. 1.

Bishop, J.M. (1989) Stochastic searching networks, Proceedings of the IEE International Conference on Artificial Neural Networks. pp. 329-331, Oct 1989.

Bonabeau, E.; Dorigo, M. & Theraulaz, G. (1999) Swarm Intelligence: From Natural to Artificial Systems. Oxford University Press.

Chan, F. T. S. & Tiwari, M. K. (2007) Swarm Intelligence: focus on ant and particle swarm optimization, *I-Tech Education and Publishing*. December 2007. ISBN 978-3-902613-09-7.

Clerc, M. Particle swarm optimization (2006), *International Scientific and Technical Encyclopedia*, ISBN-10: 1905209045.

Conn, A. R.; Coulman, P. K.; Haring, R. A.; Morrill, G. L.; Visweswariah, C. (1996), Optimization of custom MOS circuits by transistor sizing, *Proceedings of ICCAD96*. pp. 174-190, November, 1996. San Jose.

Cooren, Y.; Fakhfakh, M. , Loulou, M. & Siarry, P. (2007) Optimizing second generation current conveyors using particle swarm optimization, *Proceedings of the 19th IEEE International Conference on Microelectronics*. December 29-31, 2007. Cairo, Egypt.

Dastidar, T.R.; Chakrabarti, P. P. & Ray, P. (2005). Synthesis System for Analog Circuits Based on Evolutionary Search and Topological Reuse, *IEEE Transactions on Evolutionary Computation*, Vol. 9, No. 2, April 2005. pp. 211-224, ISSN 1089-778X.

Doig, A.H. Land (1960), An automatic method for solving discrete programming problem, *Econometrica*, Vol. 28, pp. 497.

Dorigo, M.; DiCaro G. & Gambardella, L. M. (1999) Ant algorithms for discrete optimization, *Artificial life journal* Vol. 5. pp. 137-172.

Dréo, J.; Petrowski, A.; Siarry, P.; Taillard, E. (2006) *Metaheuristics for Hard Optimization: methods and case studies*, Springer. ISBN: 354023022X.

Fakhfakh M., Loulou M. & Tlelo-Cuautle E. (2007) Synthesis of CCIIs and Design of Simulated CCII based Floating Inductances, *Proceedings of the 14th IEEE International Conference on Electronics, Circuits and Systems*. December 2007. Marrakech, Morocco.

Ferri, G.; Guerrinin, N. & Piccirilli, M. C. (2002) Low voltage current conveyor-based biquad filter, *Proceedings of the IEEE International Symposium on Industrial Electronics*. Vol. 4. pp. 1331-1334.

Glover, F. (1989) Tabu search- part I, *ORSA Journal on Computing*. Vol. 1, N° 3. Summer 1989.

Glover, F. (1990) Tabu search- part II, *ORSA Journal on Computing*. Vol. 2, N° 1. Winter 1990.

Gray, P. R.; Meyer, R. G.(1982) MOS operational amplifier design-a tutorial overview, *IEEE Solid-State Circuits*, Vol. 17, Issue 6, December 1982. pp. 969-982.

Grimbleby, J. B. (2000) Automatic analogue circuit synthesis using genetic algorithms, *Proceedings of the IEE Circuits, Devices and Systems*, December 2000, Vol. 147, Issue: 6. pp: 319-323

Kennedy, J & Eberhart, R. C. (1995) Particle swarm optimization, *Proceedings of the IEEE International Conference On Neural Networks*, pp 1942-1948, WA, Australia.

Kirkpatrick, S.; Gelatt, C. D. & Vecchi, M. P. (1983) Optimization by simulated annealing, *Journal of Science*, 220:671-220-680.

Medeiro, F.; Rodríguez-Macías, R.; Fernández, F.V.; Domínguez-astro, R.; Huertas, J.L.& Rodríguez-Vázquez, A. Global Design of Analog Cells Using Statistical Optimization Techniques, *Analog Integrated Circuits and Signal Processing*, Vol. 6, No. 3, November 1994. pp. 179-195, ISSN 0925-1030.

Nelder, J.A. & Mead, R. (1965) A simplex method for function optimization, *Computer journal*, Vol. 7, pp. 308-313.

Rajput, S. S. & Jamuar, S. S. (2007) Advanced applications of current conveyors: a tutorial, *Journal of active and passive electronic devices*, Vol 2, pp 143-164.

Schmid, H. (2000) Approximating the Universal Active Element, *IEEE Transactions on Circuits and Systems-II: Analog and Digital Signal Processing*, vol. 47, N°. 11, Nov. 2000.

Scniederjans, M.J.(1995) Goal Programming methodology and applications, Kluwer Publishers.

Sedra, A.& Smith, K. C. (1970) A second generation current conveyor and its applications, *IEEE Transactions on Circuit Theory*, pp. 132-134, February 1970.

Siarry(a), P.; Berthiau, G.; Durdin, F. & Haussy, J. (1997) Enhanced simulated annealing for globally minimizing functions of many-continuous Variables, *ACM Transactions on Mathematical Software*, Vol. 23, N°. June 1997. pp 209-228.

Siarry(b), P.; Michalewicz, Z. (2007) Advances in Metaheuristics for Hard Optimization, Springer; December 2007. ISBN 3540729593.

Smith, K. C. & Sedra, A. (1968) The current conveyor-a new circuit building block, *Proceedings of the. IEEE (Letters)*, vol 56, pp. 1368-1369, August 1968.

E. G. Talbi, E. G. (2002) A Taxonomy of Hybrid Metaheuristics, *Journal of Heuristics*, N°8 pp 541-564.

Tlelo-Cuautle, E.; Duarte-Villaseñor, M.A.(2008), Evolutionary electronics: automatic synthesis of analog circuits by GAs, In *Success in Evolutionary Computation, Series: Studies in Computational Intelligence*, Yang, A.; Shan, Y.& Bui, L. T. (Eds.), pp. 165-187, Vol. 92, ISBN: 978-3-540-76285-0, Springer-Verlag, Berlin.

Toumazou, C.& Lidgey, F. J. (1993), In Analog IC Design: The current mode approach, Haigh, D. G. (Ed.), *IEEE circuit and systems series* 2.

Tulunay, G.& Balkir, S. (2004) A Compact Optimization Methodology for Single Ended LNA, *Proceedings of the IEEE International Symposium on Circuits and Systems*, ISCAS 2004.

11

Particle Swarm Optimization Applied for Locating an Intruder by an Ultra-Wideband Radar Network

Rodrigo M. S. de Oliveira, Carlos L. S. S. Sobrinho, Josivaldo S. Araújo and Rubem G. Farias
Federal University of Pará (UFPA)
Brazil

1. Introduction

As it was shown by the authors in a previous work, the Finite-Difference Time-Domain (FDTD) method is adequate to solve numerically Maxwell's Equations for simulating the propagation of Ultra-Wideband (UWB) pulses in complex environments. These pulses are important in practice in high-resolution radar and GPS systems and in high performance (wideband) wireless communication links, because they are immune to selective frequency fading related to complex environments, such as residences, offices, laboratories among others. In this case, it is necessary to use spread spectrum techniques for transmission, in order to avoid interferences to other wireless systems, such as cell phone networks, GPS, Bluetooth and IEEE802.11. It is worth to mention that by combining these techniques to UWB pulses; it is possible to obtain a signal with power spectrum density under noise threshold, what is a very interesting characteristic for this application.

The proposed simulated environment is a building consisting of several rooms (laboratories) separated by masonry. Internal and external walls are characterized by specific widths and electrical parameters. Wood doors were included in the analysis domain. The analysis region is then limited by U-PML (Uniaxial Perfectly Matched Layers) technique and the system is excited by omni-directional antennas. In order to make the simulations more real, Additive White Gaussian Noise was considered. Aiming at verifying the robustness of the radar network, objects are included in the domain in a semi-random spatial distribution, increasing the contribution of the wave scattering phenomena. Omni-directional antennas were used to register transient electric field in specific points of the scenery, which are adequate for the propose of this work. From those transient responses, it is possible to determine the time intervals the electromagnetic signal requires to travel through the paths transceiver-intruder-transceiver and transceiver-intruder-receivers, forming, this way, a non-linear system of equations (involving circle and ellipses equations, respectively).

In order to estimate the intruder position, the PSO method is used and a new methodology was conceived. The main idea is to apply PSO to determine the equidistant point to the circle and to the two ellipses generated by using the data extracted from received transient signals (those three curves usually does not have a single interception point for highly

scattering environments). The equidistant point, determined via PSO, is the position estimative for single radar.
For a radar network, which is necessary for a large area under monitoring, the transmitters should operate in TDM (Time-Division Multiplexing) mode in order to avoid interference among them. For each possible transceiver-receivers combination, an estimate is obtained and, from the set of estimations, statistical parameters are calculated and used in order to produce a unique prediction of the intruder's position.

2. The FDTD Method and its Applications

The FDTD Method (Finite-Difference Time-Domain) had its first application in the solution of Maxwell's equations, in 1966, when Kane Yee used it in the analysis of spread of electromagnetic waves through bidimensional structures (Yee, 1966). This technique defines the spacial positioning of the components of the electric and magnetic fields in such a way that Ampère and Faraday laws are satisfied, and it approaches the derivates, constituents of those equations, by centered finite differences, in which the updating of the components of the electric fields is alternately verified in relation to those of the magnetic fields, by forming this way what is known as the algorithm of Yee. The method constitutes a solution of complete wave, in which the reflection, refraction, and diffraction phenomena are implicitly included.
Years passed by and, along with them, several scientific advances contributed to the establishment of this method as an important tool in the analysis and synthesis of problems in electromagnetism, among them it is noted: new high speed computers and auto-performance computer networks; the expansion of the method for the solution of problems in the 3D space, with the inclusion of complex materials, and the condition of stability (Taflove & Brodwin, 1975); development of truncation techniques of the region of analysis, known as ABC´s (Absorbing Boundary Conditions), such as the operators of Bayliss-Turkel Bayliss, & Turkel, (1980), Mur of first and second orders (Mur, 1981), Higdon technique (Ridon, 1987), Liao (Liao, 1987), PML of Berenger (Berenger, 1994), and the UPML of Sacks (Sacks et al., 1995).
The FDTD method, for its simplicity of application, strength and application in all spectrum of frequencies, has been used in the solution of antenna problems (Zhang et al., 1988), circuit analysis in high frequencies (Fornberg et al., 2000), radars (Muller et al., 2005), photonic (Goorjian & Taflove, 1992), communication systems (Kondylis et al., 1999), periodic structures (Maloney & Kesler, 1998), medicine (Manteuffell & Simon, 2005) , electric grounding system (Tanabe, 2001) , etc.

2.1 The Yee's Algorithm

Equations (1) and (2) represent the equations of Maxwell in its differential form, where **E** and **H** are the vectors intensity of electric and magnetic fields, respectively, μ is the magnetic permeability, ε is the electric permittivity of the medium and **J** is the current density vector. For the solution of these equations by the FDTD method, Kane Yee (Yee, 1966) proposed that the components of **E** (E_x, E_y, E_z) and **H** (H_x, H_y, H_z) were positioned in the space as it shown in Fig. 1.

$$\nabla x\mathbf{E} = -\mu\frac{\partial \mathbf{H}}{\partial t} \tag{1}$$

$$\nabla x\mathbf{H} = \varepsilon\frac{\partial \mathbf{E}}{\partial t} + \mathbf{J}. \tag{2}$$

Such procedure is justified by the necessity of agreement with the mathematical operators indicated in the equations above.

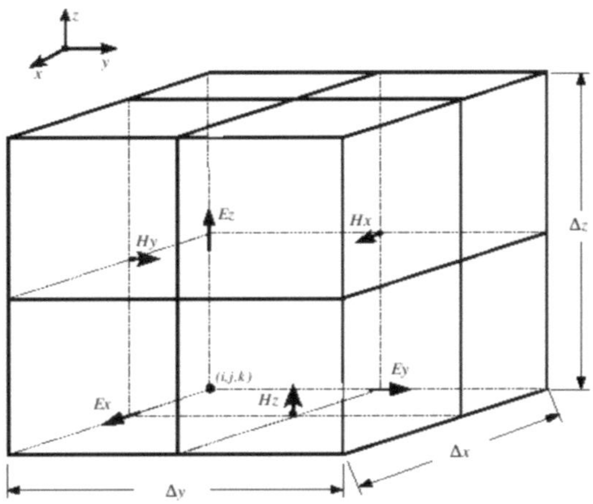

Figure 1. The Yee's Cell

This way, by expanding the curl operators in (1) and (2), it results in the following scalar equations

$$\frac{\partial H_x}{\partial t} = \frac{1}{\mu}\left(\frac{\partial E_Y}{\partial z} - \frac{\partial E_z}{\partial y}\right), \tag{3.a}$$

$$\frac{\partial H_y}{\partial t} = \frac{1}{\mu}\left(\frac{\partial E_z}{\partial x} - \frac{\partial E_x}{\partial z}\right), \tag{3.b}$$

$$\frac{\partial H_z}{\partial t} = \frac{1}{\mu}\left(\frac{\partial E_x}{\partial y} - \frac{\partial E_y}{\partial x}\right), \tag{3.c}$$

and

$$\frac{\partial E_x}{\partial t} = \frac{1}{\varepsilon}\left(\frac{\partial H_y}{\partial z} - \frac{\partial H_z}{\partial y} - \sigma E_x\right) \tag{4.a}$$

$$\frac{\partial E_y}{\partial t} = \frac{1}{\varepsilon}\left(\frac{\partial H_x}{\partial z} - \frac{\partial H_z}{\partial x} - \sigma E_y\right), \tag{4.b}$$

$$\frac{\partial E_z}{\partial t} = \frac{1}{\varepsilon}\left(\frac{\partial H_y}{\partial x} - \frac{\partial H_x}{\partial y} - \sigma E_z\right), \tag{4.c}$$

respectively.

The derivates in (3) and (4) are then approximated by central finite differences, in the following way

$$\frac{\partial F}{\partial l} \simeq \frac{F(l+\frac{1}{2}\Delta l)-F(l-\frac{1}{2}\Delta l)}{\Delta l} \tag{5}$$

where F represents any component of either electric or magnetic field and l can be x, y, z or t. By applying (5) in (3) and (4), it results in the updating equations of the components of fields given by (6)-(7), as follows.

$$H_x^{n+\frac{1}{2}}(i,j,k) = H_x^{n-\frac{1}{2}}(i,j,k) + \frac{\Delta_t}{\mu}\left[\frac{E_y^n(i,j,k+1)-E_y^n(i,j,k)}{\Delta_z} - \frac{E_z^n(i,j+1,k)-E_z^n(i,j,k)}{\Delta_y}\right], \tag{6.a}$$

$$H_y^{n+\frac{1}{2}}(i,j,k) = H_y^{n-\frac{1}{2}}(i,j,k) + \frac{\Delta_t}{\mu}\left[\frac{E_z^n(i+1,j,k)-E_z^n(i,j,k)}{\Delta_x} - \frac{E_x^n(i,j,k+1)-E_x^n(i,j,k)}{\Delta_z}\right], \tag{6.b}$$

$$H_z^{n+\frac{1}{2}}(i,j,k) = H_z^{n-\frac{1}{2}}(i,j,k) + \frac{\Delta_t}{\mu}\left[\frac{E_x^n(i,j+1,k)-E_x^n(i,j,k)}{\Delta_y} - \frac{E_y^n(i+1,j,k)-E_y^n(i,j,k)}{\Delta_x}\right], \tag{6.c}$$

and

$$E_x^{n+1}(i,j,k) = E_x^n(i,j,k)\left(\frac{1-\sigma\frac{\Delta_t}{2\varepsilon}}{1+\sigma\frac{\Delta_t}{2\varepsilon}}\right) + \frac{\Delta_t}{\varepsilon\left(1+\sigma\frac{\Delta_t}{2\varepsilon}\right)}\left[\frac{H_z^{n+1/2}(i,j,k)-H_z^{n+1/2}(i,j-1,k)}{\Delta_y} - \frac{H_y^{n+1/2}(i,j,k)-H_y^{n+1/2}(i,j,k-1)}{\Delta_z}\right], \tag{7.a}$$

$$E_y^{n+1}(i,j,k) = E_y^n(i,j,k)\left(\frac{1-\sigma\frac{\Delta_t}{2\varepsilon}}{1+\sigma\frac{\Delta_t}{2\varepsilon}}\right) + \frac{\Delta_t}{\varepsilon\left(1+\sigma\frac{\Delta_t}{2\varepsilon}\right)}\left[\frac{H_x^{n+1/2}(i,j,k)-H_x^{n+1/2}(i,j,k-1)}{\Delta_z} - \frac{H_y^{n+1/2}(i,j,k)-H_y^{n+1/2}(i-1,j,k)}{\Delta_x}\right], \tag{7.b}$$

$$E_z^{n+1}(i,j,k) = E_z^n(i,j,k)\left(\frac{1-\sigma\frac{\Delta_t}{2\varepsilon}}{1+\sigma\frac{\Delta_t}{2\varepsilon}}\right) +$$

$$+\frac{\Delta_t}{\varepsilon\left(1+\sigma\frac{\Delta_t}{2\varepsilon}\right)}\left[\frac{H_y^{n+1/2}(i,j,k)-H_y^{n+1/2}(i-1,j,k)}{\Delta_x} - \frac{H_x^{n+1/2}(i,j,k)-H_x^{n+1/2}(i,j-1,k)}{\Delta_y}\right], \tag{7.c}$$

where i,j,k and n are integers; i,j,k are indexes for the spatial coordinates x, y and z and n is the temporal index for the time t, in such way that $x = i\Delta_x$, $y = j\Delta_y$, $z = k\Delta_z$ and $t = n\Delta_t$ (Δ_x, Δ_y and Δ_z are the spatial increments and Δ_t is the time step).

2.2 Precision and Stability

The precision represents how close the obtained result is to the exact result, and the stability is the guarantee that the solution of the problem will not diverge. In order to precision and stability to be guaranteed, the following criteria are adopted in this work (Taflove & Hagness 2005):

$$\Delta_{x,y,z} \leq \frac{\lambda_{min}}{10}$$

and

$$\Delta_t \leq \frac{1}{v_{max}\sqrt{\frac{1}{(\Delta_x)^2}+\frac{1}{(\Delta_y)^2}+\frac{1}{(\Delta_z)^2}}}.$$

which means that the minimum wave length existing in the work environment has to be characterized by, at least, 10 cells (Taflove & Hagness 2005). Depending on the application, this number can be superior to 100, and the time increment will be limited by the maximum distance to be travelled, by the respective wave, in the cell of Yee (Taflove & Hagness 2005).

2.3 The Sacks' Uniaxial Perfecttly Matched Layers

One of the problems of the numeric methods is the fact that they do not offer resources that permits the interruption of the spacial iterative process. This causes the method to be limited, mainly when the solution of open problems is taken into account. In order to solve this problem, several techniques have been developed, among them there is the UPML (Uniaxial perfecttly matched layers) (Sacks et al., 1995), which was used in this work. This method takes into account, around the region of analysis (Fig.2), layers perfectly matched, constituted by anisotropic media and with loss, which are characterized by the following equations of Maxwell, in the frequency domain.

$$\nabla x\mathbf{E} = -j\omega\mu[s]\mathbf{H} \tag{8}$$

$$\nabla x\mathbf{H} = j\omega\varepsilon[s]\mathbf{E}, \tag{9}$$

where the tensor $[s]=\begin{bmatrix} \frac{s_y s_z}{s_x} & 0 & 0 \\ 0 & \frac{s_x s_z}{s_y} & 0 \\ 0 & 0 & \frac{s_x s_y}{s_z} \end{bmatrix}$, with $s_\alpha = 1+\frac{\sigma_\alpha}{j\omega\varepsilon_0}$, in which σ_α is the attenuation electric conductivity in the directions α = x, y, z, introducing the anisotropy in the medium. **E** and **H** are the vectors intensity of electric and magnetic field in the frequency domain, respectively.

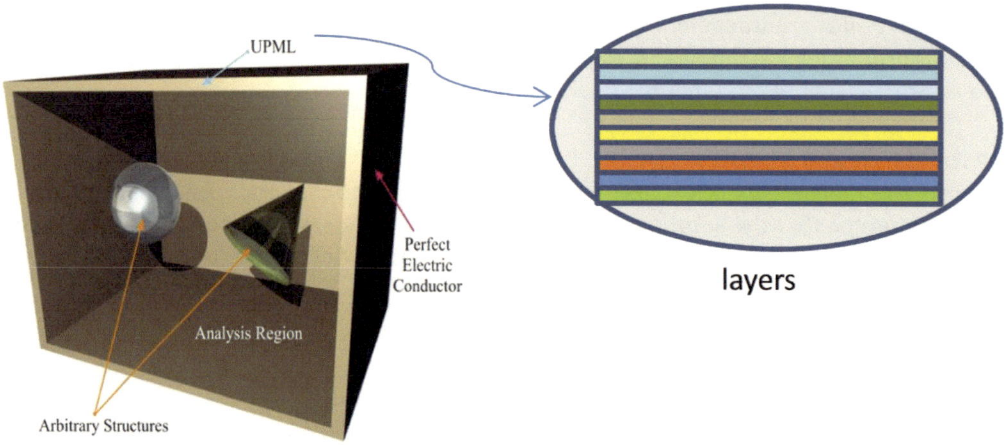

Figure 2. The analysis region limited by UPML

In order to avoid the use of convolution in the transformation of the equations above into the time domain, one defines the following constitutive relations:

$$D_x = \varepsilon\left(\frac{s_y}{s_x}E_x\right), D_y = \varepsilon\left(\frac{s_z}{s_y}E_y\right), D_z = \varepsilon\left(\frac{s_x}{s_z}E_z\right); \quad (10)$$

$$B_x = \mu\left(\frac{s_y}{s_x}H_x\right), B_y = \mu\left(\frac{s_z}{s_y}H_y\right), B_z = \mu\left(\frac{s_x}{s_z}H_z\right), \quad (11)$$

where D_x, D_y, D_z and B_x, B_y, B_z are the components of the vectors electric flux density (**D**) and magnetic (**B**), respectively. In order to find the updating equations for the components of the electric field, the updating equations for D_x, D_y and D_z, have to be found first, which is done by the substitution of [s] in (9), considering (10). Next, the components of **E** are found through eq. (10). The same procedure is done in order to find the components of **H** (Taflove & Hagness, 2005).

3. Particle Swarm Optimization and Radar Applications

3.1 Basic Radar Theory Overview

The main reason for using radars is to determine the spatial position of an object. This is performed by transmitting electromagnetic pulses through space, which will be scattered by the target and by other objects. Transient responses obtained at certain points in space are used to determine the target's position.

In particular, multistatic radars can be composed by a transceiver (transmitter and receiver at the same point - Tx/Rx1) and, at least, two remote receivers (Rx2 and Rx3), such as illustrated by Fig. 4. The signal leaves the transceiver and reaches the target, which reflects it toward the receivers and the transceiver as well.

From the transceiver perspective, the signal takes a certain amount of time for returning. This only means that the target could be at any point of a circle centered at the transceiver's coordinates (Fig. 4). Longer the time, larger is the circumference. From the receiver perspective, the signal travels from the transmitter, it reaches the target and then it arrives at the receiver coordinates. This only means that the target is at the locus defined by an ellipse with foci at the transceiver's and at the receiver's coordinates (Fig. 3). Of course, longer the propagation time, greater is the total path (calculated by using time and the propagating speed) and larger is the ellipse's semiminor axis. The solution of the system of equations this way composed provides the target's position.

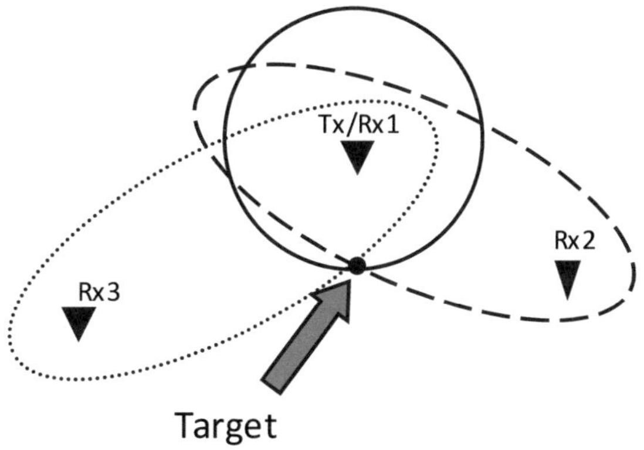

Figure 3. Ideal multistatic radar

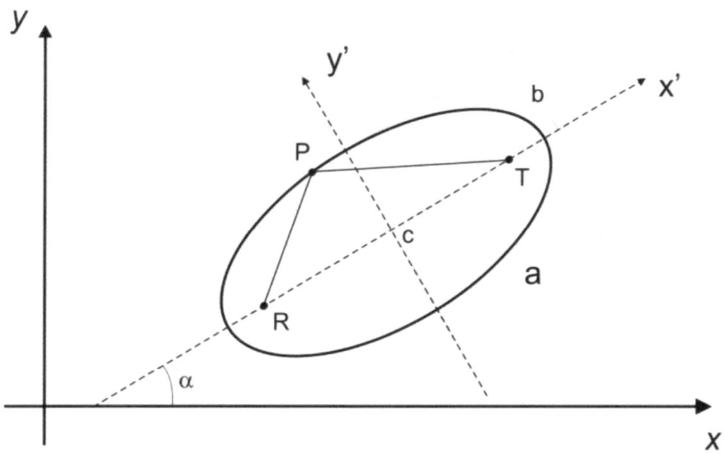

Figure 4. The ellipse's parameters

Fig. 4 shows the ellipse's basic parameters (T indicates the transceiver position, R indicates the receiver's, position and P defines the intruder's location).

The ellipse equation is given by

$$F_n(x,y) = A_n^2(x,y) + B_n^2(x,y) - C_n^2 = 0, \tag{12}$$

where

$$A_n\,(x,y) = a_n\left[(y - y_{c_n})\cos\alpha_n - (x - x_{c_n})\sin\alpha_n\right], \tag{13}$$

$$B_n\,(x,y) = b_n\left[(x - x_{c_n})\cos\alpha_n - (y - y_{c_n})\sin\alpha_n\right] \tag{14}$$

and

$$C_n = a_n b_n, \tag{15}$$

in which a is the semimajor axis, b is the semiminor axis, x_c and y_c are the coordinates of the center C of the ellipse, and α is the angle from the x-axis to the ellipse's semimajor axis. Here, n is the receiver identifier (index). The parameters x_{C_n}, y_{C_n}, a_n, b_n and α_n are calculated by

$$x_{c_n} = \frac{1}{2}(x_T + x_{R_n}), \tag{16}$$

$$y_{c_n} = \frac{1}{2}(y_T + y_{R_n}), \tag{17}$$

$$a_n = \frac{1}{2}(d_{TPR_n}), \tag{18}$$

$$b_n = \frac{1}{2}\left(\sqrt{d_{TPR_n}^2 - d_{TR_n}^2}\right), \tag{19}$$

$$d_{TR_n} = \sqrt{(x_T - x_{R_n})^2 + (y_T - y_{R_n})^2}, \tag{20}$$

$$\alpha_n = tan^{-1}\left(\frac{y_T - y_{R_n}}{x_T - x_{R_n}}\right). \tag{21}$$

were x_T and y_T are the coordinates of the transmitter, x_R and y_R are the coordinates of the receiver R and d_{TR} is the distance from the receiver to the transmitter. Finally, d_{TPR} is given by the sum of the lengths of the segments $\overline{TP}$ and $\overline{TR}$ (the total path length), estimated from the propagation time.

The calculation of the propagation time is performed by two steps: 1) by sending a pulse and registering the transient response at the transceiver and at the receivers and 2) by sending a second pulse and subtracting the new obtained registers from the previously recorded set. Of course, it is assumed that the target is in movement; otherwise the data obtained from steps 1) and 2) would be identical. If the pulse is UWB, it is possible to detect the movement of the heart of a human intruder, meaning he would be a detectable target even if he kept perfectly static.

3.2 Particle Swarm Optimization

The particle swarm optimization (PSO) method is a modern heuristic optimization algorithm, based on group movement of animals, such as fishes, birds and insects. The movement of each animal (individual or particle) can be seen as a resultant vector of personal and collective characteristics (vector components).

Proposed in (Kennedy & Eberhart, 1995), this method consists on the optimization of an objective function trough the exchange of information among the particles (individuals), resulting in a non-deterministic, but robust and efficient algorithm, which can be easily implemented computationally.

In an initial moment, all the particles are positioned randomly in the searching space, in which the solution must be. The movement of each particle is the result of a vector sum of three distinct terms: the first contribution is related to the inertia of the particle (a particle's personal component), the second is related to the best position occupied by the particle (a personal component - memory) and the third is relative to the best position found by the group (group contribution – cooperation). Each particle position (a multidimensional vector) corresponds to an alternative solution for the problem (combination of the multidimensional vector). Each alternative solution must be evaluated.

Thus, at a given time step, a particle i changes its position from $\vec{X}_i$ to $\vec{X}_i^{new}$ according to

$$\vec{X}_i^{new} = \vec{X}_i + \vec{\Delta}_{x,i} \quad , \tag{22}$$

in which $\vec{\Delta}_{x,i}$ is the updated position increment for particle i, that is, it is the vector representing the position change for particle i and it is given by

$$\vec{\Delta}_{x,i} = \vec{\Delta}_{x,i}^{old} + U.W_{m,i}(\vec{b}_i - X_i) + U.W_{c,i}(\vec{b}_g - X_i) \tag{23}$$

The heights $W_{m,i}$ (memory) and $W_{c,i}$ (cooperation) are previously defined, U represents independent samples of a random variable uniformly distributed between zero and one, $\vec{b}_i$ is the best solution found by the particle i and $\vec{b}_g$ is the best solution found by the swarm, up to the current interaction.

The initial values for the displacements, i.e. $\vec{\Delta}_{x,i}^{old}$, are randomly chosen among the real values limited by $-\vec{\Delta}_{x}^{\max}$ and $\vec{\Delta}_{x}^{\max}$, in order to avoid large values and the consequent divergence from the solution. It is worth to mention that it is necessary to avoid such large values during the interactions. It was observed that usually the method results in divergence or in low precision due to this tendency. There are, however, some methods for minimize these problems, such as:

1. The employment of a descending function, affecting the inertial term, such as an evanescent exponential function of time;
2. The use of terms for reduction of the velocity at each interaction, known as constriction terms.
3. Simply to limit each velocity component to the interval $[-\vec{\Delta}_{x}^{\max}, \vec{\Delta}_{x}^{\max}]$.

All the methods have been tested, and, although all of them were efficient, the last one was applied here.

3.3 Estimation of the Intruder's Position with PSO

After obtaining the time responses with the FDTD method, the radar theory can be employed. The parameters of the three curves (a circle and two ellipses) are calculated from the differences of the time responses (with and without the intruder), and the obtained system, when solved, deliveries the intruder's position estimation. However, the case where the three curves have a common point (Fig. 5a) does not always happen and the more frequent case is illustrated by Fig. 5b. This way, the objective of the PSO algorithm is to locate the point with the minimal distance from the three curves simultaneously. This defines the objective function, which is mathematically given by

$$F_i = d_iC_{min} + d_iE^1_{min} + d_iE^2_{min}, \tag{24}$$

in which d_iC_{min} is the minimal distance from particle i to the circle and $d_iE^{\kappa}_{min}$ is the minimal distance from particle i to the ellipse κ.
This way, the PSO algorithm acts towards the minimization of the objective function F_i.

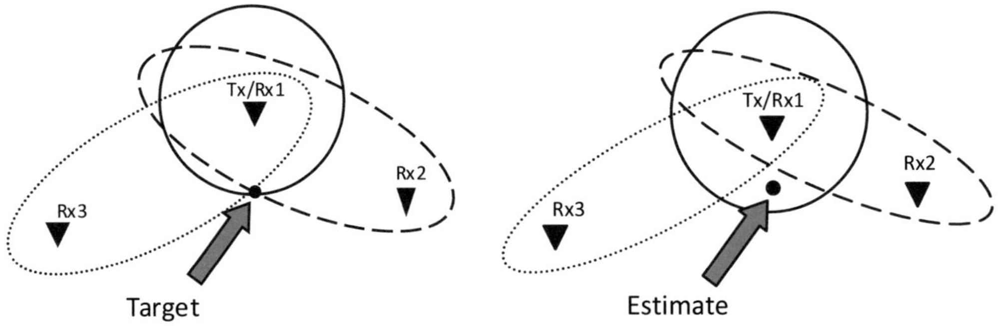

(a) (b)

Figure 5. Ideal radar configuration and (b) real radar configuration and the position estimate (objective of the PSO Locator)

In order to create a more realistic situation, additive Gaussian white noise (AWGN) has been added to the FDTD time responses. A sample of noise $\mathbf{R}(\xi)$ is generated by

$$\mathbf{R}(\xi) = \sigma_a \sqrt{2\ln\left[1/(1-\mathbf{U}(\xi_j))\right]} \cos\left[2\pi\mathbf{U}(\xi_k)\right], \tag{25}$$

in which $\sigma_a = 0.02$ for the present work, and $U(\xi)$ has the same meaning of U in (23).

3.4 Estimation of the numerical velocity for distance calculations.

FDTD Method introduces numerical dispersion and numerical anisotropy for the propagating waves. This means that velocity of propagation is a function of frequency and of the propagation direction (Taflove & Brodwin, 1975.a). Due to this numerical characteristic of the FDTD methodology, it is not appropriate to use the light free space velocity. Besides that, the dielectric walls promote delays on the signals, affecting the average velocity. This way, as detailed in (Muller et al., 2005), and effective velocity was determined experimentally for calculating the ellipses parameters (distances). The idea is to measure the propagating time in multiple points around the source, with and without walls, and take an average of the obtained velocities (Muller et al., 2005).

It is worth to mention that the procedure presented in (Muller et al., 2005) takes automatically into account numerical dispersion and anisotropy and the delays caused by walls. In real applications, obviously only walls' delays must be considered for the correct operation of the radar system.

4. Environment and Parameters of Simulation

In this work, the indoor environment considered for the simulations is shown in Fig. 6. In that building, there are two distinct kinds of walls, characterized by different electrical parameters, which are: the relative electric permittivity of the exterior walls is $\varepsilon_r = 5.0$ and those of the interior walls have $\varepsilon_r = 4.2$. In both of them, the chosen conductivity is $\sigma = 0.02$ S/m. Everywhere else, the relative permittivity is equal to unity, except in the UPML. The thickness of walls are 27 (external) and 12 (internal) centimeters.

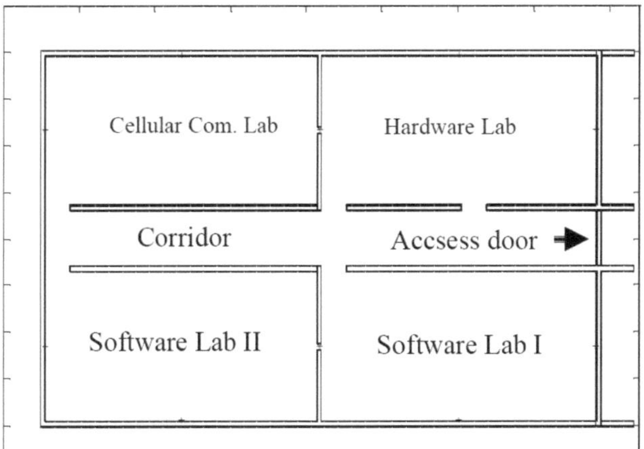

Figure 6. Layout of the building (floor plan)

The simulations are performed using a 2D-FDTD method for nondispersive isotropic media (analysis region), based on Yee's formulation. It is worse to mention that only perpendicular polarization relative to the plan in Fig. 6 is considered in the transmitter antenna. Here, an uniform mesh with 1000×1000 cells was used. The square-shaped cells have 1.5 cm ($\Delta_x = \Delta_y = \Delta_s$) of width, which is equivalent to approximately one-tenth of the free-space wavelength of the excitation pulse in the reference frequency f_o = 2 GHz. The time increment was obtained from the spacial cell dimension , in order to assure the numerical stability of the method. The value used in this paper is given by

$$\Delta t = 0.7\frac{\Delta s}{c\sqrt{2}} \tag{26}$$

where c is the speed of light in vacuum. Equation (26) is the Courant's condition (Taflove & Brodwin, 1975.a).

The absorbing boundaries are very important elements in the FDTD mesh (see section 2). Their purpose is to limit the computational domain and, thus, to simulate propagation in an open environment, with minimum reflection. In order to achieve this, an anisotropic perfectly matched layer-absorbing medium (UPML) based on a lossy uniaxial medium is used. The parameters of the UPML are: Thickness d = 10 cells, maximum attenuation conductivity σ_{max} = 15 S/m, and order of polynomial variation m=4.

The waveform used as an excitation source, in order to scan the environment, is the Gaussian monocycle, shown in Fig. 7.

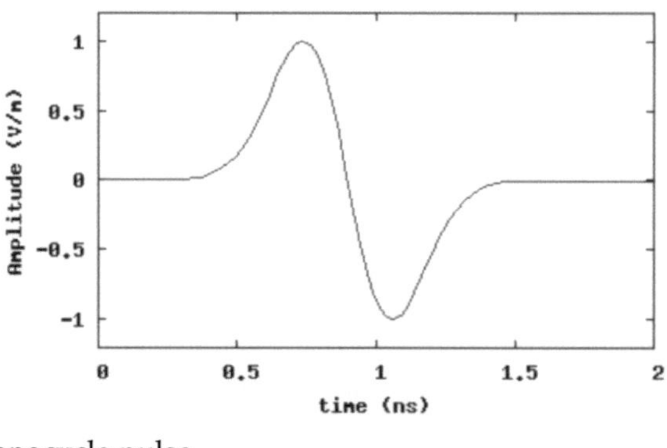

Figure 7. Gaussian monocycle pulse

This is the type of pulse is used, for example, in PulsON system (Petroff & Withington, 2001). It is obtained from the following Gaussian function:

$$g(t) = A_0 Exp\left[\frac{-(t-t_0)^2}{\tau^2}\right] \tag{27}$$

where A_0 is the maximum amplitude of the excitation source, t_0 is the time when the maximum amplitude occurs, and τ is the time-decay constant. The Gaussian monocycle is the first derivative of this function, that is:

$$p(t) = -A_p\sqrt{\frac{2e}{\tau^2}}(t-t_0)exp\left[-\frac{(t-t_0)^2}{\tau^2}\right], \tag{28}$$

Where $e \approx 2.71828$ and A_p is the peak amplitude of the monocycle. A_p and A_0 are related by

$$A_0 = A_p \tau \sqrt{\frac{e}{2}} \tag{29}$$

The Gaussian monocycle is an ultra-wideband signal, with the bandwidth and central frequency dependent on the duration of the monocycle. In the frequency domain, the spectrum obtained from its Fourier transform is given by

$$p(f) = A_p \tau^2 \sqrt{\frac{\pi e}{2}} exp\left[1-(\pi\tau f)^2\right] exp(-j2\pi t_0 f) \tag{30}$$

and the central frequency of the monocycle can be calculated using the following equation:

$$f_0 = \frac{1}{\tau\sqrt{2\pi^2}} \tag{31}$$

The monocycle spectrum is shown by Fig. 8. Observe the significant power is distributed up to the frequency 2 GHz, which is the frequency used for determining Yee's spatial increment Δs .

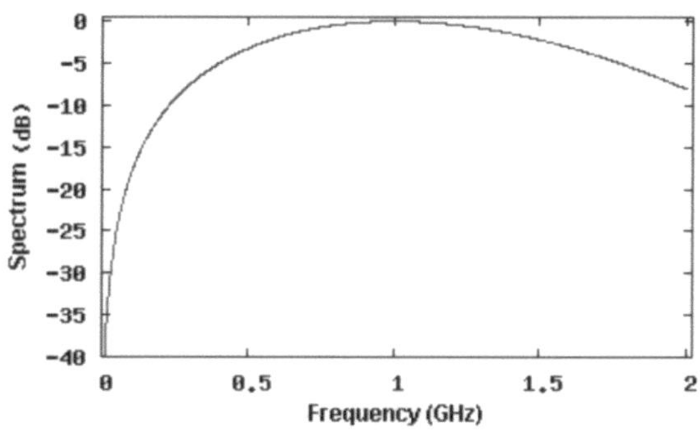

Figure 8. The Gaussian monocycle spectrum

To complete the environment description, the only missing item is the target. It was chosen to be a cylinder with a 0.25 m radius (in fact, only its transversal section is considered, since the mesh has two dimensions), with the aim of representing a human body. The relative permittivity considered is $\varepsilon_r = 50$ and the conductivity $\sigma = 1.43$ *S/m* (Gandhi & Lazzi, 1996).

5. Results

For our numerical simulations, we chose different positions of the target in order to investigate some critical situations in the sense of errors of the position estimation. For computer implementation, we need to choose also some parameters, which have not been specified yet. For PSO, we define the following weights for particles: $W_m = W_c = 10^{-2}$ and the maximum value for the parameter $\vec{\Delta}_{x,i}$ is 10^{-2}. These parameters have been defined empirically. The total number of particles is 100 and the maximum number of PSO iterations is 2000. An unfavorable situation of the target position is shown in Fig. 9. The transceivers are denoted by TRX1 and TRX2. The remote receivers are denoted by RX2,..., RX9. When a transceiver is transmitting, its receiver is denoted by RX1. The transceivers are activated in different time windows in accordance with TDM (time division multiplexing) scheme. The target, in this case, is on the line connecting the two transceivers, and it is situated outside the rooms where the transceivers are mounted.

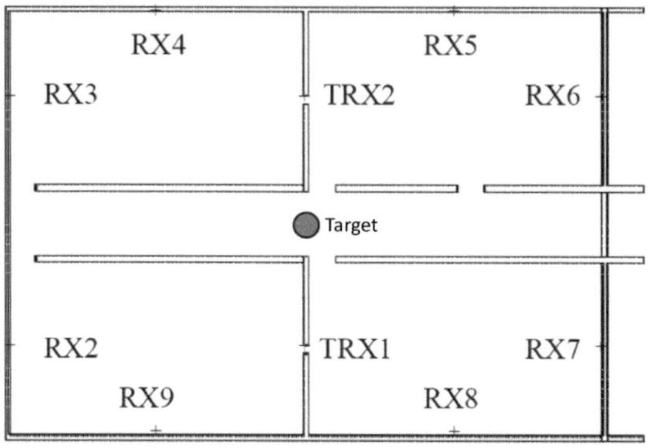

Figure 9. An unfavorable position for the target and the radar elements' positions

The transmitting antennas are initially positioned in small windows in the walls (Fig. 9). Because of the diffraction in these windows, we can expect a larger estimation error as compared to the more favorable configurations. Fig. 10 shows the set ellipses for this case. There is a considerable dispersion of the ellipses. The estimated error for this situation is about 17 cm, but even in this case one can still consider the precision of the target position estimation as rather good. Of course, more favorable conditions generate results with better precision.

In this work, the final estimation of the position is obtained from statistically treating the responses obtained from all the possible combinations of multistatic radars (one transceiver and two receivers). The mean and standard deviation of the estimates are calculated. All the estimative outside the standard deviation, around the mean value, are not considered in the calculation of the final mean, which is the final output of the estimator.

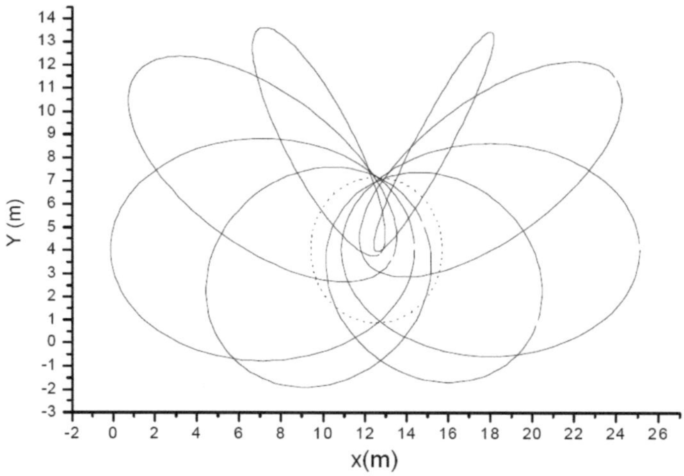

Figure 10. The set of ellipses obtained for locating the target

Fig. 11 shows the convergence of the PSO method for a single multistatic radar (the transceiver and two receivers). It is evident that the algorithm can be employed for solving this kind of problem, as far as the particles clearly move to the correct target's position. Similar behavior was observed in many other experiments.

Fig. 12 shows the transient electric field obtained by receiver 4 (see Fig. 9), in the presence of the target and in its absence. It is clear the perturbation caused in the reference signal by the dielectric cylinder. The perturbation (difference between the signals) is plotted in Fig. 13, from which the temporal information necessary for defining the ellipse with focus in that receiver and in the transceiver (when disturbance's amplitude is different from zero).

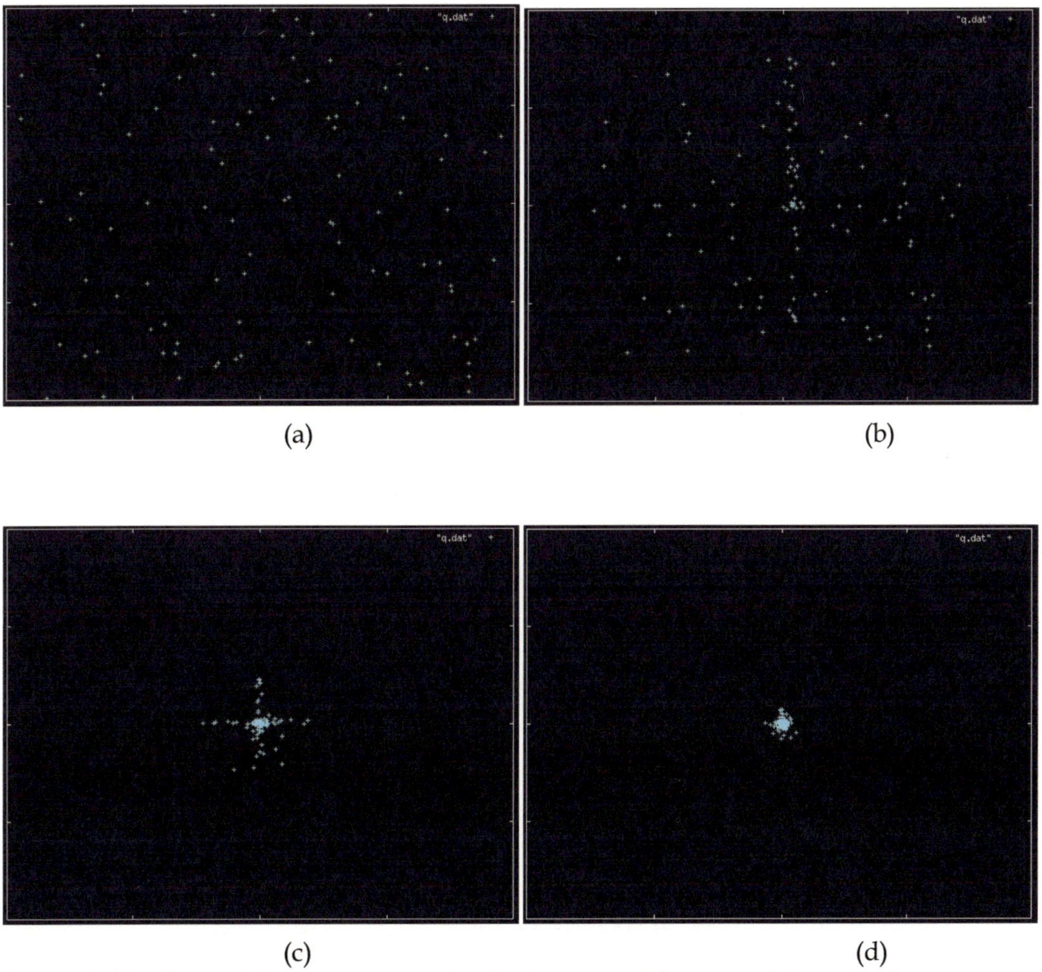

Figure 11. PSO's particles convergence for the location of the target (a) randomly distributed particles; (b) particles' positions after 100 interactions; (c) particles' positions after 500 interactions and (d) particles' positions after 700 interactions

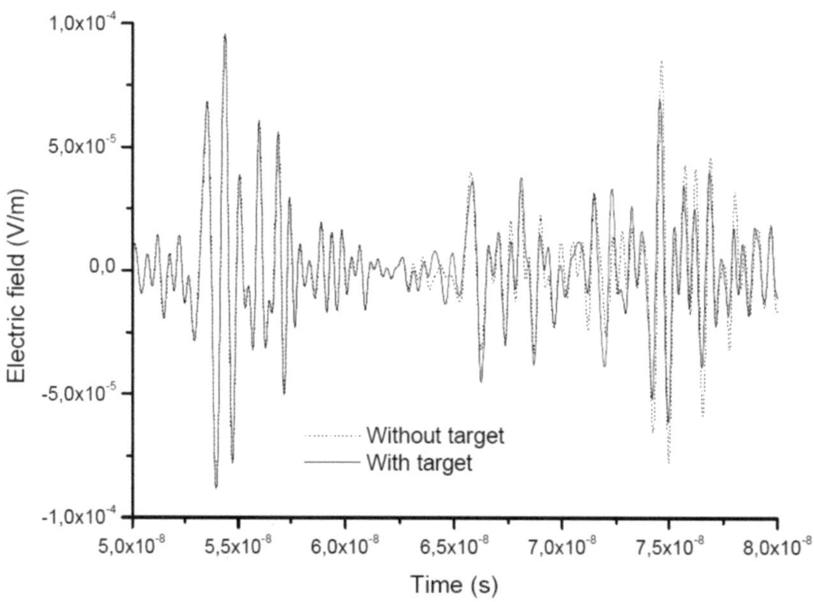

Figure 12. Electric field data obtained by the receiver 4 (with and with no target)

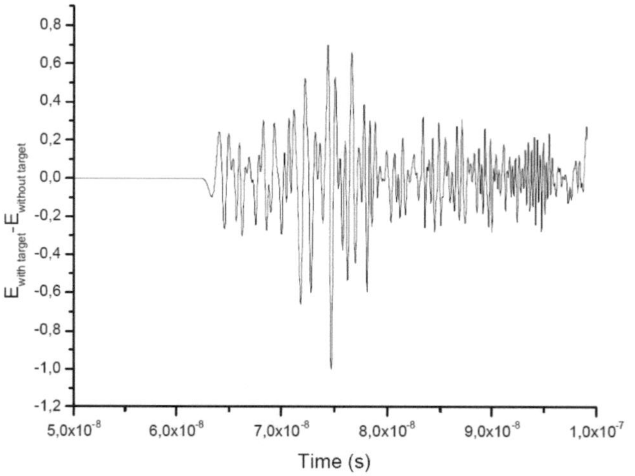

Figure 13. Difference between the signals depicted in Fig. 12 (disturbance caused by the target)

Fig. 14(a) shows the configuration used for executing a second numerical experiment. In this case, the transceivers TRX1 and TRX2, represented by rhombuses, are positioned away from the walls. The receivers (represented by triangles) and the target (square) were positioned exactly as in the previous case (Fig. 9). For the case illustrated by Fig. 15(a), in which it is used only the transceiver TRX1, the PSO estimation is represented by the star (the estimated position was (432.98,410.92)) . The central cell of the target is (460,450) and, this way, the surface of the target was pointed out, as it is clearly shown by Fig. 15(a). Similar behavior was observed for the case illustrated by Fig. 15(b), in which only the transceiver TRX2 is used. It is worth to mention that the identified points of the target's surface is, for each simulation, closer to the correspondent used transceiver. This behavior is expected, as long as reflection is used for determining the propagation time used for calculating the circle's and the ellipses' parameters.

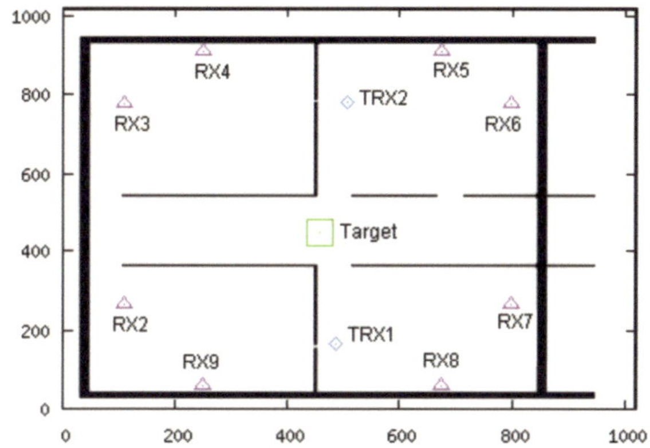

Figure 14. Configuration used for the second experiment (axis represent the Yee's cells indexes)

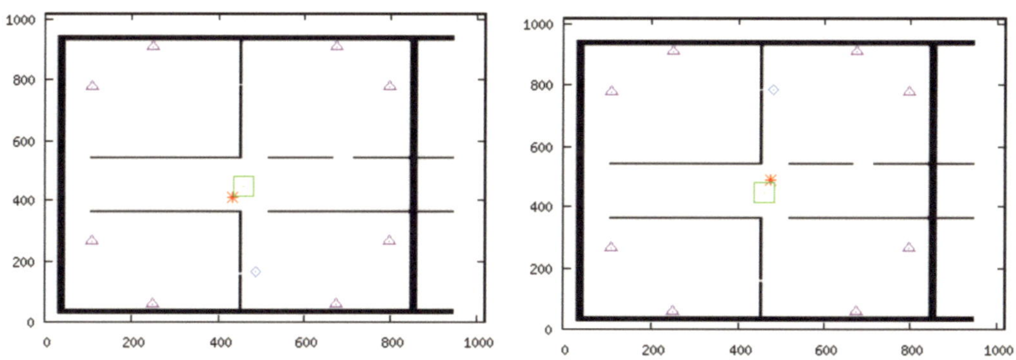

(a) (b)

Figure 15. The PSO estimation for the second experiment (a) result obtained by using TRX1 and (b) result obtained by using TRX2

In order to increase the complexity of the environment, and for testing a more general situation, scatters were introduced in the environment and the situation previously analyzed was used as base for the configuration shown by Fig. 16, which defines the third experiment. Each scatter consists of a dielectric material with electrical conductivity of 0.02 S/m and permittivity of $5.\varepsilon_0$. The diameters of the dielectric scatters are around 18 centimeters. Such scatters create a chaotic electromagnetic environment, generating multiple reflections, refractions and delays on the propagation of the wave. As far as difference of electromagnetic transients are considered for calculating the propagation periods, such effects are suppressed and the obtained results are very similar to the previous experiment responses, as shown by Figs. 16(a) and 16(b).

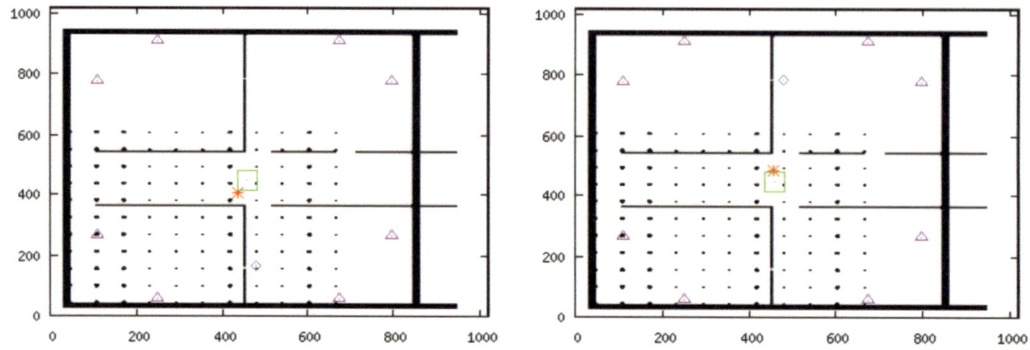

(a) (b)

Figure 16. The PSO estimation for the third experiment (with dielectric scatters) (a) result obtained by using TRX1 and (b) result obtained by using TRX2

6. Final Remarks

We have presented in this work some results of numerical simulations of a radar array based on UWB pulses. The registers of the electric field have been obtained numerically using the FDTD method. In order to define the localization curves we have used the concept of optic rays. The solutions of the system of the nonlinear equations (which usually does not exist) defined for every combination of a transceiver and 2 remote receivers give an estimation of the target position. The solution, in those cases, are defined by determining the closest point in the space to the circle and for the two ellipses, for a single multistatic radar. The final estimation for the array of two transceivers and eight receivers is fulfilled by PSO method. We have shown that PSO is a useful tool for this type of problem. The proposed methodology seems to be robust, as long as the presence of dielectric scatters, which promotes a complex (chaotic) electromagnetic environment, does not substantially affects the performance of the position estimator.

7. Acknowledgements

Authors would like to acknowledge the support provided by Federal University of Pará (UFPA), for all infrastructure provided.

8. References

Bayliss, A. & Turkel, E. (1980). Radiation Boundary Conditions for wave-like equation, *Comm. Pure Appl. Math.*, vol. 23, pp. 707-725

Berenger, J. (1994). A perfectly matched layer for the absorption of electromagnetic waves, *J. Computational Physics*, vol. 114, pp. 185-200

Fornberg, P.E.; Byers, A.; Piket-May, M. & Holloway, C.L.(2000). FDTD modeling of printed circuit board signal integrity and radiation, *IEEE International Symposium on Electromagnetic Compatibility*

Gandhi, O. P.; Lazzi G. & Furse, C. M (1996). *Electromagnetic absorption in the human head and neck for mobile telephones at 835 and 1900 MHz,* IEEE Trans. Microwave Theory and Tech., vol. MTT-44, No. 10.

Goorjian, P.M. & Taflove, A. (1992). Direct time integration of Maxwell's equation in nonlinear dispersive media for propagation and scattering of femtosecond electromagnetic solitons, *Optics Lett.*, vol. 17, pp. 180-182.

Liao , Z.; Wong, H.; Yang, B.P. & Yuan, Y.F. (1984). A Transmitting boundary for transient wave analysis, *Scientia Sinica*, vol. XXVII (series A), pp. 1063-1076

Maloney, J.G. & Kesler, M.P. (1998). Analysis of periodic structures. *Advances in Computational Electrodynamics*, A. Taflove, Artech House, 1998.

Manteuffell, D. & Simon W., FDTD calculation of the SAR induced in the human head by mobile phones: new standards and procedures for the numerical assessment, *IWAT 2005 (IEEE International Workshop on Antenna Technology)*, pp. 137-140.

Muller, F.C.B.F.; Farias, R.G.; Sobrinho, C.L.S.S. & Dmitriev, V. (2005). Multistatic radar with ultra wideband pulses: FDTD simulation, *International Microwave and Optoelectronic Conference*, Brasilia (Brazil)

Mur, G. (1981). Absorbing boundary conditions for the finite-difference approximation of the time-domain electromagnetic field equation, *IEEE Trans. Electromagnetic Compatibility*, vol. 23, pp. 377-382

Petroff,A. & Withington, P. (2001). PulsOn technology overview, 2001, *http://w.w.w.timedomain.com/ files/downloads/techpapers/PulsONOverview7_01.pdf.*

Ridon, R. (1987). Numerical absorbing boundary conditions for the wave equations, *Mathematics of computation*, vol. 49, pp. 65-90

Sacks, Z.; Kingsland, D.; Lee R. & Lee, J. (1995). A perfectly matched anisotropic absorber for use as an absorbing boundary condition, *IEEE Trans. Antennas and Propagation*, vol. 43, pp. 1460-1463

Taflove A. & Brodwin, M.E. (1975.a). Computation of the electromagnetic fields and induced temperatures within a model of the microwave-irradiated human eye, *IEEE Transaction on Microwave Theory Tech.*, vol. 23, pp. 888-896

Taflove, A & Hagness, S.C. (2005). *Computational Electromagnetics, The Finite-Difference Time-Domain Method*, 3rd ed., Artech House Inc..

Taflove A. & Brodwin, M.E. (1975.b). Numerical solution of steady-state electromagnetic scattering problems using the time-dependent Maxwell's equations, *IEEE Transaction on Microwave Theory Tech.*, vol. 23, pp. 623-630

Tanabe, K.(2001). Novel method for analyzing the transient behavior of grounding systems based on the finite-difference time-domain method, *Power Engineering Review*, vol. 21, no. 9, pp. 1128-1132

Kennedy, J. & Eberhart, R. C., Particle swarm optimization, *IEEE International Conference on Neural Networks (ICNN)*, Vol. IV, pp.1942-1948, Perth, Australia.

Kondylis, G.; DeFlaviis F. & Pottie, G. (1999). Indoor channel characterization for wireless communications using reduced finite difference time domain (R-FDTD), *IEEE VTC Fall 99*, Amsterdam.

Yee, k. (1996). Numerical solution of initial boundary value problems involving Maxwell's equations in isotropic media, *IEEE Trans. Antennas and Propagation*, vol. 14, pp. 302-307

Zhang X.; Fang, J.; Mei, K.K. & Liu, Y. (1988). Calculation of dispersive characteristics of microstrips by the Time-Domain Finite-Difference method, *IEEE Transaction on Microwave Theory Tech.*, vol. 36, pp. 263-267

Federal University of Pará
Electrical Engineering, CEP: 68455-700, Tucuruí, Pará, Brazil
Computer Engineering, CEP: 66075-900, Belém, Pará, Brazil
rmso@ufpa.br, leonidas@ufpa.br, josivaldo@lane.ufpa.br, rgfarias@ufpa.br

12

Application of Particle Swarm Optimization in Accurate Segmentation of Brain MR Images

Nosratallah Forghani[1], Mohamad Forouzanfar[1,2], Armin Eftekhari[1], Shahab Mohammad-Moradi[1] and Mohammad Teshnehlab[1]
[1]*K.N. Toosi University of Technology*, [2]*University of Tehran*
[1,2]*Iran*

1. Introduction

Medical imaging refers to the techniques and processes used to obtain images of the human body for clinical purposes or medical science. Common medical imaging modalities include ultrasound (US), computerized tomography (CT), and magnetic resonance imaging (MRI). Medical imaging analysis is usually applied in one of two capacities: i) to gain scientific knowledge of diseases and their effect on anatomical structure in vivo, and ii) as a component for diagnostics and treatment planning (Kannan, 2008).

Medical US uses high frequency broadband sound waves that are reflected by tissue to varying degrees to produce 2D or 3D images. This is often used to visualize the fetus in pregnant women. Other important uses include imaging the abdominal organs, heart, male genitalia, and the veins of the leg. US has several advantages which make it ideal in numerous situations. It studies the function of moving structures in real-time, emits no ionizing radiation, and contains speckle that can be used in elastography. It is very safe to use and does not appear to cause any adverse effects. It is also relatively cheap and quick to perform. US scanners can be taken to critically ill patients in intensive care units, avoiding the danger caused while moving the patient to the radiology department. The real time moving image obtained can be used to guide drainage and biopsy procedures. Doppler capabilities on modern scanners allow the blood flow in arteries and veins to be assessed. However, US images provides less anatomical detail than CT and MRI (Macovski, 1983).

CT is a medical imaging method employing tomography (Slone et al., 1999). Digital geometry processing is used to generate a three-dimensional image of the inside of an object from a large series of two-dimensional X-ray images taken around a single axis of rotation. CT produces a volume of data which can be manipulated, through a process known as windowing, in order to demonstrate various structures based on their ability to block the X-ray beam. Although historically the images generated were in the axial or transverse plane (orthogonal to the long axis of the body), modern scanners allow this volume of data to be reformatted in various planes or even as volumetric (3D) representations of structures. CT was the first imaging modality to provide in vivo evidence of gross brain morphological abnormalities in schizophrenia, with many CT reports of increase in cerebrospinal fluid (CSF)-filled spaces, both centrally (ventricles), and peripherally (sulci) in a variety of psychiatric patients.

MRI is a technique that uses a magnetic field and radio waves to create cross-sectional images of organs, soft tissues, bone and virtually all other internal body structures. MRI is based on the phenomenon of nuclear magnetic resonance (NMR). Nuclei with an odd number of nucleons, exposed to a uniform static magnetic field, can be excited with a radio frequency (RF) pulse with the proper frequency and energy. After the excitation pulse, NMR signal can be recorded. The return to equilibrium is characterized by relaxation times T1 and T2, which depend on the nuclei imaged and on the molecular environment. Mainly hydrogen nuclei (proton) are imaged in clinical applications of MRI, because they are most NMR-sensitive nuclei (Haacke et al., 1999). MRI possesses good contrast resolution for different tissues and has advantages over computerized tomography (CT) for brain studies due to its superior contrast properties. In this context, brain MRI segmentation is becoming an increasingly important image processing step in many applications including: i) automatic or semiautomatic delineation of areas to be treated prior to radiosurgery, ii) delineation of tumours before and after surgical or radiosurgical intervention for response assessment, and iii) tissue classification (Bondareff et al., 1990).

Several techniques have been developed for brain MR image segmentation, most notably thresholding (Suzuki & Toriwaki, 1991), edge detection (Canny, 1986), region growing (Pohle & Toennies, 2001), and clustering (Dubes & Jain, 1988). Thresholding is the simplest segmentation method, where the classification of each pixel depends on its own information such as intensity and colour. Thresholding methods are efficient when the histograms of objects and background are clearly separated. Since the distribution of tissue intensities in brain MR images is often very complex, these methods fail to achieve acceptable segmentation results. Edge-based segmentation methods are based on detection of boundaries in the image. These techniques suffer from incorrect detection of boundaries due to noise, over- and under-segmentation, and variability in threshold selection in the edge image. These drawbacks of early image segmentation methods, has led to region growing algorithms. Region growing extends thresholding by combining it with connectivity conditions or region homogeneity criteria. However, only well defined regions can be robustly identified by region growing algorithms (Clarke et al., 1995).

Since the above mentioned methods are generally limited to relatively simple structures, clustering methods are utilized for complex pathology. Clustering is a method of grouping data with similar characteristics into larger units of analysis. Expectation–maximization (EM) (Wells et al., 1996), hard c-means (HCM) and its fuzzy equivalent, fuzzy c-means (FCM) algorithms (Li et al., 1993) are the typical methods of clustering. A common disadvantage of EM algorithms is that the intensity distribution of brain images is modeled as a normal distribution, which is untrue, especially for noisy images. Since Zadeh (1965) first introduced fuzzy set theory which gave rise to the concept of partial membership, fuzziness has received increasing attention. Fuzzy clustering algorithms have been widely studied and applied in various areas. Among fuzzy clustering techniques, FCM is the best known and most powerful method used in image segmentation. Unfortunately, the greatest shortcoming of FCM is its over-sensitivity to noise, which is also a drawback of many other intensity-based segmentation methods. Since medical images contain significant amount of noise caused by operator, equipment, and the environment, there is an essential need for development of less noise-sensitive algorithms.

Many extensions of the FCM algorithm have been reported in the literature to overcome the effects of noise, such as noisy clustering (NC) (Dave, 1991), possibilistic c-means (PCM)

(Krishnapuram & Keller, 1993), robust fuzzy c-means algorithm (RFCM) (Pham, 2001), bias-corrected FCM (BCFCM) (Ahmed et al., 2002), spatially constrained kernelized FCM (SKFCM) (Zhang & Chen, 2004), and so on. These methods generally modify most equations along with modification of the objective function. Therefore, they lose the continuity from FCM, which inevitably introduce computation issues.

Recently, Shen et al. (2005) introduced a new extension of FCM algorithm, called improved FCM (IFCM). They introduced two influential factors in segmentation that address the neighbourhood attraction. The first parameter is the feature difference between neighbouring pixels in the image and the second one is the relative location of the neighbouring pixels. Therefore, segmentation is decided not only by the pixel's intensity but also by neighbouring pixel's intensities and their locations. However, the problem of determining optimum parameters constitutes an important part of implementing the IFCM algorithm for real applications. The implementation performance of IFCM may be significantly degraded if the attraction parameters are not properly selected. It is therefore important to select suitable parameters such that the IFCM algorithm achieves superior partition performance compared to the FCM. In (Shen et al., 2005), an artificial neural network (ANN) was employed for computation of these two parameters. However, designing the neural network architecture and setting its parameters are always complicated which slow down the algorithm and may also lead to inappropriate attraction parameters and consequently degrade the partitioning performance (Haykin, 1998).

In this paper we investigate the potential of genetic algorithms (GAs) and particle swarm optimization (PSO) to determine the optimum values of the neighborhood attraction parameters. We will show both GAs and PSO are superior to ANN in segmentation of noisy MR images; however, PSO obtains the best results. The achieved improvements are validated both quantitatively and qualitatively on simulated and real brain MR images at different noise levels.

This paper is organized as follows. In Section 2, common clustering algorithms, including EM, FCM, and different extensions of FCM, are introduced. Section 3 presents new parameter optimization methods based on GAs and PSO for determination of optimum degree of attraction in IFCM algorithm. Section 4 is dedicated to a comprehensive comparison of the proposed segmentation algorithms based on GAs and PSO with related recent techniques. The paper in concluded in Section 5 with some remarks.

2. Clustering Algorithms

According to the limitation of conventional segmentation methods such as thresholding, edge detection, and region growing, clustering methods are utilized for complex pathology. Clustering is an unsupervised classification of data samples with similar characteristics into larger units of analysis (clusters). While classifiers are trained on pre-labeled data and tested on unlabeled data, clustering algorithms take as input a set of unlabeled samples and organize them into clusters based on similarity criteria. The algorithm alternates between dividing the data into clusters and learning the characteristics of each cluster using the current division. In image segmentation, a clustering algorithm iteratively computes the characteristics of each cluster (e.g. mean, standard deviation) and segments the image by classifying each pixel in the closest cluster according to a distance metric. The algorithm alternates between the two steps until convergence is achieved or a maximum number of iterations is reached (Lauric & Frisken, 2007). In this Section, typical methods of clustering including EM algorithm, FCM algorithm, and extensions of FCM are described.

2.1 EM Algorithm

The EM algorithm is an estimation method used in statistics for finding maximum likelihood estimates of parameters in probabilistic models, where the model depends on unobserved latent variables (Wells et al., 1994). In image segmentation, the observed data are the feature vectors x_j associated with pixels j, while the hidden variables are the expectations E_{ji} for each pixel j that it belongs to each of the given clusters i.
The algorithm starts with an initial guess at the model parameters of the clusters and then re-estimates the expectations for each pixel in an iterative manner. Each iteration consists of two steps: the expectation (E) step and the maximization (M) step. In the E-step, the probability distribution of each hidden variable is computed from the observed values and the current estimate of the model parameters (e.g. mean, covariance). In the M-step, the model parameters are re-estimated assuming the probability distributions computed in the E-step are correct. The parameters found in the M step are then used to begin another E step, and the process is repeated.
Assuming Gaussian distributions for all clusters, the hidden variables are the expectations E_{ji} that pixel j belongs to cluster i. The model parameters to estimate are the mean, the covariance and the mixing weight corresponding to each cluster. The mixing weight is a measure of a cluster's strength, representing how prevalent the cluster is in the data. The E and M step of the EM algorithm are as follows.
E-step:

$$E_{ji}^{t} = P(i|x_j, \theta_i^t) = \frac{P(x_j|i, \theta_i^t)\, \pi_i^t}{\sum_{k=1}^{c} P(x_j|k, \theta_k^t)\, \pi_k^t} \tag{1}$$

M-step:

$$\pi_i^{t+1} = \frac{1}{n}\sum_{j=1}^{n} E_{ji}^{t} \tag{2}$$

$$v_i^{t+1} = \frac{1}{n\pi_i^{t+1}}\sum_{j=1}^{n} E_{ji}^{t} x_j \tag{3}$$

$$\Sigma_i^{t+1} = \frac{1}{n\pi_i^{t+1}}\sum_{j=1}^{n} E_{ji}^{t}(x_j - v_i^{t+1})(x_j - v_i^{t+1})^T \tag{4}$$

where θ_i^t are the model parameters of class i at time t and π_i^t is the mixing weight of class i at time t. Note that $\sum_{i=1}^{c} \pi_i^t = 1, \forall t$. $P(i|x_j)$ is the a posteriori conditional probability that pixel j is a member of class i, given its feature vector x_j. $P(i|x_j)$ gives the membership value of pixel j to class i, where i takes values between 1 and c (the number of classes), while j takes values between 1 and n (the number of pixels in the image). Note that $\sum_{k=1}^{c} P(k|x_j) = 1$. $P(x_j|i)$ is the conditional density distribution, i.e., the probability that pixel j has feature vector x_j given that it belongs to class i. If the feature vectors of class i have a Gaussian distribution, the conditional density function has the form:

$$P(x_j|i) = \frac{1}{(2\pi)^{\frac{D}{2}} det^{\frac{1}{2}}(\Sigma_i)} e^{-\frac{1}{2}(x_j-v_i)^T \Sigma_i (x_j-v_i)} \quad (5)$$

where v_i and Σ_i are the mean feature vector and the covariance matrix of class i. The mean and the covariance of each class are estimated from training data. D is the dimension of the feature vector. The prior probability of class i is:

$$P(i) = \frac{|w_i|}{\sum_{k=1}^{c}|w_k|} \quad (6)$$

where $|w_i|$ is a measure of the frequency of occurrence of class i and $\sum_{k=1}^{c}|w_k|$ is a measure of the total occurrence of all classes. In image segmentation, $|w_i|$ is usually set to the number of pixels which belong to class i in the training data, and $\sum_{k=1}^{c}|w_k|$ to the total number of pixels in the training data.

The algorithm iterates between the two steps until the log likelihood increases by less than some threshold or a maximum number of iterations is reached. EM algorithm can be summarized as follows (Lauric & Frisken, 2007):

1. Initialize the means v_i^0, the covariance matrices Σ_i^0 and the mixing weights π_i^0. Typically, the means are initialized to random values, the covariance matrices to the identity matrix and the mixing weights to $1/c$.
2. E-step: Estimate E_{ji} for each pixel j and class i, using (1).
3. M-step: Estimate the model parameters for class i, using (2)-(4).
4. Stop if convergence condition $\left(\log\prod_{j=1}^{n} E_{ji}^{t+1} - \log\prod_{j=1}^{n} E_{ji}^{t}\right) \leq \epsilon$ is achieved. Otherwise, repeat steps 2 to 4.

A common disadvantage of EM algorithms is that the intensity distribution of brain images is modeled as a normal distribution, which is untrue, especially for noisy images.

2.2 FCM Algorithm

Let $X = \{x_1, \dots, x_n\}$ be a data set and let c be a positive integer greater than one. A partition of X into c clusters is represented by mutually disjoint sets $X_1, \dots, X_c$ such that $X_1 \cup \dots \cup X_c = X$ or equivalently by indicator function $\mu_1, \dots, \mu_c$ such that $\mu_i(x) = 1$ if x is in X_i and $\mu_i(x) = 0$ if x is not in X_i, for all $i = 1, \dots, c$. This is known as clustering X into c clusters $X_1, \dots, X_c$ by hard c-partition $\{\mu_1, \dots, \mu_c\}$. A fuzzy extension allows $\mu_i(x)$ taking values in the interval $[0, 1]$ such that $\sum_{i=1}^{c}\mu_i(x) = 1$ for all x in X. In this case, $\{\mu_1, \dots, \mu_c\}$ is called a fuzzy c-partition of X. Thus, the FCM objective function J_{FCM} is defined as (Bezdek, 1981):

$$J_{FCM}(\mu, v) = \sum_{i=1}^{c}\sum_{j=1}^{n} \mu_{ij}^m d^2(x_j, v_i) \quad (7)$$

where $\mu = \{\mu_1, \dots, \mu_c\}$ is a fuzzy c-partition with $\mu_{ij} = \mu_i(x_j)$, the weighted exponent m is a fixed number greater than one establishing the degree of fuzziness, $v = \{v_1, \dots, v_c\}$ is the c cluster centers, and $d^2(x_j, v_i) = \|x_j - v_i\|^2$ represents the Euclidean distance or its generalization such as the Mahalanobis distance. The FCM algorithm is an iteration through the necessary conditions for minimizing J_{FCM} with the following update equations:

$$v_i = \frac{\sum_{j=1}^{n} \mu_{ij}^m x_j}{\sum_{j=1}^{n} \mu_{ij}^m} \qquad (i = 1, \ldots, c) \tag{8}$$

and

$$\mu_{ij} = \frac{1}{\sum_{k=1}^{c} \left(\frac{d(x_j, v_i)}{d(x_j, v_k)} \right)^{2/(m-1)}} \tag{9}$$

The FCM algorithm iteratively optimizes $J_{FCM}(\mu, v)$ with the continuous update of μ and v, until $|\mu^{(l+1)} - \mu^l| \leq \varepsilon$, where l is the number of iterations.
From (7), it is clear that the objective function of FCM does not take into consideration any spatial dependence among X and deals with each image pixel as a separate point. Also, the membership function in (9) is mostly decided by $d^2(x_j, v_i)$, which measures the similarity between the pixel intensity and the cluster center. Higher membership depends on closer intensity values to the cluster center. It therefore increases the sensitivity of the membership function to noise. If an MR image contains noise or is affected by artifacts, their presence can change the pixel intensities, which will result in an incorrect membership and improper segmentation.
There are several approaches to reduce sensitivity of FCM algorithm to noise. The most direct way is the use of low pass filters in order to smooth the image and then applying the FCM algorithm. However low pass filtering, may lead to lose some important details. Different extensions of FCM algorithm were proposed by researchers in order to solve sensitivity to noise. In the following Subsections we will introduce some of these extensions.

2.2.1 NC algorithm

The most popular approach for increasing the robustness of FCM to noise is to modify the objective function directly. Dáve (1991) proposed the idea of a noise cluster to deal with noisy clustering data in the approach known as NC. Noise is effectively clustered into a separate cluster which is unique from signal clusters. However, it is not suitable for image segmentation, since noisy pixels should not be separated from other pixels, but assigned to the most appropriate clusters in order to reduce the effect of noise.

2.2.2 PCM algorithm

Another similar method, developed by Krishnapuram and Keller (1993), is called PCM, which interprets clustering as a possibilistic partition. Instead of having one term in the objective function, a second term is included, forcing the membership to be as high as possible without a maximum limit constraint of one. However, it caused clustering being stuck in one or two clusters. The objective function of PCM is defined as follows:

$$J_{PCM}(\mu, v) = \sum_{i=1}^{c} \sum_{j=1}^{n} \mu_{ij}^m d^2(x_j, v_i) + \sum_{i=1}^{c} \eta_i \sum_{j=1}^{n} (1 - \mu_{ij})^m \tag{10}$$

where η_i are suitable positive numbers. The first term demands that the distances from the feature vectors to the prototypes be as low as possible, whereas the second term forces the μ_{ij} to be as large as possible, thus avoiding the trivial solution.

2.2.3 RFCM algorithm

Pham presented a new approach of FCM, named the robust RFCM (Pham, 2001). A modified objective function was proposed for incorporating spatial context into FCM. A parameter controls the tradeoff between the conventional FCM objective function and the smooth membership functions. However, the modification of the objective function results in the complex variation of the membership function. The objective function of RFCM is defined as follows:

$$J_{RFCM}(\mu, v) = \sum_{j\in\Omega}\sum_{i=1}^{c} \mu_{ij}^{m} d^2(x_j, v_i) + \frac{\beta}{2}\sum_{j\in\Omega}\sum_{i=1}^{c} \mu_{ij}^{m} \sum_{r\in N_j}\sum_{s\in M_i} \mu_{rs}^{m} \tag{11}$$

where N_j is the set of neighbors of pixel j in Ω, and $M_i = \{1, \dots, c\}\backslash\{i\}$. The parameter β controls the trade-off between minimizing the standard FCM objective function and obtaining smooth membership functions.

2.2.4 BCFCM algorithm

Another improved version of FCM by the modification of the objective function was introduced by Ahmed et al. (2002). They proposed a modification of the objective function by introducing a term that allows the labeling of a pixel to be influenced by the labels in its immediate neighborhood. The neighborhood effect acts as a regularizer and biases the solution toward piecewise-homogeneous labeling. Such regularization is useful in segmenting scans corrupted by salt and pepper noise. The modified objective function is given by:

$$J_{PCM}(\mu, v) = \sum_{i=1}^{c}\sum_{j=1}^{n} \mu_{ij}^{m} d^2(x_j, v_i) + \frac{\alpha}{N_R}\sum_{i=1}^{c}\sum_{j=1}^{n} \mu_{ij}^{m}\left(\sum_{x_r\in N_j} d^2(x_r, v_i)\right) \tag{12}$$

where N_j stands for the set of neighbors that exist in a window around x_j and N_R is the cardinality of N_j. The effect of the neighbors term is controlled by the parameter α. The relative importance of the regularizing term is inversely proportional to the signal-to-noise ratio (SNR) of the MRI signal. Lower SNR would require a higher value of the parameter α.

2.2.5 SKFCM algorithm

The SKFCM uses a different penalty term containing spatial neighborhood information in the objective function, and simultaneously the similarity measurement in the FCM, is replaced by a kernel-induced distance (Zhang & Chen, 2004). We know every algorithm that only uses inner products can implicitly be executed in the feature space F. This trick can also be used in clustering, as shown in support vector clustering (Hur et al., 2001) and kernel FCM (KFCM) algorithms (Girolami, 2002; Zhang & Chen, 2002). A common ground of these algorithms is to represent the clustering center as a linearly-combined sum of all $\emptyset(x_j)$, i.e. the clustering centers lie in feature space. The KFCM objective function is as follows:

$$J_{KFCM}(\mu, v) = \sum_{i=1}^{c}\sum_{j=1}^{n} \mu_{ij}^{m} d^2\left(\emptyset(x_j), \emptyset(v_i)\right) \tag{13}$$

where $\emptyset$ is an implicit nonlinear map. Same as BCFCM, the KFCM-based methods inevitably introduce computation issues, by modifying most equations along with the modification of the objective function, and have to lose the continuity from FCM, which is well-realized with many types of software, such as MATLAB.

2.2.6 IFCM algorithm

To overcome these drawbacks, Shen et al. (2005) presented an improved algorithm. They found that the similarity function $d^2(x_j, v_i)$ is the key to segmentation success. In their approach, an attraction entitled neighborhood attraction is considered to exist between neighboring pixels. During clustering, each pixel attempts to attract its neighboring pixels toward its own cluster. This neighborhood attraction depends on two factors; the pixel intensities or feature attraction λ, and the spatial position of the neighbors or distance attraction ξ , which also depends on the neighborhood structure. Considering this neighborhood attraction, they defined the similarity function as below:

$$d^2(x_j, v_i) = \|x_j - v_i\|^2(1 - \lambda H_{ij} - \xi F_{ij}) \tag{14}$$

where H_{ij} represents the feature attraction and F_{ij} represents the distance attraction. Magnitudes of two parameters λ and ζ are between 0 and 1; adjust the degree of the two neighborhood attractions. H_{ij} and F_{ij} are computed in a neighborhood containing S pixels as follow:

$$H_{ij} = \frac{\sum_{k=1}^{S} \mu_{jk} g_{jk}}{\sum_{k=1}^{S} \mu_{jk}} \tag{15}$$

$$F_{ij} = \frac{\sum_{k=1}^{S} \mu_{ik}^2 q_{jk}^2}{\sum_{k=1}^{S} \mu_{ik}^2} \tag{16}$$

with

$$g_{jk} = |x_j - x_k|, \quad q_{jk} = (a_j - a_k)^2 + (b_j - b_k)^2 \tag{17}$$

where $(a_j,\ b_j)$ and $(a_k,\ b_k)$ denote the coordinate of pixel j and k, respectively. It should be noted that a higher value of λ leads to stronger feature attraction and a higher value of ξ leads to stronger distance attraction. Optimized values of these parameters enable the best segmentation results to be achieved. However, inappropriate values can be detrimental. Therefore, parameter optimization is an important issue in IFCM algorithm that can significantly affect the segmentation results.

3. Parameter Optimization of IFCM Algorithm

Optimization algorithms are search methods, where the goal is to find a solution to an optimization problem, such that a given quantity is optimized, possibly subject to a set of constrains. Although this definition is simple, it hides a number of complex issues. For example, the solution may consist of a combination of different data types, nonlinear constrains may restrict the search area, the search space can be convoluted with many candidate solutions, the characteristics of the problem may change over time, or the quantity being optimized may have conflicting objectives (Engelbrecht, 2006).

As mentioned earlier, the problem of determining optimum attraction parameters constitutes an important part of implementing the IFCM algorithm. Shen et al. (2005) computed these two parameters using an ANN through an optimization problem. However, designing the neural network architecture and setting its parameters are always complicated tasks which slow down the algorithm and may lead to inappropriate attraction parameters and consequently degrade the partitioning performance. In this Section we introduce two new algorithms, namely GAs and PSO, for optimum determination of the attraction parameters. The performance evaluation of the proposed algorithms is carried out in the next Section.

3.1. Structure of GAs

Like neural networks, GAs are based on a biological metaphor, however, instead of the biological brain, GAs view learning in terms of competition among a population of evolving candidate problem solutions. GAs were first introduced by Holland (1992) and have been widely successful in optimization problems. Algorithm is started with a set of solutions (represented by chromosomes) called population. Solutions from one population are taken and used to form a new population. This is motivated by a hope, that the new population will be better than the old one. Solutions which are selected to form new solutions (offspring) are selected according to their fitness; the more suitable they are the more chances they have to reproduce. This is repeated until some condition is satisfied. The GAs can be outlined as follows.

1. [Start] Generate random population of *P* chromosomes (suitable solutions for the problem).
2. [Fitness] Evaluate the fitness of each chromosome in the population with respect to the cost function J.
3. [New population] Create a new population by repeating following steps until the new population is complete:
   a. [Selection] Select two parent chromosomes from a population according to their fitness (the better fitness, the bigger chance to be selected).
   b. [Crossover] With a crossover probability, cross over the parents to form a new offspring (children). If no crossover was performed, offspring is an exact copy of parents.
   c. [Mutation] With a mutation probability, mutate new offspring at each locus (position in chromosome).
   d. [Accepting] Place new offspring in a new population.
4. [Loop] Go to step 2 until convergence.

For selection stage a roulette wheel approach is adopted. Construction of roulette wheel is as follows (Mitchel, 1999):

1. Arrange the chromosomes according to their fitness.
2. Compute summations of all fitness values and calculate the total fitness.
3. Divide each fitness value to total fitness and compute the selection probability (p_k) for each chromosome.

4. Calculate cumulative probability (P_k) for each chromosome.

In selection process, roulette wheel spins equal to the number population size. Each time a single chromosome is selected for a new population in the following manner (Gen & Cheng, 1997):

1. Generate a random number r from the rang $[0,\ 1]$.
2. If $r \leq P_1$, then select the first chromosome, otherwise select the k-th chromosome such that $q_{k-1} < r < q_k$.

The mentioned algorithm is iterated until a certain criterion is met. At this point, the most fitted chromosome represents the corresponding optimum values. The specific parameters of the introduced structure are described in Section 4.

3.2. Structure of PSO

Team formation has been observed in many animal species. For some animal species, teams or groups are controlled by a leader, for example a pride of lions, a troop of baboon, and a troop of wild buck. In these societies the behavior of individuals is strongly dictated by social hierarchy. More interesting is the self-organizing behavior of species living in groups where no leader can be identified, for example, a flock of birds, a school of fish, or a herd of sheep. Within these social groups, individuals have no knowledge of the global behavior of the entire group, nor they have any global information about the environment. Despite this, they have the ability to gather and move together, based on local interactions between individuals. From the simple, local interaction between individuals, more complex collective behavior emerges, such as flocking behavior, homing behavior, exploration and herding. Studies of the collective behavior of social animals include (Engelbrecht, 2006):

1. Bird flocking behavior;
2. Fish schooling behavior;
3. The hunting behavior of humpback whales;
4. The foraging behavior of wild monkeys; and
5. The courtship-like and foraging behavior of the basking shark.

PSO, introduced by Kennedy and Eberhart (1995), is a member of wide category of swarm intelligence methods (Kennedy & Eberhart, 2001). Kennedy originally proposed PSO as a simulation of social behavior and it was initially introduced as an optimization method. The PSO algorithm is conceptually simple and can be implemented in a few lines of code. A PSO individual also retains the knowledge of where in search space it performed the best, while in GAs if an individual is not selected for crossover or mutation, the information contained by that individual is lost. Comparisons between PSO and GAs are done analytically in (Eberhart & Shi, 1998) and also with regards to performance in (Angeline, 1998). In PSO, a swarm consists of individuals, called particles, which change their position $\bar{x}_i(t)$ with time t. Each particle represents a potential solution to the problem and flies around in a multidimensional search space. During flight each particle adjusts its position according to its own experience, and according to the experience of neighboring particles, making use of the best position encountered by itself and its neighbors. The effect is that particles move towards the best solution. The performance of each particle is measured according to a pre-defined fitness function, which is related to the problem being solved.

To implement the PSO algorithm, we have to define a neighborhood in the corresponding population and then describe the relations between particles that fall in that neighborhood. In this context, we have many topologies such as: star, ring, and wheel. Here we use the ring topology. In ring topology, each particle is related with two neighbors and attempts to imitate its best neighbor by moving closer to the best solution found within the neighborhood. The local best algorithm is associated with this topology (Eberhart et al., 1996; Corne et al., 1999):

1. [Start] Generate a random swarm of P particles in D-dimensional space, where D represents the number of variables (here D = 2).
2. [Fitness] Evaluate the fitness $f(\bar{x}_i(t))$ of each particle with respect to the cost function J.
3. [Update] Particles are moved toward the best solution by repeating the following steps:
   a. If $f(\bar{x}_i(t)) < pbest_i$ then $pbest_i = f(\bar{x}_i(t))$ and $\bar{x}_{pbest_i} = \bar{x}_i(t)$, where $pbest_i$ is the current best fitness achieved by the i-th particle and $\bar{x}_{pbest_i}$ is the corresponding coordinate.
   b. If $f(\bar{x}_i(t)) < lbest_i$ then $lbest = f(\bar{x}_i(t))$, where $lbest_i$ is the best fitness over the topological neighbors.
   c. Change the velocity v_i of each particle:

$$\bar{v}_i(t) = \bar{v}_i(t-1) + \rho_1\left(\bar{x}_{pbest_i} - \bar{x}_i(t)\right) + \rho_2\left(\bar{x}_{lbest_i} - \bar{x}_i(t)\right) \qquad (18)$$

   where ρ_1 and ρ_2 are random accelerate constants between 0 and 1.
   d. Fly each particle to its new position $\bar{x}_i(t) + \bar{v}_i(t)$.
4. [Loop] Go to step 2 until convergence.

The above procedures are iterated until a certain criterion is met. At this point, the most fitted particle represents the corresponding optimum values. The specific parameters of the introduced structure are described in Section 4.

4. Experimental Results

This Section is dedicated to a comprehensive investigation on the proposed methods performance. To this end, we will compare the proposed algorithms with FCM, PCM (Krishnapuram & Keller, 1993), RFCM (Pham, 2001), and an implementation of IFCM algorithm based on ANN (ANN-IFCM) (Shen et al., 2005).

Our experiments were performed on three types of images: 1) a synthetic square image; 2) simulated brain images obtained from Brainweb[1]; and 3) real MR images acquired from IBSR[2]. In all experiment the size of the population (P) is set to 20 and the cost function J_{FCM} with the similarity index defined in (14) is employed as a measure of fitness. Also, a single point crossover with probability of 0.2 and an order changing mutation with probability of 0.01 are applied. The weighting exponent m in all fuzzy clustering methods was set to 2. It has been observed that this value of weighting exponent yields the best results in most brain MR images (Shen et al., 2005).

4.1 Square Image

A synthetic square image consisting of 16 squares of size 64 × 64 is generated. This square image consists of 4 classes with intensity values of 0, 100, 200, and 300, respectively. In order to investigate the sensitivity of the algorithms to noise, a uniformly distributed noise in the

[1] http://www.bic.mni.mcgill.ca/brainweb/

[2] http://www.cma.mgh.harvard.edu/ibsr/

interval (0, 120) is added to the image. The reference noise-free image and the noisy one are illustrated in Figures 1 (a) and (b), respectively.
In order to evaluate the segmentation performance quantitatively, some metrics are defined as follows:

1. Under segmentation (UnS), representing the percentage of negative false segmentation:

$$UnS = \frac{N_{fp}}{N_n} \times 100 \tag{19}$$

2. Over segmentation (OvS), representing the percentage of positive false segmentation:

$$OvS = \frac{N_{fn}}{N_p} \times 100 \tag{20}$$

3. Incorrect segmentation (InC), representing the total percentage of false segmentation:

$$InC = \frac{N_{fp} + N_{fn}}{N} \times 100 \tag{21}$$

where N_{fp} is the number of pixels that do not belong to a cluster and are segmented into the cluster. N_{fn} is the number of pixels that belong to a cluster and are not segmented into the cluster. N_p is the number of all pixels that belong to a cluster, and N_n is the total number of pixels that do not belong to a cluster.
Table 1 lists the above metrics calculated for the seven tested methods. It is clear that FCM, PCM, and RFCM cannot overcome the degradation caused by noise and their segmentation performance is very poor compared to IFCM-based algorithms. Among IFCM-based algorithms, the PSO-based is superior to the others. For better comparison, the segmentation results of IFCM-based methods are illustrated in Figures 1(c)-(e); where the segmented classes are demonstrated in red, green, blue and black colors.

Evaluation parameters	FCM	PCM	RFCM	ANN-IFCM	GAs-IFCM	PSO-IFCM
UnS(%)	9.560	25.20	6.420	0.0230	0.0210	0.0110
OvS(%)	23.79	75.00	16.22	0.0530	0.0468	0.0358
InC(%)	14.24	43.75	9.88	0.0260	0.0220	0.0143

Table 1. Segmentation evaluation of synthetic square image

Since the segmentation results of IFCM-based algorithms are too closed to each other, we define another metric for better comparison of these methods. The new metric is the similarity index (SI) used for comparing the similarity of two samples defined as follows:

$$SI = 2 \times \frac{A \cap B}{A + B} \times 100 \tag{22}$$

where A and B are the reference and the segmented images, respectively. We compute this metric on the squared segmented image at different noise levels. The results are averaged over 10 runs of the algorithms. Figure 2 illustrates the performance comparison of different IFCM-based methods. The comparison clearly indicates that both GAs and PSO are superior to ANN in optimized estimation of λ and ξ. However, best results are obtained using the PSO algorithm.

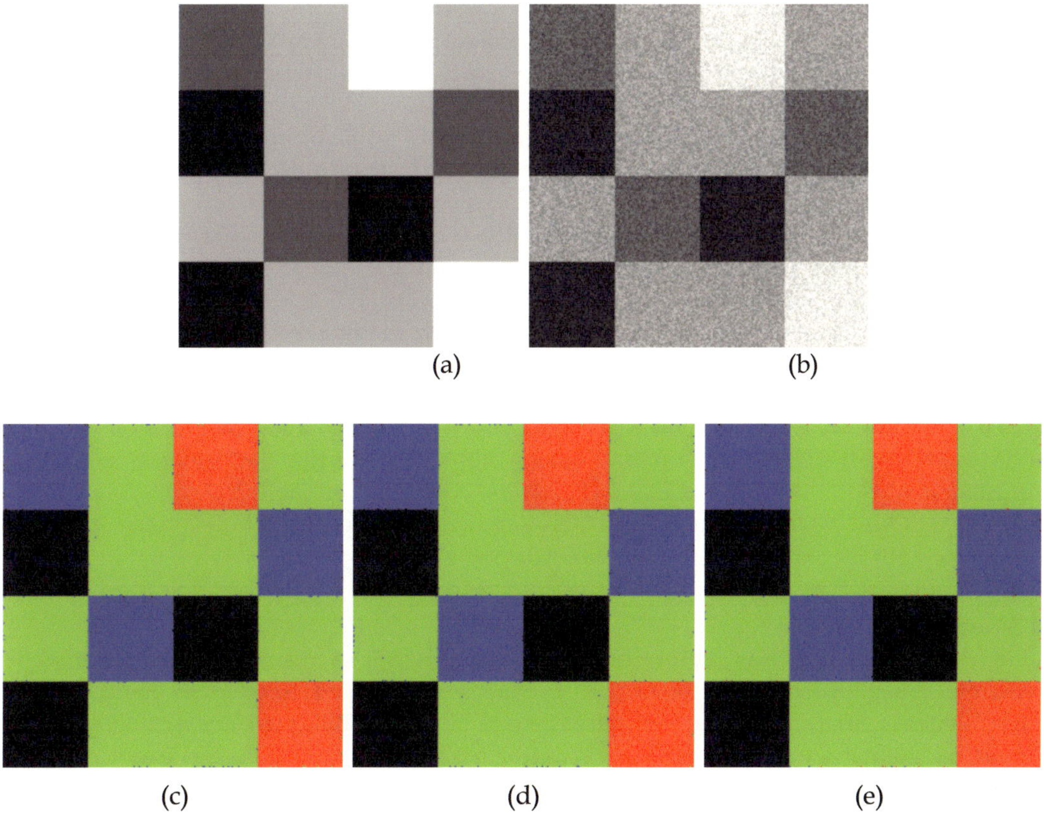

Figure 1. Segmentation results on a synthetic square image with a uniformly distributed noise in the interval (0, 120). (a) Noise-free reference image, (b) Noisy image, (c) ANN-IFCM, (d) GAs-IFCM, (e) PSO-IFCM

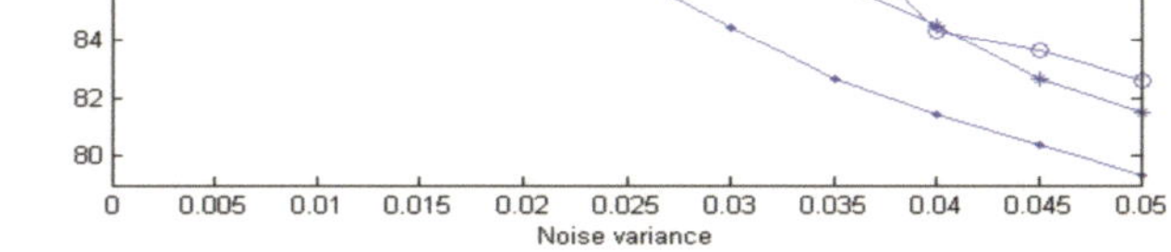

Figure 2. Performance comparison of IFCM-based methods using the SI metric at different noise levels

4.2 Simulated MR images

Generally, it is impossible to quantitatively evaluate the segmentation performance of an algorithm on real MR images, since the ground truth of segmentation for real images is not available. Therefore, only visual comparison is possible. However, Brainweb provides a simulated brain database including a set of realistic MRI data volumes produced by an MRI simulator. These data enable us to evaluate the performance of various image analysis methods in a setting where the truth is known.

In this experiment, a simulated T_1-weighted MR image (181 × 217 × 181) was downloaded from Brainweb. 7% noise was applied to each slice of the simulated image. The 100th brain region slice of the simulated image is shown in Figure 3(a) and its discrete anatomical structure consisting of cerebral spinal fluid (CSF), white matter, and gray matter is shown in Figure 3(b). The noisy slice was segmented into four clusters: background, CSF, white matter, and gray matter (the background was neglected from the viewing results) using FCM, PCM, RFCM, and the IFCM-based methods. The segmentation results after applying IFCM-based methods are shown in Figures 3(c)-(e). Also, the performance evaluation parameters of FCM, PCM, RFCM, and IFCMs are compared in Table 2. Again, it is obvious that the PSO-IFCM has achieved the best segmentation results. These observations are consistent with the simulation results obtained in the previous Section.

4.3 Real MR images

Finally, an evaluation was performed on real MR images. A real MR image (coronal T_1-weighted image with a matrix of 256 × 256) was obtained from IBSR the Center of Morphometric Analysis at Massachusetts General Hospital. IBSR provides manually guided expert segmentation results along with brain MRI data to support the evaluation and development of segmentation methods.

Figure 4(a) shows a slice of the image with 5% Gaussian noise and Figure 4(b) shows the manual segmentation result provided by the IBSR. For comparison with the manual segmentation result, which included four classes, CSF, gray matter, white matter, and others, the cluster number was set to 4. The segmentation results of FCM algorithm is shown in Figure 4(c), while segmentation of IFCM-based methods are shown in Figures 4(d)-(f). Table 3 lists the evaluation parameters for all methods. PSO-IFCM showed a significant improvement over other IFCMs both visually and parametrically, and eliminated the effect of noise, considerably. These results nominate the PSO-IFCM algorithm as a good technique for segmentation of noisy brain MR images in real application.

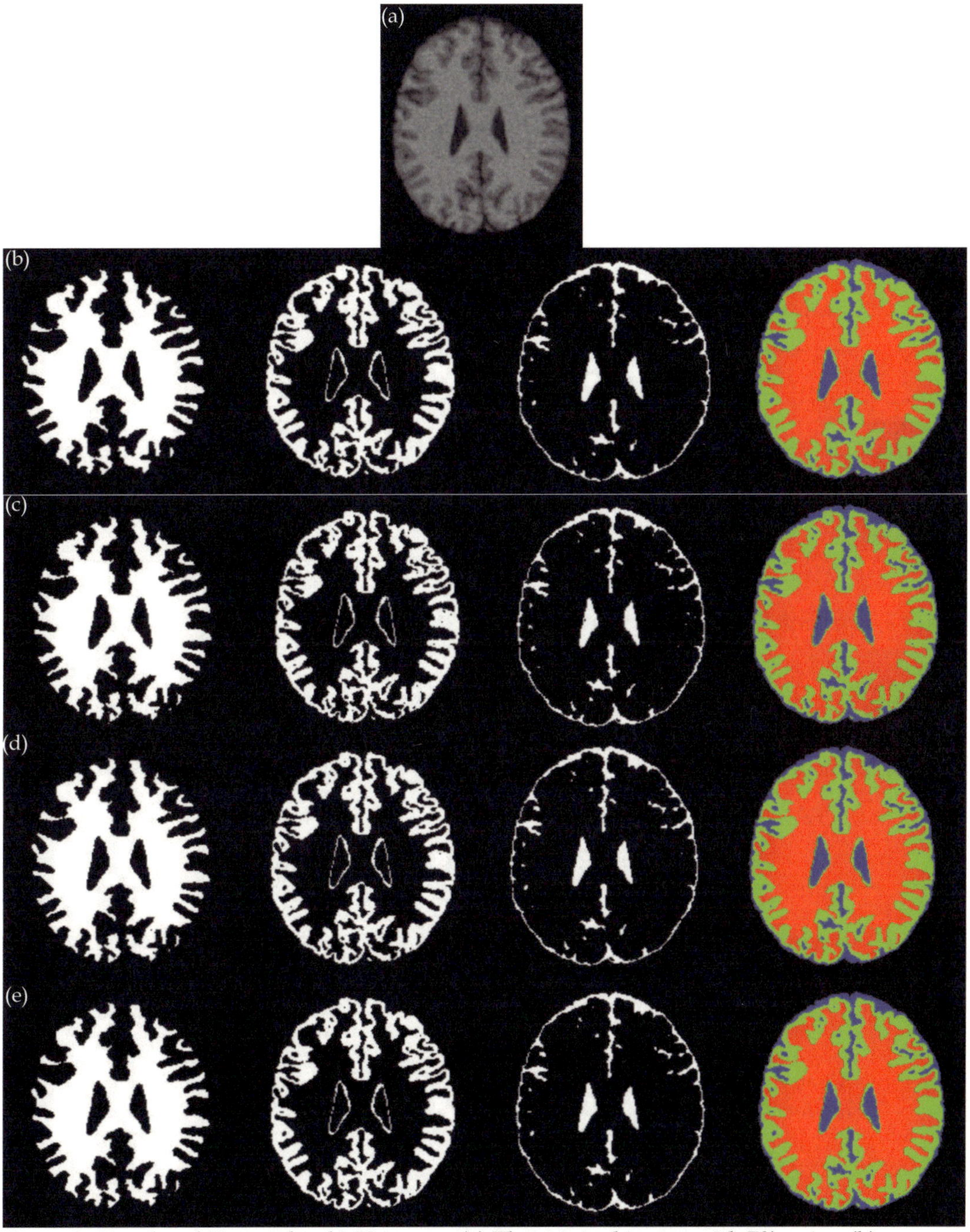

Figure 3. Simulated T_1-weighted MR image. (a) The original image with 7% noise, (b) Discrete anatomical model (from left to right) white matter, gray matter, CSF, and the total segmentation, (c) Segmentation result of ANN-IFCM, (d) Segmentation result of GAs-IFCM, (e) Segmentation result of PSO-IFCM

class	Evaluation parameters	FCM	PCM	RFCM	ANN-IFCM	GAs-IFCM	PSO-IFCM
CSF	UnS(%)	0.50	0	0.47	0.20	0.16	0.11
	OvS(%)	7.98	100	7.98	6.82	5.91	4.36
	InC(%)	0.76	34.0	0.73	0.57	0.45	0.31
White matter	UnS(%)	1.35	0	1.11	0.95	0.91	0.78
	OvS(%)	11.08	100	10.92	7.31	7.02	5.56
	InC(%)	2.33	10.16	2.11	1.59	1.39	1.06
Gray matter	UnS(%)	0.75	15.86	0.76	0.54	0.48	0.29
	OvS(%)	7.23	0	5.72	2.65	2.61	2.13
	InC(%)	1.68	13.57	1.47	0.93	0.87	0.71
Average	UnS(%)	0.87	5.29	0.78	0.56	0.52	0.39
	OvS(%)	8.76	66.67	8.21	5.59	5.18	4.02
	InC(%)	1.59	19.24	1.44	1.03	0.90	0.69

Table 2. Segmentation evaluation on simulated T_1-weighted MR

class	Evaluation parameters	FCM	ANN-IFCM	GAs-IFCM	PSO-IFCM
CFS	UnS(%)	11.1732	11.1142	10.6406	10.1619
	OvS(%)	44.4444	45.1356	41.4939	40.9091
	InC(%)	12.4009	12.7177	11.7791	11.2965
	SI(%)	87.5991	87.6305	88.2209	88.7035
White matter	UnS(%)	3.3556	2.7622	0.9783	1.5532
	OvS(%)	14.8345	9.6177	3.1523	9.0279
	InC(%)	6.2951	4.5178	1.5350	3.4673
	SI(%)	93.7049	95.4822	98.4650	96.5327
Gray matter	UnS(%)	5.9200	3.8073	3.8469	3.5824
	OvS(%)	36.9655	35.9035	31.4066	30.5603
	InC(%)	16.9305	15.1905	13.6211	13.1503
	SI(%)	83.0695	87.6305	86.3789	86.8497
Average	UnS(%)	5.7635	5.1014	4.5606	4.4094
	OvS(%)	24.2163	22.7491	20.7562	20.2043
	InC(%)	9.3831	8.4900	7.6465	7.3856
	SI(%)	90.6169	91.5100	92.3535	92.6144

Table 3. Segmentation evaluation on Real T_1-weighted MR image

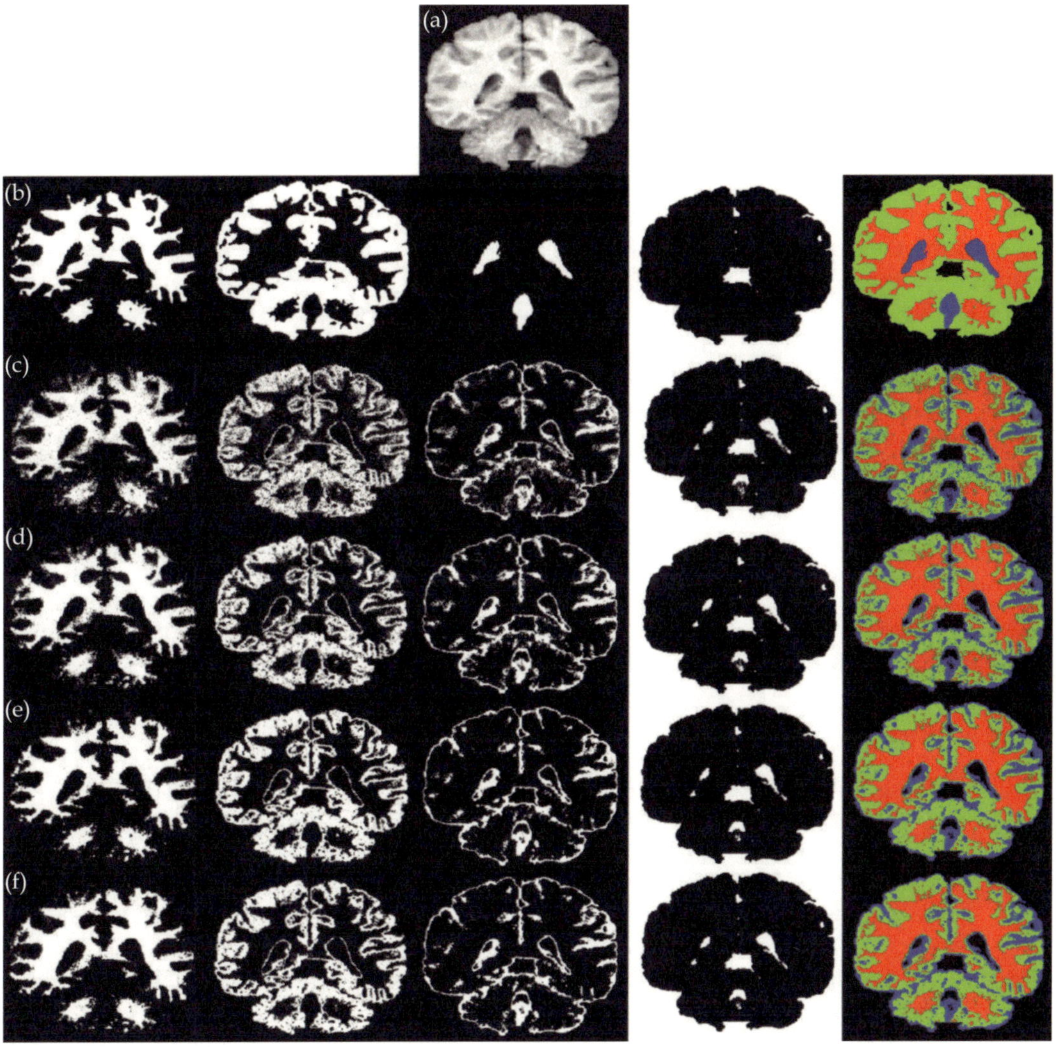

Figure 4. Real T_1-weighted MR image. (a) The original image with 5% noise, (b) Discrete anatomical model (from left to right) white matter, gray matter, CSF, others, and the total segmentation, (c) Segmentation results of FCM, (d) Segmentation result of ANN-IFCM, (e) Segmentation result of GAs-IFCM, (f) Segmentation result of PSO-IFCM

5. Conclusion and Future Work

Brain MRI segmentation is becoming an increasingly important image processing step in many applications including automatic or semiautomatic delineation of areas to be treated prior to radiosurgery, delineation of tumors before and after surgical or radiosurgical intervention for response assessment, and tissue classification. A traditional approach to segmentation of MR images is the FCM clustering algorithm. The efficacy of FCM algorithm considerably reduces in the case of noisy data. In order to improve the performance of FCM algorithm, researchers have introduced a neighborhood attraction, which is dependent on the relative location and features of neighboring pixels. However, determination of the degree of attraction is a challenging task which can considerably affect the segmentation results.

In this context, we introduced new optimized IFCM-based algorithms for segmentation of noisy brain MR images. We utilized GAs and PSO, to estimate the optimized values of neighborhood attraction parameters in IFCM clustering algorithm. GAs are best at reaching a near optimal solution but have trouble finding an exact solution, while PSO's group interactions enhances the search for an optimal local solution. We tested the proposed methods on three kinds of images; a square image, simulated brain MR images, and real brain MR images. Both quantitative and quantitative comparisons at different noise levels demonstrated that both GAs and PSO are superior to the previously proposed ANN method in optimizing the attraction parameters. However, best segmentation results were achieved using the PSO algorithm. These results nominate the PSO-IFCM algorithm as a good technique for segmentation of noisy brain MR images. It is expected that a hybrid method combining the strengths of PSO with GAs, simultaneously, would result to significant improvements that will be addressed in a future work.

6. Acknowledgement

The authors would like to thank Youness Aliyari Ghassabeh for the constructive discussions and useful suggestions.

7. References

Ahmed, M.N.; Yamany, S.M.; Mohamed, N.; Farag, A.A. & Moriarty, T. (2002). A modified fuzzy c-means algorithm for bias field estimation and segmentation of MRI data, *IEEE Trans. Med. Imag.*, vol. 21, pp. 193–199, Mar. 2002

Angeline, P.J. (1998). Evolutionary Optimization Versus Particle Swarm Optimization: Philosophy and Performance Differences, *Evolutionary Programming VII, Lecture Notes in Computer Science 1447*, pp. 601-610, Springer, 1998

Bezdek, J.C. (1981). *Pattern Recognition with Fuzzy Objective Function Algorithms*, Plenum Press, New York, 1981

Bondareff, W.; Raval, J.; Woo, B.; Hauser, D.L. & Colletti, P.M. (1990). Magnetic resonance and severity of dementia in older adults, *Arch. Gen. Psychiatry*, vol. 47, pp. 47-51, Jan. 1990

Canny, J.A. (1986). Computational approach to edge detection, *IEEE Trans. Patt. Anal. Machine Intell.*, vol. 8, pp. 679-698, 1986

Clarke, L.P. et al. (1995). MRI segmentation: Methods and applications, *Magn. Reson. Imag.*, vol. 13, pp. 343-368, 1995

Corne, D.; Dorigo, M. & Glover, F. (1999). *New Ideas in Optimization*, McGraw Hill, 1999

Dave, R.N. (1991). Characterization and detection of noise in clustering, Pattern Recogn. Lett., vol. 12, pp. 657–664, 1991

Dubes, R. & Jain, A. (1988). *Algorithms That Cluster Data*, Prentice Hall, Englewood Cliffs, 1988

Eberhart, R.C.; Dobbins R.W. & Simpson, P. (1996). *Computation Intelligence PC Tools*, Academic Press, 1996

Eberhart R.C. & Shi, Y. (1998). Comparison between Genetic Algorithms and Particle Swarm Optimization, *Evolutionary Programming VII, Lecture Notes in Computer Science 1447*, pp. 611-616, Springer, 1998

Engelbrecht, A.P. (2006). *Fundamentals of Computational Swarm Intelligence*, John Wiley, 2006.

Gen, M. & Cheng, R. (1997). *Genetic Algorithms and Engineer Design*, John Wiley, 1997

Girolami, M. (2002). Mercer kernel-based clustering in feature space. *IEEE Trans. Neural Networks*, vol. 13, pp. 780-784, 2002

Haacke, E. M.; Brown, R.W.; Thompson, M.L. & Venkatesan, R. (1999). *Magnetic Resonance Imaging: Physical Principles and Sequence Design*, John Wiley, 1999

Haykin, S. (1998). *Neural Networks: A Comprehensive Foundation*, Prentice Hall, 1998

Holland, J.H. (1992). *Adaptation in Natural and Artificial Systems*, MIT Press Cambridge, MA, USA, 1992

Hur, A.B.; Horn, D.; Siegelmann, H.T. & Vapnik, V. (2001). Support vector clustering. *J. Mach. Learn. Res.*, vol. 2, pp. 125—37, 2001

Kannan, S.R. (2008). A new segmentation system for brain MR images based on fuzzy techniques, *Applied Soft Computing*, in press

Kennedy, J. & Eberhart, R.C. (1995). Particle Swarm Optimisation, *Proceedings of IEEE International Conference on Neural Networks, IV*, pp. 1942-1948, 1995

Kennedy, J. & Eberhart, R.C. (2001). *Swarm Intelligence*, Morgan Kaufman Publishers ,2001

Krishnapuram R.R. & Keller, J.M. (1993). A possibilistic approach to clustering, *IEEE Trans. Fuzzy Syst.*, vol. 1, pp. 98–110, May 1993

Lauric, A. & Frisken, S. (2007). Soft Segmentation of CT Brain Data, Tufts University, Medford, MA, USA, Tech. Rep. 2007

Li, C.L.; Goldgof, D.B. & Hall, L.O. (1993). Knowledge-based classification and tissue labeling of MR images of human brain, *IEEE Trans. Med. Imag.*, vol. 12, pp. 740–750, Apr. 1993

Macovski, A. (1983). *Medical Imaging Systems*, Prentice-Hall, New Jersey, 1983

Mitchel, M. (1999). *An Introduction to Genetic Algorithms*, MIT Press, 1999

Pham, D.L. (2001). Spatial models for fuzzy clustering, *Comput. Vis. Imag. Understand.*, vol. 84, pp. 285–297, 2001

Pohle, R. & Toennies, K.D. (2001). Segmentation of medical images using adaptive region growing, *Proc. SPIE Med. Imag.*, vol. 4322, pp. 1337–1346, 2001

Shen, S.; Sandham, W.; Granat, M. & Sterr, A. (2005). MRI fuzzuy segmentation of brain tissue using neighborhood attraction with neural-network optimization, *IEEE Trans. Information Technology in Biomedicine*, vol. 9; pp 459-467, Sep. 2005

Slone, R.M.; Fisher, A.J.; Pickhardt, P.J.; Guitierrez, F. & Balfe D.M. (1999). *Body CT : a practical approach*, McGraw-Hill, Health Professions Division, New York, 1983

Suzuki, H. & Toriwaki, J. (1992). Automatic segmentation of head MRI images by knowledge guided thresholding, *Comput. Med. Imag. Graph.*, vol. 15, pp. 233–240, 1991

Wells, W.; Kikinis, R.; Grimson, F. & Jolesz, EA. (1994). Statistical intensity correction and segmentation of magnetic resonance image data, *Proc. SPIE Vis. Biomed. Comput.*, 1994

Wells, W.M., III; Grimson, W.E.L.; Kikinis, R. & Jolesz, F.A. (1996). Adaptive segmentation of MRI data, *IEEE Trans. Med. Imag.*, vol. 15, pp. 429–442, Aug. 1996

Zadeh, L.A. (1965). Fuzzy sets, *Inform. Control*, vol. 8, pp. 338–353, Jun. 1965

Zhang, D.Q. & Chen, S.C. (2002). Fuzzy clustering using kernel methods. *Proceedings of the International Conference on Control and Automation*, Xiamen, China, June, 2002

Zhang, D.Q. & Chen, S.C. (2004). A novel kernelized fuzzy c-means algorithm with application in medical image segmentation, *Artif. Intell. Med.*, vol. 32, pp. 37-52, 2004

13

Swarm Intelligence in Portfolio Selection

Shahab Mohammad-Moradi[1], Hamid Khaloozadeh[1], Mohamad Forouzanfar[1,2], Ramezan Paravi Torghabeh[1] and Nosratallah Forghani[1]
[1]K.N. Toosi University of Technology, [2]University of Tehran
[1,2]Iran

1. Introduction

Portfolio selection problems in investments are among the most studied in modern finance, because of their computational intractability. The basic perception in modern portfolio theory is the way that upon it investors construct diversified portfolio of financial securities so as to achieve improved tradeoffs between risk and return.

Portfolio optimization is a procedure for generating the composition that best achieves the portfolio manager's objectives. One of the first to apply mathematical programming models to portfolio management was the quadratic programming model of Markowitz (1952), who proposed that risk be represented as the variance of the return (a quadratic function), which is to be minimized subject to achieving a minimum expected return on investment (a linear constraint). This single-period model is explained in detail by Luenberger (1998). The inputs of this analysis are security expected returns, variances, and covariance for each pair of securities, and these are all estimated from past performances of the securities. However, it is not realistic for real ever-changing asset markets. In addition, it would be so difficult to find the efficient portfolio when short sales are not allowed.

Mathematical programming (e.g., linear programming, integer linear programming, nonlinear programming, and dynamic programming) models have been applied to portfolio management for at least half a century. For a review on the application of mathematical programming models to financial markets refer to Board and Sutcliffe (1999).

Several portfolio optimization strategies have been proposed to respond to the investment objectives of individuals, corporations and financial firms, where the optimization strategy is selected according to one's investment objective. Jones (2000) gives a framework for classifying these alternative investment objectives.

Although the most obvious applications of portfolio optimization models are to equity portfolios, several mathematical programming methods (including linear, mixed integer, quadratic, dynamic, and goal programming) have also been applied to the solution of fixed income portfolio management problems since the early 1970s.

Recently, many Evolutionary Computation (EC) techniques (Beyer, 1996) such as Genetic Algorithm (GA), Particle Swarm Optimization (PSO) (Xu et al., 2006), (Delvalle et al., 2007) have been applied to solve combinatorial optimization problems (Angeline, 1995). These techniques use a set of potential solutions as a population, and find the optimal solution through cooperation and contest among the particles of the population. In comparison, in

optimization problems with computation complexity, EC techniques find often optimal solution faster than traditional algorithms (Pursehouse and Fleming, 2007).
In this study, the portfolio selection problem is concerned, in case that expected return rates are stochastic variables and the breeding swarm algorithm is applied to solve this problem. The First, the stochastic portfolio model and reliable decision are presented. The Second, the global evolutionary computation algorithm-breeding swarm is proposed in order to overcome the computational complexity and local and global searching limitation of traditional optimization methods. Finally, a numerical example of portfolio selection problem is given. Findings endorse the effectiveness of the newly proposed algorithm in comparison to particle swarm optimization method. The results show that the breeding swarm approach to portfolio selection has high potential to achieve better solution and higher convergence.

2. Stochastic Portfolio Model

The mean-variance model of Markowitz, to find an efficient portfolio is led to solve the following optimization problem (Markowitz, 1952):

$$\begin{array}{ll} \textit{minimize} & \sigma^2(R'X) \\ \textit{subject to} & \begin{cases} \rho(X) = \rho \\ e'(X) = 1 \end{cases} \end{array} \tag{1}$$

where $\rho(X)$ is the reward on the portfolio X, ρ is a constant target reward for a specific investor, and e' is the transpose of the vector $e \in \Re^n$ of all 1s. The risk, $\sigma^2(R'X)$, of portfolio $X \in \Re^n$ is defined as the variance of its return $R'X$. R is the random vector of return rates. The expectation of R will be denoted by $\overline{R}$, that is, $E(R) = \overline{R}$. Conveniently, we set: $X = (x_1, x_2, ..., x_n)'$, $\overline{R} = (\overline{r}_1, \overline{r}_2, ..., \overline{r}_n)'$, $e = (1, 1, ..., 1)'$.
This model can be rewritten by the following quadratic programming:

$$\begin{array}{ll} \textit{min} & X'\Sigma X \\ \textit{s.t.} & R'X = \rho \\ & e'(X) = 1 \end{array} \tag{2}$$

where Σ is the covariance matrix of the random variables R.
In real ever-changing asset markets, returns of risky assets are not constant over the time. So we need to estimate $E(\overline{R})$ and $\Sigma = (\sigma_{ij})_{n \times n}$ in practical. The notion of efficient portfolio is a relative concept. The dominance between two portfolios can be defined in many different ways, and each one is expected to produce a different set of efficient portfolios. Only efficient portfolios are presented to the investor to make his/her final choice according to his/her taste toward risk. All investors in the same class, say risk averters, when the return of portfolio satisfy the expected value select the security with the lowest risk. According to above perceptions, the stochastic portfolio model can be described as:
A: Stochastic portfolio model without risk-free asset

$$\begin{aligned} \min \quad & X'\Sigma X \\ s.t. \quad & X'R \geq R_0 \\ & e'X = 1 \\ & X \geq 0 \end{aligned} \tag{3}$$

On condition that short sales are allowed, the stochastic portfolio model without risk-free asset can be described by eliminating the constraint $X \geq 0$.

B: Stochastic portfolio model with risk-free asset

$$\begin{aligned} \min \quad & X'\Sigma X \\ s.t. \quad & X'\overline{R} + (1 - X'e)R_f \geq R_0 \\ & e'X = 1 \\ & X \geq 0 \end{aligned} \tag{4}$$

where R_f is the return rate of risk-free asset.

3. Reliable Decision of Portfolio Selection

Because of randomness of the condition $X'\overline{R} \geq R_0$, the feasible solution to the model (3) and (4) maybe achievable or not. Due to the degree of probability available in model (3) and (4), we define reliability and construct a model with limited probability. The new model can be described as follows:

$$\begin{aligned} \min \quad & X'\Sigma X \\ s.t. \quad & P(X'\overline{R} \geq R_0) \geq \alpha \\ & e'X = 1 \\ & X \geq 0 \end{aligned} \tag{5}$$

in the case that a risk-free asset exists:

$$\begin{aligned} \min \quad & X'\Sigma X \\ s.t. \quad & P(X'\overline{R} + (1 - e'X)R_f \geq R_0) \geq \alpha \\ & e'X = 1 \\ & X \geq 0 \end{aligned} \tag{6}$$

The model (5) and (6) is defined as the reliable model (3) and (4), and the possible solution of (5) and (6) is named α feasible solution of model (3) and (4) and is defined as α reliable decision for the portfolio. Since α reliable decision demonstrates that the portfolio decision is stochastic decision, is more important and practical and reflect the inconsistence of asset markets.

The model (5) and (6) can be converted into the determinate decision model. Defining constant M by the following formula:

$$P\left(\frac{X'\overline{R} - X'R}{\sqrt{X'\Sigma X}} \geq M\right) = \alpha$$

The condition $P(X\overline{R} \geq R_0) \geq \alpha$ would be equivalent to the determinate condition $X'R + M\sqrt{X'MX} \geq R_0$. The proof can be so followed:

if $P(X\overline{R} \geq R_0) \geq \alpha$ *then* $P(X\overline{R} \leq R_0) \leq 1-\alpha$. Since $P(X\overline{R} \leq X'R + M\sqrt{X'\Sigma X}) = 1-\alpha$, then according to unchanging nondecreasing manner of the distribution function of random variable, we obtain $X'R + M\sqrt{X'\Sigma X} \geq R_0$. Contradictorily, if $X'R + M\sqrt{X'\Sigma X} \geq R_0$ then $P(X\overline{R} \geq R_0) \geq P(X\overline{R} \geq X'R + M\sqrt{X'\Sigma X}) = \alpha$

Hence, the model (5) and (6) can be described with determinate constraint model (7) and (8):

$$\begin{aligned} \min \quad & J = X'\Sigma X \\ s.t. \quad & X'R + M\sqrt{X'\Sigma X} \geq R_0 \\ & e'X = 1 \\ & X \geq 0 \end{aligned} \tag{7}$$

in the case that we have a risk-free asset:

$$\begin{aligned} \min \quad & J = X'\Sigma X \\ s.t. \quad & X'R + M\sqrt{X'\Sigma X} - X'eR_f \geq R_0 - R_f \\ & e'X = 1 \\ & X \geq 0 \end{aligned} \tag{8}$$

If risky assets follow normal distribution $N(R_i, \sigma_i^2)$, constant M can be obtained by following formula:

$$\frac{1}{\sqrt{2\pi}} \int_{-\infty}^{M} e^{\frac{-x^2}{2}} dx = 1-\alpha.$$

where α is reliable decision for the portfolio. Since α reliable decision demonstrates that the portfolio decision is stochastic decision, is more important and practical and reflect the inconsistence of asset markets (Xu et al., 2006).

4. Breeding Swarm Optimization Method for Stochastic Portfolio Selection

4.1 structure of Breeding Swarm Model

Angeline (1998) and Eberhart and Shi (1998) proposed that a hybrid model of GA and PSO can produce a very effective search strategy. In this context, our goal is to introduce a hybrid GA/PSO model. It has been shown that the performance of the PSO is not sensitive to the population size (Shi and Eberhart, 1999). Therefore, the PSO will work well (with a low number of particles) compared to the number of individuals needed for the GA. Since, each particle has one fitness function to be evaluated per iteration, the number of fitness function evaluations can be reduced or more iteration can be performed. The hybrid PSOs combine the traditional velocity and position update rules with the idea of breeding and subpopulations.

In this study, the hybrid model is tested and compared with the standard PSO model. This is done to illustrate that PSO with breeding strategies has the potential to achieve faster convergence and better solution. Our results show that with the correct combination of GA and PSO, the hybrid can outperform, or perform as well as, both the standard PSO and GA models. The hybrid algorithm combines the standard velocity and position update rules of PSOs (Xiao et al., 2004) with the ideas of selection, crossover and mutation from GAs. An additional parameter, the breeding ratio (Ψ), determines the proportion of the population which undergoes breeding (selection, crossover and mutation) in the current generation. Values for the breeding ratio parameter range from 0.0 to 1.0. In each generation, after the fitness values of all the individuals in the same population are calculated, the bottom ($N \cdot \Psi$), where N is the population size, is discarded and removed from the population. The remaining individual's velocity vectors are updated, acquiring new information from the population. The next generation is then created by updating the position vectors of these individuals to fill $N \cdot (1-\Psi)$ individuals in the next generation. The $N \cdot \Psi$ individuals needed to fill the population are selected from the individuals whose velocities are updated to undergo crossover and mutation and the process is repeated.

4.2 The Breeding Swarm Optimization Approach for Portfolio Selection

As mentioned in the previous section, domain of variables x_i is [0, 1] and the number of particles required for simultaneous computation is 7. These particles represent the investment rate to asset i. We considered the population size equal to 20 and then generated a random initial population. Cost function J in (7) is defined as fitness function and used for evaluation of initial chromosomes. In this stage some particles are strong and others are weak (some of them produce lower value for fitness function and vice versa). These particles are floated in a 7-dimensional (7-D) space. After ranking the particles based on their fitness functions the best particles are selected. First each particle changes its position according to its own experience and its neighbors. So, first we have to define a neighborhood in the corresponding population and then describe the relations between particles that fall in that neighborhood. In this context, we have many topologies such as: Star, Ring, and Wheel. In this study we use the ring topology. In ring topology, each particle is related with two neighbors and intends to move toward the best neighbor. Each particle attempts to imitate its best neighbor by moving closer to the best solution found within the neighborhoods. It is important to note that neighborhoods overlap, which facilitates the exchange of information between neighborhoods and convergence to a single solution. In addition, we are using mutation and crossover operators for offspring from the selected particles to generate new populations. Therefore new populations are generated using two approaches: PSO and GA. The local best of BS algorithm is associated with the following topology (Settles et al., 2005):

1. Initialize a swarm of P particles in D-dimensional space, where D is the number of weights and biases.
2. Evaluate the fitness f_p of each particle p as the J.
3. If $f_p < p_{best}$ then $p_{best} = f_p$ and $x_{pbest} = x_p$, where p_{best} is the current best fitness achieved by particle p, x_p is the current coordinates of particle p in D-dimensional weights space, and x_{pbest} is the coordinate corresponding to particle p's best fitness so far.
4. If $f_p < l_{best}$ then $l_{best} = p$, where l_{best} is the particle having the overall best fitness over all particles in the swarm.

5. Select the first K best of P particles
6. Generate new population
   A: Change K particles velocity with equation:

$$\bar{v}_i = \bar{v}_i(t-1) + \rho_1(\bar{x}_{pbest_i} - \bar{x}_i(t)) + \rho_2(\bar{x}_{lbest_i} - \bar{x}_i(t))$$

   where ρ_1, ρ_2 are accelerate constants and rand return uniform random number between 0 and 1. Then fly each particle K to $x_K + V_K$.
   B: Then each K particles are used to offspring with mutation and crossover operators.
7. Loop to step 2 until convergence.

After completion of above processes, a new population is produced and the current iteration is completed. We iterate the above procedures until a certain criterion is met. At this point, the best fitted particle represents the optimum values of x_i.

5. Experimental Results

In this part we present experimental results to illustrate the effectiveness of breeding swarm optimization method for the stochastic portfolio selection. The problem of portfolio selection is considered here with seven risky assets. In addition, we only examine model (7) by the breeding swarm optimization, but the optimal solution can be obtained for model (8) by the same algorithm. The return rate and covariance chart of returns are shown in Table 1 (Xu et al., 2006). Denote $F^{\bullet}$ as the obtained result of the risk of portfolio, $R^{\bullet}$ as the obtained result of the return of the portfolio.

5.1 Simulation Results

We used the following values for parameters in our experiments: the size of the population is 20, and for each experimental setting, 20 trials were performed. For the stochastic model, the expected portfolio return rate is $R_0 = 0.175$, $M = 0.42$. Finally, the optimal portfolio of assets is obtained as follows. By 2000 iterations we found:
$X^{\bullet} = \{\ 0.8076, 0.3918, 0.0019, 0.0213, 0.0066, 0.2985, 0.0245\ \}$, the risk of portfolio is: $\sigma^2(X^{\bullet}) = 0.0018$, the return of the portfolio is: $R(X^{\bullet}) = 0.1716$.
By 5000 iteration we obtained the following result for the optimal portfolio:
$X^{\bullet} = \{0.9137, 0.385, 0.0115, 0.0018, 0.2997, 0.0089\}$, the risk of portfolio is: $\sigma^2(X^{\bullet}) = 0.0011$, the return of the portfolio is: $R(X^{\bullet}) = 0.1812$.

5.2 Illustration and Analysis

The efficiency of the breeding swarm algorithm for portfolio selection, can be appraised from $F^{\bullet}$ (the risk of portfolio), $R^{\bullet}$ (the return of portfolio), number of iterations and the convergence rate. The results of simulation for two different iteration numbers are listed in Table 2., Fig. 1., Fig. 2., and Fig. 3.. In Table 2. the precision of the solutions for different iteration numbers is showed. From Fig. 1., Fig. 2., and Fig. 3. it can be found that the breeding swarm algorithm has so fast convergence rate for different iteration numbers.

These figures show the average fitness function of risk in 20 trials in three different iterations.

Return	Covariance						
	1	2	3	4	5	6	7
0.120	0.141	-0.189	0.167	0.188	-0.186	-0.194	0.161
0.090	-0.189	0.260	-0.220	-0.248	0.253	0.255	-0.216
0.100	0.167	-0.220	0.224	0.238	-0.217	-0.238	0.209
0.100	0.188	-0.248	0.238	0.270	-0.247	-0.260	0.220
0.009	-0.186	0.253	-0.238	-0.260	0.256	0.279	-0.230
0.115	-0.194	0.255	-0.238	-0.260	0.256	0.279	-0.230
0.110	0.161	-0.216	0.209	0.220	-0.217	-0.230	0.209

Table 1. Return rate and covariance chart (Xu et al., 2006)

Iterations	Best $F^{\bullet}$	Best $R^{\bullet}$	Average $F^{\bullet}$	Average $R^{\bullet}$
2000	0.0018	0.1716	0.0038	0.1588
5000	0.0011	0.1812	0.0026	0.1638

Table 2. BS Algorithm Evaluation Results

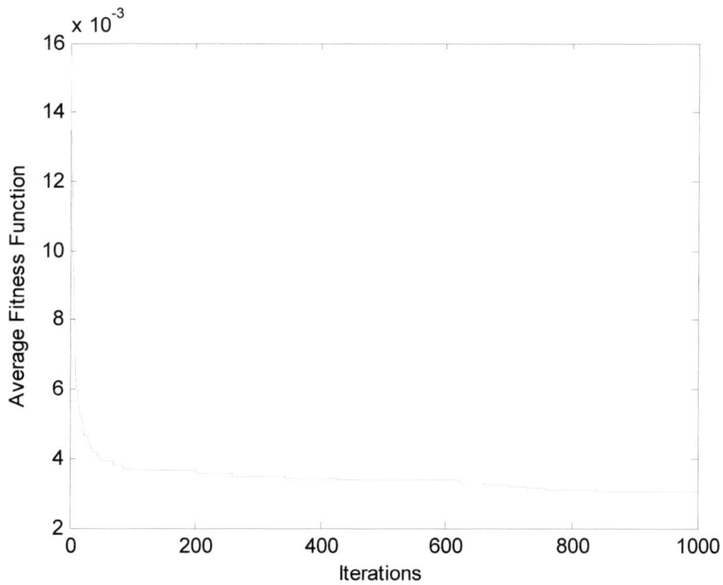

Figure 1. The performance and convergence rate with 1000 iterations

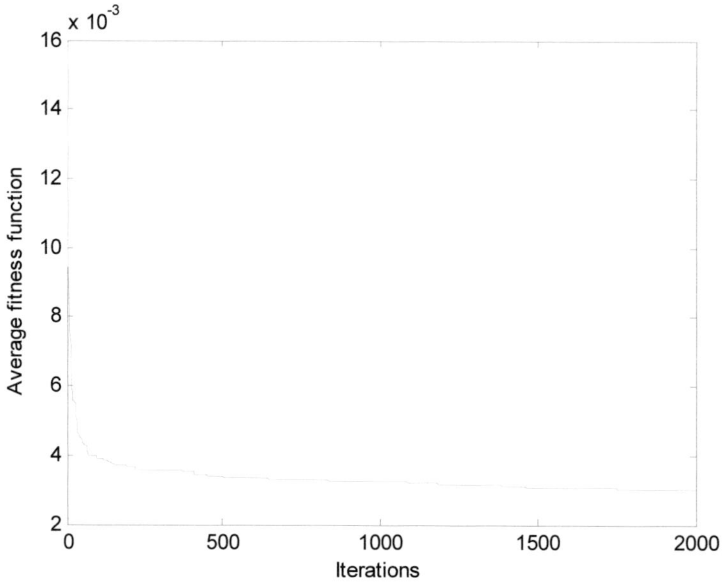

Figure 2. The performance and convergence rate with 2000 iterations

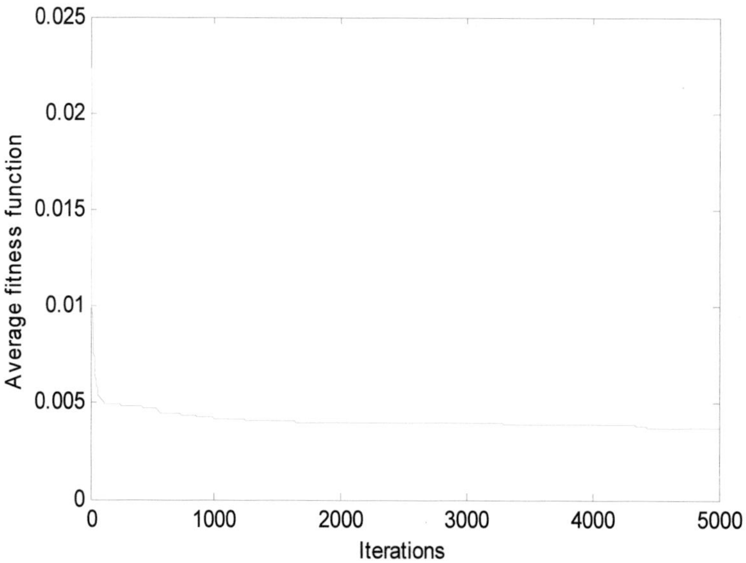

Figure 3. The performance and convergence rate with 5000 iterations

It is obvious from the figures that the BS algorithm has achieved to its efficient solution by nearly 1000 iterations. These results approve that the BS algorithm can find the solution of portfolio selection problem with high accuracy and convergence rate. The best results of Limited Velocity Particle Swarm Optimization (LVPSO) approach (Xu et al., 2006) are summarized in Table 3 to compare with our results.

Method	Iterations	Average Iterations	Best F*	Best R*	Average F*	Average R*
LVPSO (Xu et al., 2006)	7544	5006	0.009311	0.112622	0.009926	0.111531
	5415	3444	0.010612	0.110619	0.011098	0.107835
BS	5000	4850	0.001100	0.181200	0.002600	0.163800
	2000	1920	0.001800	0.171600	0.003800	0.158800

Table 3. Compare best results of two approaches LVPSO and BS

6. Conclusion

In this study, a new optimization method is used for portfolio selection problem which is powerful to select the best portfolio proportion with minimum risk and high return. One of the advantages of this hybrid approach is the high speed of convergence to the best solution, because it uses both advantages of GA and PSO approaches. Simulation results demonstrate that the BS approach can achieve better solutions to stochastic portfolio selection compared to PSO method.

7. References

Angeline P. (1995), Evolution Revolution:An Introduction to the Special Track on Genetic and Evolutionary Programming, *IEEE Expert: Intelligent Systems and Their Applications*, 10. 3., 6-10

Angeline P. (1998), Evolutionary Optimization Versus Particle Swarm Optimization: Philosophy and Performance Differences, *In e. a. V. William Porto, editor, Lecture Notes in Computer Science, In Proceedings of the 7th International Conference on Evolutionary Programming VII, 1447, pp.* 601–610, 1998, Springer-Verlag, London, UK

Beyer H-G (1996), *Toward a theory of evolution strategies: Self-adaptation, Evolutionary Computation*, 3.,3., 311-347

Board, J. & C. Sutcliffe (1999), *The Application of Operations Research Techniques to Financial Markets, Stochastic Programming e-print series*, http://www.speps.info

DelValle Y., G. K. Venayagamoorthy, S. Mohagheghi, J.-C. Hernandez & R.G. Harley (2007), *Particle Swarm Optimization: Basic Concepts, Variants and Applications in Power Systems*, Evolutionary Computation, IEEE Transactions, PP.,99., 1-1

Eberhart R. & Y. Shi (1998), Comparison Between Genetic Algorithms and Particle Swarm Optimization, In e. a. V. William Porto, editor, Springer, Lecture Notes in Computer Science, *In Proceedings of the 7th International Conference on Evolutionary Programming VII, 1447, pp.* 611–616, Springer-Verlag, London, UK

Jones Frank J. (2000), *An Overview of Institutional Fixed Income Strategies, in Professional Perspectives on Fixed Income Portfolio Management*, Fabozzi Frank J. Associates, Pennsylvania, pp. 1-13

Luenberger David G. (1998), *Investment science*, Oxford University Press, New York, pp. 137-162 and pp. 481-483

Markowitz, H. (1952), *Portfolio selection*, Journal of Finance, 7., 1., pp. 77-91, March 1952

Purshouse R.C. & P.J. Fleming (2007), *Evolutionary Computation*, IEEE Transactions ,11., 6., pp. 770 - 784

Settles M. , P. Nathan & T. Soule (2005), *Breeding Swarms: A New Approach to Recurrent Neural Network Training, GECCO'05,* 25–29 June 2005, Washington DC, USA

Shi Y. & R. C. Eberhart (1999), Empirical Study of Particle Swarm Optimization, *In Proceedings of the 1999 Congress of Evolutionary Computation,* 3: 1945-1950, IEEE Press

Xiao X., E. R. Dow, R. Eberhart, Z. Ben Miled & R. J. Oppelt (2004), *Concurrency and Computation: Practice & Experience,* 16., 9., pp. 895 - 915

Xu F. & W. Chen (2006), Stochastic Portfolio Selection Based on Velocity Limited Particle Swarm Optimization, *In Proceedings of the 6th World Congress on Intelligent Control and Automation,* 21-23 June 2006, Dalian, China

14

Enhanced Particle Swarm Optimization for Design and Optimization of Frequency Selective Surfaces and Artificial Magnetic Conductors

Simone Genovesi[1], Agostino Monorchio[1] and Raj Mittra[2]
[1]*Microwave and Radiation Laboratory, Dept. of Information Engineering, University of Pisa,*
[2]*Electromagnetic Communication Lab, PennState University*
[1]*Italy,* [2]*USA*

1. Introduction

Optimization methods are invaluable tools for the engineer who has to face the increasing complexity in the design of electromagnetic devices, or has to deal with inverse problems. Basically, an objective function $f(x)$ is defined where x is the set of parameters that has to be optimized in order to satisfy the imposed requirements. In design problems the parameters defined in x completely describe the features of the device (a printed antenna for example), and $f(x)$ is a measure of the system performance (gain or return loss). However, the objective function for a real-world problem may be nonlinear, may have many local extrema and may even be nondifferentiable. Numerous optimization methods that have been proposed in the literature can be divided into two groups – deterministic and stochastic. The former performs a local search which yields results that are highly influenced by the starting point, and sometimes requires the objective function to be differentiable. They might lead to a rapid convergence to a local extremum, as opposed to the global one and impose constraints on the solution domain that may be difficult to handle. The latter are largely independent of the initial conditions and place few constraints on the solution domain. They carry out a global search, and are able to deal with solution spaces with discontinuities, as well as a large number of dimensions and hence many potential local minima and maxima. Among the stochastic methods, for instance Monte Carlo and Simulated Annealing techniques, a particular subset also referred to as evolutionary algorithms have been recently growing in importance and interest. This class comprises the Genetic Algorithms (GA) (Goldberg, 1989), the Ant Colony Optimization (ACO) (Dorigo and Stutzle, 2004) and the Particle Swarm Optimization (PSO).
The PSO algorithm has been originally proposed by Kennedy and his colleagues (Kennedy and Eberhart, 1995) and it is inspired by a zoological metaphor of the social behavior of animals (birds, insects, or fishes) that are organized in groups (flocks, swarms, or schools). All of the basic units of the swarm, called particles (or agents) are trial solutions for the problem to be optimized, and are free to fly through the multidimensional search-space toward the optimal solution. The search-space represents the global set of potential results, where each dimension of this space corresponds to a

parameter of the problem to be determined. The swarm is largely self-organized, and coordination arises from the different interactions among agents. Each member of the swarm exploits the solution space by taking into account the experience of the single particle as well as that of the entire swarm. This combined and synergic use of information yields a promising tool for solving design problems that require the optimization of a relatively large number of parameters.
The organization of this chapter is as follows: Section 2 describes the implementation of a PSO algorithm employed in the design of Frequency Selective Surfaces. A parallelization of the PSO method is described in Section 3 that makes efficient use of all the available hardware resources to overcome the computational burden incurred in the process. A useful procedure for increasing the convergence rate is described in Section 4 and numerical results are provided to illustrate the reliability and efficiency of the new algorithm. Finally, concluding remarks are given in Section 5.

2. Optimization of Frequency Selective Surfaces

In this section the problem of synthesizing Frequency Selective Surfaces (FSSs) is addressed by using a specifically derived particle swarm optimization procedure, which is able to handle, simultaneously, both real and binary parameters. After a brief introduction of the nature of the FSSs and the applications in which they are employed, the PSO method developed for their optimization is described and a representative numerical example is given to demonstrate the effectiveness of this tool.

2.1 Frequency Selective Surfaces

At the end of the 18th century the American physicist David Rittenhouse (Rittenhouse, 1786), found that the light spectrum is decomposed into lines of different brightness and color, while observing a street lamp through his silk handkerchief. This was the first proof of the fact that non-continuous and periodic surfaces show different transmission properties for different frequencies of incident wave. The first device which takes advantage of this phenomenon is the parabolic reflector of wire sections, built by Marconi and Franklin in 1919 and, since then, FSSs have been further investigated and exploited for use in many practical applications. For instance, FSSs find use as subreflectors in dual frequency Cassegrainian systems and in radomes designed for antennas, where FSSs are used as pass band or stop band filters. They are employed to reduce the Radar Cross Section (RCS) of antennas outside their operating frequency band, and provide a reflective surface for beam focusing in reflector antenna system, realize waveguide filters and artificial magnetic conductors. At microwaves FSSs protect humans from harmful electronic radiation, as for instance, in the case of a microwave oven , in which the FSS printed on the screen doors totally reflects microwave energy at 2.45 GHz while allowing light to pass through. Recently, the FSSs have been employed at infrared (IR) frequencies for beam-splitters, filters and polarizers.
An FSS is either a periodic array of metallic patches printed on a substrate, or a conducting sheet periodically perforated with apertures. Their shape, size, periodicity, thickness of the metal screen and the dielectric substrate determine their frequency and angular response (Mittra et al., 1988; Munk, 2000).

2.2 Particle Swarm Optimization with mixed parameters

In the basic PSO algorithm, each agent in the swarm flies in an n-dimension space, and the position at a certain instant i is identified by the vector of the coordinates X:

$$X(i)=[x_1(i),x_2(i),\dots,x_n(i)]. \quad (1)$$

Each $x_n(i)$ component represents a parameter of the physical problem that has to be optimized. At the beginning of the process, each particle is randomly located at a position, and moves with a random velocity, both in direction and magnitude. The particle is free to fly inside the n-dimensional space defined by the user, within the constraints of the n boundary conditions, which limit the extent of the search space and, hence, the values of the parameters during the optimization process. At the generic time step i+1, the velocity is expressed by the following equation:

$$v_l(i+1)=w^*\ v_l(i)+c_1{}^*\mathrm{rand}()^*(p_{\mathrm{best},l}(i)-x_l(i))+c2^*\mathrm{rand}()^*(g_{\mathrm{best},l}(i)-x_l(i)), \quad (2)$$

where $v_l(i)$ is the velocity along the l direction at the time step i; w is the inertial weight; c_1 and c_2 are the cognitive and the social rate, respectively; $p_{\mathrm{best},l}(i)$ is the best position along the l direction found by the agent during its own wandering up to i-th; $g_{\mathrm{best},l}(i)$ is the best position along the l direction discovered by the entire swarm; and rand() is a generator of random numbers uniformly distributed between 0 and 1. The position of each particle is then simply updated according to the equation:

$$x_l(i+1)= x_l(i)+ v_l(i)^*\Delta t \quad (3)$$

where $x_l(i)$ is the current position of the agent along the direction l at the iteration i-th, and Δt is the time step. An interesting insight into the basic PSO algorithm details may be found in (Robinson and Rahmat-Samii, 2002). This basic procedure is suitable for solving optimization problems involving real parameters. However, for the case of the FSS design, we need to manage not only the real but also the binary parameters in order to describe the shape of the unit cell (Manara et al., 1999). Therefore it is necessary to incorporate both of these features into the algorithm (Fig. 1). A discrete binary version of the PSO was first introduced by Kennedy and Eberhart (Kennedy and Eberhart, 1997), in which the concept of velocity loses its physical meaning and assumes the value of a probability instead. More specifically, the position along a direction can now be either 0 or 1, and the velocity represents the probability of change for the value of that bit. In light of this, the expression in (2) has to be modified by imposing the condition that the value of $v_l(i)$ must be in the interval [0.0, 1.0], and enforcing the constraint that any value outside this interval be unacceptable. As a consequence, a function T is defined to map the results of (2) within the allowed range. If w=1 and c_1= c_2=2, $v_l(i)$ is within the interval [-4, 5]. The T function linearly compresses this dynamic range into the desired set [0, 1] and then the position is updated by using the following rule:

$$\begin{aligned}&\text{if } (\mathrm{rand}() < \mathrm{T}(v_l(i)) \text{ then} \\ &\qquad x_l(i)= \mathrm{NOT}(x_l(i)) \\ &\text{else} \\ &\qquad x_l(i)= x_l(i)\end{aligned} \quad (4)$$

where *rand()* is the same random function adopted in (2) and the operator NOT indicates the binary negation of x_l.

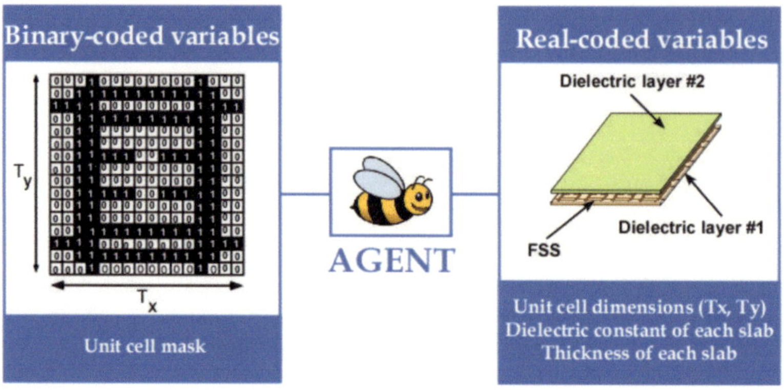

Figure 1. Each agent represents number and type of the parameters involved in the optimization process

This implies that if the random number is less than the probability expressed by the velocity, then the bit is changed. Hence, the faster the particle moves in that direction, the larger is the possibility of change.

The parameters that can be optimized by the algorithm for the design of an FSS structure are the shape of the unit cell, its dimensions, the permittivities of dielectric layers and their thicknesses. The size of the multi-dimensional space in which the particle moves is variable, and it is related to the different options given to the user. In fact, the number and the kind of the parameters depend on the choices offered at the beginning of the optimization process. First of all, the two real-valued parameters that can be tuned according to the imposed requirements are the dimensions of the unit cell along the main directions of periodicity (T_x, T_y). For each dielectric substrate, it is possible to choose the value of the permittivity from a predefined database, using integer parameters in this case. Consequently, the particle is only allowed to assume integer values, and a finite number of these values in the search direction. As for the thickness, it can be either chosen from a database (integer parameter) or be a real value within the imposed boundary for that component. The shape of the unit cell is completely defined as a binary parameter, where '1' implies the presence of perfect electric conductor and '0' designates an absence of conductor. The discretization adopted for the FSS binary mask can be 16×16 for a total of 256 binary parameters. This number reduces to 64 and 36, for a four-fold or eight-fold symmetry imposed to the unit cell, respectively. The analysis of the entire FSS structure is performed via an MoM code, employing roof top basis functions (Manara et al., 1999). The objective function (also referred to as the fitness function), which is employed to test the performance of the solution proposed by the PSO, is based on the mean square error between the reflection coefficient (or the transmission one) of the synthesized structure and the frequency mask which translates the requirements imposed by the user in one (or more) frequency band and for a set of incidence angles. It is apparent that in this case the aim is to minimize the fitness value and therefore we are in search of a the global minimum.

In order to demonstrate the capabilities of the PSO algorithm, a frequency mask is imposed to have a transmission coefficient less than -15 dB in the 0.1 GHz - 2.0 GHz band , less than – 10 dB within the 10.0 GHz-12-0 GHz and to be transparent in the 5.0 GHz - 6.0 GHz band.

The algorithm has to optimize the shape of the unit cell and the thickness and dielectric constant values of two dielectric slabs which contains the FSS. The unit cell designed by the PSO is a square and has a period of 1 cm. The two dielectric slab have permittivities of ε_r=3.3 and ε_r=7.68, and thicknesses of 0.2 cm and 0.1 cm, respectively. The result is shown in Fig.2 as well as the unit cell shape represented in the binary variables.

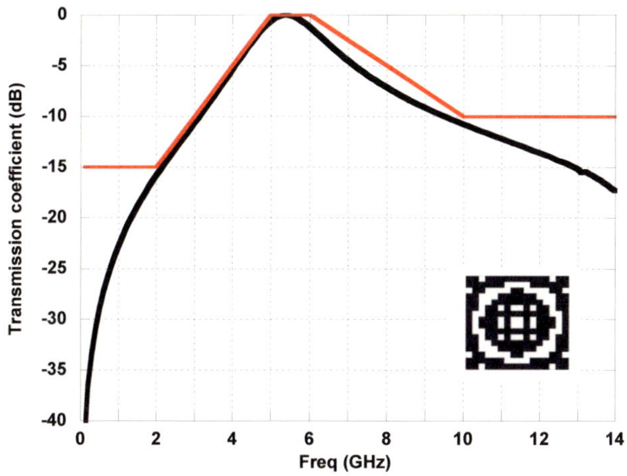

Figure 2. Comparison between the mask expressing the requirements imposed by the user (red line) and the transmission coefficient of the FSS optimized by the PSO algorithm (black line). In the inset the unit cell is reported

3. Parallel Particle Swarm Optimization

There have been many attempts in the past toward increasing the convergence of the PSO algorithm by modifying it (Clerc and Kennedy, 2002; Shi and Eberhart, 1999). This section will focus on an alternative approach, that involves an enhancement in the performance via the implementation of a parallel version of the PSO algorithm (PPSO) which is designed to address the CPU time issue. The parallel version can be useful, for example, for designing FSSs requiring a unit cell geometry with a fine discretization (e.g., 32×32), or for synthesizing a dual-screen version, both of which demand a significant computational effort, which is not easily handled by a single processor, at least within a reasonable time frame. The basic structure the parallel PSO algorithm is reported in Fig. 3(a). Starting from the observation that the updating of the velocity and the position of the agents, together with the evaluation of the scores of the fitness values to determine p_{best} and g_{best}, requires a relatively small fraction of the time needed to compute the fitness function; hence the evaluation of the objective function is the only operation that is parallelized. The basic idea is to make a partitioning of the swarm among all the CPUs. The global partitioning strategy is clearly shown Fig. 3(b), where the case of four processors used in the optimization is considered for a swarm comprising eight particles.

A partition (two agents) of the swarm is assigned to each processor, which evaluates the fitness function of the given set of particles at each stage of iteration. Upon finishing these tasks, the processors communicate with each other to broadcast the best location they have found individually (red lines in Fig.4).

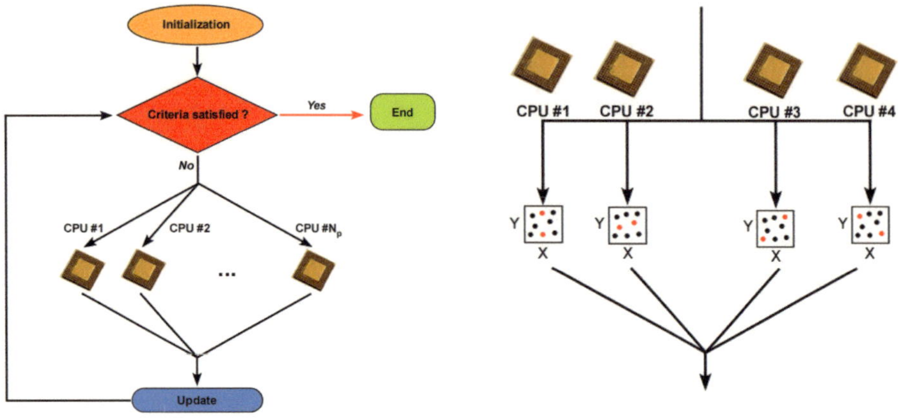

(a) (b)

Figure 3. PPSO implementation: (a) Flow chart; (b) detail of work subdivision among all the available processors. Each CPU considers only the agents assigned (red dots)

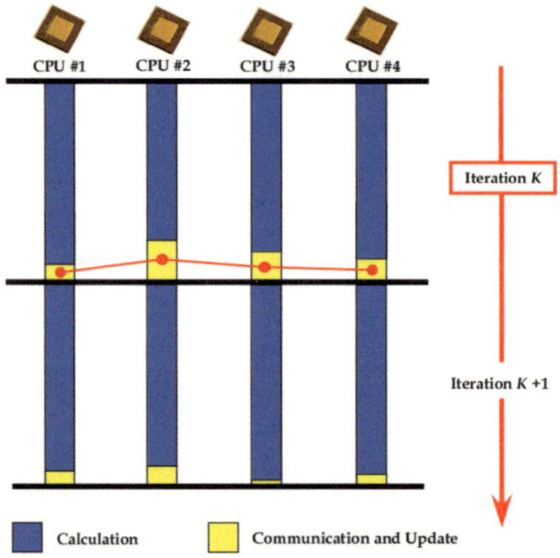

Figure 4. At iteration K, after the computation (blue), all the CPUs communicate to the others their results (red lines) and each processor perform the ranking to find the g_{best} (yellow)

Since the configuration analyzed by each processor is different, the time they require for their computation (highlighted in blue in Fig. 4) may vary slightly between the processors, even if the wait-time experienced by the faster processors is relatively small. All the processors have their own information, at the end of each evaluation step, as well as the latest information from the others about the best areas; hence, it is relatively easy to find the g_{best}. There is no master processor to carry out the ranking task and, hence, only a single transfer of information is needed at each iteration step. As is evident from Fig. 5, the general trend is a decrease of the overall simulation time.

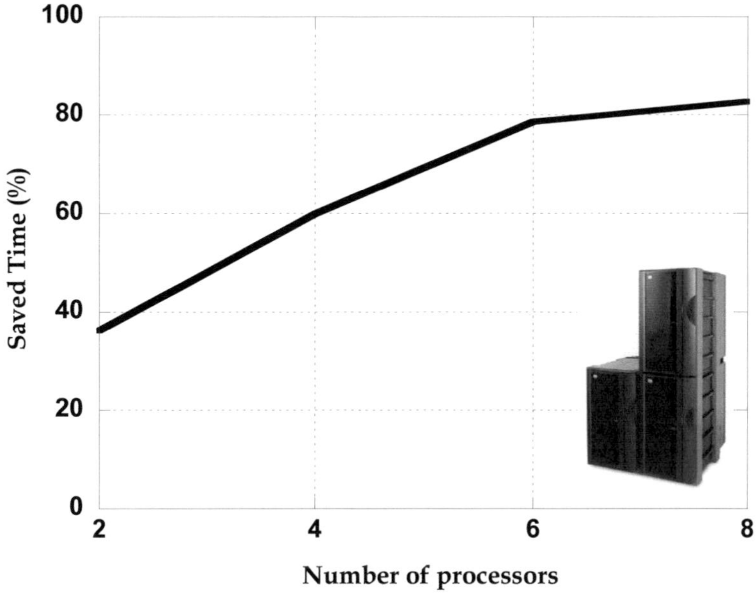

Figure 5. General trend of the saved time achieved by employing the PPSO approach

4. Space partitioning for increasing convergence rate

The problems of control of parameters and their tuning has been widely investigated (Clerc and Kennedy, 2002; Shi, and Eberhart, 2001) in the context of PSO, who have dealt with open issues such as premature convergence and stagnation into local minima. Furthermore, the effect of changing the neighborhood topology has been discussed extensively (Clerc, 1999; Kennedy, 1999; Lovbjerg et al., 2001; Abdelbar et al., 2005). However, to the best of our knowledge, the initialization of the position of the particles within the search space has not been subject of the same attention. The initialization of the position of the particles has a deep impact on the rate of convergence a in PSO and, therefore, has to be carefully taken into account. Since the agents are randomly located in most cases, it is possible that some areas may have higher densities of particles than others, especially if the multidimensional domain is large. Of course, this inhomogeneity in the distributions of the agents does not prevent them from pursuing the goal but can affect the time required for approaching the final solution. We propose to circumvent this difficulty by subdividing the solution space into sub-domains within which groups of agents are initially located in order to guarantee the homogeneous distribution of agents all over the computational domain. Each particle cooperates only with those particles in its own group independently from the other groups. After a fixed number of iterations, the sub-boundaries are removed, the best positions found by each group are scored and the actual global best location is revealed to all. It is demonstrated that the first part of the optimization process, managed by particles inside the sub-boundaries, improves the speed with which we find the optimal solution and hence increases the convergence rate of the process. The efficiency of the proposed implementation, referred to enhanced PSO in this Section, has been verified through the optimization of commonly employed test functions as well as of a complex electromagnetic problem, *viz.*, the design of Artificial Magnetic Conductors (AMCs).

4.1 Space partitioning

We now discuss the space partitioning scheme using a slightly modified notation than used in Section 2. Let us denote to the position of the generic agent k at a certain instant i by using the vector X given by:

$$X^k(i)=[x^k_1(i),x^k_2(i),\ldots,x^k_n(i)], \tag{5}$$

and let $p^k_{best,n}$ be the best position along the direction n found by the agent k during its own wandering up to the i-th time step, and let $g_{best,n}$ be the best position along the direction n, discovered by the entire swarm at time step i. The particle is free to fly inside the defined n–dimensional space, within the constraints imposed by the n boundary conditions, which delimit the extent of the search space between a minimum ($x_{n,min}$) and maximum ($x_{n,MAX}$) and, hence, the values of the parameters during the optimization process. Accordinlgy, at the generic time step i+1, the velocity of the simple particle k along each direction is updated by following the rule:

$$v^k_n(i+1)=w^*\, v^k_n(i)+c_1{}^*\text{rand}()^*(p^k_{best,n}(i)-x^k_n(i))+c2^*\text{rand}()^*(g_{best,n}(i)-x^k_n(i)), \tag{6}$$

```
Define the allowed range of each dimension (boundaries)
Set i=1
for k=1, number_of_agents
   for n=1, number_of_dimensions
      Random initialization of x^k_n(i) within the allowed range [x_n,min ; x_n,MAX]
      Random initialization of  v^k_n(i) proportional to the dynamic of dim. n
   next n
next k
for j=1, number_of_iterations
   for k=1, number_of_agents
      Evaluate fitness^k(i), the fitness of agent k at instant i
   next k
   Rank the fitness values of all agents
   for k=1, number_of_agents
      if fitness^k(i) is the best value ever found by agent k then
         p^k_best,n(i)= x^k_n(i)
      end if
      if fitness^k(i) is the best value ever found by all agents then
         g_best,n(i)= x^k_n(i)
      end if
   next k
Update agent velocity by using (6) and limit if required
Update agent position, check it with respect to the Boundaries
i=i+1
next j
```

Figure 6. PSO implementation with initialization by using boundary conditions

To refresh the memory of the standard particle swarm optimization algorithm, we present its pseudocode in Fig. 6, since it is useful to understand the novelty introduced by the initialization of the sub-boundaries. The solution we propose is based on the simple observation that there exists a high probability that the initial step, which entails a random position of all the agents, can determine a non-uniform coverage of the search domain. This fact affects the convergence rate, especially if the domain is large compared to the number of agents involved in the search process. Even if the algorithm is able to find the optimal solution, the process could be speeded up by adopting an approach which will be detailed in this section. The underlying concept upon which the algorithm is based is to distribute the agents uniformly at the start of the optimization process. The agents are organized into equal groups and these groups are then forced to exploit a sector of the domain defined by the sub-boundaries. This concept is described in Fig. 7 for a three-dimensional domain.

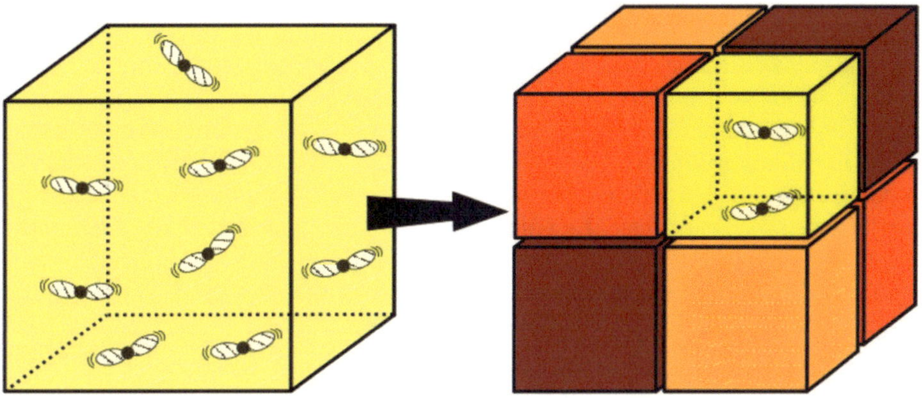

Figure 7. The domain defined by the boundaries is split into sectors defined by sub-boundaries within groups of agents wandering in search of the best location

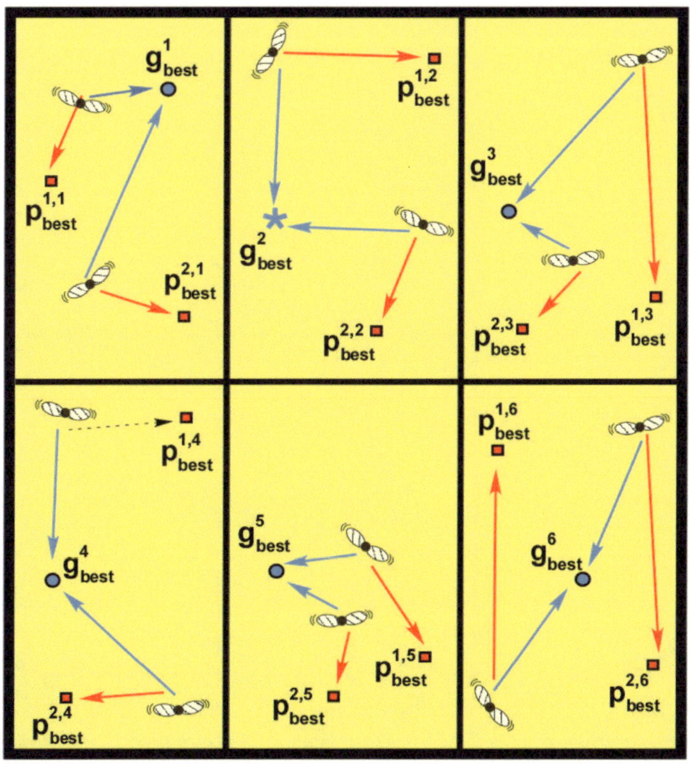

Figure 8. After the last iteration in sub-domain mode, and before starting the entire domain discovery, each particle is attracted by its own sub-domain best (blue dots) and its local best (red squares). The blue star in sector 2 is the best of all the sectors' bests

The domain is subdivided into sectors (or sub-domains) by using sub-boundaries that split one or more dimensions into equal intervals. The number of sub-boundaries cannot exceed the number of agents but, as it will be evident later, they should not produce groups that contain very few agents. During the initial stages, each group flies inside the assigned sub-domain and, hence, each group g has its own "sub-domain best" (indicated by $g^{g}_{best,n}$). Furthermore, each agent k in the group g has its own position $x^{k,g}$ and the local best location ($p^{k,g}_{best}$). The sub-boundaries pose impassable limits and consequently, none of the agents of one group can cross these boundaries to enter another sector. This guarantees that the number of agents in each sector is constant and so that the homogeneity of their spread within the multidimensional domain is preserved. Once the number of iterations dedicated to this process is exceeded, the barriers imposed by the sub-boundaries are removed and the particles are free to fly all over the entire domain. The "global best" is then chosen from those found in the sectors by the groups while the "local best" position of each agent is preserved. The operation executed at the exact instant of the passage from the sub-boundary conditions to the global boundary conditions is described in Figs. 8 and 9 for a two-dimensional case. To illustrate the differences introduced in this modified version of the PSO, its pseudocode is presented in Fig. 10.

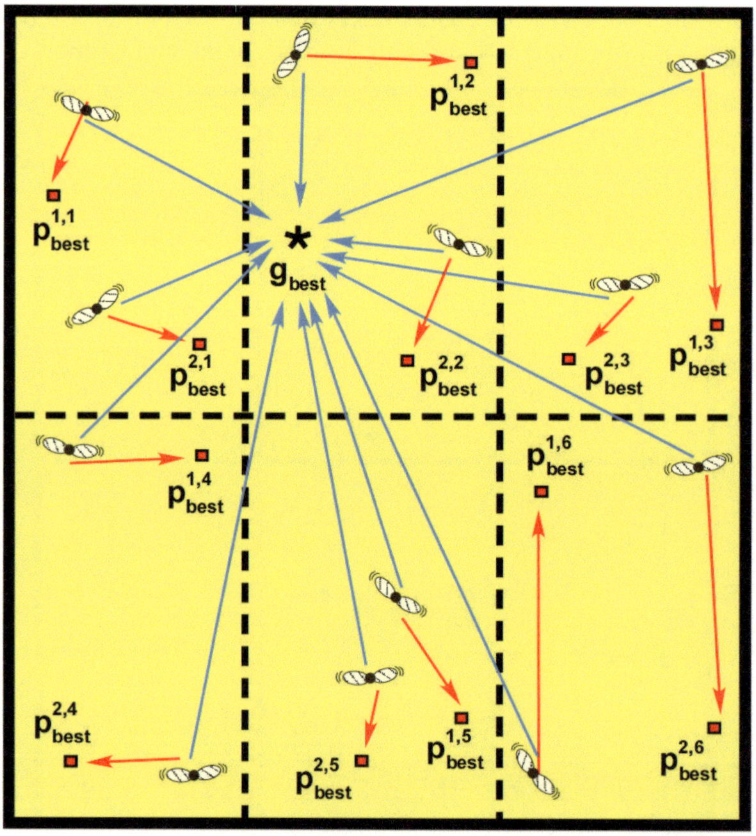

Figure 9. Opening the sub-boundaries: all the agents gain the information about the global best as soon as the barriers imposed by the sub-boundaries are removed. They are attracted both by that location as well as by the own local best previously found

To point out the changes in the results obtained by using this new PSO implementation, we have optimized several functions used as test beds for studying the performance of optimizers (Clerc and Kennedy, 2002). In particular, the following functions have been considered. The first type is the Rastrigin function defined as:

$$f_1(x) = \sum_{i=1}^{N} \left(x_i^2 - 10\cos(2\pi x_i) + 10 \right), \tag{7}$$

with ($-5.12 < x_i < 5.12$). The second type is the Griewank function ($-600 < x_i < 600$):

$$f_2(x) = \frac{1}{4000}\sum_{i=1}^{N} x_i^2 - \prod_{i=1}^{N} \cos\left(\frac{x_i}{\sqrt{i}} \right) + 1 . \tag{8}$$

The last function considered is the Rosenbrock function:

$$f_3(x) = \sum_{i=1}^{N} \left(100\left(x_{i+1} - x_i^2 \right)^2 + \left(x_i - 1 \right)^2 \right). \tag{9}$$

with ($-50 < x_i < 50$).

All the introduced functions have a global minimum equal to zero. Several simulations have been run for each of these functions, both with the standard PSO algorithm as well as with the new proposed one.

Three different sizes of the swarm have been considered, comprising of 16, 20 and 32 agents, respectively. Furthermore, to better understand the influence of the sub-boundary initialization, we have addressed the problem with a variable number of sectors (2, 4, 8, and 16) and, hence, different number of groups. As mentioned previously each sector contains only one group. The maximum allowed number of iterations to reach the minimum has been set to 150. Except for the boundary case, we have run half of the total amount of iterations with active sub-boundaries. This choice is to be regarded only as a suggestion , which is important for efficient cooperation of all the agents acting together – one of the most important features of the PSO algorithm. The results for N=3 are shown in Table I.

The first value expresses the average number of iterations necessary to approach the minimum with a tolerance of less than 0.01. The abbreviation N.R. (not reached) means that this requirement has not been satisfied up to the 150-*th* iteration. The second value within the brackets is the number of fitness evaluations which indicates the number of calls to the solver. We have deliberately omitted to consider the case of 20 agents and 8 sectors because it is not possible to have groups with the same number of agents. From the above results, it is possible to state that the initialization with the sub-boundaries not only helps us to reach the convergence more rapidly, but also that the more we increase the number of divisions the less we improve the performance. Moreover, in the case of 16 groups the efficiency drops dramatically and the results are even worse than without sub-boundaries. This fact suggests a logical conclusion, *viz.*, that there is a limit to the improvement that we can achieve by increasing the number of subdomains beyond a certain point. Of course, the number of sectors is also limited by the number of agents, since a group has to be composed at least by two agents. The above results lead us to conclude that the initialization with the sub-boundaries helps us to reach the convergence more rapidly, but we have to prevent the use of very small groups. Therefore, even if a group has to be composed at least by two agents, these results suggested us to use a minimum of 4 agents in each group.

```
Set i=1
for g=1, number_of_groups
   for k=1, number_of_agents_in_the_group
      for n=1, number_of_dimensions
         Random initialization of x^{k,g}_n(i) within the range of  subdomain
#g
         Random initialization of v^{k,g}_n(i) prop. to the dynamic of subd. #g
      next n
   next k
next g
do while (Sub_boundary_case)
   Flag_set_global_best = FALSE
   for g=1, number_of_groups
      for k=1, number_of_agents_in_the_group
         Evaluate fitness^{k,g}(i), the fitness of agent k in group g at instant i
      next k
   next g
   for g=1, number_of_groups
      Rank the fitness values of all agents included only in group g
   next g
   for g=1, number_of_groups
      for k=1, number_of_agents_in_the_group
         if fitness^{k,g}(i) is the best value ever found by agent k in group g then
            p^{k,g}_{best,n}(i)= x^{k,g}_n(i)
         end if
         if fitness^{k,g}(i) is the best value ever found by all agents then
            g^g_{best,n}(i)= x^{k,g}_n(i)
         end if
      next k
   next g
   i=i+1
   if (i >= sub_boundaries_iterations) then Sub_boundary_case= FALSE
end do
if (Flag_set_global_best = FALSE) then
      Flag_set_global_best = TRUE
      Rank all the g^g_{best,n}(i) and set the actual g_{best,n}(i)
else
      follow, with the actual value of i, the procedure showed in Fig.6
end if
```

Figure 10. Pseudocode of the modified PSO. During the preliminary iterations the agents seek together, organized in groups, in an area defined by the sub-boundaries. After this stage, they are set free and can move all over the solution space

Rastrigin function

# of agents	No Sub-Boundaries	2 Groups	4 Groups	8 Groups	16 Groups
16	N.R.	142 (2272)	117 (1872)	98 (1568)	N.R.
20	N.R.	110 (2200)	70 (1400)	–	–
32	N.R.	60 (1920)	40 (1280)	34 (1088)	138 (4416)

Griewanck function

# of agents	No Sub-Boundaries	2 Groups	4 Groups	8 Groups	16 Groups
16	122 (1952)	110 (1760)	93 (1488)	80 (1280)	130 (4160)
20	96 (1920)	84 (1680)	74 (1480)	–	–
32	80 (2560)	52 (1664)	45 (1440)	38 (1216)	112 (3584)

Rosenbrock function

# of agents	No Sub-Boundaries	2 Groups	4 Groups	8 Groups	16 Groups
16	44 (704)	31 (496)	18 (288)	15 (240)	58 (1856)
20	30 (600)	23 (460)	12 (240)	–	–
32	19 (608)	14 (448)	7 (224)	7 (224)	55 (1760)

Table 1. Results obtained by using sub-boundaries initialization in solving benchmark functions

4.2 Artificial Magnetic Conductor case study

In recent years, much attention has been devoted to the problem of designing Artificial Magnetic Conductors (AMC) that find a variety of applications, especially in the field of low-profile antennas (Sievenpiper et al., 1999; Kern et al. 2005). The zero-phase reflection coefficient at the resonance frequency allows one to place the source close to the artificial magnetic ground plane, and this offers the possibility of reducing the total dimension of the device. In order to realize an AMC ground plane, one can exploit the use of planar architectures which incorporate an FSS printed on a grounded dielectric slab (Kern et al. 2005). As shown in Fig. 6(a), once the number and the configuration of the dielectric layers have been chosen, it is necessary to design the FSS unit cell, choose the values of dielectric constants as well as the thickness of each dielectric slab so as to realize the AMC behavior at the desired frequency.

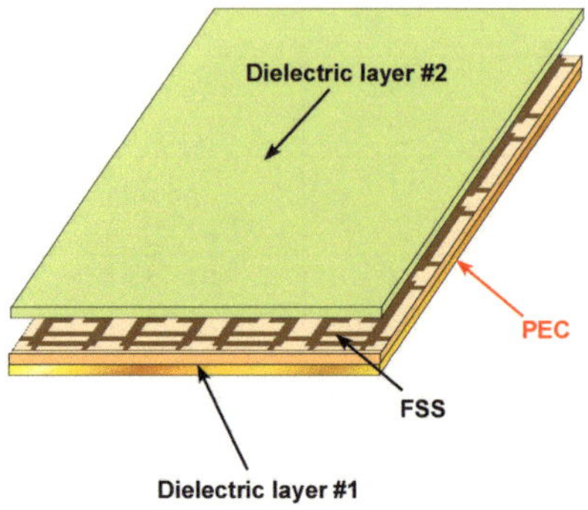

Figure 11. Geometry of an AMC screen A FSS is printed on a dielectric substrate backed by a perfect electric conductor (PEC)

A quantity proportional to the root mean square of the difference between the actual electric field reflection coefficient (Γ_E) and the desired one (Re{Γ_{AMC}}=1, Im{Γ_{AMC}}=0), for both TE and TM modes, is used to evaluate the performance of the structure. In order to evaluate the performance of the PSO enhanced with sub-boundaries we have run several simulations, each one carrying out 300 iterations, with different number of sectors. Our aim is to design an AMC screen acting as a PMC at 2.5 GHz, optimizing both the unit cell and the characteristic of two dielectric slabs (a superstrate and a substrate). At each simulation (except for the case with no sub-boundaries), one half of these iterations are carried out by using sub-boundaries and the average value of the fitness considered is the one of the best sector. The number of particles in the swarm is 32. The results are summarized in Fig. 12 where we show the convergence rate for each sub-domain configuration.

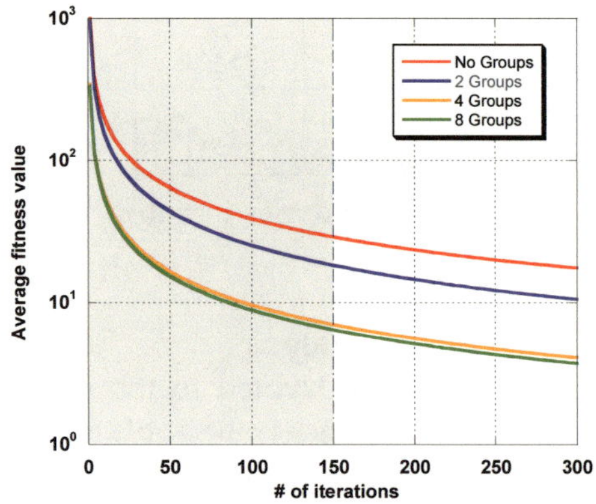

Figure 12. Trend of the convergence rates for four different cases. The grey zone represents the part of the iteration run by using sub-boundaries (except for the no-groups case)

We note that there is an improvement in the performance as we increase the number of groups and that, as in the previous case, the advantages of this approach are not directly proportional to the number of sub-boundaries utilized. In fact, we gain an advantage over the conventional PSO when we use two groups and the performance is better if we change the number of groups to four. However, it is not worthwhile to go beyond this value and to further subdivide the domain into eight groups. Moreover the sub-boundary approach is not applied to the binary map in this case and, hence, it reduces the impact of further subdivisions of the domain. As an example, in Fig. 13 we show an AMC screen, together with its electromagnetic performance, obtained in the case of a swarm initialized by using 4 groups.

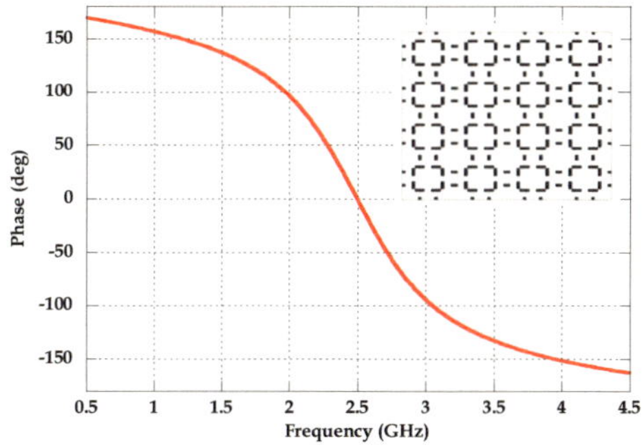

Figure 13. Phase of the reflection coefficient vs. frequency for the AMC screen shown in the inset. The phase response is reported for normal incidence

5. Conclusion

In this chapter, we have address the problem of efficiently synthesizing Frequency Selective Surfaces by using PSO. We have presented our specifically derived particle swarm optimization procedure which is able to handle, simultaneously, both real and binary parameters. We proposed a parallel version of the PSO algorithm to face challenging problems, which may require hardware resources and computational time that cannot be handled by a single CPU. Finally, we have introduced a novel strategy for the initialization of the agents' position within the multidimensional solution domain to further improve the convergence rate. This new procedure has been shown to be reliable with benchmark functions and has been successfully applied to the synthesis of Artificial Magnetic Conductors.

6. References

Abdelbar, A. M., Abdelshahid, S. & Wunsch D. C. (2005). Fuzzy PSO: a generalization of particle swarm optimization, *Proc. IEEE Int. Joint Conf. Neural Networks (IJCNN '05)*, Vol. 2, pp. 1086-1091.

Clerc, M. (1999). The swarm and the queen: towards a deterministic and adaptive particle swarm optimization, *Proc. Evolutionary Computation (CEC 99)*, Vol. 3, pp. 1951-1957.

Clerc, M. & Kennedy, J. (2002). The particle swarm-explosion, stability, and convergence in a multidimensional complex space, *IEEE Trans. Evol. Comput.*, Vol. 6, No. 1, pp. 58-73.

Dorigo, M. & Stutzle, T. (2004). *Ant Colony Optimization*, MIT Press, ISBN 0262042193.

Goldberg, D. E. (1989). *Genetic Algorithms in Search, Optimization and Machine Learning*, Addison-Wesley, Reading, MA.

Kennedy, J. & Eberhart, R.C. (1995). Particle Swarm Optimization, *Proceedings of IEEE International Conference on Neural Networks*, Vol. 4, pp. 1942-1948. Piscataway, NJ.

Kennedy, J. & Eberhart, R.C. (1997). A discrete binary version of the particle swarm algorithm, *IEEE Int. Conf. Systems, Man, and Cybernatics*, Vol. 5, pp. 4104-4108.

Kennedy, J. (1999). Small worlds and mega-minds: effects of neighborhood topology on particle swarm performance, *Proc. Evolutionary Computation (CEC 99)*, Vol.3, pp. 1931-1938.

Kern, D. J., Werner, D., Monorchio, A., Lanuzza, L. & Wilhelm M. (2005). The Design Synthesis of Multiband Artificial Magnetic Conductors Using High Impedance Frequency Selective Surfaces, *IEEE Trans. On Antennas Propag.*, Vol.53, No.1.

Lovbjerg, M., Rasmussen,T. K. & Krink T. (2001). Hybrid particle swarm optimizer with breeding and subpopulations, *Proc. 3rd Genetic and Evol. Comp. Conf. GECCO-2001.*

Manara, G., Monorchio, A & Mittra, R. (1999). Frequency selective surface design based on genetic algorithm, *Electronic Letters*, Vol. 35, pp.1400-1401.

Mittra, R.; Chan, C. & Cwik, T. (1988). Techniques for Analyzing Frequency Selective Surfaces-A Review, *IEEE Proceedings*, Vol. 76, Issue 12, pp.1593-1615.

Munk, B. A. (2000). *Frequency Selective Surfaces – Theory and Design*, Wiley, New York.

Rittenhouse, D. (1786). An optical problem, proposed by Mr. Hopkins, and solved by Mr. Rittenhouse, *Transaction of the American Philosophical Society*, Vol. 2, pp. 201-206.

Robinson, J. & Rahmat-Samii, Y. (2002). Particle Swarm Optimization in Electromagnetics, *IEEE Trans. Antennas Propag.*, Vol. 52, No. 2, pp. 397-407.

Shi, Y. & Eberhart, R. C. (1999). Empirical study of particle swarm optimization, *Proc. Evolutionary Computation (CEC 99)*, Vol. 3, pp. 1945–1950.

Shi, Y. & Eberhart, R. C. (2001). Fuzzy adaptive particle swarm optimization, *Proc. Evolutionary Computation (CEC 01)*, Vol. 1, pp. 101-106.

Sievenpiper, D., Zhang, L., Broas, R., Alexopolous, N. & Yablonovitch E. (1999). High impedance frequency selective surfaces with a forbidden frequency band, *IEEE Trans. Microwave Theory Tech.*, Vol.47, No. 11, pp. 2059-2074.

15

Search Performance Improvement for PSO in High Dimensional Space

Toshiharu Hatanaka[1], Takeshi Korenaga[1], Nobuhiko Kondo[2] and Katsuji Uosaki[3]
[1]*Department of Information and Physical Sciences, Osaka University*
[2]*Institute of Intelligent Information and Communications Technology, Konan University*
[3]*Department of Management and Information Sciences, Fukui University of Technology*
Japan

1. Introduction

Particle swarm optimisation (PSO) was developed by Kennedy and Eberhart in 1995 (Kennedy & Eberhart, 1995) inspired by the collective behaviour of natural birds or fish. PSO is a stochastic optimisation technique that uses a behaviour of population composed by many search points called particle. In spite of easy implementation in computer algorithms, it is well known as a powerful numerical optimizer. In the typical PSO algorithms, a set of particles searches the optimal solution in the problem space efficiently, by sharing the common attractor called global best. There are many modified versions of PSO by improving convergence property to a certain problem. While, a standard PSO is defined by Bratton and Kennedy (Bratton & Kennedy, 2007) to give a real standard for PSO studies. PSO seems as one of the evolutionary computations (ECs), and it has been shown that PSO is comparable to a genetic algorithm (Angeline, 1998). Thus, a lot of studies have demonstrated the effectiveness of PSO family in optimizing various continuous and discrete optimization problems. And a plenty of applications of PSO, such as the neural network training, PID controller tuning, electric system optimisation have been studied and achieved well results (Kennedy, 1997).
However, PSO is often failed in searching the global optimal solution in the case of the objective function has a large number of dimensions. The reason of this phenomenon is not only existence of the local optimal solutions, the velocities of the particles sometimes lapsed into the degeneracy, so that the successive range is restricted in the sub-plain of the whole search hyper-plain. The sub-plane that is defined by finite number of particle velocities is a partial space in the whole search space. The issue of local optima in PSO has been studied and proposed several modifications on the basic particle driven equation (Parsopoulos et al., 2001; Hendtlass, 2005; Liang et al., 2006). There used a kind of adaptation technique or randomized method (e.g. mutation in evolutionary computations) to keep particles velocities or to accelerate them. Although such improvements work well and have ability to avoid fall in the local optima, the problem of early convergence by the degeneracy of some dimensions is still remaining, even if there are no local optima. Hence the PSO algorithm does not always work well for the high-dimensional function.

From this point of view, the purpose of this paper is to improve performance of the PSO algorithm in case of high-dimensional optimization. To avoid such convergence with finite number of particles, we propose a novel PSO model, called as the Rotated Particle Swarm (RPS), where we introduce a coordinate conversion method. The numerical simulation results show the RPS is efficient in optimizing high-dimensional functions.

The remaining parts of this chapter organized as the following. In Section 2, PSO is briefly introduced, and then the early convergence phenomenon is illustrated. The proposed novel PSO model is shown in Section 3. Some results of the numerical studies for the benchmark problems are presented in Section 4, and we mention about some remarks in the last section.

2. Particle Swarm Optimization

Each particle, it is a member of the population, has its own position x and velocity v. A velocity decides a movement direction of a particle. The particles fly around the problem space, searching for the position of optima. Each particle memorizes two positions in order to find a favourite position in the search space. One is its own best position called the personal best and the other is the global best that is the best among all particles, denoted by $\boldsymbol{p}$ and g, respectively. Then, $p^{(i)}$ indicates the best position found by i-th particle from the first time step and $g^{(i)}$ indicates the best position among all p_i in the neighbour particle of i-th particle. Neighbour particle is defined by the topology of particles, which represents the network structure of population. Memories are utilized in adjusting the velocity to find better solutions.

In one of the standard versions of PSO algorithm, the velocity and position are updated at each time step, according to the following two equations,

$$v_d^{(i)} = \chi(v_d^{(i)} + \phi_{1,d} r_{1,d} (p_d^{(i)} - x_d^{(i)}) + \phi_{2,d} r_{2,d} (g_d^{(i)} - x_d^{(i)})) \tag{1}$$

$$x_d^{(i)} = x_d^{(i)} + v_d^{(i)} \tag{2}$$

Here, χ is the constriction coefficient, which prevents explosion of the velocity and balances between exploration and exploitation. The coefficients $r_{1,d}$ and $r_{2,d}$ are random values uniformly distributed over the range [0, 1]. These parameters are often set as $\varphi_{1,d} = \varphi_{2d} = 2.05$ and $\chi = 0.7298$ (Kenndy & Clerc, 2002). $v_d^{(i)}$ indicates d-th element of velocity vector of i-th particle, and $x_d^{(i)}$ indicates d-th element of position. $p_d^{(i)}$ and $g_d^{(i)}$ represent d-th elements of $p^{(i)}$ and $g^{(i)}$ respectively.

Some theoretical analyses of particle trajectories derived from Eq. (1) and (2) have been performed, where PSO algorithm is simplified (e.g., only one particle, one dimension, no stochastic elements) (Ozcan & Mohan, 1998; Ozcan & Mohan, 1999; Kenndy & Clerc, 2002). In those studies, it is shown that each particle oscillates around the weighted average position of its $\boldsymbol{p}$ and g, and settle down in an equilibrium state where velocities are considerably small until new $\boldsymbol{p}$ or g is found by particle. Note that the particles converge are not always local or global optima. We consider the effect of this kind of convergence property on high-dimensional optimization. Now, we present the experimental results where a standard PSO algorithm is applied to high-dimension Sphere function. Sphere function is one of the standard test functions without local optima. It is defined as follows,

$$f_1(x) = \sum_{d=1}^{D} x_d^2 \tag{3}$$

where D represents the number of dimensions.
Population size is set to 20 particles. Star topology, where all particles are interconnected, is used. The average fitness (function value) for 10 dimensions case at each time step over 10 trials is shown in Fig.1.

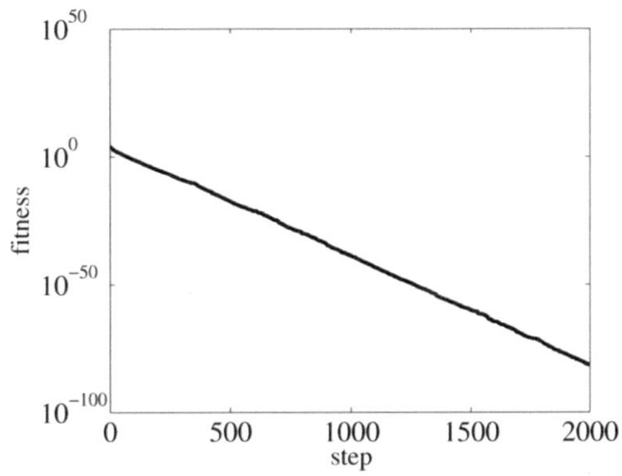

Figure 1. Function value of the global best particle, in case of dimension size D=10

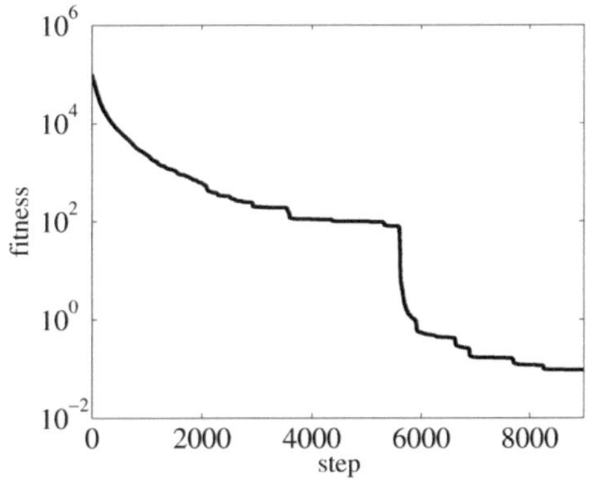

Figure 2. Function value of the global best particle, in case of dimension size D=100

Figure 2 shows the average fitness in the same conditions except for the dimension. In this case, a dimension is 100. The function value in 10 dimensions keeps decreasing as the search proceeds, while the improvement of the fitness value in 100 dimensions gets slow. Note that both vertical and horizontal axes are not same order. For higher dimension, the convergence speed is very low, or it does not converge.
We examined the other topologies such as four clusters, pyramid or ring. They have low connectivity to keep diversity in population. Though they yield better results than the Star topology, performance gets worse as the dimension of dimensions increases. When PSO

does not work well in optimizing high-dimensional function like this result, it is frequently observed that diversity of positions and memories of the whole population in some dimensions gets lost without trapping local optima.
It is conjectured that such premature convergence occurs because the velocity updating by Eq. (1) depends only on information of the same dimension. Once the diversity of positions and memories of certain dimension gets low, particles have difficulty in searching in the direction of the dimension. In the next section, we propose the novel velocity model that utilizes information of other dimensions.

3. Rotated Particle Swarm

Now, to consider the conventional way to update the velocity, we rewrite Eq. (1) by vectors and matrixes, such as,

$$v_i = \chi(v_i + \Phi_1(p_i - x_i) + \Phi_2(g_i - x_i)), \tag{4}$$

where

$$\Phi_1 = diag(\phi_{1,1}r_{1,1}, \phi_{1,2}r_{1,2}, \ldots, \phi_{1,D}r_{1,D}) \tag{5}$$

$$\Phi_2 = diag(\phi_{2,1}r_{2,1}, \phi_{2,2}r_{2,2}, \ldots, \phi_{2,D}r_{2,D}). \tag{6}$$

Fig.3 illustrates sample space by $\Phi_1(p^{(i)} - x^{(i)})$, the second term of Eq. (1), in 2 dimensions.

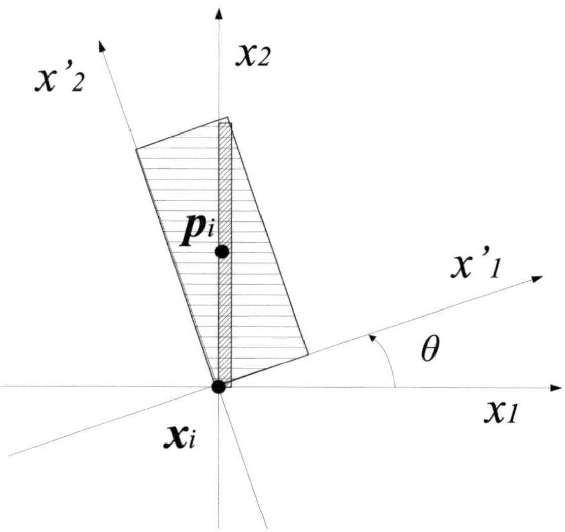

Figure 3. Geometric illustration of sample space by $\Phi_1(p^{(i)} - x^{(i)})$ in 2 dimensions

In $x_1 - x_2$ coordinate system where x_i and p_i are aligned parallel to the axis, the sample space has only one degree of freedom. On the other hand, the sample space is two-dimensional in the $x_1' - x_2'$ coordinate system. The same can be said about $\Phi_2(g^{(i)} - x^{(i)})$. The original PSO algorithm was designed by emulating birds seeking food. Birds probably never change the strategy to seek according to whether food exists in the true north or in the northeast. Consequently, particles can search optima even if axes are rotated. We introduce the coordinate conversion to the velocity update.

Before the values are sampled by $\Phi_1(p^{(i)} - x^{(i)})$ and $\Phi_2(g^{(i)} - x^{(i)})$, the coordinate system is rotated. Thus information of other dimensions is employed in calculating each component of velocity. In the proposed method, the velocity update equation Eq. (5) is substituted into

$$v_i = \chi(v_i + A^{-1}\Phi_1 A(p_i - x_i) + A^{-1}\Phi_2 A(g_i - x_i)) \tag{7}$$

where A is $D \times D$ matrix to rotate the axes. For the remainder of this paper, we refer to the PSO algorithm with this proposed velocity update method as the Rotated Particle Swarm (RPS). The RPS is designed for high-dimensional optimization. Therefore matrix computation is time-consuming if axes are arbitrarily rotated. To avoid it, in this study, certain number of axes are randomly selected without duplication and paired respectively. Only pairs of selected axes are rotated by θ. Most of the elements of A determined by this means are zero. For example, if $D = 5$ and selected pairs of axes are $x_1 - x_2$ and $x_3 - x_5$,

$$A = \begin{pmatrix} \cos\theta & -\sin\theta & 0 & 0 & 0 \\ \sin\theta & \cos\theta & 0 & 0 & 0 \\ 0 & 0 & \cos\theta & 0 & -\sin\theta \\ 0 & 0 & 0 & 1 & 0 \\ 0 & 0 & \sin\theta & 0 & \cos\theta \end{pmatrix} \tag{8}$$

4. Numerical Simulation

The following well-known test functions, i.e. Sphere function, Quatric function (De Jong F4), Rosenbrock function, Griewank Function, and Rastrigin function) are used to evaluate convergence property of the proposed method.

Sphere function:
$$f_1(x) = \sum_{d=1}^{D} x_d^2 \tag{9}$$

Quatric function:
$$f_2(x) = \sum_{d=1}^{D} d x_d^4 \tag{10}$$

Rosenbrock function:
$$f_3(x) = \sum_{d=1}^{D-1} 100(x_{d+1} - x_d^2)^2 + (x_d - 1)^2 \tag{11}$$

Griewank function:
$$f_4(x) = \frac{1}{4000}\sum_{d=1}^{D} x_d^2 - \prod_{d=1}^{D} \cos\left(\frac{x_d}{\sqrt{d}}\right) + 1 \tag{12}$$

Rastrigin function:
$$f_5(x) = \sum_{d=1}^{D} x_d^2 + 10 - 10\cos(2\pi x_d) \tag{13}$$

Sphere function, Quatric function and Rosenbrock function are unimodal. The others are multimodal functions. Rosenbrock function has dependence among variables.
For each function, search range and initialization rage were defined as listed in Table.1. Rosenbrock function has its global optimum at $[1, 1]^D$ and the others have at the origin. We use asymmetric initialization method, in which initial population is distributed only in a portion of the search range (Angeline, 1998). Optimal population size is problem-dependent. In this study, population size is set to 20 which is commonly used (Bergh & Engelbrecht, 2001). The canonical PSO and the RPS are tested with Star and Von Neumann topology. Von Neumann topology is grid-structured and has been shown to outperform other topologies in various problems (Kennedy & Mendes, 2002). In the RPS algorithm, the angle of rotation θ is set to $\pi/5$ and number of axes to be rotated is 40% of number of dimensions. The number of dimension D is set to 30, 100, and 400. Each experiment is run 20 times in each condition and the fitness at each time step is averaged.
In the results of Sphere function shown in Fig.3 - 5, in these figures, the bold lines show the convergence properties of the conventional PSO and the thin lines show the convergence properties of the proposed PSO. The solid lines indicate using the star topology and the dash lines indicate using Von-Neumann topology.
We can see a great difference in convergence ability between the RPS and the canonical PSO. Especially in D=400 though it becomes difficult for the canonical PSO to keep converging to the optimum, the fitness of RPS keeps decreasing. Similarly, in the case of Quatric, Rosenbrock and Griewank shown in Fig.6-14, for every functions, a convergence speed and final obtained fitness of the RPS get relatively good compared with the canonical PSO as the number of dimension increases.

Function	Search range	Range of the initial population
Sphere	$[-50, 50]^D$	$[25, 40]^D$
Quatric	$[-20, 20]^D$	$[10, 16]^D$
Rosenbrock	$[-100, 100]^D$	$[50, 80]^D$
Griewank	$[-600, 600]^D$	$[300, 500]^D$
Rastrigin	$[-5.12, 5.12]^D$	$[1, 4.5]^D$

Table 1. Search range and initialization for each function

5. Conclusion

The purpose of this study is to improve the early convergence of the particle swarm optimization in high-dimensional function optimization problems by the degeneracy. We have proposed the novel particle driven model, called Rotated Particle Swarm (RPS). It employs a coordinate conversion where information of other dimensions is utilized to keep diversity of each dimension. It is very simple technique and it is able to apply to any modified PSO model. The experimental results have shown that the proposed RPS is more efficient in optimizing high-dimensional functions than a standard PSO. The proposed RPS indicated remarkable improvement in convergence for high-dimensional space, especially in unimodal functions. An appropriate selection of rotated angles and dimensions are the future study, however it is envisioned that the performance of the proposed algorithm has robustness for such parameter settings. To compare the proposed method to the other modifications and to develop more powerful algorithm by combining with local optima technique are now under investigation.

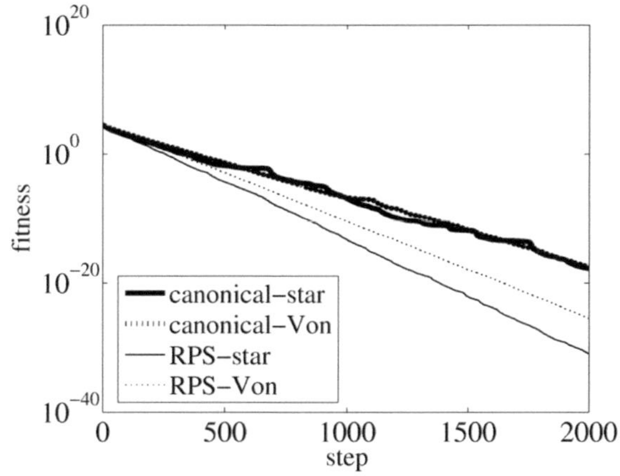

Figure 4. Sphere function (D=30)

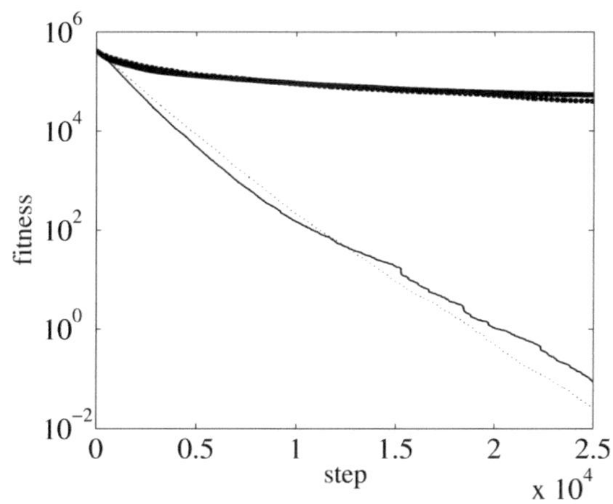

Figure 5. Sphere function (D=100)

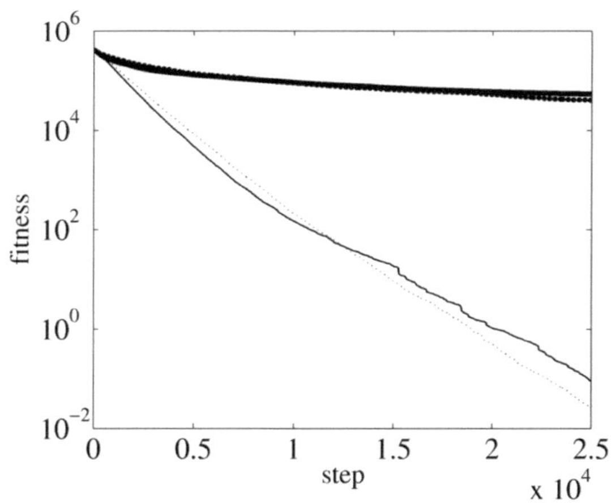

Figure 6. Sphere function (D=400)

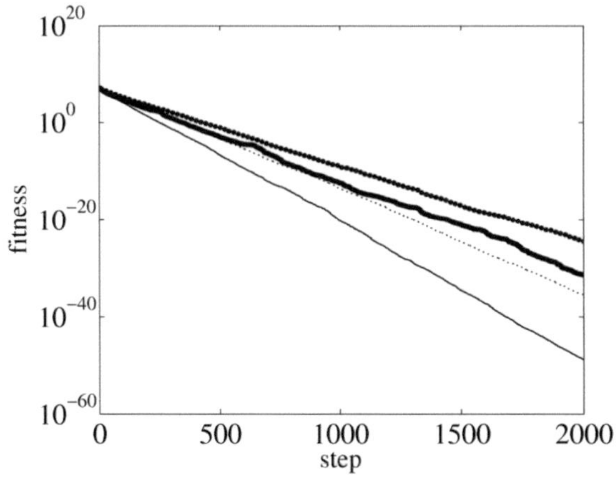

Figure 7. Quatric function (D=30)

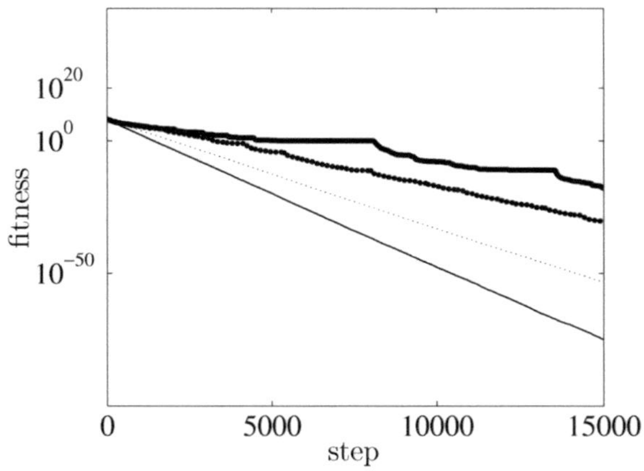

Figure 8. Quatric function (D=100)

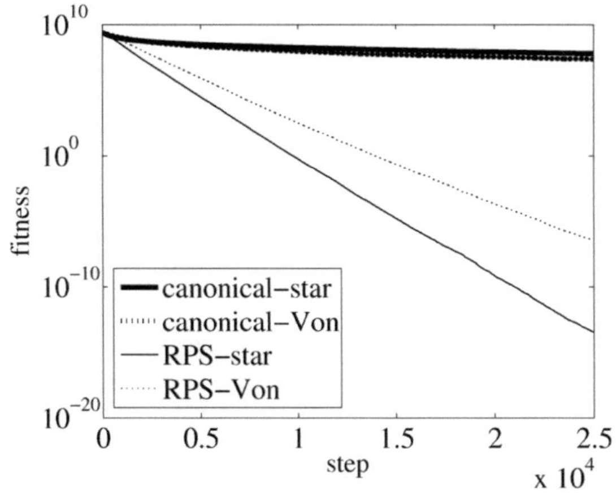

Figure 9. Quatric function (D=400)

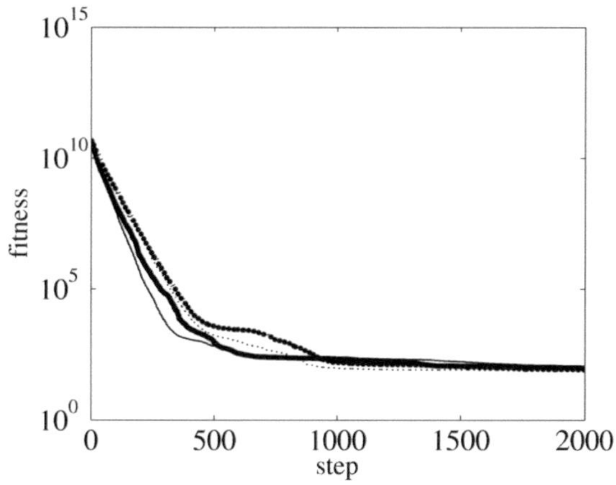

Figure 10. Rosenbrock function (D=30)

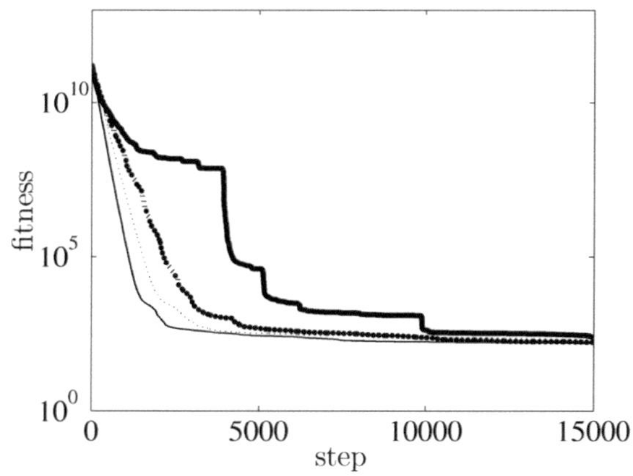

Figure 11. Rosenbrock function (D=100)

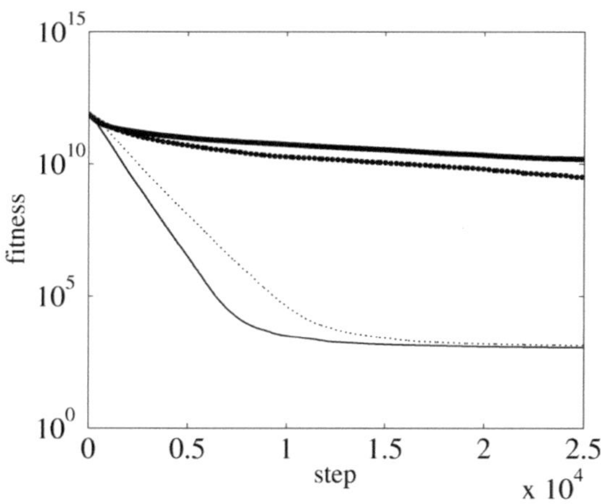

Figure 12. Rosenbrock function (D=400)

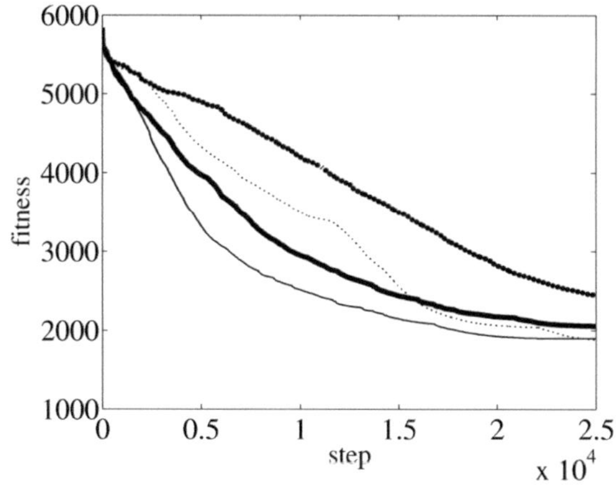

Figure 13. Griewank function (*D*=30)

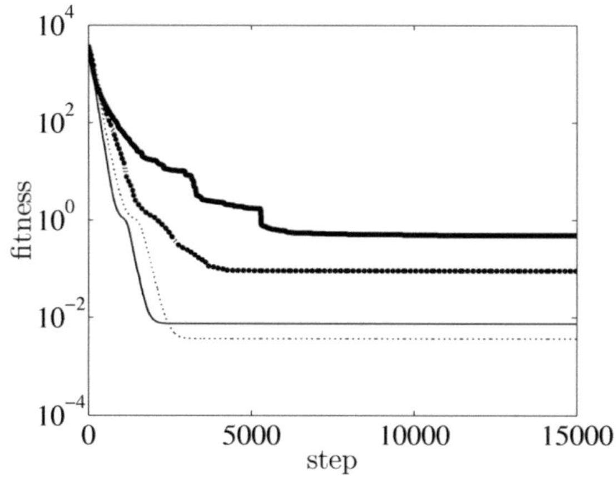

Figure 14. Griewank function (*D*=30)

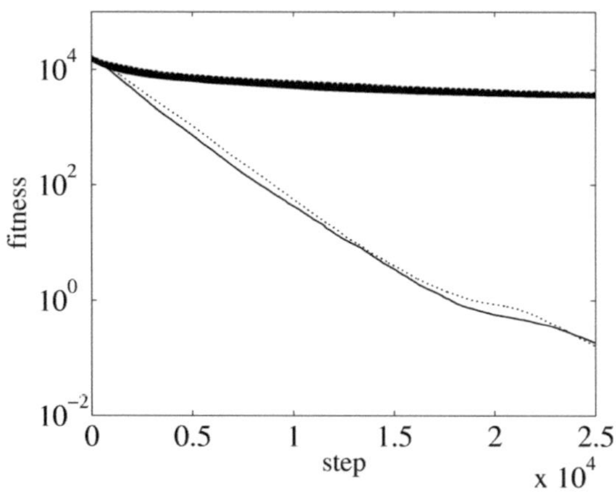

Figure 15. Griewank function (*D*=30)

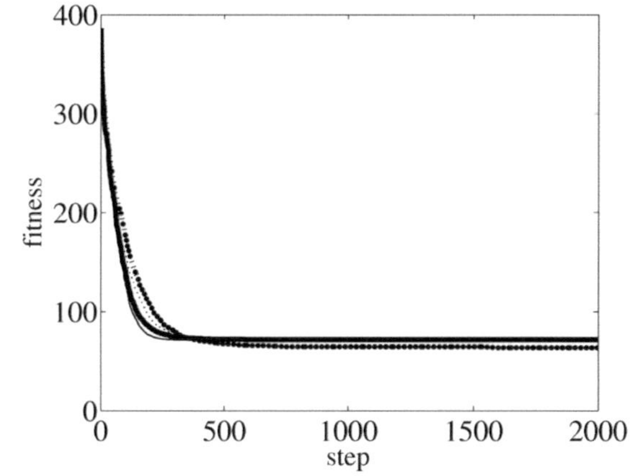

Figure 16. Rastrigin function (*D*=30)

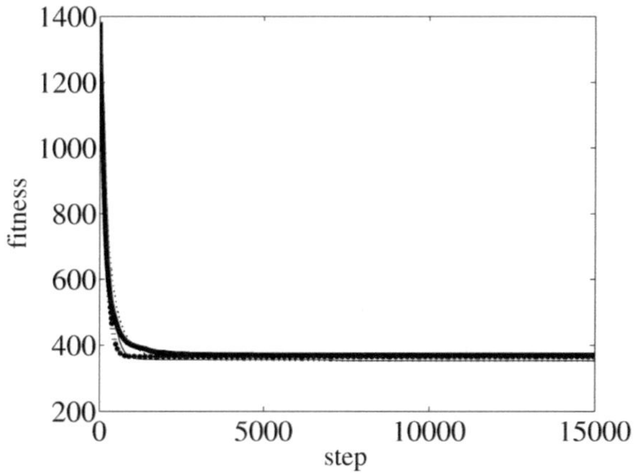

Figure 17. Rastrigin function (*D*=100)

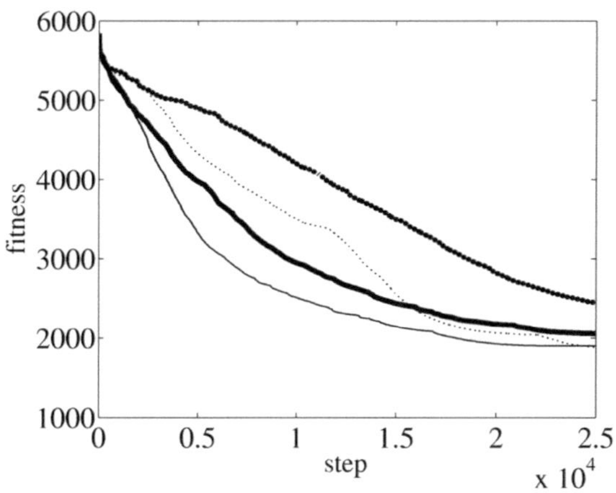

Figure 18. Rastrigin function (*D*=400)

6. References

Angeline, P.J. (1998). Evolutionary Optimization Versus Particle Swarm Optimization: Philosophy and Performance Differences, *Evolutionary Programming VII, in Lecture Notes in Computer Science*, Vol. 1447, pp. 601-610, 3-540-64891-7, Springer, London

Bratton, D. & Kennedy, J. (2007). Defining a Standard for Particle Swarm Optimization, *Proceedings of Swarm Intelligence Symposium 2007*, pp. 120-127, 1-4244-0708-7, Honolulu. April 2007

Hendtlass, T. (2005). A particle swarm algorithm for high dimensional, multi-optima problem spaces, *Proceedings of Swarm Intelligence Symposium 2005*. pp. 149-154, Pasadena, June 2005

Kennedy, J. (1997). The particle swarm: Social Adaptation of Knowledge, *Proceedings of IEEE International Conference on Evolutionary Computation*, pp.303-308, 0-7803-3949-5, Indianapolis, April 1997

Kenndy, J. & Clerc, M. (2002). The particle swarm: Explosion, stability, and convergence in a multidimensional complex space, *IEEE Transactions on Evolutionary Computation*, Vol. 6, No. 1, 58-73, 1089-778X

Kennedy, J. & Eberhart, R.C. (1995). Particle Swarm Optimization, *Proceedings of IEEE International Conference on Neural Networks*, pp. 1942-1948, 0-7803-2768-3, Perth, November 1995

Kennedy, J. & Mendes, R. (2002). Population structure and particle swarm performance, *Proceedings of 2002 IEEE Congress on Evolutionary Computation*, Vol. 2, pp.1671-1676, Honolulu, May 2002

Kennedy, J. & Spears, W.M. (1998). Matching algorithms to problems: An experimental test of the particle swarm and some genetic algorithms on the multimodal problem generator, *Proceedings of IEEE International Conference on Evolutionary Computation*, pp. 78--83, 0-7803-4869-9, Anchorage, May 1998

Liang, J.J., Qin, A.K., Suganthan, P.N. & Baskar, S. (2006). Comprehensive learning particle swarm optimizer for global optimization of multimodal functions, *IEEE Transactions on Evolutionary Computation*, Vol.10, No.3, 281-295, 1089-778X

Ozcan, E. & Mohan, C.K. (1998). Analysis of a Simple Particle Swarm Optimization System, *Intelligent Engineering Systems Through Artificial Neural Networks*, Vol. 8, pp. 253-258, 0-7918-0051-2

Ozcan, E. & Mohan, C.K. (1999). Particle swarm optimization: Surfing the waves, *Proceedings of 1999 IEEE Congress on Evolutionary Computation*, Vol. 3, pp.1939-1944, Washington, July 1999

Parsopoulos, K., Plagianakos, V. P. , Magoulas, G. D. & Vrahatis, M. N. (2001). Stretching technique for obtaining global minimizers through particle swarm optimization, Proceedings of the Particle Swarm Optimization Workshop, pp. 22-29, Indianapolis, 2001

van den Bergh, F. & A.P. Engelbrecht, A.P. (2001). Effects of Swarm Size on Cooperative Particle Swarm Optimizers, *Proceedings of the Genetic and Evolutionary Computation Conference*, pp.892-899, San Francisco, July 2001

16

Finding Base-Station Locations in Two-Tiered Wireless Sensor Networks by Particle Swarm Optimization*

Tzung-Pei Hong[1, 2], Guo-Neng Shiu[3] and Yeong-Chyi Lee[4]
[1]*Department of Computer Science and Information Engineering, National University of Kaohsiung*
[2]*Department of Computer Science and Engineering, National Sun Yat-sen University*
[3]*Department of Electrical Engineering, National University of Kaohsiung*
[4]*Department of Information Management, Cheng-Shiu University*
Taiwan

1. Abstract

In wireless sensor networks, minimizing power consumption to prolong network lifetime is very crucial. In the past, Pan *et al.* proposed two algorithms to find the optimal locations of base stations in two-tiered wireless sensor networks. Their approaches assumed the initial energy and the energy-consumption parameters were the same for all application nodes. If any of the above parameters were not the same, their approaches could not work. Recently, the PSO technique has been widely used in finding nearly optimal solutions for optimization problems. In this paper, an algorithm based on particle swarm optimization (PSO) is thus proposed for general power-consumption constraints. The proposed approach can search for nearly optimal BS locations in heterogeneous sensor networks, where application nodes may own different data transmission rates, initial energies and parameter values. Experimental results also show the good performance of the proposed PSO approach and the effects of the parameters on the results. The proposed algorithm can thus help find good BS locations to reduce power consumption and maximize network lifetime in two-tiered wireless sensor networks.
Keywords: wireless sensor network, network lifetime, energy consumption, particle swarm optimization, base station.

2. Introduction

Recently, a two-tiered architecture of wireless sensor networks has been proposed and become popular [1]. It is motivated by the latest advances in distributed signal processing

---

* This is a modified and expanded version of the paper "A PSO heuristic algorithm for base-station locations," presented at The Joint Conference of the Third International Conference on Soft Computing and Intelligent Systems and the Seventh International Symposium on Advanced Intelligent Systems, 2006, Japan.

and source coding and can offer a more flexible balance among reliability, redundancy and scalability of wireless sensor networks. A two-tiered wireless sensor network, as shown in Figure 1, consists of sensor nodes (SNs), application nodes (ANs), and one or several base stations (BSs).

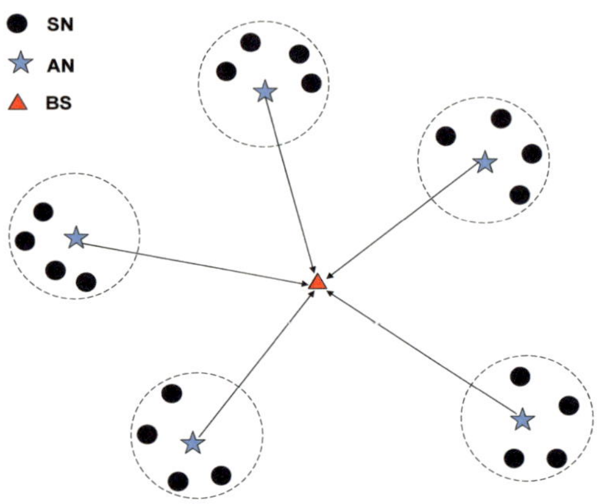

Figure 1. A two-tiered architecture of wireless sensor networks

Sensor nodes are usually small, low-cost and disposable, and do not communicate with other sensor nodes. They are usually deployed in clusters around interesting areas. Each cluster of sensor nodes is allocated with at least one application node. Application nodes possess longer-range transmission, higher-speed computation, and more energy than sensor nodes. The raw data obtained from sensor nodes are first transmitted to their corresponding application nodes. After receiving the raw data from all its sensor nodes, an application node conducts data fusion within each cluster. It then transmits the aggregated data directly to the base station or via multi-hop communication. The base station is usually assumed to have unlimited energy and powerful processing capability. It also serves as a gateway for wireless sensor networks to exchange data and information to other networks. Wireless sensor networks usually have some assumptions for SNs and ANs. For instance, each AN may be aware of its own location through receiving GPS signals [11] and its own energy.

In the past, many approaches were proposed to efficiently utilize energy in wireless networks. For example, appropriate transmission ways were designed to save energy for multi-hop communication in ad-hoc networks [16][10][5][19][7][6][20]. Good algorithms for allocation of base stations and sensors nodes were also proposed to reduce power consumption [12][15][16][8][9]. Thus, a fundamental problem in wireless sensor networks is to maximize the system lifetime under some given constraints. Pan *et al.* proposed two algorithms to find the optimal locations of base stations in two-tiered wireless sensor networks [13]. Their approaches assumed the initial energy and the energy-consumption parameters were the same for all ANs. If any of the above parameters were not the same, their approaches could not work.

In this paper, an algorithm based on particle swarm optimization (PSO) is proposed to find the base-station locations for general power-consumption constraints. The PSO technique was proposed by Eberhart and Kennedy in 1995 [2][3] and has been widely used in finding solutions for optimization problems. Some related researches about its improvement and applications has also been proposed [4][14][17][18]. It maintains several particles (each represents a solution) and all the particles continuously move in the search space according to their own local optima and the up-to-date global optimum. After a lot of generations, the optimal solution or an approximate optimal solution is expected to be found. The proposed approach here can search for nearly optimal BS locations in heterogeneous sensor networks. Experimental results also show the performance of the proposed PSO approach on finding the BS locations and the effects of the parameters on the results.

The remaining parts of this paper are organized as follows. Some related works about finding the locations of base stations in a two-tiered wireless networks is reviewed in Section 3. An algorithm based on PSO to discover base stations in a two-tiered wireless networks is proposed in Section 4. An example to illustrate the proposed algorithm is given in Section 5. Experimental results for demonstrating the performance of the algorithm and the effects of the parameters are described in Section 6. Conclusions are stated in Section 7.

3. Review of Related Works

As mentioned above, a fundamental problem in wireless sensor networks is to maximize the system lifetime under some given constraints. Pan *et al.* proposed two algorithms to find the optimal locations of base stations in two-tiered wireless sensor networks [13]. The first algorithm was used to find the optimal locations of base stations for homogenous ANs, and the second one was used for heterogeneous ANs. Homogenous ANs had the same data transmission rate and heterogeneous ANs might have different data transmission rates. In their paper, only the energy in ANs was considered. If a single SN ran out of energy, its corresponding AN might still have the capability to collect enough information. However, if an AN ran out of energy, the information in its coverage range would be completely lost, which was dangerous to the whole system.

Let d be the Euclidean distance from an AN to a BS, and r be the data transmission rate. Pan *et al.* adopted the following formula to calculate the energy consumption per unit time:

$$p(r,d) = r(\alpha_1 + \alpha_2 d^b), \tag{1}$$

where a_1 is a distance-independent parameter, a_2 is a distance-dependent parameter, and b is the Euclidean dimension. The energy consumption thus relates to Euclidean distances and data transmission rates.

Pan *et al.* assumed each AN had the same a_1, a_2 and initial energy. For homogenous ANs, they showed that the center of the minimal circle covering all the ANs was the optimal BS location (with the maximum lifetime).

4. A General Base-Station Allocation Algorithm Based on PSO

The ANs produced by different manufacturers may own different data transmission rates, initial energies and parameter values. When different kinds of ANs exist in a wireless network, it is hard to find the optimal BS location. In this section, a heuristic algorithm based on PSO to search for optimal BS locations under general constraints is proposed. An initial set of particles is first randomly generated, with each particle representing a possible BS location. Each particle is also allocated an initial velocity for changing its state. Let $e_j(0)$ be the initial energy, r_j be the data transmission rate, a_{j1} be the distance-independent parameter, and a_{j2} be the distance-dependent parameter of the j-th AN. The lifetime l_{ij} of an application node AN_j for the i-th particle is calculated by the following formula:

$$l_{ij} = e_j(0)/r_j(\alpha_{j1} + \alpha_{j2}d_{ij}^b), \tag{2}$$

where d_{ij}^b is the b-order Euclidian distance from the j-th AN to the i-th particle. The fitness function used for evaluating each particle is thus shown below:

$$fitness\,(i) = \overset{m}{\underset{j=1}{Min}}\, l_{ij}, \tag{3}$$

where m is number of ANs. That is, each particle takes the minimal lifetime of all ANs as its fitness value. A larger fitness value denotes a longer lifetime of the whole system, meaning the corresponding BS location is better. The fitness value of each particle is then compared with that of its corresponding *pBest*. If the fitness value of the i-th particle is larger than that of $pBest_i$, $pBest_i$ is replaced with the i-th particle. The best $pBest_i$ among all the particles is chosen as the *gBest*. Besides, each particle has a velocity, which is used to change the current position. All particles thus continuously move in the search space. When the termination conditions are achieved, the final *gBest* will be output as the location of the base station. The proposed algorithm is stated below.

The proposed PSO algorithm for finding the best BS location:

- Input: A set of ANs, each AN_j with its location (x_j, y_j), data transmission rate r_j, initial energy $e_j(0)$, parameters a_{j1} and a_{j2}.
- Output: A BS location that will cause a nearly maximal lifetime in the whole system.
- Step 1: Initialize the fitness values of all *pBests* and the *gBest* to zero.
- Step 2: Randomly generate a group of n particles, each representing a possible BS location. Locations may be two-dimensional or three-dimensional, depending on the problems to be solved.
- Step 3: Randomly generate an initial velocity for each particle.
- Step 4: Calculate the lifetime l_{ij} of the j-th AN for the i-th particle by the following formula:

  $$l_{ij} = e_j(0)/r_j(\alpha_{j1} + \alpha_{j2}d_{ij}^b),$$

  where $e_j(0)$ is the initial energy, r_j is the data transmission rate, a_{j1} is a distance-independent parameter, a_{j2} is a distance-dependent parameter of the j-th AN, and d_{ij}^b is the b-order Euclidean distance from the i-th particle (BS) to the j-th AN.
- Step 5: Calculate the lifetime of the whole sensor system for the i-th particle as its fitness value ($fitness_i$) by the following formula:

  $$fitness(i) = \overset{m}{\underset{j=1}{Min}}\, l_{ij},$$

  where m is number of ANs and i = 1 to n.
- Step 6: Set $pBest_i$ as the current i-th particle if the value of *fitness(i)* is larger than the current fitness value of $pBest_i$.
- Step 7: Set *gBest* as the best *pBest* among all the particles. That is, let:

$$\text{fitness of } pBest_k = max_{i=1}^{n} \text{ fitness of } pBest_i,$$

and set $gBest=pBest_k$.

- Step 8: Update the velocity of the i-th particle as:

$$V_{id}^{new} = w \times V_{id}^{old} + c_1 \times Rand_1() \times (pBest_{id} - x_{id}) + c_2 \times Rand_2() \times (gBest_d - x_{id})$$

  where x_{id}^{new} is the new velocity of the i-th particle at the d-th dimension, x_{id}^{old} is the current velocity of the i-th particle at the d-th dimension, w is the inertial weight, c_1 is the acceleration constant for particles moving to *pBest*, c_2 is the acceleration constant for particles moving to *gBest*, $Rand_1()$ and $Rand_2()$ are two random numbers among 0 to 1, x_{id} is the current position of the i-th particle at the d-th dimension, $pBest_{id}$ is the value of $pBest_i$ at the d-th dimension, and $gBest_d$ is the value of *gBest* at the d-th dimension.
- Step 9: Update the position of the i-th particle as:

$$x_{id}^{new} = x_{id}^{old} + V_{id}^{new},$$

  where x_{id}^{new} and x_{id}^{old} are respectively the new position and the current position of the i-th particle at the d-th dimension.
- Step 10: Repeat Steps 4 to 9 until the termination conditions are satisfied.

In Step 10, the termination conditions may be predefined execution time, a fixed number of generation or when the particles have converged to a certain threshold.

5. An Example

In this section, a simple example in a two-dimensional space is given to explain how the PSO approach can be used to find the best BS location that will generate the nearly maximal lifetime in the whole system. Assume there are totally four ANs in this example and their initial parameters are shown in Table 1, where "Location" represents the two-dimensional coordinate position of an AN, "Rate" represents the data transmission rate, and "Power" represents the initially allocated energy. All a_{j1}'s are set at 0 and all a_{j2}'s at 1 for simplicity.

AN	Location	Rate	Power
1	(1, 10)	5	10000
2	(11, 0)	5	10000
3	(8, 7)	4	6400
4	(4, 3)	4	6400

Table 1. The initial parameters of ANs in the example

For the example, the proposed PSO algorithm proceeds as follows.

- Step 1: The initial fitness values of all *pBests* and the *gBest* are set to zero.
- Step 2: A group of n particles are generated at random. Assume n is set at 3 in this example for simplicity. Also assume the three initial particles randomly generated are located at (4, 7), (9, 5) and (6, 4). Figure 2 shows the positions of the given ANs and the initial particles, where the triangles represent the particles and the circles represent the ANs.

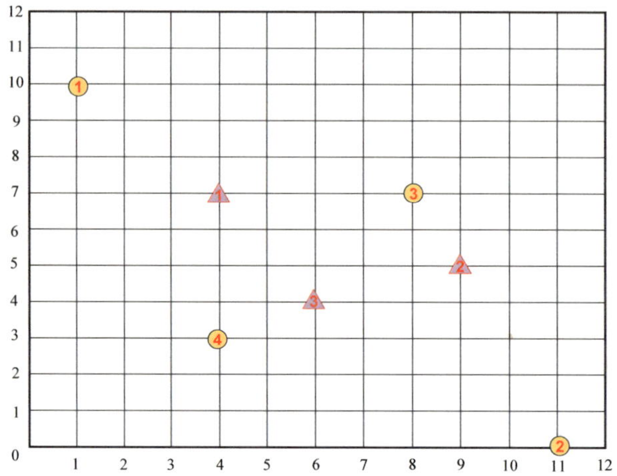

Figure 2. The positions of the given ANs and the initial particles

- Step 3: An initial velocity is randomly generated for each particle. In this example assume the initial velocity is set at zero for simplicity.
- Step 4: The lifetime of each AN for a particle is calculated. Take the first AN for the first particle as an example. Its lifetime is calculated as follows:

$$l_{11} = 10000/5[(4-1)^2 + (7-10)^2] = 111.11.$$

The lifetimes of all ANs for all particles are shown in Table 2.

Particle \ AN	1(1, 10)	2(11, 0)	3(8, 7)	4(4, 3)
1(4, 7)	111.11	20.41	100	100
2(9, 5)	22.47	68.97	320	55.17
3(6, 4)	32.79	48.78	123.08	320

Table 2. The lifetimes of all ANs for all particles

- Step 5: The lifetime of the whole sensor system for each particle is calculated as the fitness value. Take the first particle as an example. Its fitness is calculated as follows:

$$Fitness(1) = Min\{l_{11}, l_{12}, l_{13}, l_{14}\} = Min\{111.11, 20.41, 100, 100\} = 20.41.$$

In the same way, the fitness values of all the particles are calculated and shown in Table 3.

Particle	Location	Fitness
1	(4, 7)	20.41
2	(9, 5)	22.47
3	(6, 4)	32.79

Table 3. The fitness values of all the particles

- Step 6: The fitness value of each particle is compared with that of its corresponding *pBest*. If the fitness value of the *i*-th particle is larger than that of $pBest_i$, $pBest_i$ is replaced with the *i*-th particle. In the first generation, the fitness values of all the *pBest*s are zero, smaller than those of the particles. The particles are then stored as the new *pBest*s. The resulting *pBest*s are shown in Table 4, where the field "appearance generation" represents the generation number in which a particle is set as the current *pBest*.

Particle	Location	Fitness	Appearing Generation
1	(4, 7)	20.41	1
2	(9, 5)	22.47	1
3	(6, 4)	32.79	1

Table 4. The *pBest*s after the first generation

- Step 7: The best $pBest_i$ among all the particles is chosen as the *gBest*. In this example, $pBest_3$ has the largest fitness value and is set as the *gBest*.
- Step 8: The new velocity of each particle is updated. Assume the inertial weight w is set at 1, the acceleration constant c_1 for particles moving to *pBest* is set at 2, and the acceleration constant c_2 for particles moving to *gBest* is set at 2. Take the first particle as an example to illustrate the step. Its new velocity is calculated as follows:

$$\begin{aligned} V_{1x}^{new} &= w \times V_{1x}^{old} + c_1 \times Rand_1() \times (pBest_{1x} - x_{1x}) \\ &+ c_2 \times Rand_2() \times (gBest_d - x_{1x}) \\ &= 1 \times 0 + 2 \times 0.5(4-4) + 2 \times 0.25(6-4) \\ &= 1, \text{ and} \\ V_{1y}^{new} &= w \times V_{1y}^{old} + c_1 \times Rand_3() \times (pBest_{1y} - x_{1y}) \\ &+ c_2 \times Rand_4() \times (gBest_d - x_{1y}) \\ &= 1 \times 0 + 2 \times 1(7-7) + 2 \times 0.125(4-7) \\ &= -0.75, \end{aligned}$$

where the four random numbers generated are 0.5, 0.25, 1 and 0.125, respectively. In the same way, the new velocities of the other two particles can be calculated. The results are shown in Table 5.

Particle	Old Location	Velocity
1	(4, 7)	(1, -0.75)
2	(9, 5)	(-1.2, -0.2)
3	(6, 4)	(0, 0)

Table 5. The new velocities of all the three particles

- Step 9: The position of each particle is updated. Take the first particle as an example. Its new position is calculated as follows:

$$\begin{aligned} x_{1x}^{new} &= x_{1x}^{old} + V_{1x}^{new} \\ &= 4 + 1 \\ &= 5, \text{ and} \\ x_{1y}^{new} &= x_{1y}^{old} + V_{1y}^{new} \\ &= 7 + (-0.75) \\ &= 6.25. \end{aligned}$$

In the same way, the new positions of all the other two particles can be found. The results are shown in Table 6.

Particle	Old Location	Velocity	New Location
1	(4, 7)	(1, -0.75)	(5, 6.25)
2	(9, 5)	(-1.2, -0.2)	(7.8, 4.8)
3	(6, 4)	(0, 0)	(6, 4)

Table 6. The new positions of all the three particles

- Step 10: Steps 4 to 9 are then repeated until the termination conditions are satisfied. The lifetime evolution along with different generations is shown in Figure 3.

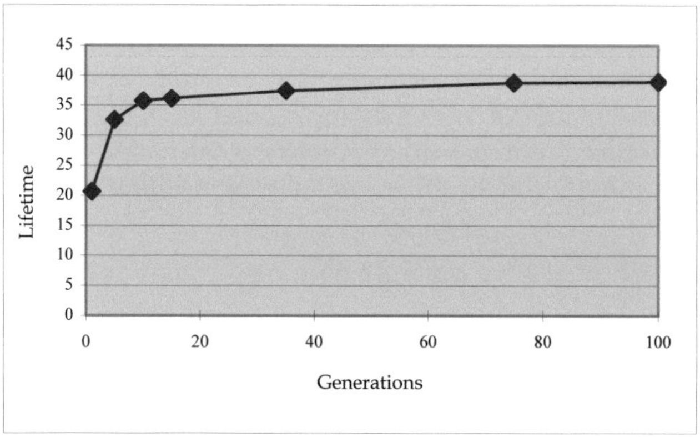

Figure 3. The evolution of the maximal lifetime for the example

6. Experimental Results

Experiments were made to show the performance of the proposed PSO algorithm on finding the optimal positions of base stations. They were performed in C language on an AMD PC with a 2.0GHz processor and 1G main memory and running the Microsoft Window XP operating system. The simulation was done in a two-dimensional real-number space of 1000*1000. That is, the ranges for both x and y axes were within 0 to 1000. The data transmission rate was limited within 1 to 10 and the range of initial energy was limited between 100000000 to 999999999. The data of all ANs, each with its own location, data transmission rate and initial energy, were randomly generated. Note that the data transmission rates and the initial energy amounts of real-life sensors may not fall in the above range. But the proposed approach is still suitable since the lifetime is proportional to the initial energy amount and inversely proportional to the transmission rate.

Experiments were first made to show the convergence of the proposed PSO algorithm when the acceleration constant (c_1) for a particle moving to its *pBest* was set at 2, the acceleration constant (c_2) for a particle moving to its *gBest* was set at 2, the inertial weight (w) was set at 0.6, the distance-independent parameter (a_{j1}) was set at zero, and the distance-dependent parameter (a_{j2}) was set at one. The experimental results of the resulting lifetime along with different generations for 50 ANs and 10 particles in each generation are shown in Figure 4.

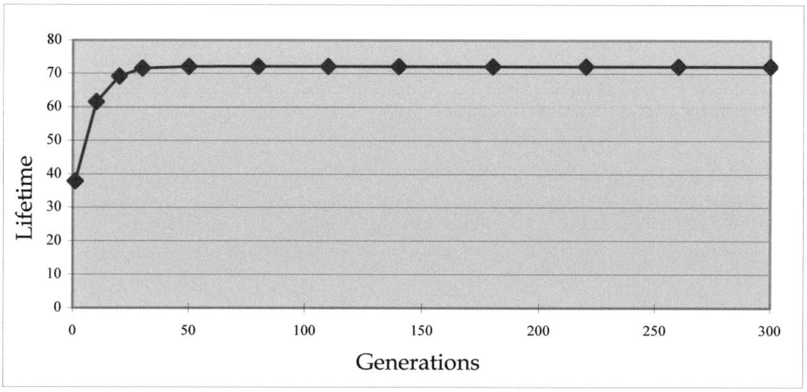

Figure 4. The lifetime for 50 ANs and10 particles

It is easily seen from Figure 4 that the proposed PSO algorithm could converge very fast (below 50 generations). Next, experiments were made to show the effects of different parameters on the lifetime. The influence of the acceleration constant (c_1) for a particle moving to its *pBest* on the proposed algorithm was first considered. The process was terminated at 300 generations. When $w = 1$ and $c_2 = 2$, the nearly optimal lifetimes for 50ANs and 10 particles along with different acceleration constants (c_1) are shown in Figure 5.

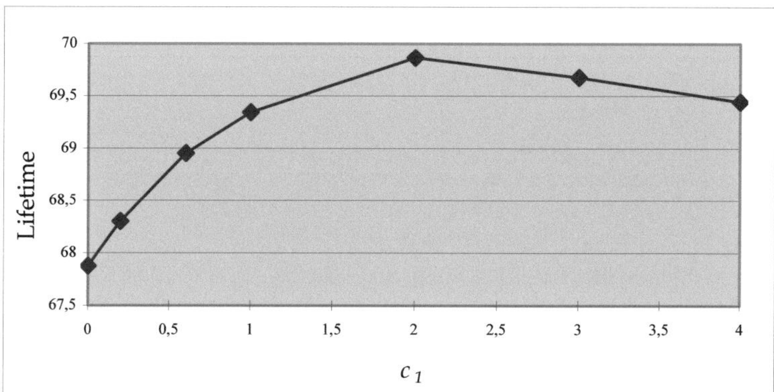

Figure 5. The lifetimes along with different acceleration constants (c_1)

It can be observed from Figure 5 that the lifetime first increased and then decreased along with the increase of the acceleration constant (c_1). When the value of the acceleration constant (c_1) was small, the velocity update of each particle was also small, causing the convergence speed slow. The proposed PSO algorithm might thus not get the optimal solution after the predefined number of generations. On the contrary, when the value of the acceleration constant (c_1) was large, the velocity change would be large as well, causing the particles to move fast. It was then hard to converge. In the experiments, the optimal c_1 value was about 2. Next, experiments were made to show the effects of the acceleration constant (c_2) for a particle moving to its *gBest* on the proposed algorithm. When $w = 1$ and $c_1 = 2$, the experimental results are shown in Figure 6.

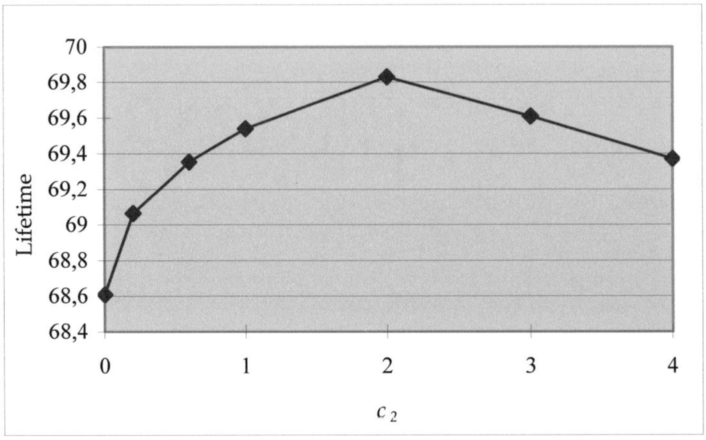

Figure 6. The lifetimes along with different acceleration constants (c_2)

It can be observed from Figure 6 that the lifetime first increased and then decreased along with the increase of the acceleration constant (c_2). The reason was the same as above. In the experiments, the optimal c_2 value was about 2. Next, experiments were made to show the effects of the inertial weight (w) on the proposed algorithm. When $c_1 = 2$ and $c_2 = 2$, the experimental results are shown in Figure 7.

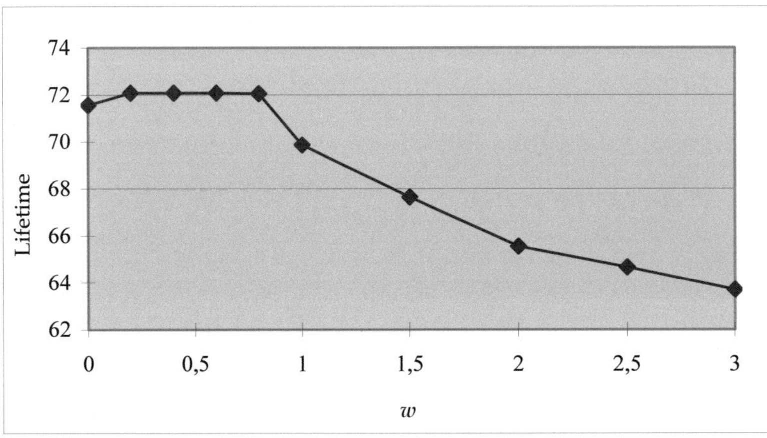

Figure 7. The lifetimes along with different inertial weights (w)

It can be observed from Figure 7 that the proposed algorithm could get good lifetime when the inertial weight (w) was smaller than 0.6. The lifetime decreased along with the increase of the inertial weight (w) when w was bigger than 0.6. This was because when the value of the inertial weight was large, the particles would move fast due to the multiple of the old velocity. It was then hard to converge. Next, experiments were made to show the relation between lifetimes and numbers of ANs. The experimental results are shown in Figure 8.

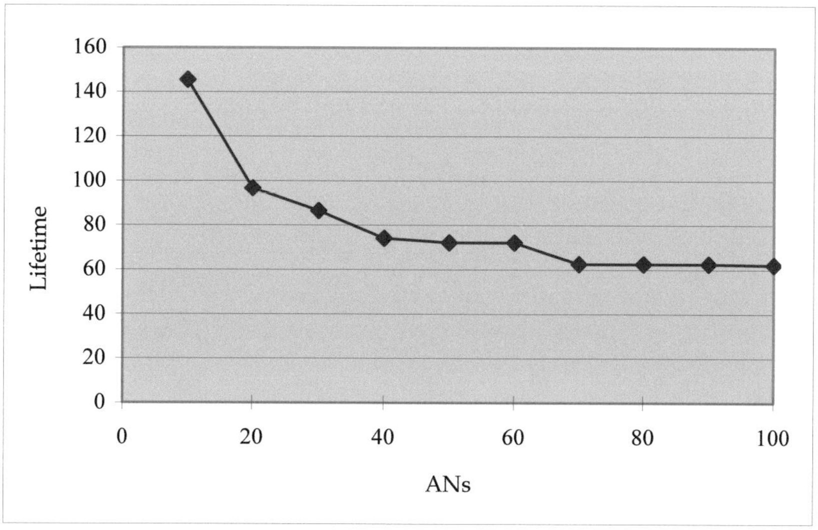

Figure 8. The lifetimes along with different numbers of ANs

It can be seen from Figure 8 that the lifetime decreased along with the increase of the number of ANs. It was reasonable since the probability for at least an AN in the system to fail would increase when the number of ANS grew up. The execution time along with different numbers of ANs is shown in Figure 9.

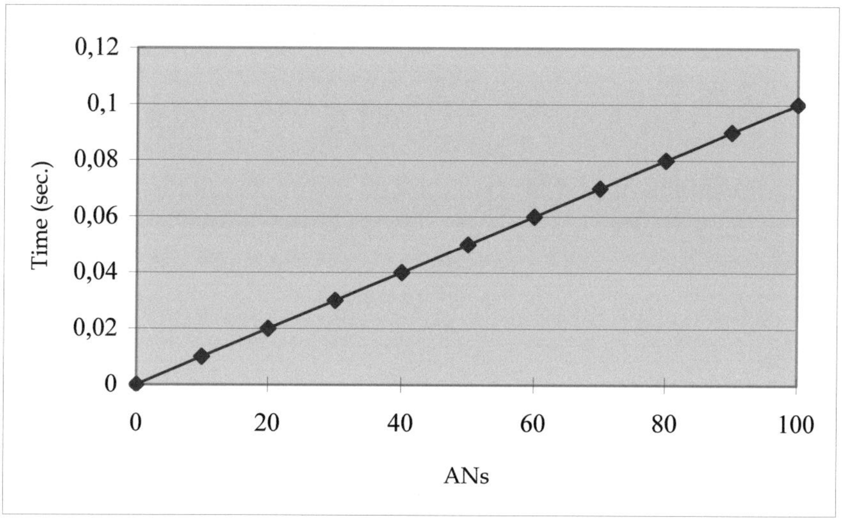

Figure 9. The execution time along with different numbers of ANs

It can be observed from Figure 9 that the execution time increased along with the increase of numbers of ANs. The relation was nearly linear. Experiments were then made to show the relation between lifetimes and numbers of particles for 50 ANs and 300 generations. The internal weight was set at 1. The experimental results are shown in Figure 10.

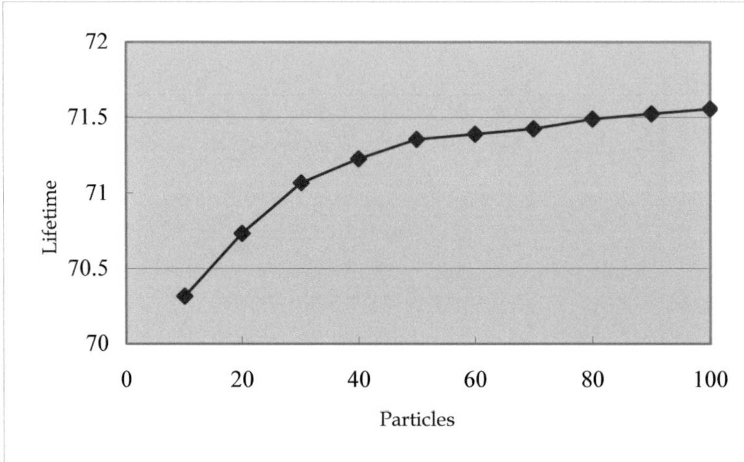

Figure 10. The lifetimes along with different numbers of particles

It can be seen from Figure 10 that the lifetime increased along with the increase of numbers of particles for the same number of generations. The execution time along with different numbers of particles for 300 generations is shown in Figure 11.

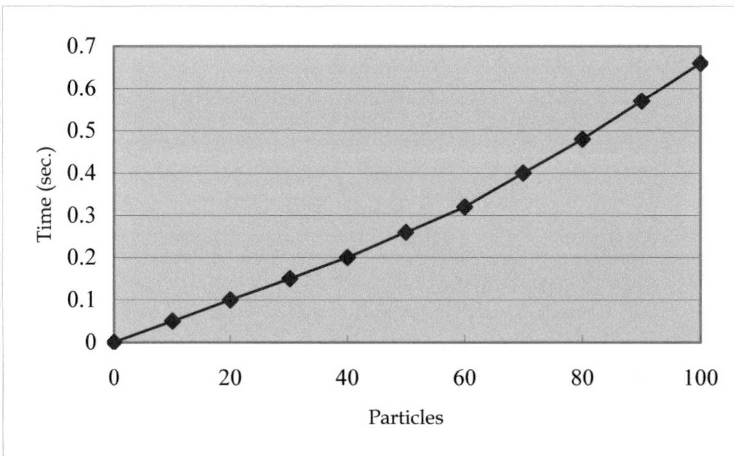

Figure 11. The execution time along with different numbers of particles for 50 ANs

Method	Lifetime
The proposed PSO algorithm	72.0763
The exhaustive grid search (grid size = 1)	72.0048
The exhaustive grid search (grid size = 0.1)	72.0666
The exhaustive grid search (grid size = 0.01)	72.0752

Table 7. A lifetime comparison of the PSO approach and the exhaustive grid searc

It can be observed from Figure 11 that the execution time increased along with the increase of numbers of particles. The relation was nearly linear. This was reasonable since the execution time would be approximately proportional to the number of particles.
Note that no optimal solutions can be found in a finite amount of time since the problem is NP-hard. For a comparison, an exhaustive search using grids was used to find nearly optimal solutions. The approach found the lifetime of the system when a BS was allocated at any cross-point of the grids. The cross-point with the maximum lifetime was then output as the solution. A lifetime comparison of the PSO approach and the exhaustive search with different grid sizes are shown in Table 7.
It can be observed from Table 7 that the lifetime obtained by our proposed PSO algorithm was not worse than those by the exhaustive grid search within a certain precision. The lifetime by the proposed PSO algorithm was 72.0763, and was 72.0048, 72.0666 and 72.0752 for the exhaustive search when the grid size was set at 1, 0.1 and 0.01, respectively. For the exhaustive grid search, the smaller the grid size, the better the results.

7. Conclusion

In wireless sensor networks, minimizing power consumption to prolong network lifetime is very crucial. In this paper, a two-tiered wireless sensor networks has been considered and an algorithm based on particle swarm optimization (PSO) has been proposed for general power-consumption constraints. The proposed approach can search for nearly optimal BS locations in heterogeneous sensor networks, where ANs may own different data transmission rates, initial energies and parameter values. Finding BS locations is by nature very similar to finding the food locations originated from PSO. It is thus very easy to model such a problem by the proposed algorithm based on PSO. Experiments have also been made to show the performance of the proposed PSO approach and the effects of the parameters on the results. From the experimental results, it can be easily concluded that the proposed PSO algorithm converges very fast when compared to the exhaustive search. It can also be easily extended to finding multiple base stations.

8. Acknowledgement

This research was supported by the National Science Council of the Republic of China under contract NSC 97-2221-E-390-023. We also like to thank Mr. Cheng-Hsi Wu for his help in making part of the experiments.

9. References

J. Chou, D. Petrovis and K. Ramchandran, A distributed and adaptive signal processing approach to reducing energy consumption in sensor networks, *The 22nd IEEE Conference on Computer Communications (INFOCOM)*, pp. 1054-1062, San Francisco, USA, March, 2003. [1]

R. C. Eberhart and J. Kennedy, A new optimizer using particles swarm theory, *The Sixth International Symposium on Micro Machine and Human Science*, pp. 39-43, Nagoya, Japan, October, 1995. [2]

R. C. Eberhart and J. Kennedy, Particle swarm optimization, *The IEEE International Conference on Neural Networks*, Vol. 4, pp. 1942-1948, Perth, Australia, November, 1995. [3]

Z. L. Gaing, Discrete particle swarm optimization algorithm for unit commitment, *The IEEE Power Engineering Society General Meeting*, Toronto, Canada, July, 2003. [4]

W. Heinzelman, J. Kulik, and H. Balakrishnan, Adaptive protocols for information dissemination in wireless sensor networks, *The Fifth ACM International Conference on Mobile Computing and Networking*, pp. 174-185, Seattle, USA, August, 1999. [5]

W. Heinzelman, A. Chandrakasan, and H. Balakrishnan, Energy-efficient communication protocols for wireless microsensor networks, *The Hawaiian International Conference on Systems Science,* Hawaii, USA, January, 2000. [6]

C. Intanagonwiwat, R. Govindan and D. Estrin, Directed diffusion: a scalable and robust communication paradigm for sensor networks, *The ACM International Conference on Mobile Computing and Networking*, Boston, USA, August, 2000. [7]

Vikas Kawadia and P. R. Kumar, Power control and clustering in ad hoc networks, *The 22nd IEEE Conference on Computer Communications (INFOCOM),* San Francisco, USA, March, 2003. [8]

N. Li, J. C. Hou and L. Sha, Design and analysis of an mst-based topology control algorithm, *The 22nd IEEE Conference on Computer Communications (INFOCOM)*, San Francisco, USA, March, 2003. [9]

S. Lee, W. Su and M. Gerla, Wireless ad hoc multicast routing with mobility prediction, *Mobile Networks and Applications*, Vol. 6, No. 4, pp. 351-360, 2001. [10]

D. Niculescu and B. Nath, Ad hoc positioning system (APS) using AoA, *The 22nd IEEE Conference on Computer Communications (INFOCOM)*, pp. 1734-1743, San Francisco, USA, March, 2003. [11]

J. Pan, Y. Hou, L. Cai, Y. Shi and X. Shen, Topology control for wireless sensor networks, *The Ninth ACM International Conference on Mobile Computing and Networking*, pp. 286-299, San Diego, USA, September, 2003. [12]

J. Pan, L. Cai, Y. T. Hou, Y. Shi and S. X. Shen, Optimal base-station locations in two-tiered wireless sensor networks, *IEEE Transactions on Mobile Computing*, Vol. 4, No. 5, pp. 458-473, 2005. [13]

Y. Q. Qin, D. B. Sun, N. Li and Y. G. Cen, Path planning for mobile robot using the particle swarm optimization with mutation operator, *The IEEE Third International Conference on Machine Learning and Cybernetics*, pp. 2473-2478, Shanghai, China, August, 2004. [14]

V. Rodoplu and T. H. Meng, Minimum energy mobile wireless networks, *IEEE Journal on Selected Areas in Communications,* Vol. 17, No. 8, 1999. [15]

R. Ramanathan and R. Hain, Topology control of multihop wireless networks using transmit power adjustment, *The 19th IEEE Conference on Computer Communications (INFOCOM)*, Tel Aviv, Israel, March, 2000. [16]

Y. Shi and R. C. Eberhart, A modified particle swarm optimizer, *The IEEE International Conference on Evolutionary Computation*, pp. 69-73, Anchorage, USA, May, 1998, [17]

A. Stacey, M. Jancic and I. Grundy, Particle swarm optimization with mutation, *The IEEE Congress on Evolutionary Computation*, pp. 1425-1430, Canberra, Australia, December, 2003. [18]

D. Tian and N. Georganas, Energy efficient routing with guaranteed delivery in wireless sensor networks, *The IEEE Wireless Communication and Networking Conference,* Orleans, USA, March, 2003. [19]

F. Ye, H. Luo, J. Cheng, S. Lu and L. Zhang, A two-tier data dissemination model for large scale wireless sensor networks, *The ACM International Conference on Mobile Computing and Networking,* Atlanta, USA, September, 2002. [20]

17

Particle Swarm Optimization Algorithm for Transportation Problems

Han Huang[1] and Zhifeng Hao[2]
[1]School of Software Engineering, South China University of Technology
[2]College of Mathematical Science, South China University of Technology
P. R. China

1. Brief Introduction of PSO

Particle swarm optimization (PSO) is a newer evolutionary computational method than genetic algorithm and evolutionary programming. PSO has some common properties of evolutionary computation like randomly searching, iteration time and so on. However, there are no crossover and mutation operators in the classical PSO. PSO simulates the social behavior of birds: Individual birds exchange information about their position, velocity and fitness, and the behavior of the flock is then influenced to increase the probability of migration to regions of high fitness. The framework of PSO can be described as Figure 1.

1. Initialize K Particles $X_1, X_2, ..., X_K$, calculating $pbest_1, ..., pbest_K$ and $gbest, t=1$;
2. For $i=1,...,K$ and $j=1,...,N$, update particles and use X_i to refresh $pbest_i$ and $gbest$; (shown as equation 1 and 2)
3. $t=t+1$; If $t > \max\_gen$, output $gbest$ and exit; else, return Step 2.

Figure 1. The framework of classical PSO

In the optimal size and shape design problem, the position of each bird is designed as variables x, while the velocity of each bird v influences the incremental change in the position of each bird. For particle d Kennedy proposed that position x^d be updated as:

$$x^d_{t+1} = x^d_t + v^d_{t+1} \tag{1}$$

$$v^d_{t+1} = v^d_t + c_1 r_1 (p^d_t - x^d_t) + c_2 r_2 (p^g_t - x^d_t) \tag{2}$$

Here, p^d_t is the best previous position of particle d at time t, while p^g_t is the global best position in the swarm at time t. r_1 and r_2 are uniform random numbers between 0 and 1, and $c_1 = c_2 = 2$.

2. Particle Swarm Optimization for linear Transportation Problem

2.1 Linear and Balance Transportation Problem

The transportation problem (TP) is one of the fundamental problems of network flow optimization. A surprisingly large number of real-life applications can be formulated as a TP. It seeks determination of a minimum cost transportation plan for a single commodity from a number of sources to a number of destinations. So the LTP can be described as: Given there are n sources and m destinations. The amount of supply at source i is a_i and the demand at destination j is b_j. The unit transportation cost between source i and destination j is c_{ij}. x_{ij} is the transport amount from source i to destination j, and the LTP model is:

$$\min \quad z=\sum_{i=1}^{n}\sum_{j=1}^{m}c_{ij}x_{ij}$$

$$\text{s.t.} \quad \sum_{j=1}^{m}x_{ij} \le a_i \qquad i=1,2,\ldots,n \tag{3}$$

$$\sum_{i=1}^{n}x_{ij} \ge b_j \qquad j=1,2,\ldots,m\cdot$$

$$x_{ij} \ge 0; \qquad i=1,2,\ldots,n; j=1,2,\ldots,m$$

TP has been paid much attention to and classified into several types of transmutation. According to the nature of object function, there are four types: (1) linear TP and nonlinear TP. (2) single objective TP and multi objective. Based on the type of constraints, there are planar TP and solid TP. The single object LTP dealt with in this paper is the basic model for other kinds of transportation problems.
A special LTP called balanced LTP is considered as follows:

$$\min \quad z=\sum_{i=1}^{n}\sum_{j=1}^{m}c_{ij}x_{ij}$$

$$\text{s.t.} \quad \sum_{j=1}^{m}x_{ij} = a_i \qquad i=1,2,\ldots,n \tag{4}$$

$$\sum_{i=1}^{n}x_{ij} = b_j \qquad j=1,2,\ldots,m.$$

$$\sum_{i=1}^{n}a_i=\sum_{j=1}^{m}b_j$$

$$x_{ij} \ge 0; \qquad i=1,2,\ldots,n; j=1,2,\ldots,m$$

The fact that a $n \times m$ LTP can be changed into a $n \times (m+1)$ balanced LTP, can be found in operational research because the demand at destination $m+1$ could be calculated by $b_{m+1} = \sum_{i=1}^{n} a_i - \sum_{j=1}^{m} b_j$ with the condition $\sum_{i=1}^{n} a_i \geq \sum_{j=1}^{m} b_j$.

2.2 Initialization of PSO for Linear and Balance Particle Swarm Optimization

A particle $X = \begin{bmatrix} x_{11} & \dots & x_{1m} \\ \dots & \dots & \dots \\ x_{n1} & \dots & x_{nm} \end{bmatrix}$ stands for a solution to LTP. There are nm particles initialized to form nm initial solutions in the initialization. Every element of set N can be chosen as the first assignment to generate the solutions dispersedly, which is good for obtaining the optimal solution in the iteration.

If a LTP is balanced, the following procedure can be used to obtain an initial solution:

```
program GetOnePrimal (var X: Particle, first: int)
  var   i,j,k: integer;
     N: Set of Integer;
  begin
    k :=0;
     N := {1,2,…,nm};
     repeat
         if k=0 then
             k:=first ;
         else
             k:= a random element in N;
         i := ⌊(k-1)/m⌋+1 ;
         j := ((k-1) mod m) +1;
         xij := min {ai, bj};
         ai := ai - xij;
         bi := bi - xij;
         N := N \ {k};
     until N is empty
  end.
```

And the initialization of PSO-TP can be designed as follows:

```
program Initialization
  var   i : integer;
  begin
   Get a balanced LTP;
         i := 1;
         repeat
               GetOnePrimal (Xi, i);
               i := i+1;
         until i > nm
  end.
```

2.3 Updating Rule of PSO for Linear and Balance Particle Swarm Optimization

In PSO algorithm, a new solution can be obtained by using the position updating rule as equations 2 and 3. However, the classical rule is unable to meet such constraints of TP as $\sum_{j=1}^{m} x_{ij} = a_i$ and $\sum_{i=1}^{n} x_{ij} = b_j$. A new rule is designed to overcome this shortcoming. For particle d , we propose that position X^d $(n \times m)$ be updated as

$$V^d_{t+1} = \begin{cases} \varphi_1(P^d_t - X^d_t) + \varphi_2(P^g_t - X^d_t) & t=0 \\ \lambda_1 V^d_t + \lambda_2[\varphi_1(P^d_t - X^d_t) + \varphi_2(P^g_t - X^d_t)] & t>0 \end{cases} \tag{5}$$

$$X^d_{t+1} = V^d_{t+1} + X^d_t \tag{6}$$

where $P^g_t \neq X^d_t$ and $P^d_t \neq X^d_t$.

If $P^g_t = X^d_t$ and $P^d_t \neq X^d_t$, $\varphi_1 = 1$. If $P^g_t \neq X^d_t$ and $P^d_t = X^d_t$, $\varphi_2 = 1$. If $P^g_t = X^d_t$ and $P^d_t = X^d_t$, $\lambda_1 = 1$.

$P^d_t (n \times m)$ is the best previous position of particle d at time t, while $P^g_t (n \times m)$ is the global best position in the swarm at time t. φ_1 and φ_2 are uniform random numbers in (0, 1), meeting $\varphi_1 + \varphi_2 = 1$, while λ_1 is a uniform random number between [0.8, 1.0) and $\lambda_2 = 1 - \lambda_1$.

$$if \quad t=0,\ X^d_{t+1} = V^d_{t+1} + X^d_t$$

$$= \varphi_1(P^d_t - X^d_t) + \varphi_2(P^g_t - X^d_t) + X^d_t = (\varphi_1 P^d_t + \varphi_2 P^g_t) - (\varphi_1 X^d_t + \varphi_2 X^d_t) + X^d_t$$

$$\sum_{j=1}^{m} x^d{}_{ij}(t+1)$$

$$= \varphi_1 \sum_{j=1}^{m} p^d{}_{ij}(t) + \varphi_2 \sum_{j=1}^{m} p^g{}_{ij}(t) - (\varphi_1 \sum_{j=1}^{m} x^d{}_{ij}(t) + \varphi_2 \sum_{j=1}^{m} x^d{}_{ij}(t)) + \sum_{j=1}^{m} x^d{}_{ij}(t)$$

$$= \varphi_1 a_i + \varphi_2 a_i - (\varphi_1 a_i + \varphi_2 a_i) + a_i = a_i$$

$$\sum_{i=1}^{n} x^d{}_{ij}(t+1)$$

$$= \varphi_1 \sum_{i=1}^{n} p^d{}_{ij}(t) + \varphi_2 \sum_{i=1}^{n} p^g{}_{ij}(t) - (\varphi_1 \sum_{i=1}^{n} x^d{}_{ij}(t) + \varphi_2 \sum_{i=1}^{n} x^d{}_{ij}(t)) + \sum_{i=1}^{n} x^d{}_{ij}(t)$$

$$= \varphi_1 b_j + \varphi_2 b_j - (\varphi_1 b_j + \varphi_2 b_j) + b_j = b_j$$

$$if \quad t > 0,$$

$$X^d{}_{t+1} = V^d{}_{t+1} + X^d{}_t$$

$$= \lambda_1 V^d{}_t + \lambda_2 [\varphi_1 (P^d{}_t - X^d{}_t) + \varphi_2 (P^g{}_t - X^d{}_t)] + X^d{}_t$$

$$= \lambda_1 V^d{}_t + \lambda_2 [(\varphi_1 P^d{}_t + \varphi_2 P^g{}_t) - (\varphi_1 X^d{}_t + \varphi_2 X^d{}_t)] + X^d{}_t$$

$$= \lambda_1 (X^d{}_t - X^d{}_{t-1}) + \lambda_2 [(\varphi_1 P^d{}_t + \varphi_2 P^g{}_t) - (\varphi_1 X^d{}_t + \varphi_2 X^d{}_t)] + X^d{}_t$$

$$\sum_{j=1}^{m} x^d{}_{ij}(t+1) = \lambda_1 (\sum_{j=1}^{m} x^d{}_{ij}(t) - \sum_{j=1}^{m} x^d{}_{ij}(t-1)) + \lambda_2 (\varphi_1 a_i + \varphi_2 a_i - (\varphi_1 a_i + \varphi_2 a_i)) + a_i$$

$$= \lambda_1 (a_i - a_i) + 0 + a_i = a_i$$

$$\sum_{i=1}^{n} x^d{}_{ij}(t+1)$$

$$= \lambda_1 (\sum_{i=1}^{n} x^d{}_{ij}(t) - \sum_{i=1}^{n} x^d{}_{ij}(t-1)) + \lambda_2 (\varphi_1 b_j + \varphi_2 b_j - (\varphi_1 b_j + \varphi_2 b_j)) + b_j$$

$$= \lambda_1 (b_j - b_j) + 0 + b_j = b_j$$

Therefore, X^d_{t+1} would meet the condition that $\sum_{j=1}^{m} x^d_{ij}(t+1) = a_i$ and $\sum_{i=1}^{n} x^d_{ij}(t+1) = b_j$ with the function of Formulae 5 and 6. However, the new rule cannot ensure the last constraint that $x_{ij} \geq 0, i = 1,..,n, j = 1,...,m$. In the following section, an extra operator is given to improve the algorithm.

2.4 Negative Repair Operator

A particle of PSO-TP (Formula 7) will be influenced by the negative repair operator if $x_{ki} < 0, k = 1,...,n, i = 1,...,m$, which is indicated as follows:

$$X = \begin{bmatrix} x_{11} & \cdots & x_{1i} & \cdots & x_{1m} \\ \cdots & \cdots & \cdots & \cdots & \cdots \\ x_{k1} & \cdots & x_{ki} & \cdots & x_{km} \\ \cdots & \cdots & \cdots & \cdots & \cdots \\ x_{l1} & \cdots & x_{li} & \cdots & x_{lm} \\ \cdots & \cdots & \cdots & \cdots & \cdots \\ x_{n1} & \cdots & x_{ni} & \cdots & x_{nm} \end{bmatrix} \quad (7)$$

---

program RepairOnePos (var X: Particle, k,i: int)
begin

select the maximum element signed as x_{li} in Col. i;

$x_0 := x_{ki}$, $x_{li} := x_{li} - |x_0|$, $x_{ki} := 0$;

change elements in Row.k into $x_{kj} := \begin{cases} x_{kj} & x_{kj} = 0 \\ x_{kj} - \dfrac{|x_0|}{u} & x_{kj} > 0 \end{cases}$;

(u is the number of times when the following condition $x_{kj} > 0, j = 1,...,m$ is met)

change elements in Row. l into $x_{lj} := \begin{cases} x_{lj} & x_{kj} = 0 \\ x_{lj} + \dfrac{|x_0|}{u} & x_{kj} > 0 \end{cases}$;

end.

As a result, the procedure of negative repair operator can be described as:

```
program NegativeRepair (var X: Particle)
var   i,j: integer;
begin
   if some element of X is negative then
        repeat
          If xij<0 is found then
                 RepairOnePos (X, i, j);
        until Every element of X is not negative
end.
```

2.5 PSO Mutation

Mutation is a popular operator in Genetic Algorithm, and a special PSO mutation is designed to help PSO-TP change the partial structure of some particles in order to get new types of solution. PSO-TP cannot fall into the local convergence easily because the mutation operator can explore the new solution.

program PSOMutation (var X: Particle)

begin

Obtain p and q randomly meeting $0<p<n$ and $0<q<m$;

Select p rows $\{i_1,\ldots i_p\}$ and q lines $\{j_1,\ldots j_q\}$ randomly from matrix X to form a small matrix Y (y_{ij},i=1,…,p,j=1,…,q);

$$a^y{}_i = \sum_{j\in\{j_1,\ldots,j_q\}} x_{ij} \qquad (i = i_1,\ldots,i_p)$$

$$b^y{}_j = \sum_{i\in\{i_1,\ldots,i_p\}} x_{ij} \qquad (j = j_1,\ldots,j_q)$$

Use a method like the one in initialization to form the initial assignment for Y;

Update X with Y;

end.

2.6 The Structure of PSO-TP

According to the setting above, the structure of PSO-TP is shown as:

```
program PSO-TP (problem: balanced LTP of n×m size, pm: float)
var t:integer;
begin
  t:=0;
  Initialization;
```

Obtain $P^g{}_0(n \times m)$ and $P^d{}_0(n \times m)$(d=1,…,n×m);

repeat

t:=t+1;

Calculate $X^d{}_t$ with Formula 5 and 6 (d=1,…,n×m);

NegativeRepair($X^d{}_t$)(d=1,…,n×m);

Carry out PSOMutation($X^d{}_t$) by the probability pm;

Update $P^g{}_t(n \times m)$ and $P^d{}_t(n \times m)$(d=1,…,n×m);

until meeting the condition to stop

end.

3. Numerical Results

There are two experiments in this section: one is comparing PSO-TP with genetic algorithm (GA) in some integer instances and the second is testing the performance of PSO-TP in the open problems. Both of the experiments are done at a PC with 3.06G Hz, 512M DDR memory and Windows XP operating system. GA and PSO-TP would stop when no better solution could be found in 500 iterations, which is considered as a virtual convergence of the algorithms. The probability of mutation in PSO-TP is set to be 0.05.

Problem\ five runs	PSO-TP Min	PSO-TP Ave	GA Min	GA Ave	PSO-TP Time(s)	GA Time(s)
P1 (3*4)	152	152	152	153	0.015	1.72
P2 (4*8)	287	288	290	301	0.368	5.831
P3 (3*4)	375	375	375	375	0.028	0.265
P4 (3*4)	119	119	119	119	0.018	1.273
P5 (3*4)	85	85	85	85	0.159	0.968
P6*(15*20)	596	598	-	-	36.4	-

Table 1. Comparison Between PSO-TP and GA

As Table 1 shows, both the minimum cost and average cost obtained by PSO-TP are less than those of GA. Furthermore, the time cost of PSO-TP is much less than that of GA. In order to verify the effectiveness of PSO-TP, 9 real number instances are computed and the results are shown in Table 2. Since GA is unable to deal with the real number LTP directly, only PSO-T is tested.

Problem\five runs	Optimal Value	PSO-TP Average	PSO-TP Time(s)
No.1	67.98	67.98	0.02
No.2	1020	1020	0.184
No.4	13610	13610	0.168
No.5	1580	1580	0.015
No.6	98	98	0.023
No.7	2000	2000	0.015
No.8	250	250	<0.001
No.9	215	215	0.003
No.10	110	110	0.012

Table 2. Performance of PSO-TP in open problems

According to the results in Table 2, PSO-TP can solve the test problems very quickly. The efficiency of PSO-TP may be due to the characteristic of PSO algorithm and the special operators. Through the function of the new position updating rule and negative repair operator, the idea of PSO is introduced to solve LTP successfully. The nature of PSO can accelerate the searching of the novel algorithm, which would also enable PSO-TP to get the local best solution. What's more, the PSO mutation as an extra operator can help PSO-TP to avoid finishing searching prematurely. Therefore, PSO-TP can be a novel effective algorithm for solving TP.

4. Particle Swarm Optimization for Non-linear Transportation Problem

4.1 Non-linear and Balance Transportation Problem

The unit transportation cost between source i and destination j is $f_{ij}(x_{ij})$ where x_{ij} is the transportation amount from source i to destination j, and TP model is:

$$\min \quad z = \sum_{i=1}^{n}\sum_{j=1}^{m} f_{ij}(x_{ij})$$

$$\text{s.t.} \quad \sum_{j=1}^{m} x_{ij} \le a_i \qquad i = 1,2,\ldots,n \tag{8}$$

$$\sum_{i=1}^{n} x_{ij} \ge b_j \qquad j = 1,2,\ldots,m \cdot$$

$$x_{ij} \ge 0; \qquad i = 1,2,\ldots,n; j = 1,2,\ldots,m$$

According to the nature of object function, there are four types: linear TP in which the function $f_{ij}(x_{ij})$ is linear and nonlinear TP in which $f_{ij}(x_{ij})$ is non-linear, as well as single objective and multi-objective TP. Based on the types of constraints, there are planar TP and solid TP. The single object NLTP is dealt with in this paper. In many fields like railway transportation, the relation between transportation amount and price is often non-linear, so NLTP is an important for application.

4.2 Framework of PSO for Non-linear TP

In the population of PSO-NLTP, an individual $X_i = \begin{bmatrix} x_{11} & \cdots & x_{1m} \\ \cdots & \cdots & \cdots \\ x_{n1} & \cdots & x_{nm} \end{bmatrix}$ stands for a solution to NLTP (Exp. 2), where $n \times m$ is the population size. There are $n \times m$ individuals initialized to form $n \times m$ initial solutions in the initialization. The initialization and mutation are the same as the ones in PSO-LTP (Section 2.2 and 2.5).
And the framework of PSO-NLTP is given:

Algorithm: PSO-NLTP
Input: NLTP problem (Exp. 8)
begin
    Initialization;
    Setting parameters;
  repeat
    Updating rule;
    Mutation;
    Updating the current optimal solution
  until meeting the condition to stop
end.
Output: Optimal solution for NLTP

In the parameter setting, The parameters of PSO-NLTP are all set adaptively: as the population size is $n \times m$, the size of mutation matrix Y is set randomly meeting 0<p<n and 0<q<m and the mutation probability P_m is calculated by $P_m = 0.005 \times N_t$, where $N_t = 1$ when $X_{best}^{(t)}$ is updated and $N_t = N_t + 1$ when $X_{best}^{(t)}$ remains the same as $X_{best}^{(t-1)}$.

4.3 Updating Rule of PSO-NLTP

As one of the important evolutionary operator, recombination is designed to optimize the individuals and make them meet the constraints of supply and demand as $\sum_{j=1}^{m} x_{ij} = a_i$ and

$\sum_{i=1}^{n} x_{ij} = b_j$ (Exp. 4). At the beginning of an iteration, every individual is recombined by the following expression.

$$X_i^{(t+1)} = \varphi_1 X_i^{(t)} + \varphi_2 X_{best}^{(t)} + \varphi_3 X_{random}^{(t)} \tag{9}$$

$X_{best}^{(t)}$ is the best particle found by PSO-NLTP form iteration 0 to t. $X_{random}^{(t)}$ is the particle formed randomly (by sub-algorithm GetOnePrimal in section 2.2) for the updating rule of $X_i^{(t)}$. φ_1, φ_2 and φ_3 are the weight terms meeting $\varphi_1 + \varphi_2 + \varphi_3 = 1$, which are calculated as Exp 4-6 show, where $f(X_i^{(t)})$ is the cost of the solution for TP (Exp. 4).

$$\varphi_1 = f(X_i^{(t)})^{-1} / \left(f(X_i^{(t)})^{-1} + f(X_{best}^{(t)})^{-1} + f(X_{random}^{(t)})^{-1} \right) \tag{10}$$

$$\varphi_2 = f(X_{best}^{(t)})^{-1} / \left(f(X_i^{(t)})^{-1} + f(X_{best}^{(t)})^{-1} + f(X_{random}^{(t)})^{-1} \right) \tag{11}$$

$$\varphi_3 = f(X_{random}^{(t)})^{-1} / \left(f(X_i^{(t)})^{-1} + f(X_{best}^{(t)})^{-1} + f(X_{random}^{(t)})^{-1} \right) \tag{12}$$

$X_i^{(t+1)}$ can be considered as a combination of $X_i^{(t)}$, $X_{best}^{(t)}$ and $X_{random}^{(t)}$ based on the their quality, and proved to meet the constraints of supply and demand.

$$\sum_{j=1}^{m} x_{ij}^{(t+1)} = \sum_{j=1}^{m} (\varphi_1 x_{ij}^{(t)} + \varphi_2 x_{i,j,best}^{(t)} + \varphi_3 x_{i,j,random}^{(t)})$$

$$= \varphi_1 \sum_{j=1}^{m} x_{ij}^{(t)} + \varphi_2 \sum_{j=1}^{m} x_{i,j,best}^{(t)} + \varphi_3 \sum_{j=1}^{m} x_{i,j,random}^{(t)}$$

$$= \varphi_1 a_i + \varphi_2 a_i + \varphi_3 a_i = a_i \quad (i = 1, \ldots, n)$$

$$\sum_{i=1}^{n} x_{ij}^{(t+1)} = \sum_{i=1}^{n} (\varphi_1 x_{ij}^{(t)} + \varphi_2 x_{i,j,best}^{(t)} + \varphi_3 x_{i,j,random}^{(t)})$$

$$= \varphi_1 \sum_{i=1}^{n} x_{ij}^{(t)} + \varphi_2 \sum_{i=1}^{n} x_{i,j,best}^{(t)} + \varphi_3 \sum_{i=1}^{n} x_{i,j,random}^{(t)}$$

$$= \varphi_1 b_j + \varphi_2 b_j + \varphi_3 b_j = b_j \quad (j = 1, \ldots, m)$$

Furthermore, the recombination rule can also ensure the positive constraint that
$$x_{ij}^{(t+1)} = \varphi_1 x_{ij}^{(t)} + \varphi_2 x_{i,j,best}^{(t)} + \varphi_3 x_{i,j,random}^{(t)} \geq 0, i = 1,..,n, j = 1,...,m.$$

4.4 Numerical Results

There are 56 NLTP instances computed in the experiment, of which the results are shown in this section. The experiment is done at a PC with 3.06G Hz, 512M DDR memory and Windows XP operating system. The NLTP instances are generated by replacing the linear cost functions of the open problems with the non-linear functions. The methods which are effective for linear TP cannot deal with NLTP for the complexity of non-linear object function. The common NLTP cost functions are indicated in Table 1.

Problem	Transportation Cost Functions
No.1	$f_{ij}(x_{ij}) = c_{ij} x_{ij}^2$
No.2	$f_{ij}(x_{ij}) = c_{ij} \sqrt{x_{ij}}$
No.3	$f_{ij}(x_{ij}) = \begin{cases} c_{ij}(\frac{x_{ij}}{S}), & if\ 0 \leq x_{ij} < S \\ c_{ij}, & if\ S < x_{ij} \leq 2S \\ c_{ij}(1 + \frac{x_{ij} - 2S}{S}), & if\ 2S < x_{ij} \end{cases}$
No.4	$f_{ij}(x_{ij}) = c_{ij} x_{ij} [\sin(x_{ij} \frac{5\pi}{4S}) + 1]$

Table 3. NLTP cost functions [15]

The comparison between PSO-NLTP and EP with penalty strategy only indicates whether the recombination of PSO-NLTP is better at dealing with the constraints of NLTP (Exp. 8) than penalty strategy of EP. There cannot be any conclusion that PSO-NLTP or EP is better than the other because they are the algorithms for different applications. The three algorithms are computed in 50 runs independently, and the results are in Table 4 and Table 5. They would stop when no better solution could be found in 100 iterations, which is considered as a virtual convergence of the algorithms.

NLTP instances in Table 4 are formed with the non-linear functions (shown in Table 3) and the problems. And the instances in Table 5 are formed with the non-linear functions and the problems. We set $S = \sum_{i=1}^{n} a_i / 10$ in function No.3 and $S = 1$ in function No.4 in the experiment.

Problem	PSO-NLTP Average	GA Average	EP Average	PSO-NLTP Time(s)	GA Time(s)	EP Time(s)
No.1-1	8.03	8.10	8.36	0.093	0.89	0.109
No.1-2	112.29	114.25	120.61	0.11	0.312	0.125
No.1-4	1348.3	1350.8	1476.1	0.062	0.109	0.078
No.1-5	205.9	206.3	216.1	0.043	0.125	0.052
No.1-6	12.64	12.72	13.53	0.062	0.75	0.078
No.1-7	246.9	247.6	256.9	0.088	0.32	0.093
No.1-8	84.72	84.72	87.5	<0.001	0.015	<0.001
No.1-9	44.64	44.65	46.2	<0.001	0.046	<0.001
No.1-10	24.85	24.97	25.83	<0.001	0.032	<0.001
No.2-1	155.3	155.3	168.5	<0.001	0.016	<0.001
No.2-2	2281.5	2281.5	2696.2	<0.001	0.015	<0.001
No.2-4	28021	28021	30020.2	<0.001	0.015	<0.001
No.2-5	3519.3	3520.4	3583.1	<0.001	0.015	<0.001
No.2-6	264.9	266.5	314.4	<0.001	0.015	<0.001
No.2-7	4576.9	4584.5	5326.0	0.009	0.052	0.012
No.2-8	432.8	432.8	432.8	<0.001	0.015	<0.001
No.2-9	386.3	386.3	386.3	<0.001	0.031	<0.001
No.2-10	195.3	195.3	226.0	<0.001	0.006	<0.001
No.3-1	309.9	310.0	346.6	<0.001	0.093	0.001
No.3-2	4649.2	4650	5415.2	<0.001	0.921	0.012
No.3-4	65496.7	66123.3	68223.3	<0.001	0.105	<0.001
No.3-5	7038.1	7066.6	7220.9	<0.001	1.015	0.001
No.3-6	540	540	672.5	0.001	0.062	0.002
No.3-7	9171.0	9173.2	9833.3	<0.001	0.312	<0.001
No.3-8	1033.4	1033.4	1066.7	<0.001	0.012	<0.001
No.3-9	933.3	933.4	1006.4	0.002	0.147	0.015
No.3-10	480	480	480	0.016	0.046	0.004
No.4-1	107.6	107.8	118.2	0.063	0.159	0.078
No.4-2	1583.5	1585.2	1622	0.062	0.285	0.093
No.4-4	19528.4	19531.3	20119	0.075	0.968	0.068
No.4-5	2466.9	2468.2	2880.2	0.072	0.625	0.046
No.4-6	151.7	152.1	161.9	0.093	1.046	0.167
No.4-7	3171.1	3173.8	3227.5	0.047	0.692	0.073
No.4-8	467.1	467.1	467.1	<0.001	0.036	<0.001
No.4-9	376.3	376.3	382.5	<0.001	0.081	0.003
No.4-10	205.9	205.9	227.6	0.026	0.422	0.031

Table 4. Comparison I between PSO-NLTP, GA and EP with penalty strategy

Problem	PSO-NLTP Average	GA Average	EP Average	PSO-NLTP Time(s)	GA Time(s)	EP Time(s)
No.1-11	1113.4	1143.09	1158.2	0.031	0.065	0.046
No.1-12	429.3	440.3	488.3	0.187	1.312	0.203
No.1-13	740.5	740.5	863.6	0.09	2.406	0.781
No.1-14	2519.4	2529.0	2630.3	0.015	0.067	0.016
No.1-15	297.2	297.9	309.2	0.046	0.178	0.058
No.1-16	219.92	220.8	234.6	0.040	1.75	0.060
No.2-11	49.7	51.9	64.2	<0.001	0.001	<0.001
No.2-12	78.4	78.4	104.5	0.001	0.025	<0.001
No.2-13	150.2	150.4	177.9	<0.001	0.015	<0.001
No.2-14	118.6	118.2	148.4	<0.001	0.001	<0.001
No.2-15	64.5	64.5	64.5	<0.001	0.031	<0.001
No.2-16	47.1	47.8	53.4	<0.001	0.015	<0.001
No.3-11	13.3	13.3	13.3	0.015	0.734	0.031
No.3-12	21.0	21.0	26.3	0.018	0.308	0.036
No.3-13	37.2	37.4	43.5	0.171	1.906	0.156
No.3-14	37.5	37.8	46.7	0.011	0.578	0.008
No.3-15	28.3	28.1	33	0.009	0.325	0.013
No.3-16	22.5	23.0	29.6	<0.001	0.059	0.015
No.4-11	8.6	8.8	37.4	0.001	0.106	0.001
No.4-12	20.0	23.1	40.8	0.253	2.328	0.234
No.4-13	49.0	52.3	72.1	0.109	2.031	0.359
No.4-14	47.7	51.2	82.2	0.003	0.629	0.006
No.4-15	11.97	12.06	36.58	0.019	0.484	0.026
No.4-16	2.92	3.08	8.1	0.031	0.921	0.045

Table 5. Comparison II between PSO-NLTP, GA and EP with penalty strategy

As Table 4 and Table 5 indicate, PSO-NLTP performs the best of three in the items of average transportation cost and average computational cost. The NLTP solutions found by EP with penalty strategy cost more than PSO-NLTP and GA, which indicates recombination of PSO-NLTP and crossover of GA handle the constraints of NLTP (Exp. 4) better than the penalty strategy. However, EP with penalty strategy cost less time than GA to converge because the crossover and mutation operator of GA is more complicated. PSO-NLTP can cost the least to obtain the best NLTP solution of the three tested methods. Its recombination makes the particles feasible and evolutionary for optimization. The combination of updating rule and mutation operators can play a part of global searching quickly, which makes PSO-NLTP effective for solving NLTPs.

5. Discussions and Conclusions

Most of the methods that solve linear transportation problems well cannot handle the non-linear TP. An particle swarm optimization algorithm named PSO-NLTP is proposed in the present paper to deal with NLTP. The updating rule of PSO-NLTP can make the particles of the swarm optimally in the feasible solution space, which satisfies the constraints of NLTP. A mutation operator is added to strengthen the global optimal capacity of PSO-NLTP. In the experiment of computing 56 NLTP instances, PSO-NLTP performs much better than GA and EP with penalty strategy. All of the parameters of PSO-NLTP are set adaptively in the iteration so that it is good for the application of the proposed algorithm. Moreover, PSO-NLTP can also solve linear TPs.

The design of the updating rule of PSO can be considered as an example for solving optimization problems with special constraints. The operator is different from other methods such as stochastic approach, greedy decoders and repair mechanisms, which are to restrict the searching only to some feasible sub-space satisfying the constraints. It uses both the local and global heuristic information for searching in the whole feasible solution space. Furthermore, through the initial experimental result, it performs better than the penalty strategy which is another popular approach for handling constraints.

6. References

Papamanthou C., Paparrizos K., and Samaras N., Computational experience with exterior point algorithms for the transportation problem, *Applied Mathematics and Computation*, vol. 158, pp. 459-475, 2004. [1]

Vignaux G.A. and Michalewicz Z., A genetic algorithm for the linear transportation problem, *IEEE Transactions on Systems, Man, and Cybernetics*, vol. 21, no. 2, MARCWAPRIL, pp.445-452, 2004. [2]

Hitchcock F., The distribution of a product from several sources to numerous location, *Journal of Mathematical Physics*, vol. 20, pp. 224-230, 1941. [3]

Michalewicz Z., et al, A non-Standard Genetic Algorithm for the Nonlinear Transportation Problems, *ORSA Journal on Computing*, vol. 3, no. 4, pp.307-316, 1991. [4]

Li Y.Z., Ida K.C. and Gen M., Improved genetic algorithm for solving multi objective solid transportation problem with fuzzy numbers, *Computers ind. Engng*, vol. 33, no.3-4, pp. 589-592, 1997. [5]

Gen M., et al, Solving bicriteria solid transportation problem by genetic algorithms, *Proceedings of the 16th International Conference on computers and industrial engineering*, Ashikaga, Japan, pp.572-575, 1994. [6]

Dantzig G.B., Application of the simplex method to a transportation problem, in: T.C. Koopmans (Ed.), *Activity of production and application*, John Wiley & Sons, NY, pp. 359-373, 1951. [7]

Orlin J.B., Plotkin S.A. and Tardos E., Polynomial dual network simplex algorithms, *Math. Program*, vol. 60, pp. 255-276, 1993. [8]

Paparrizos K., An exterior point simplex algorithm for general linear problems, *Ann. Oper. Res.*, vol. 32, pp. 497-508, 1993. [9]

Papamanthou C., Paparrizos K. and Samaras N., Computational experience with exterior point algorithms for the transportation problem, *Applied Mathematics and Computation*, vol. 158, pp. 459-475, 2004. [10]

Sharma R.R.K. and Sharma K.D., A new dual based procedure for the transportation problem, *European Journal of Operational Research*, vol. 122, pp. 611-624, 2000. [11]

Yang X. and Gen M., Evolution program for bicriteria transportation problem, *Proceedings of the 16th International Conference on computers and industrial engineering*, Ashikaga, Japan, pp. 451-454, 1994. [12]

Kennedy J. and Eberhart R.C., Particle swarm optimization, in *Proc IEEE Int. Conf. Neural Networks*, Perth, Austalia,pp. 1942-1948, Nov. 1995. [13]

Kennedy J., The particle swarm: Social adaptation knowledge, in *Proc. 1997 Int. Conf. Evolutionary Computation*, Indianapolis, IN, pp. 303-308, Apr. 1997. [14]

Fourie P.C. and Groenwold A.A., The particle swarm optimization algorithm in size and shape optimization, *Struct Multidisc Optim*, vol. 23, pp. 259-267, 2000. [15]

Shi Y.H. and Eberhart R.C., A modified particle swarm optimizer, *Proc. Int. Conf. On Evolutionary Computation*, pp.69-73, 1998. [16]

18

A Particle Swarm Optimisation Approach to Graph Permutations

Omar Ilaya and Cees Bil
RMIT University
Australia

1. Introduction

In many real-world applications, the arrangement, ordering, and selection of a discrete set of objects from a finite set, is used to satisfy a desired objective. The problem of finding optimal configurations from a discrete set of objects is known as the *combinatorial optimisation problem*. Examples of combinatorial optimisation problems in real-world scenarios include network design for optimal performance, fleet management, transportation and logistics, production-planning, inventory, airline-crew scheduling, and facility location.

While many of these combinatorial optimisation problems can be solved in polynomial time, a majority belong to the class of NP -hard (Aardal et al., 1997). To deal with these hard combinatorial optimisation problems, approximation and heuristic algorithms have been employed as a compromise between solution quality and computational time (Festa and Resende, 2008). This makes heuristic algorithms well-suited for applications where computational resources are limited. These include dynamic ad-hoc networks, decentralised multi-agent systems, and multi-vehicle formations. The success of these heuristic algorithms depends on the computational complexity of the algorithm and their ability to converge to the optimal solution (Festa and Resende, 2008). In most cases, the solutions obtained by these heuristic algorithms are not guaranteed optimal.

A recently developed class of heuristic algorithms, known as the *meta-heuristic algorithms*, have demonstrated promising results in the field of combinatorial optimisation. Meta-heuristic algorithms represent the class of all-purpose search techniques that can be applied to a variety of optimisation problems including combinatorial optimisation. The class of meta-heuristic algorithms include (but not restricted to) simulated annealing (SA), tabu search, evolutionary algorithms (EA) (including genetic algorithms), ant colony optimisation (ACO) (Aguilar, 2001), bacterial foraging (Passino, 2002), scatter search, and iterated local search.

Recently, a new family of computationally efficient meta-heuristic algorithms better posed at handling non-linear constraints and non-convex solution spaces have been developed. From this family of meta-heuristic algorithms, is particle swarm optimisation (PSO) (Kennedy and Eberhart, 1995). Like other biologically inspired meta-heuristic algorithms, PSO is an adaptive search technique that is based on the social foraging of insects and animals. In PSO, a population of candidate solutions are modelled as a swarm of particles. At each iteration, the particles update their position (and solution) by moving stochastically towards regions previously visited by the individual particle and the collective swarm. The simplicity, robustness, and adaptability of PSO, has found application in a wide-range of optimisation problems over continuous search spaces. While PSO has proven to be successful on a variety of continuous functions, limited success has been demonstrated to adapt PSO to more complex richer spaces such as combinatorial optimisation.

In this chapter, the concepts of the standard PSO model are extended to the discrete combinatorial space and a new PSO is developed to solve the combinatorial optimisation problem. The chapter is organised as follows: In Section 2, a brief review of related works to solving the combinatorial optimisation space using meta-heuristics is presented. In Section 3, the standard PSO model is introduced. The nature of the combinatorial optimisation problem is then presented in Section 4 before the concepts of the standard PSO model are adapted to the combinatorial space in Section 5. Section 6 analyses the stability and performance of the newly developed algorithm. The performance of the newly developed algorithm is then compared to the performance of a traditional genetic algorithm in Section 7 before Section 8 concludes with final remarks.

2. Related Works

In recent years, variants of traditional PSO have been used to solve discrete and combinatorial optimisation problems. A binary PSO was first developed in (Kennedy and Eberhart, 1997) to solve discrete optimisation problems. In the binary PSO, each particle encoded a binary string in the solution space. A particle moved according to a probability distribution function determined using the Hamming distance between two points in the binary space. The early concepts introduced by the binary PSO appeared in later PSO algorithms for combinatorial optimisation such as in (Shi et al., 2006); (Tasgetiren et al., 2004); (Liu et al., 2007b); (Pang et al., 2004); (Martínez García and Moreno Pérez, 2008); (Song et al., 2008); and (Wang et al., 2003). Tasgetiren et al. (Tasgetiren et al., 2004) introduced the smallest position value rule (SPV) to enable the continuous PSO algorithm to be applied the class of sequencing and combinatorial problems. In SPV, each particle assigns a position value in continuous space to each dimension in the discrete space. At each iteration, the position value is updated according to the traditional velocity update equation and the sequence of objects is re-sorted according to the values assigned to the continuous space. The method proposed by (Tasgetiren et al., 2004) is similar to the random keys in GA (Bean, 1994). Following a similar method to (Kennedy and Eberhart, 1997), Wang et al. (Wang et al., 2003) introduced the concept of a swap operator to exchange dimensions in the particle position. In (Wang et al., 2003), each particle encoded a permutation of objects and a transition from one position to the next was achieved by exchanging elements in the permutation. To account for both the personal best positions and global best positions, Wang et al. extended the concept of swap operator to swap sequence. The swap sequence was used to move a particle from one position to the next by successively applying a sequence of swap operators. Using this approach, the notion of velocity on the combinatorial space was defined; and the Hamming distance was used to exclusively determine the motion of a particle. Premature convergence was addressed by randomly applying the swap operator to the particle. Similar approaches to Wang et al. include (Shi et al., 2006); (Martínez García and Moreno Pérez, 2008); and (Bonyadi et al., 2007), where a swap sequence was also constructed through the concatenation of successive swap operators. The ordering of these swap operators influences the position of the particle at the end of each iteration. In (Wang et al., 2003); (Shi et al., 2006); (Martínez García and Moreno Pérez, 2008); and (Bonyadi et al., 2007), the swap sequence is constructed by first applying the swap operators that move the particle to it's personal best, followed by the swap operators that move the particle to it's global best. For sufficiently small perturbations, the particles will tend towards the global best position of the swarm and stimulate the loss of solution diversity. This invariably leads to the rapid convergence of the algorithm and poor solution quality. For large complex optimisation problems, the PSO must compromise the local and global search strategies effectively to find high-quality (if not optimal) solutions rapidly. In addition, the PSO framework must be sufficiently robust to adapt to a wide variety of discrete and combinatorial optimisation problems. In this chapter, a generalised combinatorial optimisation framework is introduced that builds on the works of (Wang et al., 2003); (Shi et al., 2006); (Tasgetiren et al., 2004); and (Kennedy and Eberhart, 1997) to develop a new combinatorial optimisation PSO. In the following section, a brief introduction into the traditional PSO is presented before the main results of this chapter are developed.

3. The Standard Particle Swarm Optimisation Model

Let $\mathcal{P}$ denote a D-dimensional problem, and $f(x): X \rightarrow \mathbb{R}$ an objective function for the problem that maps X to the set of real numbers. Without loss of generality, consider the following optimisation problem $x^* \in X \Leftrightarrow x^* = \arg\min_{x \in X} f(x) \;\; \forall x \in X$. In traditional PSO, a solution i is represented by a particle in a swarm P moving through D-dimensional space with position vector $x_k^i = (x_k^i(1), \ldots, x_k^i(d), \ldots, x_k^i(D))$ for any time k. At each iteration, the particles adjust their velocity v_k^i along each dimension according to the previous best position of the i-th particle p_k^i and the best position of the collective swarm p_k^g (see Fig. 1). The position x_k^i for the i-th particle is updated according to the following velocity function:

$$v_{k+1}^i = w \cdot v_k^i + c_1 \cdot r_1 \cdot (p_k^i - x_k^i) + c_2 \cdot r_2 \cdot (p_k^g - x_k^i) \tag{1a}$$

$$x_{k+1}^i = x_k^i + v_k^i \tag{1b}$$

where $r_1, r_2 \in [0,1]$ are random variables affecting the search direction, $c_1, c_2 \in \mathbb{R}$ are configuration parameters weighting the relative confidence in the personal best solutions and the global best solutions respectively, and w is an inertia term influencing the momentum along a given search direction. Algorithm 1 summarises the iterative nature of the PSO algorithm.

The terms c_1 and c_2 are the main configuration parameters of the PSO that directly influence the convergence of the algorithm. For large values of c_1, exploration of particles is bounded to local regions of the best previously found solutions p_k^i. This maintains population diversity and is favourable when the problem is characterised by non-linear and non-convex solution spaces. In contrast, large c_2 values will encourage particles to explore regions closer to the global best solution p_k^g at each iteration. Generally, this search strategy will converge faster and is practical for convex solution spaces with unique optima. Adjusting the inertia term w affects the relative weighting of the local and global searches. A large w encourages the particles to explore a larger region of the solution space at each iteration and maximise global search ability, whilst a smaller w will restrict the particles to local search at each iteration (Shi and Eberhart, 1998b).

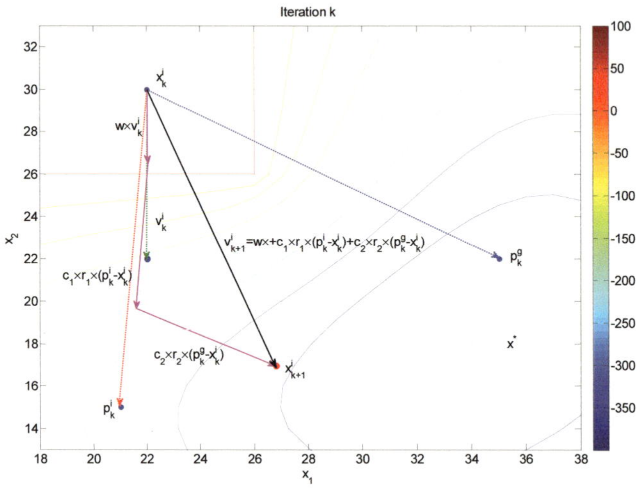

Figure 1. Particle position and velocity on a two-dimensional vector space

---

for all particle i **do**
    initialise position x_k^i randomly in the search space
end for
while termination criteria not satisfied **do**
    for all particle i **do**
        set personal best p_k^i as the best position found by the particle so far
        set global best p_k^g as the best position found by the swarm so far
    end for
    for all particle i **do**
        update velocity according to
        $v_{k+1}^i = w \cdot v_k^i + c_1 \cdot r_1 \cdot (p_k^i - x_k^i) + c_2 \cdot r_2 \cdot (p_k^g - x_k^i)$
        update position according to
        $x_{k+1}^i = x_k^i + v_k^i$
    end for
end while

Algorithm 1. Traditional PSO

4. Problem Description and Model Construction

The combinatorial optimisation problem for PSO is now discussed. Let $X = \{x^1, x^2, \ldots, x^i, \ldots\}$ denote the finite set of solutions to the combinatorial optimisation problem with objective function $f : X \to \mathbb{R}$. Assume the objective of the combinatorial optimisation problem is to find $x^* \in X$, such that $x^* \in X \Leftrightarrow x^* = \arg\min_{x \in X} f(x) \quad \forall x \in X$. Consider the case where a solution $x^i \in X$ to the combinatorial optimisation problem is given by the linear ordering of elements in the set $[n]=\{1,2,\ldots,n\}$, such that $\forall x^i \in X$, $x^i = (x^i(1), x^i(2), \ldots, x^i(n)) \in \{1,2,\ldots,n\}$. Then $|X| = n!$. Each integer value in the list encodes the relative ordering of a set of objects and is referred to as a *permutation* of objects (Bóna, 2004). These include cities in a tour, nodes in a network, jobs in a schedule, or vehicles in a formation. For convenience, a permutation is represented using *two-line form*. Let $g:[d] \to [n]$ be a bijection on the ordered list. If $[n]$ describes the list of numbers $[n]=\{1,\ldots,n\}$, then $[d]=\{1,\ldots,n\}$ and g is also a permutation of the set $[n]$ (Bóna, 2004).

Example 1.

As an example, consider the following permutation $\{3,4,1,5,2\}$. The function $g:[5] \to [5]$ defined by $g(1)=3$, $g(2)=4$, $g(3)=1$, $g(4)=5$, and $g(5)=2$ is also permutation of $[5]$ (Bóna, 2004). In two-line form, the set $[5]$ can be written as:

$$g = \begin{matrix} 1 & 2 & 3 & 4 & 5 \\ 3 & 4 & 1 & 5 & 2 \end{matrix}$$

where it is implied that g maps 1 to 3, 2 to 4, 3 to 1, 4 to 5, and 5 to 2.

5. Fitness Landscape

In order to adapt PSO to the combinatorial space, it is convenient to define a metric space characteristic of the combinatorial optimisation problem. Let $\mathcal{N}: X \to 2^X$ denote a syntactic neighbourhood function that attaches to each solution $x^i \in X$ the neighbouring set of solutions $x^j \in \mathcal{N}_i(x^i) \subseteq X$ that can be reached by applying a unitary syntactic operation moving $x^i \mapsto x^j$ (Moraglio and Poli, 2004). Denote this unitary syntactic operator by φ and assume that the operation is reversible, i.e. $x^j \in \mathcal{N}_i(x^i) \Leftrightarrow x^i \in \mathcal{N}_j(x^j)$. Such a neighbourhood can be associated to an undirected *neighbourhood graph* $G=(V,E)$, where V is the set of vertices representing the solutions $x^i \in X$, and E the set of edges representing the transformation paths for permutations. By definition, the combinatorial space endowed with a neighbourhood structure $\mathcal{N}_i(x^i)$ and induced by a distance function $h_{ij}(x^i,x^j)$ is a *metric space*. Formally, the definition of a metric or distance function is any real valued function $h_{ij}(x^i,x^j)$ that conforms to the axioms of identity, symmetry, and triangular inequality, i.e.:

1. $h_{ij}(x^i,x^j) \geq 0$ and $h_{ij}(x^i,x^i)=0$ (identity);
2. $h_{ij}(x^i,x^j) = h_{ij}(x^j,x^i)$ (symmetric);
3. $h_{ij}(x^l,x^j) \leq h_{li}(x^l,x^i) + h_{ij}(x^i,x^j)$ (triangle inequality);
4. if $i \neq j$, then $h_{ij}(x^i,x^j) > 0$.

A neighbourhood structure $\mathcal{N}_i(x^i)$ induced by a distance function $h_{ij}(x^i,x^j)$ can then be formally expressed as:

$$\mathcal{N}_i(x^i) = \{x^j \mid x^j \in X, h_{ij}(x^i,x^j) \leq s\} \tag{2}$$

where $s \in \mathbb{R}$. On a combinatorial space with syntactic operator φ, any configuration x^i can be transformed into any other x^j by applying the operator φ a finite number of times ($1 < s \leq n$) (Misevicius et al., 2004). In such a case, the distance metric $h_{ij}(x^i, x^j)$ is given by the Hamming distance:

$$h_{ij}(x^i, x^j) = \sum_{l=1}^{n} \operatorname{sgn}\left|x^i(d) - x^j(d)\right|$$

and s represents the minimum number of exchanges to transform x^i into x^j. Other distance metrics can be similarly defined (see (Ronald, 1997); (Ronald, 1998); and (Moraglio and Poli, 2004) references therein for a comprehensive treatment on distance metrics defined on the combinatorial space).

For generality, only the *deviation distance metric* (Ronald, 1998) will be considered hereafter. While other distance metrics can be defined for discrete and combinatorial spaces, the decision to use the deviation distance metric is trivial with respect to algorithmic design. Other problem-specific metrics can be substituted into the developed algorithm with little influence on the procedural implementations of the algorithm.

The deviation distance metric provides a measure of the relative distance of neighbouring elements between two permutations x^i and x^j. In problems where the adjacency of two elements influences the cost of the objective function $f(x)$, such as in TSP and flow-shop scheduling, the deviation distance function provides an appropriate choice of metric for the problem space (Ronald, 1998). Formally, the positional perturbation Δ_a of one element value $x^i(d_1)$ to its matching value in $x^j(d_2)$, such that $x^i(d_1) = x^j(d_2) = a$, $a \in [n]$, is given by the following:

$$\Delta_a = \left|d_1 - d_2\right| \tag{3}$$

For convenience, Δ_a is normalised $\overline{\Delta}_a \in [0,1]$:

$$\overline{\Delta}_a = \frac{\Delta_a}{n-1} \tag{4}$$

The deviation distance $h_{ij}(x^i, x^j)$ is then defined as the sum of the $\overline{\Delta}_a$ values:

$$h_{ij}(x^i, x^j) = \sum_{a}^{n} \overline{\Delta}_a \tag{5}$$

From Eq. (5) a large position deviation induces a greater distance in the metric space. The notion of position deviation is now used to construct the combinatorial optimisation PSO.

6. Proposed Algorithm

In Section 4.1, the concept of a syntactic operator φ was discussed as a method of transforming one configuration x^i to another $x^j \in \mathcal{N}_i(x^i)$. In the following section, the parallel between a syntactic operator φ and the motion of a particle i in the combinatorial space is described. Let $x^i \in X$ encode a permutation of $[d]$ objects in D-dimensional space. The position $x^i \in X$ of a particle i in the D-dimensional space corresponds to a permutation of $[d]$ objects. Define φ by a two-way perturbation (transformation) operator $\varphi := SO(d_1, d_2)$ as the *swap operator* that exchanges elements d_1 and d_2 in solution x^i, such that $X \to X$, $d_1, d_2 \in \{1,2,\ldots D\}$, $d_1 \neq d_2$. Applying the swap operator to the permutation x^i, the following solution is derived:

$$x_{k+1}^i = x_k^i \oplus SO(d_1, d_2) \tag{6}$$

where $x^i(d_1) = x^j(d_2) = a$, and $x_k^j, x_k^{i+1}, x^j \in \mathcal{N}_i(x_k^i)$, and the notation $\oplus$ is used to denote x_{k+1}^i is obtained from x_k^i by applying the perturbation $SO(d_1, d_2)$. In the combinatorial optimisation PSO, x_k^i and $x_k^j \in \mathcal{N}_i(x_k^i) \subseteq X$, $x_k^i \neq x_k^j$ encode two permutations in the combinatorial optimisation problem and represents positions in the combinatorial search space. Applying the notions of swap operator to PSO, the swap operator $SO(d_1, d_2)$ for a particle i can be interpreted as a motion of the particle x_k^i to a position x_k^j displaced from x_k^i by the deviation distance $h_{ij}(x_k^i, x_k^j)$. Consider the case when $x_k^j \notin \mathcal{N}_i(x_k^i)$. Then, the following transition $x_k^i \mapsto x_k^j$ is not possible by Eq. (6) alone. Define the following *swap sequence* (Knuth, 1998):

$$SS = \{SO_1, SO_2, \ldots, SO_n\} \tag{7}$$

where SS is the concatenation of swap operators and the order of the swap operators SO_i, $i = 1, \ldots, n$ is influential to the final position x_{k+1}^i. The minimum number of swap operators required to move $x_k^i \mapsto x_k^j$ is given by the Hamming distance and is referred to as the *basic swap sequence* (Knuth, 1998).

Suppose particle i moves according to $x_k^i \mapsto p_k^i$. The basic swap sequence transforming x_k^i to p_k^i can be determined by moving along each dimension of the initial position x_k^i and applying the Partially Mapped Crossover function (PMX) (Goldberg and Lingle, 1985) to each dimension along x_k^i. The PMX function maps each dimension in the current position x_k^i to the corresponding dimension in p_k^i (see Fig. 2). A swap operator is invoked if the object in the d_1-th dimension of the p_k^i solution and the x_k^i are inconsistent. The d_1-th element in x_k^i is then swapped with the d_2-th element in x_k^i such that $x_k^i(d_2) = p_k^i(d_1)$. Algorithm 2 summarises the basic swap operator used to move $x_k^i \mapsto p_k^i$

1: **while** $d(x^i, x^j) \neq 0$
2:     **if** $x_k^i(d_1) \neq x_k^j(d_1)$ **then**
3:         find d_2 such that $x_k^i(d_2) = x_k^j(d_1) = a_1$, and $d_1, d_2 \in \{1, \ldots, D\}$
4:             set $SO_j(d_1, d_2)$ and store as j-th entry in SS
5:     **else, end if**
4: **end while**

Algorithm 2. Basic Swap Operator

Note, applying the algorithm from left-right gives $d_2 > d_1$, $d_1, d_2 \in \{1,2,\ldots,D\}$.

Example 2.

Consider the following two solutions $x^i = \binom{1\ 2\ 3\ 4\ 5}{1\ 2\ 3\ 4\ 5}$ and $x^j = \binom{1\ 2\ 3\ 4\ 5}{2\ 3\ 1\ 5\ 4}$ represented in two-line form. Applying Algorithm 2 from left to right, the first swap operator is invoked if $x^i(1) \neq x^j(1)$. Since $x^i(1) = 1$ and $x^j(1) = 2$, the following mapping is observed between object $1 \to 2$. The first swap operator is then given by the exchange of elements 1 and 2 in x^i, $SO_1(1,2)$. Following $SO_1(1,2)$, particle i is now at position $x' = \binom{1\ 2\ 3\ 4\ 5}{2\ 1\ 3\ 4\ 5}$. Comparing x' to x^j, the following mapping $1 \leftrightarrow 3$ is now observed between object $x'(2)$ and $x^j(2)$. The next mapping is then given by $SO_2(2,3)$ taking x' to $x'' = \binom{1\ 2\ 3\ 4\ 5}{2\ 3\ 1\ 4\ 5}$. Repeating this procedure, the swap sequence SS that takes x^i to x^j is then given by $SS = \{SO_1(1,2), SO_2(2,3), SO_3(4,5)\}$ such that $x^j = x^i \oplus SS$.

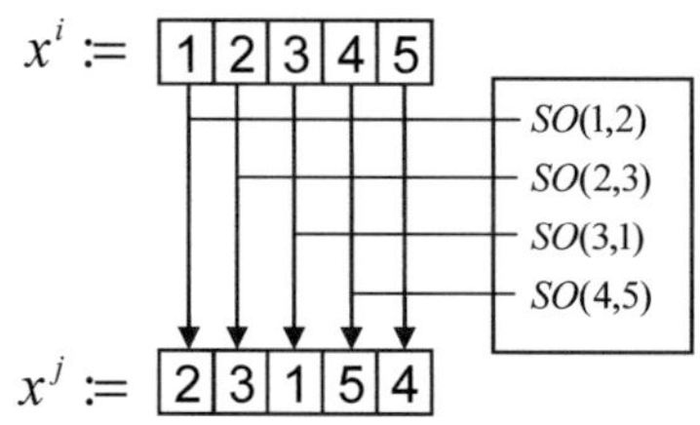

Figure 2. Partially-mapped crossover (PMX)

In traditional PSO, the motion of a particle is influenced by the personal best position p_k^i and global best of the swarm p_k^g. In the combinatorial optimisation PSO, each position encodes a permutation to the combinatorial optimisation problem. If the personal best and global best positions are not coincident, i.e. $p_k^i \neq p_k^g$, then the swap sequences SS_1 and SS_2 that moves the i-th particle along the transformations $x_k^i \mapsto p_k^i$ and $x_k^i \mapsto p_k^g$ respectively, are not equivalent, i.e. $SS_1 \neq SS_2$. Application of SS_1 or SS_2 will yield $x_{k+1}^i = p_k^i$ or $x_{k+1}^i = p_k^g$ and will cause the particles to converge towards the personal best solution, or the global best solution respectively. This leads to rapid convergence and sub-optimal solution quality. The local search induced by the exclusive application of SS_1, and the global search induced by the exclusive application of SS_2 is now combined to develop a velocity update function with similar characteristics to the original PSO algorithm.

In the traditional PSO algorithm, the velocity of a particle is composed of three parts; the *momentum term*, i.e. $v \cdot w$, the *cognitive velocity* $c_1 \cdot r_1 \cdot (p_k^i - x_k^i)$, and the *social velocity* $c_2 \cdot r_2 \cdot (p_k^g - x_k^i)$. Using the notions of *momentum, cognitive velocity,* and *social velocity,* the following decoupled velocity update for a particle in the combinatorial space with deviation distance metric Δ_a is defined:

$$v_{k+1}^{l,i} = w \cdot v_k^{l,i} + c_1 \cdot (\Delta_a'(x_k^i, p_k^i)) \tag{8a}$$

$$v_{k+1}^{g,i} = w \cdot v_k^{g,i} + c_2 \cdot (\Delta'_a(x_k^i, p_k^g)) \tag{8b}$$

where w, c_1, and c_2 have the same meanings as the original PSO algorithm. For convenience, denote Eq. (8a) as the *local velocity* and Eq. (8b) as the *global velocity*. Equation (8a) and (8b) preserve the same tuning parameters as the original PSO without the random variables $r_1, r_2 \in [0,1]$. The decision to omit the random variables is trivial, but will become apparent in the proceeding section.

Recall, the position of each particle x_k^i, $\forall i \in P$ is a vector in the D-dimensional combinatorial space $x_k^i \in X$ and moves along the dimensions of the D-dimensional hypercube by exchanging elements via the swap operator $SO(d_1, d_2)$. The velocity of each particle v_k^i, $\forall i \in P$ is a vector in the D-dimensional *continuous* space $v_k^i \in \mathbb{R}^D$ and describes the local gradient of the fitness landscape using the deviation distance metric. Using the velocity $v_k^i \in \mathbb{R}^D$, a probability mapping is described that invokes the swap operator and preserves the contributions of both the local velocity and global velocity. Let $\Pr(x^i(d) \mid p^i(d))$ and $\Pr(x^i(d) \mid p^g(d))$ denote the sampling probability of the i-th particle for dimension d in the particle when the individual best is $p^i(d)$ and global best is $p^g(d)$ respectively. Then, the probability that $x^i(d)$ moves to $p^i(d)$ and $p^g(d)$ is given by the following statements:

$$\Pr(x_k^i(d) \mid p_k^i(d)) := v_k^{l,i} \tag{9a}$$

$$\Pr(x_k^i(d) \mid p_k^g(d)) := v_k^{g,i} \tag{9b}$$

Since $p^i(d)$ and $p^g(d)$ is a mapping for $x^i(d) \mapsto p^i(d)$ and $x^i(d) \mapsto p^g(d)$ respectively, the probability that the swap operator $SO_j(d_1, d_2)$ is invoked by moving $x^i(d) \mapsto p^i(d)$ or $x^i(d) \mapsto p^g(d)$ using Algorithm 2 is defined using the local and global velocities respectively:

$$\Pr(SO(d_1, d_2)) := v_k^{l,i} \tag{10a}$$

$$\Pr(SO(d_1, d_2)) := v_k^{g,i} \tag{10b}$$

where $x^i(d_2) = p^i(d_1)$ or $x^i(d_2) = p^g(d_1)$ for $x^i(d) \mapsto p^i(d)$ and $x^i(d) \mapsto p^g(d)$ respectively. Following Eq. (10a) and Eq. (10b), the velocity $v_k^i(d)$ describes the probability that an element in $x_k^i(d)$ will swap with the corresponding element in $x_k^j(d)$ and invoke Algorithm 2, then the velocity on each dimension $d \in D$ must be bounded over the interval $v_k^i(d) \in [0,1]$. The velocities described in Eq. (10a) and Eq. (10b) are normalised according to:

$$v_{k+1}^{l,i} = \frac{v_{k+1}^{l,i}}{\arg\max\{v_{k+1}^{l,i}, v_{k+1}^{g,i}\}} \tag{11a}$$

$$v_{k+1}^{g,i} = \frac{v_{k+1}^{g,i}}{\arg\max\{v_{k+1}^{l,i}, v_{k+1}^{g,i}\}} \tag{11b}$$

Normalising the velocities with respect to both the personal best and global best velocity profiles is used to prioritise the order of swap operations and preserve the probability map. Once an element $x_k^i(d_1)$ has been swapped with the corresponding element $x_k^i(d_2)$ in $p_k^i(d_1)$, the associated velocity $v_k^i(d_2)$ at element $x_k^i(d_2)$ is set to zero if $x_k^i(d_2) = p_k^i(d_2)$ to prevent cyclic behaviour.

Using the definition of the sample probability in Eq. (10a) and Eq. (10b) for the personal best and global best respectively, the swap sequence induced by the combinatorial optimisation PSO can now be described. From Eq. (8a) and Eq. (8b), large deviation distances incur a large velocity. This observation is complimentary to the original concepts of the traditional PSO algorithm. Following Eq. (10a) and Eq. (10b) a large velocity will induce a greater probability that a swap operation is invoked with either the personal best or global best. Using this concept, a swap sequence can be defined using the relative probabilities of the personal best and global best velocity profiles. Consider the case when $v_k^{l,i}(d) > v_k^{g,i}(d)$. Then, the probability of exchanging $x_k^i(d) \mapsto p_k^i(d)$ is greater than the probability of exchanging $x_k^i(d) \mapsto p_k^g(d)$. In the swap sequence, the larger of the two probabilities will receive a higher priority in the swap sequence and take precedence over the lower probability swap operations. At a given iteration, particle i will move according to the following swap sequence:

$$x_{k+1}^i = x_k^i \oplus SS \tag{12}$$

where $SS = (SO_1(x_k^i(d), p_k^i(d)), SO_2(x_k^i(d), p_k^g(d)))$ if $v_k^{l,i} > v_k^{g,i}$. Algorithm 3 describes the implementation of the swap sequence SS.

0: **for all** $d \in D$ **do**
1:     **if** $v_k^{l,i}(d) > v_k^{g,i}(d)$ **do**
2:         invoke swap operator $SO_j(d_1, d_2)$ for $x_k^i \mapsto p_k^i$ using Algorithm 2
3:             **if** $x_k^i(d_2) = p_k^i(d_2)$ **do**
4:                 set $v_k^{l,i}(d_2) = 0$
5:             **else, end if**
6:         **goto** 8
7:     **otherwise if** $v_k^{g,i}(d) > v_k^{l,i}(d)$ **do**
8:         invoke swap operator $SO_j(d_1, d_2)$ for $x_k^i \mapsto p_k^g$ using Algorithm 2
9:             **if** $x_k^i(d_2) = p_k^g(d_2)$ **do**
10:                 set $v_k^g(d_2) = 0$
11:             **else, end if**
12:         **goto** 2
13:     **end if**
14: **end for**

Algorithm 3. Swap Sequence

Following the definition of the basic swap sequence and swap sequence in Algorithm 2 and Algorithm 3 respectively, the proposed combinatorial PSO algorithm can now be defined. Algorithm 4 describes the procedural implementation of the swap sequence within the context of the traditional PSO algorithm.

7. Algorithmic Analysis

The behaviour of each particle in the swarm can be viewed as a traditional line-search procedure dependent on a stochastic step size and a stochastic search direction. Both the stochastic step size and search direction depend on the selection of social and cognitive parameters. In addition, the stochastic search direction is driven by the best design space locations found by each particle and by the swarm as a whole. Unlike traditional line-search procedures however, PSO uses information from neighbouring particles to influence the search direction at each iteration. This exchange of information plays an important role in the stability and performance of the swarm. In the following section, the spectral properties of algebraic graph theory are used to show that for a fully interconnected swarm, the particles will reach a consensus on the equilibrium. The analysis begins by considering the original PSO algorithm with velocity and position update given by Eq. (1a) and Eq. (1b).

---

for all particle i **do**
    initialise position x_k^i randomly in the search space
end for
while termination criteria not satisfied **do**
    for all particle i **do**
        set personal best p_k^i as the best position found by the particle so far
        set global best p_k^g as the best position found by the swarm so far
    end for
    for all particle i **do**
        update local velocity according to
        $v_{k+1}^{l,i} = w \cdot v_k^{l,i} + c_1 \cdot (\Delta_v'(x_k^i, p_k^i))$
        update global velocity according to
        $v_{k+1}^{g,i} = w \cdot v_k^{g,i} + c_2 \cdot (\Delta_v'(x_k^i, p_k^g))$
        normalise local velocity according to
        $v_{k+1}^{l,i} = v_k^{l,i} / \arg\max\{v_k^{l,i}, v_k^{g,i}\}$
        normalise global velocity according to
        $v_{k+1}^{g,i} = v_k^{g,i} / \arg\max\{v_k^{l,i}, v_k^{g,i}\}$
        update position according to
        $x_{k+1}^i = x_k^i \oplus SS$
        where SS is determined from Algorithm 3
    end for
end while

Algorithm 4. Combinatorial Optimisation PSO

Without loss of generality, consider the following objective function for the combinatorial optimisation problem:

$$x^* = \arg\min_{x\in X} f(x) \ \forall x \in X$$

Then, the personal best p_k^i is the current best solution of the i-th particle found so far; i.e. $p_k^i = \arg\min_\tau x_\tau^i$, $\forall \tau \in (0,k]$; and the global best p_k^g is the current best solution of the global swarm found so far; i.e. $p_k^g = \arg\min_\tau x_\tau^i$, $\forall \tau \in (0,k]$, $\forall i \in N$. The swarm of particles is said to have reached an equilibria if and only if all the particles have reached a consensus on the value of p_k^g, i.e., $p_k^l = p_k^g = p^e$. For asymptotic convergence, all the particles in the swarm must globally asymptotically reach a consensus on the global best solution, such that $x^e = \lim_{k\to+\infty} x_k^i$, and $x_k^{e,i} = x_k^{e,j} = \min(X), \forall i,j \in X, i \neq j$. For convenience, Eq. (1a) and Eq. (1b) are combined into compact matrix form:

$$\begin{bmatrix} x_{k+1}^i \\ v_{k+1}^i \end{bmatrix} = \begin{bmatrix} -(c_1r_1+c_2r_2) & w \\ -(c_1r_1+c_2r_2) & w \end{bmatrix} \cdot \begin{bmatrix} x_k^i \\ v_k^i \end{bmatrix} + \begin{bmatrix} c_1r_1 & c_2r_2 \\ c_1r_1 & c_2r_2 \end{bmatrix} \cdot \begin{bmatrix} p_k^i \\ p_k^g \end{bmatrix} \tag{13}$$

which can be considered as a discrete-dynamic system representation of the original PSO algorithm.

7.1 Equilibrium of the PSO

Before the main analysis results are presented, a brief introduction into algebraic graph modelling of swarms is presented. The information flow in the swarm of particles can be represented using an interconnected graph $G = (V,E)$, where V is the enumerated set of particles $x_k^i \in V$, $i \in \{1,\ldots,N\}$ in the swarm, and $E \subseteq V \times V$ is the set of edge relations between neighbouring particles. The *order* $|V|$ and *size* $|E|$ of the graph G physically represents the number of particles in the swarm and the number of edge connections. For a fully connected swarm, each particle communicates with every other particle in the population, and the graph is said to be complete. This is the case of the original PSO algorithm. The connectivity of a graph is described by the square matrix A, with size $|V|$, and elements a_{ij} describing the connectivity of adjacent vertices x^i and x^j, such that:

$$a_{ij} = \begin{cases} 1, & \text{if } (x^i, x^j) \in E \\ 0, & \text{otherwise} \end{cases} \tag{14}$$

The matrix A uniquely defines the connectivity of the graph G and is referred to as the *adjacency matrix*. Associated with the adjacency matrix A is the *graph Laplacian* L, and its *Laplacian potential* Ψ_G:

$$L = \Lambda^{-1}(\Lambda - A) \tag{15}$$

$$\Psi_G = \frac{1}{2} x^T L x \tag{16}$$

where Λ is the square matrix containing the out-degree of each vertex along the diagonal, and x is the concatenation of particles in the swarm. A well-known property of the Laplacian potential is that it is positive semi-definite and satisfies the following sum-of-squares property (Godsil and Royle, 2001):

$$x^T L x = \sum_{i,j \in E} A_{ij} \left(x^j - x^i\right)^2, \quad x \in \mathbb{R}^n \tag{17}$$

Using Eq. (17), the objective is to show that the personal best positions of each particle reaches a consensus (by way of equilibria) coincident to the global best of the swarm, i.e. $p_k^i = p_k^g$, $\forall \in P$. Eq. (16) becomes:

$$p^T L p = \sum_{i,j \in E} A_{ij} \left(p_k^j - p_k^i\right)^2, \quad p_k^i \in \mathbb{R}^n \tag{18}$$

where p is the concatenated states of the personal best of each of the particles in the swarm. The closed-loop dynamics of the global best position evolve according to the following continuous-time dynamic equation:

$$\dot{p} = -Lp = -\nabla \Psi_G \tag{19}$$

The equilibrium points of Eq. (19) correspond to stationary points of Ψ_G and the region outside of these points, the potential is strictly decreasing (Moreau, 2004); i.e., if x^e is an equilibrium of Eq. (18), then $Lx^e = 0$. From Eq. (16):

$$\Psi_G(p^e) = \frac{1}{2}(p^e)^T L p^e = 0 \tag{20}$$

Following the connectivity of G, $p_i^e = p_j^e = c, \forall i, j \in N$, i.e. $p^e = (c, \ldots, c)^T, c \in X$. Since the Laplacian potential equals zero at equilibrium, then $p^g = \min(p)$ is an invariant quantity, Given the invariance property of $\min(p)$, then $\min(p^e) = \min(p(0))$, and $\min(p^e) = c$. This implies $p_k^{e,i} = \min(p(0))$, $\forall i \in P$ (Olfati-Saber and Murray, 2003). This leads to the following observations for the particle dynamics in Eq. (1a) and Eq. (1b) that are consistent with the works of (Clerc and Kennedy, 2002); (Trelea, 2003); and (Kadirkamanathan et al., 2006):

1. The system dynamics are stochastic and order two;
2. The system does not have an equilibrium point if $p_k^g \neq p_k^l$;
3. If $p_k^l = p_k^g = p^e$ is time invariant, there is a unique equilibrium at $v^e = 0$, $x^e = p^e$.

An equilibrium point thus exists only for the best particle whose local best solution is the same as the global best solution (Kadirkamanathan et al., 2006).

Consider the case for a given particle i when the external input is constant (as is the case when no personal or global better positions are found). From Eq. (15) the eigenvalues of $-L$

are negative in the complex plane. Then, for particle i, the position asymptotically converges to the point x^e in the eigenspace associated to the global minimum found by the swarm of particles (Olfati-Saber and Murray, 2003). Such a position x^e is not necessarily a local or global minimiser of the combinatorial optimisation problem. Instead, it will improve towards the optimum x^* if a better individual or global position is found. Discovery of better individual or global positions can be improved by increasing the population diversity of the swarm through the introduction of chaos or turbulence (Kennedy and Eberhart, 1995). In the following section, a non-stationary Markov chain is constructed to integrate the discrete syntactic swap operators introduced in Section 5 to the continuous time-dynamics of the traditional PSO

7.2 Non-Stationary Markov Model of combinatorial PSO

Markov chains are important in the theoretical analysis of evolutionary algorithms operating on discrete search spaces (Poli et al., 2007) and have been used to model the probabilistic convergence of population-based meta-heuristic algorithms (see (Rudolph, 1996); (Cao and Wu, 1997); (Poli and Langdon, 2007); and (Greenwood and Zhu, 2001) for examples of their implementation). While traditional PSO has operated on a continuous search space, the combinatorial PSO operates on a discrete combinatorial space. This makes Markov chains a suitable method of modelling and analysing the behaviour of the combinatorial PSO. The use of Markov chains on bare-bones PSO has previously been investigated by (Poli and Langdon, 2007) where the continuous search space was discretised using a hypercube sampling. In the following section, a non-stationary Markov chain is used to model the combinatorial PSO and account for the newly introduced swap operator.

Let X denote the finite state space describing the set of permutation encodings with $r = |X| = n!$ possible solutions. Let $P \subset X$ be a population of solutions from X with size $|P| = N$. Then a finite Markov chain $\Gamma \subseteq X$ describes a probabilistic trajectory over the finite state space X (Rudolph, 1996) with $\mathbf{N} = \binom{m+n!-1}{n!-1}$ possible populations as states; i.e.:

$$X = \{S_1, S_2, \ldots, S_{\mathbf{N}}\} \tag{21}$$

The probability $q_{k-1,k}^{mn} := \Pr_{mn}(\Gamma^k = S_n | \Gamma^{k-1} = S_m)$ of transitioning from state $S_m \in X$ to $S_n \in X$, $m,n \in \mathbf{N}$ at step k is called the *transition probability* from m to n at step k. The transition probability of a finite Markov chain can be gathered into a *transition matrix* $Q_k = \{q_{k-1,k}^{mn}\}$ (Rudolph, 1994), where each dimension $q_{k-1,k}^{mn} \in [0,1]$. In a *stationary Markov chain* the probabilities remain fixed, and the Markov chain is said to be *homogenous;* i.e., $Q = Q_k = \{q_{k-1,k}^{mn}\}$, $\forall k = 1,2,\ldots$, and $m,n = 1,2,\ldots,\mathbf{N}$. In the case of the combinatorial PSO, the probabilities of the swap operator are updated according to Eq. (8a) and Eq. (8b). This results in a *non-stationary Markov chain*. The transition probabilities of non-stationary Markov chains are calculated by considering how the population incidence vector S_j describes the composition of the next iteration (Cao and Wu, 1997). Denote $z_k^{l,i} = \Pr(x_k^i | p_k^i) = v_k^{l,i}$ as the sampling probability when the personal best is p_k^i; likewise, denote $z_k^{g,i} = \Pr(x_k^i | p_k^g) = v_k^g$ as the sampling probability when the global best is p_k^g. The probability that a particle i will move according to $x_k^i \mapsto p_k^i$ or $x_k^i \mapsto p_k^g$ x_k^i is given by $z_k^i = (p_k^i \cup p_k^g)$. From Algorithm 3, the dimension for $z_k^{l,i} = \Pr(x_k^i | p_k^i)$ and $z_k^{g,i} = \Pr(x_k^i | p_k^g)$ is calculated independently using Eq. (8a) and Eq. (8b) and the probability of a particle sampling p_k^i or p_k^g is given by:

$$\Pr(p_k^i \cup p_k^g) = \prod_{d=1}^{D} \Pr\left(p_k^i(d) \cup p_k^g(d) \middle| p_k^i(d), p_k^g(d)\right) \tag{22a}$$

$$\Pr(p_k^i \cup p_k^g) = \prod_{d=1}^{D} \Pr(p_k^i(d)) + \Pr(p_k^g(d)) - \Pr(p_k^i(d)) \cdot \Pr(p_k^g(d)) \tag{22b}$$

Since personal bests can only change if there is a fitness improvement, only certain state transitions can occur. That is, a transition from state $S_m \mapsto S_n$ is possible only if the fitness of at least one particle in the swarm improves (Poli and Langdon, 2007). Because of the independence of the particles (over one time step), the state transition probability for the whole PSO is given by:

$$q_{k-1,k}^{mn} = \prod_i \Pr(p_k^i \cup p_k^g) \tag{23}$$

From Sec. 6.1, the local velocity $v_k^{l,i}$ and global velocity $v_k^{g,i}$ will tend to zero as $k \to +\infty$. This implies $\lim_{k\to\infty} q_{k-1,k}^{mn} = \lim_{k\to\infty} v_k^{l,i} = \lim_{k\to\infty} v_k^{g,i} = 0$, $m,n = 1,2,\ldots,\mathbf{N}$. Therefore, the swap operator preserves the convergent behaviour of traditional PSO and the combinatorial PSO converges to the equilibrium pair (x^e, v^e).

8. Numerical Examples

8.1 The Travelling Salesman Problem

To test the efficiency of the proposed algorithm, the combinatorial optimisation PSO is tested on the travelling salesman problem (TSP). TSP is an invaluable test problem that belongs to the class of NP -hard combinatorial optimisation problems. The objective of TSP is to find a minimum-cost tour that visits a set of n cities and returns to an initial point (Applegate et al., 2006). Mathematically, TSP is a combinatorial optimisation problem on an undirected graph $G = (V, E)$. Each city $c_i \in [n]$, $i = 1,2,\ldots,n$, is represented by a vertex $v_i \in V$ in the graph $G = (V, E)$ with cost of travel between adjacent cities given by $h_{ij} \in E$. A solution to TSP can be represented as a sequence of cities encoded by a permutation $x \in X$. Mathematically, the objective of TSP is given by the following optimisation problem:

$$x^* \in X \Leftrightarrow x^* = \arg\min_{x \in X} \sum_{d=1}^{n-1} h_{ij}(x(d), x(d+1)) + h_{ij}(x(n), x(1)) \tag{24}$$

Various problems, including path-finding, routing, and scheduling, can be modelled as a TSP. A repository of test-instances (and their solutions) is available through the TSPLIB library (Reinelt, 1991). In the following section, the combinatorial PSO is tested on several instances of the TPSLIB library. Table 1 summarises the test instances of TSPLIB used to validate and compare the combinatorial PSO.

Name	Dimension	Optimal $f(x)$	Optimal Solution
burma	14	30.8785	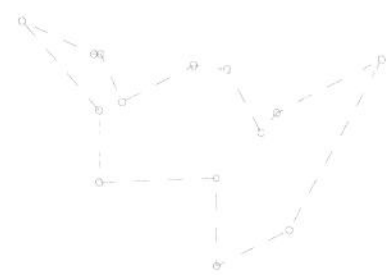
gr17	17	2085	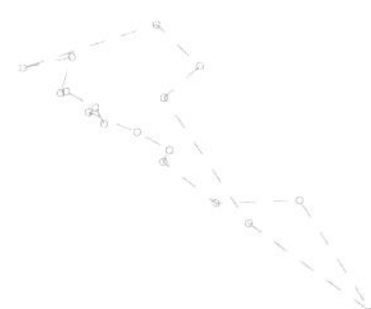
gr24	24	1272	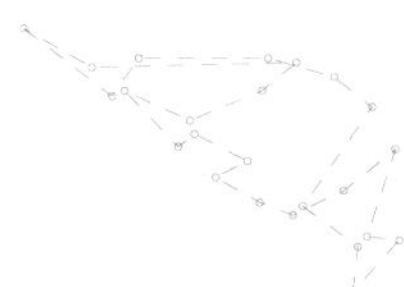
eil51	51	426	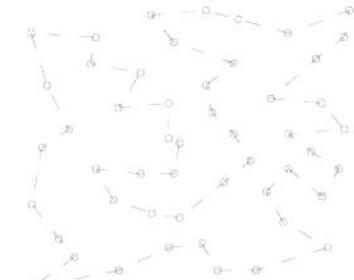

Table 1. Test instances taken from TSPLIB (Reinelt, 1991) used for the validation of the combinatorial PSO

8.2 Optimisation Results and Discussion

In the following experiments, the combinatorial PSO is applied to each case of the TSP in Table 1. The parameters used in each experiment are selected based on the findings reported in the literature (Zhang et al., 2005); (Shi and Eberhart, 1998a); (Zheng et al., 2003); (Clerc and Kennedy, 2002); and (Eberhart and Shi, 2000). While the inertia weight, cognitive and social parameters are sensitive to the problem domain in traditional PSO, a parametric analysis of their influence on the combinatorial PSO is beyond the scope of this chapter. For illustrative purposes, the parameters given in Table 2 are considered throughout the remainder of this chapter. The influence of these parameters on the performance of the combinatorial PSO remains the subject of future research.

Parameter	Value
w	0.8
c_1	2.025
c_2	2.025

Table 2. Combinatorial PSO parameters

To demonstrate the relative efficiency of the proposed algorithm, the performance of the combinatorial PSO is compared to a genetic algorithm. Each TSP experiment was trialled 100 times using randomly generated individuals. In both algorithms, a population of $P = 30$ was maintained for each iteration. The fitness values obtained by the combinatorial PSO and the GA over the 100 trials are presented in Table 3. Table 4 compares the success rate of the PSO and GA for each of the problems. Figure 3 compares the percentage of the solution space explored by the combinatorial PSO and the GA. This is determined as the number of unique solutions tested $x_k^i \in X$, $\forall i \in P$, $k = 1,\ldots,1000$ by the PSO and GA versus the size of the solution space $|X| = n!$.

Problem	Optimal Solution	Minimum		Maximum		Average	
		PSO	GA	PSO	GA	PSO	GA
burma	30.87	30.87	30.87	30.87	34.62	30.87	31.20
gr17	2085	2085	2085	2687	2489	2141.55	2175.02
gr24	1272	1272	1282	1632	1810	1453.52	1488.68
eil51	426	494.80	495.46	687.52	671.85	573.55	573.95

Table 3. Performance of the proposed algorithm compared to a traditional genetic algorithm for combinatorial optimisation

From Table 3, the combinatorial PSO outperformed the GA in all problem instances, except for the 51 variable eil51 problem. In this case, both the GA and combinatorial PSO failed to find the best solution over the 100 trials. Examination of Fig. 3 suggests that both the combinatorial PSO and GA were only able to search a small percentage ($<< 1\%$) of the total solution space over the 1000 iterations. This suggests, that both the combinatorial PSO and GA experience a loss of solution diversity over the optimisation procedure. Figure 3 also indicates that the GA was able to cover a larger percentage of the solution space for each trial than the combinatorial PSO. This suggests that the combinatorial PSO suffers from the same rapid convergence and stagnation issues of traditional PSO. Loss of solution diversity and rapid convergence is a well-known problem in traditional PSO. In traditional PSO, the performance of the algorithm deteriorates as the number of iterations increases. Once the algorithm has slowed down (becomes stagnant), it is usually difficult to achieve a better fitness value; particularly for high-dimensionality problem spaces.

Problem	Success Rate (%)	
	PSO	GA
burma	100	92
gr17	36	17
gr24	4	0
eil51	0	0

Table 4. Success rate of the combinatorial PSO and GA

Recently, several methods have been proposed to improve solution diversity and avoid stagnation in traditional PSO. These methods include the use of chaos variables (Fieldsend and Singh, 2002); (Kennedy and Eberhart, 1995); and (He et al., 2004); variable neighbourhood topologies (Kennedy, 1999); and (Liu et al., 2007a); and mutation operators (Liu et al., 2007b); and (Andrews, 2006). Many of these techniques have had varying levels of success on the traditional PSO algorithm. It is expected, that these same strategies can be adapted to the combinatorial PSO. Future work aims to investigate the potential to implement these algorithmic improvements to the combinatorial PSO and solve for larger scale combinatorial optimisation problems.

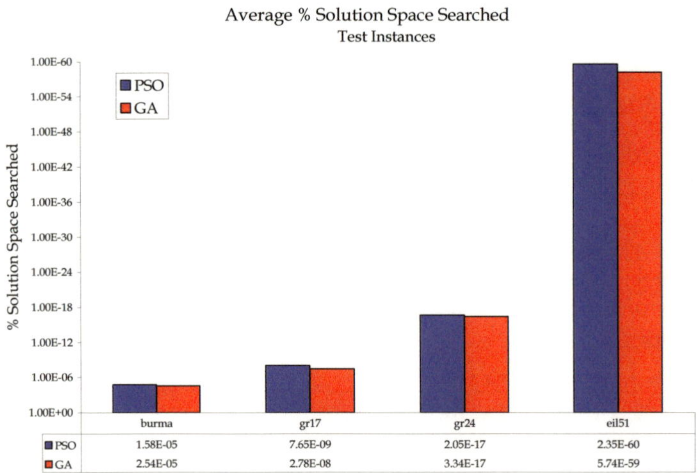

Figure 3. Comparison of the solution space searched by the combinatorial PSO and the GA

9. Conclusion

The PSO's simplicity, robustness, and low computational costs, makes it an ideal method for continuous optimisation problems. Previous efforts to adapt the traditional PSO algorithm to combinatorial spaces have shown varying levels of success. In this chapter, a new combinatorial optimisation PSO that builds on previous works is introduced. A distance metric was introduced to define a metric space for the combinatorial optimisation problem and a syntactic swap operator introduced. Motion was induced by associating a probability sampling function to the velocity profile of a particle on the combinatorial space and invoking the defined swap operator. The proposed algorithm was tested on several instances of TSPLIB and compared to the performance of a GA. Preliminary test results demonstrated superior performance over the GA in all test cases. For larger set sizes, the proposed algorithm failed to converge to the optimal solution. Examination of the sampled solution space suggested that the proposed algorithm suffered from the same rapid convergence and stagnation issues observed in traditional PSO. Further research is needed to clarify the effect of the various tuning parameters on the performance of the proposed algorithm, and their influence on loss of solution diversity. The generalised approach to the algorithm's development allows for the consideration of other metrics on discrete spaces, and the implementation of further algorithmic improvements. Future work aims to investigate methods to mitigate the stagnation issues of the proposed algorithm and extending the combinatorial optimisation PSO's capabilities to other discrete optimisation problems.

10. References

Aardal, K., Hoesel, S. v., Lenstra, J. K. and Stougie, L. (1997). *A Decade of Combinatorial Optimization.* Department of Information and Computing Sciences, Utrecht University, UU-CS-1997-12,

Aguilar, J. (2001). A General Ant Colony Model to solve Combinatorial Optimization Problems. *Revista Colombiana De Computación,* 2, 7 - 18.

Andrews, P. S. (2006). An Investigation into Mutation Operators for Particle Swarm Optimization, *Proceedings of IEEE Congress on Evolutionary Computation,* pp. 1044 - 1051, Vancouver BC, Canada, July,

Applegate, D. L., Bixby, R. E., Chvátal, V. e. and Cook, W. J. (2006). *The Traveling Salesman Problem,* Princeton University Press, New Jersey.

Bean, J. (1994). Genetic Algorithms and Random Keys for Sequencing and Optimization. *ORSA Journal on Computing,* 6, 154 - 160.

Bóna, M. (2004). *Combinatorics of Permutations,* Chapman & Hall/CRC, New York.

Bonyadi, M. R., Azghadi, S. M. R. and Hosseini, H. S. (2007). Solving Traveling Salesman Problem Using Combinational Evolutionary Algorithm, In *Artificial Intelligence and Innovations 2007: From Theory to Applications,* Vol. 247 (Eds, Boukis, C., Pnevmatikakis, L. and Polymenakos, L.) Springer, Boston, pp. 37 - 44.

Cao, Y. J. and Wu, Q. H. (1997). Convergence Analysis of Adaptive Genetic Algorithms, *Proceedings of Genetic Algorithms in Engineering Systems: Innovations and Applications,* pp. 85 - 89, 2 - 4 September,

Clerc, M. and Kennedy, J. (2002). The Particle Swarm - Explosion, Stability, and Convergence in a Multidimensional Complex Space. *IEEE Transactions on Evolutionary Computation,* 6, 58 - 73.

Eberhart, R. C. and Shi, Y. (2000). Comparing Inertia Weights and Constriction Factors in Particle Swarn Optimization, *Proceedings of IEEE Congress on Evolutionary Computation*, pp. 84-88, San Diego, CA,

Festa, P. and Resende, M. G. C. (2008). *Hybrid Grasp Heuristics.* AT&T Labs Research, Florham Park, July

Fieldsend, J. E. and Singh, S. (2002). A Multi-Objective Algorithm Based Upon Particle Swarm Optimisation, an Efficient Data Structure and Turbulence, *Proceedings of UK Workshop on Computational Intelligence*, pp. 37 - 44, UK,

Godsil, C. and Royle, G. (2001). *Algebraic Graph Theory,* Springer-Verlag, New York.

Goldberg, D. and Lingle, J. R. (1985). Alleles, Loci and the TSP, *Proceedings of First International Conference on Genetic Algorithms and Their Applications*, pp. 154 - 159, Hillsdale, Hew Jersey,

Greenwood, G. W. and Zhu, Q. J. (2001). Convergence in Evolutionary Programs with Self-Adaptation. *Evolutionary Computation,* 2, 147 - 157.

He, S., Wu, Q. H., Wen, J. Y., Saunders, J. R. and Paton, R. C. (2004). A Particle Swarm Optimizer with Passive Congregation. *Biosystems,* 78, 135 - 147.

Kadirkamanathan, V., Selvarajah, K. and Fleming, P. J. (2006). Stability Analysis of the Particle Dynamics in Particle Swarm Optimizer. *IEEE Transactions on Evolutionary Computation,* 10, 245 - 255.

Kennedy, J. (1999). Small Worlds and Mega-Minds: Effects of Neighborhood Topology on Particle Swarm Performance, *Proceedings of Congress on Evolutionary Computation*, pp. 1931 - 1938, Washington DC, USA,

Kennedy, J. and Eberhart, R. (1995). Particle Swarm Optimization, *Proceedings of IEEE International Conference on Neural Networks*, pp. 1942-1948, 27th November - 1 December, 1995,

Kennedy, J. and Eberhart, R. C. (1997). A Discrete Binary Version of the Particle Swarm Algorithm, *Proceedings of IEEE International Conference on Systems, Man, and Cybernetics*, pp.

Knuth, D. E. (1998). *The Art of Computer Programming,* Addison-Wesley, Reading.

Liu, H., Abraham, A. and Grosan, C. (2007a). A Novel Variable Neighborhood Particle Swarm Optimization for Multi-Objective Flexible Job-Shop Scheduling Problems, *Proceedings of 2nd International Conference on Digital Information Management*, pp. 138 - 145, October,

Liu, J., Fan, X. and Qu, Z. (2007b). An Improved Particle Swarm Optimization with Mutation Based on Similarity, *Proceedings of Third International Conference on Natural Computation*, pp. Haikou, China,

Martínez García, F. J. and Moreno Pérez, J. A. (2008). *Jumping Frogs Optimization: A New Swarm Method for Discrete Optimization.* Department of Statistics, O. R. and Computing, University of La Laguna, Tenerife, Spain, DEIOC 3/2008,

Misevicius, A., Blažauskas, T., Blonskis, J. and Smolinskas, J. (2004). An Overview of Some Heuristic Algorithms for Combinatorial Optimization Problems. *Information Technology and Control,* 30, 21 - 31.

Moraglio, A. and Poli, R. (2004). Topological Interpretation of Crossover, In *Genetic and Evolutionary Computation - GECCO 2004*, Vol. 3102/2004 Springer Berlin/Heidelberg, Berlin/Heidelberg, pp. 1377 - 1388.

Moreau, L. (2004). Stability of Continuous-Time Distributed Consensus Algorithms, *Proceedings of 43rd IEEE Conference on Decision and Control*, pp. 3998 - 4003, Atlantis, Paradise Island, Bahamas, December,

Olfati-Saber, R. and Murray, R. M. (2003). Consensus Protocols for Networks of Dynamic Agents, *Proceedings of American Control Conference*, pp. 951-956,

Pang, W., Wang, K.-p., Zhou, C.-g. and Dong, L.-j. (2004). Fuzzy Discrete Particle Swarm Optimization for Solving Traveling Salesman Problem, *Proceedings of 4th International Conference on Computer and Information Technology (CIT04), IEEE Computer Society*, pp.

Passino, K. M. (2002). Biomimicry of Bacterial Foraging for Distributed Optimization and Control. *IEEE Control Systems Magazine*, 22, 52 - 67.

Poli, R. and Langdon, W. B. (2007). Markov Chain Models of Bare-Bones Particle Swarm Optimizers, *Proceedings of 9th Annual Conference on Genetic and Evolutionary Computation*, pp. 142 - 149, London, England, 7 - 11 July,

Poli, R., Langdon, W. B., Clerc, M. and Stephens, C. R. (2007). Continuous Optimisation Theory Made Easy? Finite-Element Models of Evolutionary Strategies, Genetic Algorithms and Particles Swarm Optimizers, In *Foundations of Genetic Algorithms*, Vol. 4436/2007 Springer Berlin/Heidelberg, Berlin, pp. 165 - 193.

Reinelt, G. (1991). TSPLIB - Traveling Salesman Problem Library. *ORSA Journal on Computing*, 3, 376 - 384.

Ronald, S. (1997). Distance Functions for Order-Based Encodings, *Proceedings of IEEE International Conference on Evolutionary Computation*, pp. 49 - 54, Indianapolis, USA,

Ronald, S. (1998). More Distance Functions for Order-Based Encodings, *Proceedings of IEEE Conference on Evolutionary Computation*, pp. 558 - 563, IEEE Press

Rudolph, G. (1994). Convergence Analysis of Canonical Genetic Algorithms. *IEEE Transactions on Neural Networks*, 5, 96 - 101.

Rudolph, G. (1996). Convergence of Evolutionary Algorithms in General Search Spaces, *Proceedings of IEEE International Conference on Evolutionary Computation*, pp. 50 - 54, Nagoya, Japan, 20 - 22 May,

Shi, X. H., Zhou, Y., Wang, L. M., Wang, Q. X. and Liang, Y. C. (2006). A Discrete Particle Swarm Optimization Algorithm for Travelling Salesman Problem, In *Computational Methods*(Eds, Liu, G. R., Tan, V. B. C. and Han, X.) Springer Netherlands, Netherlands, pp. 1063 - 1068.

Shi, Y. and Eberhart, R. C. (1998a). A Modified Particle Swarm Optimiser, *Proceedings of IEEE International Conference on Evolutionary Computation*, pp. Anchorage, Alaska, May,

Shi, Y. and Eberhart, R. C. (1998b). Parameter Selection in Particle Swarm Optimization, *Proceedings of 7th International Conference on Evolutionary Programming*, pp. 591 - 600,

Song, X., Chang, C. and Cao, Y. (2008). New Particle Swarm Algorithm for Job Shop Scheduling Problems, *Proceedings of 7th World Congress on Intelligent Control and Automation*, pp. 3996 - 4001, Chongqing, China, 25 - 27 June,

Tasgetiren, M. F., Sevkli, M., Liang, Y. C. and Gencyilmaz, G. (2004). Particle Swarm Optimization Algorithm for Permutation Flowshop Sequencing Problem, In *Ant Colony, Optimization and Swarm Intelligence,* Vol. 3172/2004 Springer Berlin/Heidelberg, Berlin, pp. 382 - 389.

Trelea, I. C. (2003). The Particle Swarm Optimization Algorithm: Convergence Analysis and Parameter Selection. *Information Processing Letters,* 85, 317 - 325.

Wang, K.-p., Huang, L., Zhou, C. G. and Pang, W. (2003). Particle Swarm Optimization for Traveling Salesman Problem, *Proceedings of Second International Conference on Machine Learning and Cybernetics,* pp. 1583 - 1585, Xi'an, China, November,

Zhang, L.-p., Yu, H.-j. and Hu, S.-X. (2005). Optimal Choice of Parameters for Particle Swarm Optimization. *Journal of Zhejiang University Science,* 6, 528-534.

Zheng, Y.-L., Ma, L.-H., Zhang, L.-Y. and Qian, J.-X. (2003). On the Convergence Analysis and Parameter Selection in Particle Swarm Optimization, *Proceedings of Second International Conference on Machine Learning and Cybernetics,* pp. 1802 - 1807, Xi'an, China, November,

19

Particle Swarm Optimization Applied to Parameters Learning of Probabilistic Neural Networks for Classification of Economic Activities

Patrick Marques Ciarelli, Renato A. Krohling and Elias Oliveira
Universidade Federal do Espírito Santo
Brazil

1. Introduction

Automatic text classification and clustering are still very challenging computational problems to the information retrieval (IR) communities both in academic and industrial contexts. Currently, a great effort of work on IR, one can find in the literature, is focused on classification and clustering of generic content of text documents. However, there are many other important applications to which little attention has hitherto been paid, which are as well very difficult to deal with. One example of these applications is the classification of companies based on the descriptions of their economic activities, also called mission statements, which represent the business context of the companies' activities, in other words, the business economic activities from free text description by the company's founders.

The categorization of companies according to their economic activities constitute a very important step towards building tools for obtaining correct information for performing statistical analysis of the economic activities within a city or country. With this goal, the Brazilian government is creating a centralized digital library with the business economic activity descriptions of all companies in the country. This library will serve the three government levels: Federal; the 27 States; and more than 5.000 Brazilian counties. We estimate that the data related to nearly 1.5 million companies will have to be processed every year (DNRC, 2007) into more than 1.000 possible different activities. It is important to highlight that the large number of possible categories makes this problem particularly complex when compared with others presented in the literature (Jain et al., 1999; Sebastiani, 2002).

In this paper, we proposed a slightly modified version of the standard structure of the probabilistic neural network (PNN) (Specht, 1990) so that we could deal with the multi-label problem faced in this work. We compared the PNN performance trained by a canonical Particle Swarm Optimization (PSO) and a Bare Bones Particle Swarm Optimization (BBPSO). Our results show that, in the categorization of free text descriptions of economic activities, the PNN trained by BBPSO got slightly better results than the PNN trained by PSO.

This work is organized as follows. In Section 2, we detail more the characteristics of the problem and its importance for the government institutions in Brazil. Related works are mentioned in Section 3. We describe our probabilistic neural network algorithm in Section 4. Section 5 describes the Particle Swarm Optimization algorithm and a special version named Bare Bones Particle Swarm Optimization. In Section 6, the experimental results are discussed. Finally, we present our conclusions and indicate some future paths for future research in Section 7.

2. The Problem of Multi-label Text Categorization

In many countries, companies must have a contract (Articles of Incorporation or Corporate Charter, in USA) with the society where they can legally operate. In Brazil, this contract is called a social contract and must contain the statement of purpose of the company - this statement of purpose describe the business activities of the company and must be categorized into a legal business activity by Brazilian government officials. For that, all legal business activities are cataloged using a table called National Classification of Economic Activities, for short, CNAE (CNAE, 2003).

To perform the categorization, the government officials (at the Federal, State and County levels) must find the semantic correspondence between the company economic activities description and one or more entries of the CNAE table. There is a numerical code for each entry of the CNAE table and, in the categorization task, the government official attributes one or more of such codes to the company at hand. This can happen on the foundation of the company or in a change of its social contract, if that modifies its economic activities.

The work of finding the semantic correspondence between the company economic activities description and a set of entries into the CNAE table are both very difficult and labor-intensive task. This is because of the subjectivity of each local government officials who can focus on their own particular interests so that some codes may be assigned to a company, whereas in other regions, similar companies, may have a totally different set of codes. Sometimes, even inside of the same state, different level of government officials may count on a different number of codes for the same company for performing their work of assessing that company. Having inhomogeneous ways of classifying any company everywhere in all the three levels of the governmental administrations can cause a serious distortion on the key information for the long time planning and taxation. Additionally, the continental size of Brazil makes this problem of classification even worse.

In addition, the number of codes assigned by the human specialist to a company can vary greatly, in our dataset we have seen cases where the number of codes varied from 1 up to 109. However, in the set of assigned codes, the first code is the main code of that company. The remaining codes have no order of importance.

Due to this task is up to now decentralized, we might have the same job being performed many times by each of the three levels of the government officials. Nevertheless, it is known that there has been not enough staff to do this job properly.

For all these reasons, the computational problem addressed by us is mainly that of automatically suggesting the human classifier the semantic correspondence between a textual description of the economic activities of a company and one or more items of the CNAE table. Or, depending on the level of certainty the algorithms have on the automatic classification, we may consider bypassing thus the human classifier.

2.1 Metrics for Evaluating of Multi-label Text Categorization

Typically, text categorization is mainly evaluated by the Recall and Precision metrics in the single-labled cases (Baeza-Yates & Ribeiro-Neto, 1998). Nonetheless, other authors have already proposed different metrics for multi-label categorization problems (Schapire & Singer, 2000; Zhang & Zhou, 2007).

Formalizing the problem we have at hand, text categorization may be defined as a task of assigning documents to a predefined set of categories, or classes (Sebastiani, 2002). In multi-label text categorization a document may be assigned to one or more categories. Let D be the domain of documents, $C = \{c_1, c_2, \ldots, c_{|C|}\}$ a set of predefined categories, and $W = \{d_1, d_2, \ldots, d_{|W|}\}$ an initial set of documents previously categorized by some human specialists into subsets of categories of C.

In multi-label learning, the training (-and validation) set $TV = \{d_1, d_2, \ldots, d_{|TV|}\}$ is composed of a number of documents, each associated with a subset of categories in C. TV is used to train and validate (actually, to tune eventual parameters of) a categorization system that associates the appropriate combination of categories to the characteristics of each document in the TV. The test set $Te = \{d_{|TV|+1}, d_{|TV|+2}, \ldots, d_{|W|}\}$, on the other hand, consists of documents for which the categories are unknown to the automatic categorization systems. After being trained, as well as tuned, by the TV, the categorization systems are used to predict the set of categories of each document in Te.

A multi-label categorization system typically implements a real-valued function of the form $f : D \times C \rightarrow \Re$ that returns a value for each pair $\langle d_j, c_i \rangle \in D \times C$ that, roughly speaking, represents the evidence for the fact that the test document d_j should be categorized under the category $c_i \in C_i$, where $C_i \subset C$. The real-valued function $f(.,.)$ can be transformed into a ranking function $r(.,.)$, which is an one-to-one mapping onto $\{1, 2, \ldots, |C|\}$ such that, if $f(d_j, c_1) > f(d_j, c_2)$, then $r(d_j, c_1) < r(d_j, c_2)$. If C_i is the set of proper categories for the test document d_j, then a successful categorization system tends to rank categories in C_i higher than those not in C_i. Additionally, we also use a threshold parameter so that those categories that are ranked above the threshold τ (i.e., $c_k \mid f(d_j, c_k) \geq \tau$) are the only ones to be assigned to the test document.

We have used five multi-label metrics discussed by Zhang & Zhou (2007) to evaluate the categorization performance of PNN: *hamming loss*, *one-error*, *coverage*, *ranking loss*, and *average precision*. We now present each of these metrics:

- **Hamming Loss (hloss$_j$)** evaluates how many times the test document d_j is misclassified, i.e., a category not belonging to the document is predicted or a category belonging to the document is not predicted.

$$\text{hloss}_j = \frac{1}{|C|} |P_j \Delta C_i| \tag{1}$$

where $|C|$ is the number of categories and Δ is the symmetric difference between the set of predicted categories P_j and the set of appropriate categories C_i of the test document d_j. The predicted categories are those with rank higher than the threshold τ.

- **One-error (one-error$_j$)** evaluates if the top ranked category is present in the set of proper categories C_i of the test document d_j.

$$\text{one-error}_j = \begin{cases} 0 & \text{if } \arg\max_{c \in C} f(d_j, c) \in C_i \\ 1 & \text{otherwise} \end{cases} \tag{2}$$

where $\arg\max_{c \in C} f(d_j, c)$ returns the top ranked category for the test document d_j.

- **Coverage (coverage$_j$)** measures how far we need to go down the rank of categories in order to cover all the possible categories assigned to a test document.

$$\text{coverage}_j = \max_{c \in C_i} r(d_j, c) - 1 \tag{3}$$

where $\max_{c \in C_i} r(d_j, c)$ returns the maximum rank for the set of appropriate categories of the test document d_j.

- **Ranking Loss (rloss$_j$)** evaluates the fraction of category pairs $\langle c_k, c_l \rangle$, for which $c_k \in C_i$ and $c_l \in \overline{C}_i$, that are reversely ordered for the test document d_j:

$$\text{rloss}_j = \frac{\left|\left\{(c_k, c_l) | f(d_j, c_k) \le f(d_j, c_l)\right\}\right|}{|C_i||\overline{C}_i|} \tag{4}$$

where $(c_k, c_l) \in C_i \times \overline{C}_i$, and $\overline{C}_i$ is the complementary set of C_i in C.

- **Average Precision (avgprec$_j$)** evaluates the average of precisions computed after truncating the ranking of categories after each category $c_i \in C_i$ in turn:

$$\text{avgprec}_j = \frac{1}{|C_i|} \sum_{k=1}^{|C_i|} \text{precision}_j(R_{jk}) \tag{5}$$

where R_{jk} is the set of ranked categories that goes from the top ranked category until a ranking position k where there is a category $c_i \in C_i$ for d_j, and $\text{precision}_j(R_{jk})$ is the number of pertinent categories in R_{jk} divided by $|R_{jk}|$.

For p test documents, the overall performance is obtained by averaging each metric, that is, $\text{hloss} = \frac{1}{p}\sum_{j=1}^{p} \text{hloss}_j$, $\text{one-error} = \frac{1}{p}\sum_{j=1}^{p} \text{one-error}_j$, $\text{coverage} = \frac{1}{p}\sum_{j=1}^{p} \text{coverage}_j$,

$\text{rloss} = \frac{1}{p}\sum_{j=1}^{p} \text{rloss}_j$, $\text{avgprec} = \frac{1}{p}\sum_{j=1}^{p} \text{avgprec}_j$. On the one hand, the smaller the value of *hamming loss, one-error, coverage* and *ranking loss,* the better the performance of the categorization system. On the other hand, for the *average precision,* the larger the value the better the performance. So, the problem can be formulated as an optimization problem, where the performance is optimal when hloss = one-error = rloss = 0 and avgprec = 1.

In the next section are mentioned some related works regarding the problem of economic activities classification.

3. Related Works

The authors in (Souza et al., 2007) are among the first to tackle the problem of economic activities classification. In their work they compared the results achieved between a Nearly Neighbors algorithm approach and a Weightless Neural Network, called VG-RAM WNN, using a metric to evaluate the performance equivalent to 1 - one-error, defined in Section 2.1. In the first algorithm they got the performance of 63.36%, while VG-RAM WNN showed to be slightly better, with a performance of 67.56%. However, the use of a single metric seemed to be not enough for evaluating multi-labled problems.

A different approach was performed by (Oliveira et al., 2007). In this work were used 83 arrays of small standard PNN for classification, whose main metrics used were Recall and Precision. However, it was noted to be very difficult to merge the results returned of each neural network array node. Thus the performance of the array as a whole was harmed. Although it has found a reasonable value for the Recall, the value for the Precision was very low, since almost every neural networks returned at least one class to each instance of test.

A PNN with a slightly modified architecture to treat problems of multi-label classification was proposed in (Oliveira et al., 2008). Such neural network presents advantage over the array of small standard PNN approach, used in (Oliveira et al., 2007), because only one PNN is used to solve the problem of multi-label classification. Whereas, in the previous approach, we need to build many neural networks (83 in that case) which complicate the process of optimization.

The results achieved in (Oliveira et al., 2008) using the proposed PNN were better than the achieved using the Multi-label k-Nearest Neighbors (ML-kNN) algorithm. The ML-kNN was considered to be the best algorithm for all the database used in (Zhang & Zhou, 2007). In order to evaluate the performance of the algorithms, the authors in that work used the metrics presented in the Section 2. Moreover, the parameters of these algorithms were optimized using a Genetic Algorithm (GA).

The cited previous works used the same database that we present in this work, but the division of the database was performed in a different way for each work, making it difficult conducting a comparison of results among them. However, in this work we will divide the database in a similar way to used in (Oliveira et al., 2008), making possible a comparison among results.

Another very close multi-label problem to one we are presenting in this paper, concern with the economic activities classification, is that of patent categorization (Li et al., 2007). Our problem and that are both based on free text descriptions of variety topics. So a large volume of patents documents, are usually, up to these days, manually classified by the patent offices, this is a labor-intensive and time-consuming task. A patent document may cite another patent document, or articles, for comparing or contrasting reasons. Therefore, besides using the content categorization approach, the authors in (Li et al., 2007) proposed to extract and use the direct hyperlink citation relationships among patent documents in order to improve the quality of the whole process of classification. Hyperlink citation is a similar strategy some researchers have been widely applied to web page classification studies. The experiments were conducted on a nanotechnology-related patent dataset from the USPTO. The training dataset contained 13,913 instances, and the testing data set 4,358 data instances. The average of category for document was 36, and the total of categories was up to 426. The results by the K_{Gra} kernel proposed approach yielded 86.67% accuracy overcome the 81% of manually processing and the results of previous work (Koster et al., 2003).

In the following, we describe a slightly modified Probabilistic Neural Network (PNN) used to solve the optimization problem of text categorization.

4. Probabilistic Neural Network Architecture

The Probabilistic Neural Network was first proposed by Donald Specht in 1990 (Specht, 1990). This is an artificial neural network for nonlinear computing, which approaches the Bayes optimal decision boundaries. This is done by estimating the *probability density function* of the training dataset using the Parzen nonparametric estimator (Parzen, 1962).

The literature has shown that this type of neural network can yield similar results, sometimes superior, in pattern recognition problems when compared with others techniques (Fung et al., 2005; Patra et al., 2002).

The original Probabilistic Neural Network algorithm was designed for single-label problems. Thus, we slightly modified its standard architecture, so that it is now capable of solving multi-label problem addressed in this work.

In our modified version, instead of four, the Probabilistic Neural Network is now composed of only three layers: the *input* layer, the *pattern* layer and the *summation* layer, as depicted in Figure 1. Thus like the original, this version of Probabilistic Neural Network needs only one training step, thus its training is very fast compared to the others feedforward neural networks (Duda et al., 2001; Haykin, 1998). The training consists in assigning each training sample w_i of class C_i to a neuron of pattern layer of class C_i. Thus the weight vector of this neuron is the characteristics vector of the sample.

For each pattern x passed by the input layer to a neuron in the pattern layer, it computes the output for x. The computation is performed by Equation 6.

$$F_{k,i}(x) = \frac{1}{2\pi\sigma^2} \exp\left(\frac{x^t w_{ki} - 1}{\sigma^2} \right) \tag{6}$$

where x is the pattern characteristics input vector, and the w_{ki} is the kth sample for a neuron of class C_i, $k \in N_i$, whereas N_i is the number of neurons of C_i. In addition, x was normalized so that $x^t x = 1$ and $w_{ki}{}^t w_{ki} = 1$. The parameter σ is the Gaussian standard deviation, which determines the receptive field of the Gaussian curve.

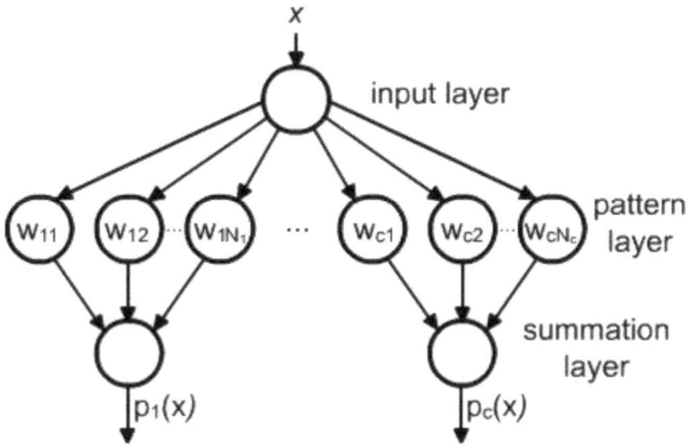

Figure 1. The modified Probabilistic Neural Network architecture

The next step is the summation layer. In this layer, all weight vectors are summed according to Equation 7, in each cluster C_i producing $p_i(x)$ values, where $|C|$ is the total number of classes.

$$p_i(x) = \sum_{k=1}^{N_i} F_{k,i}(x) \tag{7}$$

$$k = 1,2,\ldots,N_i; \quad i = 1,2,\ldots,|C|$$

Finally, for the selection of the classes, which will be assigned by neural network to each sample, we consider the most likely classes pointed out by the summation layer based on a chosen threshold.

Differently from other types of neural networks, such as the feedforward one (Haykin, 1998), the probabilistic neural network proposed needs few parameters to be configured: the σ, (see Equation 6) and the determination of threshold value. The σ is used to narrow the receptive field of the Gaussian curve in order to strictly select only the more likely inputs for a given class. Other advantages of the probabilistic neural networks is that it is easy to add new classes, or new training inputs, into the already running structure, which is good for on-line applications (Duda et al., 2001). Moreover, it is reported in the literature (Duda et al., 2001) that it is also easy to implement this type of neural network in parallel. On the other hand, one of its drawbacks is the great number of neurons in the pattern layer, which can be, nevertheless, mitigated by an optimization on the number of the neuron (Georgiou et al., 2004; Mao et al., 2000).

Next, we propose a PSO algorithm to find out the σ parameters and tune the PNN automatically.

5. The Canonical and the Bare Bones Particle Swarm Optimization

Particle Swarm Optimisation (PSO) has its origins in the simulation of bird flocking developed by Reynolds (1987) and was further developed in the context of optimization by Eberhart and Kennedy (Eberhart & Kennedy, 1995; Kennedy & Eberhart, 1995). PSO is initialised with a population of random solutions. Each potential solution in PSO is also

associated with a randomised velocity, and the potential solutions, are called *particles*, that move in the search space. Each particle keeps track of its coordinates in the problem space, which are associated with the best solution (fitness) it has achieved so far. This value is called *pbest*. Another *best* value that is tracked by the *global* version of the particle swarm optimizer is the overall best value, and its location, obtained so far by any particle in the population. This location is called *gbest*.
The particle swarm optimization concept consists of, at each time step, changing the velocity of each particle moving toward its *pbest* and *gbest* locations (global version of PSO). Acceleration is weighted by random terms, with separate random numbers being generated for acceleration toward *pbest* and *gbest* locations, respectively. The PSO algorithm consists basically in updating the velocities and positions of the particle, respectively as follows in Equations 8 and 9 (Clerc & Kennedy, 2002):

$$v_i(t+1) = \lambda\left[v_i(t) + c_1 rand_1\left(p_{best_i} - x_i(t)\right) + c_2 rand_2\left(g_{best} - x_i(t)\right)\right] \tag{8}$$

$$x_i(t+1) = x_i(t) + v_i(t+1) \tag{9}$$

$$\text{with } \lambda = \frac{2}{\left|\sqrt{2 - \varphi - \sqrt{\varphi^2 - 4\varphi}}\right|}, \quad \text{where } \varphi = c_1 + c_2, \quad \varphi > 4$$

where:

- $x_i = [x_{i1}, x_{i2}, \ldots, x_{in}]^T$ is the position of the ith particle in the n-dimensional search space;
- $v_i = [v_{i1}, v_{i2}, \ldots, v_{in}]^T$ is the velocity of the ith particle;
- p_{best_i} is the best previous i^{th} particle position;
- g_{best} is the best particle among all particles;
- λ is the constriction factor;
- c_1 and c_2 are positive constants;
- $rand_1$ and $rand_2$ are random numbers in the range [0;1] generated using the uniform probability distribution.

Usually, when the constriction factor is used, φ is set to 4.1 ($c_1 = c_2 = 2.05$), and the constriction factor λ is 0.729. In this paper, it is assumed minimization problems unless stated otherwise.
In the meantime different versions of PSO have been proposed by (Krohling & Coelho, 2006). In this work we focus on the Bare Bones PSO (Kennedy, 2003). The Bare Bones PSO (BBPSO) eliminates the velocity item and the Gaussian distribution is used to sampling the search space based on the global best (gbest) and the personal best (pbest) particle. So, the Equations 8 and 9 are replaced by Equation 10:

$$N = \left(\mu_i, \sigma_i^2\right) \tag{10}$$

$$\text{with } \mu_i = \frac{\left(g_{best} + p_{best_i}\right)}{2}, \quad \sigma_i = \left|g_{best} - p_{best_i}\right|$$

where N denotes the Gaussian distribution.

This version of PSO presents some advantages over other versions because its reduced numbers of parameters of the algorithms to be tuned. The BBPSO is described in the Listing 1.

```
PSO and BBPSO Algorithms
Input parameters: swarm size P
FOR each particle i
// random initialization of a population of particles with positions x_i using uniform
// probability distribution.
  x_i = \underline{x_i} + (\overline{x_i} - \underline{x_i})·u_i  // \underline{x_i} and \overline{x_i} stands for the lower and upper bound,
//respectively, and u_i is a random number.
  p_best_i = x_i
  compute f(x_i) // fitness evaluation.
  p_gbest := arg min{f(x_i)} // global best particle.
END FOR
DO
  FOR each particle i
    update the position x_i according to Equations 8 and 9 if PSO
    update the position x_i according to Equation 10 if BBPSO
    compute f(x_i) // fitness evaluation
    IF f(x_i) < f(p_best_i) THEN // update of the personal best.
      p_best_i = x_i
    IF f(x_i) < f(p_gbest) THEN // update the global best.
      p_gbest = p_best_i
  END FOR
WHILE termination condition not met.
Output: p_gbest, f(p_gbest).
```

Listing 1 PSO and BBPSO Algorithms.

6. Experimental Results

We employed a series of experiments to compare PNNs optimized using canonical PSO and BBPSO. We used a dataset containing 3264 documents of free text business descriptions of Brazilian companies categorized into a subset of 764 CNAE categories. This dataset was obtained from real companies placed in Vitoria County in Brazil. The CNAE codes of each company in this dataset were assigned by Brazilian government officials trained for this task. Then we evenly partitioned the whole dataset into four subsets of equal size of 816 documents. We joined to this categorizing dataset the brief description of each one of the 764 CNAE categories, totalizing 4028 documents. Hence, in all training (-and validation) set, we adopted the 764 descriptions of CNAE categories and a subset of 816 business description documents, and, as the test set, the other three subsets of business descriptions totalizing 2448 documents.

6.1 Categorization of Free-text Descriptions of Economic Activities

We pre-processed the dataset via term selection - a total of 1001 terms were found in the database after removing stop words and trivial cases of gender and plural; only words appearing in the CNAE table were considered. After that, each document in the dataset was described as a multidimensional vector using the Bag-of-Words representation (Dumais et al., 1998), i.e., each dimension of the vector corresponds to the number of times a term of the vocabulary appears in the corresponding document. Table 1 summarizes the characteristics of this dataset (dataset available at http://www.inf.ufes.br/~elias/vitoria.tar.gz).

#C	#t	Training set				Test/validation set			
		NTD	DC	CD	RC	NTD	DC	CD	RC
764	1001	4.65	0.00	1.00	100.00	10.92	74.48	4.27	85.21

Table 1. Characteristics of the CNAE dataset

In this Table #C denotes the number of categories, #t denotes the number of terms in the vocabulary, NTD denotes the average number of terms per document, DC denotes the percentage of documents belonging to more than one category, CD denotes the average number of categories for each document, and RC denotes the percentage of rare categories, i.e., those categories associated with less than 1% of the documents of the dataset. The training set is composed by 764 categories descriptions belonging at CNAE table, where each description is concerning just one category and there is only one description by category (one to one relationship), resulting in CD equal 1 and DC equal 0. As there are 764 instances of training and just one instance for category, the index RC is equal 100%. On the other hand, the test/validation set is composed by 3264 instances, where 74.48% of instances are assigned to more than one category and the average number of categories of each instance is more than 4 per document. However, like we said in Section 2, this number vary greatly. Moreover, we can note that RC value is high since there are few instances by category.

The PNNs parameters σ, in Equation 6, were optimized for each class of the dataset and just one threshold τ value for the whole neural network, resulting in 765 parameters, i. e., each particle is represented by a 765-dimensional vector. This is a quite huge amount of parameters for optimization.

To tune these parameters we divided the training set (-and validation) set into a training set, which was used to inductively build the categorizer, and a validation set, which was used to evaluate the performance of the categorizer in the series of experiments aimed at parameter optimization. The training set is composed of 764 descriptions of CNAE classes and the validation set of 816 business description documents described previously. As a result, we carried out a sequence of experiments with PSO and BBPSO. For each one of these algorithms was carried out 48 experiments:

- 4 experiments each using algorithm with 100 particles and 500 iterations;
- 4 experiments each using algorithm with 50 particles and 500 iterations;
- 40 experiments each using algorithm with 50 particles and 100 iterations.

The two first experiments set were used to evaluate the performance of the algorithms for different population sizes. The last 40 experiments were used for a statistical analysis.

In Figures 2 and 3 are shown the performance of the PNN optimized in function of the number of iterations for 100 and 50 particles, respectively. Where is written in the legend 1st subset means that the first subset was used for validation and the 764 descriptions were used for training, in a similar way this is valid for others cases. The continuous lines are the results of the canonical PSO algorithm and the dotted lines are the results of the BBPSO algorithm. Here, the performance value is a linear combination of the several metrics, where these metrics were described in the Section 2. Thus, performance is the sum of the hamming loss, one error, coverage, ranking loss and $\overline{\text{average precision}}$, where $\overline{\text{average precision}} = 1 -$ average precision. The coverage value was divided by the factor $|C|-1$ to normalize it and keep it in the same scale of the others metrics. A strategy for optimization could be the use of weighted metrics, however in this work was regarded the same value of importance for every metrics.

In both figures the smaller the value of the performance, the better the performance of the neural network. We can observe in both figures that the BBPSO algorithm presented better results than the canonical PSO algorithm. Although the determination of the optimal swarm size is beyond the scope of this work, can be noted that exist no big differences between the results obtained with 100 particles and 50 particles. Moreover, there is a large gain of performance until the 100th iteration and a gain slower in the next iterations. Because of this and since the experiments require substantial amount of run time, we carry out others experiments using 50 particles and 100 iterations for statistical analysis purposes.

In the Table 2 are shown the best, mean, median, standard deviation and worst results obtained in the validation with PSO and BBPSO. The results in bold indicate the best results found for each subset. We can observe in Table 2 that BBPSO finds slightly better results than the canonical PSO.

After tuning, the multi-label categorizers were trained with the 764 descriptions of CNAE categories and tested with the 2448 documents of the test set. The Table 3 shows the best, mean, median, standard deviation and worst results found in the validation with PSO and BBPSO. In this table, where is written 1st means the 1st subset for validation and the others subsets for test, in a similar way this is valid for the other subsets. Again, the results in bold are the best results found for each subset. Similarly as occurred in Table 2, Table 3 also shows that the BBPSO performs slightly better than the PSO.

The mean of results achieved for each metric are shown in Table 4 and 5 for the PNN trained by canonical PSO and BBPSO, respectively. Comparing the results found in this tables we noticed that there weren't significant differences among them, this indicates that the proposed PNN presents certain robustness on the dataset used for training/validation.

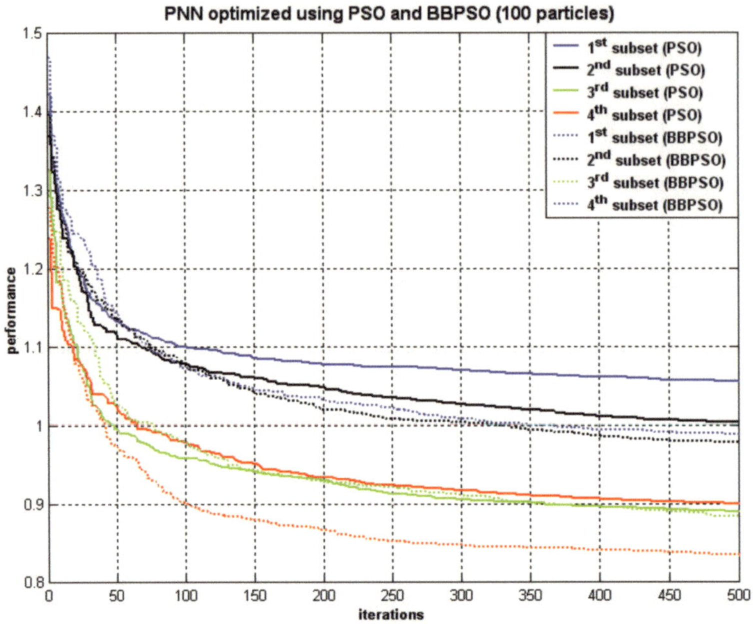

Figure 2. Experimental results of validation of the PNN using PSO and BBPSO with 100 particles and 500 iterations

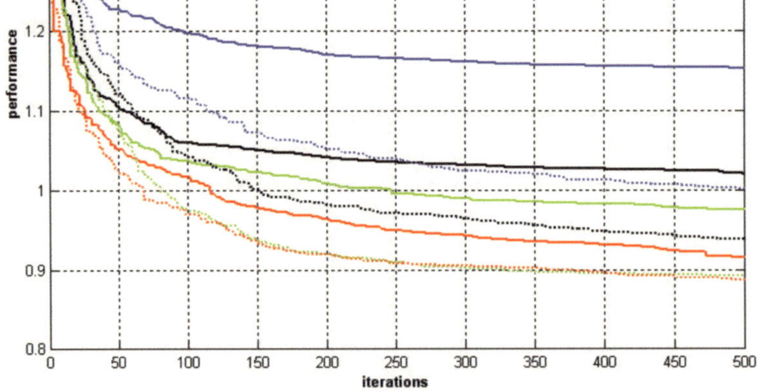

Figure 3. Experimental results of validation of the PNN using PSO and BBPSO with 50 particles and 500 iterations

Subset	Algorithm	Best	Mean	Median	Std. Deviation	Worst
1st	PSO	1.1334	1.1744	1.1617	0.0292	1.2194
	BBPSO	**1.0789**	**1.1107**	**1.1163**	**0.0187**	**1.1344**
2nd	PSO	1.0596	1.0971	1.1003	**0.0176**	1.1241
	BBPSO	**1.0334**	**1.0652**	**1.0671**	0.0192	**1.0864**
3rd	PSO	1.0320	1.0475	1.0488	**0.0087**	1.0608
	BBPSO	**0.9622**	**0.9902**	**0.9842**	0.0217	**1.0257**
4th	PSO	0.9741	1.0060	1.0072	0.0202	1.0435
	BBPSO	**0.9363**	**0.9553**	**0.9558**	**0.0110**	**0.9746**

Table 2. Information about the validation phase

Subset	Algorithm	Best	Mean	Median	Std. Deviation	Worst
1st	PSO	1.1465	1.1766	1.1671	0.0284	1.2332
	BBPSO	**1.1204**	**1.1361**	**1.1358**	**0.0146**	**1.1689**
2nd	PSO	1.1190	1.1632	1.1679	0.0217	1.1853
	BBPSO	**1.1107**	**1.1429**	**1.1432**	**0.0209**	**1.1798**
3rd	PSO	1.1537	1.1873	1.1912	0.0203	1.2202
	BBPSO	**1.1375**	**1.1632**	**1.1633**	**0.0184**	**1.2026**
4th	PSO	1.1841	1.2260	1.2260	0.0345	1.3057
	BBPSO	**1.1555**	**1.1810**	**1.1826**	**0.0167**	**1.2094**

Table 3. Information about the test phase

Subeset	Hamming loss	One-error	Coverage	Ranking loss	Average precision
1st	0.0056	0.3708	144.3723	0.0835	0.4725
2nd	0.0056	0.3688	142.2521	0.0874	0.4850
3rd	0.0055	0.3756	143.9365	0.0912	0.4737
4th	0.0056	0.3857	154.7565	0.0937	0.4619

Table 4. Results achieved with PNN trained by canonical PSO

Subeset	Hamming loss	One-error	Coverage	Ranking loss	Average precision
1st	0.0056	0.3544	143.9079	0.0749	0.4875
2nd	0.0056	0.3592	145.8953	0.0805	0.4937
3rd	0.0055	0.3648	147.5607	0.0842	0.4847
4th	0.0056	0.3634	155.6463	0.0874	0.4794

Table 5. Results achieved with PNN trained by BBPSO

A comparison among the results obtained in this work with the found in (Oliveira et al., 2008) is done in Table 6. The results mentioned are the mean of the four subsets for each metric, and for those in bold are the best results found for each one of the metrics. It is important to highlight that such comparison is a little unfair, since the GA algorithm was executed with 80 individuals and 100 generations whereas the PSO and BBPSO were simulated with 50 particles and 100 iterations. Nevertheless, the results achieved to PNNs are similar. Furthermore, the approach using PSO and BBPSO got the best value of coverage and one-error, respectively. We can note that there is a discrepant difference among the performance of MLkNN and the performance obtained with the PNNs.

Again we can note a certain robustness of the PNN, because its performance didn't change significantly when trained by a PSO, BBPSO or GA algorithm.

Metrics	PNN-PSO	PNN-BBPSO	PNN-GA	ML-kNN-GA
Hamming loss	0.0055	0.0055	0.0055	0.0055
One-error	0.3752	**0.3604**	0.3736	0.4952
Coverage	**146.3293**	148.2525	156.4150	303.9029
Ranking loss	0.0889	0.0817	**0.0798**	0.1966
Average precision	0.4732	0.4863	**0.4880**	0.3813

Table 6. Comparison among different approaches of classification

7. Conclusions

The problem of classifying a large number of economic activities descriptions from free text format every day is a huge challenge for the Brazilian governmental administration. This problem is crucial for the long term planning in all three levels of the administration in Brazil. Therefore, an either automatic or semi-automatic manner of doing that is needed for making it possible and also for avoiding the problem of subjectivity introduced by the human classifier.

In this work, we presented an experimental evaluation of the performance of Probabilistic Neural Network on multi-label text classification. We performed a comparative study of probabilistic neural network trained by PSO and BBPSO, using a multi-label dataset for the categorization of free-text descriptions of economic activities. The approach using PSO and BBPSO were compared with GA and it was noted that there weren't significant differences among them.

To our knowledge, this is one of the first few initiatives on using probabilistic neural network for text categorization into a large number of classes as that used in this work and the results are very promising. One of the advantages of probabilistic neural network is that it needs only one parameter to be configured. In addition, the BBPSO employed is an almost parameter free algorithm, just the number of particles needs to be specified.

A direction for future work is to boldly compare the probabilistic neural network performance against other multi-label text categorization methods. Examining the correlation on assigning codes to a set of descriptions of economic activities may further improve the performance of the multi-label text categorization methods. We are planning on doing that in future work.

8. Acknowledgments

We would like to thank Andréa Pimenta Mesquita, CNAE classifications coordinators at Vitoria City Hall, for providing us with the dataset we used in this work. We would also like to thank Min-Ling Zhang for all the help with the ML-KNN categorization tool. Thank to all the colleagues, especially Alberto Ferreira De Souza, Claudine Badue, Felipe M. G. França and Priscila Machado Vieira Lima for their technical support and valuable comments on this work. This work is partially supported by the Internal Revenue Brazilian Service (Receita Federal do Brasil) and Fundação Espírito Santense de Tecnologia— FAPES-Brasil (grant 41936450/2008) for their support of this research work. Furthermore, R. A. Krohling thanks the partial funding of his research work provided by FAPES/MCT/CNPq (grant 37286374/2007).

9. References

Baeza-Yates, R. & Ribeiro-Neto, B. (1998). *Modern Information Retrieval.* Addison-Wesley, New York, 1st edition.

Clerc, M. & Kennedy, J. (2002). The Particle Swarm: Explosion Stability and Convergence in a Multi-dimensional Complex Space. *IEEE Transactions on Evolutionary Computation*, vol. 6:58 - 73.

CNAE (2003). Classificação Nacional de Atividades Econômicas Fiscal. *IBGE - Intituto Brasileiro de Geografia e Estatística*, Rio de Janeiro, RJ, 1.1 edition. http://www.ibge.gov.br/concla.

DNRC (2007). *Ranking das Juntas Comerciais Segundo Movimento de Constituição, Alteração e Extinção e Cancelamento de Empresas.* Ministério do Desenvolvimento, Indústria e Comércio Exterior - Secretaria do Desenvolvimento da Produção, Departamento Nacional de Registro do Comércio (DNRC).

Duda, R. O.; Hart, P. E. & Stork, D. G. (2001). *Pattern Classification.* Wiley-Interscience, New York, 2nd edition.

Dumais, S. T.; Platt, J.; Heckerman, D. & Sahami, M. (1998). Inductive Learning Algorithms and Representation for Text Categorization. In *Proceedings of the 7th ACM International Conference on Information and Knowledge Management*, pages 148–155, Bethesda, MD.

Eberhart, R. C. & Kennedy, J. (1995). A New Optimizer Using Particle Swarm Theory. *Proceedings of the Sixth International Symposium on Micro Machine and Human Science*, pages 39 - 43.

Fung, C. C.; Iyer, V.; Brown, W. & Wong, K. W. (2005). Comparing the Performance of Different Neural Networks Architectures for the Prediction of Mineral Prospectivity. *Proceedings of International Conference on Machine Learning and Cybernetics*, 1:pages 394 - 398.

Georgiou, V. L.; Pavlidis, N. G.; Parsopoulos, K. E.; Alevizos, P. D. & Vrahatis, M. N. (2004). Optimizing the Performance of Probabilistic Neural Networks in a Bioinformatic Task. *Proceedings of the EUNITE Conference*, pages pages 34 - 40.

Haykin, S. (1998). *Neural Networks - A Comprehensive Foundation.* Prentice Hall, New Jersey, 2nd edition.

Jain, A. K.; Murty, M. N. & Flynn, P. J. (1999). Data Clustering: a Review. *ACM Computing Surveys*, 31(3):264–323.

Kennedy, J. (2003). Bare Bones Particle Swarms. *Proceedings of the IEEE Swarm Intelligence Symposium*, pages 80 - 87.

Kennedy, J. & Eberhart, R. C. (1995). Particle Swarm Optimization. *Proceedings of the IEEE International Conference on Neural Networks* IV, pages 1942 - 1948.

Koster, C. H. A.; Seutter, M. & Beney, J. (2003). Multi-classification of Patent Applications with Winnow. *Ershov Memorial Conference*, vol. 2890, pages 546 - 555.

Krohling, R. A. & Coelho, L. S. (2006). Co-evolutionary Particle Swarm Using Gaussian Distribution to Solving Constraint Optimization Problems. *IEEE Transactions on Systems, Man and Cybernetics*, part B, vol. 36:1407 - 1416.

Li, X.; Chen, H.; Zhang, Z. & Li, J. (2007). Automatic Patent Classification using Citation Network Information: an Experimental Study in Nanotechnology. *Proceedings of the 2007 Conference on Digital Libraries*, pages 419 - 427.

Mao, K. Z.; Tan, K. C. & Ser, W. (2000). Probabilistic Neural-Network Structure Determination for Pattern Classification. *IEEE Transactions on Neural Networks*, 11:1009–1016.

Oliveira, E.; Ciarelli, P. M.; Souza, A. F. & Badue, C. (2008). Using a Probabilistic Neural Network for a Large Multi-label Problem. *10th Brazilian Symposium on Neural Networks*, pages 1 - 6.

Oliveira, E.; Ciarelli, P. M. & Lima, F. O. (2007). The Automation of the Classification of Economic Activities from Free Text Descriptions using an Array Architecture of Probabilistic Neural Network. *VIII Simpósio Brasileiro de Automação Inteligente*, pages 1 - 5.

Parzen, E. (1962). On Estimation of a Probability Density Function and Mode. *The Annals of Mathematical Statistics*, 33:pages 1065 – 1076.

Patra, P. K.; Nayak, M.; Nayak, S. K. & Gobbak, N. K. (2002). Probabilistic Neural Network for Pattern Classification. *IEEE Proceedings of the 2002 International Joint Conference on Neural Networks*, volume 2, pages 1200–1205.

Reynolds, C. W. (1987). Flocks, Herds, and Schools: A Distributed Behavioral Model. *Computer Graphics*, vol. 21(4):25 – 34.

Schapire, R. E. & Singer, Y. (2000). BoosTexter: A Boosting-based System for Text Categorization. *Machine Learning*, 39(2/3):135–168.

Sebastiani, F. (2002). Machine Learning in Automated Text Categorization. *ACM Computing* Surveys, 34(1):1–47.

Specht, D. F. (1990). Probabilistic Neural Networks. *Neural Networks*, 3(1):109–118.

Souza, A. F.; Pedroni, F.; Oliveira, E.; Ciarelli, P. M.; Henrique, W. F. & Veronese, L. (2007). Automated Free Text Classification of Economic Activities using VG-RAM Weightless Neural Networks. *7th International Conference on Intelligent Systems Design and Applications*, pages 1 - 5.

Zhang, M.-L. & Zhou, Z.-H. (2007). ML-KNN: A Lazy Learning Approach to Multi-Label Learning. *Pattern Recognition.*, 40:2038–2048.

20

Path Planning for Formations of Mobile Robots using PSO Technique

Martin Macaš[1], Martin Saska[2], Lenka Lhotská[1], Libor Přeučil[1] and Klaus Schilling[2]
[1]*Dep. Of Cybernetics, Czech Technical University,* [2] *University of Wuerzburg*
[1]*Czech Republic,* [2]*Germany*

1. Introduction

Multi-robotics systems are currently subject of major interest in the robotics literature. In the leading journals can be found hundreds of articles, published in the last few years, concerning applications and theoretical studies of small groups maintaining in fixed formation (Fua et al., 2007; Kaminka et al., 2008) as well as swarms of thousands robots (Derenick & Spletzet, 2007; Daigle et. al, 2008).

The large systems can be moreover represented by work published in (Peasgood et al., 2008) where collision free trajectories to reach individual goals are designed for 100 robots. The method using graph and spanning tree representation is developed for utilization in underground mine environment. In another example (Kloetzer & Belta,2007), a large swarm of robots is controlled using hierarchical abstractions. Inter-robot collision avoidance and environment containment are there guaranteed applying centralized communication architecture. Finally work presented in (Milutinovi & Lima, 2006) applies a Stochastic Hybrid Automation model for modeling and control of multi-agent population composed of a large number of agents. In this method probabilistic description of task allocation as well as distribution of the population over the work space is considered. As an example of common multi-robots application highway traffic coordination can be mentioned. In (Pallotino et al., 2007) is presented decentralized approach using traffic rules for control of tens vehicles. The method enables dynamically adding and removing of the vehicles and is based only on local communication which makes the algorithm scalable.

Algorithms designed for smaller groups of robots are usually aimed at maintaining of vehicles in a predefined formation for the purpose of cooperative tasks accomplishing (as can be e.g. box pushing (Vig & Adams, 2006), load carrying (Tanner et al., 2003), snow shoveling (Saska et al., 2008) or aircraft as well as satellites cooperative mapping (Ren & Beard, 2003; Kang & Sparks, 2000). Another interesting application of formation driving is presented in (Fahimi, 2007) where autonomous boats are maintained in formations under sliding mode, which provides faster movement. The hot research topics in formations of autonomous robots, investigated nowadays, include e.g. data fusion: (Kaminka et al., 2008) represents the sensing capabilities using a monitoring multigraph. This approach allows the robots to adjust to sensory failures by switching of control graphs on-line. An application of data fusion can be cooperative localization of mobile formations: (Mourikis & Roumeliotis,

2006b) addresses a problem of resource allocation which provides the sensing frequencies, for each sensor on very robot, required in order to maximize the positioning accuracy of the group. This work is extended by a performance analysis providing upper bound on the robots' expected positioning uncertainty which is determined as a function of the sensors' noise covariance and relative position measurements (Moutikis & Roumeliotis, 2006a). Another separate branch of the research relevant to the formations of mobile robots is solving how to achieve the desired formation. An approach considering this task without assigning specific configuration to specific robots is published in (Kloder & Hutchinson, 2006) where a new representation for the configuration space of permutation-invariant multi-robot groups is described.

This chapter is focussed on the path planning and formation driving of autonomous car-like robots. In the literature formation driving approaches are divided into the three main groups: virtual structure, behavioral techniques, and leader-following methods. In the virtual structure approaches is the entire formation regarded as a single structure where to each vehicle is given a set of control to follow the desired trajectory of formation as a rigid body (Beard et al., 2001; Lalish et al., 2006). In behavior based methods the desired behaviors are designated for each agent and the final control is derived as a weighted sum with respect to the importance of each task (for basic ideas see (Langer et al., 1994; Parker, 1998). These classical methods have been extended for maintaining of shape of formations using desired patterns (Lawton et al., 2003; Balch & Arkin, 1998). In the leader-following approaches, a robot or even several robots are designated as leaders, while the others are following them (Desai et al., 2001; Das et al., 2003). Example of the methods using multiple leaders is presented in (Fredslund & Mataric, 2002) where due to limited communication the followers are leaded by their closest neighbors. Unfortunately all these results are focused on the following of a leader's trajectory which is assumed as an input of the methods. It is supposed that the trajectory is designed by a human operator or by a standard path planning method modified for formation requirements. In the literature there is no adequate method providing flexible control inputs for the followers as well as designing an optimal path for the leader of formation responding to the environment which is necessary for fully autonomous systems.

This chapter proposes a path planning approach developed for leader-following formations of car-like robots which is an extension of work (published by the authors' team in (Saska et al., 2006)) designed for single robot. In this extended method a reference path calculated by the leader should be feasible for all following robots without changing a relative distance in the formation. This requirement can be satisfied using a solution which is composed of smoothly connected cubic splines and can be calculated on-line. Qualities of the result like the length and minimal radius of the resulting path as well as the distance to obstacles are merged into a discontinuous penalty function.

The resulting global minimization problem is solved with Particle Swarm Optimization (PSO). Since the original PSO scheme has been developed, many various modifications were proposed that more or less improve the method. In context of our optimization problem, we are strongly limited by the requirement on low time complexity. Therefore, every modification that could be used here must not lead to any slow down of the convergence. This fact suspend some sequential hybridization of PSO and any other optimization technique. Also, any sub-swarm based and multi-start algorithms are not suitable. It will be shown that the original global-best PSO performs well and even significantly better than genetic algorithms. Nevertheless, the chapter shows some comparison of PSO with limited maximum velocity and constricted PSO that can improve the result in case of small swarm and number of iterations.

2. Formation Control

The formation driving method described in this section is based on a leader-follower approach, in which the followers should follow a leader's trajectory. The method was developed by Barfoot and Clark (Barfoot et al., 2002; Barfoot & Clark, 2004) and later improved for following of trajectories with arbitrary shape within our team (Saska et al., 2006; Hess et al., 2007). In this chapter there will be published only the parts of formation control necessary for understanding of restrictions applied in the path planning while a detailed description of control inputs for each vehicle can be found in (Saska et al., 2006; Hess et al., 2007).
In the description of the method as well as in the final experiments, known map of environment and utilization of car-like robots with limits for maximum velocity v_r and minimum turning radius R_r will be assumed. Furthermore, around each vehicle will be considered distance d_r from its center in which the obstacles have to be avoided (d_r is usually a function of robot's width).

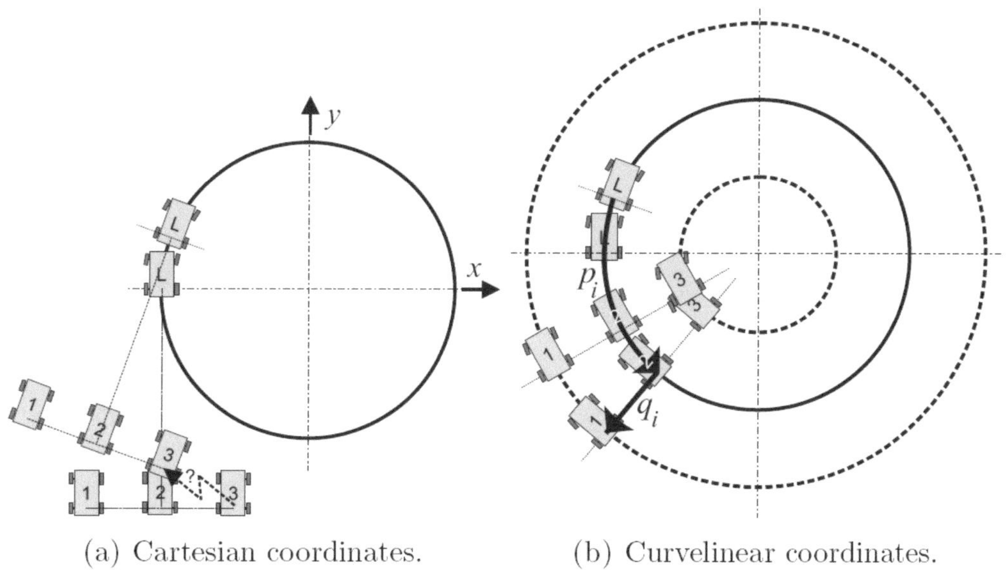

(a) Cartesian coordinates. (b) Curvelinear coordinates.

Figure 1. Two subsequence snapshots of formation driving using fixed position of followers in Cartesian (a) and Curvelinear (b) coordinates. Solid lines denote path of leader while paths of followers are denoted by dashed lines

Important fact of the formation driving of car-like robots that needs to be considered is caused by impossibility to change heading of the robot on spot. Due to this feature formations with fixed relative distance in Cartesian coordinates cannot be used, because such structure makes smooth movement of the followers impossible (simple example is shown in Fig. 1. Therefore we utilized an approach in which the followers are maintained in relative distance to the leader in curvelinear coordinates with two axes p and q, where p traces movement of leader and q is perpendicular to p as is demonstrated in Fig. 1b. The positive direction of p is defined from actual position of the leader back to the origin of its movement and the positive direction of q is defined in the left half plane in direction of forward movement.

The shape of formation is then uniquely determined by states $\psi_L(t_{p_i(t)})$ in *travelled distance* $p_i(t)$ from actual position of the leader along its trajectory and by *offset distance* $q_i(t_{p_i(t)})$ between positions of the leader and the ith follower in perpendicular direction from the leaders' trajectory. The parameters $p_i(t)$ and $q_i(t)$ defined for each follower i can be varying during the mission and $t_{p_i(t)}$ is time when the leader was at the *travelled distance* $p_i(t)$ behind the actual position. $\psi_L(t)=\{x_L(t), y_L(t), \Theta_L(t)\}$ denotes the configuration of a leader robot at time t, and similarly $\psi_i=\{x_i(t), y_i(t), \Theta_i(t)\}$, with $i\in\{1,\ldots,n_r\}$, denote the configuration for each of the n_r follower robots at time t. The Cartesian coordinates x_t, y_t for an arbitrary configuration $\psi(t)$ define the position of a robot and $\Theta(t)$ denotes its heading.

To convert the state of the followers in curvelinear coordinates to the state in rectangular coordinates $\psi_i(t)$ the following equations can be applied:

$$\begin{aligned} x_i(t) &= x_L(t_{p_i(t)}) - q_i(t_{p_i(t)})\sin(\theta_L(t_{p_i(t)})) \\ y_i(t) &= y_L(t_{p_i(t)}) + q_i(t_{p_i(t)})\cos(\theta_L(t_{p_i(t)})) \\ \theta_i(t) &= \theta_L(t_{p_i(t)}), \end{aligned} \tag{1}$$

where $\psi_L(t_{p_i(t)})=\{x_L(t_{p_i(t)}), y_L(t_{p_i(t)}), \Theta_L(t_{p_i(t)})\}$ is state of the leader in time $t_{p_i(t)}$.

Applying the leader following approach using p,q coordinates we can easily determine inadmissible interval of turning radius for the leader of formation as $R_f^-(t); R_f^+(t)$, where

$$\begin{aligned} R_f^-(t) &= \max_{i=1,..,n_r}(-R_r + q_i(t)) \\ R_f^+(t) &= \min_{i=1,..,n_r}(R_r + q_i(t)). \end{aligned} \tag{2}$$

These restrictions must be applied due to the different turning radius of the robots on the different position in the formation during turning. It is obvious that the robot following inner track should go slower and with smaller turning radius than the robot further from the centre of turning.

Since the leader trajectory has to be collision free for the leader but also for the followers, the shape of the formation should be included to the avoidance behaviour. The extended obstacle free distance for the leaders' planning can be then expressed as

$$d_f(t) = d_r + \max_{i=1,\ldots,n_r} |q_i(t)|. \tag{3}$$

Remark 2.1 Time dependence and asymmetry of the formation will be for simplification of the algorithm description omitted and the variables will be considered as constants:

$$\begin{aligned} d_f &= \max_{0<t<T} d_f(t), \\ |R_f| &= \min(\min_{0<t<T} R_f^+(t), \min_{0<t<T} -R_f^-(t)) \end{aligned} \tag{4}$$

where T is total time of the formation movement.

3. Path Description and Evaluation

The path planning for the leader of formation can be realized by a search in the space of functions. In this approach the space is reduced to a sub-space which only contains strings of cubic splines. The mathematic notation of a cubic spline (Ye & Qu, 1999) is

$$g(s) \quad = \quad As^3 - Bs^2 + Cs + D, \tag{5}$$

where s is within the interval $< 0;1 >$ and A, B, C, D are constants. The whole string of the splines is then in 2D case uniquely determined by $8n$ variables (n denotes the amount of splines in the string). The initial and desired state (position and orientation) of the formation is specified by 8 equations, while continuity of first and second derivative in the whole path, which is important for the formation driving as is shown in (Saska et al., 2006), is guaranteed by $6(n-1)$ equations.

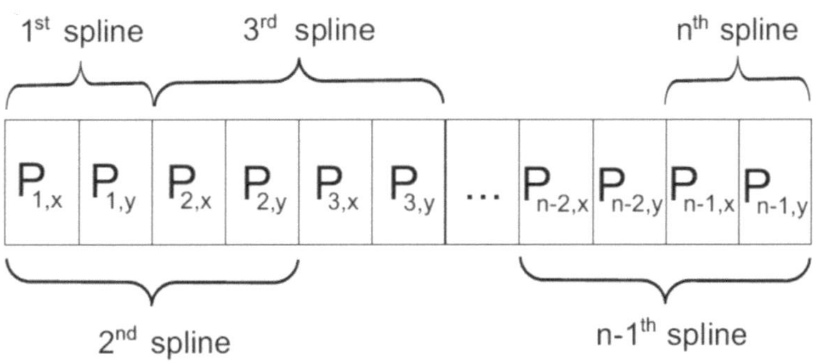

Figure 2. Path representation

Therefore, only $2(n-1)$ degree of freedom define the whole path, which conforms to positions of the points in the spline connections. The whole path representation used in our method is shown in Fig. 2.

Each solution achieved by the global optimization method is evaluated by a cost function. The global minimum of this function corresponds to a smooth and short path that is safe (there is sufficient distance to obstacles). The cost function was in introduced method used in the form

$$f = f_{length} + f_{distance} + f_{radius}. \tag{6}$$

where part f_{length} corresponds to the length of the path which in 2D case can be computed by

$$f_{length} = \int_0^1 \sqrt{(g'_x(s))^2 + (g'_y(s))^2 dt}. \tag{7}$$

The component $f_{distance}$ (Fig. 3a) penalizes the paths close to an obstacle and it is defined by equation

$$f_{distance} = \begin{cases} d^{-2}, & \text{if } d_f < d \\ d^{-2} + p_{df}, & \text{if } d_r < d < d_f \\ d^{-2} + p_{df} + p_{dr}, & \text{if } d < d_r \end{cases} \tag{8}$$

where p_{df} penalizes solutions with a collision that can be avoided by a change in the formation and p_{dr} penalizes paths with a collision of the leader. Parameter d denotes minimal distance of the path to the closest obstacle and can be expressed as

$$d = \min_{o \in O} \min_{t \in <0;1>} ||o - g(s)||, \tag{9}$$

where O is set of all obstacles in the workspace of the robots.

The part of the cost function f_{radius} (Fig. 3b), that is necessary because of using the car-like robots as well as due to presented formation driving approach, is computed according

$$f_{radius} = \begin{cases} r^{-2}, & \text{if } R_f < r \\ r^{-2} + p_{rf}, & \text{if } R_r < r < R_f \\ r^{-2} + p_{rf} + p_{rr}, & \text{if } r < R_r \end{cases} \tag{10}$$

where solutions penalized only by p_{rf} can be repaired by a formation changing, while paths with radius smaller than R_r do not meet even requirements for a single robot. Parameter *r* is minimal radius along the whole path and it is defined by

$$r = \min_{t \in <0;1>} \frac{\begin{vmatrix} g'_x(s) & g'_y(s) \\ g''_x(s) & g''_y(s) \end{vmatrix}}{(g'_x(s)^2 + g'_y(s)^2)^{\frac{3}{2}}}. \tag{11}$$

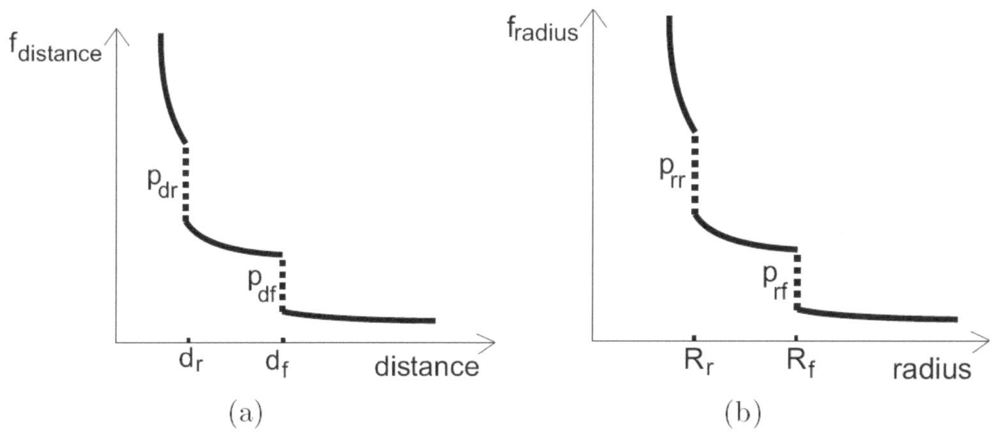

Figure 3. (a) $f_{distance}$, (b) f_{radius} - components of cost function with denoted penalizations

4. Particle Swarm Optimization

Each particle *i* is represented as a*D*-dimensional position vector $\vec{x}_i(t)$ and has a corresponding instantaneous velocity vector $\vec{v}_i(t)$. The position vector encodes robot path according to the schema depicted in Fig. 2. In our simple case of three splines (two spline connections), the position vector is 4-dimensional and $\vec{x}_i(t) = \{P_{1,x}, P_{1,y}, P_{2,x}, P_{2,y}\}$. Furthermore, each particle remembers its individual best value of fitness function and position $\vec{p}_i(t)$ that has resulted in that value. During each iteration *t*, the velocity update rule (12) is applied on each particle in the swarm:

$$\begin{aligned} \vec{v}_i(t) = {} & w\vec{v}_i(t-1) + \\ & + \varphi_1 R_1(\vec{p}_i - \vec{x}_i(t-1)) + \\ & + \varphi_2 R_2(\vec{p}_g - \vec{x}_i(t-1)). \end{aligned} \tag{12}$$

The $\vec{p}_g(t)$ is the best position of the entire swarm and represents the social knowledge. Another alternative can be "local best PSO", where the best position from a local neighborhood is used instead of $\vec{p}_g(t)$. We chose the "global-best PSO" because of faster convergence that is consistent with our requirement on low time complexity. The parameter w is called inertia weight and during all iterations decreases linearly from $w_{start}=0.8$ to $w_{end}=0$. The symbols R_1 and R_2 represent the diagonal matrices with random diagonal elements drawn from a uniform distribution between 0 and 1. The parameters φ_1 and φ_2 are scalar constants that weight influence of particles' own experience and the social knowledge. The parameters were set $\varphi_1 = \varphi_2 = 2$ in compliance with literature recommendation.
Next, the position update rule (13) is applied:

$$\vec{x}_i(t) = \vec{x}_i(t-1) + \vec{v}_i(t) \tag{13}$$

If any component of $\vec{v}_i(t)$ is less than $-V_{\max}$ or greater than $+V_{\max}$, the corresponding value is replaced by $-V_{\max}$ or $+V_{\max}$, respectively. The $V_{\max}$ is maximum velocity parameter. This parameter (as well as the velocity and position vectors) is related to the spatial dimensions of the planning area. For the area with 80000×40000 pixels, some preliminary tests showed that $V_{\max} = 3000$ was suitable setting.
The update formulas (12) and (13) are applied during each iteration and the $\vec{p}_i(t)$ and $\vec{p}_g(t)$ values are updated simultaneously. The algorithm stops if maximum number of iterations is achieved.
There are some specific moments in our application. The swarm initialization is the most important one. The particular components of the particle positions have the direct interpretations. They are coordinates of 2-D points in the robot workspace. Therefore, it is suitable to initialize the position vectors into a rectangle with one corner in the start position and the opposite corner in the goal position. However, there can be some different initialization strategies (e.g. initializing the spline connection points over the whole workspace or on the line connecting the start and the goal position.
For our particular scenarios, we choose the initial position to be uniform random numbers from *<30000;40000>*. The same initialization was used for genetic algorithm described below.

5. Genetic Algorithm

The PSO has been compared to the most commonly used nature-inspired method - genetic algorithm (GA). In all experiments, the same GA scheme with stochastic uniform selection, scattered crossover and gaussian mutation was used (Vose, 1999). The particular settings have been chosen experimentally.

In the stochastic uniform selection a line is laid out in which each parent corresponds to a section of the line of length proportional to its scaled value. The algorithm moves along the line in equal sized steps and allocates a parent from the section it lands on. The "scattered" crossover selects randomly the genes to be recombined. The Gaussian mutation adds a random number drawn from Gaussian distribution with zero mean and variance linearly decreasing from $0.5r_0$ to $0.125r_0$, where r_0 is the the initial range (for our experiments, $r_0 = 40000 - 30000 = 10000$). Moreover, elitism has been used that copies two best individuals from the previous generation into the new generation if a better individual was not created in the new generation. This prevents the loss of best solution and accelerates the convergence.

6. Implementation Details

Great number of evaluations is required by available optimization methods and therefore computational complexity of the cost function is key factor for real time applications. The most calculation-intensive part of the equation (6) is $f_{distance}$. It is done by big amount and complexity of obstacles from which the distance needs to be computed. In the presented method a distance grid map of the environment is pre-computed. Each cell in such matrix denotes minimum distance of relevant place to the closest obstacle according to equation (8). The regions outside the polygon denoting walls of the building or inside the obstacles could be signed by infinite value, because they are infeasible for the formation movement. Nevertheless due to the simple initialization used in this chapter all particles in the initial swarm can be intersecting an obstacle and therefore evaluated by the same value $f_{distance} = \infty$.

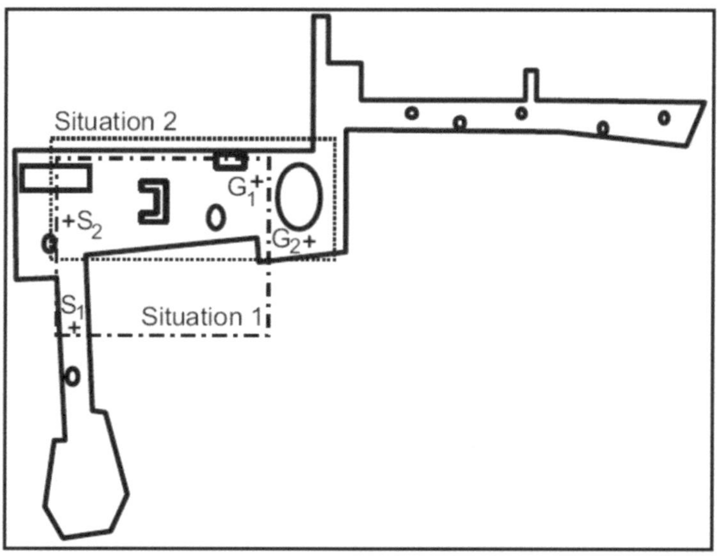

Figure 4. Map of utilized workspace with denoted zoomed areas of the scenarios: Situation 1 and Situation 2

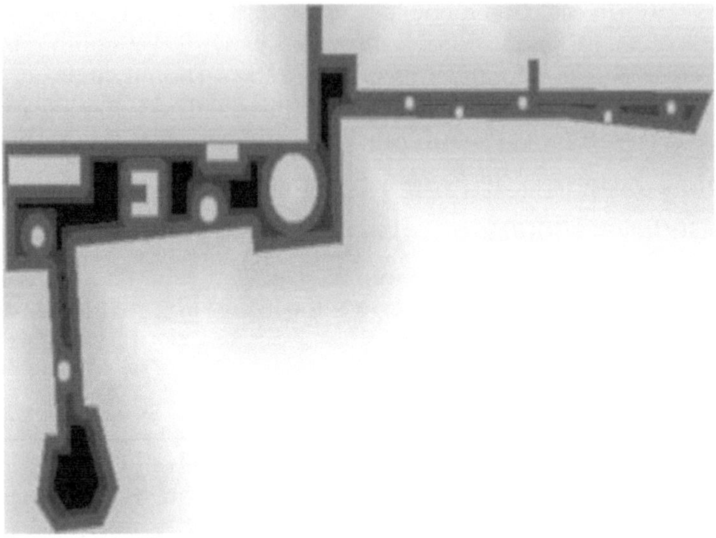

Figure 5. Distance map used for computing of the cost function. Black color denotes the regions where $f_{distance} = 0$ and white color denotes the region with maximum values of $f_{distance}$

In such case even the smartest optimization method degrades to a random search. A solution could be to artificially add a rising of $f_{distance}$ outside the polygon from the walls of building (similarly inside the circular obstacles the increase will be from the borders to the center of obstacle) which enables the optimization method to reach the feasible space. Big advantage of such grid-map approach is possibility to use obstacles with arbitrarily complicated shape, that is usually done be autonomous mapping technique. An occupancy grid that is obtained by a range finder can be used as well. An example of the robot workspace with obstacles that was used for experiments is depicted on the Fig. 4 and the appropriate distance map is drawn in the Fig. 5.

7. Experiments

This section summarizes various types of experiments in static environment for two scenarios (Situation 1 and Situation 2) depicted in Fig. 4. First, the results obtained by PSO are discussed and further, the PSO is compared to genetic algorithm. The presented tests have been realized in the environment of computer science building in Wuerzburg (map is depicted in Fig. 4) which is frequently used for hardware experiments of indoor mobile robots.

7.1 PSO Results

Parameters of the PSO method were adjusted in agreement with (Saska et al., 2006), where the algorithm was used in similar application. As the test scenario were chosen situations with several local extremes corresponding to feasible as well as unfeasible paths for the leader. In Fig. 6 are presented two solutions of the Situation 1 designed by PSO method. The path evaluated by cost $f=13.02$ is close to the global optimal solution and is feasible for the formation maintaining fixed shape. Contrariwise the second path (*f=28.71*) is close to one of the local optimal solutions and it is feasible only for a single robot. For the formation driving it means that the shape of the formation must be temporarily changed during the passage around the obstacles as well as in the loop replacing sharp unfeasible curve next to the corner of the room. We should note that the loop was created automatically by the path planning method. Such manoeuvres could be useful e.g. in crossroads of narrow corridors where straightforward movement is impossible due to the restriction of turning radius.

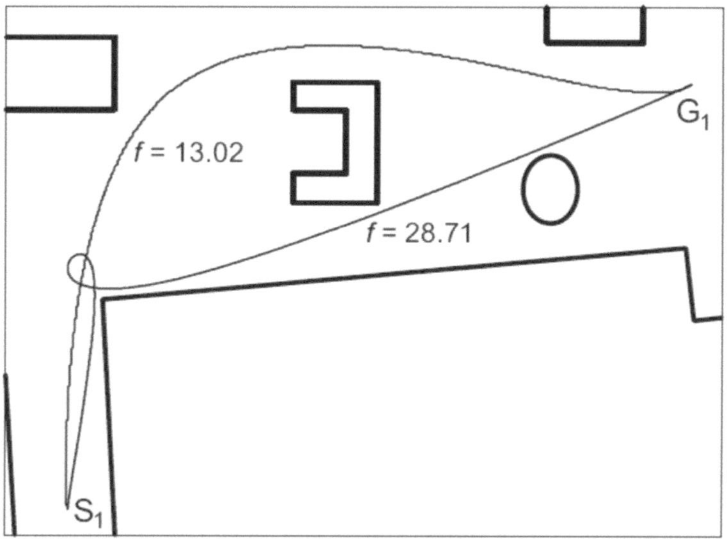

Figure 6. Two different solutions of Situation 1 obtained by PSO

Results of the second scenario, Situation 2, are shown in Fig. 7 where the solution with *f=13.82* is feasible for the complete formation whereas the second solution (*f=18.31*) requires small changes of the positions of outer followers. The second path is shorter than the first solution, which is close to the global minimum of the cost function (6). Therefore the second solution could be preferred in the application where the shape of formation can be easily modified.

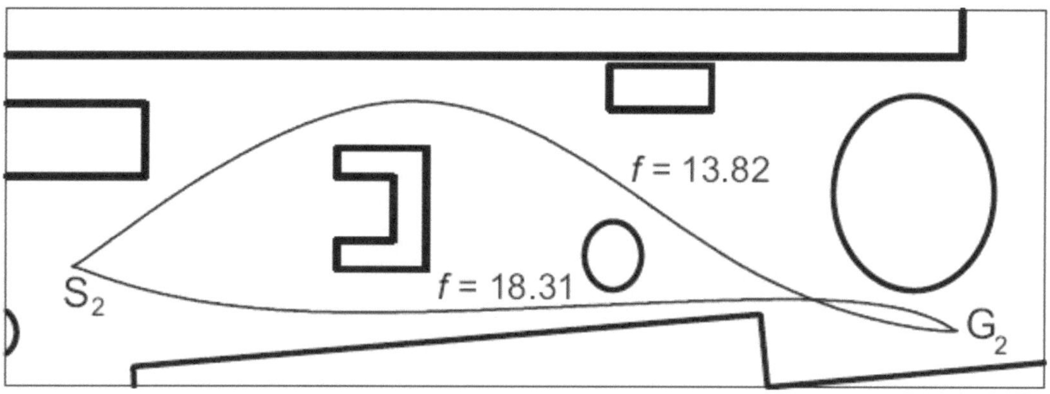

Figure 7. Two different solutions of Situation 2 obtained by PSO

7.2 Comparison with GA

The two scenarios described above were used for the comparison of PSO and GA. For both methods, the swarm (population) size was *30* and the number of iterations (generations) was *300*. Such an excessive number of cost function evaluations enables better evaluation of results and the chance of the algorithm to converge into an optimum.

	min	mean	std	max
PSO	13.00	18.05	7.74	32.6
GA	13.01	39.41	155.33	1181.4

Table 1. The minimum, mean, standard deviation and maximum of the set of minimum cost values found by particular runs for Situation 1. Set of results from 100 repeated runs was used

$f_{min} \in$	$(-\infty; 14>$	$(14; 40>$	$(40; 300>$	$(300; +\infty)$
PSO	70	30	0	0
GA	80	16	2	2

Table 2. Situation 1 - absolute occurrences of different values of final $f_{\min}$ in the set of 100 results of independent runs

Because of statistical purposes, *100* runs of each method (with different random initialization) has been launched. The main quality criterion used is the minimum cost function $f_{\min}$ found at a particular moment. First, we took final values of the minimum cost value found in particular runs. Basic statistical properties computed from the 100 runs are depicted in Table 1. Although the mean best PSO solutions is lower than the mean best GA solution, the difference is not statistically significant (two-sample t-test with significance level *0.05* was used to investigate the significance of difference between the methods). However, high standard deviation and high maximum (worst result) obtained for GA results shows that in some runs, the genetic algorithm found extremely poor result that do not belong to any of the two optima shown in Fig. 6. This is especially evident from the Table 2, where the histogram of best solutions is depicted. The second column corresponds to the global minimum of cost function that lies under the value $f=14$. The numbers are absolute occurrences (of totally 100 runs) of the final minimum fitness values that are lower than *14*. The third column describes hits to the local optima (that lies somewhere around *28*). The other two columns correspond to quite poor (probably unusable) solutions. One can observe that for the Situation 1 the GA finds these bad solutions in *4* of totally *100* cases. On the other hand the PSO always finds at least the local minimum and is more susceptible to getting stuck in the local optimum. This fact is probably a tax on the faster convergence. The higher convergence rate of PSO can be observed from Fig. 8b, where the mean temporal evolution of $f_{\min}$ is depicted. One can see that the curve for PSO decreases and reaches minimum much more rapidly than the curve measured for GA.

The results for Situation 2 are similar. This time, the mean result for GA is significantly worse (Table 3). In histogram (Table 4 and Fig. 9a), one can observe that GA again was unable to find neither the global optimum (*f<16*) nor the local optimum ($f \in (16;19)$)in *5* of totally *100* cases. Moreover, it found the global optima fewer times than the PSO. Again, the convergence of PSO is much faster for the Situation 2.

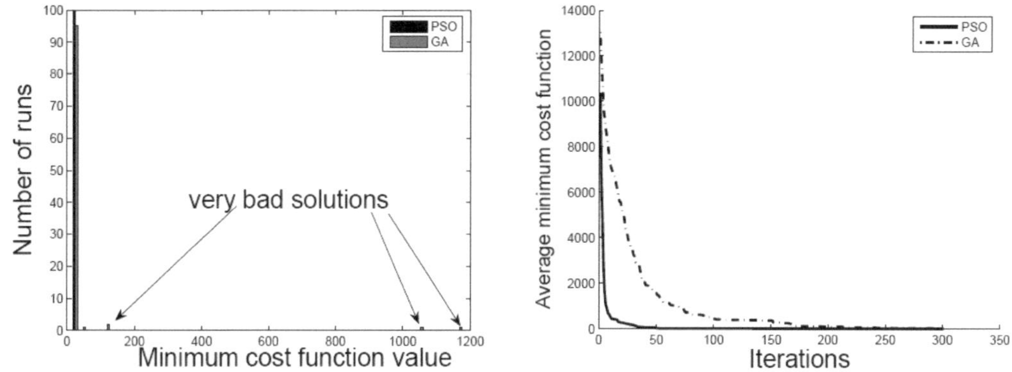

(a) (b)

Figure 8. The results for Situation 1. The histogram of final $f_{\min}$ values obtained from 100 runs (a) and the temporal evolution of $f_{\min}$ values averaged over 100 runs (b)

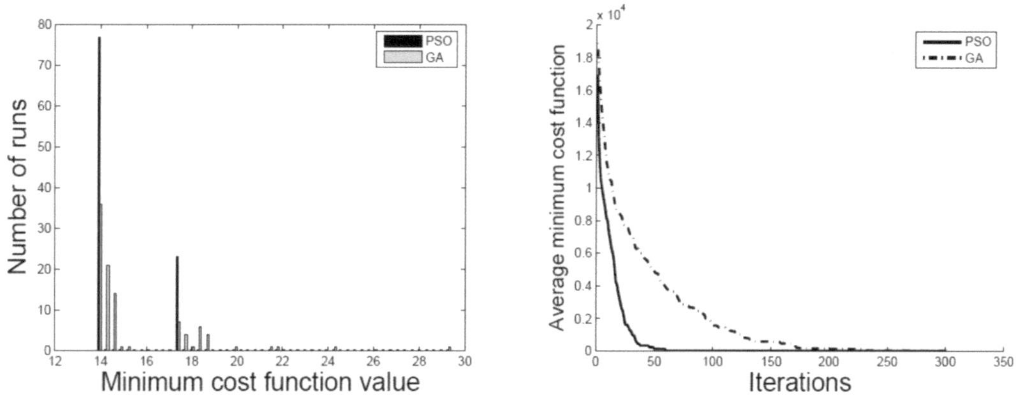

(a) (b)

Figure 9. The results for Situation 2. The histogram of final $f_{\min}$ values obtained from 100 runs (a) and the temporal evolution of $f_{\min}$ values averaged over 100 runs (b)

	min	mean	std	max
PSO	13.80	14.66	1.53	17.53
GA	13.87	15.49	2.54	29.45

Table. 3 The minimum, mean, standard deviation and maximum of the set of minimum cost values found by particular runs for Situation 2. Set of results from 100 repeated runs was used

$f_{min} \in$	$(-\infty; 16 >$	$(16; 19 >$	$(19; +\infty >$
PSO	77	23	0
GA	73	22	5

Table 4. Situation 2 - absolute occurrences of different values of final *fmin* in the set of 100 results of independent runs

The conclusion of this section is that the PSO finds the solution much faster than GA . Moreover, the GA sometimes produces unusable poor solution. Both the PSO and GA parameters were tuned experimentally in some preliminary testing.

7.3 Constriction and Dynamic Inertia Weight

It has been already mentioned above that an acceptable modification of the PSO method must be very simple and should lead to improvement of algorithm's convergence rate. In this section, two very simple modifications are compared to the basic PSO described in Section 4. The first modification is the PSO with constriction coefficient (CCPSO) and the second is PSO with adaptive dynamic inertia weight (AIWPSO) (Fan & Chang, 2007).
The constriction coefficient was derived from an eigenvalue analysis of swarm dynamics (Clerk, 1999). The method is used to balance exploration and exploitation trade-off. The velocity update Equation (12) is modified:

$$\vec{v}_i(t) = \chi[w\vec{v}_i(t-1) + \varphi_1 R_1(\vec{p}_i - \vec{x}_i(t-1)) + \\ + \varphi_2 R_2(\vec{p}_g - \vec{x}_i(t-1))] \tag{14}$$

where χ is the constriction coefficient, which is computed from values of φ_1 and φ_2. We used $\varphi_1 = \varphi_2 = 2.1$ and

$$\chi = \frac{2}{|2 - \varphi - \sqrt{(\varphi^2 - 4\varphi)}|}, \tag{14}$$

where $\varphi = \varphi_1 + \varphi_2$. The advantage is that the velocity clamping does not need to be used.
The second modification - PSO with adaptive dynamic inertia weight (AIWPSO) (Fan & Chang, 2007) is based on dynamically changing inertia weight $w = w(t)$. The principal modification is the nonlinear modification of the inertia weight. The nonlinear function is given by: $w=(d)^r w_{start}$, where d is the decrease rate and has been set experimentally to $d = 0.95$ and r changes through time according to the following rules: 1. $r \leftarrow r+1$ if the best cost function value (minimal value in the swarm) decreased (improved) and 2. $r \leftarrow r-1$ if the best cost function value increased or remained the same. This mechanism wishes to make particles fly more quickly toward the potential optimal solution, and then through decreasing inertia weight to perform local refinement around the neighbourhood of the optimal solution.
The comparison has been done using the Situation 2 described above. The results of 100 runs are depicted on Fig. 10. For all runs, only 15 particles and 100 iterations were used. The results show that in average, better results are obtained by CCPSO, although the CCPSO has

slower convergence than PSO. On the other hand, the difference of the final best solutions is not significant. The PSO reached the global optimum area (*f*<20) in 73 runs and the final minimum cost value averaged over 100 runs was *73.25*. The CCPSO reached the global optimum area in 71 runs and the final minimum cost value averaged over 100 runs was *117.62*. One can also see that the AIWPSO did not perform well. It found the global optimum area in 54 runs and the final minimum cost value averaged over 100 runs was *1159.00*.

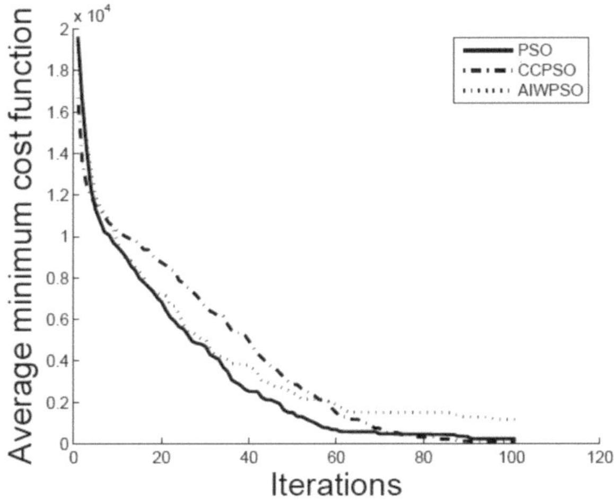

Figure 10. Comparison of three PSO modifcations. The temporal evolution of $f_{\min}$ values averaged over 100 runs

7.4 Simulation of Formation Driving

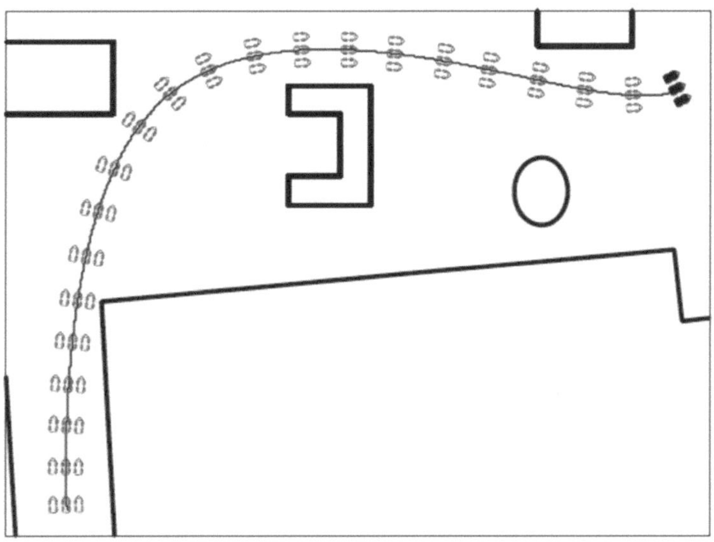

Figure 11. Simulation of formation movement

For demonstration of the formation movement was chosen the feasible solution designed by PSO in situation 1. The path planning as well as the formation driving were adjusted for the formation of three robots in the line that is perpendicular to the leader's path. In the Fig. 11 is zoomed part of the workspace with delineated positions of the robots during task execution. Robots were controlled by an approach that was presented by our team in (Hess et al. 2007).

8. Conclusion and Future Work

This chapter gave concrete recommendations about the use of PSO based spline-planner. Namely, a suitable PSO method with recommended parameter values is resumed and its main advantages and disadvantages are critically discussed. The original PSO with velocity clamping and linearly decreasing inertia weight performed well and was able to find better solution in shorter time than genetic algorithm. Because of strong limitations on time consumption, we do not recommend any complex modification. Among the two tested modification, the PSO with constriction coefficient could compete with the original PSO version. Finally, it was shown, how problematic is the use of PSO for formation path planning. In our cases, the only feasible paths corresponded to global optima of the cost function. A promising future direction is the modified random initialization of the swarm that can be adjusted in number of ways. The good initialization is simple instrument for improving the speed of the planning process that is for real time planning and dynamical environment response crucial.

9. Acknowledgments

The research was supported by the research program No. MSM6840770012 Transdisciplinary Research in the Area of Biomedical Engineering II of the CTU in Prague, sponsored by the Ministry of Education, Youth and Sports of the Czech Republic.

10. References

Balch, T., & Arkin, R. C. (1998, December). Behaviour-based formation control for multi-robot teams. *IEEE Transactions on Robotics andAutomation, 14*(6), 926–939.

Barfoot, T. D., & Clark, C. M. (2004, February). Motion planning for formations of mobile robots. *Robotics and Autonomous Systems, 46*, 65–78.

Barfoot, T. D., Clark, C. M., Rock, S. M., & D'Eleuterio, G. M. T. (2002, october). *Kinematic path-planning for formations of mobile robots with a nonholonomic constraint.*

Beard, R., Lawton, J., & Hadaegh, F. (2001, November). A coordination architecture for spacecraft formation control. *IEEE Transactions on Control Systems Technology, 9*(6), 777 - 790.

Clerc, M. (1999). The swarm and the queen: Towards a deterministic and adaptive particle swarm optimization. In *Proceedings of the ieee congress on evolutionary computation* (Vol. 3, pp. 1951- 1957).

Daigle, M. J., Koutsoukos, X. D., & Biswas, G. (2007, April). Distributed diagnosis in formations of mobile robots. *IEEE Transactions on Robotics, 23*(2), 353 - 369.

Das, A., Fierro, R., Kumar, V., Ostrowski, J., Spletzer, J., & Taylor, C. (2003, October). A vision-based formation control framework. *IEEE Transactions on Robotics and Automation, 18*(5), 813825.

Derenick, J., & Spletzer, J. (2007, December). Convex optimization strategies for coordinating large-scale robot formations. *IEEE Transactions on Robotics, 23*(6), 1252-1259.

Desai, J., Ostrowski, J., & Kumar, V. (2001, December). Modeling and control of formations of nonholonomic mobile robots. *IEEE Transactions on Robotics and Automation, 17*(6), 905908.

Fahimi, F. (2007, June). Sliding-mode formation control for underactuated surface vessels. *IEEE Transactions on Robotics, 23*(3), 617 - 622.

Fan, S.-K. S., & Chang, J.-M. (2007). A modified particle swarm optimizer using an adaptive dynamic weight scheme. In *Hcii (12)* (p. 56-65). Springer.

Fredslund, J., & Mataric, M. (2002, October). A general algorithm for robot formations using local sensing and minimal communication. *IEEE Transactions on Robotics and Automation, special issue on Advances in Multi-Robot Systems, 18*(5), 837846.

Fua, C., Ge, S., Duc Do, K., & Lim, K.-W. (2007). Multirobot formations based on the queue-formation scheme with limited communication. *IEEE Transactions on Robotics, 23*(6), 1160-1169.

Hess, M., Saska, M., & Schilling, K. (2007, September). *Enhanced motion planning for dynamic formations of nonholonomic mobile robots.*

Kaminka, G., Schechter-Glick, R., & Sadov, V. (2008, April). Using sensor morphology for multirobot formations. *IEEE Transactions on Robotics, 24*(2), 271 - 282.

Kang, W., Xi, N., & Sparks, A. (2000). *Formation control of autonomous agents in 3d workspace.*

Kennedy, J., & Eberhart, R. (1995). Particle swarm optimization. In *Proceedings international conference on neural networks ieee* (Vol. 4, pp. 1942–1948).

Kloder, S., & Hutchinson, S. (2006, August). Path planning for permutation-invariant multirobot formations. *IEEE Transactions on Robotics, 22*(4), 650-665.

Kloetzer, M., & Belta, C. (2007, April). Temporal logic planning and control of robotic swarms by hierarchical abstractions. *IEEE Transactions on Robotics, 23*(2), 320 - 330.

Lalish, E., Morgansen, K., & Tsukamaki, T. (2006). *Formation tracking control using virtual structures and deconfliction.*

Langer, D., Rosenblatt, J., & Hebert, M. (1994, December). A behavior-based system for off-road navigation. *IEEE Transactions on Robotics and Automation, 10*(6), 776–783.

Lawton, J., Beard, R., & Young, B. (2003, December). A decentralized approach to formation maneuvers. *IEEE Transactions on Robotics and Automation, 19*(6), 933941.

Milutinovi, D., & Lima, P. (2006, December). Modeling and optimal centralized control of a large-size robotic population. *IEEE Transactions on Robotics, 22*(6), 1280 - 1285.

Mourikis, A., & Roumeliotis, S. (2006a, october). Optimal sensor scheduling for resource-constrained localization of mobile robot formations. *IEEE Transactions on Robotics, 22*(5), 917 - 931.

Mourikis, A., & Roumeliotis, S. (2006b, August). Performance analysis of multirobot cooperative localization. *IEEE Transactions on Robotics, 22*(4), 666 - 681.

Pallottino, L., Scordio, V., Bicchi, A., & Frazzoli, E. (2007, December). Decentralized cooperative policy for conflict resolution in multivehicle systems. *IEEE Transactions on Robotics, 23*(6), 1170 - 1183.

Parker, L. (1998, April). Alliance: an architecture for fault tolerant multirobot cooperation. *IEEE Transactions on Robotics and Automation, 14*(2), 220–240.

Peasgood, M., Clark, C., & McPhee, J. (2008, April). A complete and scalable strategy for coordinating multiple robots within roadmaps. *IEEE Transactions on Robotics, 24*(2), 283 - 292.

Ren, W., & Beard, R. (2003, June). *A decentralized scheme for spacecraft formation flying via the virtual structure approach.* Saska, M., Hess, M., & Schilling, K. (2007, December). *Path planning and motion coordination for compact vehicle-formations.* Guimaraes, Portugal.

Saska, M., Hess, M., & Schilling, K. (2008, May). *Efficient airport snow shoveling by applying autonomous multi-vehicle formations.* Pasadena, USA.

Saska, M., Macas, M., Preucil, L., & Lhotska, L. (2006). Robot path planning using partical swarm optimization of Ferguson splines. *Proc. IEEE/ETFA'06,* 833-839.

Tanner, H., Loizou, S., & Kyriakopoulos, K. (2003). Nonholonomic navigation and control of cooperating mobile manipulators. *IEEE Transactions on Robotics and Automation., 19*(1), 53-64.

Vig, L., & Adams, J. (2006, August). Multi-robot coalition formation. *IEEE Transactions on Robotics, 22*(4).

Vose, M. D. (1999). *The simple genetic algorithm: Foundations and theory.* MIT Press, Cambridge.

Ye, J., & Qu, R. (1999). *Fairing of parametric cubic splines.* Elseviers.

21

Simultaneous Perturbation Particle Swarm Optimization and Its FPGA Implementation

Yutaka Maeda and Naoto Matsushita
Kansai University
Japan

1. Introduction

The particle swarm optimization technique is one of the promising tools to find a proper optimum for an unknown function optimization. Especially, global search capability of the method is very powerful. The particle swarm optimization utilizes common knowledge of the group and individual experiences effectively. That is, direction for the best estimator that a particle has ever reached, direction for the best one that all particles have ever found and momentum are successfully combined to determine the next direction. At the same time, the method does not utilize gradient of the objective function. Only values of the objective function are used. In many applications, it is difficult or impossible to obtain the gradient of an objective function. Then, the particle swarm optimization can take advantage of the merit.

However, this means that the method does not use local information of the function. Even if a particle is close to a global optimal, the particle moves based on three factors described above. In this case, it seems better to search neighbour area carefully. To do so, local information such as gradient is necessary.

On the other hand, the simultaneous perturbation method is a kind of stochastic gradient method. The scheme can obtain the local information of the gradient without direct calculation of the gradient. The simultaneous perturbation estimates the gradient using a kind of finite difference technique. However, even if dimension of the parameters are large, the simultaneous perturbation requires only two values of the target function. Therefore, we can apply this to high dimensional optimization problems in effect.

As mentioned now, since the simultaneous perturbation is a stochastic gradient method, we cannot expect global search capability. That is, this method cannot give a global optimal but a local one.

Combination of the particle swarm optimization and the simultaneous perturbation optimization will yield interesting algorithms which have advantages of these two approaches. There are some ways to combine the particle swarm optimization and the simultaneous perturbation method. In this paper, we propose four new algorithms based on combinations of the particle swarm optimization and the simultaneous perturbation. Some results for test functions are also shown.

Moreover, hardware implementation of these kinds of algorithms is interesting research target. Especially, the particle swarm optimization has plural search points which are candidates of optimum. If we can evaluate these search points in parallel processing system, we can realize intriguing optimization scheme as a hardware system. From this point of view, we implemented the particle swarm optimization using the simultaneous perturbation by using field programmable gate array (FPGA). This paper presents detailed description on the implementation of the simultaneous perturbation particle swarm optimization.

2. Particle swarm optimization and simultaneous perturbation

2.1 Particle swarm optimization

The particle swarm optimization is proposed by Eberhart and Kennedy (Kennedy & Eberhart, 1995). This scheme realizes an intelligent interesting computational technique. Intelligence come out swarm behaviour of creatures are successfully modelled as an optimization scheme (Bonabeau et al., 1999)(Engelbrecht, 2006). Many applications of the particle swarm optimization for some fields are reported (Juang, 2004)(Parsopoulos & Vrahatis, 2004)(Bo et al., 2007)(Fernandez et al., 2007)(Nanbo, 2007)(del Valle et al., 2008). Our problem is to find a minimum point of an objective function $f(x) \in \Re^1$ with an adjustable n-dimensional parameter vector $x \in \Re^n$. The algorithm of the particle swarm optimization is described as follows;

$$x_{t+1} = x_t + \Delta x_t \tag{1}$$

$$\Delta x_{t+1} = \chi(\omega \Delta x_t + \phi_1(p_t - x_t) + \phi_2(n_t - x_t)) \tag{2}$$

where, the parameter vector x_t denote an estimator of the minimum point at the t-th iteration. Δx_t is called a velocity vector, that is, a modifying vector for the parameter vector. This term becomes so-called momentum for the next iteration.

p_t is the best estimator that this particle has ever reached, n_t is the best one that all the particles have ever found until the t-th iteration. The coefficients ϕ_1 and ϕ_2 are two positive random numbers in a certain range to decide a balance between the individual best estimator and the swarm best one. Uniform distribution with upper limitation is used in this work. ω denotes a coefficient to adjust the effect of the inertia, χ is a gain coefficient for the update.

As shown in Eq.(2), in the particle swarm optimization algorithm, each individual changes their position based on the balance of three factors; velocity, the individual best estimator and the group best estimator. All the particle change their position using Eq.(2).

2.2 Simultaneous perturbation

The simultaneous perturbation optimization method is very simple stochastic gradient method which does not require the gradient of an objective function but only two values of the function. The simultaneous perturbation was introduced by J.C.Spall in 1987 (Spall, 1987). Convergence of the algorithm was proved in the framework of the stochastic approximation method (Spall, 1992). Y.Maeda also have independently proposed a learning rule of neural networks based on the simultaneous perturbation method and reported a comparison between the simultaneous perturbation type of learning rule of neural networks, the simple finite difference type of learning rule and the ordinary backpropagation method (Maeda et al.,1995). J.Alespector et al. and G.Cauwenberghs also individually proposed a parallel gradient descent method and stochastic error descent algorithm, respectively, which are identical to the simultaneous perturbation learning rule (Cauwenberghs, 1993) (Alespector et al., 1993). Many applications of the simultaneous perturbation are reported in the fields of neural networks (Maeda, 1997) and their hardware implementation (Maeda, 2003) (Maeda, 2005). The simultaneous perturbation method is described as follows;

$$x_{t+1} = x_t - a\Delta g_t \tag{3}$$

$$\Delta g_t^i = \frac{f(\boldsymbol{x}_t + \boldsymbol{c}_t) - f(\boldsymbol{x}_t)}{c_t^i} \quad (i = 1, \cdots, n) \tag{4}$$

Where, a is a positive constant, c and c_t^i are a perturbation vector and its *i*-th element which is determined randomly. Δg_t^i represents the *i*-th element of Δg_t . c_t^i is independent with different element and different iteration. For example, the segmented uniform distribution or the Bernoulli distribution is applicable to generate the perturbation. Δg_t becomes an estimator of the gradient of the function.
As is shown in Eq.(4), this method requires only two values of the target function despite of dimension of the function. That is, even if the dimension n of the evaluation function is so large, two value of the function gives the partial derivative of the function with respect to all the parameters, although ordinary finite difference requires many values of the function. Combination with the particle swarm optimization is very promising approach to improve performance of the particle swarm optimization.

3. Combination of particle swarm optimization and simultaneous perturbation

We can obtain a global optimal using the particle swarm optimization. However, unfortunately, since the particle swarm optimization itself does not have a capability searching the neighbor of the position, and it may miss the optimal point near the present position. As a result, efficiency of the particle swarm optimization may be limited in some cases.
On the other hand, the simultaneous perturbation estimates gradient of the position. The simultaneous perturbation method searches only local area based on the estimated gradient. If we can add the local search capability of the simultaneous perturbation to global search one of the particle swarm optimization, we will have a useful optimization method with good global search capability and efficient local search ability at the same time. Therefore, combination of the particle swarm optimization and the simultaneous perturbation is promising and interesting approach.
Combined methods of the particle swarm optimization and the simultaneous perturbation is proposed by Maeda (Maeda, 2006). In this work, the update algorithm which is a combination of particle swarm optimization and the simultaneous perturbation is applied for all the particles uniformly. In other words, the same update algorithm is used for all particles.
In population, there are plural particles and we know the best one. The best individual is the best candidate for a global optimal at that iteration. A possibility that the particle is close to

the global optimal is high. We change the movement rule depending on a situation of the particles. Especially, the best particle has a specific meaning;
From this point of view, we propose some schemes which are combinations of the particle swarm optimization and the simultaneous perturbation.

3.1 Scheme 1

We directly combine the idea of the particle swarm optimization and the simultaneous perturbation. In this method, the momentum term of Eq.(2) is replaced by the simultaneous perturbation term. The estimated gradient generated by Eq.(4) is used to change the direction of modification. The main equation is shown as follows;

$$\Delta x_{t+1}=\chi(-a\Delta g_t+\phi_1(p_t-x_t)+\phi_2(n_t-x_t)) \tag{5}$$

Where the i-th element of Δg_t is defined by Eq.(4). a is a coefficient to adjust the effect of the estimated gradient.
Since the information is estimated by the simultaneous perturbation method, the algorithm does not use the gradient of the function directly but utilizes only two values of the objective function. Therefore, this scheme contains twice observations or calculations for the objective function. However, this number of the observations does not depend on the dimension n of the function. Local information of the gradient of the function is added to the ordinary particle swarm optimization effectively. Fig.l shows elements to generate modifying quantity in the first algorithm.

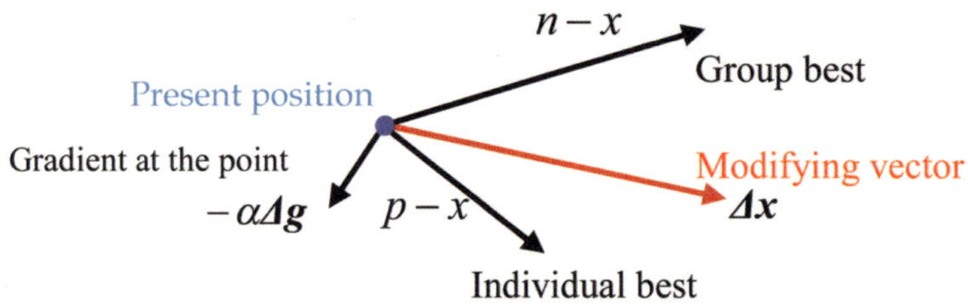

Figure 1. Modifying vector of the algorithm 1

3.2 Scheme 2

In the algorithm 1, all individuals have the same characteristics. That is, Eq.(5) is applied for all particles. However, if the best particle is close to the global minimum, and this is likely, the best particle had better search neighbor of the present point carefully. Then, modification based on the original particle swarm optimization is not suitable for this particle. The gradient type of method is suitable.
Therefore, in this algorithm 2, the simultaneous perturbation method of Eqs.(3) and (4) are applied only to the best particle. All the other individuals are updated by the ordinary particle swarm optimization shown in Eqs.(l) and (2).

3.3 Scheme 3

In this algorithm 3, the particle swarm optimization and the simultaneous perturbation are mixed. That is, in every iteration, half of individuals in the population are updated by the particle swarm optimization, left half particles are modified only by the simultaneous perturbation.

All the individuals select the particle swarm optimization or the simultaneous perturbation randomly with probability of 0.5 in every iteration.

It is interesting what level of performance does such a simple mixture of the particle swarm optimization and the simultaneous perturbation has. Changing ratio of the particle swarm optimization and the simultaneous perturbation is another option.

3.4 Scheme 4

We have another option to construct new algorithm. Basically, we use the algorithm 3. However, the best individual is updated only by the simultaneous perturbation. The reason is as same as that of the algorithm 2. The best particle has a good chance to be a neighbor of a global minimum. Therefore, we always use the simultaneous perturbation for the best particle.

4. Comparison

In order to evaluate performance of these algorithms, we use the following test functions. These functions have their inherent characteristics about local minimum or slope.

- Rastrigin function
- Rosenbrock function
- 2^n-minima function

Comparisons are carried out for ten-dimensional case, that is, n=10 for all test functions. Average of 50 trials is shown. 30 particles are included in the population. Change of average means that an average of the best particle in 30 particles at the iteration for 50 trials are shown. For the simultaneous perturbation term, the perturbation c is generated by uniform distribution in the interval [0.01 0.5] for the scheme 1 to 4. These setting are common for the following test functions.

1. **Rastrigin function**

The function is described as follows;

$$f(x) = 10n + \sum_{i=1}^{n} (x_i^2 - 10\cos(2\pi x_i)) \tag{6}$$

The shape of this function is shown in Fig.2 for two-dimensional case. The value of the global minimum of the function is 0. Searched area is -5 up to +5 for the function. We found the best setting of the particle swarm optimization for the function χ=1.0 and ω=0.9. Upper limitation of ϕ_1 and ϕ_2 are 2.0 and 1.0, respectively. Using the setting (See Table 1), we compare these four methods and the ordinary particle swarm optimization.

As shown in the figure, this function contains many local minimum points. It is generally difficult to find a global minimum using the gradient type of the method. It is difficult also for the particle swarm optimization to cope with the function. The past experiences will not give any clue to find the global minimum. This is one of difficult functions to obtain the global minimum.

Change of the best particle is also depicted in Fig.3. The horizontal axis is number of observations for the function. The ordinary particle swarm optimization requires the same number of observations with the number of particles in the population. Since the scheme 1 contains the simultaneous perturbation procedure, the scheme uses twice number of the observations. However, this does not change, even if the dimension of the parameters increases.

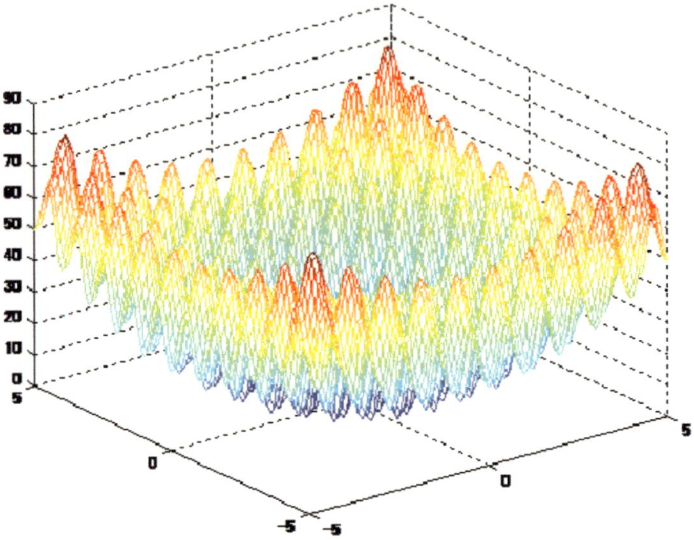

Figure 2. Rastrigin function

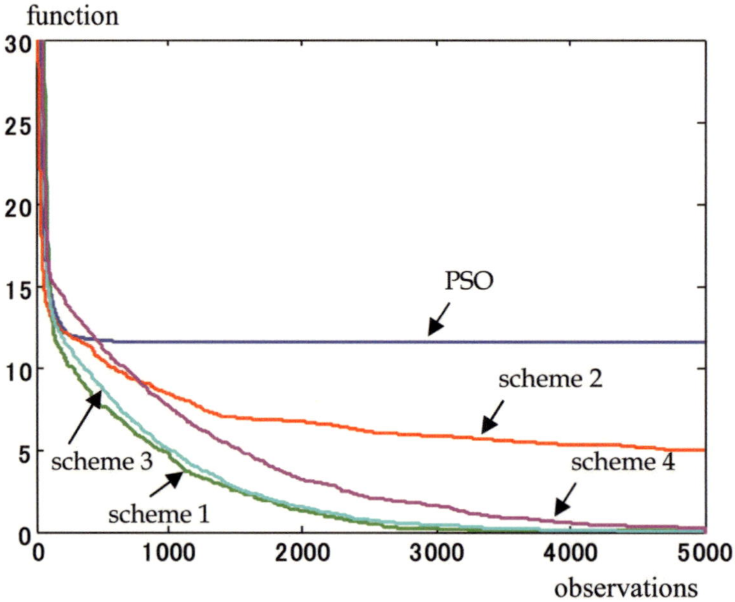

Figure 3. Change of the best particle for Rastrigin function

ϕ_1	ϕ_2	χ	ω	Scheme 1	Scheme 2	Scheme 3	Scheme 4
2.0	1.0	1.0	0.9	$\alpha = 0.000003$	$\alpha = 0.00003$	$\alpha = 0.000006$	$\alpha = 0.000003$

Table 1. Parameters setting for Rastrigin function

The scheme 2 has the number of the observations of the ordinary particle swarm optimization plus one, because only the best particle uses the simultaneous perturbation. The scheme 3 requires 1.5 times of number of the observation of the particle swarm optimization, because half of the particles in the population utilize the simultaneous perturbation. The scheme 4 basically uses the same number of the observations with the scheme 3. In our work, we take these different situations into account. For this function, scheme 1,3 and 4 have relatively good performance.

2. Rosenbrock function

Shape of the function is shown in Fig.4 for two-dimensional case. The value of the global minimum of the function is 0. Searched area is -2 up to +2. Parameters are shown in Table 2. Since the Rosenbrock has gradual descent, the gradient method with suitable gain coefficient will easily find the global minimum. However, we do not know the suitable gain coefficient so that the gradient method will be inefficient in many cases. On the other hand, the particle swarm optimization is beneficial for this kind of shape, because the momentum term accelerates moving speed and plural particles will be able to find the global minimum efficiently.

Change of the best particle is depicted in Fig.5. From Fig.5, we can see that the scheme 2 and the ordinary particle swarm optimization have relatively good performance for this function. As we mentioned, the ordinary gradient method has not good performance, the particle swarm optimization is suitable. If we add local search for the best particle, the performance will increase. The results illustrate this. The scheme 1 does not have the momentum term, it is replaced by the estimated gradient term by the simultaneous perturbation. The momentum term accelerates convergence and the gradient term does not work well for flat slope. It seems that this results in this slow convergence.

$$f(x)=\sum_{i=1}^{n-1}\left[100(x_i^2-x_{i+1})^2+(x_i-1)^2\right] \tag{7}$$

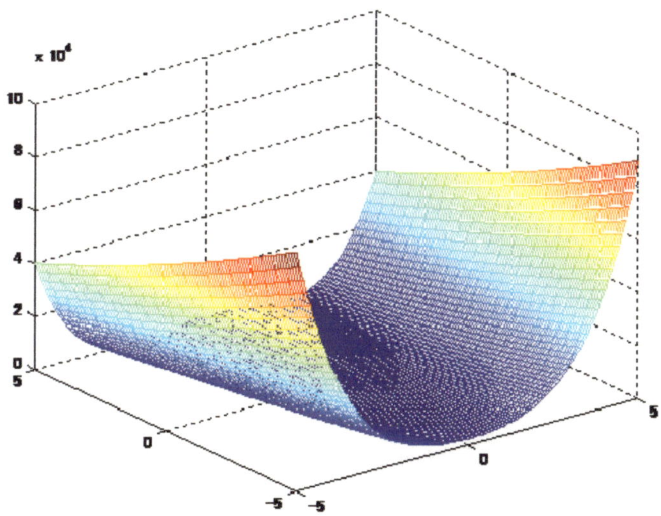

Figure 4. Rosenbrock function

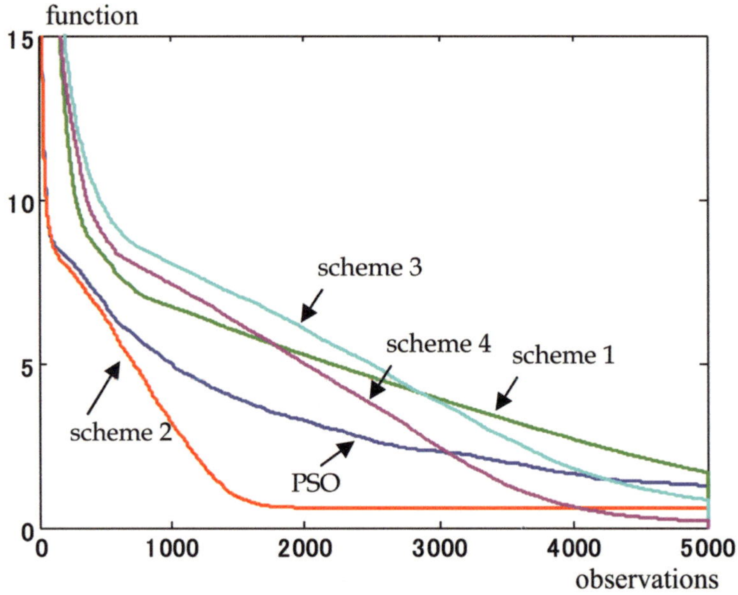

Figure 5. Change of the best particle for Rosenbrock function

ϕ_1	ϕ_2	χ	ω	Scheme 1	Scheme 2	Scheme 3	Scheme 4
1.5	1.0	1.0	0.9	$\alpha = 0.0000007$	$\alpha = 0.00000008$	$\alpha = 0.000000006$	$\alpha = 0.00000001$

Table 2. Parameters setting for Rosenbrock function

3. 2^n-minima function

The 2^n-minima function is

$$f(x) = \sum_{i=1}^{n} \left[x_i^4 - 16x_i^2 + 5x_i \right] \tag{8}$$

Shape of the function is shown in Fig.6. Searched area is -5 up to +5. Table 3 shows parameters setting. The value of the global minimum of the function is -783.32.

The function has some local minimum points and relatively flat bottom. This deteriorates search capability of the gradient method. Change of the best particle is also depicted in Fig.7. The scheme 4 has relatively good performance for this case. The function has flat bottom including a global minimum. In order to search the global minimum, it seems that the swarm search is useful. Searching the global minimum using many particles is efficient. Simultaneously, local search is necessary to find exact position of the global minimum. It seems that the scheme 4 matched for the case.

As a result, we can say that the gradient search is important and combination with the particle swarm optimization will give us a powerful tool.

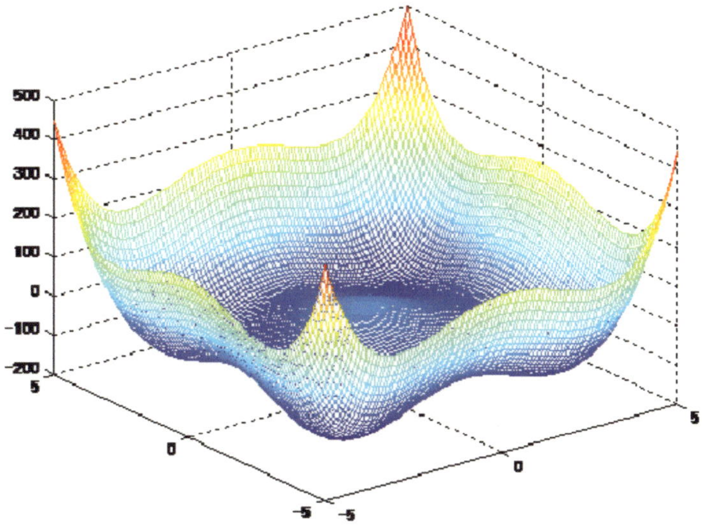

Figure 6. 2^n-minima function

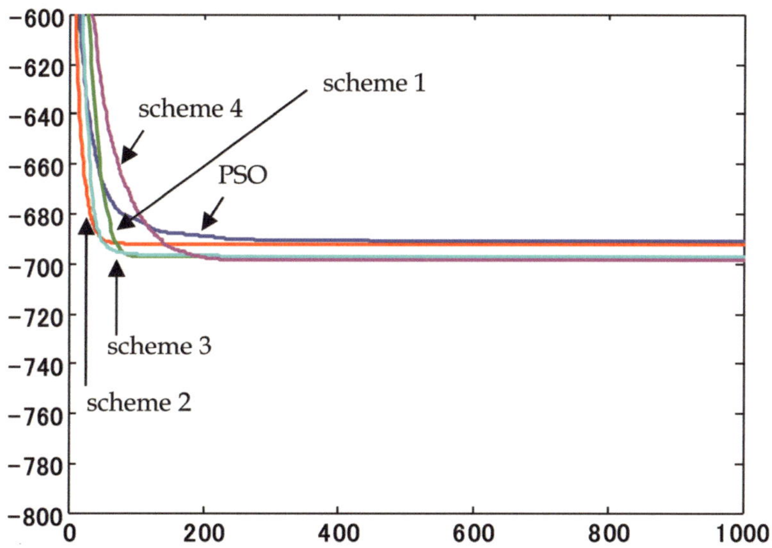

Figure 7. Change of the best particle for 2^n-minima function

ϕ_1	ϕ_2	χ	ω	Scheme 1	Scheme 2	Scheme 3	Scheme 4
2.0	1.5	1.0	0.9	$\alpha = 0.00009$	$\alpha = 0.0008$	$\alpha = 0.0008$	$\alpha = 0.000005$

Table 3. Parameters setting for 2^n-minima function

5. FPGA implementation

Now, we implement the simultaneous perturbation particle swarm optimization using FPGA. Then we can realize one feature of parallel operation of the particle swarm optimization. This results in higher operation speed for optimization problems.
We adopted VHDL (VHSIC Hardware Description Language) in basic circuit design for FPGA. The design result by VHDL is configured on MU200 - SX60 board with EP1S60F1020C6 (Altera) (see Fig.8). This FPGA contains 57,120 LEs with 5,215,104 bit user memory.

Figure 8. FPGA board MU200-SX60 (MMS)

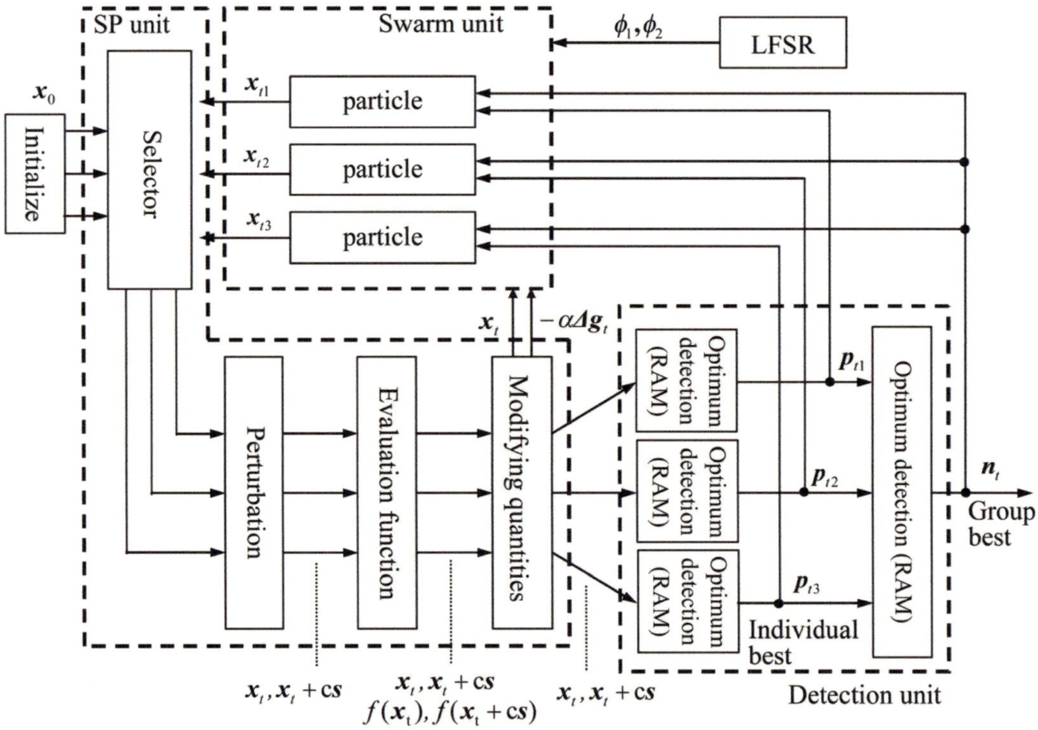

Figure 9. Configuration of the SP particle swarm optimization system

Visual Elite (Summit) is used for the basic deign. Synplify Pro (Synplicity) carried out the logical synthesis for the VHDL. QuartusII (Altera) is used for wiring.Overall system configuration is shown in Fig.9. Basically, the system consists of three units; swarm unit, detection unit and simultaneous perturbation unit.

In this system, we prepared three particles. These particles works parallel to obtain values of a target function, and are updated their positions and velocity. Therefore, even if the system has many particles, this does not effect on the overall operation speed. Number of the particles in this system is restricted by the scale of target FPGA. We should economize the design, if we would like to contain many particles.

The target function with two parameters x_1 and x_2 is defined as follow;

$$f(\boldsymbol{x}) = 16 + \sum_{i=1}^{2}(x_i^2 - 8(1 - 4x_i^2 + \frac{1}{4}x_i^4 - \frac{1}{128}x_i^6 + \frac{1}{8192}x_i^8)) \tag{9}$$

Based on Rastrigin function, we assume this test function with optimal value of 0 and 8th order. We would like to find the optimal point (0.0 0.0) in the range [-5.5 5.5]. Then optimal value of the function is 0. Fig. 10 shows shape of the function.

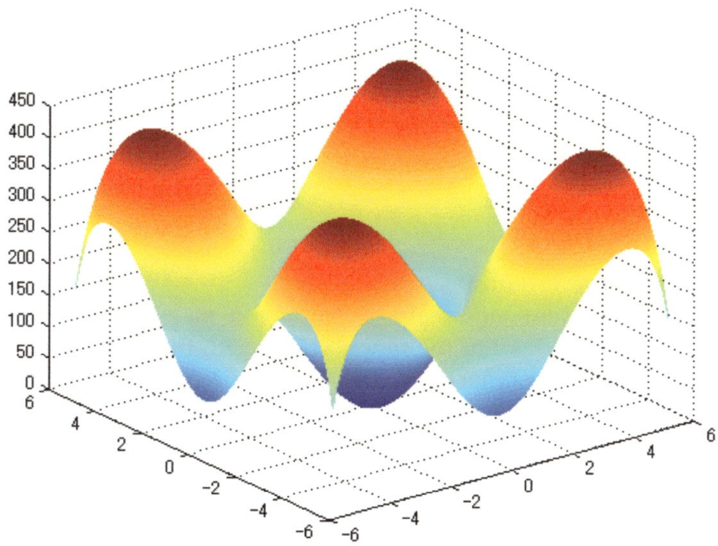

Figure 10. Shape of the target function

5.1 Swarm unit

Swarm unit includes some particles which are candidate of the optimum point. Candidate values are memorized and updated in these particle parts.

Configuration of the particle part is shown in Fig. 11. This part holds its position value and velocity. At the same time, modifying quantities for all particles are sent by the simultaneous perturbation unit. The particle part updates its position and velocity based on these modifying quantities.

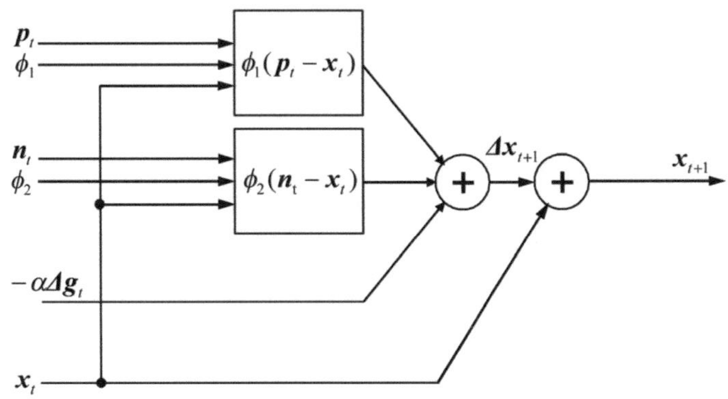

Figure 11. Particle part

5.2 Detection unit

The detection unit finds and holds the best estimated value for each particle. We refer this estimator as individual best. And based on the individual best values of the each particle, the unit searches the best one that all the particles have ever found. We call it the group best. The individual best values and the group best value are stored in RAM. For iteration, new positions for all particles are compared with corresponding values stored in RAM. If new position is better, it is stored, that is, the individual best value is updated. Moreover, these are used to determine the group best value.

These individual best values and the group best value are used in the swarm unit to update the velocity.

5.3 Simultaneous perturbation unit

The simultaneous perturbation unit realizes calculation of evaluation function for each particle, estimation of the gradient of the function based on the simultaneous perturbation. As a result, the unit produces estimated gradient for all the particles. The results are sent to the swarm unit.

5.4 Implementation result

Single precision floating point expression IEEE 574 is adopted to express all values in the system. Ordinary floating point operations are used to realize the simultaneous perturbation particle swarm optimization algorithm.

We searched the area of [-5.5 5.5]. Initial positions of the particles were determined randomly from (2.401, 2.551), (-4.238, 4.026) or (-3.506, 1.753). Initial velocity was all zero. Then we defined value of χ is 1. Coefficients ϕ_1 and ϕ_2 in the algorithm were selected from 2i(=2), 2°(=1), 2-i(=0.5), 2-2(=0.25), 2-3(=0.125), 2-4(=0.0625), 2-5(=0.03125) or 2-6(=0.015625). This simplifies multiplication of these coefficients. The multiplication can be carried out by addition for exponent component.

Design result is depicted in Fig.12. 84% of LE is used for all this system design. We should economize the scale of the design, if we would like to implement much more particles in the system. Or, we can also adopt time-sharing usage of the single particle part. Then total operation speed will deteriorate.

Flow Status	Successful - Tue Apr 24 16:28:30 2007
Quartus II Version	6.0 Build 178 04/27/2006 SJ Full Version
Revision Name	SP_PSO_ver2
Top-level Entity Name	SP_PSO_ver2
Family	Stratix
Device	EP1S60F1020C6
Timing Models	Final
Met timing requirements	No
Total logic elements	47,877 / 57,120 (84 %)
Total pins	13 / 782 (2 %)
Total virtual pins	0
Total memory bits	0 / 5,215,104 (0 %)
DSP block 9-bit elements	40 / 144 (28 %)
Total PLLs	0 / 12 (0 %)
Total DLLs	0 / 2 (0 %)

Figure 12. Design result

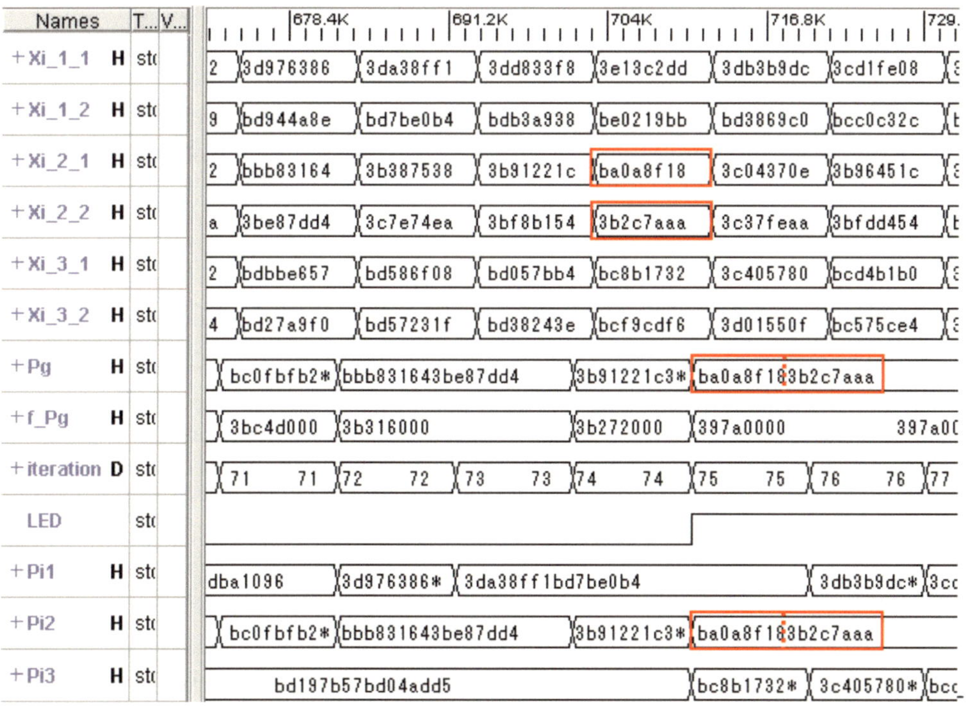

Figure 13. Simulation result

Fig.13 shows a simulation result by Visual Elite. Upper six signals xi_1_1 upto xi_3_2 denote values of parameters x_1 and x_2 of three particles, respectively. Lower three signals HI upto Pi3 are individual best values of three particles at the present iteration. x_1 and x_2 values are consecutively memorized. Between these, the best one becomes group best shown in Pg signal. f_Pg is the corresponding function value. In Fig.13 between three particle, the second particle of Pi2 became the group best value of Pg. We can find END flag of "LED" at 75th iteration.

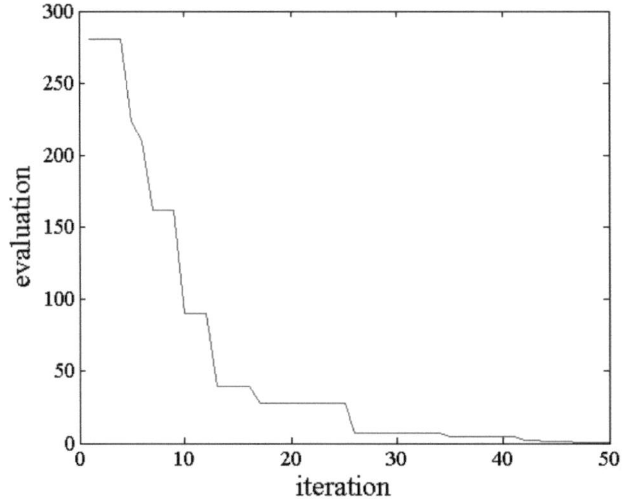

Figure 14. Operation result

Fig.14 shows a change of the evaluation function of the best of the swarm for iteration. The system easily finds the optimum point with three particles. About 50 iteration, the best particle is very close to global optimum. As mentioned before, after 75 iteration, the system stoped with an end condition.

6. Conclusion

In this paper, we presented hardware implementation of the particle swarm optimization algorithm which is combination of the ordinary particle swarm optimization and the simultaneous perturbation method. FPGA is used to realize the system. This algorithm utilizes local information of objective function effectively without lack of advantage of the original particle swarm optimization. Moreover, the FPGA implementation gives higher operation speed effectively using parallelism of the particle swarm optimization. We confirmed viability of the system.

7. Acknowledgement

This work is financially supported by Grant-in-Aid for Scientific Research (No.19500198) of the Ministry of Education, Culture, Sports, Science and Technology (MEXT) of Japan, and the Intelligence system technology and kansei information processing research group,

Organization for Research and Development of Innovative Science and Technology, Kansai University, and "Academic Frontier" Project of MEXT of Japan for Kansai University.

8. References

Alespector, J.; Meir, R.; Yuhas, B.; Jayakumar, A. & Lippe,D. (1993). A Parallel Gradient Descent Method for Learning in Analog VLSI Neural Networks, In: *Advances in neural information processing systems,* Hanson, S., Cowan, J., Lee, C. (Eds.), 836-844, Vol.5, Morgan Kaufmann Publisher, Cambridge, MA

Bo Y.; Yunping C. & Zunlian Z.(2007). Survey on Applications of Particle Swarm Optimization in Electric Power Systems, IEEE International Conference on Control and Automation, pp. 481-486

Bonabeau, E.; Dorigo, M. & Theraulaz, G. (1999). Swarm intelligence: from natural to artificial systems, Oxford University Press, 0-19-513159-2, NY

Cauwenberghs, G. (1993). A Fast Stochastic Error-descent Algorithm for Supervised Learning and Optimization,' In: *Advances in neural information processing systems,* Hanson, S., Cowan, J., Lee, C. (Eds.), 244-251, Vol.5, Morgan Kaufmann Publisher, Cambridge, MA

del Valle, Y.; Venayagamoorthy, G.K.; Mohagheghi, S.; Hernandez, J.-C. & Harley, R.G.(2008). Particle Swarm Optimization: Basic Concepts, Variants and Applications in Power Systems, *IEEE transactions on evolutionary computation,* Vol. 12, No. 2,171-195

Engelbrecht, A.P.(2006). Fundamentals of Computational Swarm Intelligence, John Wiley & Sons Ltd., West Sussex, 0-470-09191-6

Fernandez, P. M.; Rubio, B. A.; Garcia, R. P.; Garcia, S.G. & Gomez, M. R.(2007). Particle-Swarm Optimization in Antenna Design: Optimization of Log-Periodic Dipole Arrays, *IEEE Antennas and Propagation Magazine,* Vol. 49, No. 4,34-47

Juang, C. (2004). A Hybrid of Genetic Algorithm and Particle Swarm Optimization for Recurrent Network Design, *IEEE Transaction on System, Man, and Cybernetics – Part B: Cybernetics,* Vol. 34, No.2,997-1006,

Kennedy, J. & Eberhart, R. (1995). Particle Swarm Optimization, Proceedings of the IEEE Conference on Neural Networks, pp.1942-1948,

Maeda, Y., Hirano, H. & Kanata, Y. (1995). A Learning Rule of Neural Networks Via Simultaneous Perturbation and Its Hardware Implementation, *Neural Networks,* Vol.8, No.2,251-259,

Maeda, Y. & de Figueiredo, R. J. P. (1997). Learning Rules for Neuro-controller Via Simultaneous Perturbation, *IEEE Transaction on Neural Networks,* Vol.8, No.5,1119-1130, Maeda,

Y. & Tada, T. (2003). FPGA Implementation of a Pulse Density Neural Network with Learning Ability Using Simultaneous Perturbation, *IEEE Transaction on Neural Networks,* Vol.14, No.3, 688-695,

Maeda, Y. & Wakamura, M. (2005). Simultaneous Perturbation Learning Rule for Recurrent Neural Networks and Its FPGA Implementation, *IEEE Transaction on Neural Networks,* Vol. 16, No.6,1664-1672,

Maeda, Y. & Kuratani, T. (2006). Simultaneous Perturbation Particle Swarm Optimization, 2006 IEEE Congress on Evolutionary Computation, pp. 2687-2691,

Nanbo, J. & Rahmat-Samii, Y.(2007). Advances in Particle Swarm Optimization for Antenna Designs: Real-Number, Binary, Single-Objective and Multiobjective Implementations, *IEEE Transactions on Antennas and Propagation*, Vol. 55, No. 3, Part 1,556-567

Parsopoulos, K. E. & Vrahatis, M. N. (2004). On the Computation of All Global Minimizers Through Particle Swarm Optimization, *IEEE Transaction on Evolutionary Computation*, Vol. 8, No.3,211-224,

Spall, J. C. (1987). A Stochastic Approximation Technique for Generating Maximum Likelihood Parameter Estimation, Proceedings of the 1987 American Control Conference, pp.1161-1167, Spall, J. C. (1992). Multivariate Stochastic Approximation Using a Simultaneous Perturbation Gradient Approximation, *IEEE Transaction on Automatic Control*, Vol. 37, No.3,332-341,

22

Particle Swarm Optimization with External Archives for Interactive Fuzzy Multiobjective Nonlinear Programming

Takeshi Matsui, Masatoshi Sakawa, Kosuke Kato and Koichi Tamada
Hiroshima University
Japan

1. Introduction

In general nonlinear programming problems to find a solution which minimizes an objective function under given constraints, one whose objective function and constraint region are convex is called a convex programming problem. For such convex programming problems, there have been proposed many efficient solution method as the successive quadratic programming method and the general gradient method. Unfortunately, there have not been proposed any decisive solution method for nonconvex programming problems. As practical solution methods, meta-heuristic optimization methods as the simulated annealing method and the genetic algorithm have been proposed.

In recent years, however, more speedy and more accurate optimization methods have been desired because the size of actual problems has been increasing.

As a new optimization method, particle swarm optimization (PSO) was proposed (Kennedy & Eberhart, 1995). PSO is a search method simulating the social behavior that each individual in the population acts by using both the knowledge owned by it and that owned by the population, and they search better points by constituting the population. The authors proposed a revised PSO (rPSO) by incorporating the homomorphous mapping and the multiple stretching technique in order to deal with shortcomings of the original PSO as the concentration to local solution and the inapplicability of constrained problems (Matsui et al., 2008).

In recent years, with the diversification of social requirements, the demand for the programs with multiple objective functions, which may be conflicting with each other, rather than a single-objective function, has been increasing (e.g. maximizing the total profit and minimizing the amount of pollution in a production planning). Since there does not always exist a complete optimal solution which optimizes all objectives simultaneously for multiobjective programming problems, the Pareto optimal solution or non-inferior solution, is defined, where a solution is Pareto optimal if any improvement of one objective function can be achieved only at the expense of at least one of the other objective functions. For such multiobjective optimization problems, fuzzy programming approaches (e.g. (Zimmermann, 1983), (Rommelfanger, 1996), considering the imprecise nature of the DM's judgments in multiobjective optimization problems, seem to be very applicable and promising. In the application of the fuzzy set theory into multiobjective linear programming problems started

(Zimmermann, 1978), it has been implicitly assumed that the fuzzy decision or the minimum-operator of (Bellman & Zadeh ,1970) is the proper representation of the DM's fuzzy preferences. Thereby, M. Sakawa et al. have proposed interactive fuzzy satisficing methods to derive satisficing solutions for the decision maker along with checking the local preference of the decision maker through interactions for various multiobjective programming problems (Sakawa et al, 2002).

In this paper, focusing on multiobjective nonlinear programming problems, we attempt to derive satisficing solutions through the interactive fuzzy satisficing method. Since problems solved in the interactive fuzzy satificing method for multiobjective nonlinear programming problems are nonlinear programming problems, we adopt rPSO (Matsui et al, 2008) as solution methods to them. In particular, we consider measures to improve the performance of rPSO in applying it to solving the augmented minimax problem.

2. Multiobjective nonlinear programming problems

In this paper, we consider multiobjective nonlinear programming problem as follows:

$$\begin{aligned} &\text{minimize} && f_l(\boldsymbol{x}),\ l=1, 2, \ldots, k \\ &\text{subject to} && g_i(\boldsymbol{x}) \leq 0,\ i=1, 2, \ldots, m \\ &&& l_j \leq x_j \leq u_j,\ j=1, 2, \ldots, n \\ &&& \boldsymbol{x} = (x_1, x_2, \ldots, x_n)^T \in R^n \end{aligned} \tag{1}$$

where $f_l(\cdot)$, $g_i(\cdot)$ are linear or nonlinear functions, l_j and u_j are the lower limit and the upper limit of each decision variable x_j. In addition, we denote the feasible region of (1) by X.

3. An interactive fuzzy satisficing method

In order to consider the imprecise nature of the decision maker's judgments for each objective function in (1), if we introduce the fuzzy goals such as ``$f_l(\boldsymbol{x})$ should be substantially less than or equal to a certain value'', (1) can be rewritten as:

$$\underset{\boldsymbol{x}\in X}{\text{maximize}} \quad (\mu_1(f_1(\boldsymbol{x})), \ldots, \mu_k(f_k(\boldsymbol{x}))) \tag{2}$$

where $\mu_l(\cdot)$ is the membership function to quantify the fuzzy goal for the l th objective function in (1).

Since (2) is regarded as a fuzzy multiobjective decision making problem, there rarely exists a complete optimal solution that simultaneously optimizes all objective functions. As a reasonable solution concept for the fuzzy multiobjective decision making problem, M. Sakawa defined M-Pareto optimality on the basis of membership function values by directly extending the Pareto optimality in the ordinary multiobjective programming problem (Sakawa, 1993). In the interactive fuzzy satisficing method, in order to generate a candidate for the satisficing solution which is also M-Pareto optimal, the decision maker is asked to specify the aspiration levels of achievement for all membership functions, called the reference membership levels (Sakawa, 1993). For the decision maker's reference membership levels $\bar{\mu}_l$, l=1, ..., k, the corresponding M-Pareto optimal solution, which is nearest to the requirements in the minimax sense or better than it if the reference membership levels are attainable, is obtained by solving the following augmented minimax problem (3).

$$\underset{x \in X}{\text{minimize}} \quad \max_{l=1,\dots,k} \left\{ (\bar{\mu}_l - \mu_l(f_l(\boldsymbol{x}))) + \rho \sum_{i=1}^{k} (\bar{\mu}_i - \mu_i(f_i(\boldsymbol{x}))) \right\} \tag{3}$$

where ρ is a sufficiently small positive number.

We can now construct the interactive algorithm in order to derive the satisficing solution for the decision maker from the M-Pareto optimal solution set. The procedure of an interactive fuzzy satisficing method is summarized as follows.

Step 1:

Under a given constraint, minimal value and maximum one of each objective function are calculated by solving following problems.

$$\underset{x \in X}{\text{minimize}} \quad f_l(\boldsymbol{x}),\ l=1, 2, \dots, k \tag{4}$$

$$\underset{x \in X}{\text{maximize}} \quad f_l(\boldsymbol{x}),\ l=1, 2, \dots, k \tag{5}$$

Step 2:

In consideration of individual minimal value and maximum one of each objective function, the decision maker subjectively specifies membership functions $\mu_l(f_l(\boldsymbol{x}))$, $l=1, \dots, k$ to quantify fuzzy goals for objective functions. Next, the decision maker sets initial reference membership function values $\bar{\mu}_l$, $l=1, \dots, k$.

Step 3:

We solve the following augmented minimax problem corresponding to current reference membership function values (3).

Step 4:

If the decision maker is satisfied with the solution obtained in Step 3, the interactive procedure is finished. Otherwise, the decision maker updates reference membership function values $\bar{\mu}_l$, $l=1, 2, \dots, k$ based on current membership function values and objective function values, and return to Step 3.

4. Particle swarm optimization

Particle swarm optimization (Kennedy & Eberhart, 1995) is based on the social behavior that a population of individuals adapts to its environment by returning to promising regions that were previously discovered (Kennedy & Spears, 1998). This adaptation to the environment is a stochastic process that depends on both the memory of each individual, called particle, and the knowledge gained by the population, called swarm. In the numerical implementation of this simplified social model, each particle has four attributes: the position vector in the search space, the velocity vector and the best position in its track and the best position of the swarm. The process can be outlined as follows.

Step 1:

Generate the initial swarm involving N particles at random.

Step 2:

Calculate the new velocity vector of each particle, based on its attributes.

Step 3:

Calculate the new position of each particle from the current positon and its new velocity vector.

Step 4:

If the termination condition is satisfied, stop. Otherwise, go to Step 2.

To be more specific, the new velocity vector of the *i*-th particle at time *t*, $\boldsymbol{v}_i^{t+1}$ is calculated by the following scheme introduced by (Shi & Eberhart, 1998).

$$\boldsymbol{v}_i^{t+1} := \omega^t \boldsymbol{v}_i^t + c_1 R_1^t (\boldsymbol{p}_i^t - \boldsymbol{x}_i^t) + c_2 R_2^t (\boldsymbol{p}_g^t - \boldsymbol{x}_i^t) \tag{6}$$

In (6), R_1^t and R_2^t are random numbers between 0 and 1, p_i^t is the best position of the *i*-th particle in its track and p_g^t is the best position of the swarm. There are three problem dependent parameters, the inertia of the particle ω^t, and two trust parameters c_1, c_2. Then, the new position of the *i*-th particle at time *t*, x_i^{t+1}, is calculated from (7).

$$x_i^{t+1} := x_i^t + v_i^{t+1} \tag{7}$$

where x_i^t is the current position of the *i*-th particle at time *t*. The *i*-th particle calculates the next search direction vector $\boldsymbol{v}_i^{t+1}$ by (6) in consideration of the current search direction vector $\boldsymbol{v}_i^t$, the direction vector going from the current search position x_i^t to the best position in its track p_i^t and the direction vector going from the current search position x_i^t to the best position of the swarm p_g^t, moves from the current position x_i^t to the next search position x_i^{t+1} calculated by (7). The parameter ω^t controls the amount of the move to search globally in early stage and to search localy by decreasing ω^t gradually.

The searching procedure of PSO is shown in Fig. 1.

Comparing the evaluation value of a particle after movement, $f(\boldsymbol{x}_i^{t+1})$, with that of the best position in its track, $f(p_i^t)$, if $f(\boldsymbol{x}_i^{t+1})$ is better than $f(p_i^t)$, then the best position in its track is updated as $p_i^t := x_i^{t+1}$. Futhermore, if $f(p_i^{t+1})$ is better than $f(p_g^t)$, then the best position in the swarm is updated as $p_g^{t+1} := p_i^{t+1}$.

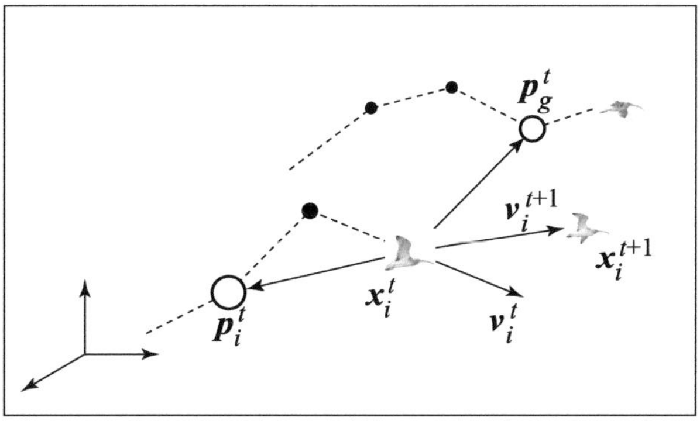

Figure 1. Movement of a particle in PSO

In the original PSO method, however, there are drawbacks that it is not directly applicable to constrained problems and it is liable to stopping around local optimal solutions.
To deal with these drawbacks of the original PSO method, we incorporate the bisection method and a homomorphous mapping to carry out the search considering constraints.
In addition, we proposed the multiple stretching technique and modified move schemes of particles to restrain the stopping around local optimal solutions (Matsui et al., 2008).
Thus, we applied rPSO for interactive fuzzy multiobjective nonlinear programming problems and proposed multiobjective revised PSO (MOrPSO) method incorporating move scheme to the nondominated particle in order to search effectively for the augmented minimax problmes (Matsui et al., 2007). In the application of large-scale augmented minimax problem, MOrPSO method is superior than rPSO method on efficiency. On the other hand, MOrPSO method is inferior on accuracy.

5. Improvement of MOrPSO

We show the results of the applicaltion of the original rPSO (Matsui et al., 2008) and MOrPSO (Matsui et al., 2007) to the augmented minimax problem for multiobjective nonlinear programming problem with l = 2, n = 55 and m = 100 in Table 1. In these experiments we set the swarm size N = 70, the maximal search generation number $T_{\max}$ = 5000. In addition, we use the following membership functions: $\bar{\mu}_1 = 1.0$, $\bar{\mu}_2 = 1.0$.

method	objective function value (minimize)			computational time (sec)
	best	average	worst	
rPSO	0.3464	0.4471	0.5632	144.45
MOrPSO	0.3614	0.4095	0.4526	129.17

Table 1. Results of the application to the augmented minimax problem

From Table 1, MOrPSO method is superior than rPSO method on efficiency in the average value, the worst one and computational time. However, the best value of MOrPSO method is worse than that of rPSO method, MOrPSO method is inferior on accuracy. We consider the case that the search accuracy turns worse incorporating the direction to nondominated particle (approximate M-Pareto optimal solution) in MOrPSO method.

In this paper, we improve the search accuracy incorporating external archives to record nondominated particles in the swarm. Here, as recorded nondominated particle increases in archives, computational time increases in order to judge whether a particle is nondominated.

Therefore, there is many computational time that we record all the nondominated particles to archives. Thus we divide membership function space with hypercube shown in Fig. 2 and record a number of nondominated particle included in each hypercube.

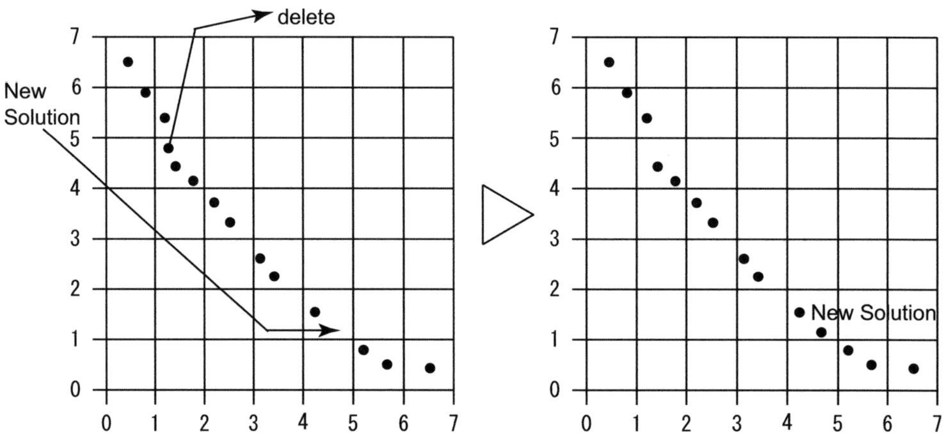

Figure 2. reduction of archives with grid (l=2)

When a number of nondominated particle recorded in archives is greater than a fixed number, we delete one particle from hypercube with many numbers of nondominated particle and record new solution (particle). We consider that can reduce computational time and express approximate M-Pareto optimal front by a few particles incorporating reduction of archives. We show the results of the application of MOrPSO method incorporating reduction of archives (MOrPSO-1) to the above same problem in Table 2.

method	objective function value (minimize)			computational time (sec)
	best	average	worst	
MOrPSO-1	0.4379	0.4708	0.5030	166.78

Table 2. Results of the application to the augmented minimax problem

From Table 2, it is clear that all of the best, average, worst value and computational time obtained by MOrPSO-1 are worse than those obtained by MOrPSO. We consider that a particle moves using nondominated particle which is not useful since all nondominated particles in archives are used in search. Thus, in the membership function space, we consider that information of a particle exsiting far from the reference membership value is hard to contribute to search and introduce threshold value for selection of nondominated particle as shown in Fig. 3.

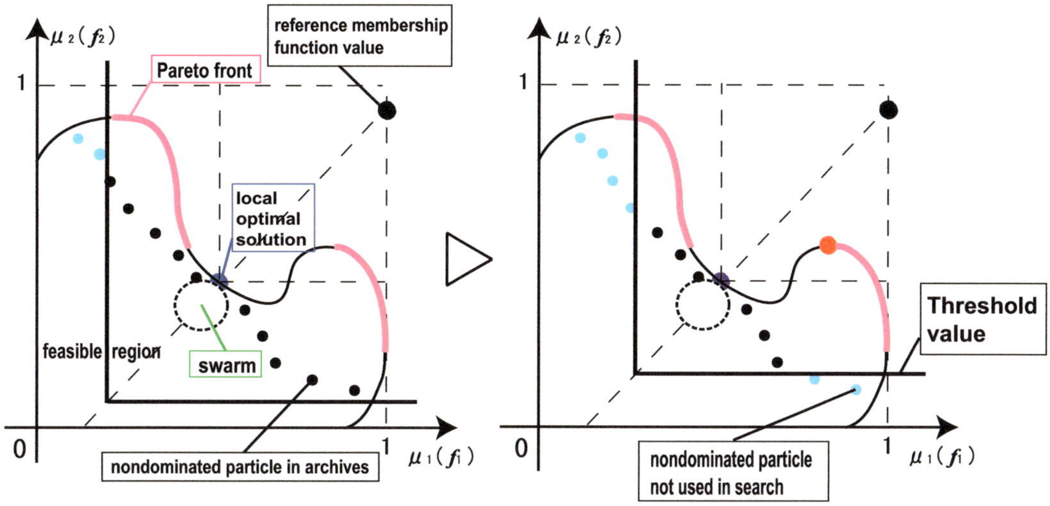

Figure 3. Limit of nondominated particle by threshold value (l=2)

We show the results of the application of MOrPSO method incorporating limitation by threshold value (MOrPSO-2) to the above same problem in Table 3.

method	objective function value (minimize)			computational time (sec)
	best	average	worst	
MOrPSO-2	0.2993	0.3430	0.3777	165.71

Table 3. Results of the application to the augmented minimax problem

From Table 3, in the application of MOrPSO method incorporating limitation by threshold value (MOrPSO-2), we can get better solutions in the sense of best, average and worst than those obtained by rPSO and MOrPSO.

In order to show the efficiency of the proposed PSO, we consider the multiobjective nonlinear programming problem with l = 2 and n = 100. In these experiments, we set the swarm size N = 100, the maximal search generation number T_{max} = 5000. In addition, we use the following reference membership function values: $\bar{\mu}_1 = 1.0$, $\bar{\mu}_2 = 1.0$.

method	objective function value (minimize)			computational time (sec)
	best	average	worst	
rPSO [6]	0.2547	0.2783	0.3251	26.91
MOrPSO [7]	0.1950	0.2033	0.2208	32.58
MOrPSO-2	0.2018	0.2320	0.2711	28.11

Table 4. Results of the application to the augmented minimax problem

From Table 4, it is clear that all of the best, average, worst value and computational time obtained by MOrPSO-2 are worse than those obtained by MOrPSO. We consider that it occurs to make no use of the information of nondominiated particle in search since there is a few nondominiated particle information stored in archives of MOrPSO-2 and only the best value of each objective function and the best value limb of the augmented minimax problem are saved. Therefore, we propose MOrPSO with external archives (MOrPSO-EA) using nondominated particle in the swarm same as MOrPSO in order to store various nondominated particle as possible in normal search. And the results of the application are shown in Table 5.

method	objective function value (minimize)			computational time (sec)
	best	average	worst	
MOrPSO	0.1950	0.2033	0.2208	32.58
MOrPSO-EA	0.1746	0.1787	0.1842	29.01

Table 5. Results of the application to the augmented minimax problem

From Table 5, in the application of MOrPSO-EA, we can get better solutions in the sense of best, average and worst than those obtained by MOrPSO.

6. Numerical examples

In MOrPSO, it searches globaly in the early generation and localy decreasing ω^t. However, we consider that necessity to search globaly in the early generation is low after the second time since the information of nondominated particle to current generation is stored in archives in proposed MOrPSO. Therefore, we consider that the proposed MOrPSO can search localy in the early generation.

In order to show the efficiency of the proposed MOrPSO, we consider the multiobjective nonlinear programming problem with l = 2 and n = 100 and m = 55. In these experiments, we set the maximal search generation number of MOrPSO and the proposed MOrPSO (MOrPSO-EA) in the 1st interactive $T_{\max}$ = 5000 and in the 2nd and 3rd interactive $T_{\max}$ = 3000. We show the results of the application are shown in Table 6 and 7.

interactive	1st	2nd	3rd
$\bar{\mu}_1$	1.0	1.0	0.85
$\bar{\mu}_2$	1.0	0.7	0.7
$\mu_1(x)$	0.6157	0.8003	0.7575
$\mu_2(x)$	0.6157	0.5003	0.6075
minimax value	0.3844	0.1997	0.0925
time (sec)	127.20	128.89	131.25

Table 6. Interactive fuzzy programming through MOrPSO

interactive	1st	2nd	3rd
$\bar{\mu}_1$	1.0	1.0	0.85
$\bar{\mu}_2$	1.0	0.7	0.7
$\mu_1(x)$	0.7183	0.8458	0.8042
$\mu_2(x)$	0.7183	0.5458	0.6542
minimax value	0.2817	0.1542	0.0458
time (sec)	157.37	98.58	101.16

Table 7. Interactive fuzzy programming through MOrPSO-EA (proposed)

From Table 6 and 7, MOrPSO-EA is superior than MOrPSO on accuracy. In addition, we can decrease total computational time by reducing the maximal search generation number.

6. Conclusion

In this research, we focused on multiobjective nonlinear programming problems and proposed a new MOrPSO technique which is accuracy for in applying the interactive fuzzy satisficing method. In particular, considering the features of augmented minimax problems solved in the interactive fuzzy satisficing method, we incorporated use of external archives, reduction of archives and the limitation of threshold value. Finally, we showed the efficiency of the proposed MOrPSO by applying it to numerical examples.

7. References

R.E. Bellman & L.A. Zadeh. (1970). Decision making in a fuzzy environment, *Management Science*, Vol. 17, pp. 141-164

C.A.C Coello, G.T. Pulido, M.S. Lechuga. (2004). Handling multiple objectives with particle swarm optimization, *IEEE Transactions on Evolutionary Computation*, Vol. 8, No. 3, pp. 256-279

V.L. Huang, A.K. Qin, K. Deb, E. Zitzler, P.N. Suganthan, J.J. Liang, M. Preuss, S. Huband. (2007). Problem definitions for performance assessment on multi-objective optimization algorithms, *http://www.ntu.edu. sg/home/EPNSugan/index-files/CEC-07/CEC-07-TR-13-Feb.pdf*

J. Kennedy & R.C. Eberhart. (1995). Particle Swarm Optimization, *Proceedings of IEEE International Conference on Neural Networks*, pp. 1942-1948

T. Matsui, K. Kato, M. Sakawa, T. Uno, K. Morihara. (2008). Nonlinear Programming Based on Particle Swarm Optimization, In: *Advances in Industrial Engineering and Operations Research*, Alan H. S. Chan, Sio-Iong Ao (Ed.), pp. 173-183, Springer, New York, 2008.

T. Matsui, M. Sakawa, K. Kato, T. Uno, K. Tamada. (2007). An interactive fuzzy satisficing method through particle swarm optimization for multiobjective nonlinear programming problems, *Proceedings of the 2007 IEEE Symposium Series on Computational Intelligence*, pp. 71-76

H. Rommelfanger. (1996). Fuzzy linear programming and applications, *European Journal of Operational Research*, vol. 92, pp. 512-528

M. Sakawa. (1993). *Fuzzy Sets and Interactive Multiobjective Optimization*, Plenum Press, New York

M. Sakawa, K. Kato, T. Suzuki. (2002). An interactvie fuzzy satisficing method for multiobjective non-convex programming problems through genetic algorithms, *Proceedings of 8th Japan Society for Fuzzy Theory and Systems Chugoku / Shikoku Branch Office Meeting*, pp. 33-36

Y.H. Shi & R.C. Eberhart. (1998). A modified particle swarm optimizer, *Proceedings of IEEE International Conference on Evolutionary Computation*, pp. 69-73

H.-J. Zimmermann. (1978). Fuzzy programming and linear programming with several objective functions, *Fuzzy Sets and Systems*, Vol. 1 pp. 45-55

H.-J. Zimmermann. (1983). Fuzzy mathematical programming, *Computers & Operations Research*, Vol. 10, pp. 291-298

23

Using Opposition-based Learning with Particle Swarm Optimization and Barebones Differential Evolution

Mahamed G.H. Omran
Gulf University for Science and Technology
Kuwait

1. Introduction

Particle swarm optimization (PSO) (Kennedy & Eberhart, 1995) and differential evolution (DE) (Storn & Price, 1995) are two stochastic, population-based optimization methods, which have been applied successfully to a wide range of problems as summarized in Engelbrecht (2005) and Price et al. (2005).

A number of variations of both PSO and DE have been developed in the past decade to improve the performance of these algorithms (Engelbrecht, 2005; Price et al. 2005). One class of variations includes hybrids between PSO and DE, where the advantages of the two approaches are combined. The barebones DE (BBDE) is a PSO-DE hybrid algorithm proposed by Omran et al. (2007) which combines concepts from the barebones PSO (Kennedy 2003) and the recombination operator of DE. The resulting algorithm eliminates the control parameters of PSO and replaces the static DE control parameters with dynamically changing parameters to produce an almost parameter-free, self-adaptive, optimization algorithm.

Recently, opposition-based learning (OBL) was proposed by Tizhoosh (2005) and was successfully applied to several problems (Rahnamayan et al., 2008). The basic concept of OBL is the consideration of an estimate and its corresponding opposite estimate simultaneously to approximate the current candidate solution. Opposite numbers were used by Rahnamayan et al. (2008) to enhance the performance of Differential Evolution. In addition, Han and He (2007) and Wang et al. (2007) used OBL to improve the performance of PSO. However, in both cases, several parameters were added to the PSO that are difficult to tune. Wang et al. (2007) used OBL during swarm initialization and in each iteration with a user-specified probability. In addition, Cauchy mutation is applied to the best particle to avoid being trapping in local optima. Similarly, Han and He (2007) used OBL in the initialization phase and also during each iteration. However, a constriction factor is used to enhance the convergence speed.

In this chapter, OBL is used to improve the performance of PSO and BBDE without adding any extra parameter. The performance of the proposed methods is investigated when applied to several benchmark functions. The experiments conducted show that OBL improves the performance of both PSO and BBDE.

The remainder of the chapter is organized as follows: PSO is summarized in Section 2. DE is presented in Section 3. Section 4 provides an overview of BBDE. OBL is briefly reviewed in

Section 5. The proposed methods are presented in Section 6. Section 7 presents and discusses the results of the experiments. Finally, Section 8 concludes the chaper.

2. Particle Swarm Optimization

Particle swarm optimization (PSO) is a stochastic, population-based optimization algorithm modeled after the simulation of social behavior of bird flocks. In a PSO system, a swarm of individuals (called *particles*) fly through the search space. Each particle represents a candidate solution to the optimization problem. The position of a particle is influenced by the best position visited by itself (i.e. its own experience) and the position of the best particle in its neighborhood (i.e. the experience of neighboring particles). Particle position, $\mathbf{x}_i$, are adjusted using

$$\mathbf{x}_i(t+1) = \mathbf{x}_i(t) + \mathbf{v}_i(t+1) \tag{1}$$

where the velocity component, $\mathbf{v}_i$, represents the step size. For the basic PSO,

$$v_{i,j}(t+1) = wv_{i,j}(t) + c_1 r_{1,j}(t)(y_{i,j}(t) - x_{i,j}(t)) + c_2 r_{2,j}(t)(\hat{y}_j(t) - x_{i,j}(t)) \tag{2}$$

where w is the inertia weight (Shi & Eberhart, 1998), c_1 and c_2 are the acceleration coefficients, $r_{1,j}, r_{2,j} \sim U(0,1)$, $\mathbf{y}_i$ is the personal best position of particle i, and $\hat{\mathbf{y}}_i$ is the neighborhood best position of particle i.

The neighborhood best position $\hat{\mathbf{y}}_i$, of particle i depends on the neighborhood topology used (Kennedy, 1999; Kenedy & Mendes, 2002). If a fully-connected topology is used, then $\hat{\mathbf{y}}_i$ refers to the best position found by the entire swarm. That is,

$$\hat{y}_i(t) \in \{y_0(t), y_1(t), \ldots, y_s(t)\} = min\{f(y_0(t)), f(y_1(t)), \ldots, f(y_s(t))\} \tag{3}$$

where s is the swarm size.

The resulting algorithm is referred to as the global best (*gbest*) PSO. A pseudo-code for PSO is shown in Alg. 1.

```
for each particle i ∈ 1,...,s do
  Randomly initialize x_i
  Set v_i to zero
  Set y_i = x_i
endfor
Repeat
  for each particle i ∈ 1,...,s do
    Evaluate the fitness of particle i, f(x_i)
    Update y_i
    Update ŷ using equation (3)
    for each dimension j ∈ 1,...,N_d do
      Apply velocity update using equation (2)
    endloop
    Apply position update using equation (1)
  endloop
Until some convergence criteria is satisfied
```

Algorithm 1. General pseudo-code for PSO

Van den Bergh and Engelbrecht (2006) and Clerc and Kennedy (2002) proved that each particle converges to a weighted average of its personal best and neighborhood best position, that is,

$$\lim_{t \to +\infty} x_{i,j}(t) = \frac{c_1 y_{i,j} + c_2 \hat{y}_{i,j}}{c_1 + c_2}$$

This theoretically derived behavior provides support for the barebones PSO developed by Kennedy (2003). It replaces Eqs. 1 and 2 with

$$x_{i,j}(t+1) = N\left(\frac{y_{i,j}(t) + \hat{y}_j(t)}{2}, \left|y_{i,j}(t) - \hat{y}_j(t)\right|\right)$$

Particle positions are therefore randomly selected from a Gaussian distribution with the mean given as the weighted average of the personal best and global best positions, i.e. the swarm attractor. Note that exploration is facilitated via the deviation, $y_{i,j}(t)-\hat{y}_j(t)$, which approaches zero as t increases. In the limit, all particles will converge on the attractor point.
Kennedy (2003) also proposed an alternative version of the barebones PSO where Eqs. 1 and 2 are replaced with

$$x_{i,j}(t+1) = \begin{cases} N\left(\frac{y_{i,j}(t) + \hat{y}_j(t)}{2}, \left|y_{i,j}(t) - \hat{y}_j(t)\right|\right) & \text{if } U(0,1) > 0.5 \\ y_{i,j}(t) & \text{otherwise} \end{cases}$$

Based on the above equation, there is a 50% chance that the j-th dimension of the particle dimension changes to the corresponding personal best position. This version of PSO biases towards exploiting personal best positions.

3. Differential Evolution

Differential evolution (DE) is an evolutionary algorithm proposed by Storn and Price (1995). While DE shares similarities with other evolutionary algorithms (EA), it differs significantly in the sense that distance and direction information from the current population is used to guide the search process. DE uses the differences between randomly selected vectors (individuals) as the source of random variations for a third vector (individual), referred to as the *target* vector. Trial solutions are generated by adding weighted difference vectors to the target vector. This process is referred to as the mutation operator where the target vector is mutated. A recombination, or crossover step is then applied to produce an offspring which is only accepted if it improves on the fitness of the parent individual.
The basic DE algorithm is described in more detail below with reference to the three evolution operators: mutation, crossover, and selection.
Mutation: For each parent, $\boldsymbol{x}_i(t)$, of generation t, a trial vector, $\boldsymbol{v}_i(t)$, is created by mutating a target vector. The target vector, $\boldsymbol{x}_{i_3}(t)$, is randomly selected, with $i \neq i_3$. Then, two

individuals $\boldsymbol{x}_{i_1}(t)$, and $\boldsymbol{x}_{i_2}(t)$ are randomly selected with $i_1 \neq i_2 \neq i_3 \neq i$, and the difference vector, $\boldsymbol{x}_{i_1}$ - $\boldsymbol{x}_{i_2}$, is calculated. The trial vector is then calculated as

$$\boldsymbol{v}_i(t) = \boldsymbol{x}_{i_3}(t) + F(\boldsymbol{x}_{i_1}(t) - \boldsymbol{x}_{i_2}(t)) \tag{4}$$

where the last term represents the mutation step size. In the above, F is a scale factor used to control the amplification of the differential variation. Note that $F \in (0, \infty)$.

Crossover: DE follows a discrete recombination approach where elements from the parent vector, $\boldsymbol{x}_i(t)$, are combined with elements from the trial vector, $\boldsymbol{v}_i(t)$, to produce the offspring, $\boldsymbol{\mu}_i(t)$. Using the binomial crossover,

$$\mu_{ij}(t) = \begin{cases} v_{ij}(t) & \text{if } U(0,1) < P_r \quad \text{or} \quad j = r \\ x_{ij}(t) & \text{otherwise} \end{cases}$$

where $j = 1, \ldots, N_d$ refers to a specific dimension, N_d is the number of genes (parameters) of a single chromosome, and $r \sim U(1,\ldots, N_d)$. In the above, p_r is the probability of reproduction (with $p_r \in [0, 1]$).

Thus, each offspring is a stochastic linear combination of three randomly chosen individuals when $U(0, 1) < p_r$; otherwise the offspring inherits directly from the parent. Even when p_r = 0, at least one of the parameters of the offspring will differ from the parent (forced by the condition $j = r$).

Selection: DE evolution implements a very simple selection procedure. The generated offspring, $\boldsymbol{\mu}_i(t)$, replaces the parent, $\boldsymbol{x}_i(t)$, only if the fitness of the offspring is better than that of the parent.

4. Barebones Differential Evolution

Both PSO and DE have their strengths and weaknesses. PSO has the advantage that formal proofs exist to show that particles will converge to a single attractor. The barebones PSO utilizes this information by sampling candidate solutions, normally distributed around the formally derived attractor point. Additionally, the barebones PSO has no parameters to be tuned. On the other hand, DE has the advantage of not being biased towards any prior defined distribution for sampling mutational step sizes and its selection operator follows a hill-climbing process. Mutational step sizes are determined as differences between individuals in the current population. One of the problems which both PSO and DE share is that control parameters need to be optimized for each new problem.

The barebones DE combines the strengths of both the barebones PSO and DE to form a new, efficient hybrid optimization algorithm. For the barebones DE, position updates are done as follows:

$$x_{i,j}(t) = \begin{cases} p_{i,j}(t) + r_{2,j} \times (x_{i_1,j}(t) - x_{i_2,j}(t)) & \text{if } U(0, 1) > p_r \\ y_{i_3,j}(t) & \text{otherwise} \end{cases} \tag{5}$$

where

$$p_{i,j}(t) = r_{1,j}(t)\, y_{i,j}(t) + (1 - r_{1,j}(t))\, \hat{y}_{i,j}(t) \quad (6)$$

with i_1, i_2, $i_3 \sim U(1,\ldots,s)$, $i_1 \neq i_2 \neq i$, $r_{1,j}$, $r_{2,j} \sim U(0,1)$ and p_r is the probability of recombination.

Referring to Eq. 6, $\boldsymbol{p}_i(t)$ represents the particle attractor as a stochastic weighted average of personal best and global best positions, borrowing from the barebones PSO (Kennedy 2003). Referring to Eq. 5, the mutation operator of DE is used to explore around the current attractor, $\boldsymbol{p}_i(t)$, by adding a difference vector to the attractor. Crossover is done with a randomly selected personal best, $\boldsymbol{y}_{i_3}$, as these personal bests represent a memory of best solutions found by individuals since the start of the search process. Also note that the scale factor is a random variable. Using the position update in Eq. 6, for a proportion of (1- p_r) of the updates, information from a randomly selected personal best, $\boldsymbol{y}_{i_3}$, is used (facilitating exploitation), while for a proportion of p_r of the updates step sizes are mutations of the attractor point, $\boldsymbol{p}_i$ (facilitating exploration). Mutation step sizes are based on the difference vector between randomly selected particles, $\boldsymbol{x}_{i_1}$ and $\boldsymbol{x}_{i_2}$. Using the above, the BBDE achieves a good balance between exploration and exploitation. It should also be noted that the exploitation of personal best positions does not focus on a specific position. The personal best position, $\boldsymbol{y}_{i_3}$, is randomly selected for each application of the position update.

5. Opposition-based Learning

Opposition-based learning (OBL) was first proposed by Tizhoosh (2005) and was successfully applied to several problems (Rahnamayan et al., 2008). Opposite numbers are defined as follows:

Let $x \in [a,b]$, then the opposite number x' is defined as

$$x' = a + b - x$$

The above definition can be extended to higher dimensions as follows:

Let $P(x_1, x_2, \cdots, x_n)$ be an n-dimensional vector, where $x_i \in [a_i,b_i]$ and i=1, 2, …, n. The opposite vector of P is defined by $P'(x_1', x_2', \cdots, x_n')$ where

$$x_i' = a_i + b_i - x_i$$

6. Proposed Methods

In this chapter, OBL is used to enhance the performance of PSO and BBDE without adding any extra parameter. Two variants are proposed as follows:

6.1 Improved PSO (iPSO)

An improved version of PSO is proposed such that in each iteration the particle with the lowest fitness, $\boldsymbol{x}_b$, is replaced by its opposite (the *anti-particle*) as follows,

$$x_{b,j} = LB_j + UB_j - x_{b,j}$$

where $x_{b,j} \in [LB_j, UB_j]$, $j=1,2,\ldots,N_d$ and N_d is the dimension of the problem.

The velocity and personal experience of the anti-particle are reset. The global best solution is also updated. A pseudo-code for *i*PSO is shown in Alg. 2.

The rationale behind this approach is the basic idea of opposition-based learning: if we begin with a random guess, which is very far away from the existing solution, let say in worst case it is in the *opposite location*, then we should look in the *opposite direction*. In our case, the guess that is "very far away from the existing solution" is the particle with the lowest fitness.

The main difference between *i*PSO on one side and the approaches proposed by Han and He (2007) and Wang et al. (2007) on the other side, is that we did not introduce any extra parameter to the original PSO. In addition, *i*PSO uses only OBL to enhance the performance of PSO while (Han & He, 2007; Wang et al. 2007) use OBL combined with other techniques (e.g. Cauchy mutation).

for each particle $i \in 1,\ldots,s$ **do**
  for each dimension $j \in 1,\ldots,N_d$ **do**
    $\boldsymbol{x}_{i,j} = LB_j + r_j \times (UB_j - LB_j)$
  endloop
endfor
for each particle $i \in 1,\ldots,s$ **do**
  Set $\boldsymbol{v}_i$ to zero
  Set $\boldsymbol{y}_i = \boldsymbol{x}_i$
endfor
Repeat
  for each particle $i \in 1,\ldots,s$ **do**
    Evaluate the fitness of particle *i*, $f(\boldsymbol{x}_i)$
    Update $\boldsymbol{y}_i$
    Update $\hat{\boldsymbol{y}}$ using equation (3)
    for each dimension $j \in 1,\ldots,N_d$ **do**
      Apply velocity update using Eq. (2)
    endloop
    Apply position update using equation (1)
  endloop
  Let $\boldsymbol{x}_b$ be the particle with the lowest fitness
  for each dimension $j \in 1,\ldots,N_d$ **do**
    $\boldsymbol{x}_{b,j} = LB_j + UB_j - \boldsymbol{x}_{b,j}$
  endloop
  $\boldsymbol{v}_b = \boldsymbol{0}$
  $\boldsymbol{y}_b = \boldsymbol{x}_b$
  if $f(\boldsymbol{x}_b) < f(\hat{\boldsymbol{y}})$
    $\hat{\boldsymbol{y}} = \boldsymbol{x}_b$
  endif
Until some convergence criteria is satisfied

Algorithm 2. General pseudo-code for *i*PSO

6.2 Improved BBDE (iBBDE)

Similar to *i*PSO, BBDE is modified such that in each iteration the particle with the lowest fitness, x_b, is replaced by its opposite. The personal experience of the anti-particle is also reset. The global best solution is updated.

7. Experimental Results

This section compares the performance of the proposed methods with that of *gbest* PSO and BBDE discussed in Section 2 and 4, respectively. For the PSO algorithms, $w = 0.72$ and $c_1 = c_2 = 1.49$. These values have been shown to provide very good results (van den Berg, 2002). In addition $s = 50$ for all methods. All functions were implemented in 30 dimensions.

The following functions have been used to compare the performance of the different approaches. These benchmark functions provide a balance of unimodal, multimodal, separable and non-separable functions.

For each of these functions, the goal is to find the global minimizer, formally defined as

$$\text{Given } f\colon \Re^{N_d} \rightarrow \Re$$

$$\text{find } \boldsymbol{x}^* \in \Re^{N_d} \text{ such that } f(\boldsymbol{x}^*) \leq f(\boldsymbol{x}), \forall \boldsymbol{x} \in \Re^{N_d}$$

The following functions were used:

A. *Sphere* function, defined as

$$f(\boldsymbol{x}) = \sum_{i=1}^{N_d} x_i^2$$

where $\boldsymbol{x}^* = \boldsymbol{0}$ and $f(\boldsymbol{x}^*) = 0$ for $-100 \leq x_i \leq 100$.

B. *Rosenbrock* function, defined as

$$f(x) = \sum_{i=1}^{N_d-1} \left(100\left(x_i - x_{i-1}^2\right)^2 + \left(x_{i-1} - 1\right)^2\right)$$

where $\boldsymbol{x}^* = (1,1,\ldots,1)$ and $f(\boldsymbol{x}^*) = 0$ for $-2 \leq x_i \leq 2$.

C. *Rotated hyper-ellipsoid* function, defined as

$$f(\boldsymbol{x}) = \sum_{i=1}^{N_d} \left(\sum_{j=1}^{i} x_j\right)^2$$

where $\boldsymbol{x}^* = \boldsymbol{0}$ and $f(\boldsymbol{x}^*) = 0$ for $-100 \leq x_i \leq 100$.

D. *Rastrigin* function, defined as

$$f(\boldsymbol{x})=\sum_{i=1}^{N_d}\left(x_i^2-10\cos(2\pi x_i)+10\right)$$

where $\boldsymbol{x}^*=\boldsymbol{0}$ and $f(\boldsymbol{x}^*)=0$ for $-5.12\le x_i\le 5.12$.

E. *Ackley*'s function, defined as

$$f(x)=-20\exp\left(-0.2\sqrt{\frac{1}{30}\sum_{i=1}^{N_d}x_i^2}\right)$$
$$-\exp\left(\frac{1}{30}\sum_{i=1}^{N_d}\cos(2\pi x_i)\right)+20+e$$

where $\boldsymbol{x}^*=\boldsymbol{0}$ and $f(\boldsymbol{x}^*)=0$ for $-32\le x_i\le 32$.

F. *Griewank* function, defined as

$$f(\boldsymbol{x})=\frac{1}{4000}\sum_{i=1}^{N_d}x_i^2-\prod_{i=1}^{N_d}\cos\left(\frac{x_i}{\sqrt{i}}\right)+1$$

where $\boldsymbol{x}^*=\boldsymbol{0}$ and $f(\boldsymbol{x}^*)=0$ for $-600\le x_i\le 600$.

G. *Salomon* function, defined as

$$f(x)=-\cos\left(2\pi\sum_{i=1}^{N_d}x_i^2\right)+0.1\sqrt{\sum_{i=1}^{N_d}x_i^2}+1$$

where $\boldsymbol{x}^*=\boldsymbol{0}$ and $f(\boldsymbol{x}^*)=0$ for $-100\le x_i\le 100$.

Sphere, Rosenbrock and Rotated hyper-ellipsoid are unimodal, while Rastrigin, Ackley, Griewank and Salomon are difficult multimodal functions where the number of local optima increases exponentially with the problem dimension.

The results reported in this section are averages and standard deviations over 30 simulations. In order to have a fair comparison, each simulation was allowed to run for 50,000 evaluations of the objective function.

Table 1 summarizes the results obtained by applying the two PSO approaches to the benchmark functions. In general, the results show that *i*PSO performed better than (or equal to) *gbest* PSO. Figure 1 illustrates results for selected functions. The figure shows that *i*PSO generally reached good solutions faster than PSO. Similarly, Table 2 shows that *i*BBDE generally outperformed BBDE. Figure 2 illustrates results for selected functions. Thus, Tables 1 and 2 suggest that using the simple idea of replacing the worst particle is the main reason for improving the performance of PSO and BBDE. In additon, we can conclude that opposition-based learning improved the performance of both PSO and BBDE without requiring any extra parameter.

	PSO	*iPSO*
Sphere	0(0)	0(0)
Rosenbrock	22.191441 (1.741527)	20.645323 (0.426212)
Rotated hyper-ellipsoid	2.021006 (1.675313)	0.355572 (0.890755)
Rastrigin	48.487584 (14.599249)	27.460845 (11.966896)
Ackley	1.096863 (0.953266)	0(0)
Griewank	0.015806 (0.022757)	0.006163 (0.009966)
Salomon	0.446540 (0.122428)	0.113207 (0.034575)

Table 1. Mean and standard deviation (±SD) of the function optimization results

	BBDE	*iBBDE*
Sphere	0(0)	0(0)
Rosenbrock	25.826400 (0.216660)	25.942146 (0.209437)
Rotated hyper-ellipsoid	15.409460 (20.873456)	0.905987 (1.199178)
Rastrigin	34.761833 (28.598884)	0(0)
Ackley	0(0)	0(0)
Griewank	0.000329 (0.001800)	0(0)
Salomon	0.166540 (0.047946)	0.149917 (0.050826)

Table 2. Mean and standard deviation (±SD) of the function optimization results

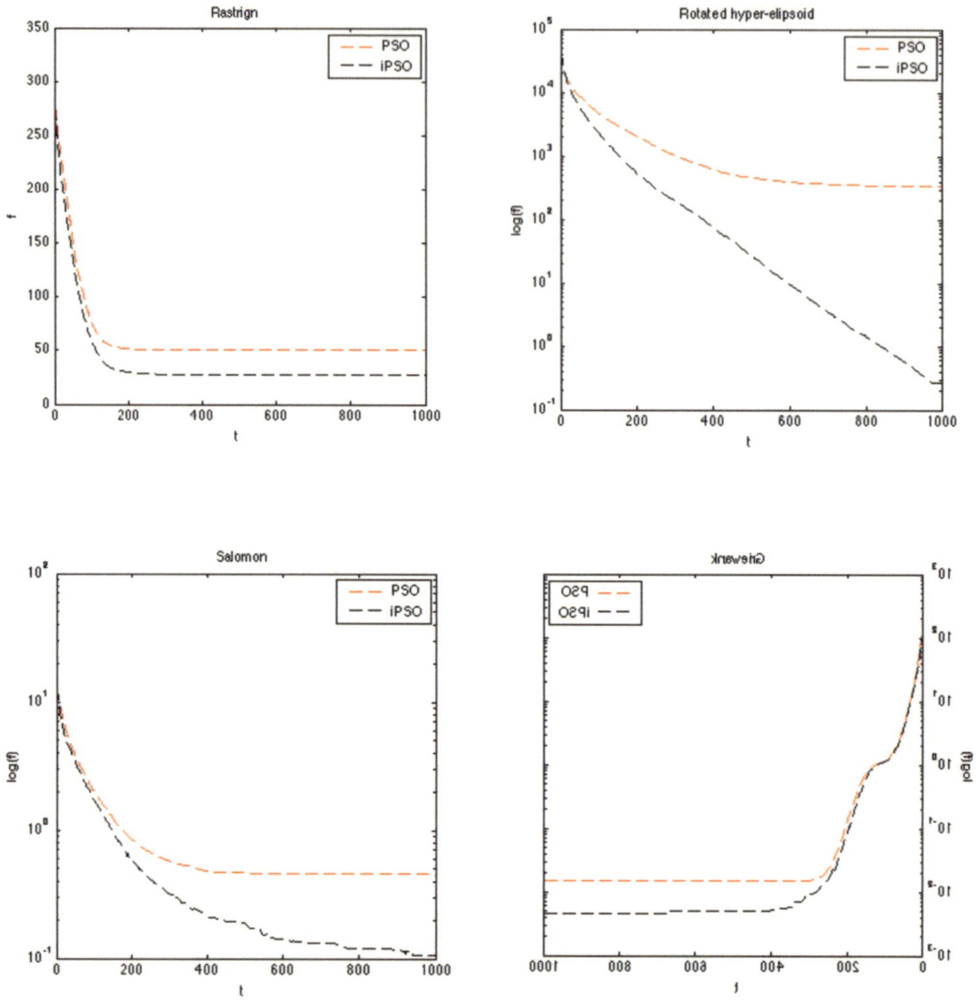

Figure 1. Performance Comparison of PSO and *i*PSO when applied to selected functions

7. Conclusion

Opposition-based learning was used in this chapter to improve the performance of PSO and BBDE. Two opposition-based variants were proposed (namely, *i*PSO and *i*BBDE). The *i*PSO and *i*BBDE algorithms replace the least-fit particle with its anti-particle. The results show that, in general, *i*PSO and *i*BBDE outperformed PSO and BBDE, respectively. In addition, the results show that using OBL enhances the performance of PSO and BBDE without requiring additional parameters. The ideas introduced in this chapter could also be used with any PSO/BBDE variant.

Future research will investigate the effect of noise on the performance of the proposed approaches. Furthermore, a scalability study will be conducted. Finally, applying the proposed approaches to real-world problem will be investigated.

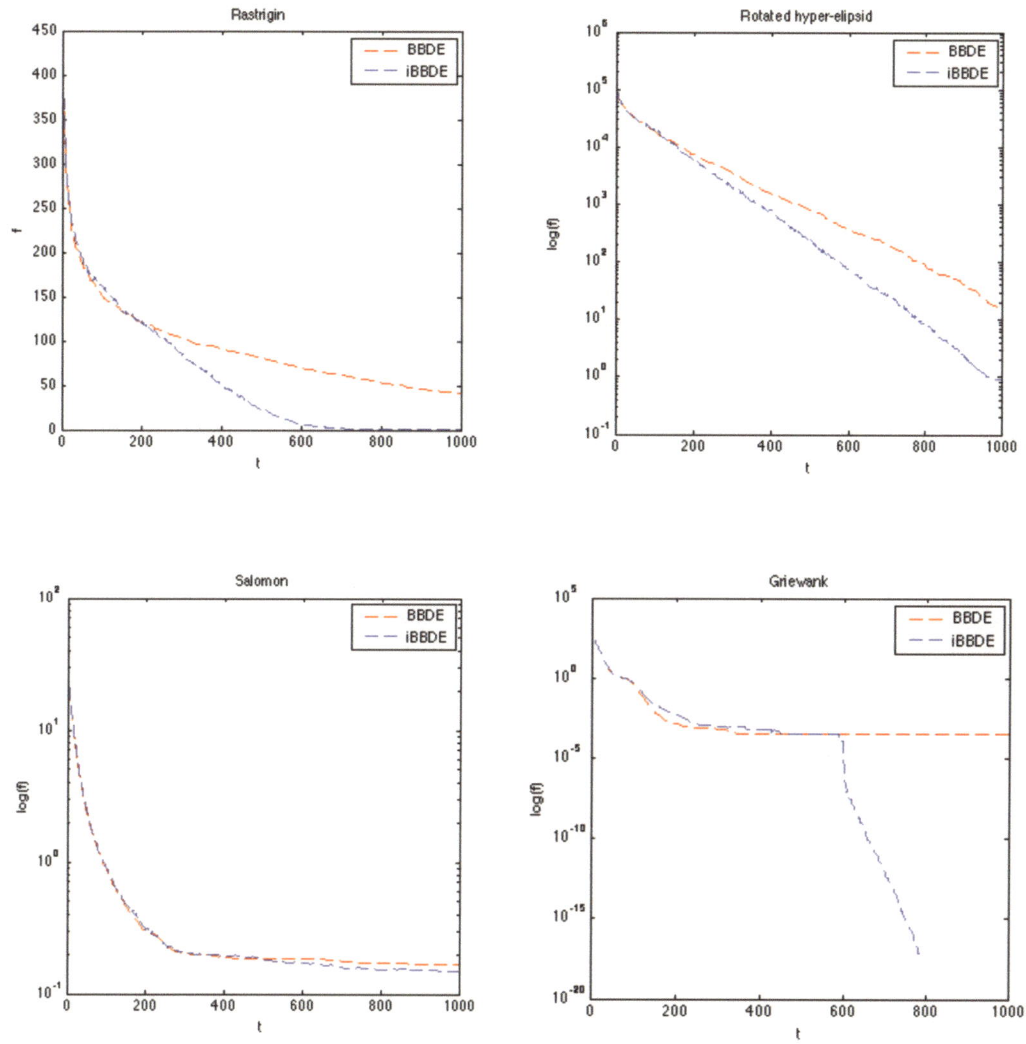

Figure 2. Performance Comparison of BBDE and *i*BBDE when applied to selected functions

8. References

Clerc, M. & Kennedy, J. (2002). The Particle Swarm-Explosion, Stability, and Convergence in a Multidimensional Complex Space. *IEEE Transactions on Evolutionary Computation*, Vol. 6, No. 1, pp. 58-73.

Engelbrecht, A. (2005). *Fundamentals of Computational Swarm Intelligence*, Wiley & Sons.

Han, L. & He, X. (2007). A novel Opposition-based Particle Swarm Optimization for Noisy Problems. *Proceedings of the Third International Conference on Natural Computation*, IEEE Press, Vol. 3, pp. 624 - 629.

Kennedy, J. (1999). Small Worlds and Mega-Minds: Effects of Neighborhood Topology on Particle Swarm Performance. *Proceedings of the IEEE Congress on Evolutionary Computation*, Vol. 3, pp. 1931-1938.

Kennedy, J. (2003). Bare Bones Particle Swarms. *Proceedings of the IEEE Swarm Intelligence Symposium*, pp. 80-87.

Kennedy, J. & Eberhart, R. (1995). Particle Swarm Optimization. *Proceedings of the IEEE International Joint Conference on Neural Networks*, pp. 1942-1948.

Kennedy, J. & Mendes, R. (2002). Population Structure and Particle Performance. *Proceedings of the IEEE Congress on Evolutionary Computation*, pp. 1671-1676, IEEE Press.

Omran, M., Engelbrecht, A. & Salman, A. (2007). Differential evolution based on particle swarm optimization. *Proceedings of the IEEE Swarm Intelligence Symposium*, pp. 112-119.

Price, K.; Storn, R. & Lampinen, J. (2005). *Differential Evolution: A Practical Approach to Global Optimization*, Springer.

Rahnamayan, S.; Tizhoosh, H. & Salama, M. (2008). Opposite-based Differential Evolution. *IEEE Trans. On Evolutionary Computation*, Vol. 12, No. 1, pp. 107-125.

Shi, Y. & Eberhart, R. (1998). A Modified Particle Swarm Optimizer. *Proceedings of the IEEE Congress on Evolutionary Computation*, pp. 69-73.

Storn, R. & Price, K. (1995). Differential evolution - A Simple and efficient adaptive scheme for global optimization over continuous spaces. *Technical Report TR-95-012*, International Computer Science Institute.

Tizhoosh, H. (2005). Opposition-based Learning: A New Scheme for Machine Intelligence. *Proceedings Int. Conf. Comput. Intell. Modeling Control and Autom*, Vol. I, pp. 695-701.

van den Bergh, F. (2002). An Analysis of Particle Swarm Optimizers. *PhD thesis*, Department of Computer Science, University of Pretoria, Pretoria, South Africa, 2002.

van den Bergh, F. & Engelbrecht, A. (2006). A Study of Particle Swarm Optimization Particle Trajectories. *Information Sciences*, Vol. 176, No. 8, pp. 937-971.

Wang, H.; Liu, Y.; Zeng, S.; Li, H. & Li, C. (2007). Opposition-based Particle Swarm Algorithm with Cauchy Mutation. *Proceedings of the IEEE Congress on Evolutionary Computation*, pp. 4750-4756.

24

Particle Swarm Optimization: Dynamical Analysis through Fractional Calculus

E. J. Solteiro Pires[1], J. A. Tenreiro Machado[2] and P. B. de Moura Oliveira[1]
[1]*Universidade de Trás-os-Montes e Alto Douro,*
[2]*Instituto Superior de Engenharia do Porto*
Portugal

1. Introduction

This chapter considers the particle swarm optimization algorithm as a system, whose dynamics is studied from the point of view of fractional calculus. In this study some initial swarm particles are randomly changed, for the system stimulation, and its response is compared with a non-perturbed reference response. The perturbation effect in the PSO evolution is observed in the perspective of the fitness time behaviour of the best particle. The dynamics is represented through the median of a sample of experiments, while adopting the Fourier analysis for describing the phenomena. The influence upon the global dynamics is also analyzed. Two main issues are reported: the PSO dynamics when the system is subjected to random perturbations, and its modelling with fractional order transfer functions.

2. Particle Swarm Optimization Basics

Evolutionary algorithms have been successfully applied to solve complex optimization engineering problems. Together with genetic algorithms, the particle swarm optimization (PSO) algorithm, proposed by (Kennedy & Eberhart, 1995), has achieved considerable success in solving optimization problems. While PSO algorithms and related variants have been extensively studied (Clerk & Kennedy, 2002), the influence of perturbations signals over the operation conditions is not yet well known.

The PSO algorithm was proposed originally by Kennedy and Eberhart (1995). This optimization technique is inspired in the way swarms behave and its elements move in a synchronized way, both as a defensive tactic and for searching food. An analogy is established between a particle and a swarm element. The particle movement is characterized by two vectors, representing its current position x and velocity v. Since 1995, many techniques were proposed to refine and/or complement the original canonical PSO algorithm, namely regarding it's tuning parameters (Shi and Eberhat, 1999) and by considering hybridization with other evolutionary techniques (Lovbjerg et al., 2001).

In this study a standard elementary PSO algorithm is considered (see Fig. 1). The basic algorithm begins by initializing the swarm randomly in the search space. As it can be seen in Fig. 1, where t and $t + 1$ represent two consecutive iterations, the position x of each particle is changed during the iterations by adding a new velocity v. This velocity is evaluated by

summing an increment to the previous velocity value. The increment is a function of two components representing the cognitive and the social knowledge.
The cognitive knowledge of each particle is included by evaluating the difference between the current position x and its best position so far b. The social knowledge of each particle is incorporated through the difference between its current position x and the best swarm global position achieved so far g. The cognitive and social knowledge factors are multiplied by randomly uniformly generated terms φ_1 and φ_2, respectively. The particles velocity is restricted, in order to keep velocities from exploding, through the inertia term I (Clerk and Kennedy, 2002).

```
Initialize Swarm
 forAll particles
  calculate fitness f
 endfor
Repeat
 forAll particles
  v_{t+1}=Iv_t+φ1(b-x_t)+ φ2(g-x_t)
  x_{t+1}=x_t+v_{t+1}
 endfor
 forAll particles
  calculate fitness f
 endfor
until Stopping criteria
```

Figure 1. Particle swarm optimization algorithm

3. Fractional Calculus

Fractional Calculus (FC) goes back to the beginning of the theory of differential calculus. Nevertheless, the application of FC just emerged in the last two decades, due to the progress in the area of chaos that revealed subtle relationships with the FC concepts. In the field of dynamical systems theory some work has been carried out but the proposed models and algorithms are still in a preliminary stage of establishment.
The fundamentals aspects of FC theory are addressed in (Gement, 1938; Méhauté, 1991; Oustaloup, 1991; Podlubny, 1999). Concerning FC applications research efforts can be mentioned in the area of viscoelasticity, chaos, fractals, biology, electronics, signal processing, diffusion, wave propagation, percolation, modelling, control and irreversibility (Ross, 1974; Tenreiro Machado, 2001; Torvik, 1984; Vinagre, 2002; Westerlund, 2002).
The FC is a generalization of the classical differential calculus to a non-integer order $\alpha \in \mathbf{C}$. Since its foundation has been the subject of distinct approaches. Due to this reason there are several alternative definitions of fractional derivatives. For example, the Laplace definition of a derivative of order $\alpha \in \mathbf{C}$ of the signal $x(t)$, $D^{\alpha}[x(t)]$, is a 'direct' generalization of the classic integer-order scheme yielding equation (1):

$$L\{D^{\alpha}[x(t)]\} = s^{\alpha} X(s) \tag{1}$$

for zero initial conditions, where s represents the Laplace operator. This means that frequency-based analysis methods have a straightforward adaptation.

An alternative approach, based on the concept of fractional differential, is the Grünwald-Letnikov definition given by equation (2) where h represents the time increment.

$$D^{\alpha}[x(t)] = \lim_{h \to 0}\left[\frac{1}{h^{\alpha}}\sum_{k=0}^{+\infty}\frac{(-1)^k \Gamma(\alpha+1)x(t-kh)}{\Gamma(k+1)(\alpha-k+1)}\right] \quad (2)$$

An important property revealed by equation (2) is that while an integer-order derivative implies just a finite series, the fractional-order derivative requires an infinite number of terms. This means that integer derivatives are 'local' operators in opposition with fractional derivatives which have, implicitly, a 'memory' of all past events.

The characteristics revealed by fractional-order models make this mathematical tool well suited to describe phenomena such as irreversibility and chaos, because of its inherent memory property. In this line of thought, the propagation of perturbations and the appearance of long-term dynamic phenomena in a population of individuals subjected to an evolutionary process seems to be a case where FC tools fit adequately, as shown in (Solteiro Pires et al.; 2003, Solteiro Pires et al., 2006) for genetic algorithms.

4. PSO Swarm Optimization Dynamic analysis

4.1 Problem statement

This section introduces the problem formulation adopted in the study of the PSO dynamic systems. Moreover, the dynamical phenomena involved in the signal propagation within the PSO population is analyzed. For a statistical sample of n independent cases, a particle is randomly initialized, in every experiment, and replaces the corresponding particle of the initial reference population. The experiments reveal a fractional dynamics of the perturbation propagation during the evolution which can be described by system theory tools.

The PSO algorithm, called in this report the 'system', is applied in the optimization of: a quadratic function, the Eason function and the Bohachevsky function.

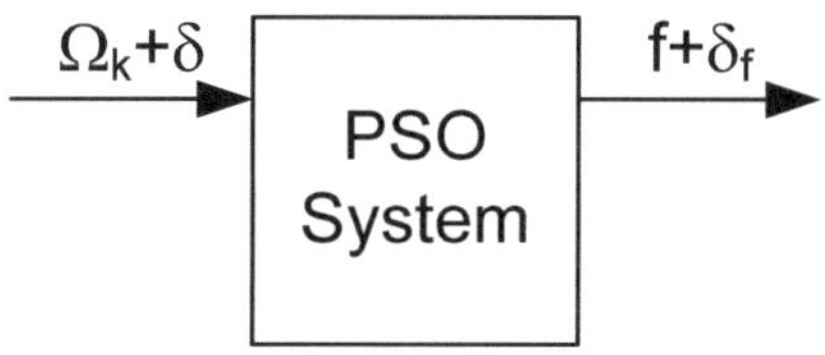

Figure 2. Perturbation of the PSO system

In the first test function case, the objective function consists in minimizing the quadratic function (3) which is adopted as a case study due to it's simplicity.

$$f(x) = x^2 \quad (3)$$

This function has only one parameter and its global optimum value is located at $f(x)|_{opt} = 0$. The variable interval is $x \in [-100,100]$ and the algorithm uses an encoding scheme with real numbers to codify the particles. A PSO is executed during a period of $T_m = 10000$ iterations with $\{\varphi_1, \varphi_2\} \sim U[0, 1.5]$.

The influence of several factors can be analyzed in order to study the dynamics of the PSO system, particularly the inertia factor I or the φ_i factors, $i = \{1, 2\}$. This effect can vary according to the population size, fitness function and iteration number used. As mentioned previously, one particle of the initial population is changed randomly. The inertia parameter influence is studied to analyze the effect of the perturbation for the values of $I = \{0.50, 0.55, ..., 0.80\}$ *versus* the swarm population size pop = {6, 8,..., 12}. The variation of the best global particle fitness evolution is taken as the system output signal as illustrated in Fig. 2.

4.2 The PSO dynamics

Initially, the PSO system is executed without any initial perturbation signal, during $T_m = 10000$ iterations, for a predefined inertia weight value I and swarm population size. The data regarding this test is stored, namely the global particle fitness and the stochastic parameters. This experiment will serve as a reference test. The *optimization* system perturbation consists in replacing the first initial particle of the stored reference swarm population, in every algorithm execution, by another particle randomly generated. Indeed, this stimulus to the system, results in a swarm fitness modification δf which is evaluated. This perturbation test is repeated for $n = 10000$ cases. It is important to state that the remaining test conditions, namely the stochastic reference stored values, remain unchanged along the n experiments. Therefore, the variation of the resulting PSO swarm fitness perturbation, during the evolution, can be viewed as the output signal which varies during the successive iterations.

The output signal consists in the difference between the population fitness with and without the initial perturbation, that is, $\delta f(T) = f_{pert}(T) - f(T)$. Figure 3a) shows the output signal $\delta f(T)$, for one particle replacement, in the iteration domain. In each experiment the Fourier transform of the signal perturbation, $F[\delta f(T)]$ (see Fig. 3b)) is evaluated in order to analyze the dynamics.

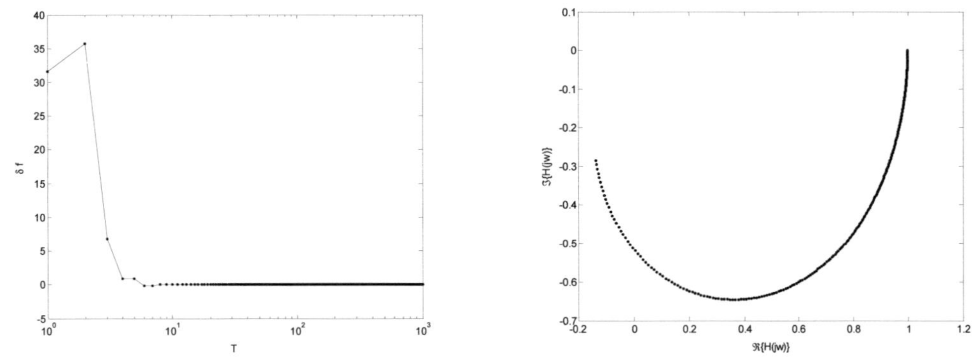

a) Iteration domain b) Polar diagram

Figure 3. Output signal for an initial perturbation. Experiment with $I = 0.7$ and a swarm population size of $pop = 12$ elements.

With the output signal Fourier description it is possible to evaluate the corresponding normalized transfer function (4):

$$H(j\omega) = \frac{F\{\delta f(T)\}(j\omega)}{F\{\delta f(T)\}(\omega = 0)} \quad (4)$$

where w represents the frequency, T the discrete time evolution (number of iterations used) and $j = \sqrt{-1}$. The transfer function H(jw) for this experiment is depicted in Figure 3b). Finally it is obtained a 'representative' transfer function, by using the median of the statistical sample (Tenreiro Machado & Galhano, 1998) of n experiments (see Figure 4).

Figure 5 shows the archieved results for inertial values of I = {0.50, 0.55,..., 0.80}. The medians of the transfer functions calculated previously (*i.e.*, for the real and the imaginary parts for each frequency) are taken as the final result of the numerical transfer function H(jw).

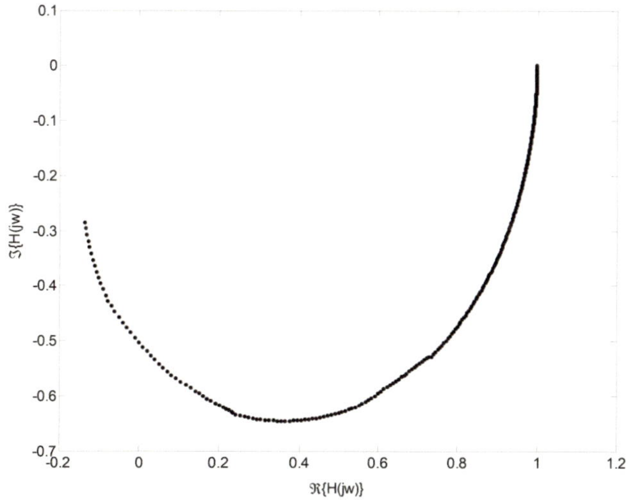

Figure 4. Median transfer function H(jw) of n = 10000 experiments for an inertial term I = 0.7 and pop = 12 elements.

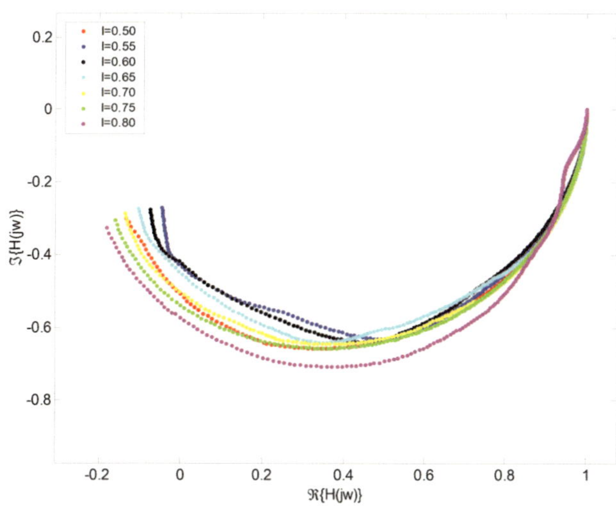

Figure 5. Median transfer function H(jw), of the n experiments for I = {0.50, 0.55,..., 0.80} for a population swarm of pop = 12 elements.

Varying the swarm population number of elements in the interval $pop \in [6, 12]$ results in a family of transfer functions. For a swarm size greater than 12 elements there is no difference between the reference test and the perturbation tests. It can be concluded that with large swarms an element has a negligible impact upon the search and, consequently, the performance of the algorithm is independent of the initial swarm. On the other hand, in small swarms, an element has a large impact on the evolution; therefore, it is necessary a large number of perturbation tests to lead to a convergence towards the statistical sample median. From the tests it can be observed that for $I = 0.8$ the median is very irregular because the system is close to the instability region (den Bergh and Engelbrecht, 2006).

4.3 Dynamical analysis

In this section the median of the numerical transfer functions is approximated by analytical expressions with gain $k = 1$ and one pole $a \in \mathrm{R}^+$ of fractional order $\alpha \in \mathrm{R}^+$, given by equation (5):

$$\mathrm{G}(\mathrm{j}\omega) = \frac{k}{\left(\frac{\mathrm{j}\omega}{a}+1\right)^{\alpha}} \tag{5}$$

Since the normalized Fourier transform (H) is used, it yields $k = 1$. In order to estimate the transfer function parameters $\{a, \alpha\}$ another PSO algorithm is used, which is named the *identification* PSO. The *identification* PSO is executed during $T_{\mathrm{ide}} = 200$ iterations with a 100 particle swarm size. The PSO parameters are: $\{\varphi_1, \varphi_2\}\sim\mathrm{U}[0, 1.5]$, $I = 0.6$, and the transfer function parameters intervals are $a \in [4 \times 10^{-3}, 50]$ and $\alpha \in [0, 100]$.
To guide the PSO search, the fitness function $\mathrm{f}_{\mathrm{ide}}$ is used to measure the distance between the numerical median $\mathrm{H}(\mathrm{j}w_k)$ and the analytical expression $\mathrm{G}(\mathrm{j}w_k)$:

$$\mathrm{f}_{\mathrm{ide}}(\mathrm{j}\omega) = \sum_{k=1}^{nf} \left\| \mathrm{H}(\mathrm{j}\omega_k) - \mathrm{G}(\mathrm{j}\omega_k) \right\| \tag{6}$$

where nf is the total number of sampling points and w_k, $k = \{1,\ldots,nf\}$, is the corresponding vector of frequencies.
As explained previously, the *optimization* PSO has stochastic dynamics. Therefore, every time the PSO system is executed with a different initial particle replacement, it leads to a slightly different transfer function. Consequently, in order to obtain numerical convergence (Tenreiro Machado & Galhano, 1998) $n = 10000$ perturbation experiments are performed with different replacement particles, while all the other particles remain unchanged. The *optimization* PSO dynamics transfer function is evaluated by computing the normalized signals Fourier transform (FT) (equation 4). The transfer functions medians determined previously (*i.e.*, for the real and the imaginary parts, and for each frequency) are taken as the final result of the numerical transfer function $\mathrm{H}(\mathrm{j}w)$.
Figure 6 and 7 show, superimposed, the normalized median transfer function $\mathrm{H}(\mathrm{j}w)$ and the corresponding identified transfer function $\mathrm{G}(\mathrm{j}w)$, both as polar and amplitude diagrams, respectively. As it can be observed from these figures the fractional order transfer function,

identified by the PSO, captures the *optimization* PSO dynamics quite well, apart from the high frequency range (not represented).

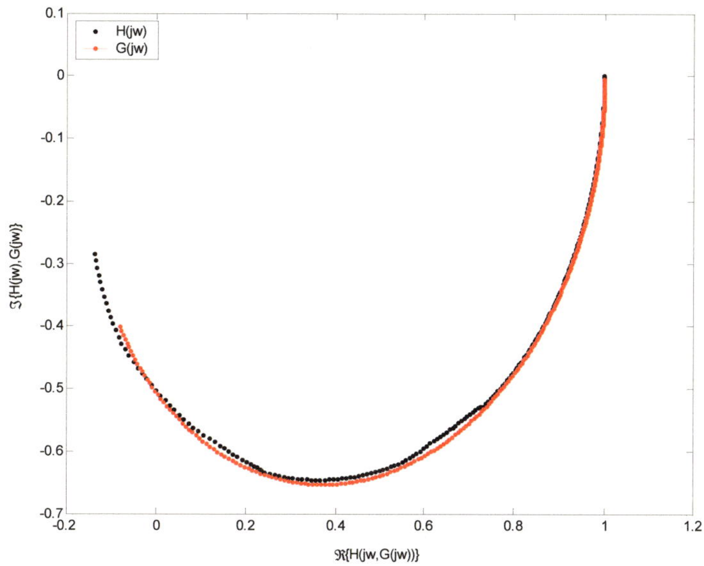

Figure 6. Polar Diagram of H(jw) and G(jw) for I = 0.70 and a swarm size of pop = 12 elements

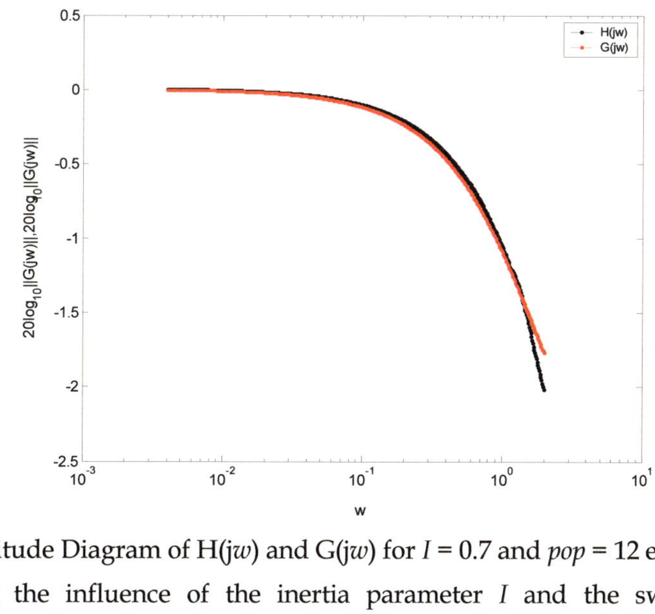

Figure 7. Amplitude Diagram of H(jw) and G(jw) for I = 0.7 and pop = 12 elements

For evaluating the influence of the inertia parameter I and the swarm size, several simulations are performed ranging from I = 0.50 up to I = 0.80 and the number of swarm elements from pop = 6 up to pop = 12, respectively. The estimated parameters for $\{a, \alpha\}$ are depicted in Figure 8 and 9, respectively.

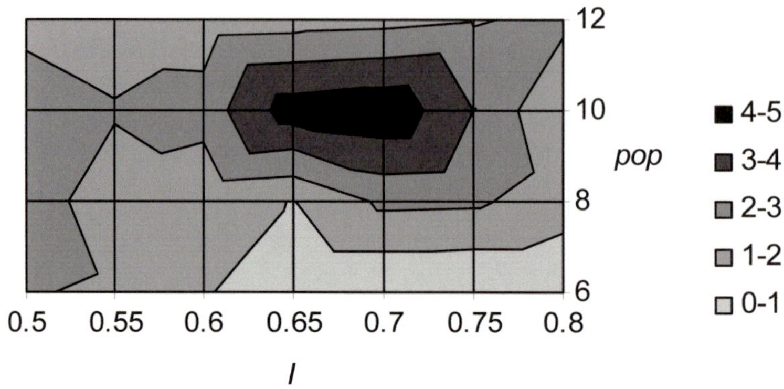

Figure 8. Parameter *a versus* {*I*, *pop*}

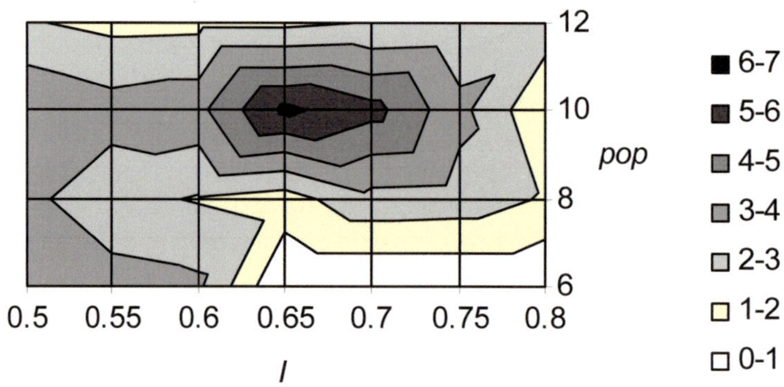

Figure 9. Parameter α *versus* {*I*, *pop*}

The results reveal that the transfer function parameters {*a*, α} have some dependence with the inertia coefficient *I* and the swarm size *pop*. It can be observed that the transfer function parameters have maximum values at $I = 0.65$ and for $pop = 10$ elements. Moreover, it can be seen that there is a correlation between parameters *a* and α.

In what concerns the transfer function, by enabling the zero/pole order to vary freely we get non-integer values for α. The alternative adoption of integer-order transfer functions would lead to a larger number of zero and poles to get the same quality in the fitting of curves.

5. Other illustrative examples

In this section additional experiments are presented, in which the PSO system is deployed to optimize: the Easom function (7) and the Bohachevsky function (8).

$$f(x_1, x_2) = -\cos(x_1)\cos(x_2)e^{-(x_1-\pi)^2-(x_2-\pi)^2} \tag{7}$$

$$f(x_1, x_2) = x_1^2 + x_2^2 - 0.3\cos(3\pi x_1) - 0.4\cos(4\pi x_1) + 0.7 \quad (8)$$

These functions (7,8) are more complex than the quadratic function used in previous section. In these cases, a swarm of *pop* = 20 elements was used in the experimental tests while varying the inertial parameter in the set $I = \{0.5, 0.6, \ldots, 0.8\}$. The polar diagrams illustrated by Figures 10 and 11 were obtained for the Easom and the Bohachevsky fitness functions, respectively.

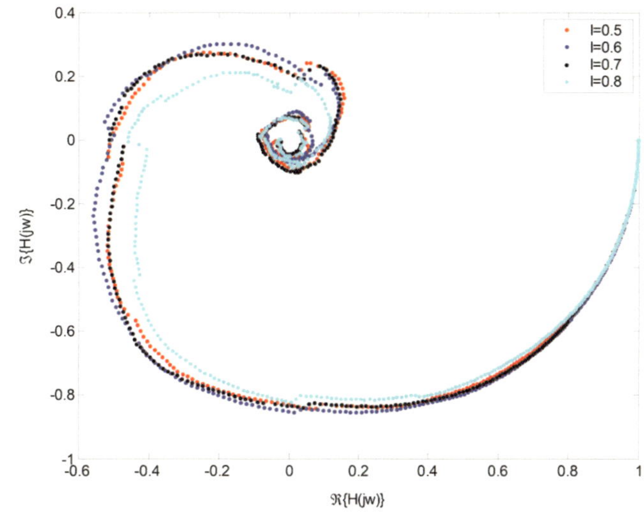

Figure 10. Median transfer function H(j*w*) of the *n* experiments for the Easom function and *pop* = 20 elements

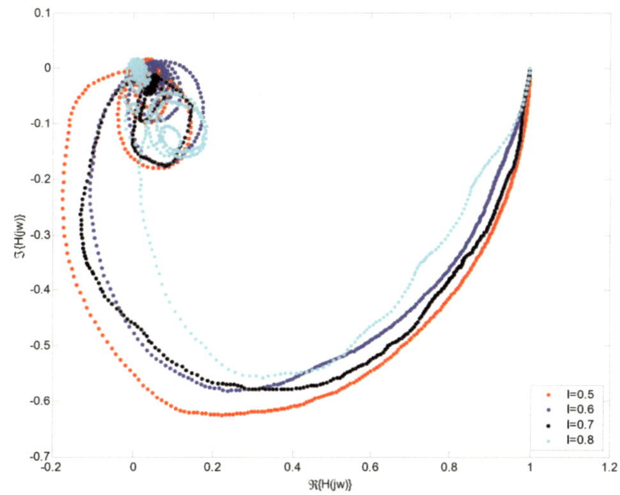

Figure 11. Median transfer function H(j*w*), of the *n* experiments for the Bohachevsky function and *pop* = 20 elements

The approximations are carried out by the same *identification* PSO described previously. However, in these experiments, the medians of the numerical transfer functions are approximated by analytical expressions incorporating a time delay T_d (9).

$$G(j\omega) = \frac{e^{-j\omega T_d}}{\left(\frac{j\omega}{a}+1\right)^{\alpha}} \tag{9}$$

The polar diagrams confirm the existence of a time delay T_d, which represents the perturbation propagation in the swarm evolution. Moreover, in these experiments the dynamics follows the behavior of a low-pass filter too. The parameters obtained by the *identification* PSO can be observed in Figure 12. The results reveal that the transfer function parameters $\{a, \alpha, T_d\}$ have some dependence with the inertia coefficient I.

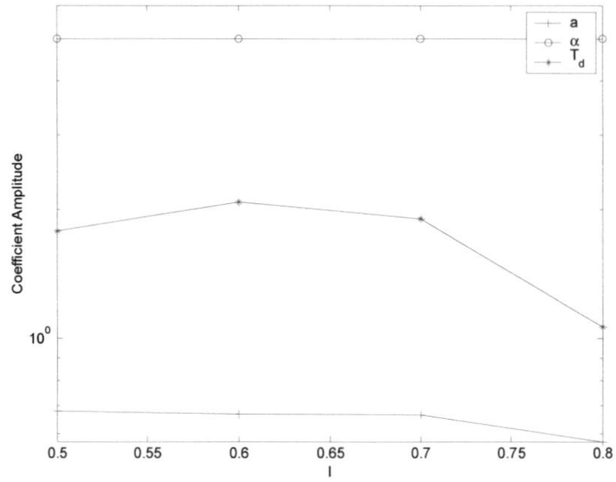

a) Easom function

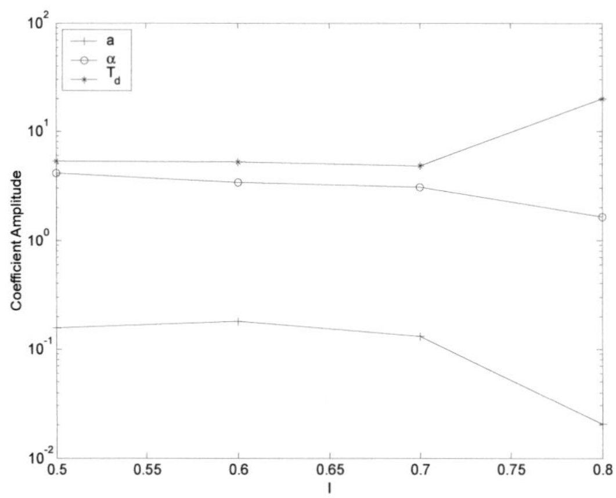

b) Bohachevsky function

Figure 12. Parameters $\{a, \alpha, T_d\}$ of G(jw)

6. Conclusion

This work analyzed the signal propagation and the phenomena involved in the discrete time evolution of a particle swarm optimization algorithm. The particle swarm algorithm was deployed as an optimization tool using three different functions as tests cases. The *optimization* PSO system was subjected to a statistical sample of tests. In each test a particle of a reference swarm was replaced by a randomly generated particle and the global population fitness perturbation effect measured. A second PSO algorithm was used to identify the parameters of a fractional order transfer function. The results indicate that the fractional calculus provides a good understanding of the effects corresponding to the propagation of the perturbations signals over the operating conditions.

7. Acknowledgment

The authors would like to acknowledge the GECAD Unit.

8. References

Clerc, M.; Kennedy, J. (2002). The particle swarm - explosion, stability, and convergence in a multidimensional complex space. *IEEE Transactions on Evolutionary Computation*, 6, 1, (2002) 58-73.

den Bergh, F. V.; Engelbrecht, A (2006). P., A study of particle swarm optimization particle trajectories, *Inf. Sci.*, 176, 8, (2006) 937-971.

Gement, A. (1938). On fractional differentials. *Proc. Philosophical Magazine*, 25, (2008) 540-549.

Kennedy, J.; Eberhart, R. (1995). Particle swarm optimization, *Proceedings of the 1995 IEEE International Conference on Neural Networks*, pp. 1942-1948, Perth, Australia, IEEE Service Center, Piscataway, NJ, 1995.

Lovbjerg, M.; Rasmussen, T. K.; Krink, T. (2001). Hybrid particle swarm optimiser with breeding and subpopulations, *Proceedings of the Genetic and Evolutionary Computation Conference (GECCO)*, pp. 469-476, San Francisco, California, USA, July 2001, Morgan Kaufmann.

Méhauté, A. L. (1991). *Fractal Geometries: Theory and Applications*, Penton Press.

Oustaloup, A. (1991). *La Commande CRONE: Commande Robuste d'Ordre Non Intier*, Hermes.

Podlubny, I. (1999) *Fractional Diferential Equations*, Academic Press, San Diego.

Ross, B. (1974), Fractional Calculus and its applications, *Lecture Notes in Mathematics*, 457, Springer Berlin, (1974).

Shi, Y.; Eberhart, R. C. (1999). Empirical study of particle swarm optimization, *Proceedings of the Congress of Evolutionary Computation*, pp. 1945-1950, Mayflower Hotel, Washington D.C., USA, July 1999, IEEE Press, 1999.

Solteiro Pires, E. J.; Tenreiro Machado, J. A.; de Moura Oliveira, P. B. (2003). Fractional order dynamics in a GA planner. *Signal Processing*, 83, 11, (2003) 2377-2386.

Solteiro Pires, E. J.; Tenreiro Machado, J. A.; de Moura Oliveira, P. B. (2006). Dynamical modelling of a genetic algorithm. *Signal Processing*, 86, 10, (2006) 2760-2770.

Tenreiro Machado, J. A. (1997). Analysis and design of fractional-order digital control systems. *Journal System Analysis-Modelling-Simulation*, 27, (1997) 107-122.

Tenreiro Machado, J. A. (2001) System modelling and control through fractional-order algorithms. *FCAA – Jornal of Fractional Calculus and Ap. Analysis*, 4, (2001) 47-66.

Tenreiro Machado, J. A.; Galhano, A. M. S. F. (1998). A statistical perspective to the fourier analysis of mechanical manipulators. *Journal Systems Analysis-Modelling-Simulation,* 33 (1998), 373-384.

Torvik, P. J.; L. Bagley, R. (1984). On the appearance of the fractional derivative in the behaviour of real materials. *ASME Journal of Applied Mechanics,* 51 (june 1984), 294-298.

Vinagre, B. M.; Petras, I.; Podlubny, I.; Chen, Y. Q. (2002). Using fractional order adjustment rules and fractional order reference models in model-reference adaptive control, *Nonlinear Dynamics,* 29 (July 2002), 269-279.

Westerlund, S. (2002). *Dead Matter Has Memory! Causal Consulting.* Kalmar, Sweden.

25

Discrete Particle Swarm Optimization Algorithm for Flowshop Scheduling

S.G. Ponnambalam[1], N. Jawahar[2] and S. Chandrasekaran[3]
[1]*Monash University*, [2]*Thiagarajar College of Engineering*
[3]*S R M V Polytechnic College*
[1]*Malaysia*, [2,3]*India*

1. Introduction

In the context of manufacturing systems, scheduling refers to allocation of resources over time to perform a set of operations. Manufacturing systems scheduling has many applications ranging from manufacturing, computer processing, transportation, communication, health care, space exploration, education, distribution networks, etc. Scheduling is a process by which limited resources are allocated over time among parallel or sequential activities. Solving such a problem amounts to making discrete choices such that an optimal solution is found among a finite or a countably infinite number of alternatives. Such problems are called combinatorial optimization problems. Typically, the task is complex, limiting the practical utility of combinatorial, mathematical programming and other analytical methods in solving scheduling problems effectively. Manufacturing system entails the acquisition and allocation of limited resources to production activities so as to reduce the manufacturing cycle time and in-process inventory and to satisfy customer demand in specified time. Successful achievement of these objectives lies in efficient scheduling of the system. Scheduling plays an important role in shop floor planning. A schedule shows the planned time when processing of a specific job will start on a machine. It also indicates when a job will get completed on a machine. Scheduling is a decision-making process of sequencing a set of operations on different machines in a manufacturing unit. The objective of scheduling is generally to improve the utilization of resources and profitability of production lines. Scheduling problem is characterized by three components namely:

1. Number of machines, number of jobs and the processing time for each job using appropriate machine
2. A set of constraints such as operation precedence constraint for a given job and operation non-overlapping constraint for a given machine
3. A target function called objective function consisting of single or multiple criteria that must be optimized.

Traditionally, scheduling researchers has shown interest in optimizing a single-objective or performance measure while scheduling, which is not a reality. Practical scheduling problems acquire consideration of several objectives as desired by the scheduler. When multiple criteria are considered, scheduler may wish to generate a schedule which performs better with respect to all the measures under study, such solution does not exist. This chapter presents the application of Discrete Particle Swarm Optimisation Algorithm for solving flowshop scheduling problem (FSP) under single and multiple objective criteria.

2. Flowshop Scheduling

2.1 Description of FSP

In discrete parts manufacturing industries, jobs with multiple operations use machines in the same order. In such case, machines are installed in series. Raw materials initially enter the first machine and when a job has finished its processing on the first machine, it goes to the next machine. When the next machine is not immediately available, job has to wait till the machine becomes available for processing. Such a manufacturing system is called a flowshop, where the machines are arranged in the order in which operations are to be performed on jobs. A flowshop is a conventional manufacturing system where machines are arranged in the order of performing operations on jobs. The technological order, in which the jobs are processed on different machines, is unidirectional. In a flowshop, a job i with a set of m operations $i_1, i_2, i_3, ..., i_m$ is to be completed in a predetermined sequence. In short, each operation except the first has exactly one direct predecessor and each operation except the last one has exactly one direct successor as shown in Figure 1. Thus each job requires a specific immutable sequence of operations to be carried out for it to be complete. This type of structure is sometimes referred as linear precedence structure (Baker, 1974). Further, once started, an operation on a machine cannot be interrupted.

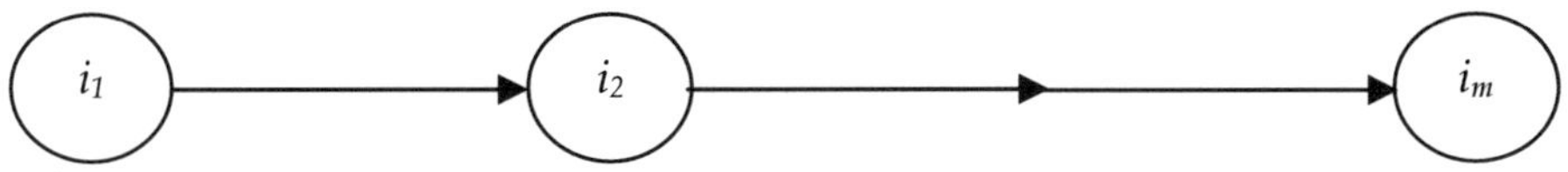

Figure 1. Work Flow in Flowshop

2.2 Characteristics of FSP

Flowshop consists of m machines and there are n different jobs to be optimally sequenced through these machines. The common assumptions used in modelling the flowshop problems are as follows:

- All n jobs are available for processing at time zero and each job follows identical routing through the machines.
- Unlimited storage exists between the machines. Each job requires m operations and each operation requires a different machine.
- Every machine processes only one job at a time and every job is processed by one machine at a time.
- Setup-times for the operations are sequence-independent and are included in processing times.
- The machines are continuously available.
- Individual operations cannot be pre-empted.

Further it is assumed that:

- Each job must be processed to completion.
- In-process inventory is allowed when necessary.

- There is only one machine of each type in the shop.
- Machines are available throughout the scheduling period.
- There is no randomness and the scheduling problem under study is a deterministic scheduling problem. In particular
  - The number of jobs is known and fixed.
  - The number of machines is known and fixed.
  - The processing times are known and fixed, and
  - All other quantities needed to define a particular problem are known and fixed.

The general structure of typical n job m machine FSP is shown in Figure 2.

Job	Processing order			
	M_1	M_2	M_3	M_m
J_1	Pt_1	Pt_2	Pt_3	Pt_m
J_2	Pt_1	Pt_2	Pt_3	Pt_m
J_3	Pt_1	Pt_2	Pt_3	Pt_m
..	..	..	..	..
..	..	..	..	..
J_n	Pt_1	Pt_2	Pt_3	Pt_m

where Pt - processing time of job J in machine M

Figure 2. General Structure of Flowshop

2.3 Solution approaches for FSP

Computational complexity of a problem is the maximum number of computational steps needed to obtain an optimal solution. For example if there are n jobs and m available machines, the available number of schedule to be evaluated to get an optimal solution is $(n!)^m$. In a permutation flow based manufacturing system, the number of available schedules is $n!$. Based on the complexity of the problem, all problems can be classified into two classes, called P and NP in the literature. Class P consists of problems for which the execution time of the solution algorithms grows polynomially with the size of the problem. Thus, a problem of size m would be solvable in time proportional to m^k, when k is an exponent. The time taken to solve a problem belonging to the NP class grows exponentially, thus this time would grow in proportion to t^m, where t is some constant. In practice, algorithms for which the execution time grows polynomially are preferred. However, a widely held conjecture of modern mathematics is that there are problems in NP class for which algorithms with polynomial time complexity will never be found (French, 1982). These problems are classified as NP – hard problems. Unfortunately, most of the practical scheduling problems belong to the NP – hard class (Rinnooy Kan, 1976). Many scheduling problems are polynomially solvable, or NP-hard in that it is impossible to find an optimal solution here without the use of an essentially enumerative algorithm. FSP is a widely researched combinatorial optimization problem, for which the computational effort increases exponentially with problem size (Jiyin Liu & Colin Reeves, 2001; Brucker, 1998; Sridhar & Rajendran, 1996; French, 1982). In FSP, the computational complexity increases with increase in problem size due to increase in number of jobs and/or number of machines.

To find exact solution for such combinatorial problems, a branch and bound or dynamic programming algorithm is often used when the problem size is small. Exact solution methods are impractical for solving FSP with large number of jobs and/or machines. For the large-sized problems, application of heuristic procedures provides simple and quick method of finding best solutions for the FSP instead of finding optimal solutions. A heuristic is a technique which seeks (and hopefully finds) good solutions at a reasonable computational cost. A heuristic is approximate in the sense that it provides a good solution for relatively little effort, but it does not guarantee optimally. A heuristic can be a rule of thumb that is used to guide one's action. Heuristics for the FSP can be a constructive heuristics or improvement heuristics. Various constructive heuristics methods have been proposed by Johnson, 1954; Palmer, 1965; Campbell et al., 1970; Dannenbring 1977 and Nawaz et al. 1983. Literature shows that constructive heuristic methods give very good results for NP-hard combinatorial optimization problems. This builds a feasible schedule from scratch and the improvement heuristics try to improve a previously generated schedule by applying some form of specific improvement methods. An application of heuristics provides simple and quick method of finding best solutions for the FSPs instead of finding optimal solutions (Ruiz & Maroto, 2005; Dudek et al. 1992). Johnson's algorithm (1954) is the earliest known heuristic for the FSP, which provides an optimal solution for two-machine problem to minimize makespan. Palmer (1965) developed a very simple heuristic in which for every job a "slope index" is calculated and then the jobs are scheduled by non-increasing order of this index. Ignall & Schrage (1965) applied the branch and bound technique to the flowshop sequencing problem. Campbell et al. (1970) developed a heuristic algorithm known as CDS algorithm and it builds $m-1$ schedules by clustering the m original machines into two virtual machines and solving the generated two machine problem by repeatedly using Johnson's rule. Dannenbring's (1977) Rapid Access heuristic is a mixture of the previous ideas of Johnson's algorithm and Palmer's slope index. Nawaz et al.'s (1983) NEH heuristic is based on the idea that jobs with high processing times on all the machines should be scheduled as early in the sequence as possible. NEH heuristics seems to be the performing better compared to others. Heuristic algorithms are conspicuously preferable in practical applications. Among the most studied heuristics are those based on applying some sort of greediness or applying priority based procedures including, e.g., insertion and dispatching rules. The main drawback of these approaches, their inability to continue the search upon becoming trapped in a local optimum, leads to consideration of techniques for guiding known heuristics to overcome local optimality (Jose Framinan et al. 2003). And also the heuristics has the problems like

1. Lack of comprehensiveness
2. Little robustness of conclusions
3. Weak/partial experimental design

For these reasons, one can investigate the application of metaheuristic search methods for solving optimization problems. It is a set of algorithmic concepts that can be used to define heuristic methods applicable to wide set of varied problems. The use of metaheuristics has significantly produced good quality solutions to hard combinatorial problems in a reasonable time. It is defined as an iterative generation process which guides a subordinate heuristic by combining intelligently different concepts for exploring and exploiting the search space, learning strategies are used to structure information in order to find efficiently near-optimal solutions (Osman & Laporte, 1996). The fundamental properties which characterize metaheuristics are as follows (Christian Blum & Andrea Roli, 2003):

- The goal is to efficiently explore the search space in order to find (near-) optimal solutions.
- Techniques which constitute metaheuristic algorithms range from simple local search procedures to complex learning processes.
- Metaheuristic algorithms are approximate and usually non-deterministic.
- They may incorporate mechanisms to avoid getting trapped in confined areas of the search space.
- The basic concepts of metaheuristics permit an abstract level description.
- Metaheuristics are not problem-specific.
- Metaheuristics may make use of domain-specific knowledge in the form of heuristics that are controlled by the upper level strategy.
- Today's more advanced metaheuristics use search experience (embodied in some form of memory) to guide the search.

Metaheuristics or Improvement heuristics are extensively employed by researchers to solve scheduling problems (Chandrasekaran et al. 2006; Suresh & Mohanasundaram, 2004; Hisao Ishibuchi et al. 2003; Lixin Tang & Jiyin Liu, 2002; Eberhart & Kennedy, 1995). Improvement methods such as Genetic Algorithm (Chan et al. 2005; Ruiz et al. 2004; Sridhar & Rajendran, 1996), Simulated Annealing algorithm (Ogbu & Smith, 1990), Tabu Search algorithm (Moccellin & Nagamo, 1998) and Particle Swarm Optimization algorithm (Rameshkumar et al. 2005; Prabhaharan et al. 2005; Faith Tasgetiren et al. 2004) have been widely used by researchers to solve FSPs. Metaheuristic algorithms such as Simulated Annealing (SA) and Tabu Search (TS) methods are single point local search procedures where, a single solution is improved continuously by an improvement procedure. Algorithms such as Genetic Algorithm (GA), Ant Colony Optimization (ACO) algorithm and Particle Swarm Optimization (PSO) algorithm belongs to population based search algorithms. These are designed to maintain a set of solution transiting from a generation to the next. The family of metaheuristics includes, but is not limited to, GA, SA, ACO, TS, PSO, evolutionary methods, and their hybrids.

2.4 Performance measures considered

Measures of schedule performance are usually functions of the set of completion times in a schedule. Performance measures can be classified as regular and non-regular. A regular measure is one in which the penalty function is non-decreasing in terms of job completion times. Some examples of regular performance measures are makespan, mean flowtime, total flowtime, and number of tardy jobs. Performance measures, which are not regular, are termed non-regular. That is, such measures are not an increasing function with respect to job completion times. Some examples of non-regular measures are earliness, tardiness, and completion time variance. In this chapter, the performance measures namely minimization of makespan, total flowtime and completion time variance is considered for solving flowshop scheduling problems. Makespan (C_{max}) has been considered by many scheduling researchers (Ignall & Scharge, 1965; Campbell et al. 1970; Nawaz et al.1983; Framinan et al. 2002; Ruiz & Maroto, 2005). Makespan is defined as the time required for processing all the jobs or the maximum time required for completing a given set of jobs. Minimization of makespan ensures better utilization of the machines and leads to a high throughput (Framinan et al. 2002; Ruiz & Maroto, 2005). Makespan is computed using equation (1).

$$C_{max} = \max\{C_i, i = 1,2,........,n\} \quad (1)$$

The time spend by a job in the system has been defined as its flow time. Total flowtime is defined as the sum of completion time of every job or total time taken by all the jobs. Total flowtime (F_{Σ}) of the schedule is computed using equation (2). Minimizing total flowtime results in minimum work-in-process inventory (Chandrasekharan Rajendran & Hans Ziegler, 2005).

$$F_{\Sigma} = \sum_{i=1}^{n} C_i \quad (2)$$

Completion time variance is defined as the variance about the mean flowtime and is computed using equation (3). Minimizing completion time variance (V_T) serves to minimize variations in resource consumption and utilization (Gowrishankar et al. 2001; Gajpal & Rajendran, 2006; Viswanath Kumar Ganesan et al. 2006).

$$V_T = \frac{1}{n}\sum_{i=1}^{n}(C_i - \overline{F})^2 \quad (3)$$

where $\overline{F} = \frac{F_T}{n}$ is the mean flowtime.

3. Particle Swarm Optimization Algorithm

3.1 Features of PSO

Particle Swarm Optimization (PSO) algorithm is an evolutionary computation technique developed by Eberhart & Kennedy in 1995 inspired by social behavior of bird flocking or fish schooling. PSO is a stochastic, population-based approach for solving problems (Kennedy & Eberhart, 1995). It is a kind of swarm intelligence that is based on social-psychological principles and provides insights into social behavior, as well as contributing to engineering applications. PSO algorithm has been successfully used to solve many difficult combinatorial optimization problems. PSO algorithm is problem-independent, which means little specific knowledge relevant to a given problem is required. All we have to know is the fitness evaluation of each solution. This advantage makes PSO more robust than many search algorithms. In the last couple of years the particle swarm optimization algorithm has reached the level of maturity necessary to be interesting from an engineering point of view. It is a potent alternative optimizer for complex problems and possesses many attractive features such as:

- Ease of implementation: The PSO is implemented with just a few lines of code, using only basic mathematical operations.
- Flexibility: Often no major adjustments have to be made when adapting the PSO to a new problem.
- Robustness: The solutions of the PSO are almost independent of the initialization of the swarm. Additionally, very few parameters have to be tuned to obtain quality solutions.

- Possibility to combine discrete and continuous variables. Although some authors present this as a special feature of the PSO (Sensarma et al., 2002), others point out that there are potential dangers associated with the relaxation process necessary for handling the discrete variables (Abido, 2002). Simple round-off calculations may lead to significant errors.
- Possibility to easily tune the balance between local and global exploration.
- Parallelism: The PSO is inherently well suited for parallel computing. The swarm population can be divided between many processors to reduce computation time.

3.2 Applications of PSO

In recent years, PSO has been successfully applied in many areas. Currently, PSO has been implemented in a wide range of research areas such as functional optimization, pattern recognition, neural network training, fuzzy system control etc. and obtained significant success. PSO is widely applied and focused by researchers due to its profound intelligence background and simple algorithm structure. Many proposals indicate that PSO is relatively more capable for global exploration and converges more quickly than many other heuristic algorithms. It solves a variety of optimization problems in a faster and cheaper way than the evolutionary algorithms in the early iterations. One of the reasons that PSO is attractive is that there are very few parameters to adjust. One version, with very slight variation (or none at all) works well in a wide variety of applications. PSO has been used for approaches that can be used across a wide rage of applications, as well as for specific applications focused on a specific requirement. PSO has been applied to the analysis of human tremor. The diagnosis of human tremor, including Parkinson's disease and essential tremor, is a very challenging area. PSO has been used to evolve a neural network that distinguishes between normal subjects and those with tremor. Inputs to the network are normalized movement amplitudes obtained from an actigraph system. The method is fast and accurate (Eberhart & Hu, 1999). While development of computer numerically controlled machine tools has significantly improved productivity, there operation is far from optimized. None of the methods previously developed is sufficiently general to be applied in numerous situations with high accuracy. A new and successful approach involves using artificial neural networks for process simulation and PSO for multi-dimensional optimization. The application was implanted using computer-aided design and computer-aided manufacturing (CAD/CAM) and other standard engineering development tools as the platform (Tandon, 2000). Another application is the use of particle swarm optimization for reactive power and voltage control by a Japanese electric utility (Yoshida et al., 1999). PSO has also been used in conjunction with a back propagation algorithm to train a neural network as a state-of-charge estimator for a battery pack for electric vehicle use. Determination of the battery pack state of charge is an important issue in the development of electric and hybrid / electric vehicle technology. The state of charge is basically the fuel gauge of an electric vehicle. A strategy was developed to train the neural network based on a combination of particle swarm optimization and the back propagation algorithm. Finally, one of the most exciting applications of PSO is that by a major American corporation to ingredient mix optimization. In this work, "ingredient mix" refers to the mixture of ingredients that are used to grow production strains of microorganisms that naturally secrete of manufacture something of interest. Here, PSO was used in parallel with traditional industrial optimization methods. PSO provided an optimized ingredient mix that provided over twice the fitness as the mix found using traditional methods, at a very different location in ingredient space. PSO was shown to be robust: the occurrence of an ingredient becoming contaminated hampered the search for a few iterations but in the end did not result in poor final results. PSO, by its nature, searched a much larger portion of the problem space than the traditional method. Generally speaking, particle swarm optimization, like the other evolutionary computation algorithms, can be applied to solve most optimization problems and problems that can be converted to optimization problems. Among the application areas with the most potential are system design, multi-objective optimization, classification, pattern recognition, biological system modelling, scheduling (planning), signal processing, games, robotic applications, decision making, simulation and identification. Examples include fuzzy controller design, job shop scheduling, real time robot path planning, image segmentation, EEG signal simulation, speaker verification, time-frequency analysis, modelling of the spread of antibiotic resistance, burn diagnosing, gesture recognition and automatic target detection, to name a few (Eberhart & Shi, 2001).

3.3 Working of PSO

PSO is initialized with a swarm of random feasible solutions and searches for optima by updating velocities and positions. PSO algorithm is initialized with a set of several random particles called a swarm. A set of moving particles (the swarm) is initially thrown inside the multi-dimensional search space. Each particle is a potential solution, which has the ability to remember its previous best position and current position, and it survives from generation to generation. Each particle has the following features:

- It has a position and a velocity
- It knows its neighbours, best previous position and objective function value.
- It remembers its best previous position.

At each time step, the behavior of a given particle is a compromise between three possible choices

- To follow its own way
- To go towards its best previous position
- To go towards the best neighbour's best previous position, or forwards the best neighbour.

The swarm is typically modelled by particles in multi-dimensional space that have a position and a velocity. These particles fly through hyperspace and have two essential reasoning capabilities: their memory of their own best position and knowledge of their neighborhood's best, "best" simply meaning the position with the smallest objective value. Members of a swarm communicate good positions to each other and adjust their own position and velocity based on these good positions. PSO shares many similarities with evolutionary computation techniques such as GA, SA, TS and ACO algorithms. The PSO system is initialized with a swarm of random solutions and searches for optima by updating generations. The advantages of PSO are that PSO is easy to implement and there are few parameters to adjust. PSO has been successfully applied in many areas: function optimization, artificial neural network training, fuzzy system control, and other areas where GA can be applied. Most of evolutionary techniques have the following procedure:

1. Random generation of an initial population
2. Reckoning of a fitness value for each subject. It will directly depend on the distance to the optimum.

3. Reproduction of the population based on fitness values.
4. If requirements are met, then stop. Otherwise go back to step 2.

Evolutionary Algorithms use a population of potential solutions (points) of the search space. These solutions (initially randomly generated) are evolved using different specific operators which are inspired from biology. Through cooperation and competition among the potential solutions, these techniques often can find near-optimal solutions quickly when applied to complex optimization problems. There are some similarities between PSO and Evolutionary Algorithms:

1. Both techniques use a population (which is called *swarm* in the PSO case) of solutions from the search space which are initially random generated;
2. Solutions belonging to the same population interact with each other during the search process;
3. Solutions are evolved using techniques inspired from the real world.

PSO shares many common points with GA. Both algorithms start with a group of a randomly generated population; both have fitness values to evaluate the population. Both update the population and search for the optimum with random techniques. Both systems do not guarantee success. However, PSO does not have genetic operators like crossover and mutation. Particles update themselves with the internal velocity. The information sharing mechanism in PSO is significantly different. In GA, chromosomes share information with each other. So the whole population moves like one group towards an optimal area. In PSO, only global or local best particle gives out the information to others. It is a one-way information sharing mechanism. Compared with GA, all the particles tend to converge to the best solution quickly even in the local version in most cases/ PSO optimization algorithm uses a set of particles called a swarm, similar to chromosomes in a binary-coded Genetic Algorithm (GA). PSO and ACO are optimization algorithms based on the behavior of swarms (birds, fishes) and ants respectfully. However, the particles are multidimensional points in real space during the optimization. The PSO optimization run starts with a user-specified swarm size and objective function used to evaluate objection function values, called fitness in GA terminology. The particles are initialized randomly within the variable bounds and they search for the optimum (maximum or minimum) in the search space with some communication between particles. For a maximization (or minimization) problem, the particles will move towards the particle with the highest (or least) objective function value using a position update equation, that is stochastic. This is how randomness in introduced to PSO algorithm. This position update method is similar to the use of crossover and mutation operations used to generate new individuals in a new generation in the GA. However, the PSO differs in that, updates of particle position usually involve the best particles (global or in the neighborhood) of each particle. The position updating tends to always exploit the best solution found so far. While this may lead to premature convergence, when all particles positions become equal to that of the best particle (i.e., no diversity), there are schemes designed to prevent such premature convergence. In the PSO literature, several neighborhood schemes have been developed for the particle updating (Merkle and Middendorf, 2000). This chapter aims to develop a metaheuristic algorithm called PSO algorithm which is suitable for solving FSPs with the objective of minimising three performance measures namely makespan, total flowtime and completion time variance. Firstly, a single objective PSO is proposed and the above performance measures are considered individually. Performance of the proposed single objective PSO is tested by solving a large set of benchmark FSPs available in the literature having number of jobs varying from 5 to 500 and number of machines from 5 to 20.

3.4 Structure of PSO Algorithm

The pseudo-code of the simple PSO algorithm and its general framework are given in Figures 3 and 4 respectively.
The basic elements of PSO algorithm are summarized below:

Particle: X_i^t denotes the ith particle in the swarm at iteration *t* and is represented by *n* number of dimensions as $X_i^t = [x_{i1}^t, x_{i2}^t, .., x_{in}^t]$, where x_{ij}^t is the position value of the ith particle with respect to the jth dimension ($j = 1,2,...,n$).

Population: pop^t is the set of NP particles in the swarm at iteration *t*, i.e., $pop^t = [X_1^t, X_2^t, ..., X_{NP}^t]$.

Sequence: We introduce a new variable π_i^t, which is a permutation of jobs implied by the particle X_i^t. It can be described as $\pi_i^t = [\pi_{i1}^t, \pi_{i2}^t, .., \pi_{in}^t]$, where π_{ij}^t is the assignment of job *j* of the particle *i* in the permutation at iteration *t*.

```
Initialize swarm
Initialize velocity
Initialize position
Initialize parameters
      Evaluate particles
      Find the local best
      Find the global best
Do
{
            Update velocity
            Update position
            Evaluate
            Update local best
            Update global best
} ( until termination)
```

Figure 3. Pseudocode of the PSO Algorithm

Particle velocity: V_i^t is the velocity of particle *i* at iteration *t*. It can be defined as $V_i^t = [v_{i1}^t, v_{i2}^t, ..., v_{in}^t]$, where v_{ij}^t is the velocity of particle *i* at iteration *t* with respect to the jth dimension.

Local best: P_i^t represents the best position of the particle *i* with the best fitness until iteration *t*, so the best position associated with the best fitness value of the particle *i* obtained so far is called the *local best*. For each particle in the swarm, P_i^t can be determined and updated at each iteration *t*. In a minimization problem with the objective function $f(\pi_i^t)$ where π_i^t is the corresponding sequence of particle X_i^t, the local best P_i^t of the ith particle is obtained such that $f(\pi_i^t) \leq f(\pi_i^{t-1})$ where π_i^t is the corresponding permutation of local best P_i^t

and π_i^{t-1} is the corresponding sequence of local best P_i^{t-1}. To simplify, we denote the fitness function of the local best as $f_i^{pb} = f(\pi_i^t)$. For each particle, the local best is defined as $P_i^t = [p_{i1}^t, p_{i2}^t, ..., p_{in}^t]$ where p_{ij}^t is the position value of the ith local best with respect to the jth dimension ($j = 1,2,...,n$).

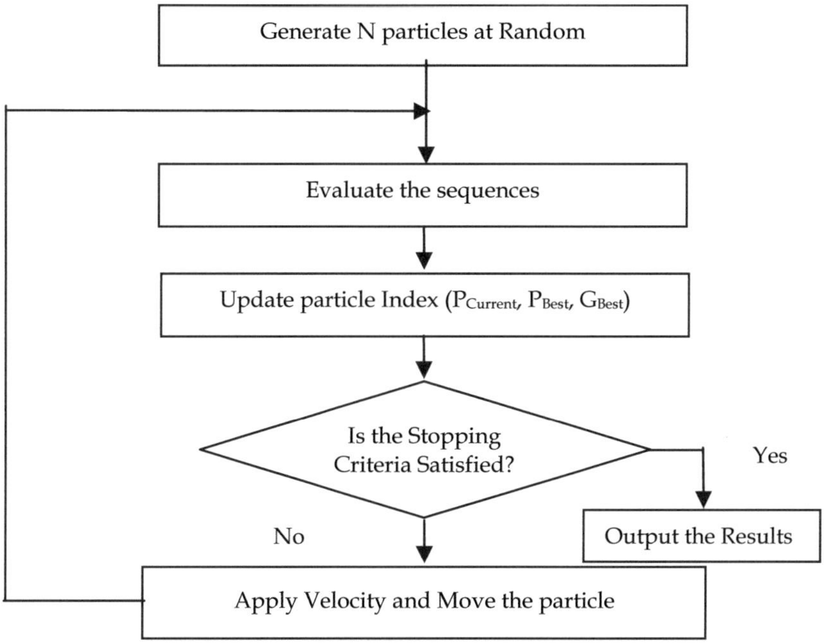

Figure 4. The Framework of PSO Algorithm

4. Discrete PSO Algorithm for Single-Objective FSP

4.1 Pseudocode of the proposed discrete PSO algorithm

Particle Swarm Optimization algorithm starts with a population of randomly generated initial solutions called particles (swarm). It is to be noted that the particle structure is taken as a string, which consists of job numbers in certain order. The order of jobs in the string represents a sequence. After the swarm is initialized, each potential solution is assigned a velocity randomly. The length of the velocity of each particle $\|v\|$ is generated randomly between *0* and *n* (Rameshkumar et al. 2005; Chandrasekaran et al. 2006) and the corresponding lists of transpositions $(i_q, j_q); q = 1, \|v_k\|$ are generated randomly for each particle. The above formulation permits exchange of jobs $(i_1, j_1), (i_2, j_2)......(i_{\|v\|}, j_{\|v\|})$ in the given order. Each particle keeps track of its improvement and the best objective function value achieved by the individual particles so far is stored as local best solution $({}^eP_k^t)$, and the overall best objective function achieved by all the particles together so far is stored as the global best solution (G_b^t). The particle velocity and position are updated continuously in all iterations. The iterative improvement process is continued afterwards to further improve the solution quality. The Pseudocode of the proposed discrete PSO algorithm is shown in Figure 5.

Initialize swarm P $t=0;$

Initialize velocity v_k^t *and position* P_k^t

Initialize parameters

Evaluate particles

Find the local best ${}^eP_k^t$ *and global best* G_b^t

Do

{

for $(k=1,N)$

Update Velocity v_k^{t+1} ;

Update Position P_k^{t+1} ;

Evaluate all particles;

Update ${}^eP_k^{t+1}$ *and* G^{t+1} , $(k=1,N)$;

$t \to t+1$;

} $(\text{while } t < t_{max})$

Figure 5. Pseudocode of the Proposed Discrete PSO Algorithm

The particle velocity and position are continuously updated using equation (4) and (5).

$$v_k^{t+1} = C_1 U_1 v_k^t + C_2 U_2 \, rand()({}^eP_k^{t+1} - P_k^{t+1}) + C_3 U_3 \, rand()(G_k - P_k^{t+1}) \quad (4)$$

$$P_k^{t+1} = P_k^t + v_k^{t+1} \quad (5)$$

where C_1, C_2 and C_3 is called acceleration constants. The acceleration constants C_1, C_2 and C_3 in equation (4) guide every particle toward local best and the global best solution during the search process. Low acceleration value results in walking far from the target, namely local best and the global best. High value results in premature convergence of the search process.

4.2 Procedural steps of the Discrete PSO Algorithm

The step by step procedure for implementing the proposed discrete PSO algorithm is as follows.

Step1: Initialize a swarm P_i with random positions and velocities in the problem space X.

Step2: For each particle, evaluate the desired optimization fitness function

Step3: Compare the fitness function with its previous best. If current value is better than previous best, then set previous best equal to current value and P_i equal to the current location X_i .

Step4: Identify the particle in the neighborhood with the best success so far, and assign its index to the variable G .

Step5: Apply local search algorithm to all the particles at the end of each iteration and evaluate for the objective function.

Step6: Change the velocity and position of the particle according to equation (4) and equation (5).

Step7: Loop to step (2) until a criterion is met (usually number of iterations).

4.3 Numerical Illustrations

An example illustrating the process of updating the velocity and the position of a sequence is explained as follows:

Velocity update: The procedure for updating the velocity of all the particles in each iteration is as follows: For example, let us assume

The sequence $P_k^t = \{2,3,4,1\}$; $C_1 = 1,\ C_2 = 2,\ C_3 = 2$; $U_1 = 0.2,\ U_2 = 0.4,\ U_3 = 0.3$; $\|V_k\| = 2$, $v = (1,4),(2,3)$; ${}^eP_k^t = (1,4,3,2)$ and $G_b^t = (3,1,4,2)$.

Velocity of the particle *k* at time step $t+1$ namely V_k^{t+1} is obtained using equation (4)

$$V_k^{t+1} = 1\text{x}\ 0.2\ [(1,4),(2,3)] \oplus 2 \text{ x } 0.4\ [(1,4,3,2) - (2,3,4,1)] \oplus 2 \text{ x } 0.3\ [(3,1,4,2) - (2,3,4,1)]$$

where [(1,4,3,2) - (2,3,4,1)] represents a velocity such that applying the resulting velocity to the current particle (2,3,4,1) yields a position (1,4,3,2).

Thus, $V_k^{t+1} = 0.2\ [(1,4), (2,3)] \oplus 0.8\ [(2,3), (1,4)] \oplus 0.6\ [(1,2), (1, 4)]$
$= ((1, 4),(2, 3),(1, 2))$

Position update: Position of the particle k at time step $t+1$ namely P_k^{t+1} is obtained using equation (5) by applying V_k^{t+1} over P_k^t as follows.

P_k^{t+1} =(2,3,4,1) + ((1,4), (2,3),(1,2));
= (1,3,4,2) + ((2,3),(1,2)); =(1,4,3,2) + (1,2);
= (4,1,3,2)

4.4 Performance Comparison

An extensive performance analysis using proposed discrete PSO algorithm is carried out by means of evaluating the performance measures by solving the benchmark FSPs of Taillard (1993). Extensive experiments are conducted to fix the parameters like number of particles, number of iterations, selection of learning coefficients and initial swarm generation. The evaluation of proposed discrete PSO algorithm is coded in Linux C and run on an Intel Pentium III 900MHz PC with 128 MB memory.

Number of iterations: Number of iterations or termination criterion is a condition that the search process will be terminated. It might be a maximum number of iteration or maximum CPU times are normally to terminate the search process (Liu & Reeves, 2001; Gowrishankar et al. 2001). In this chapter, for the single-objective optimization problems, an evaluation of *1000 x n x m* number of sequences or particles is taken as the termination criterion.

Number of particles: Experiments have been conducted to identify the optimal swarm size by solving a set of 30 different instances of Taillard (1993) for makespan objective with 20 jobs and machines varying from 5, 10 and 20 using discrete PSO algorithm. In experimentation, the performance of the algorithm is better with swarm size 80 and the same has been used throughout our evaluation.

Learning coefficients: The roll of learning coefficients or acceleration constants, namely C_1, C_2 and C_3 guide every particle towards the local best and the global best solutions during the search process. Low acceleration value results in walking far from the target, namely local best and the global best. High value results in premature convergence of the search process. Experiments have been conducted using different combinations of learning coefficients. To determine the best combinations of C_1, C_2 and C_3 values by solving a set of 30 FSPs for makespan objective with 20 jobs and machines varying from 5, 10 and 20 using

the proposed PSO algorithm. The values $C_1 = 1, C_2 = 2$ and $C_3 = 2$ shows better performance and the same, has been used throughout our study.
Velocity coefficients: The velocity update is carried out after every iteration to improve the search process. The velocity coefficients, namely U_1, U_2 and U_3 guides the search to find the optimal solution quickly. As per the experiments, the values for U_1, U_2 and U_3 are generated randomly between 0 and 1.
Initial Swarm Generation: For the generation of initial swarm one particle is generated from the results obtained by certain algorithms for the desired optimization fitness function and remaining particles of the swarm is constructed in a way that a permutation is produced randomly. The particle generated from certain algorithms is added with randomly generated particles at the beginning of the search. This insertion of the particle in initial swarm is to find better sequences in each iteration of the search. And also it improves the performance of discrete PSO algorithm in terms of finding near-optimal solutions. The algorithms selected for generating the particle for different objective functions are listed below. For makespan objective, one particle is generated using NEH heuristic of Nawaz et al. (1983) and is added to the swarm. For total flowtime objective, one particle is generated based on the heuristic developed by Rajendran. (1993) and is added to the swarm. For completion time variance objective, a particle is generated based on the algorithm developed by Gajpal & Rajendran (2006), and is added to the swarm. These algorithms have better start with the respective objectives. Performance of the proposed discrete PSO with respect to makespan objective is carried out in comparison with the benchmark solutions given by Taillard (1993) and with the results published in the literature. The quality measure namely, "Average Relative Percent Deviation" ($\overline{RPD}$) is considered for the evaluation. During comparison, the corresponding better values reported in the literature are taken. The RPD is computed using equation (6).

$$RPD = [G - C^* / C^*] \times 100 \tag{6}$$

where, G represents the global best solution obtained by the proposed algorithm for a given problem and C^* represents the upper bound value reported in the literature for the corresponding objective function. Some sample results of problems ta001-ta010 of Taillard (1993) is presented in Table 1.

Instances	Problem	Results Reported	Results Obtained	RPD
20 x 5	ta001	1278	1278	0.0000
	ta002	1359	1360	0.0736
	ta003	1081	1088	0.6475
	ta004	1293	1293	0.0000
	ta005	1235	1235	0.0000
	ta006	1195	1195	0.0000
	ta007	1239	1239	0.0000
	ta008	1206	1206	0.0000
	ta009	1230	1237	0.5691
	ta010	1108	1108	0.0000
		$\overline{RPD}$		**0.1290**

Table 1. Sample Results for Makespan

In order to evaluate the performance of the proposed discrete PSO with respect to the total flowtime objective, the results are compared with the results of the popular performing heuristics developed by Liu & Reeves (2001), M-MMAS Algorithm and PACO Algorithm (Rajendran & Ziegler, 2004). Some sample results of problems ta001-ta010 for total flowtime criteria is presented in Table 2.

Instances	Problem	Results Reported	Results Obtained	RPD
	ta001	14056 [3]	14033	-0.1636
	ta002	15151 [2]	15151	0.0000
	ta003	13403 [3]	13313	-0.6715
	ta004	15486 [2]	15459	-0.1744
	ta005	13529 [3]	13529	0.0000
20 x 5	ta006	13123 [3]	13123	0.0000
	ta007	13559 [2]	13548	-0.0811
	ta008	13968 [1]	13948	-0.1432
	ta009	14317 [2]	14315	-0.0140
	ta010	12968 [2]	12943	-0.1928
		$\overline{RPD}$		**-0.1441**

Note: Superscript (1) refers to Heuristic Algorithm (Liu & Reeves, 2001) (2) M-MMAS Algorithm (Rajendran & Ziegler, 2004) (3) PACO Algorithm (Rajendran & Ziegler, 2004)

Table 2. Sample Results for Total Flowtime

Instances	Problem	Results Reported	Results Obtained	RPD
	ta001	73040.55 [3]	72060.23	-1.3422
	ta002	90885.27 [2]	89238.17	-1.8123
	ta003	53894.49 [2]	53851.95	-0.0789
	ta004	89822.05 [4]	87104.42	-3.0256
	ta005	72350.55 [2]	72020.43	-0.4563
20 x 5	ta006	71665.73 [2]	70817.64	-1.1834
	ta007	69088.45 [2]	68367.69	-1.0432
	ta008	70214.31 [2]	69793.85	-0.5988
	ta009	73329.22 [2]	72284.98	-1.4240
	ta010	52580.03 [1]	52015.34	-1.0740
		$\overline{RPD}$		**-1.2039**

Note: Superscript (1) refers to PACO Algorithm (Rajendran & Ziegler, 2004) (2) MMAS Ant Colony Algorithm (Stuetzle, 1998) (3) NACO Algorithm with position-job insertion local search (Gajpal & Rajendran, 2006) (4) NACO Algorithm with job-index based local search (Gajpal & Rajendran, 2006)

Table 3. Sample Results for Completion Time Variance

The performance of the proposed discrete PSO algorithm with respect to completion time variance criterion, the results are compared with the results of ant colony algorithm with random-job insertion local search by Gajpal & Rajendran (2006), M-MMAS Ant Colony Algorithm by Stuetzle(1998), PACO Algorithm by Rajendran & Ziegler(2004), and three

NACO Algorithm with position-job insertion and job-index based local searches by Rajendran & Ziegler (2004). To our knowledge, the results of completion time variance objective using PSO algorithm are not available in literature, the performance of the proposed algorithm is compared with other metaheuristic results. Some sample results of problems ta001-ta010 of Taillard (1993) for completion time variance objective are presented in Table 3.

The results show that the proposed single-objective discrete PSO algorithm performs better. The negative sign in RPD values shows that the proposed discrete PSO algorithm generates better results than the results reported in the literature considered. The summary of $\overline{RPD}$ values obtained for all the FSP instances of Taillard (1993) are presented in Table 4.

Instances	Number of problems	Makespan	Total Flowtime	Completion Time Variance
20 x 5	10	0.1290238	-0.1440537	-1.2038674
20 x10	10	0.5334462	-0.0164544	-1.7613968
20 x 20	10	0.5329960	-0.0260092	-0.8586390
50 x 5	10	0.0890855	-0.2925054	-0.9330275
50 x 10	10	1.7541958	-0.0108922	-0.2059756
50 x 20	10	2.9814187	0.2434647	1.7126618
100 x 5	10	0.1713382	-0.7238382	1.2988817
100 x 10	10	0.6882989	-0.1191928	0.9198400
100 x 20	10	2.8784086	0.1476830	3.4646301
200 x 10	10	0.5498368	1.8246721	0.0000000
200 x 20	10	2.7011408	1.4120018	0.0000000
500 x 20	10	1.8172343	1.4205378	0.0000000

Table 4. $\overline{RPD}$ Values Obtained for the Various FSP Instances

The proposed discrete PSO algorithm generates good results with reasonable CPU time. CPU time taken by the proposed discrete PSO algorithm for various FSPs are presented in Table 5.

Instances	Number of Problems	Makespan	Total Flowtime	Completion Time Variance
20x5	10	0m25.164s	0m5.201s	0m6.642s
20x10	10	1m36.844s	0m12.113s	0m33.619s
20x20	10	6m22.854s	0m35.139s	2m16.764s
50x5	10	13m44.973s	0m39.888s	1m10.433s
50x10	10	55m38.305s	1m45.854s	6m19.487s
50x20	10	110m32.087s	10m33.215s	32m41.970s
100x5	10	19m42.310s	4m17.995s	10m39.676s
100x10	10	26m3.295s	9m22.616s	45m1.041s
100x20	10	62m14.918s	33m57.255s	84m4.257s
200x10	10	143m25.161s	41m33.599s	50m27.703s
200x20	10	166m27.657s	79m22.342s	129m58.384s
500x20	10	543m32.695s	792m17.371s	410m50.485s

Table 5. CPU time taken for Various FSP Instances

5. Discrete PSO Algorithm for Multi-Objective FSP

5.1 Concept and terminology

The real-world scheduling problems are multi-objective in nature. In such cases, several objectives must be simultaneously considered when evaluating the quality of the proposed solution. In multi objective decision problems one desires to simultaneously optimize more than one performance objectives such as makespan, tardiness, mean flowtime of jobs, etc. multi-objective optimization usually results in a set of non-dominated solutions instead of a single solution. The goal of multi-objective scheduling is to find a set of compromising schedules satisfying different objectives under consideration. For a given finite set of schedules generated by using a suitable algorithm for a multi-objective scheduling problem, various objective functions $f(x)=\{f_1(x),f_2(x),....,f_k(x)\}$ can be evaluated. These schedules are to be compared and a set of schedules called *non-dominated solutions* are to be identified. For those solutions, no improvement in any objective function is possible without scarifying at least one of the other objective functions. Some researchers have developed multi-objective metaheuristics for solving flowshop scheduling problems (Pasupathy et al. 2006; Prabhaharan et al. 2005; Loukil et al. 2005; Suresh & Mohanasundaram, 2004; Hisao Ishibuchi et al. 2003; Ishibuchi & Murata, 1998; Sridhar & Rajendran, 1996). A survey of multi-objective scheduling problems is given by T'kindt & Billaut (2001). A multi-objective PSO algorithm has been proposed for minimizing weighted sum of makespan and maximum earliness (Prabhaharan et al. 2005). A Pareto archived simulated annealing algorithm for multi-objective scheduling has been proposed (Suresh & Mohanasundaram, 2004). Hisao Ishibuchi et al. (2003) proposed a modified multi-objective genetic local search algorithm (MMOGLS) for multi-objective FSP. They showed that the performance of the evolutionary multi-objective optimization algorithm can be improved by hybridization with local search. They apply multi-objective GA for PFSP and the results are compared with results published in the literature. Pasupathy et al. (2005) proposed a pareto-ranking based multi-objective GA called Pareto genetic algorithm with local search (PGA-ACS) algorithm for multi-objective FSP with an objective of minimizing the makespan and total flowtime. Loukil et al. (2005) proposed multi-objective simulated annealing algorithm to tackle the multi-objective production scheduling problems.

Pareto dominance: Among a set of schedules P, a schedule $x^1 \in P$ is said to *dominate* the other schedule $x^2 \in P$, denoted as $(x^1 \phi x^2)$, if both the following conditions are true.

(i) The schedule $x^1 \in P$ is no worse than $x^2 \in P$ in all objectives.

(ii) The schedule $x^1 \in P$ is strictly better than $x^2 \in P$ in at least one objective.

When both the conditions are satisfied, x^2 is called as a dominated schedule and x^1 a non-dominated schedule. If any of the above condition is violated, the schedule x^1 does not dominate the schedule x^2. Among a set of schedules P, the non-dominated set P' are those that are not dominated by any member of the set (Deb, 2003).

Non-dominated front: The set of all non-dominated schedules.

Pareto optimal set: When the set P is the entire search space X, the resulting non-dominated set is called the Pareto optimal set.

The primary objective is to find a set of non-dominated fronts for the FSPs with the consideration of performance measures.

5.2 Proposed Multi-objective Discrete PSO Algorithm

The discrete PSO algorithm proposed for single objective FSP has been suitably modified to generate non-dominated solution set considering three performance measures simultaneously. Before presenting the proposed algorithm, the non-dominated sorting procedure, Pareto search procedure and the parameters considered are discussed below.

***Non- Domination Sorting*:** Non-domination measures are used to find non-dominated set of solutions. The following procedure is used to generate non-dominated particle or solution set from the population of particles. Consider a swarm consisting of N solutions (particles).

Step 0: Begin with $i = 1; j = i + 1$, and repeat steps 1 and 2.

Step 1: Compare solutions x^i and x^j for domination using the two conditions mentioned.

Step 2: If x^j is dominated by x^i, mark x^j as 'dominated,' increment j, and go to step 1. Otherwise mark x^i as dominated, increment i, set $j = i + 1$ and go to step 1.

All solutions that are not marked 'dominated' forms a non-dominated solution set and these are stored separately in a memory called archive.

Initialize the parameters
Generate the swarm and velocity
t = 0: // iteration counter
Evaluate all the particles
Perform non-dominated sorting to identify G_b^t
Open Archive to store G_b^t

Do {
  Update position;
  $t = t + 1$
  Evaluate
  Do non-dominated sorting to identify G_b^t
  Archive update
  Update velocity
} *while* $(t < t_{max})$: $t_{max} = 100;$
Output G_b^t

Figure 6. Iterative search loop of the multi-objective discrete PSO algorithm

***Pareto Search*:** In case of a single objective scheduling optimization, an optimal solution forms the Global best (G_b^t). Under multi-objective scheduling, with multiple objectives, G_b^t consist of a set of non-dominated solutions. Once the swarm is initialized, $G_b\,(t = o)$ is obtained after non-dominated sorting of the particles. During the subsequent iterations, position and velocity update of the particles are carried out using local best and global best. It is to be noted that one solution is randomly chosen from the archive as Global best set. During every iteration, non-dominated solution set is updated. This non-dominated solution set is added with the Archive and the combined set is sorted for non-dominance. Dominated solutions within the combined set are removed and the remaining non-dominated solutions forms $G_b\,(t = 1)$. This procedure is repeated to guide the non-dominated search process towards the Pareto region. Initially, a set of particles are generated randomly and evaluated. Then the non-dominated sorting of particles is done. Within the swarm, the non-dominated solution set i.e. G_b^t is identified and they are stored in an archive. Then the positions and velocities of the particles are updated iteratively. These current sets of non-dominated solutions are combined with the archive solutions. Non-dominated sorting of archive is done to identify the archive survival members. This process is called Archive update. During this, all dominated members of the combined set are removed. This procedure is repeated to guide the non-dominated search process towards generating a solution front close to the Pareto region. After the termination criterion is met, the solution set stored in the archive forms the result. The iterative improvement process of multi-objective PSO algorithm is presented in Figure 6.

5.3 Performance of Multi-objective Discrete PSO Algorithm

In this section, the performance measures namely minimization of makespan, total flowtime and completion time variance are considered simultaneously. It is to be noted that PSO algorithm has been very rarely studied by researchers for solving FSPs with multi-objective requirements.

Parameter Selection: Using the proposed algorithm, experiments are conducted to redesign the algorithm with appropriate parameter settings. Parameters were identified by trial and error approach for the better performance. The swarm size is taken as 80. The values of acceleration constants are fixed by trial and error as $C_1 = 1; C_2 = 2$ and $C_3 = 2$. The values of velocity coefficients U_1, U_2 and U_3 are generated randomly between 0 and 1. Termination criterion is taken as 100 iterations. The benchmark instances of Taillard (1993) form a set of 120 problems of various sizes, having 20, 50, 100, 200 and 500 jobs and 5, 10 or 20 machines have been taken and solved. When the iterative search process is continued beyond 100 iterations, solution quality is expected to improve further and the non-dominated front will converge towards the Pareto front. Some samples of non-dominated solution sets obtained during 1st, 50th and 100th iterations of selected benchmark FSPs are presented in Table 6. to Table 10.

1st Iteration			50th Iteration			100th Iteration		
C_{max}	F_Σ	V_T	C_{max}	F_Σ	V_T	C_{max}	F_Σ	V_T
2372	37335	143185.03	2418	37282	163238.72	2380	37749	121770.54
2385	37379	134831.95	2450	37645	139131.23	2395	37465	130522.04
2410	36900	148013.59	2451	38181	137003.64	2458	37187	210477.03
2412	37674	129799.71	2495	36838	186985.58	2465	37341	187537.33
2412	36970	138733.95	2518	39668	127576.64	2488	36988	148466.05
2414	36786	157977.52	2544	36566	258462.42	2493	36787	244247.03
2425	36842	155318.20	2550	36352	180610.66	2518	36639	213526.66
2432	36071	225477.25	2633	37206	175815.11	2545	36177	189031.61
2437	36855	150071.23						
2448	37604	125025.85						
2451	36764	158552.28						
2451	36600	172676.80						
2464	37521	134748.27						
2468	37875	124452.44						
2480	39012	119837.64						
2491	36170	154730.75						
2523	38802	123177.59						

Table 6. Non-dominated fronts obtained for 20 x 20 FSP (Problem ta025 of Taillard,1993)

1st Iteration			50th Iteration			100th Iteration		
C_{max}	F_{Σ}	V_T	C_{max}	F_{Σ}	V_T	C_{max}	F_{Σ}	V_T
3840	127915	674615.63	4168	138549	801359.25	4192	143728	688058.06
3923	132364	655699.19	4170	139913	794893.25	4218	142073	835741.13
3979	130656	669600.50	4181	140250	769993.81	4226	136757	870648.81
3979	132435	633633.38	4188	138913	756248.50	4241	140962	788543.19
3982	132026	666358.94	4243	137007	882535.81	4245	138443	845496.63
4018	136354	604771.06	4254	141017	750998.31	4266	137938	828836.88
4023	132426	646723.94	4284	136183	929310.25	4298	137356	866164.31
4034	135781	631409.19	4290	137714	833303.44	4324	143038	776172.63
4058	131370	652795.69	4295	135927	845500.88	4329	143586	760850.94
4081	137607	586079.44	4319	142649	731565.19	4334	141675	780154.75
4084	136148	601373.06	4320	140119	747898.00	4343	136398	868004.75

Table 7. Non-dominated fronts obtained for 50 x 20 FSP (Problem ta055 of Taillard,1993)

1st Iteration			50th Iteration			100th Iteration		
C_{max}	F_{Σ}	V_T	C_{max}	F_{Σ}	V_T	C_{max}	F_{Σ}	V_T
6719	414626	2332780.00	7079	442243	2714971.00	6977	429237	2643600.00
6736	407661	2339133.25	7122	431015	2619110.50	7187	429079	2992237.75
6754	407217	2426269.50	7125	430238	2888681.25	7222	423655	3181877.50
6759	414920	2322475.00	7279	427670	3036344.25	7266	427705	3032460.25
6772	421227	2319961.50	7307	426737	3014873.00	7287	426588	3061585.25
6776	420444	2215965.00						
6780	406735	2308902.00						
6785	417764	2299484.50						
6804	417373	2165440.25						
6934	402802	2477583.00						

Table 8. Non-dominated fronts obtained for 100 x 20 FSP (Problem ta085 of Taillard,1993)

1st Iteration			50th Iteration			100th Iteration		
C_{max}	F_{Σ}	V_T	C_{max}	F_{Σ}	V_T	C_{max}	F_{Σ}	V_T
11883	1341992	8681969.00	12169	1370395	8968974.00	12213	1382492	9226709.00
11922	1378165	8301979.00				12246	1418388	8839896.00
11935	1361242	8654574.00				12304	1390924	9191086.00
11938	1365058	8581394.00				12361	1380781	9530417.00
11964	1363602	8492216.00				12445	1379004	9589141.00
11995	1355612	8551758.00						
12020	1371423	8237680.50						
12051	1369441	8470111.00						
12115	1354810	8405068.00						

Table 9. Non-dominated fronts obtained for 200 x 20 FSP (Problem ta105 of Taillard,1993)

1st Iteration			50th Iteration			100th Iteration		
C_{max}	F_{Σ}	V_T	C_{max}	F_{Σ}	V_T	C_{max}	F_{Σ}	V_T
27361	7380460	53524660.00	27802	7498389	54440864.00	27612	7421436	53180528.00
27417	7405289	51892856.00	27811	7402468	53268448.00	27765	7458248	53042776.00
27448	7419382	51504108.00	27999	7543786	53059836.00	27870	7440681	53140668.00
27465	7394286	52016468.00	28091	7529455	52754652.00	27891	7374759	53306856.00
27534	7392887	51930096.00						
27593	7458730	51066888.00						
27603	7373445	51681608.00						
27638	7439401	51390116.00						
27680	7445450	51262332.00						
27700	7418177	51122680.00						
27729	7492150	51039416.00						

Table 10.Non-dominated fronts obtained for 500 x 20 FSP (Problem ta115 of Taillard,1993)

Normalized values of the performance measures are plotted for better visualization. Some samples of non-dominated front obtained during 1st, 50th and 100th iterations of selected benchmark FSPs are presented in Fig. 7. to Fig. 11.

6. Conclusion

Literature survey indicates that very few authors have studied the applications of multi-objective scheduling in flowshop scheduling using particle swarm optimization algorithm is scarce. This Chapter presents a discrete PSO algorithm to solve FSPs. This work has been conducted in two phases. In the first phase, a discrete PSO is proposed to solve the single-objective FSPs. In the second phase, a multi-objective discrete PSO algorithm is proposed to solve the FSPs with three objectives. The performance of the proposed single-objective discrete PSO is tested by solving a large set of benchmark FSPs. The quality measure namely "Average Relative Percent Deviation" ($\overline{RPD}$) is used to compare the solution quality obtained with the results available in the literature. It shows that the proposed discrete PSO algorithm performs better in terms of quality of results. Using the proposed algorithm, experiments are conducted to redesign the algorithm with appropriate parameter settings. The $\overline{RPD}$ for each set of instances are also shown in an efficient way. The parameters selected for solving the problems are holds good. The proposed multi-objective discrete PSO algorithm performs better in terms of yielding more number of non-dominated solutions close to Pareto front during the search. It is seen that, when the number of iterations is more, the non-dominated solution set generated is close to the Pareto front.

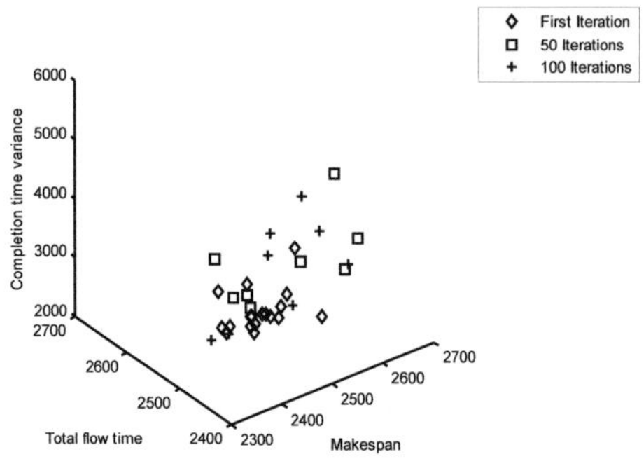

Figure 7. Non-dominated solution set obtained for 20 x 20 FSP (Problem ta025 of Taillard,1993)

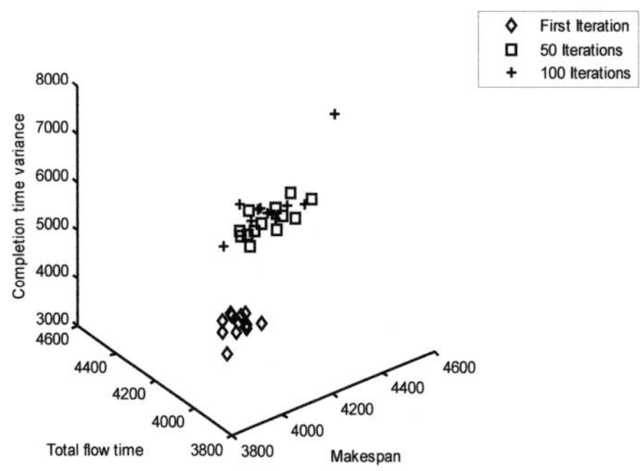

Figure 8. Non-dominated solution set obtained for 50 x 20 FSP (Problem ta055 of Taillard,1993)

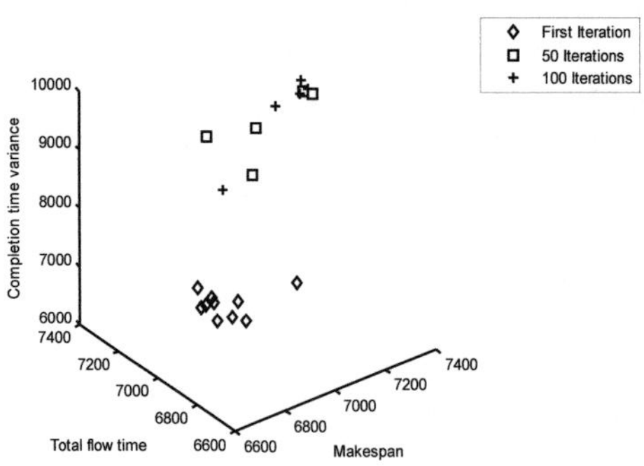

Figure 9. Non-dominated solution set obtained for 100x20 FSP (Problem ta085 of Taillard,1993)

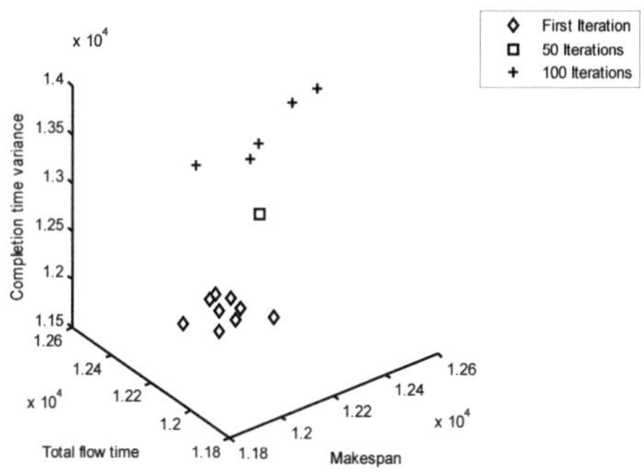

Figure 10.Non-dominated solution set obtained for 200x20 FSP (Problem ta105 of Taillard,1993)

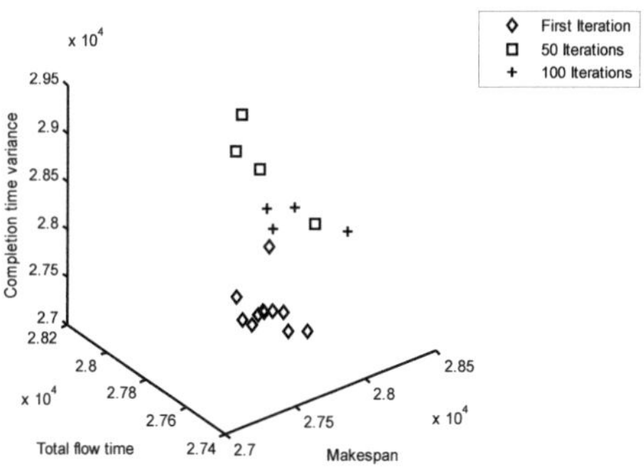

Figure 11.Non-dominated solution set obtained for 500x20 FSP (Problem ta115 of Taillard,1993)

7. References

Abido, M.A. (2002). Optimal power flow using particle swarm optimization. *Electrical Power and Energy Systems*, Vol.24, 563-571

Bagchi, T.P. (1999). *Multi-objective scheduling by Genetic Algorithms*, Kluwer Academic Publishers, Boston, Massachusetts

Baker, K.R. (1974). *Introduction to Sequencing and Scheduling*, John Wiley & Sons, New York

Brucker, P. (1998). *Scheduling Algorithms*, Springer-Verlag, Berlin

Campbell, H.G.; Dudek, R.A. & Smith, M.L. (1970). A heuristic algorithm for the n job, m machine sequencing problem, *Management Science*, Vol.16, No: 10, B630-B637

Chan, F.T.S.; Wong, T.C. & Chan, L.Y. (2005). A genetic algorithm based approach to machine assignment problem, *International Journal of Production Research*, Vol.43, No: 12, 2451-2472

Chandrasekaran, S.; Ponnambalam, S.G.; Suresh, R.K. & Vijayakumar N. (2006). An Application of Particle Swarm Optimization Algorithm to Permutation Flowshop Scheduling Problems to Minimize Makespan, Total Flowtime and Completion Time Variance, *Proceedings of the IEEE International Conference on Automation Science and Engineering, 2006 (CASE '06.)*, pp-513-518, ISBN: 1-4244-0311-1, Shanghai, China,

Chandrasekharan Rajendran. & Hans Ziegler. (2005). Two Ant-colony algorithms for minimizing total flowtime in permutation flowshops, *Computers & Industrial engineering*, Vol.48, 789-797

Christian Blum. & Andrea Roli. (2003). Metaheuristics in Combinatorial Optimization: Overview and Conceptual Comparison. *ACM Computing Surveys*, Vol. 35, No. 3, 268-309

Dannenbring, D.G. (1977). An evaluation of flowshop sequencing heuristics, *Management Science*, Vol.23, No: 11, 1174-1182

Dudek, R.A.; Panwalkar, S.S. & Smith, M.L. (1992). The lessons of flowshop scheduling research, *Operations Research*, Vol.40, No: 1, 7-13

Eberhart, R.C. & Hu, X. (1999). Human tremor analysis using particle swarm optimization. *Proceedings of the Congress on Evolutionary Computation*, pp-1927-1930, IEEE Service Center, Washington, DC, Piscataway, NJ

Eberhart, R.C. & Kennedy J. (1995). A New Optimizer Using Particles Swarm Theory, *Proceedings of the Sixth International Symposium on Micro Machine and Human Science*, pp-39-43, IEEE Service Center, Nagoya, Japan

Eberhart, R.C. & Shi, Y. (2001). Particle swarm optimization: developments, applications and resources, *Proceedings of IEEE Congress on Evolutionary Computation 2001*, Seoul, Korea

Faith Tasgetiren, S.; Mehmet Sevkli.; Yen-Chia Liang. & Gunes Gencyilmaz. (2004). Particle swarm optimization algorithm for single machine total weighted tardiness problem, *IEEE Transaction on Power and Energy Systems*, 1412-1419

Framinan, J.M. & Leisten, R. (2003). An efficient constructive heuristic for flowtime minimization in permutation flowshops, *Omega*, Vol.31, 311-317

French, S. (1982) *Sequencing and Scheduling: An introduction to the mathematics of the jobshop*, Ellis Horword Limited, Chichester, England

Gowrishankar, K.; Rajendran, C. & Srinivasan, G. (2001). Flowshop scheduling algorithms for minimizing the completion time variance and the sum of squares of completion time deviation from the common due date, *European Journal of Operational Research*, vol.132, No: 31, 643-665

Ignall, E. & Scharge, L. (1965). Application of the branch and bound technique to some flowshop-scheduling problems, *Operations Research*, Vol.13, 400-412

Ishibuchi, H.; Yoshida, T. & Murata, T. (2003). Balance between genetic search and local search in memetic algorithms for multi-objective permutation flowshop scheduling, *IEEE Transaction on Evolutionary Computation*, Vol.7 No.2, 204-223

Johnson, S.M. (1954). Optimal two-stage and three-stage production schedules with setup times included, *Naval Research Logistics Quarterly*, Vol.1 61-68

Kalyanmoy Deb. (2003). *Multi-objective Optimization Using Evolutionary Algorithms*, John Wiley & Sons, First Edition.

Kennedy, J. & Eberhart, R. (1995). Particle swarm optimization, *Proceedings of IEEE International Conference on Neural Networks-IV*, pp-1942-1948, Piscataway, NJ: IEEE service center, Perth, Australia

Kennedy, J.; Eberhart, R. & Shi, Y. (2001). *Swarm Intelligence*, Morgan Kaufmann, San Mateo,CA,USA

Liu, J. & Reeves, C.R. (2001). Constructive and composite heuristic solutions to the $P//\sum C_i$ scheduling problem, *European Journal of Operational Research.*, Vol.132, 439-452

Lixin Tang. & Jiyin Liu. (2002). A modified genetic algorithm for the flowshop sequencing problem to minimize mean flowtime, *Journal of Intelligent Manufacturing*, Vol.13, 61-67

Loukil, T.; Teghem, J. & Tuyttens, D. (2005). Solving multi-objective production scheduling problems using metaheuristics, *European Jour. of Operational Research*, Vol.161, 42-61

Merkle, D. & Middendorf, M. (2000). An ant algorithm with new pheromone evaluation rule for total tardiness problems, *Proceedings of the Evolutionary Workshops 2000*, pp-287-296, vol.1803, Lecture Notes in Computer Science, Springer

Moccellin, J.V. & Nagano, M.S. (1998). Evaluating the performance of tabu search procedures for flowshop sequencing, *Journal of the Operational Research Society*, Vol.49, 1296-1302

Nawaz, M.; Enscore Jr, E.E. & Ham, I. (1983). A Heuristic algorithm for the m-machine, n-job scquencing problem, *Omega*, Vol.11, 91-98

Ogbu, F.A. & Smith, D.K. (1990). The application of the simulated annealing algorithm to the solution of the $n/m/C_{max}$ flowshop problem, *Computers and Operations Research*, Vol.17, No: 3, 243-253

Osman, I.H. & Laporte, G. (1996). Metaheuristics: A bibliography. *Operations Research*, Vol.63, 513–623

Palmer, D. (1965). Sequencing jobs through a multi-stage process in the minimum total time-a quick method of obtaining a near optimum, *Opn. Research*, Vol.16, No: 1, 101-107

Pasupathy, T.; Chandrasekharan Rajendran. & Suresh, R.K. (2006). A multi-objective genetic algorithm for scheduling in flowshops to minimize makespan and total flowtime, *International Journal of Advanced Manufacturing Technology*, Springer-Verlag London Ltd, Vol.27, 804-815

Pinedo, M. (2002). *Scheduling: Theory, Algorithms and Systems*, Second edition,. Prentice-Hall, Englewood Cliffs, New Jersey

Prabhaharan, G.; Shahul Hamid Khan, B.; Asokan, P. & Thiyagu M. (2005). A Particle swarm optimization algorithm for permutation flowshop scheduling with regular and non-regular measures, *International Journal of Applied Management and Technology*, Vol.3, No: 1, 171-182

Rajendran, C., (1993). Heuristic algorithm for scheduling in a flowshop to minimize total flowtime, *International Journal of Production Economics*, Vol.29, 65-73

Rameshkumar, K.; Suresh, R.K. & Mohanasundaram, K.M. (2005). Discrete particle swarm optimization (DPSO) algorithm for permutation flowshop scheduling to minimize makespan, *Lecture Notes in Comp. Science*, Springer Verlag-GMBH.0302-9743. Vol.3612

Rinnooy Kan, A.H.G. (1976). *Machine Scheduling Problems: Classification, Complexity and Computations*, Nijhoff, The Hague

Ruben Ruiz. & Concepcion Maroto. (2005). A comprehensive review and evaluation of permutation flowshop heuristics, *European Journal of operational Research,* Vol.165, 479-494

Ruben Ruiz.; Concepcion Maroto. & Javier Alcaraz. (2004). Two new robust genetic algorithms for the flowshop scheduling problem, *OMEGA,* 2-16

Sensarma, P. S. ; Rahmani, M. & Carvalho, A. (2002). A comprehensive method for optimal expansion planning using particle swarm optimization, *IEEE Power Engineering Society Winter Meeting,* Vol. 2, .1317-1322

Sridhar, J. & Rajendran, C. (1996). Scheduling in flowshop and cellular manufacturing system with multiple objectives - A genetic algorithmic approach, *Production Planning and Control,* Vol.74, 374-382

Stuetzle, T. (1998). An ant approach for the flowshop problem, *Proceedings of the 6th European Congress on Intelligent Techniques and Soft Computing* (EUFIT '98), pp-1560-1564, Vol.3, Verlag Mainz, Aachen, Germany

Suresh, R.K, & Mohanasundaram, K.M, (2004). Pareto archived simulated annealing for permutation flowshop scheduling with multiple objectives, *Proceedings of the IEEE Conference on Cybermatics and Intelligent Systems,* pp-1-3, Singapore

Taillard, E. (1993). Benchmarks for basic scheduling problem, *European Journal of Operational Research,* Vol.64, 278-285

Tandon, V. (2000). Closing the gap between CAD/CAM and optimized CNC end milling. *Master's thesis,* Purdue School of Engineering and Technology, Indiana University ,Purdue University, Indianapolis.

Yoshida, H.; Kawata, K.; Fukuyama, Y. & Nakanishi, Y. (1999). A particle swarm optimization for reactive power and voltage control considering voltage stability. *Proceedings of the International Conference on Intelligent System Application to Power Systems,* pp-117-121, Rio de Janeiro, Brazil

Yuhui Shi. (2004). Particle Swarm Optimization, *IEEE Neural Networks Society,* 8-13

Yuvraj Gajpal. & Chandrasekharan Rajendran. (2006). An ant-colony optimization algorithm for minimizing the completion time variance of jobs in flowshops, *International Journal of Production Economics,* Vol. 101, No: 2, 259-272

26

A Radial Basis Function Neural Network with Adaptive Structure via Particle Swarm Optimization

Tsung-Ying Sun, Chan-Cheng Liu, Chun-Ling Lin, Sheng-Ta Hsieh and Cheng-Sen Huang
National Dong Hwa University
Taiwan, R.O.C.

1. Introduction

Radial Basis Function neural network (RBFNN) is a combination of learning vector quantizer LVQ-I and gradient descent. RBFNN is first proposed by (Broomhead & Lowe, 1988), and their interpolation and generalization properties are thoroughly investigated in (Lowe, 1989), (Freeman & Saad, 1995). Since the mid-1980s, RBFNN has been used to apply on many applications, such as pattern classification, system identification, nonlinear function approximation, adaptive control, speech recognition, and time-series prediction, and so on. In contrast to the well-known Multilayer Perceptron (MLP) Networks, the RBF network utilizes a radial construction mechanism. MLP were trained by the error Back Propagation (BP) algorithm, since the RBFNN has a faster training procedure substantially and adopts typical two-stage training scheme, it can avoid solution to fall into local optima.
A key point of RBFNN is to decide a proper number of hidden nodes. If the hidden node number of RBFNN is too small, the generated output vectors may be in low accuracy. On the contrary, it with too large number of hidden nodes may cause over-fitting for the input data, and influences global generalization performance. In conventional RBF training approach, the number of hidden node is usually decided according to the statistic properties of input data, then determine the centers and spread width for each hidden nodes by means of k-means clustering algorithm (Moddy & Darken, 1989). The drawback of this approach is that the network performance is depended on the pre-selected number of hidden nodes. If an unsuitable number is chosen, RBFNN may present a poor global generalization capability, as slow training speed, and requirement for large memory space. To solve this problem, the self-growing RBF techniques were proposed in (Karayiannis & Mi, 1997), (Zheng et al, 1999). However, the predefined parameters and local searching on solution space cause the inaccuracy of approximation from a sub-solution.
Evolutionary computation is a globally optimization technique, where the aim is to improve the ability of individual to survive. Among that, Genetic Algorithm (GA) is a parallel searching technique that mimics natural genetics and the evolutionary process. In (Back et al, 1997), they employed GA to determine the RBFNN structure so the optimal number and distribution of RBF hidden nodes can be obtained automatically. A common approach is applied GA to search for the optimal network structure among several candidates

constructed initially by the unsupervised clustering method (Chen et al, 1999). However, its results depend on the pre-selected RBFNN structures which may not be appropriate. Another method is to fix the number of RBF nodes and adopted GA to search optimal network parameters, for example, centers and spread widths for RBF hidden nodes, and the weights connected to the output layer (Aiguo & Jiren, 1998). This method requires heavy computational cost while the number of RBF hidden nodes is too large, the dimension of each chromosome has to extend to corresponding length. It will spend too much time for training. GA based self-growing RBF network training method was proposed by (Yunfei & Zhang, 2002) to overcome the mentioned drawbacks. It searches single parameter, the cluster distance factor, which can avoid organizing a large dimension in a chromosome. It performs a fast training speed and well convergences while the GA operators (reproduction, recombination, and mutation, etc.) and fitness evaluation is properly applied. However, GA-based approaches are poorer in several aspects, as premature convergence and falling into local optima, than new evolutionary computation techniques.

The particle swarm optimization (PSO) is a novel and popular search algorithm based on the simulation of the social behavior of birds within a flock in evolutionary computation. As opposed to (Yunfei & Zhang, 2002), this paper proposes a PSO based RBFNN self-structure algorithm to overcome the drawbacks that mentioned above. PSO is a swarm intelligence method that roughly models the social behavior of swarms and has been proved to be efficient on many optimization problems in science and engineering. The social behavior of PSO allows particles to stochastically return toward previously successful regions in the search space. We propose a PSO-based approach for searching the optimal cluster distance factor to provide a suitable criterion on self-structure RBFNN training. The results of simulation experiments exhibit the rapid convergence and more better optimal solutions than other related approaches. Furthermore, it yields efficient training for constructing RBFNN.

The paper is organized as follows. Section II describes structure and the training of the RBF network. Section III describes the principle and procedures of the self-structure RBF algorithm. Section IV presents the application of a PSO to search the cluster distance factor. Section V evaluates our method for modeling nonlinear function and predicting time series by RBF Network and comparing the results with the GA-RBF Network and K-means methods. Section VI is the conclusion.

2. Radial Basis Function Neural Network

Generally, a RBFNN consists of three layers: the input layer, the RBF layer (hidden layer) and the output layer. The inputs of hidden layer are the linear combinitions of scalar weights and the input vector $\mathbf{x} = [x_1, x_2, \cdots, x_n]^T$, where the scalar weights are usually assigned unity values. Thus the whole input vector appears to each neuron in the hidden layer. The incoming vectors are mapping by the radial basis functions in each hidden node. The output layer yields a vector $\mathbf{y} = [y_1, y_2, \cdots, y_m]$ for m outputs by linear combination of the outputs of the hidden nodes to produce the final output. Fig. 1 presents the structure of a single output RBF network; the network output can be obtained by

$$\mathbf{y} = f(\mathbf{x}) = \sum_{i=1}^{k} w_i \phi_i(\mathbf{x}) \tag{1}$$

where $f(\mathbf{x})$ is the final output, $\phi_i(\cdot)$ denotes the radial basis function of the i-th hidden node, w_i denotes the hidden-to-output weight corresponding to the i-th hidden node, and k is the total number of hidden nodes.

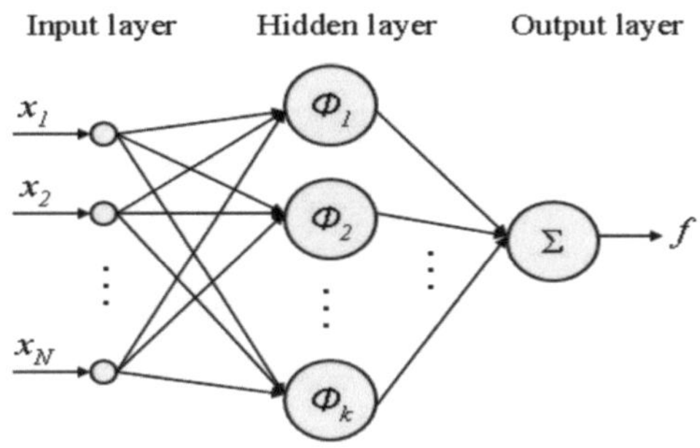

Figure 1. The structure of a RBFNN

A radial basis function is a multidimensional function that describes the distance between a given input vector and a pre-defined center vector. There are different types of radial basis function. A normalized Gaussian function usually used as the radial basis function, that is

$$\phi_i(\mathbf{x}) = \exp\left(-\frac{\|\mathbf{x}-\mu_i\|^2}{2\sigma_i^2}\right) \tag{2}$$

where μ_i and σ_i denote the center and spread width of the i-th node, respectively.

Generally, the RBFNN training can be divided into two stages:

1. Determine the parameters of radial basis functions, i.e., Gaussian center and spread width. In general, k-means clustering method was commonly used here.
2. Determine the output weight w by supervised learning method. Usually Least-Mean-Square (LMS) or Recursive Least-Square (RLS) was used.

The first stage is very crucial, since the number and location of centers in the hidden layer will influence the performance of the RBFNN directly. In the next section, the principle and procedure of self-structure RBF algorithm will be described.

3. Self-structure RBFNN

The hidden layer of an RBFNN acts as a receptive field operating on the input data space. The number of hidden node based on the distribution of the training data set. The proposed approach performs this task by defining a cluster distance factor, ε, which is the maximum distance between an input sample and a specific RBF node center and allowing the number of basis function to increase iteratively according to this factor.

The rationale of this learning is described as follows: the hidden layer starts with no hidden node and ε is pre-determined by PSO to control the clusters production. The first RBF node center μ_1 is set by choosing one data, x_1, randomly from N_T input data sample. The value of Euclidean 2-norm distance between μ_1 and the next input sample, x_2, is compared with ε.

If it is greater, a new cluster whose center location is x_2 is created as μ_2; otherwise, the elements of μ_1 are updated as

$$\mu_{1i}(\text{new}) = \mu_{1i}(\text{old}) + \alpha \left\| x_{2i} - \mu_{1i}(\text{old}) \right\|, i = 1,2,\cdots,N \tag{3}$$

where μ_{1i} and x_{2i} are the i-th component of vectors $\boldsymbol{\mu}_1$ and $\mathbf{x}_2$, respectively, $\|\cdot\|$ denotes the Euclidean distance and $0 < \alpha < 1$ is the updating ratio. Thus, this procedure is carried out on the remaining training samples. The number of clusters grows or RBF nodes center self-adjust continuously until all of the samples are processed. The proposed self-structure RBFNN algorithm can be summarized as follows:

1. Assuming that there are p clusters with their centers, $\mu_1,\cdots,\mu_p$, are generated from previous iterations. Taking a new input sample x_n to calculate the distances with the each clusters $\|x_n - \mu_i\|$, where $i = 1,\cdots,p$.
2. The cluster whose center μ_q is $\arg\min_{\mu_i}\left(\|x_n - \mu_i\|, \text{where } i = 1,\ldots,p\right)$ will be focused.
3. Comparing $\|x_n - \mu_q\|$ with the distance criterion parameter, ε. If it is greater than ε, then a new cluster center, μ_{p+1}, is created at the position of the sample point, x_n. Otherwise the elements of μ_p are updated by (3).
4. Repeating the above steps until all of the samples are processed.

For L clusters, a global spread width σ can be derived by the average of Euclidean distance between each cluster center and its nearest neighbor as

$$\sigma = \left\langle \left\| \boldsymbol{\mu}_i - \boldsymbol{\mu}_j \right\| \right\rangle \tag{4}$$

where $\langle\cdot\rangle$ denotes the expression for the average value for $1 \le i \le L$, $1 \le j \le L$ and $i \ne j$.

In (Yunfei & Zhang, 2002), the cluster distance factor, $\varepsilon \in (0,\infty)$, is obviously a critical factor to determine input space partitioning and obtains the hidden node number and locations in RBFNN. An unduly large value of ε does not reflect an enough number of cluster so it may cause a poor-generalized precision solution. On the contrary, an unduly small value of ε will create redundant clusters; therefore, it may cause overlap between RBF neurons; moreover, it may lead to poor accuracy and slow convergence either. This paper proposes a PSO-based searching approach to determine the proper value of ε; further, the optimal structure of RBF network can be obtained. And, an objective function to evaluate the effectiveness of applying PSO is proposed. Following section will describe how to employ PSO technique to search a potential optimal value ε.

4. PSO-based Self-structure RBFNN

The PSO is a population based optimization technique that was proposed by Kennedy and Eberhart in 1995 (Eberhart & Kennedy, 1995), which the population is referred to as a *swarm*. The particles express the ability of fast convergence to local and/or global optimal position(s) over a small number of generations.

4.1 Evolution of PSO

A swarm of PSO consists of a number of particles. Each particle represents a potential solution of the optimization task. All of the particles iteratively discover the probable solution. Each particle generates a position according to the new velocity and the previous positions of the particle, and it is compared with the best position which is generated by previous particles according to the cost function. The best solution is then kept; i.e., each particle accelerates in the directions of not only the local best solution but also the global best position. If a particle discovers a new probable solution, other particles will move closer to it so as to explore the region more completely in the process (Gudise & Venayagamoorthy, 2003).

Let N denotes the swarm numbers. In general, there are three attributes, current position a_{ij}, current velocity v_{ij} and past best position Pb_{ij}, for particles in the search space to present their features. Each particle in the swarm is iteratively updated according to the aforementioned attributes assuming that the objective function f is to be minimized so that the dimension consists of n particles and the new velocity of every particle is updated by (5).

$$\begin{aligned} v_{ij}(t+1) = w v_{ij}(t) + c_1 r_{1,i}(t)[Pb_{ij}(t) - a_{ij}(t)] \\ + c_2 r_{2,i}(t)[Gb_i(t) - a_{ij}(t)] \end{aligned} \tag{5}$$

where v_{ij} is the velocity of the j-th particle of the i-th swarm for all $i \in 1 \dots N$, w is the inertia weight of velocity, c_1 and c_2 denote the *acceleration coefficients*, r_1 and r_2 are two uniform random values falling in the range between (0, 1), and t is the number of generations. The new position of the i-th particle is calculated as follows:

$$a_{ij}(t+1) = a_{ij}(t) + v_{ij}(t+1) \tag{6}$$

The past best solution of each particle is updated by:

$$Pb_i(t+1) = \begin{cases} Pb_i(t), & \text{if } f(a_i(t+1)) \geq f(Pb_i(t)) \\ a_i(t+1), & \text{otherwise} \end{cases} \tag{7}$$

The global best solution Gb will be found from all of particles during previous three steps are defined as:

$$Gb\ (t+1) = \arg \min_{Pb_i} f(Pb_i(t+1)), \ \ 1 \leq i \leq n \tag{8}$$

4.2 Disturbance

Since initial particles are generated by randomly, they may not uniform enough to distribute over the solution space. Therefore, it may trap particles into local optimal solution inevitably. To avoid solution falling into the local minimal and jumping it out to find the global minimal, this paper added a mutation-like disturbance strategy into the PSO process (Sun et al, 2005). The disturbance mechanism randomly activates under a disturbance probability. While the disturbance mechanism is active, the selected particle will be randomly placed at a new position (ε value in this paper), then this particle will keep following the PSO process to search a better solution. The other non-selected particle will keep following the PSO iteration as usual and trying to find a new solution.

4.3 Objective function

For searching a suitable ε value for RBFNN training, a function of root mean squared error (RMSE) which evaluates discrepancies between the sampling data output y_n and the predictive output y_n^* is applied. Thus, the objective function for N_T sample is defined as

$$f(\varepsilon, y_n^*) = \text{RMSE}(y) = \sqrt{\frac{\sum_{k=1}^{N_T} \left(y_n(k) - y_n^*(k)\right)}{N_T}} \tag{9}$$

where $y_n^*(k)$ is the predictive output of the k-th sample data which is obtained by ε value during training.

In the section II, the relationship between self-structure RBF network training and cluster distance factor ε was discussed. If (9) can be reduced to a sufficiently small value, a suitable value of ε could be obtained to train the structure of RBFNN. Thus, the predictive RBFNN output would be closed to the sampling data output.

4.4 RBFNN structure determination by PSO

In this paper, our goal is to minimize the value of $f(\varepsilon, y_n^*)$. The objective function minimized by PSO and found potential optimal solution finally. Since we only search one parameter by PSO (i.e., the cluster distance factor ε), the swarm number i=1, and defined the particle number as $1 \le j \le m$. In the initial state of PSO, all the particles' positions a_j (i.e., initial cluster distance factor ε) were set as 0.02, v_j were set as 0, and the Pb_j and Gb_j were initialized by a random number generator in the range of [0, 1]. After particles moved by (6), each particle will find a potential solution, the new past best position would be updated by (7), and the global best position would be updated by (8). The particle would keep moving to find a better solution until it reaches the goal or meets the termination condition (Lin et al, 2005). The pseudo code of our PSO-based cluster distance factor searching approach presented in Fig. 2.

```
Create and initiate an N-dimension PSO: P
Repeat:
    Execute PSO to update P by (5) and (6)
    for each particle i ∈ [1...m]
                if f(ε_ij, y_n*) < f(Pb_ij, y_n*)
          then Pb_ij = ε_ij
                if f(Pb_ij, y_n*) < f(Gb_i, y_n*)
          then Gb_i = Pb_ij
    endfor
Until Termination condition is met
```

Figure 2. The pseudo code of PSO-based cluster distance factor searching

5. Simulations and Results

5.1 Setting of simulation

The six nonlinear functions with different complexities are tested here. These tested functions are listed as follows:

Ex.	Tested function	Range
1	$y=\dfrac{(x-2)(2x-1)}{(1+x^2)}$	$x\in[-8,12]$
2	$y=\dfrac{\sin(x)}{x}$	$x\in[-10,10]$
3	$y=1.1(1-x^2+2x^2)e^{-x^2/2}$	$x\in[-5,5]$
4	$y=0.5\sin(\dfrac{x}{2})+\dfrac{(1+\cos x)}{2}$	$x\in[-4.5,10.8]$
5	$y=\sin(\dfrac{2\pi x}{5})+\sin(\dfrac{2\pi x}{10})$	$x\in[0,10]$
6	$y=-\sin(\dfrac{\pi x}{10})+\cos(\dfrac{2\pi x}{5})$	$x\in[-10,10]$

Table 1. The six tested nonlinear functions

In order to confirm the advantages of the proposed approach, the K-means algorithm (Moddy & Darken, 1989) and GA-based self-growing RBFNN training algorithm (Yunfei & Zhang, 2002) are also carries out in these tested functions. Due to (Yunfei & Zhang, 2002) adopted Simple Genetic Algorithm (SGA) which using binary coding to train RBF structure for saving computation time, but it will loose some accuracy compared to the real-valued, i.e., this method may not present the optimal solution. So we implemented it with Real-value Genetic Algorithm (RGA) to obtain accuracy results.

For every simulation, the training data set consists of 50 input-output data samples taken at random, and the testing data set includes 75 samples different from the training data set. For the definition of parameters in the proposed approach, w, c_1 and c_2 are given 0.12, 0.25 and 0.25 respectively, and the search range of ε is bounded between 0.2 and 1, the particle number is 10. For the GA-based self-growing RBFNN training algorithm the search range of ε in the input space is also in the range from 0.2 to 1, the crossover rate P_c is given 0.8, and mutation rate P_m is given 0.01, the population size is 10. For the K-means method, the optimal number of RBF neurons in the hidden layer is chosen to be 30 by experience.

5.2 Simulation results

After simulations, the RMSE of training data, RMSE of testing data, maximal error and number of hidden node will be presented in tables for each case. In these tables, the three involved algorithms are denotes as PSO-based, GA-based (Yunfei & Zhang, 2002) and K-means (Moddy & Darken, 1989). Additionally, the real data and approximated data will be shown in the same figure; meantime, the error from each approximation will be presented by figures. There three sub-figures in each figure, the results from the left sub-figure to the right sub-figure are generated by PSO-based approach, GA-based approach and K-means approach, respectively.

Example 1.

	PSO-based	GA-based	K-means
RMSE for training data	0.0332	0.0584	0.1552
RMSE for testing data	0.0520	0.0786	0.1962
Maximal error	0.3852	0.2355	0.9508
Number of hidden node	33	29	30

Table 2. Comparison between the three approaches in example 1

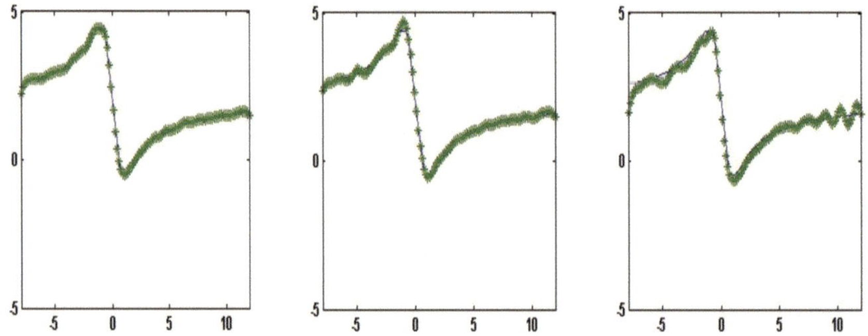

Figure 3. Curves of RBFNN output and real data in example 1. (solid-line represents the real data, dashed-line represents the output data)

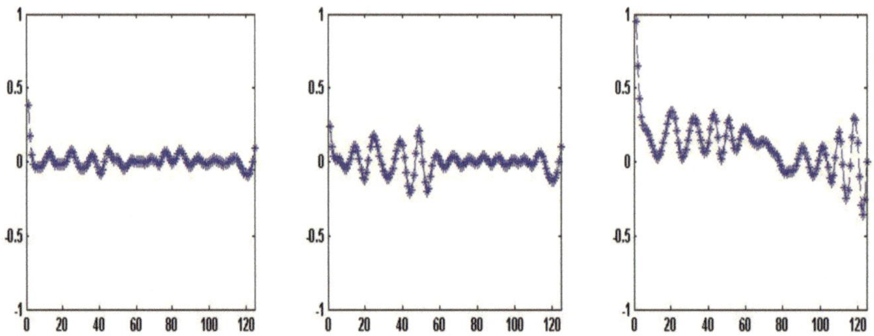

Figure 4. The errors between the real data and approximations in example 1

Example 2.

	PSO-based	GA-based	K-means
RMSE for training data	0.0035	0.0046	0.0234
RMSE for testing data	0.0099	0.0113	0.0357
Maximal error	0.0460	0.0509	0.1006
Number of hidden node	28	28	30

Table 3. Comparison between the three approaches in example 2

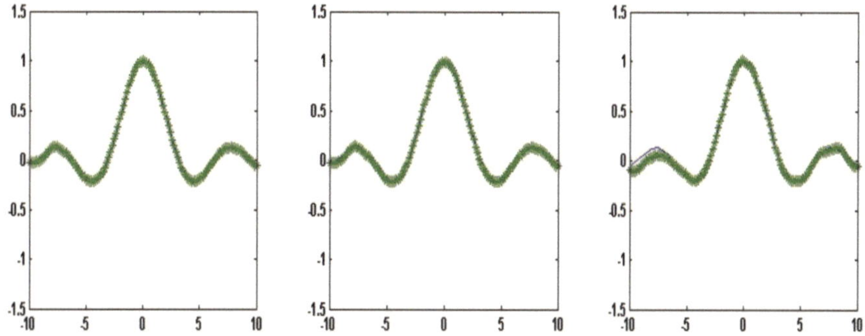

Figure 5. Curves of RBFNN output and real data in example 2. (solid-line represents the real data, dashed-line represents the output data)

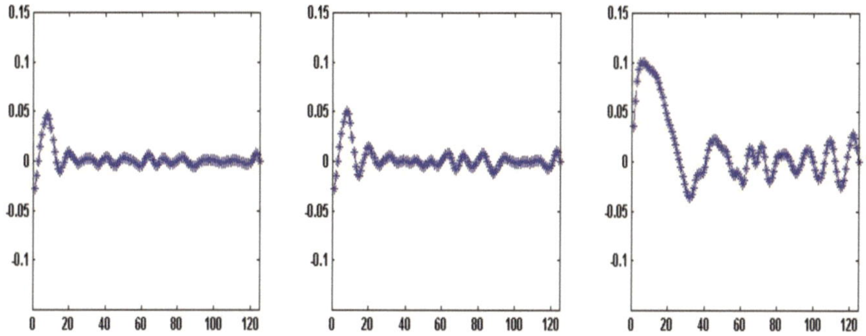

Figure 6. The errors between the real data and approximations in example 2

Example 3.

	PSO-based	GA-based	K-means
RMSE for training data	0.0056	0.0173	0.1271
RMSE for testing data	0.0057	0.0188	0.0803
Maximal error	0.0134	0.0432	0.2441
Number of hidden node	24	22	30

Table 4. Comparison between the three approaches in example 3

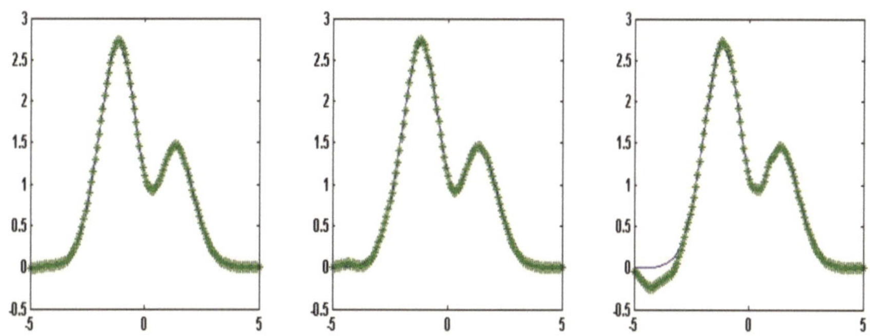

Figure 7. Curves of RBFNN output and real data in example 3. (solid-line represents the real data, dashed-line represents the output data)

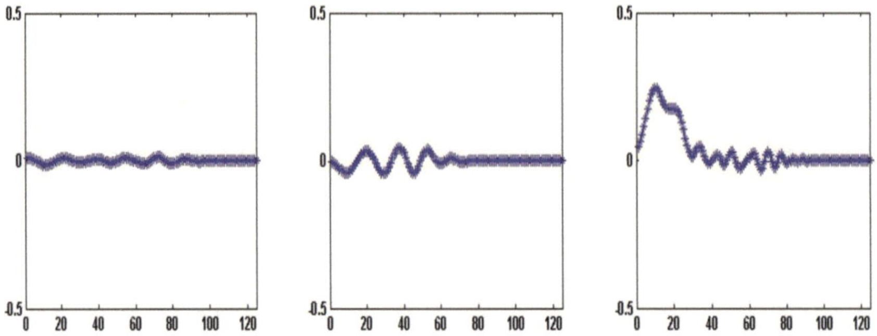

Figure 8. The errors between the real data and approximations in example 3

Example 4.

	PSO-based	GA-based	K-means
RMSE for training data	0.0079	0.0112	0.0337
RMSE for testing data	0.0192	0.0292	0.0740
Maximal error	0.1217	0.0939	0.1854
Number of hidden node	19	31	30

Table 5. Comparison between the three approaches in example 4

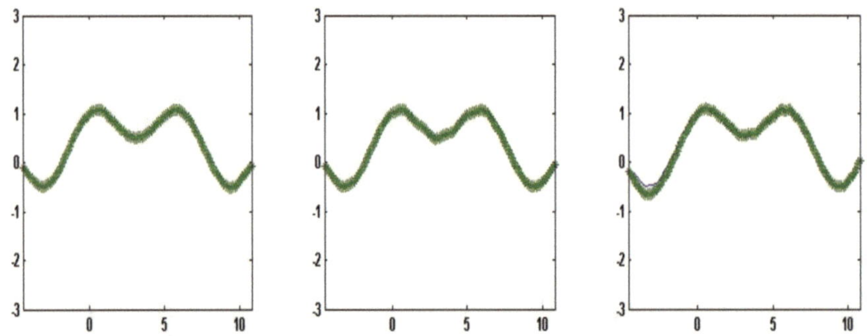

Figure 9. Curves of RBFNN output and real data in example 4. (solid-line represents the real data, dashed-line represents the output data)

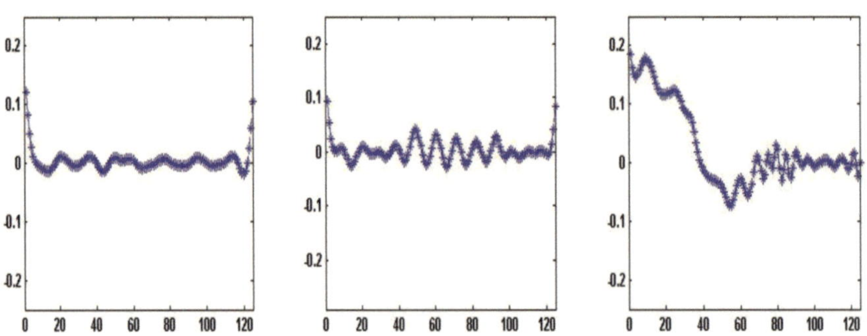

Figure 10. The errors between the real data and approximations in example 4

Example 5.

	PSO-based	GA-based	K-means
RMSE for training data	0.0460	0.0519	0.0637
RMSE for testing data	0.0546	0.0564	0.0867
Maximal error	0.3056	0.3236	0.2208
Number of hidden node	20	21	30

Table 6. Comparison between the three approaches in example 5

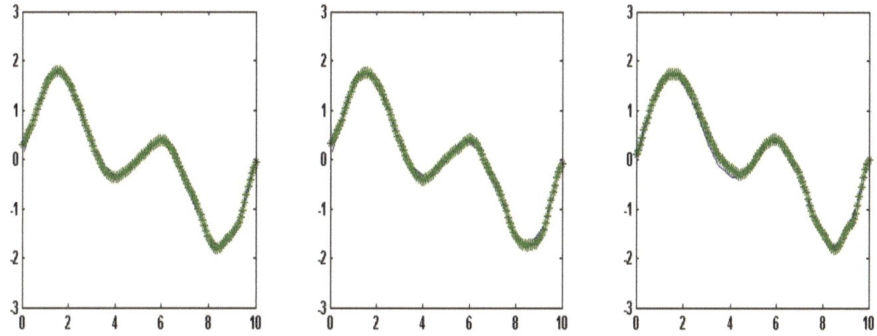

Figure 11. Curves of RBFNN output and real data in example 5. (solid-line represents the real data, dashed-line represents the output data)

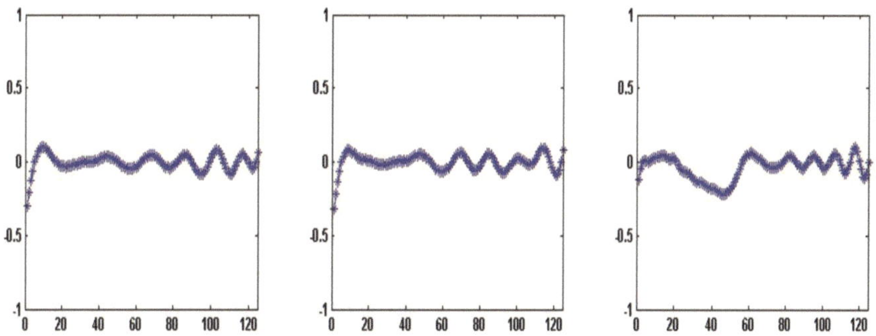

Figure 12. The errors between the real data and approximations in example 5

Example 6.

	PSO-based	GA-based	K-means
RMSE for training data	0.0079	0.0092	0.0690
RMSE for testing data	0.0439	0.0509	0.0859
Maximal error	0.2159	0.2486	0.1855
Number of hidden node	29	27	30

Table 7. Comparison between the three approaches in example 6

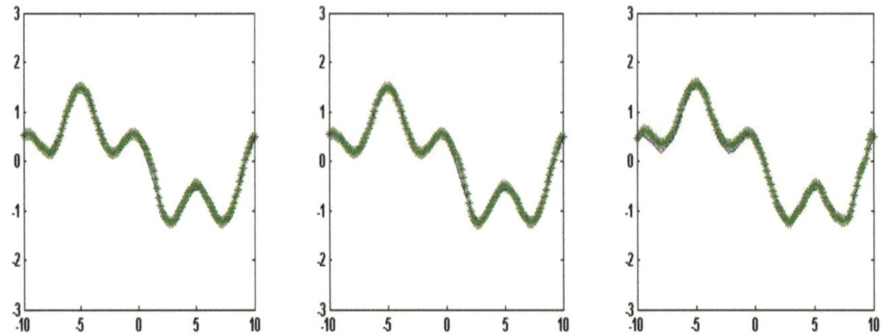

Figure 13. Curves of RBFNN output and real data in example 6. (solid-line represents the real data, dashed-line represents the output data)

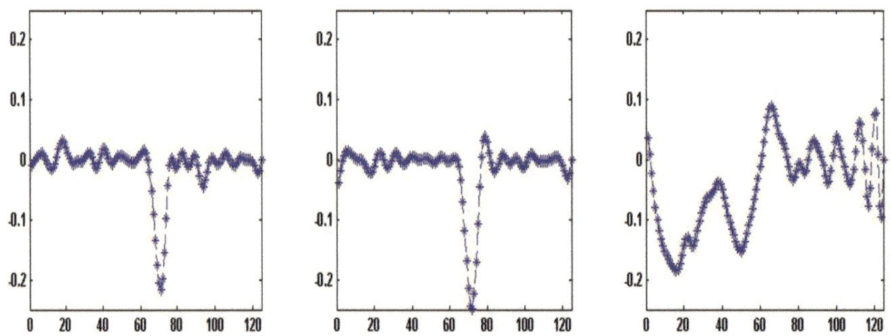

Figure 14. The errors between the real data and approximations in example 6

5.3 Discussion

In the simulation results in tables, PSO-based approach has lower RMSE for training data and testing data. It means that over fitting does not happen in the proposed approach. From figures of the curves of RBFNN output and real data, the approximated curves by PSO-based approach is closer to the real data than these by others. From figures of the approximated errors, it could be shown that PSO-based approach results small error in most of sample, whereas the K-means approach has largest error.

We know that RBFNN needs different number of hidden node and cluster radius for different complexities. K-means approach usually performs a larger error because it is not able to decide a suitable number of hidden node. Though GA-based approach decides a suitable number of hidden node, its cluster radius is not good enough to classify whole data. The proposed approach is able to find out the optimal cluster radius to further decide a number of hidden node because PSO has better capacity of global searching than GA.

6. Conclusion

This paper has presented a novel approach for self-structure RBFNN. A very important step for the RBFNN training is to decide a proper number of hidden node. If the number of hidden node does not chosen properly, the RBFNN may present poor global generalization capability, slow training speed, and the requirement of large memory space. Therefore, to decide a suitable cluster distance factor (ε) is the crucial condition for creating an optimal self-structure RBFNN. This paper proposed a PSO-based approach for searching the optimal ε ; further, RBFNN is able to determine the optimal number of hidden node automatically. For proofing benefits of the proposed PSO-based approach, the simulations consisting of six nonlinear system modeling were tested; meanwhile, GA-based approach and K-means approach were also carried out for comparison. Simulation results show that the PSO-RBFNN algorithm outperforms the GA-RBFNN and K-means methods by the minimal training RMSE and the minimal testing RMSE.

7. References

Aiguo, S. & Jiren, L. (1998). Evolving Gaussian RBF network for nonlinear time series modeling and prediction, *IEEE Electronics Letters*, Vol. 34 (12), pp. 1241-1243

Broomhead, D. S. & Lowe, D. (1988). Multivariable functional interpolation and adaptive networks, *Complex Systems*, Vol. 2, pp. 321-355

Back, T.; Hammel, U. & Schwefel, H. P. (1997). Evolutionary computation: comments on the history and current state, *IEEE Trans. on Evolutionary Computation*, Vol. 1, pp. 3-17

Chen, S.; Wu, Y. & Luk, B. L. (1999). Combined genetic algorithm optimization and regularized orthogonal least squares learning for radial basis function networks, *IEEE Trans. on Neural Networks*, Vol. 10 (5), pp. 1239-1243

Chen, S. (1995). Nonlinear time series modeling and prediction using Gaussian RBF networks with enhances clustering and RLS learning, *Electronics Letters*, Vol. 31, No. 2, pp. 117-118

Eberhart, R. C. & Kennedy, J. (1995). A new optimizer using particle swarm theory, *Proceeding of 6th Int. Symp. Micro Machine and Human Science*, pp. 39-43

Freeman, J. A. S. & Saad, D. (1995). Learning and generalization in radial basis function networks, *Neural Computation*, Vo. 9 (7), pp. 1601-1622

Gudise, V. G. & Venayagamoorthy, G. K. (2003). Comparison of Particle Swarm Optimization and Backpropagation as Training Algorithms for Neural Networks, *Proceeding of IEEE Swarm Intelligence Symposium*, pp. 110-117

Karayiannis, N.B & Mi, G.W. (1997). Growing radial basis neural networks : merging supervised and unsupervised learning with network growth techniques, *IEEE Trans. on Neural Networks*, Vol. 8 (6), pp. 1492-1506

Lin, C. L.; Hsieh, S. T.; Sun, T. Y. & Liu, C. C. (2005). PSO-based learning rate adjustment for blind source separation, *Proceeding of International Symposium on Intelligent Signal Processing and Communications Systems*, pp. 181-184

Lowe, D. (1989). Adaptive radial basis function nonlinearities, and the problem of generalization, *Procedings of IEE International Conference on Artificial Neural Networks*, pp. 171-175

Moddy, Y. & Darken, C. J. (1989). Fast learning in network of locally tuned processing unites, *Neural computation*, Vol.1, pp. 281-294

Song, A. & Lu, J. (1988). Evolving Gaussian RBF network for nonlinear time series modeling and prediction, *Electronics Letters*, Vol. 34, No.12, pp. 1241-1243

Sun, T. Y.; Hsieh, S. T. & Lin, C. W. (2005). Particle Swarm Optimization Incorporated with Disturbance for Improving the Efficiency of Macrocell Overlap Removal and Placement, *Proceeding of The 2005 International Conference on Artificial Intelligence*, pp. 122-125

Yunfei, B. & Zhang, L. (2002). Genetic algorithm based self-growing training for RBF neural Network, *IEEE Neural Networks*, Vol. 1, pp. 840-845

Zheng, N.; Zhang, Z.; Shi, G. & Qiao, Y. (1999). Self-creating and adaptive learning of RBF networks: merging soft-completion clustering algorithm with network growth technique, *Proceeding of International Joint Conference on Neural Networks*, Vol. 2, pp. 1131-1135

27

A Novel Binary Coding Particle Swarm Optimization for Feeder Reconfiguration

Men-Shen Tsai and Wu-Chang Wu
National Taipei University of Technology
Taipei, Taiwan

1. Introduction

Power distribution systems are formed by many inter-connected feeders. Each feeder is further partitioned into many load-zones by switches. These switches can be divided into two categories: normally closed sectionalizing-switches and normally opened tie-switches. During normal operation, the structure of distribution system must be maintained in radial structure by properly adjusting the status of the switches. The distribution system can be reconfigured by changing the status of these switches while maintaining the radial structure. The feeder reconfiguration serves several purposes, for example, reducing power losses, maintaining load balance and enhancing service reliability. The mean of a switch operation plan is that by changing the status of sectionalizing-switches and tie-switches, loads can be transferred from one feeder to an adjacent feeder to redistribute loads without violating the operation limitations. However, great deals of switches exist on distribution systems. The number of possible solutions for feeder reconfiguration is increased in exponential order when the number of switches on distribution system increases. Thus selecting the best switch operation plan from all feasible solutions can be considered as an NP-Complete problem. Because the status of switches can be represented as '1' or '0', the problem of feeder reconfiguration can also be regarded as '1' and '0' permutation combinatorial optimization problems.

Researchers studied the feeder reconfiguration problems using different methods in the past decades. The results of these researches provide acceptable solutions for feeder reconfiguration problems. Heuristic methods to minimize power losses and improve the searching speed were proposed in (Baran & Wu, 1989). Soft computing approaches were applied to the problem extensively as well, for example, neural network (Kim et al., 1993), simulated annealing (SA) (Chang & Kuo, 1994), genetic algorithm (GA) (Nara et al., 1992; Kitayama & Matsumoto, 1995) and evolutionary programming (EP) (Hsiao, 2004; Hsu & Tsai, 2005). Algorithms based on concept of mimicking swarm intelligent are popular in recent years. For instance, ant colony optimization (ACO) (Teng & Lui, 2003; Carpaneto & Chicco, 2004; Khoa & Phan, 2006) and particle swarm optimization (PSO) (Chang & Lu, 2002) are the algorithms that can be applied to the field of optimization problems. These algorithms are applied to the problems of power distribution system gradually.

This research will apply the concept of PSO algorithm that is a novel and suitable algorithm for solving combinatorial optimization problems. Kennedy and Eberhart (Kennedy &

Eberhart, 1995; Shi & Eberhart, 1998) proposed PSO (typical PSO) in 1995. The PSO can be treated as the branch of the evolutionary algorithms and it introduces the concept of swarm intelligent. There are many similarities between PSO and Genetic Algorithm (GA). Both algorithms produce an initial solution set randomly at first. Through iterations of the evolution process, optimal solution can be obtained. The major difference between GA and PSO is that PSO has no explicit selection, crossover and mutation operations (Eberhart & Shi, 1998). Searching process in PSO is based on the previous best solution of a particle and the best solution of the population so far to update particle's information. That means the particles will share the best information between each other and lead the particles moving toward the target. Due to the searching mechanism designed in PSO, the probability of falling into local solution for PSO algorithm can be reduced. Also, the concept of PSO is simple and is easy to implement than GA. Thus, PSO can be a powerful algorithm to aid and speed up the decision-making process for feeder reconfiguration problems to identify the best switching plan.

As mentioned previously, feeder reconfiguration problems are non-linear discrete optimization problems. However, the typical PSO is designed for continuous function optimization problems; it is not designed for discrete function optimization problems. Fortunately, Kennedy and Eberhart proposed a modified version of PSO called Binary Particle Swarm Optimization (BPSO) that can be used to solve discrete function optimization problems (Eberhart & Kennedy, 1997). Although BPSO can be applied to solve the discrete optimization problems, there are still problems when BPSO is applied for feeder reconfiguration problems. In feeder reconfiguration problems, there are a large number of tie-switches. Randomly choosing the locations of these tie-switches will cause outages or non-radial structure in distribution systems. In (Chang & Lu, 2002), BPSO is used to solve the feeder reconfiguration problems and the method they proposed avoided the problem of unsuitable numbers of tie-switches. The concept of (Chang & Lu, 2002) is based on BPSO and the moving velocity of particle is defined in terms of probabilities. Instead of BPSO used in (Chang & Lu, 2002), this research tries to construct a more feasible discrete PSO scheme based on typical PSO for feeder reconfiguration. The method proposed in this research modifies the operators of PSO's formula based on the characteristics of both the status of switches and the shift operator to construct the binary coding particle swarm optimization for feeder reconfiguration. Minimizing total line losses and load balancing without violating operation constraints and maintaining radial structure are the two objective functions in this research. The simulations will be performed and the results are used to compare the proposed method, the method proposed in (Chang & Lu, 2002) and BPSO to verify the performance and effectiveness. A distribution system in Taiwan Power Company (TPC) is used in this study to verify the stability and usefulness of the proposed algorithm.

2. Problem Statement

There are all kinds of loads on distribution systems and these loads distributed non-evenly on the distribution feeders. The uneven load distribution on feeders may cause the conductor overloading or transformer load unbalancing on distribution systems during emergency operation. Fig. 1 is a simple 3-feeder distribution system. The ampacity of each feeder is 300A. The total loads on each feeder are 105A, 250A and 200A respectively. This configuration is considered as an unbalanced distribution system when the feeder loading is concerned. The feeder reconfiguration can be performed by opening/closing of sectionalizing-switches and tie-switches on distribution systems to reduce line losses or increase the system reliability. Therefore, feeder reconfiguration can redistribute the loads and is a common practice for the distribution system operators to avoid the problems of the conductor/transformer overloading or unbalancing on distribution feeders or transformers. Fig. 2 is the result of feeder reconfiguration from Fig. 1. The loads on each feeder are 185A, 190A and 180A respectively after reconfiguration. As a result, the system is operated in a more balanced way. However, some constraints should be considered during feeder reconfiguration. These constraints include: the radial structure of distribution system must be maintained, all zones must be served, feeder capacity should not be exceeded and feeder voltage profile should be maintained. As mentioned earlier, the feeder reconfiguration problems can be treated as '1' & '0' permutation combinatorial optimization problems. '1' represents a normally closed switch; while '0' represents a normally opened switch. Considering a simple system shown in Fig. 1, the order of switch permutation is sw1, sw2, ..., sw11 in turn. Thus, the status of switch permutation of the system in Fig. 1 can be expressed as [1 1 0 1 1 1 1 0 1 1 1]. The result of feeder reconfiguration is shown in Fig. 2, and the switch permutation becomes [1 1 1 0 1 1 1 1 0 1 1].

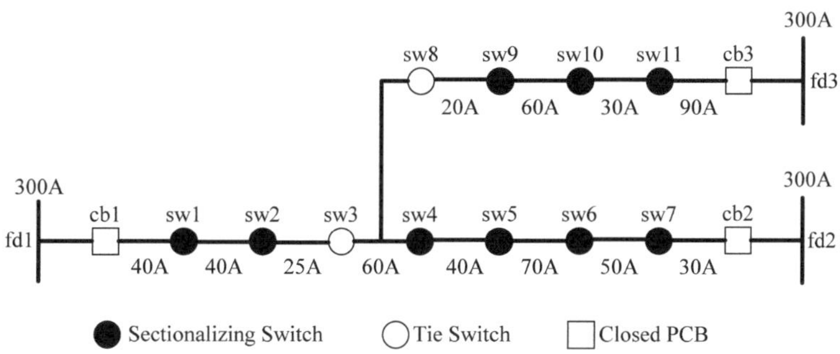

Figure 1. A simple 3-feeders distribution system

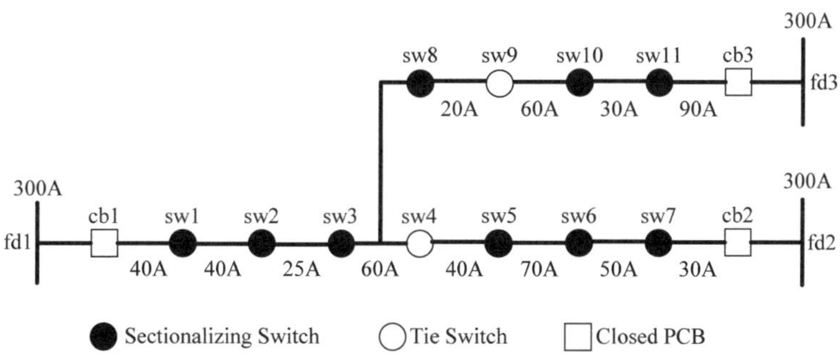

Figure 2. Result of feeder reconfiguration

Some objectives such as minimize the total line losses, minimize the numbers of operating switches, minimize voltage drop and load balance index are considered during feeder reconfiguration in general. Two objectives are considered in this research. The first is to minimize the total line losses during normal operation. By doing so, the operation of distribution system will be more economic and effective. The second objective is to distribute loads on feeders evenly. Balanced feeder loads can increase the opportunity of load transfer during emergency conditions and improve system reliability. The method proposed in this research also ensures that structure is maintained in radial and the ampacity of each conductor is kept within allowable limits. "Concentric load model" is used in this research for calculating branch currents. The line losses can be formulated as follows:

$$F_{loss} = \mathrm{Re}\left(\sum_{i=1}^{n} I_i^2 \cdot z_i\right) \tag{1}$$

where F_{loss} is the total real power losses of distribution feeders, n is the total numbers of zones in distribution system, I_i is the current magnitude of the i-th zone and z_i is the line impendence of the i-th zone. The load balance index is expressed as following:

$$F_{load\_balance} = \sum_{m=1}^{k}\sum_{n=1}^{k}(Cap_m - Cap_n)^2 \tag{2}$$

where k is number of feeder. Cap_m or Cap_n represents the total load of feeder m and n respectively. The total feeder loads can be calculated as following:

$$Cap_i = \sum_j Load_{i,j} \tag{3}$$

where, $Load_{i,j} \in Feeder_i$, i is the feeder number, and j is the load zone number within feeder i. In order to calculate the fitness value of the system represented by a particle, the method proposed in (Hsu & Tsai, 2005) is used to integrate the two object functions.

3. Particle Swarm Optimization

3.1 Typical Particle Swarm Optimization

A considerable amount of incredible social behavior and great intelligent exist in nature such as ant colonies, bird flocking, animal herding and fish schooling. Although the ability of individual is limited, the population can achieve the difficult target though cooperation with each other. Note that there is no centralized control in population. The behavior of individual depends on interacting with one another and with their environment only. These simple behaviors among individuals can lead population make themselves toward global behavior. Thus, completing a goal by aggregating the individuals and cooperating with each other that could be called swarm intelligent. Particle Swarm Optimization is one of the optimization algorithms provided with the concept of swarm intelligent. Original concept of PSO came from the study of simulating behavior of bird flocking to look for food. A possible solution for each problem can be represented as a particle that is just like a bird flocking in a D-dimensional searching space. Each individual particle has a fitness value that is evaluated by a fitness function to pick a good experience for itself and population respectively. The particles of population is initialized randomly first. A particle changed its searching direction based on two values or experiences during each iteration. The first one is the best searching experience of individual so far and it is called pbest. Another one is the best result obtained so far by any particle in the population and it is called gbest. When pbest and gbest are obtained, a particle updates its velocity and position based on (4) and (5). Lastly, the algorithm will check the results every iteration until the best solution is found or termination conditions are satisfied.

$$v_{id}^{new} = wv_{id} + c_1 \times rand() \times (pbest - x_{id}) + c_2 \times rand() \times (gbest - x_{id}) \quad (4)$$

$$x_{id}^{new} = x_{id} + v_{id}^{new} \quad (5)$$

In the above equations, v_{id} is the original velocity of the i-th particle, v_{id}^{new} is the new velocity of the i-th particle, w is the inertia weight, c_1 and c_2 are the acceleration constants, x_{id} is the original position of the i-th particle, x_{id}^{new} is the new position of the i-th particle and rand() is a random number ranging between 0 and 1.

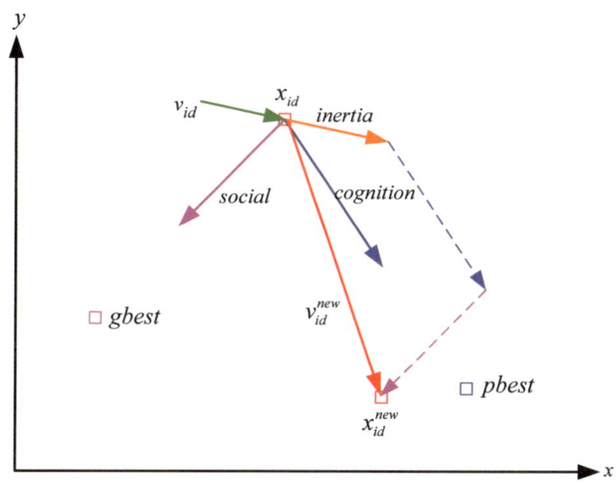

Figure 3. Searching diagram of typical PSO

In (4), the first part is the inertia (habitual behavior), which represents the particle trusts its own status at present location and provides a basic momentum. The second part is the cognition (self-knowledge) or memory, which represents the particle is attracted by its own previous best position and moving toward to it. The third part is the social (social knowledge) or cooperation, which represents the particle is attracted by the best position so far in population and moving toward to it. There are restrictions among these three parts and can be used to determine the major performance of the algorithm. The purpose of updating formula is to lead particles moving toward compound vector of inertia part, cognition part and social part. By doing so, the opportunity for particle to reach the target (optimal solution) will be increased. The inertia weight in the formula is used to adjust searching areas. A larger inertia weight will motivate the algorithm toward a global search; a smaller value will force the PSO toward a local search. The searching diagram of typical PSO is shown in Fig. 3.

3.2 Binary Particle Swarm Optimization

Kennedy and Eberhart proposed a binary version of PSO for discrete problems (Eberhart & Kennedy, 1997). In the binary PSO version, the particle's personal best and global best is still updated as in the typical version as described in (4). The elements inside x_{id}, pbest and gbest of BPSO are either `1' or `0'. Therefore, a particle flies in a search space restricted to zero and one. The speed of the particle must be constrained to the interval [0, 1]. A logistic sigmoid transformation function $S(v_{id}^{new})$ shown in (6) can be used to limit the speed of particle.

$$S(v_{id}^{new}) = \frac{1}{1+e^{-v_{id}^{new}}} \tag{6}$$

The update equation of BPSO can be done in two steps. First, (4) is used to update the velocity of the particle and the sigmoid function, (6), is used to limit the velocity in the interval [0, 1]. Second, the new position of the particle is obtained using (7) shown below:

$$\begin{aligned} &if\left(rand() < S(v_{id}^{new})\right) \ then \ x_{id}^{new} = 1 \\ &\qquad\qquad\qquad\qquad\qquad else \ x_{id}^{new} = 0 \end{aligned} \tag{7}$$

where, rand() is a uniform random number in the range [0, 1].
Since the relevant variables are derived from the changes of probabilities, the concept of BPSO is different from the typical PSO. It is hard to identify the relation between the current status and previous status of a particle. The selection of parameters, such as inertia weight, acceleration constants, etc., is also problematic.

3.3 Binary Coding Particle Swarm Optimization

Through the discussion of typical PSO and BPSO in the previous section, the PSO algorithm cannot be applied to feeder reconfiguration directly. Therefore, this research tries to construct a more feasible discrete PSO scheme based on the concept of typical PSO for feeder reconfiguration. The typical PSO must be modified based on the characteristics of distribution feeder operations. Two issues will be considered in the modification process. The first one is the problem of feeder reconfiguration is '1' & '0' permutation combinatorial optimization problem. The second issue is utilizing the shift operator that is used in computer programming languages. The shift operator and shift operator set defined in this research using these two aspects. Shift operator and shift operator set can be used to construct the binary coding particle swarm optimization for distribution feeder reconfiguration. These two definitions and the proposed binary coding PSO will be discussed.

3.3.1 Shift Operator

Suppose m sectionalizing switches (normally closed, N.C.) and n tie switches (normally opened, N.O.) exist on a distribution system. The permutation combination of the status all switches (s=m+n) is [S_1, S_2, …, S_s] and it will be called 'sequence of switch states', or SSS, in the rest of this paper. The shift operator is defined as SO (Bit_i, $Direction_{L,R}$, $Step_c$) and it means that an action will change the position of an N.O. in SSS. Bit_i is the index of i-th switch in SSS. $Direction_{L,R}$ indicates the direction of left or right shifting on the i-th switch. $Step_c$ is the number of shifting steps. The new permutation in SSS is defined as SSS'=SSS <+> SO. The symbol, '<+>', represents the shift operator. It will be applied to SSS to get a new SSS'.

A case is used to explain the operating process of shift operator. A simple distribution system shown in Fig. 4 has four feeders, nine N.C.s and three N.O.es. The SSS of this system is denoted as [1 0 1 0 1 1 1 1 1 1 0 1]. Supposing an SO(4, R, 1) is applied on this SSS. The process of operation is described as Fig. 5. When an N.O. shifts, a '1' (N.C.) needs to be set at its original position to maintain system structure.

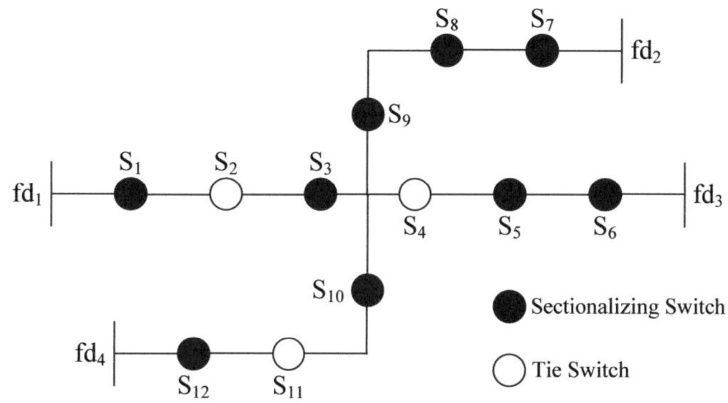

Figure 4. A simple 4-feeders distribution system

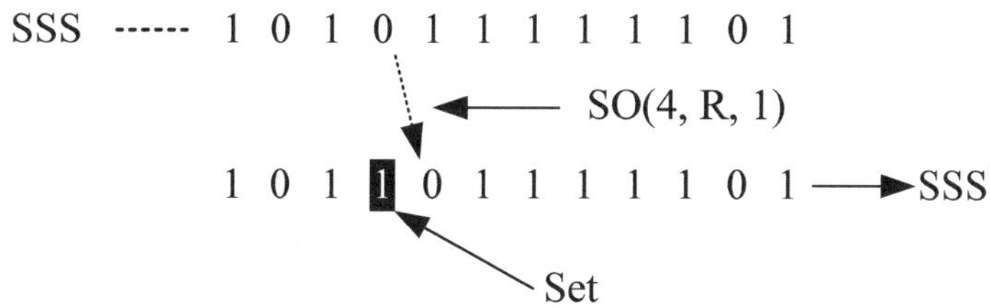

Figure 5. Basic operating process of shift operator

3.3.2 Shift Operator Set

A set with at least one or more shift operators is called shift operator set (SOS). An SOS represents all actions about how to set or shift normal open switches on distribution systems. The definition of shift operator set is shown in (8).

$$SOS = \{SO_1, SO_2, ..., SO_n\} \tag{8}$$

where n is the number of shift operators.

Considering two SSSes, SSS_1 and SSS_2, a set of shift operators which transfers SSS_1 to SSS_2 needs to be identified. Two SSSes, SSS_1=[1 0 1 0 1 1 1 1 1 1 0 1] and SSS_2=[1 1 1 1 0 1 1 0 1 0 1 1], are used to explain how the shift operators are obtained. By comparing the position of normally opened switch one by one in these two SSSes, the SOS can be acquired. The determination of the shift operator set and the result are shown as Fig. 6. In this example, SOS={ SO_1, SO_2, SO_3}= $SSS_2 \ominus SSS_1$. The symbol, '$\ominus$', is used to represent an action to get the shift operators from SSS_1 to SSS_2.

Base on the concept of above process, (pbest - x_{id}) and (gbest - x_{id}) in (4) can be rewritten as (pbest $\ominus$ x_{id}) and (gbest $\ominus$ x_{id}) respectively. The x_{id}, pbest and gbest represent different

SSSes in this sketch. This process will transfer an SSS to a new one which is closer to the best switch plan.

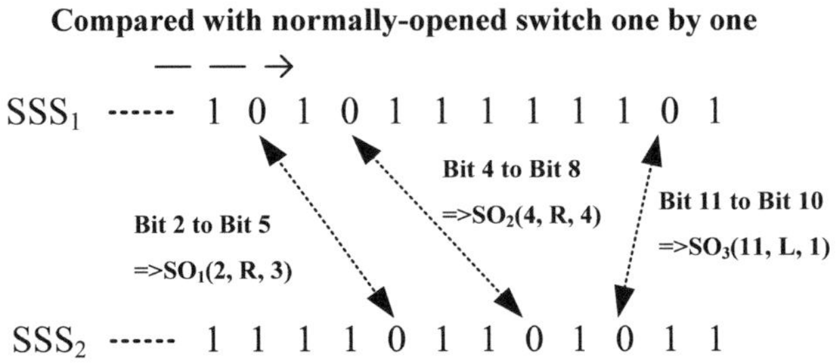

Figure 6. Decision process of shift operator set

3.3.3 Constructing Binary Coding PSO

The definition of shift operator and shift operator set are discussed in previous sections. The velocity update formulas (4) and (5) of PSO can be reestablished to solve the problem of feeder reconfiguration. The new velocity update formula for the proposed binary coding PSO is as below:

$$v_{id}^{new} = (w \otimes v_{id}) \oplus (rand() \langle\times\rangle (pbest \ominus x_{id})) \oplus (rand() \langle\times\rangle (gbest \ominus x_{id})) \tag{9}$$

$$x_{id}^{new} = x_{id} \langle + \rangle v_{id}^{new} \tag{10}$$

The symbol, '$\oplus$', shown in (9) is used for combining two shift operator sets. The symbol, '$\otimes$', is the operator that is used to shift the number of steps. The symbol, '$\langle\times\rangle$', is used to select the number of shift operator, SO, in (pbest $\ominus$ x_{id}) or (gbest $\ominus$ x_{id}) randomly. x_{id} is the original SSS of the i-th particle; pbest is the best SSS of the i-th particle; gbest is the best SSS of any particle in the population. v_{id} is the original shift operator set of the i-th particle, v_{id}^{new} is the new shift operator set of the i-th particle. x_{id}^{new} is the new SSS of the i-th particle. rand() is a random number with a range of [1, n] where n is the number of SO in SOS.

In Eq. (9), w is the inertia weight. The role of w is used for adjusting searching areas. The searching areas are reduced progressively when the number of iteration increases. The inertia weight can be calculated as (11).

$$w = \frac{iteration_{\max} - iteration_{now}}{iteration_{\max}} \times ShiftStep_{\max} \tag{11}$$

A simple example is used to show how the proposed method works. Based on the system shown in Fig. 4, x_{id}, pbest and gbest represent different SSSes are given:

x_{id} : [1 0 1 0 1 1 1 1 1 1 0 1]
pbest : [1 1 1 1 0 1 1 0 1 0 1 1]
gbest : [1 1 0 1 0 1 1 1 0 1 1 1]

The SOS can be derived from (pbest Θ x_{id}) and (gbest Θ x_{id}) as:

$$(\text{pbest} \,\Theta\, x_{id}) = \{(2, R, 3), (4, R, 4), (11, L, 1)\}$$
$$(\text{gbest} \,\Theta\, x_{id}) = \{(2, R, 1), (4, R, 1), (11, L, 2)\}$$

The three parts in (9) can be expressed as following:

$$w \otimes v_{id} = \{(2, L, 3), (4, L, 2), (11, R, 2)\}$$
$$\text{rand}() \langle\times\rangle (\text{pbest} \,\Theta\, x_{id}) = \{(2, R, 3), (4, R, 4), (11, L, 1)\}$$
$$\text{rand}() \langle\times\rangle (\text{gbest} \,\Theta\, x_{id}) = \{(2, R, 1), (11, L, 2)\}$$

According to (9), the v_{id}^{new} contains eight SOes, (2, L, 3), (2, R, 3), (2, R, 1), (4, L, 2), (4, R, 4), (11, R, 2), (11, L, 1) and (11, L, 2). Combining these eight SOes, the final v_{id}^{new} contains three SOes, (2, R, 1), (4, R, 2) and (11, L, 1). Finally the new SSS, x_{id}^{new}, will be [1 1 0 1 1 0 1 1 1 0 1 1] according to (10).

The procedure of proposed binary coding PSO is outlined as below:

a. Determine the size of population and other parameters such as number of iterations and maximum shift steps.
b. Initialize the SSS and shift operator sets randomly to produce particles.
c. Evaluate the fitness value for each particle.
d. Compare the present fitness value of i-th particle with its historical best fitness value. If the present value is better than pbest, update the information including SSS and fitness value of pbest.
e. Compare present fitness value with the best historical fitness value of any particle in population. If the present fitness value is better than gbest, update the information including SSS and fitness value for gbest.
f. Update the shift operator set and generate a new SSS of the particle according to (9) and (10), respectively.
g. If stop criterion is satisfied then stop, otherwise go to step c). In this research, the stop criterion is the iteration count reaches the maximum number of iteration.

4. Experimental Results

To verify the performance of the proposed algorithm and compare with algorithms of typical BPSO (Eberhart & Kennedy, 1997) and modified BPSO (Chang & Lu, 2002) for feeder reconfiguration problem, a four-feeder distribution system is used. This distribution system is taken from Taoyuan division, Taiwan Power Company, Taiwan. The system has 24 sectionalizing-switches, 8 tie-switches and 28 load-zones, as shown in Fig. 7. The capacity of each feeder is shown in Table 1. The objective functions are: minimizing feeder loss and load balancing index without violating operation constraints. The proposed method and the algorithms described in (Eberhart & Kennedy, 1997) and (Chang & Lu, 2002) were implemented using Java language for comparison purposes. Relevant parameters are set as follows. The size of population is 10 for all methods. Maximum number of iteration is set to 1000 for all methods as well. The inertia weight, learning factor of c_1 and c_2 for the methods

of typical BPSO (Eberhart & Kennedy, 1997) and modified BPSO (Chang & Lu, 2002) are set to 0.8, 2.0 and 2.0, respectively. The settings of these parameters can be referred to (Chang & Lu, 2002). In order to obtain the results and calculate the average performance, 10 runs were performed for each method.
The comparisons of the results from the three algorithms are shown in Table 2. The Max, Min and Average in Table 2 indicate the maximum, minimum and average fitness value, running time, losses and load balancing index values in 10 runs respectively. The typical BPSO is not able to get a better result than proposed algorithm due to the higher probability of inadequate number of tie-switches represented by particles. Although the running time of typical BPSO is less than proposed method, the average values of losses and load balancing index of typical BPSO are higher than proposed method. The modified BPSO is able to avoid the problem of inadequate number of tie-switches represented in each particle. On the other hand, the result of proposed method is better than other two methods. Beside the execution time of proposed method is two seconds longer than BPSO, all the other outcomes of proposed method are superior to other methods. The feeders which represent of maximum fitness value of feeder reconfiguration of the typical BPSO method, modified BPSO and proposed method are shown in Fig. 8, Fig. 9 and Fig. 10 respectively. Table 3 lists the comparison of total loads of each feeder obtained from the three methods. All the results indicate that the proposed method provides better and more reliable solutions than typical BPSO and modified BPSO methods for minimizing line losses and load balancing problem.

Feeder ID	F1	F2	F3	F4
Capacity (Amp)	500	500	250	500

Table 1. Capacity of each feeder

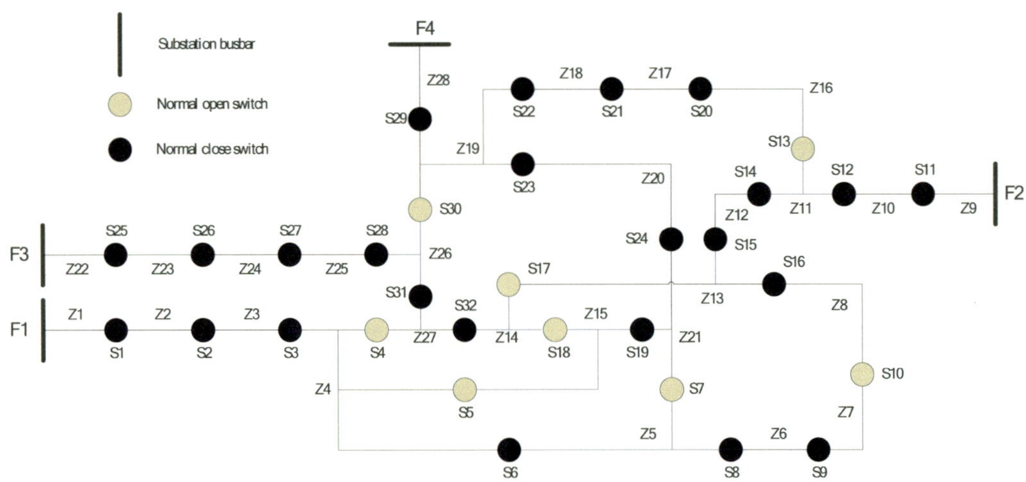

Figure 7. A 4-feeders distribution system for testing

Method		Typical BPSO	Modified BPSO	Binary coding PSO
Fitness Value	Max	0.8759	0.9121	0.9234
	Min	0.8058	0.8844	0.8898
	Average	0.8594	0.8992	0.9032
Running Time (msec)	Max	6625	11015	8734
	Min	5250	8812	8110
	Average	6212	10359	8354
Loss	Max	515kW	405kW	364kW
	Min	339kW	335kW	312kW
	Average	404kW	365kW	329kW
Load Balance Index	Max	525928	434216	264648
	Min	184712	183368	169112
	Average	329504	294859	208328

Table 2. Results and comparisons of three algorithms

Method \ Feeder ID	F1	F2	F3	F4
Original system	176	146	171	203
Typical BPSO	124	312	122	138
Modified BPSO	139	232	122	203
Binary Coding PSO	139	227	110	220

Table 3. The comparison of the feeder loading

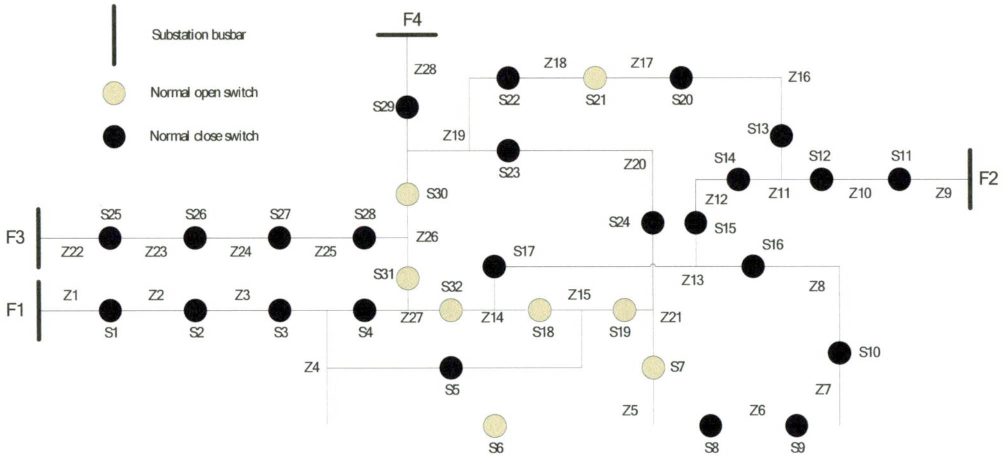

Figure 8. The final feeder configuration found by the typical BPSO method

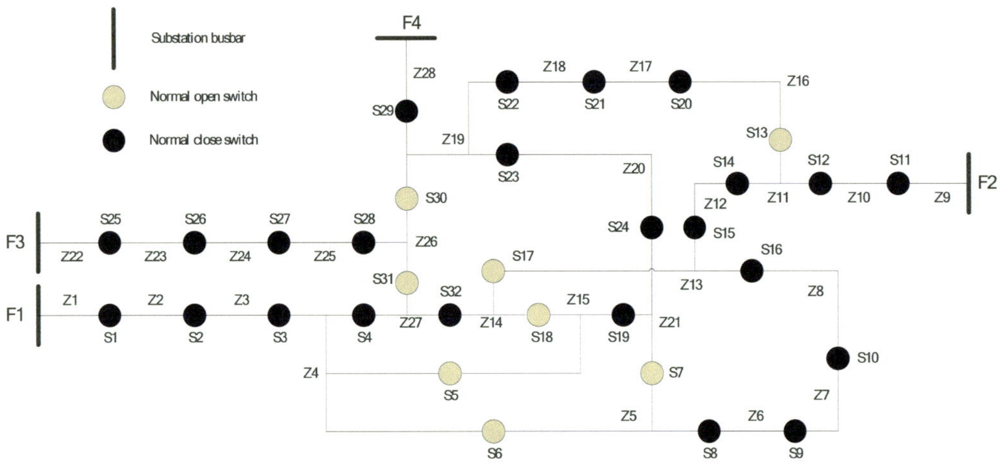

Figure 9. The final feeder configuration found by the modified BPSO method

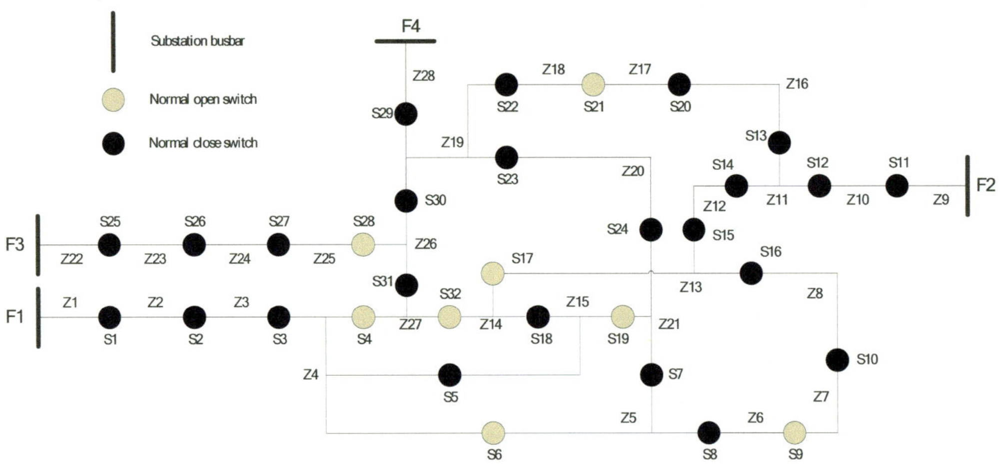

Figure 10. The final feeder configuration found by the proposed method

5. Conclusion

Particle Swarm Optimization is a novel and powerful algorithm for continuous and discrete functions optimization problems. In this work, the concept of typical PSO is modified and applied to the feeder reconfiguration problems. Feeder reconfiguration problems are non-linear discrete optimization problems in nature; and further, there are some defects to use typical BPSO directly for feeder reconfiguration. This research try to construct a binary coding particle swarm optimization based on typical PSO to solve this problem. The operators of typical PSO algorithm have been reviewed and redefined in this research to fit the application of distribution feeder reconfiguration. In addition, minimizing total line losses and load balancing without violating operation constraints are the objective functions used in this research. The experimental results show that the proposed method can solve the feeder reconfiguration problem more effectively.

6. Acknowledgement

This research was supported by the National Science Council, Taiwan under contract NSC 97-2221-E-027-110.

7. References

Baran M.E. and Wu F.F. (1989). Network Reconfiguration in Distribution Systems for Loss Reduction and Load Balancing, *IEEE Trans. on Power Delivery,* vol. 4, no.2, April 1989, pp. 1401-1407.

Chang H. C. and Kuo C. C. (1994). Network reconfiguration in distribution system using simulated annealing, *Elect. Power Syst. Res,* vol. 29, May 1994, pp. 227-238.

Chang R.F. and Lu C.N. (2002). Feeder Reconfiguration for Load Factor Improvement, *IEEE Power Engineering Society Winter Meeting,* Vol. 2, 27-31 Jan. 2002, pp.980-984.

Carpaneto E. and Chicco G. (2004). Ant-Colony Search-Based Minimum Losses Reconfiguration of Distribution Systems, *Proc. IEEE Melecon 2004,* pp.971-974, Dubrovnik, Croatia.

Eberhart R.C. and Kennedy J. (1997). A Discrete Binary Version of the Particle Swarm Algorithm, *In Proceedings of IEEE International Conference on Systems, Man, and Cybernetics,* vol. 5, pp.4104-4108, 1997.

Eberhart R.C. and Shi Y. (1998). Comparison between Genetic Algorithms and Particle Swarm Optimization, *The 7th Annual Conference on Evolutionary Programming,* San Diego, USA, 1998.

Hsiao Ying Tung. (2004). Mutiobjective Evolution Programming Method for Feeder Reconfiguration, *IEEE Trans. on Power Systems,* Vol. 19, No. 1 pp. 594-599, February 2004.

Hsu Fu-Yuan and Tsai Men-Shen. (2005). A Multi-Objective Evolution Programming Method for Feeder Reconfiguration of Power Distribution System, *Proc. of the 13th Conf. on Intelligent Systems Application to Power Systems,* pp.55-60, November 2005.

Kim H., Ko Y. and Jung K.H. (1993). Artificial Neural Networks Based Feeder Reconfiguration for Loss Reduction in Distribution Systems, *IEEE Trans. on Power Delivery,* vol. 8, no. 3, July 1993, pp. 1356-1366.

Kennedy J. and Eberhart R. C. (1995). Particle Swarm Optimization, *Proceedings IEEE Int'l. Conf. on Neural Networks, IV,* pp.1942-1948, 1995.

Kitayama M. and Matsumoto K. (1995). An Optimization Method for Distribution System Configuration Based on Genetic Algorithm, *Proceedings of IEE APSCOM,* pp. 614-619, 1995.

Khoa T.Q.D. and Phan B.T.T. (2006). Ant Colony Search based loss minimum for reconfiguration of distribution systems, *2006 IEEE Power India Conference.* Page(s): 6pp, April 2006.

Nara K., Shiose A., Kitagawa M. and Ishihara T. (1992). Implementation of Genetic Algorithm for Distribution Systems Loss Minimum Reconfiguration, *IEEE Trans. on Power Systems,* vol.7, no. 3, August 1992, pp. 1044-1051.

Shi Y. and Eberhart R.C. (1998). A modified particle swarm optimizer, *IEEE International Conference on Evolutionary Programming,* pp.69-73, May 1998, Alaska.

Teng Jen-Hao and Lui Yi-Hwa (2003). A Novel ACS-Based Optimum Switch Relocation Method, *IEEE Trans. on Power Systems,* vol. 18, no. 1, February 2003, pp.113-120.

28

Particle Swarms for Continuous, Binary, and Discrete Search Spaces

Lisa Osadciw and Kalyan Veeramachaneni
Department of Electrical Engineering and Computer Science, Syracuse University NY, U.S.A.

1. Introduction

Swarm Intelligence is an adaptive computing technique that gains knowledge from the collective behavior of a decentralized system composed of simple agents interacting locally with each other and the environment. There is no centralized command or control dictating the behavior of these agents. The local interactions among these agents cause a global pattern to emerge from which problems are solved. The foundation of swarming theory was given in 1969. Two scientists, Keller and Segel, in their paper, "Slime mold aggregation", challenged the traditional pacemaker theory [47]. They suggested that the slime mold aggregation is a result of mutual interactions among different cells rather than the traditional belief that the aggregation is directed by a pacemaker cell. This theory became the basis for swarm theory. In emergent systems, an interconnected system of rel- atively simple agents self-organize to form a more complex, adaptive, higher-level behav- ior. To attain this complex behavior, these elements follow simple rules (e.g., the rule defined by the "Social Impact Theory" [18]). Examples of such systems can be found abundant in nature including ant colonies, bird flocking, animal herding, honey bees, bac- teria, and many more. These natural systems are optimizing using certain criteria during local interactions so that the routes optimize as ants trace the way to food. The ants may be designed to achieve goals other than locating food adding more dimensions to the basic algorithm. From closely observing these highly decentralized behaviors, a "swarm-like" algorithm emerges such as the Ant Colony Optimization (ACO) and Particle Swarm Opti- mization (PSO). The ACO and PSO have been applied successfully to solve real-world optimization problems in engineering and telecommunication [8, 9]. Swarm Intelligence algorithms have many features in common with Evolutionary Algorithms. Evolutionary algorithms are population based stochastic algorithms in which the population evolves over a number of iterations using simple operations. Like EA, SI models are population- based. The system is randomly initialized with a population of individuals, i.e., potential solutions. These individuals move in search patterns over many iterations following sim- ple rules, which mimic the social and cognitive behavior of insects or animals as they try to locate a prize or optima. Unlike EA, SI based algorithms do not use evolutionary opera- tors such as crossover and mutation.

Particle Swarm Optimization algorithm (PSO) was originally by Kennedy and Eber- hart in 1995 [18], and with social and cognitive behavior, has become widely used for optimization problems found in engineering and computer science. PSO was inspired by insect swarms and has since proven to be a powerful competitor to other evolutionary algorithms such as genetic algorithms [41].

Comparisons between PSO and the standard Genetic algorithms (another kind of evolutionary algorithms) have been done analytically based on performance in [41]. Compared to Genetic algorithms the PSO tends to converge more quickly to the best solution. The PSO algorithm simulates social behavior by sharing information concerning the best solution. An attraction of some sort is formed with these "better" solutions helping improve their own best solution until all converge to the single "best" solution. Each par- ticle representing a single intersection of all search dimensions.

The particles evaluate their positions using a fitness that is in the form of a mathemati- cal measure using the solution dimensions. Particles in a local neighborhood share memo- ries of their "best" positions; then they use those memories to adjust their own velocities and, thus, positions. The original PSO formulae developed by Kennedy and Eberhart were modified by Shi and Eberhart [68] with the introduction of an inertia parameter, ω, that was shown empirically to improve the overall performance of PSO.

The number of successful applications of swarm optimization algorithms is increasing exponentially. The most recent uses of these algorithms include cluster head identification in wireless sensor networks in [69], shortest communication route in sensor networks in [9] and identifying optimal hierarchy in decentralized sensor networks.

In the next section the particle swarm for continuous search spaces is presented. The continuous particle swarm optimization algorithm has been a research topic for more than decade. The affect of the parameters on the convergence of the swarm has been well studied in. The neighborhood topolgies and different variations are presented extensively in. In this chapter we will focus on the binary and the discrete version of the algorithm. The binary version of the algorithm is presented in section 2.2 and the discrete version of the algorithm is presented in section 2.3. The binary and the discrete version of the algorithm-make the particles search in the probablistic search space. The infinite range of the velocities are transformed into a bounded probabilistic space. The transformations and the algorithms are detailed in this chapter. The affect of the parameters are briefly detailed in this chapter. The performance of these algorithms are presented on simple functions. The chapter is accompanied by a code written in MATLAB that can be used by the readers.

2. Particle Swarms for Continuous Spaces

The PSO formulae define each particle as a potential solution to a problem in a D-dimensional space with the ith particle represented as $X_i = (x_{i1}, x_{i2}, x_{i3}, ...x_{iD})$. Each particle also maintains a memory of its previous best position, designated as *pbest*, $P_i = (p_{i1}, p_{i2}, p_{i3}, ...p_{iD})$, and a velocity along each dimension represented as $V_i = (v_{i1}, v_{i2}, v_{i3}, ...v_{iD})$. In each generation, the previous best, pbest, of the particle com-bines with the best fitness in the local neighborhood, designated *gbest*. A velocity is com- puted using these values along each dimension moving the particle to a new solution. The portion of the adjustment to the velocity influenced by the individual's previous best posi- tion is considered as the cognition component, and the portion influenced by the best in the neighborhood is the social component.

In early versions of the algorithm, these formulae are

$$V_{id}^{(t+1)} = \omega \times V_{id}^{(t)} + \psi_1 \times (p_{id} - X_{id}) + \psi_2 \times (p_{gd} - X_{id}) \qquad (1)$$

$$\text{and } X_{id}^{(t+1)} = X_{id}^{(t)} + V_{id}^{(t+1)} \qquad (2)$$

Constants ψ_1 and ψ_2 determine the relative influence of the social and the cognition components, and the weights on these components are set to influence the motion to a new solution. Often this is same value to give each component (the cognition and the social learning rates) equal weight. A constant, V_{max} , is often used to limit the velocities of the particles and improve the resolution of the search space.

The algorithm is primarily used to search continuous search spaces. The pseudocode of the algorithm for the continuous search spaces is shown in Figure 1.

Algorithm PSO:

For t= 1 to the max. bound of the number on generations,

  For i=1 to the population size,

    For d=1 to the problem dimensionality,

      Apply the velocity update equation:

$$V_{id}^{t+1} = \omega \times V_{id}^{t} + \psi_1 \times (p_{id} - X_{id}) + \psi_2 \times (p_{gd} - X_{id})$$

      where P_i is the best position visited so far by X_i,

      P_g is the best position visited so far by any particle

      Limit magnitude:

$$V_{id}^{(t+1)} = min(V_{max}, max(-V_{max}, V_{id}^{(t+1)}));$$

      Update Position:

$$X_{id}^{(t+1)} = min(Max_d, max(-Min_d, X_{id}^{(t)} + V_{id}^{(t+1)}));$$

    End- for-d;

    Compute fitness of $(X_i^{(t+1)})$;

    If needed, update historical information regarding Pi and Pg;

  End-for-i;

  Terminate if Pg meets problem requirements;

End-for-t;

End algorithm.

Figure 1. Pseudocode for the Continuous PSO Algorithm

Example 1: Continuous PSO on a simple spheres function : Minimize the function

$$f(x) = \sum_{i=1}^{n} x_i^2 \text{, where } x = (x_1, x_2, x_3 .....x_n] \text{ and } x \in [-\infty, \infty].$$

The MATLAB code for the above problem as solved by the particle swarm optimiza- tion algorithm is provided along with the chapter. In the following solution 10 particles are randomly intialized in the search space. The evolution of the particles after 10, 100 and 1000 iterations in the search space are shown for a 2-D problem.

3. Binary Search Spaces

The binary version of the Particle swarm optimization is needed for discrete, binary search spaces. Many variables in the sensor management problems are binary, for example the fusion rule for binary hypothesis testing is binary valued. A sigmoid function trans- forms the infinite range of the velocities to a requisite 0 or 1. The sigmoid function is

$$s(V_{id}) = \frac{1}{1+\exp(-V_{id})} \tag{3}$$

where V_{id} is the velocity of the *ith* particle along the *dth* dimension. The velocity update equation remains the same as section 2.1. The position update equation is modified as

$$if\ \rho_{id} < s(V_{id}(t)) \text{ then } x_{id}(t) = 1\text{ ; else } x_{id}(t) = 0 \tag{4}$$

where ρ_{id} is a random number drawn from a uniform distribution between $U[0,1]$.

These formula are iterated repeatedly over each dimension of each particle, and updating the pbest vector if a better solution is found. This is similar to the PSO for continuous search spaces.

By following the above procedure, we transform the entire continuous velocity space, $[-\infty,\infty]$, is transformed into a one or zero for that dimension. The probability of 1 and probability of zero for different velocities is shown in Figure 2.

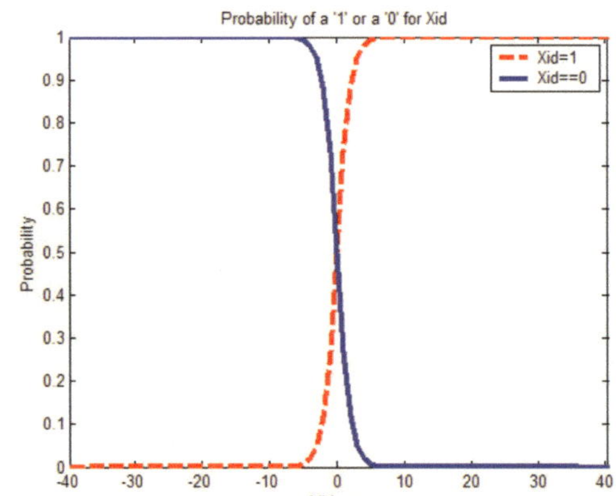

Figure 2. Probability of X_{id} =1 and X_{id}=0 given the V_{id}

Algorithm Binary PSO:

For t= 1 to the max. bound of the number on generations,

For i=1 to the population size,

For d=1 to the problem dimensionality,

Apply the velocity update equation:

$$V_{id}^{t+1} = \omega \times V_{id}^{t} + \psi_1 \times (p_{id} - X_{id}) + \psi_2 \times (p_{gd} - X_{id})$$

where P_i is the best position visited so far by X_i,
P_g is the best position visited so far by any particle
Limit magnitude:

$$V_{id}^{(t+1)} = min(V_{max}, max(-V_{max}, V_{id}^{(t+1)}));$$

Update Position:

$$s(V_{id}) = \frac{1}{1 + \exp(-V_{id})};$$

$$\rho_{id} = rand(1)$$

$$if\ \rho_{id} < s(V_{id}(t)) \text{ then } x_{id}(t) = 1 \text{; else } x_{id}(t) = 0$$

End- for-*d*;
Compute fitness of ($X_i^{(t+1)}$);
If needed, update historical information regarding *Pi* and *Pg*;
End-for-*i*;
Terminate if *Pg* meets problem requirements;
End-for-*t*;
End algorithm.

Figure 3. Pseudocode for the Binary PSO Algorithm

Example 2: Goldberg's Order-Three Problem
Groups of three bits are combined to form disjoint subsets and the fitness is evaluated using

$$f(x) = \sum_{i=1}^{\frac{n}{3}} f_3(s_i)$$

where each si is a disjoint 3-bit substring of x and

$$f_3(s_i) = \begin{cases} 0.9 & if\ |s_i| = 0 \\ 0.6 & if\ |s_i| = 1 \\ 0.3 & if\ |s_i| = 2 \\ 1.0 & if\ |s_i| = 3 \end{cases}$$ *where | si | denotes the sum of the bits in the 3-bit substring*

2. 3 Particle Swarms for Discrete Multi Valued Search Spaces

Extending this binary model of PSO, a discrete multi-valued particle swarm for any range of discrete values is described in detail. Many real world optimization problems, including signal design, power management in sensor networks, and scheduling have vari- ables which have discrete multi-values. This need is increasing as more problems are being solved by particle swarm optimization based algorithm [73, 74]. It can be argued instead that discrete variables can be transformed into an equivalent binary representation, and the binary PSO can simply be used. However, the range of the discrete variables does not typically correspond to a power of 2 for the equivalent binary representation. This then generates a range of values exceeding the real range resulting in an unbalanced convergence and more iterations than necessary. For example, a discrete variable ranging from 0 to5 [0,1,2,3,4,5] requires a minimum of three bit binary representation, which ranges between [0-7]. Special conditions need to be added reducing the algorithms efficiency to manage the values beyond the original maximum, which in this example is, 6 & 7. Another important factor is that the Hamming distances between the two discrete values, undergoes a non-linear transformation using the equivalent binary representation. This often adds to the complexity to the search process. The inefficiency emerges as an increase in the dimensions of the particle adding more variables to the search. For these reasons, a discrete multi valued PSO is more efficient and should be used for discrete ranges greater than 2.

Previously, researchers simply enhanced the performance of the binary PSO to fix the efficiency. Al-Kazemi, et al. [75], improved the original binary PSO algorithm by modifying the way particles interact. The research on designing a PSO for discrete multi-valued problems, however, has been sparse. In MVPSO [74], Jim, et al, extended the binary PSO by creating a multi dimensional particle. Each dimension of the original problem is subdivided into three dimensions for a ternary problem. Each dimension of the particle is a real valued number and is transformed into a number in the range of [0 1] using the sigmoid function. After a series of transformations, the three numbers ultimately represent the probability of having a one of three discrete values for a ternary system. The extra transformations bring us closer to the new discrete multi-valued PSO except many operations are added. The transition of a particle or position update is probabilistic similar to the binary PSO.

For discrete multi valued optimization problems, the range of variables lie between 0 and M-1, where 'M' implies an M-ary number system. The same velocity update and par- ticle representation are used in this algorithm. The position update equation is, however, change as follows.

1. Transform the velocity using

$$S_{id} = \frac{M}{1+e^{-V_{id}}} \tag{5}$$

2. A number is the generated using a normal distribution with $\mu = S_{id}$ and σ as parameters.

$$X_{id} = round(S_{id} + (M-1)\times\sigma\times randn(1)) \tag{6}$$

3. The number is rounded to the closest discrete variable with the end points fixed.

$$\text{if } X_{id} > M-1 \text{ then } X_{id} = M-1 \tag{7}$$

$$\text{and if } X_{id} < 0 \text{ then } X_{id} = 0 \tag{8}$$

4. . The velocity update equation remains the same as (1). The positions of the particles are discrete values between 0 and M-1. Now for any given S_{id}, we have an associated probability for any number between [0, M-1]. However, the probability of drawing a num- ber randomly reduces based on its distance from S_{id} according to the Figure 4. In

the subsection, the relation between Sid and the probability of a discrete variables is given.

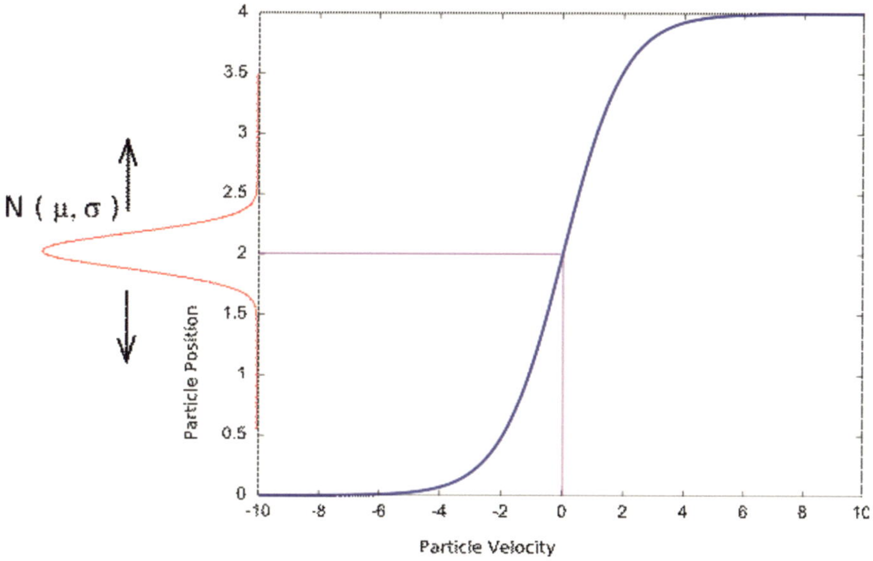

Figure 4. Transformation of the Particle Velocity to a Discrete Variable

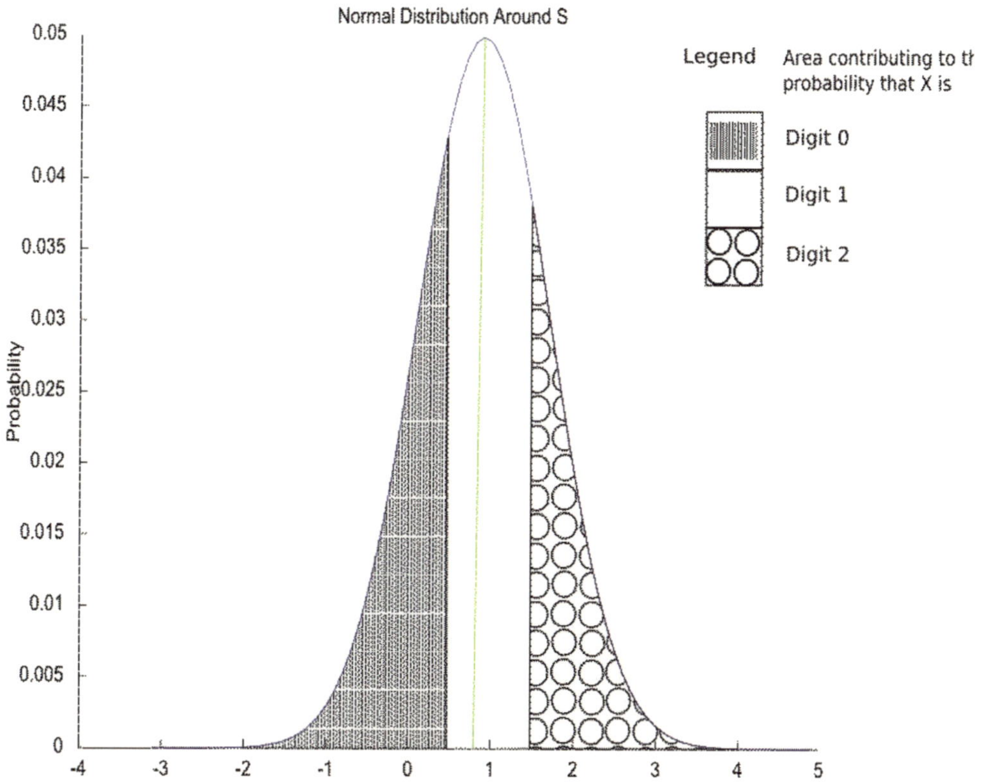

Figure 5. Probabilities of Different Digits Given a Particular S

Probability of a discrete value 'm': For a given S, a number is generated using a normal distribution with the mean as S and standard deviation σ for an M-ary system. Based on this normal distribution and equation (7), the probability for a specific discrete variables given S can be calculated based on the area under that region of the Gaussian curve. For example for a ternary system, given an S = 0.9 and σ = 0.8, the areas of the Gaussian curve that will contribute to different digits are shown in Figure 5. For a S_{id}, the probability of a discrete variable having a value 'm' is given by:
m=0,

$$P(X_{id} = 0 \mid S_{id}) = \int_{-\infty}^{0.5} g(x)\,dx$$
$$= 1 - Q\left(\frac{0.5 - S_{id}}{\sigma(M-1)}\right) \tag{9}$$

where Q is the error function. The function g(x) is

$$g(x) = \frac{1}{\sqrt{2\pi\sigma^2(M-1)^2}} \exp\left(\frac{-1}{2\sigma^2(M-1)^2}(x - S_{id})\right) \tag{10}$$

with m in the range 1 to M-2, the conditional probability of achieving X_{id} given a previous S_{id} value is

$$P(X_{id} = m \mid S_{id}) = \int_{m-0.5}^{m+0.5} g(x)\,dx$$
$$= Q\left(\frac{m - 0.5 - S_{id}}{\sigma(M-1)}\right) - Q\left(\frac{m + 0.5 - S_{id}}{\sigma(M-1)}\right) \tag{11}$$

For m = M-1, the conditional probability is

$$P(X_{id} = (M-1) \mid S_{id}) = \int_{(M-1)-0.5}^{\infty} g(x)\,dx$$
$$= Q\left(\frac{(M-1) - 0.5 - S_{id}}{\sigma(M-1)}\right) \tag{12}$$

Note that

$$\sum_{m=0}^{M} P(X_{id} = m / S_{id}) = 1 \tag{13}$$

One can significantly control the performance of the algorithm using these equations. For example, controlling the σ controls the standard deviation of the Gaussian and, hence, the probabilities of various discrete variables.

Algorithm Discrete PSO:

For t= 1 to the max. bound of the number on generations,
    For i=1 to the population size,

For d=1 to the problem dimensionality,
Apply the velocity update equation:

$$V_{id}^{t+1} = \omega \times V_{id}^{t} + \psi_1 \times (p_{id} - X_{id}) + \psi_2 \times (p_{gd} - X_{id})$$

where P_i is the best position visited so far by X_i,
P_g is the best position visited so far by any particle
Limit magnitude:

$$V_{id}^{(t+1)} = min(V_{max}, max(-V_{max}, V_{id}^{(t+1)}));$$

Update Position:

$$S_{id} = \frac{M}{1+e^{-V_{id}}};$$

$$X_{id} = round(S_{id} + (M-1) \times \sigma \times randn(1))$$

if $X_{id} > M-1$ $then$ $X_{id} = M-1$ and if $X_{id} < 0$ $then$ $X_{id} = 0$

End- for-d;
Compute fitness of $(X_i^{(t+1)})$;
If needed, update historical information regarding Pi and Pg;
End-for-i;
Terminate if Pg meets problem requirements;
End-for-t;
End algorithm.

Figure 6. Psuedo Code for Particle Swarms for Discrete Multi Valued Search Spaces

Example 3: Sastry-Veermachaneni-Osadciw Function for Ternary Systems
Groups of three digits are combined to form disjoint subsets and the fitness is evalu- ated using

$$f(x) = \sum_{i=1}^{\frac{n}{3}} f_3(s_i)$$

where each s_i is a disjoint 3-bit substring of x and

$$f_3(s_i) = \begin{cases} 1.0 & if \ |s_i| = 6 \\ 0 & if \ |s_i| = 5 \\ 0.15 & if \ |s_i| = 4 \\ 0.3 & if \ |s_i| = 3 \end{cases} \quad and \quad f_3(s_i) = \begin{cases} 0.45 & if \ |s_i| = 2 \\ 0.60 & if \ |s_i| = 1 \\ 0.75 & if \ |s_i| = 0 \end{cases}$$

where $|s_i|$ denotes the sum of the digits in the 3-digit substring.

2.4 Particle Swarms for Mixed Search Spaces

Mixed search spaces imply that the solution to the problem is composed of binary, dis- crete and continuous variables. The solution can be any combination of two. The particle swarm optimization algorithms operators work independently on each dimension making it possible for mixing different variable types into one single particle. In Genetic algo- rithms, however, the crossover operator needs to be designed independently for the differ- ent variable types. The swarm algorithm will call upon the different position update formulae based on the type of the variable. The pseudo code is given in the following fig ure.

Algorithm PSO for Mixed Search Spaces:

For t= 1 to the max. bound of the number on generations,
    For i=1 to the population size,
        For d=1 to the problem dimensionality,
            Apply the velocity update equation:

$$V_{id}^{t+1} = \omega \times V_{id}^{t} + \psi_1 \times (p_{id} - X_{id}) + \psi_2 \times (p_{gd} - X_{id})$$

where P_i is the best position visited so far by X_i,
    P_g is the best position visited so far by any particle
Limit magnitude:

$$V_{id}^{(t+1)} = min(V_{max}, max(-V_{max}, V_{id}^{(t+1)}));$$

Update Position:
if X_{id} is continuous valued

$$X_{id}^{(t+1)} = min(Max_d, max(-Min_d, X_{id}^{(t)} + V_{id}^{(t+1)}));$$

else if X_{id} is binary valued

$$s(V_{id}) = \frac{1}{1 + \exp(-V_{id})};$$

$$\rho_{id} = rand(1)$$

$$if\ \rho_{id} < s(V_{id}(t)) \text{ then } x_{id}(t) = 1; \text{else } x_{id}(t) = 0$$

elseif X_{id} is discrete valued

$$S_{id} = \frac{M}{1+e^{-V_{id}}};$$

$$X_{id} = round(S_{id} + (M-1) \times \sigma \times randn(1))$$

$$\text{if } X_{id} > M-1 \ then \ X_{id} = M-1 \text{ and if } X_{id} < 0 \ then \ X_{id} = 0$$

End- for-d;
Compute fitness of ($X_i^{(t+1)}$);
If needed, update historical information regarding Pi and Pg;
    End-for-i;
    Terminate if Pg meets problem requirements;
End-for-t;
End algorithm.

Figure 7. Pseudo code for mixed search spaces

29

Application of Particle Swarm Optimization Algorithm in Smart Antenna Array Systems

May M.M. Wagih and Hassan M. Elkamchouchi
Alexandria University, Faculty of Engineering
Egypt

1. Introduction

In wireless applications the antenna pattern is shaped so as to cancel interfering signals (placing nulls) and produce or steer a strong beam towards the wanted signal according to signal direction of arrival (DOA). Such antenna system is called smart antenna array.
This chapter presents the efficiency of Particle Swarm Optimization algorithm (PSO) compared to Genetic algorithm (GA) in solving antenna array pattern synthesis problem. Also PSO is applied to determine optimal antenna elements feed that provide null (minimum power) in the directions of the interfering signals while to maximize of radiation in the direction of the useful signal. Application for PSO algorithm in Direct Data Domain Least Squares (D3LS) approach that is used to estimate incoming signal is illustrated.
Due to environment changing the target goal is changing so modification in the algorithm is proposed to provide optimal solution for varying real time target (to track the desired users and reject interference sources). The problem is formulated and solved by means of the proposed algorithm. Examples are simulated to demonstrate the effectiveness and the design flexibility of PSO in the framework of electromagnetic synthesis of linear arrays.

2. Smart Antenna Array System Overview

The ability to communicate with people on the move has evolved remarkably since Marconi first demonstrated radio's ability to provide continuous contact with ships sailing the English Channel in 1897. There onwards, new wireless methods and services have been adopted. Smart antenna system represents one of the valuable parts that support the increasing requirement and needs to higher quality wireless services.
Smart antenna systems processes signals arriving from different directions to detect (estimate) desired signal direction of arrival DOA. Biased on the estimated DOA the beamformer optimize antenna elements weights such that the radiation pattern of the antenna array is adjusted to minimize a certain error function or to maximize a certain reward function derived by the adaptive algorithm. Figure 1. Presents block diagram for Smart antenna system. Smart antenna processing core is represented in three areas the adaptive algorithms the DOA estimation algorithm and the beamformer control.
One of the simplest geometries for an array is a linear array in which the centers of the antenna elements are aligned along a straight line. For simplicity consider the uniformly

spaced linear array of N elements and that there is M signals received. We assume that K samples are observed by the array then output vector $\mathbf{X}(n)$ is

$$\mathbf{X}(n) = \mathbf{A}(\theta)\mathbf{S}(n) + \mathbf{O}(n), \qquad n = 1,2, ... \tag{1}$$

$\mathbf{X}(n)$ is $(N \times K)$ matrix of array output signals at any given instant (sampling time) n, $\mathbf{A}(\theta)$ is $(N \times M)$ steering matrix, $\mathbf{S}(n)$ is $(M \times K)$ signal matrix, $\mathbf{O}(n)$ is noise matrix. The array steering matrix (array manifold) $\mathbf{A}(\theta)$ is

$$\mathbf{A}(\theta) = [\mathbf{a}(\theta_1), \mathbf{a}(\theta_2), \cdots\cdots \mathbf{a}(\theta_\mathrm{N})] \tag{2}$$

Where

$$\mathbf{a}(\theta_i) = \left[1, \exp\left(\frac{2\pi d \sin\theta_i}{\lambda}\right), \cdots\cdots \exp\left(\frac{2\pi d(\mathrm{N}-1)\sin\theta_\mathrm{M}}{\lambda}\right)\right], \tag{3}$$

$$i = 1,2, ... \mathrm{M}$$

$\mathbf{a}(\theta_i)$ is the response of the linear array to the ith source arriving from direction (θ_i). The array manifold is defined as the one-dimensional manifold composed of all the steering vectors as θ ranges over all possible angles i.e. $\theta \in [0, 2\pi]$.

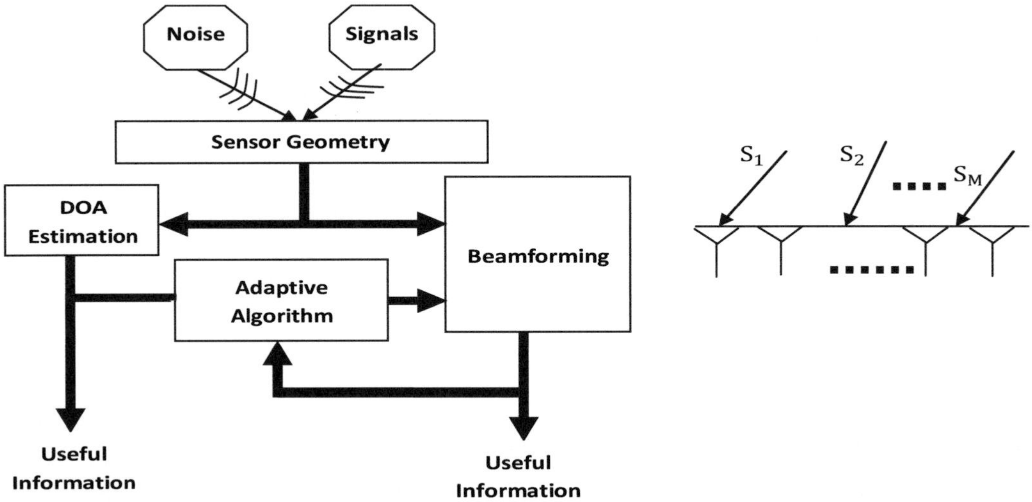

Figure 1. Block diagram of smart antenna array system and linear array signal model

The array manifold used to calibrate the array for direction finding estimation. Each element output is multiplied by a complex weight w_i^*, suggested by the adaptive algorithm then the beamformer update the phase and amplitude relation between the branches, and sum them to give information signal $\mathbf{Y}(\mathrm{n})$

$$\mathbf{Y}(n) = \mathbf{W}(n)^T\mathbf{X}(n) \tag{4}$$

$$\mathbf{W} = [w_1 \;\; w_2 \; w_3 \; ... w_N]$$

3. PSO for Smart Antenna System

The smart antenna changes their directional pattern with the help of few adjustable parameters in according to the estimation and analysis to received signal, environment and

pre-known information to improve the performance and capacity of the system. A promising way for the determination of a suitable parameter configuration for the antenna is the application of heuristic optimization procedures.
Pattern synthesis problem (beamforming) is continuous varying target real time problem that needs fast optimal solution to adjust array pattern and support for the service required. Also the controlling parameters are limited due to practical design and cost aspects. Consequently Enhancement to PSO algorithm is proposed to support for these two major needs.

3.1 PSO and Dynamic Real Environment Optimization

For real time dynamic environment problem the goal value changes, original PSO algorithm has no method for detecting this change and the particles are still influenced by their memories of the original goal position. If the change in the goal is small, this problem is self-correcting. Subsequent fitness evaluations will result in positions closer to the new goal location replacing earlier position **X** vectors, and the swarm should follow, and eventually intersect the moving goal.
However, if the movement of the goal is more pronounced, it moves too far from the swarm for subsequent fitness evaluations to return values better than the current personal best $\mathbf{P}_i^t$ vector, and the particles do not track the moving goal. A proposed attempt to rectify this problem by having the particles periodically replaces their $\mathbf{P}_i^t$ vector with their current $\mathbf{X}_i^t$ vector, thus "forgetting" their experiences to that point. This differs from a restart, in that the particles, in retaining their current location, have retained the profits from their previous experiences, but are forced to redefine their relationship to the goal at that point. Figure 2 present flow chart for the proposed PSO algorithm to support for varying dynamic target optimization problem.

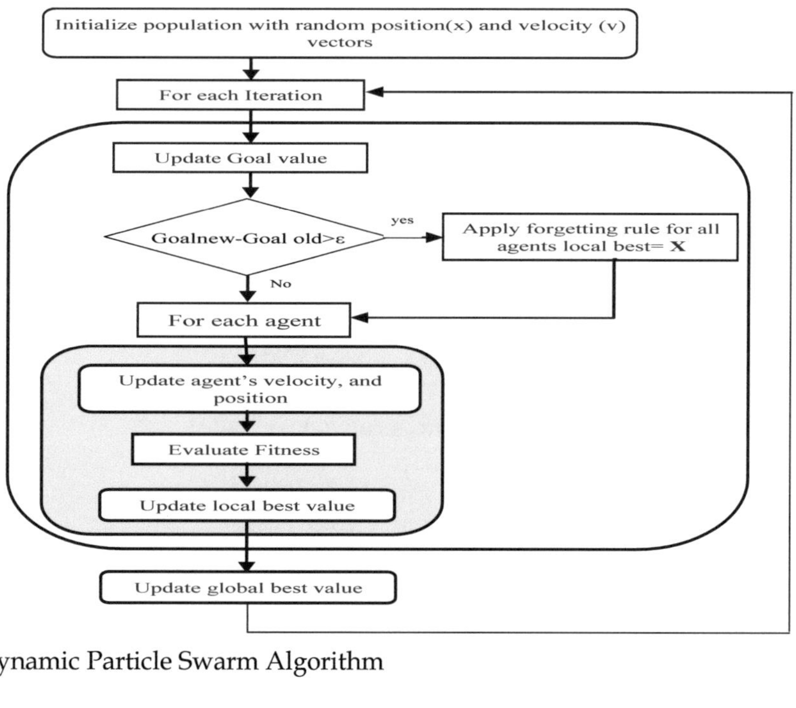

Figure 2. Dynamic Particle Swarm Algorithm

3.2 PSO and bounded search space

Constraint is usually set to the array parameters these constraints may be spatial, for example, that the interelement spacing be greater than a prescribed value or that the element positions be within specified limits. Other type of design constraint is the excitation where it may require that the elements feed is phase only or amplitude and that the current-taper ratio be less than or equal to a prescribed value.

Introducing constraint to the PSO will decrease degree of freedom. Search time will also increase if the concept of accept and after the each particle movement for each iteration according to boundaries. However, if we can convert the problem to an unconstrained one initially through using suitable transformations of the constraint parameter this will eliminate time lost in explore and probability of rejecting the particle movement. Illustration for such solution will be clear in next section while simulation.

4. PSO use for pattern synthesis

This section objects to reformulate and define antenna array adaptive beamforming in term of an optimization problem. Problem Search Space represented by array pattern controlling parameters is identified. Fitness function that measures the deviation of the optimal proposed solution from the target is defined.

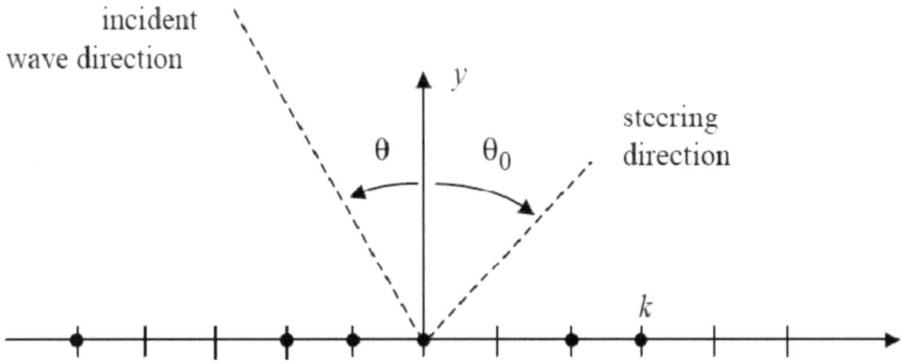

Figure 3.Linear array geometry

Let us consider the linear array of M non-uniformly spaced point source isotropic elements located along a straight line at the positions x_k , where $k = 0, \dots, M-1$. The beam pattern function $P(u)$ of the array, is defined as follows,

$$P(u) = \left| \sum_{k=0}^{M-1} w_k e^{j\frac{2\pi}{\lambda}x_k u} \right|$$

$$w_k = \propto_k \exp(j\beta_k)$$

$$p(u) = \left| \sum_{k=0}^{M-1} \propto_k e^{j(\frac{2\pi}{\lambda}x_k u + \beta_k)} \right| \tag{5}$$

Where w_k is the weight coefficient of the kth element, λ is the background wavelength, $u = \sin\theta - \sin\theta_o$, being θ and θ_o the incident angle of the impinging plane wave and the steering angle of the array, respectively. In order to generate a beam pattern (BP) that attain specific characteristics e.g., sidelobes level (SLL) lower than a fixed threshold or reproduces a

desired shape $P_{dB}^{ref}(u)$, initially we have to identify the array designing parameters and their boundaries i.e. The particle search space in PSO algorithm.
let vector ζ be defined as follow,

$$\zeta = [M, x_0, \ldots x_{M-1}; w_0 \ldots . w_{M-1}; D]^T;$$

Where, M is number of array elements, $[x_0, \ldots x_{M-1}]$ is array elements spacing vector, $[w_0 \ldots . w_{M-1}]$ is array elements feed vector generally represented as $w_k = \alpha_k \, exp\,(j\beta_k)$, finally D is array length. ζ boundary limits has to be taken in account when solving the problem to facilitate practical and cost design needs.
Then a quantized measure for the solution distance from the target required should be defined, this value will be function of the search space parameter vector ζ. Generally for antenna array pattern synthesis most of the well known target consideration is the main beam f_{MB}, total pattern f_{Bp}, sidelobe level f_{SLL}, number, location and width of nulls f_{nul}, number of array elements f_N then we can us define global antenna array fitness function f, as follows:

$$f(\zeta) = \frac{1}{c_1 f_{BP}(\zeta) + c_2 f_{MB}(\zeta) + c_3 f_{SLL}(\zeta) + c_4 f_{nul}(\zeta) + c_5 f_N(\zeta)} \tag{6}$$

Where

$$f_{BP}(\zeta) = \int_{u \in B} \left(P_{dB}(u)/Q - P_{dB}^{ref}(u) \right) du \tag{7}$$

$$f_{MB}(\zeta) = \sum_{i=1}^{mb} \left(\int_{u \in MB} \left(P_{dB}(u)/Q - P_{dB}^{ref}(u) \right) du \right) \tag{8}$$

$$f_{SLL}(\zeta) = \frac{Q}{max\{P_{dB}(u)\}} \quad for\ u_{start} \le u \le 1 \tag{9}$$

$$f_{nul}(\zeta) = \sum_{i=1}^{nl} \left(\int_{u \in BN_i} \left(P_{dB}(u)/Q - P_{dB}^{ref}(u) \right) du \right)$$

$$BN_i = u_{nul_i} \pm 0.5 \Delta u_{nul_i} \tag{10}$$

$$f_N(\zeta) = M; \tag{11}$$

Where u_{start} being a value that allows excluding the main lobe from the calculation of the SLL. Moreover, Q is a normalizing constant, B represents visible region; while $P_{dB}^{ref}(u)$ represents the desired BP shape. MB represents the range of values covering the Main beam, mb number of beams in the pattern, BN corresponds to the nulls locations and nl is number of nulls required. Finally, c_i are coefficients that identify each criteria value.
It is often necessary to impose a constraint on the interelement spacing to minimize the mutual coupling effects. For and array with an even number of elements the constraint may be expressed as follow

$$x_1 \ge \frac{d}{2}, \qquad x_i - x_{i-1} \ge d \qquad i = 2,3, \ldots \ldots M \tag{12}$$

The above constrain can be represented using the following transformation:

$$x_1 = \frac{d}{2} + (\acute{x}_1)^2$$

$$x_2 = \left(\frac{d}{2} + d \right) + (\acute{x}_1)^2 + (\acute{x}_2)^2$$

Generally

$$(x_i) = \left(i - \frac{1}{2}\right) d + \sum_{k=1}^{i} (x\'_k)^2 \quad , \qquad i = 1,2, \ldots . M$$

For odd elements number array

$$(x_i) = (i-1)d + \sum_{k=1}^{i-1} (x\'_k)^2 \quad , \qquad i = 2, \ldots . (M-1)/2 \tag{13}$$

Solving using equation 10 allows minimization to be carried out with the new primed variables, and it is readily seen that the constraints are always satisfied.
Another type of constraint on spacing's usually imposed is the one requiring the elements to lie within a specified range mainly required to avoid unacceptable practical array dimensions. Stated mathematically in the following form:

$$a_i \le x_i \le b_i \qquad\qquad i = 1,2, \ldots . M \tag{14}$$

the transformation to be used in this case is

$$x_i = a_i + (b_i - a_i) \sin^2 x\'_i \tag{15}$$

It is sometimes necessary to constrain the current taper to be within specified limits. That is,

$$I_i \le I \pm C, \qquad i = 1,2, \ldots . \tag{16}$$

It is easily verified that the transformation of the form in equation (15) will transform the constrained space into an unconstrained one

$$I_i = I + C \sin I\'_i \tag{17}$$

Next section will investigate the efficiency of the PSO for solving linear array configuration compared to other algorithms.

4.1 PSO and GA for Pattern Synthesis

To validate the PSO approach, initially we apply PSO, to find the optimized element weight to achieve the Chebyshev pattern for 10 equispaced isotropic elements with λ/2 interelement spacing antenna array of minimum SLL of 26dB, and compare its performance to GA, for solving the same problem. The sample points, are chosen 300 equally distributed points over u on a personal computer with a Pentium IV processor running at 1GHz. The target beam will be P_{dB}^{ref}

$$P_{dB}^{ref} = 2.79 \cos u + 2.49 \cos 3u - 0.97 \cos 5u + 1.35 \cos 7u + \cos 9u$$

We consider 10 elements symmetric array with amplitude excitation only i.e. $\beta_i = 0$ then

$$\zeta = \left[w_0 \ldots . w_{\left(\frac{M}{2}\right)-1}\right]^T ; \quad M = 10$$

$$w_{k+(M/2)} = w_{(M/2)-(k+1)} \qquad k = 0, \ldots M/2$$

$$f_{Bp}(\zeta) = 2 * \int_{u \in B} \left(\frac{P_{dB}(u)}{Q} - P_{dB}^{ref}(u) \right) du ; \qquad for\ 0 \le u \le 1$$

$$f_{SLL}(\zeta) = \frac{26}{max_{u_{start} \le u \le 1}\{P_{dB}(u)\}} \qquad u_{start} = 0.25$$

$$(\zeta) = \frac{1}{f_{SLL}(\bar{\zeta}) + f_{BP}(\bar{\zeta})}$$

Figure 4 presents the output pattern explored over the optimization process by one particle until it reaches the optimum solution. Corresponding proposed elements weigh for these local minima is as listed in Table 1.

Iteration No	w_0, w_9	w_1, w_8	w_2, w_7	w_3, w_6	w_4, w_5	**Max. SLL dB**
P1 (5)	0.3292	0.5337	0.7030	0.9883	1	-20
P2 (30)	0.3543	0.3243	0.5679	1	0.7044	-15
P3 (78)	0.3521	0.4688	0.7158	0.8378	1	-12
P4 (122)	0.3574	0.4850	0.7055	0.8921	1	-26

Table 1. Optimum proposed weight corresponding to one particle

Figure 4, 5 shows behavior of the fitness values for solutions explored versus the number of iterations for one particle. Dotted curve represents the gbest fitness value where it intersects with the particles. Note that although the particle has achieved good fitness value in its exploring journey it was not trapped at these local minima at P1, P2, P3, P4.

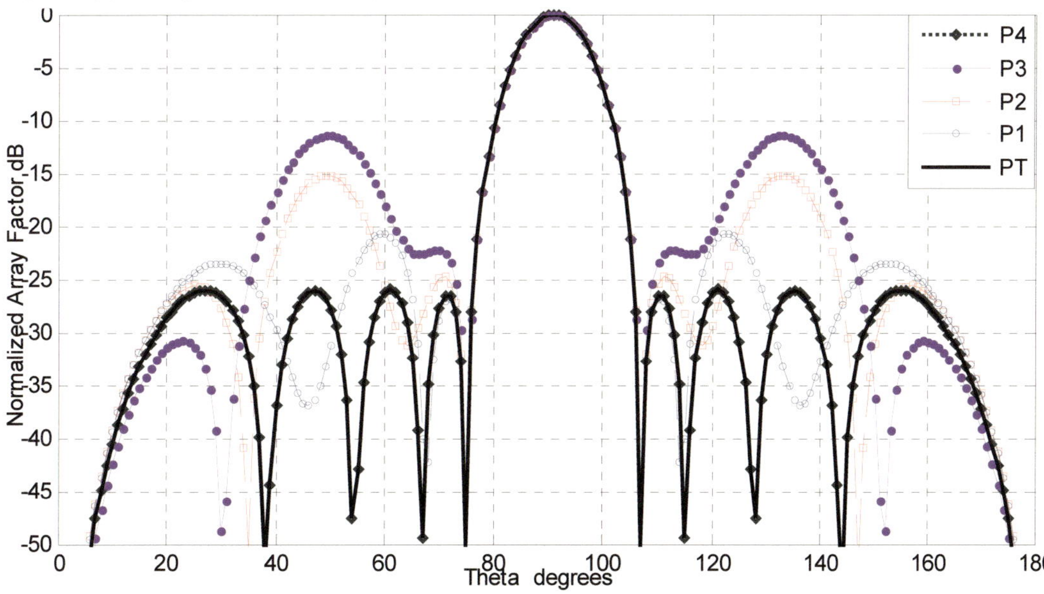

Figure 4. Explored solution for one particle at iteration 5, 30, 80, 120 compared to target pattern

Figure 6 present comparisons between the fitness error per iteration for GA and PSO algorithms solving the above problem with same initial random feed using PSO and Genetic algorithm. It can be noticed the performance difference in reaching optimum solution is not big only difference comes for the time per iteration in each algorithm. According to output in Table 1 that the optimized proposed element feeds is the same for both algorithms.

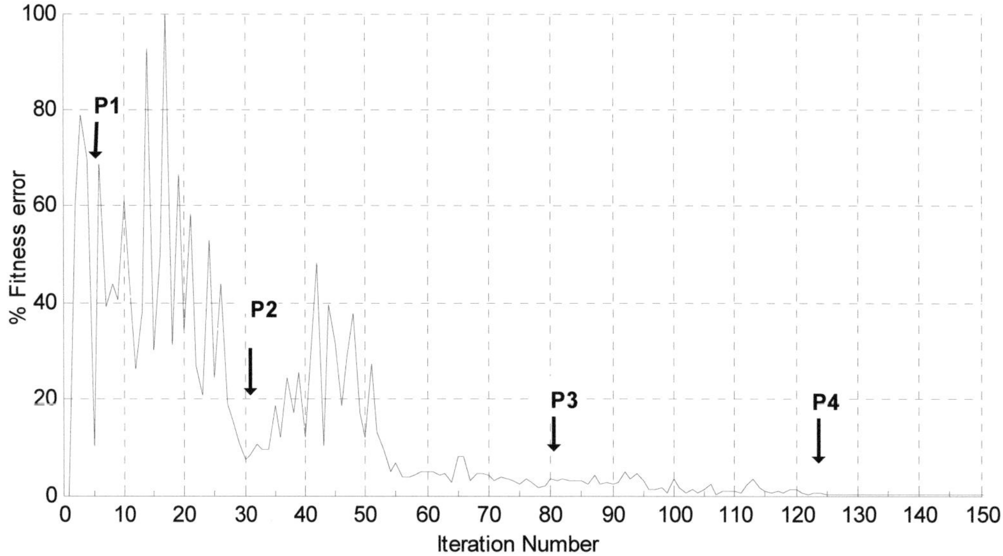

Figure 5. Behavior of the fitness function per iteration for one particle, dotted curve represent behavior of gbest fitness value per iteration

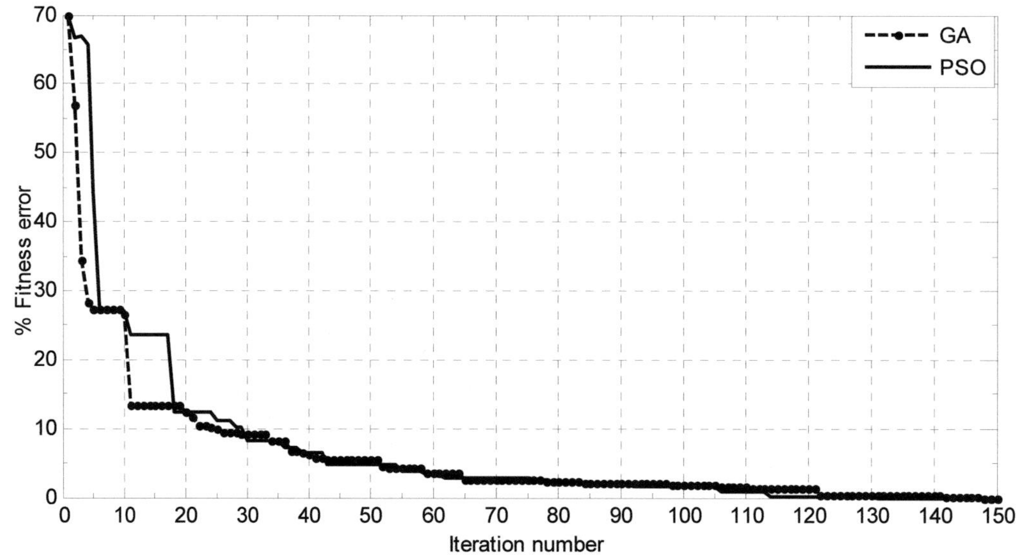

Figure 6. Fitness per iteration behavior for PSO algorithm and GA algorithm

Next section will search the capabilities of the PSO for solving array configuration. A simulation for steering single beam, introducing multiple beams in DOA and introducing nulls in the imposed directions by controlling the excitations of the array elements feed or the elements spacing represented in term of λ. also the adaptive ability of PSO for changing the problem target in runtime is presented such feature is to be useful in digital beamforming.

Algorithm/ Normalized weight	w_0, w_9	w_1, w_8	w_2, w_7	w_3, w_6	w_4, w_5	No. of Iteration	Total time min.
PSO	0.3574	0.4850	0.7055	0.8921	1.000	115	2
GA	0.3563	0.4845	0.7055	0.891	1.000	122	9

Table 2. Optimum proposed weight corresponding to PSO, GA algorithm

4.2 PSO and Pattern Synthesis Phase Control

The phase-only null synthesizing is attractive since in a phased array the required controls are available at no extra cost [Steyskal, H.,1986]. This section will illustrate different scenarios for pattern shaping using PSO to search suitable phase feed to fullfill-required pattern. Initially consider it is required to Introduce single null at direction $\theta = 50^\circ$ and SLL<30dB with same mainbeam. PSO evaluated element weighting which fulfilled the requirements of the design using fitness function equation 6.

Figure 7, shows the output pattern after 200, iteration notice that the SLL criterion is not achieved.

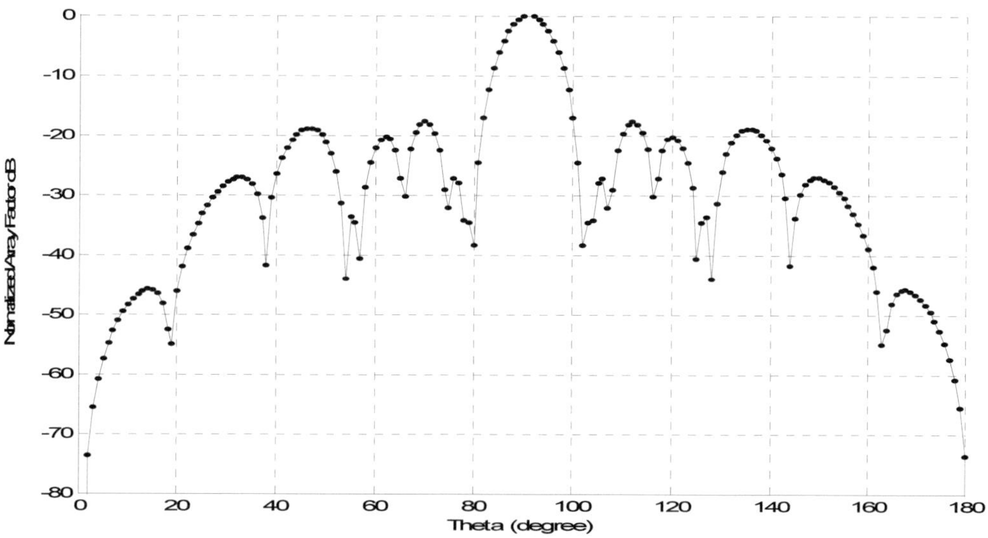

Figure 7. Pattern proposed after 200 iteration for null at 50°

Now let us consider the target is moved. Assume it is required to steer the mainbeam to be at $\theta = 110^\circ$ and presence of interference at $\theta = 150^\circ$. PSO evaluated antenna array elements' phase which fulfill these requirements of the design output proposed pattern as Figure 8a shows the output pattern after 50, iteration as can be notices although that the SLL< 20dB was not achieved as the maximum level is 18dB. Assume surrounding environment is stable so the algorithm is to continue search for better feeding solution Figure 8b shows the proposed pattern corresponding after 500 iteration maximum SLL of -22dB was achieved and also the null width and is increased. Figure 9 shows the total fitness value per iteration curve corresponding to Figure 7 and Figure 8.

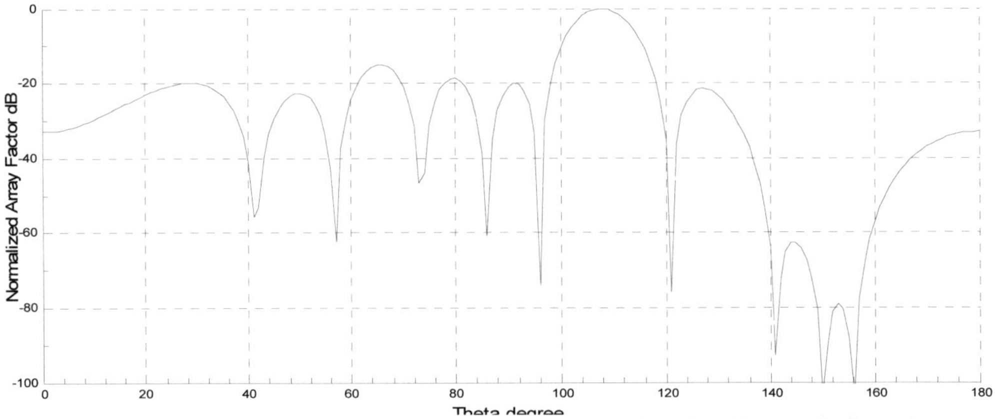

Figure 8. a) Pattern proposed for mainbeam steered to 110° and null at 150° after 50 iterations

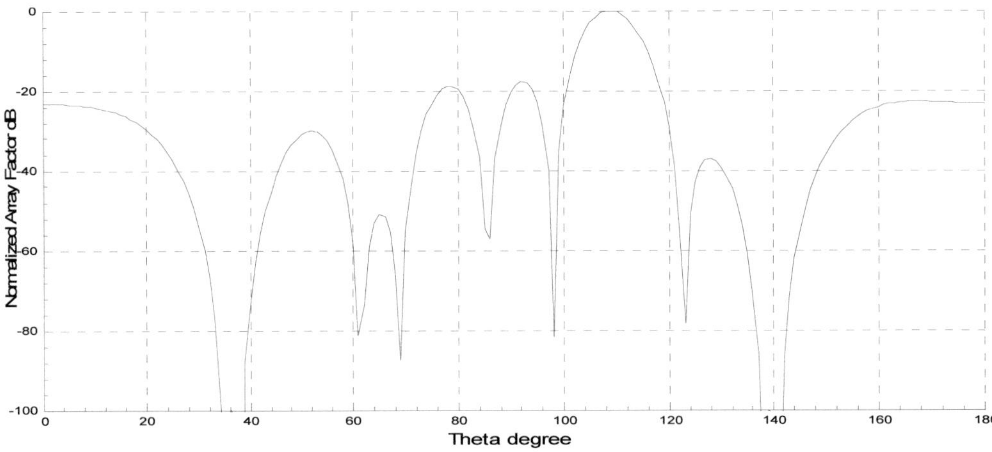

Figure 8. b) Pattern proposed for mainbeam steered to 110° and null at 150° after 500 iteration

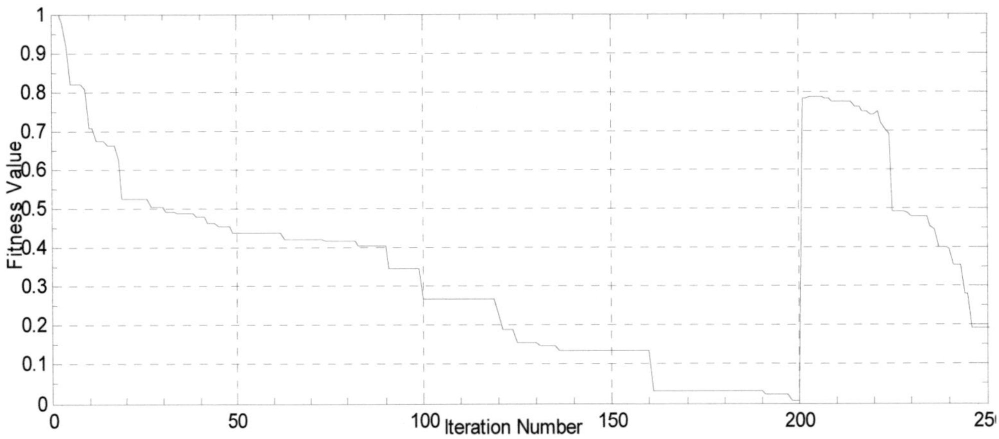

Figure 9. Fitness per iteration curve corresponding to figure 7, 8

4.3 PSO and Pattern Synthesis Phase – Position Control

The phase-only synthesis with equal element spacing requires a large number of elements compared to the amplitude only arrays. Controlling the inter element space and elements phases feed we can have the potential to circumvent this design challenge. Theoretically, the unequal spacing of antenna elements corresponds to nonuniform sampling of signals in the time domain.[H. Unz, 1960] .

The PSO is applied to search for the optimum element phases and positions of the uniform amplitude linear arrays to achieve target pattern and minimum side lobe level .We only consider symmetric arrays for the next results however same can be applied for non symmetric array. Synthesis of an unequally spaced array is carried out separately for the position-only and the position-phase cases for various limits in the distance between the elements. The number of elements considered for the PSO-based synthesis is 32; hence the number of parameters to be optimized is 16 for the position- only synthesis and 32 for the phase-position synthesis.

The PSO synthesis results of positions and phases for the cases when $d_{max} = 0.6\lambda$ and $d_{max} = \lambda$ array patterns are shown in Figure. 10 and 11, respectively. From Figure 10, we can see that the maximum SLL for the position-phase synthesis is lower than that for the position-only synthesis. In Figure 11 When $d_{max} = \lambda$, the maximum SLL of the position-phase synthesis and position-only synthesis is 23.34 and 22.53 dB, respectively

For the case $d_{max} = \lambda$, The time taken to reach -20 dB SLL was about 10 min, and the total time taken for 300 iterations was about 23 min for a swarm of 320 agents. The simulations were carried out on a PC based on an Intel Pentium-IV 3-GHz processor.

We can conclude that for smaller, $d_{max}$the element phases have a larger effect in lowering the SLL of an unequally spaced array with no significant difference in the directivity From Figures 10–11.

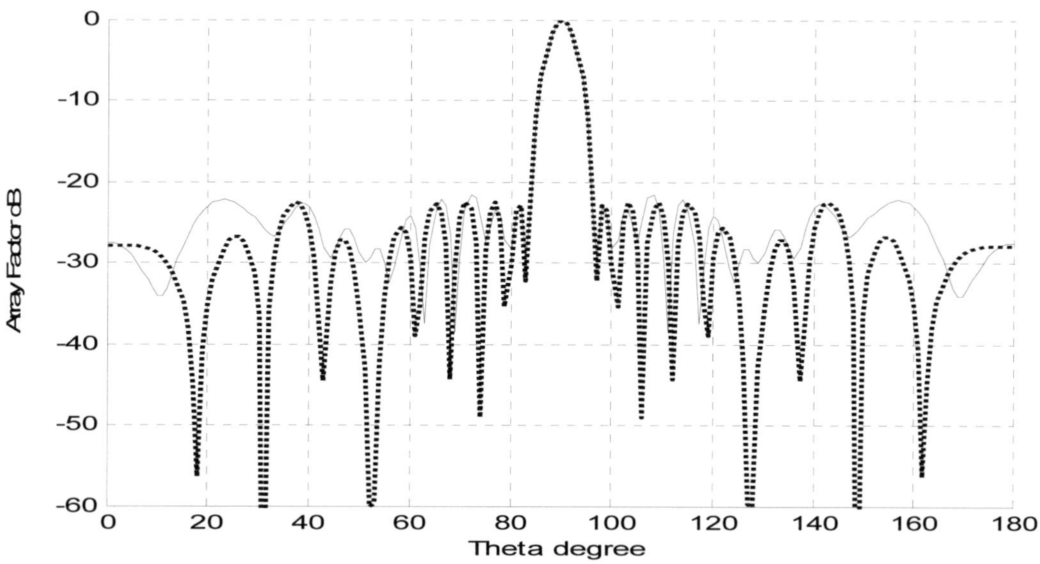

Figure 10. Array patterns for the PSO-based position-only (dashed line) the position-phase (solid line) for $d_{max} = 0.6\lambda$

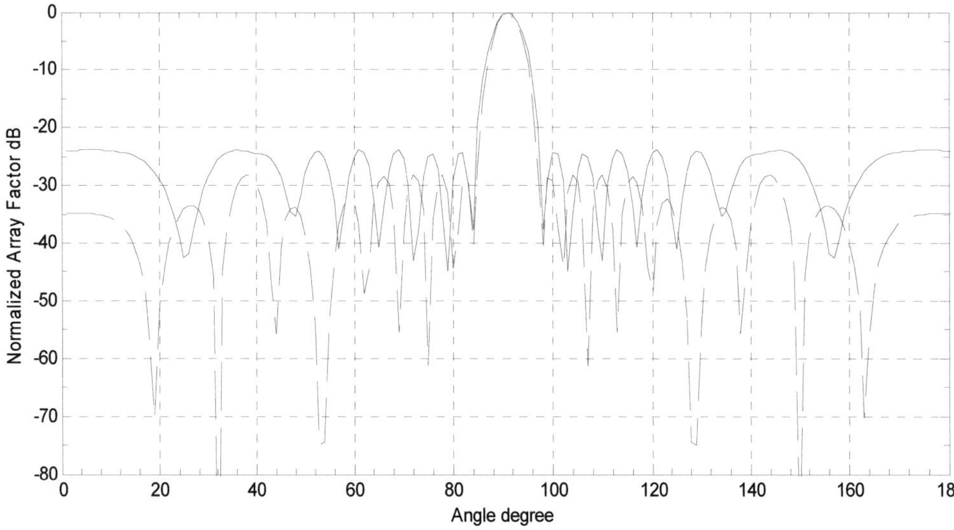

Figure 11. Array patterns for the PSO-based position-only (dashed line) the position-phase (solid line) for $d_{max} = \lambda$

We have seen that the unequally spaced array derived using the position-phase synthesis has lowered SLL compared to that of the unequally spaced arrays derived using the position-only synthesis. Let us consider the PSO-based position-phase synthesis and phase-only synthesis for designing a pencil beam array.

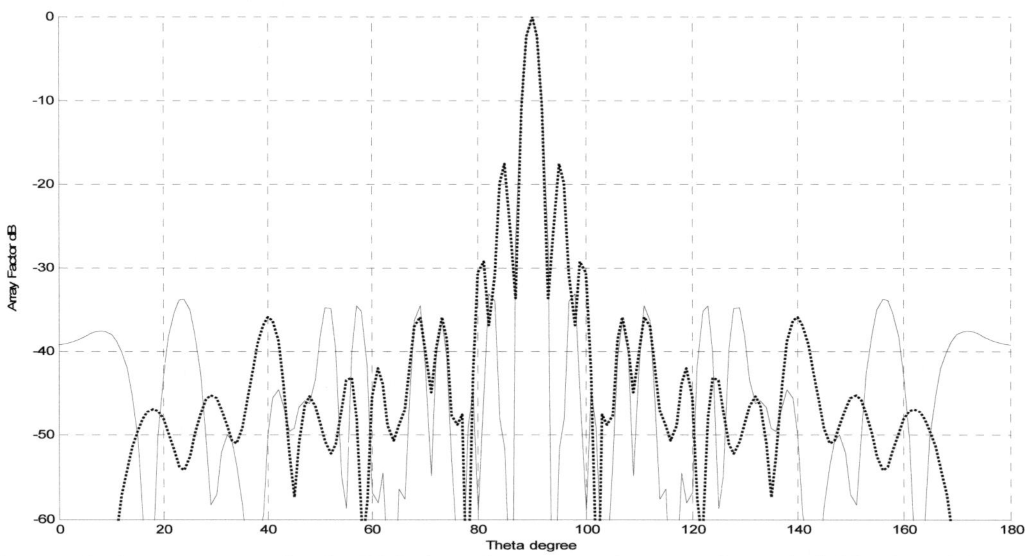

Figure 12. Array patterns for the PSO -based position-phase synthesis (solid line) and the phase-only synthesis (dashed line) of a pencil beam array of 60 elements

The number of elements has to increase to meet beam requirement we consider symmetric array of 60 elements. For the position-phase synthesis, the prior limits assumed in the minimum and maximum distance between the elements are $d_{min} = 0.5\lambda$ and $d_{max} = 0.7\lambda$, respectively. For phase-only synthesis, the uniform distances between the elements are assumed to be 0.5λ. Figure 12 shows the corresponding array patterns shows the phases and positions derived using the PSO-based phase-only synthesis and position-phase synthesis we can see that for the position-phase synthesis, the SLL is lower compared to that of the phase-only synthesis.

5. PSO Application in Smart Antenna Array Signal Estimation

Conventional adaptive beamforming algorithms are based on a stationary environment. Assume that the desired signal and interferers are not correlated. Using statistical theory, one requires several successive snapshots of the data to form a covariance matrix of the interference with independent identically distributed secondary data[B. D. Van, IEEE 1986]. The snapshots accumulation is quite time consuming. Thus when the environment becomes nonstationary, an inaccurate covariance matrix is derived, which results in that the interference cannot be rejected. Therefore the adaptive processing using a single snapshot [Markus E. Ali] is more suitable for a dynamic environment. A direct data domain least squares (D3LS) algorithm [T. K. Sarkar, 2000] has been developed to analyze the received data using a single snapshot.

Although the D3LS algorithm has certain advantages, it has some drawbacks such that the degrees of freedom are limited to nearly half. Furthermore it is shown by simulations that while the jammers can be rejected, the main lobe of the antenna beam pattern is often deviated from the direction of the desired signal and the sidelobe level is relative high.

5.1 Algorithm Formulation

Consider an array composed of N sensors separated by a distance as shown in Figure 1. We assume that narrowband signals consisting of the desired signal plus possibly coherent multipath and jammers with center frequency $f_\circ$ are impinging on the array from various angles, with the constraint. For sake of simplicity, we assume that the incident fields are coplanar and that they are located in the far field of the array.

Each received signal $x_m(k)$ includes additive, zero mean, Gaussian noise. Time is represented by the kth time sample. Thus, for $\mathrm{X(t)} = [x_1(k) \quad x_2(k) \quad x_\mathrm{N}(k)]^\mathrm{T}$

$$x(k) = [\bar{a}(\theta_1)\ \bar{a}(\theta_2) \ldots.\ \bar{a}(\theta_M)].\begin{bmatrix} s_1(k) \\ s_2(k) \\ \vdots \\ \vdots \\ s_M(k) \end{bmatrix} + \bar{n}(k) \tag{19}$$

$\bar{a}(\theta_i)$ is M-elements array steering vector for the θ_i direction of arrival, λ wavelength and d is the elements interspacing distance. $\bar{s}(k)$ is the vector of incident signals at time k and $\bar{n}(k)$ is noise vector at each array element m, zero mean, variance. Then for

$$\bar{A} = [\bar{a}(\theta_1)\ \bar{a}(\theta_2) \ldots.\ \bar{a}(\theta_D)]_{M\times D}$$

matrix of steering vectors $\bar{a}(\theta_i)$

$$\overline{\mathrm{X}} = \bar{A}.\bar{s}(k) + \bar{n}(k) \tag{20}$$

Thus, each of the D-complex signals arrives at angles θ_i and is intercepted by the M antenna elements. It is assumed the number of arriving signals D < M. It is understood that the arriving signals are time varying and thus our calculations are based upon time snapshots of

the incoming signal. Obviously if the transmitters are moving, the matrix of steering vectors is changing with time and the corresponding arrival angles are changing.
Let S_n be the complex voltage induced in the nth array element at a particular instance of time due to a signal of unity amplitude coming from a direction θ_s,

$$S_n = exp\left[j2\pi\left\{\frac{(n-1)d}{\lambda} sin(\theta_s)\right\}\right] \quad (21)$$

Let x_n be the complex voltages that are measured at the nth element due to the actual signal, jammers and thermal noise

$$x_n = \alpha_s S_n + \text{Interference} + \text{Noise} \quad (22)$$

$$x_n = \alpha_s S_n + \sum_{p=1}^{D-1} \left(A_p exp\left(j\frac{2\pi(n-1)d}{\lambda} sin(\theta_p)\right)\right) + n_n \quad (23)$$

Where α_s denotes the complex amplitude of the desired SOI, A_p and θ_p are the amplitude and direction of arrival of the p jammer signal, n_n is the thermal noise at the nth element. There are D jammers and $D < M - 1/2$. With S_n and X_n (n=0,...,M) the known received signal data, one can construct the matrix **X** and **S** such that

$$\boldsymbol{X} = \begin{bmatrix} x_0 & x_1 & \cdots & x_L \\ x_1 & x_2 & \cdots & x_{L+1} \\ \vdots & \vdots & \cdots & \vdots \\ x_L & x_{L+1} & \cdots & x_M \end{bmatrix}_{(L+1)\times(L+1)} \quad \boldsymbol{S} = \begin{bmatrix} s_0 & s_1 & \cdots & s_L \\ s_1 & s_2 & \cdots & s_{L+1} \\ \vdots & \vdots & \cdots & \vdots \\ s_L & s_{L+1} & \cdots & s_M \end{bmatrix}_{(L+1)\times(L+1)} \quad (24)$$

From equations (21) and (23) the matrix U = X − $\alpha_s \boldsymbol{S}$, represents the contribution due to signal multipaths, interferes, clutter and thermal noise (i.e., all the undesired components of the signals except SOI). In an adaptive beamforming, the adaptive weight vector w is chosen in such a way that the contribution from the jammers and thermal noise are minimized to enhance the output signal to interference plus noise ratio (SINR). Hence, the following generalized eigenvalue problem is obtained.

$$\text{UW} = (\text{X} - \alpha_s S)W = 0 \quad (25)$$

$$\overline{w} = [w_1 \ w_2 \ .... \ w_N]^T$$

Note that U(1,1) and U(1,2) elements of the interference plus noise matrix, are given by

$$U(1,1) = X_1 - \alpha S_{d1} \quad (26)$$

$$U(1,2) = X_2 - \alpha S_{d2} \quad (27)$$

Where X_1 and X_2 are the voltages received at antenna elements 1 and 2 due to the signal, jammer, clutter and noise where as S_{d1} and S_{d2} are the values of the SOI only at those elements due to a signal of unit strength, let us define Z as follow

$$z = exp\left[j2\pi\left\{\frac{d}{\lambda} sin(\theta_s)\right]\right. \quad (28)$$

Then $U(1,1) - z^{-1}U(1,2)$ contains no component of the desired signal. In general, the same is true for $U(i,j) - z^{-1}U(i,j+1), (i = 1, \dots, L+1, j = 1, \dots, L)$. Therefore one can form a square matrix F of dimension L+1, generated from U. Therefore, in such way, one can form a reduced rank matrix combined with a constraint that the gain of the subarray is C in the directionθ_s, then one can obtain equation given as follow

$$\begin{bmatrix} Z^0 & Z^1 & \cdots & Z^L \\ X_0 - Z^{-1}X_1 & \cdots & \cdots & X_L - Z^{-1}X_{L+1} \\ \vdots & \vdots & \vdots & \vdots \\ f_3 - f_4 Z^{-1} & \cdots & \cdots & X_{M-1} - Z^{-1}X_M \end{bmatrix} \begin{bmatrix} W_0 \\ W_1 \\ \vdots \\ W_L \end{bmatrix} = \begin{bmatrix} C \\ 0 \\ 0 \\ 0 \end{bmatrix} \quad (29)$$

To obtain the desired signal component, equation (5.14) is represented as

$$[F][W] = [Y] \quad (30)$$

Using any optimization algorithm to solve equation (30) for, optimum weight vector [W] that provide maximum signal gain through minimizing objective function represented as equation (31)

$$\zeta(W_i) = \frac{\|[F][W_i] - Y\|}{\|Y\|} \leq 10^{-6} \quad (31)$$

Consequently SOI the signal component α may be estimated from

$$\alpha = \frac{1}{C}\sum_{i=0}^{i=L}[W_i X_i] \quad (32)$$

The algorithm above is referred to as a "forward method" in the literature [8]. [6],[11]. note we can reformulate the problem using the same data to obtain independent estimate for the solution. This can be achieved by two methods:

a. By reversing the data sequence and then complex conjugating each term of that sequence (Backward method)
b. By combining the (forward-backwards method) to double the given data and thereby increase the number of weights (degrees of freedom) significantly over that of either the forward or backward method alone. The number of degrees of freedom can reach to $1 + (N-1)/1.5$.

to investigate the method let us we consider recovering signal using the previous presented algorithm let us consider a single tone signal with specs as table (3) received by liner array of 10 elements linear array.

	Magnitude in V	Phase	DOA in degree
Signal	1	0	45°
Jammer #1	1.25	0	75°
Jammer # 2	2	0	60°
Jammer #3	0.5	0	0°

Table 3. Incident signal characteristics

The sampling frequency is $10\,f$; Using PSO algorithm as an optimization tools to solve the optimum W_i for the objective equation (31) value for each iteration we get

W_1= (1.2996248637+j*0.0724160744), W_2=(0.9415241429+j*-0,3236468668)

W_3=(-0.9898155714+j*-0.1071454180), W_4 = (- 1.2513334352+j*0.3583762104)

Using these weights in equation 32 to get the value of SOI amplitude
The first ten samplings of the signal and the system output are compared as follow

Initial transmitted signal	Estimated signal
1	0.9999-j0.000003154
0.809+j0.5877	0.809+j0.5877
0.309+j0.951	0.309+j0.951
-0.309+j0.951	-0.309+j0951
-0.809+j0.5877	-0.809+j0.5877
-1	-0.90.999+j0000003154
-0.809-j0.587	-0.809+j0.5877
-0.309-j0.951	-0.309-j0.951
0.3090-j0.951	0.309-j0.951
0.809-j0.5877	0.80.90-j0.5877

Table 4. Output estimated signal using D3LS and PSO algorithm as an optimization method

The total CPU time taken for the above results is 1.19 sec. PSO is less computational operations compared to conjugate gradient method.

6. Conclusion

PSO application for solving different numerical problems in smart antenna is illustrated. Improvement is proposed to the algorithm to support the continuous real time varying target problem. Also a solution is proposed to overcome the case of bounded search space through introducing of transformation function. Simulation for different scenarios is solved with the aid of PSO. Synthesis of an adaptive Beamforming using the phase only control where target is dynamic over time has been presented. PSO was introduced to solve position-only and position-phase synthesis, which is a bounded search space problem. Finally an investigation for using PSO to estimate signal amplitude though D3LS approach is presented.

7. References

H. Unz, Linear arrays with arbitrarily distributed elements, *IEEE Trans. Antennas Propagat.*, vol. AP-8, pp. 222–223, Mar. 1960

B. D. Van Veen and K. M. Buckley, Beamforming: a versatile approach to spatial filtering, *IEEE SSP Mag., Apr.1988, pp. 4-24*

Markus E. Ali and Franz Schreib, Adaptive Single Snapshot Beamforming: A New Concept for the Rejection of Nonstationary and Coherent Interferers, *IEEE Trans. On Signal Processing*, Vol. 40, No. 12, Dec.1992, pp. 3055-3058.

Steyskal, H., R. A. Shore, and R. L. Haupt, Methods for null control and their effects on radiation pattern, *IEEE Trans. On Antenna and Propagation*, Vol. 34, 404–409, 1986.

2. Steyskal, H., Simple method for pattern nulling by phaseperturbation, *IEEE Trans. on Antenna and Propagation*, Vol. 31,163–166, 1983.

T. K. Sarkar and J. Koh, A Pragmatic Approach to Adaptive Antennas, *IEEE Antennas and Propagation Magazine*, Vol. 42, No. 2, Apr. 2000, pp.39-53